Active Platform: A Developer's Guide

MICROSOFT SOLUTIONS FOR NEXT GENERATION WEB SITES

Active Platform:
A Developer's Guide

MICROSOFT SOLUTIONS FOR

NEXT GENERATION WEB SITES

John Omahen

MIS:Press
A Division of Henry Holt and Company, Inc.
115 West 18th Street
New York, New York 10011
http://www.mispress.com

Copyright © 1998 by MIS:Press

Printed in the United States of America

All rights reserved. No part of this book may be reproduced or transmitted in any form or by any means, electronic or mechanical, including photocopying, recording, or by any information storage and retrieval system, without prior written permission from the Publisher. Contact the Publisher for information on foreign rights.

Limits of Liability and Disclaimer of Warranty

The Author and Publisher of this book have used their best efforts in preparing the book and the programs contained in it. These efforts include the development, research, and testing of the theories and programs to determine their effectiveness.

The Author and Publisher make no warranty of any kind, expressed or implied, with regard to these programs or the documentation contained in this book. The Author and Publisher shall not be liable in any event for incidental or consequential damages in connection with, or arising out of, the furnishing, performance, or use of these programs.

All products, names and services are trademarks or registered trademarks of their respective companies.

First Edition—1998

Library of Congress Cataloging-in-Publication Data

```
Omahen, John
   Active Platform : a developer's guide / by John Omahen
     p.      cm.
   ISBN 1-55851-578-X
     1. Internet programming. 2. ActiveX. 3. Computer.
   software Development I. Title.
   QA76.625.O45      1997
   005.2'76—dc21                                         97-45830
                                                             CIP
```

MIS:Press and M&T Books are available at special discounts for bulk purchases for sales promotions, premiums, and fundraising.

For details contact: Special Sales Director
                             MIS:Press and M&T Books
                             Divisions of Henry Holt and Company, Inc.
                             115 West 18th Street
                             New York, New York 10011

10 9 8 7 6 5 4 3 2 1

Associate Publisher: *Paul Farrell*

Managing Editor: *Shari Chappell*   **Production Editor:** *Gay Nichols*
Editor: *Debra Williams Cauley*   **Technical Editor:** *Paul Thurrott*
Copy Edit Manager: *Karen Tongish*   **Copy Editor:** *Betsy Hardinger*

Contents

Chapter 1: The Active Ingredients of a Well-Done Web Site 1

    Overview of the World Wide Web 1
    Places to Visit 2
    How Does It Work? 4
    HTML Basics 8
    Where Do We Go from Here? 13

Chapter 2: Client/Server: Who Serves Whom? 15

    Challenges of Client/Server 15
    The Benefits of Client/Server 16
        Financial Benefits 17
    The Costs of Client/Server 17
        The Network 18
        Database Needs 19
    The Dynamic Solution 19
        Tracking the State of a Process 20
        Push vs. Pull 23
    The Future of Client/Server 23
    Where Do We Go from Here? 25

Chapter 3: The Active Platform 27

    Distribution of Objects 28
    Scalabiltiy 29
    The Big Picture: Putting It Together 31
    Where to Go from Here 32

Chapter 4: The Dynamic Server Environment: The Players 33

    Extending the Platform 34
        Components of IIS 34
        Active Server Pages 35
    Safety First 38
    Hardware Considerations 41

Symmetric Multiprocessing 41
The Operating System 41
Redundant Array of Inexpensive or Independent Disks 41
Network Connections 43
Where Do We Go from Here? 43

Chapter 5: Active Server Pages 45

What Is ASP? 45
   Basic Definitions 49
   ASP Objects 50
      The Request Object 50
      The Response Object 51
      The Application Object 52
      The Server Object 52
      The Session Object 52
      ASP Object Samples 52
   Components 56
      Data Access Component 56
      Content Linking Component 56
      File System Component 56
      Browser Capabilities Component 57
      Advertisement Rotator Component 57
      Using Your Own Components 57
   Sessions 58
   Let's Create a Few Pages 59
   Tips and Troubleshooting 60
      Tips 60
      Troubleshooting 61
   Where Do We Go from Here? 62

Chapter 6: Tools for Active Platform Servers 63

Getting Data to the Client/Server World of the Web 63
Common Gateway Interface 64
   Perl 64
   Internet Database Connector 67
   ISAPI 76
A Word about Active Server Pages 80
Dynamic HTML 80

Overview 80
The Players 81
What Now? 82

Chapter 7: The Active Security Environment: Proxy Server 85

The Role of Security in Development 86
    Getting to and from the Site 86
    Security Mechanisms 87
Cisco Routers 89
    Securing the Data 96
Secure Sockets Layer 98
    Security Components of Microsoft's Proxy Server 99
Proxy Server: The Heart of Its Services 101
    Proxy Planning 101
C2 Security 101
    The Basic Services 104
Access to the Proxy World: Outbound, Inbound, and the Gateways 112
    Outbound Access 112
    Inbound Access 116
    The Proxy as a Gateway 117
Handling Increased Loads 117
Controlling the Proxy 118
    Where Is the Cache? 118
    LAT or Longitude? 120
    Client Services 121
    Logging without Carrying the Wood 121
Proxy Performance Issues and Additional Features 122
    Proxy Server Connections 123
    Screen Savers and Other Ugly Items 123
    When You're Setting Up an ISP 125
    The Charts 129
Troubleshooting Proxy Server Issues 130
Where Do You Go from Here? 132

Chapter 8: Active Data 133

The Database 133
    The Three-Story House of Databases 133
    Types of Database Models 134

Contents

    What Is a Relational Data Model? 134
    Variations on the Database Models 135
    What Is a Relational Database Management System? 136
    Ensuring Data Integrity 137
    The RDBMS Logical Data Model 138
    RDBMS Physical Data Model 143
    Using SQL 143
Database Technology 144
    The Role of the Database Administrator 145
    The Enterprise Data Model 147
Data Warehouses and Processes 148
    Data Warehousing 148
    On-Line Transaction Processing and On-Line Analytical Processing 149
    Data Mining 150
Why SQL Server? 150
    The SQL Server Tools 151
    Administrative Aspects of SQL Server 154
    Logical Aspects of SQL Server 156
    Physical Aspects of SQL Server 160
    The Warehouse 171
The Data Retrieval Method: Transact SQL 173
    Nulls 174
    JOINs 175
    CUBE 175
Where Do You Go from Here? 176

Chapter 9: Active Search: Index Server 179

The Query Process 182
    Standard Query 183
    Query Language Operators 185
    Types of Queries: Free Text, Vector Space, and Property Values 188
    Sample Query 193
Indexes 196
    Word Lists 198
    Merges 199
    Property Cache 203
    Indexing Process 204
Default Filter 205

Contents   xi

    Null Filtering 209
    Removing Filter DLLs 211
    Word Breaking 213
    Cleanup 214
Unmasking the Ifilter 214
The Catalog 217
    Catalogs and Registry Settings 220
Managing Resources 222
    Basic Administration 222
    Managing System Resources 227
    Managing Scripts 228
    Managing Virtual Roots 228
    Setting Up a Remote Virtual Root 230
Database Searching 230
Where Do You Go from Here? 230

Chapter 10: Active Money 233

E-Commerce 234
    Is Anyone Making Money? 235
    Is it Safe for Merchants and Customers? 235
    How Big Is the Potential Market? 235
    Troubles with E-commerce 237
Secure Transactions 237
    Getting the Keys 239
    Send the Request 241
    Microsoft Wallet 242
    Money in Action 245
How Commerce Server Works 246
    Commerce Server Components 248
    Order Processing Pipeline 249
    Store Builder Wizard Tools 250
    Client-Side Controls: The Wallet 251
    Buy Now Wizard 251
The Selling Process 251
    Building a Store 251
    The Store Application 260
    Setting Up a Store 263
    The Customer Shopping Process 269

xii Contents

Tips for Increasing Sales 270
    Tools 270
    Wizards 271
    Scalability 272
Where Do You Go from Here? 272

Chapter 11: Active Middleware 273

The Methodologies 274
    Two-Tier Database 274
    The Middleware Solution 276
Transaction Server 278
Transaction Processing 280
    Active Components 281
    Server Objects 282
    Transaction Server Executive 282
    Server Processes 290
    Resource Manager 291
    Resource Dispensers 292
    Microsoft Distributed Transaction Coordinator 295
    Transaction Server Explorer 299
Server and Client Issues 300
    The Client Side 300
    The Server Side 301
Applications 308
    Just-in-Time: ..How to Activate and Deactivate Objects 310
    Building a Sample Application 317
    Create the Component 317
    Create the Bank Package 318
    Install the Component 320
    Run and Monitor the Component 322
    To Maintain Integrity 322
Security and Administration 323
Where Do You Go from Here? 326

Chapter 12: How the Active Desktop Works 327

The Client 327
ActiveX 327
    ActiveX Controls 328

Active Template Library	329
Java 329	
Hello World in Java	329
The AWT Library	330
Images and Animation	331
JavaScript	333
Visual Basic and VBScript	333
VBScript	335
Where Do You Go from Here?	336

Chapter 13: ActiveX 337

What Is ActiveX?	337
ActiveX and OLE	338
Database Interactivity	339
The ActiveX Tools	339
Controls	340
Security	344
Tips for the ActiveX Developer	346
Where Do You Go from Here?	348

Chapter 14: Active Template Library 349

Why Use ATL?	349
ASP Scripts	349
When to Use ATL	350
How to Use ATL	350
Building a Sample	351
ActiveX Controls Implemented by ATL	355
The Benefit of Using ActiveX Controls	355
Threading	357
Where to Go from Here	358

Chapter 15: Visual Basic and Its Scripting Environment 359

Overview	359
VBScript	361
Basic Syntax Rules	361
Adding to the Web Page	363
More Samples	365

Contents

Controls for Visual Basic 372
Visual Basic Tips and Tricks 374
Where to Go from Here 374

Chapter 16: Java and JavaScript 375

A Few Definitions 376
Basic Java Syntax 376
Java Virtual Machine 379
Building an Applet 380
JavaBeans 381
Java and Security: Is It Safe? 381
Viruses and Attacks 382
Using a Firewall 383
Using Java for Database Connectivity 383
JavaScript 384
Variables in JavaScript 384
Functions 385
What Is an Object? 385
Security in JavaScript 386
Differences between JavaScript and JScript 386
Where to Go from Here 386

Chapter 17: Comparing the Languages 389

Java and C++ 390
Java and JavaScript 391
VBScript and JavaScript 393
VB and VBScript 395
ActiveX and Java 396
Where to Go from Here 396

Chapter 18: Creating and Managing a Next-Generation Web Site ...399

Overview 399
Purpose 400
Plan 401
Prototype 403
Promote 407
Where to Go from Here 410

Chapter 19: Web Site Case Study 411
Layout 411
Code Samples 413
   Phase 1 413
   Phase 1A: Simple Addition to the Database Using Perl 422
   Phase 1B: Java for Browser Detection 424
   Phase 2 425
   Phase 3: Incorporate More Server Products and Start Building ISAPIs 449
   Phase 4 455
Lessons Learned 456
   Basic Education in Site Development 456
   Security Issues 456
   Extranet Requirements 456
   Code Lessons 457
Where to Go from Here? 459

Chapter 20: Real-Life Security Issues 461
Netiquette 461
Confidential Issues 462
   Copyrighting and Solutions 462
   How to Prevent Hacking 464
Firewalls 466
Protecting Commerce 468
   Secure Sockets Layer 468
   Other Security Methods 468
   Encryption 469
Virtual Private Networks 469
Where to Go from Here 470

Chapter 21: 471
The Future of the Active Platform 471
   Plug and Play 472
   The Structure 473
   There Are Wolves Out There 474
   Security 476
   Costs of Doing Business 476
   Where to Go from Here 477

Appendix A 479

Setting Up IIS and NT 479
    IIS 479
        Let's Use the Internet Service Manager 480
        WWW 481
        FTP 484
        Gopher 485
        Using Scripts 486
    TCP/IP 486
    Dynamic Host configuration Protocol 487
        Creating a DHCP Scope 488
        Why DHCP? 488
        Setting Up DHCP 489
    Windows Internet Name Service 490
        Setting Up WINS 491

Appendix B 493

Resources and the CD-ROM 493
    Resources 493
        Web Sites 493
    Resources Used in the Writing of this Book 494
    What Is on the CD-ROM 495

Index 497

Chapter 1

The Active Ingredients of a Well-Done Web Site

You can visit the Louvre, go to the local Amish store to buy a hat, and talk to your favorite author—all in less than an hour using the World Wide Web. Is this Web an arachnologist's dream (you know, someone who studies spiders, Web and all—pun intended), or is it an arachnophobic's nightmare? It's neither. The Web is based on a new medium of distribution. It is not TV, but you can broadcast information using it. It is not a magazine, but you can present both words and images in print.

This chapter will cover the basics of the World Wide Web, introduce you to places to visit on the Web, and explain how the Web works, including the basics of HTML.

OVERVIEW OF THE WORLD WIDE WEB

The World Wide Web, as defined by the W3 Consortium, is a "wide-area hypermedia information retrieval initiative aiming to give universal access to a large universe of documents." In English, that means the World Wide Web is an architecture that allows computer users a simple, consistent way to access a variety of media, including text, graphics, sound files, and video clips. Formats of those files range from simple text to HTML (to be discussed later in this chapter), to GIF, JPEG AVI, Quicktime, and more.

The Web is a hypermedia environment in which media are interrelated with other media. That is what makes a Web-based Louvre visit unique. This hypermedia environment allows a developer to immerse a visitor in the experience. It is not the same thing as being there; the Web is not designed to replace personal experiences. The Web enables a museum such as the Louvre to show visitors images and their related history. But the Web enriches the process. With a click of the mouse, an image springs to life as a 3-D walk-through of a village. Click on the ìvillage center,î and a virtual actor comes alive to explain in speech and text what the visitor is viewing. Now even people who have difficulty reading can experience the same adventure that previously only historians envisioned.

2 Chapter 1

All this is possible by using a piece of software called a Web *browser*. The Web supports this interactive environment by using forms of *hypertext* to interact with users. Like regular text, hypertext can be stored, read, searched for, and edited. There is one difference: Hypertext contains connections within the text to other documents.

Suppose a person reading this chapter could use a mouse to click on the word *hypertext* in the preceding paragraph. With a system that interprets hypertext, this link—called a *hyperlink*—might lead to a definition of the word or a picture of a tutorial on hypertext or an audio file that would play back on the visitor's computer. The hyperlink to the definition might also have an underlined area that would lead to a discussion of the history of hypertext. Embedded hyperlinks can go on and on, leading to additional connections like the threads of a web. In the World Wide Web, visitors are put at the center of their own universe (see Figure 1.1).

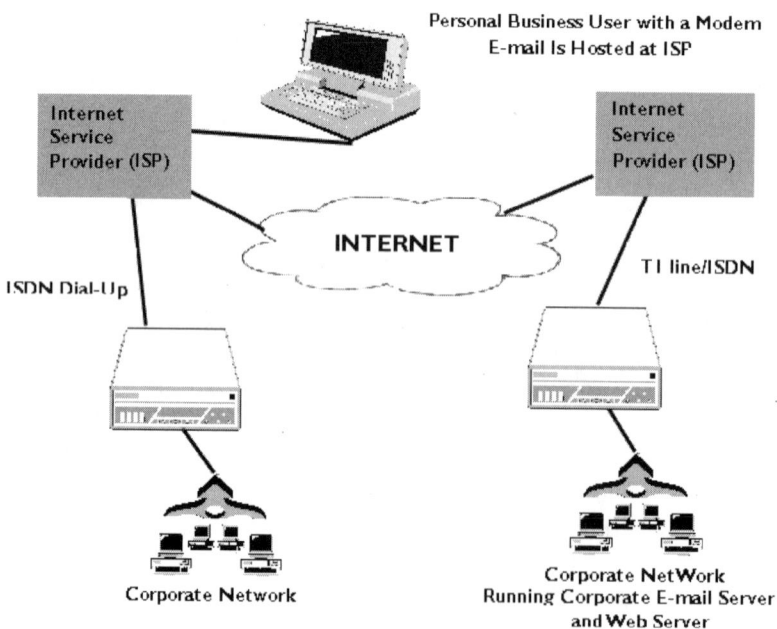

Figure 1.1 The Web.

PLACES TO VISIT

Hypermedia documents contain links not only to text documents but also to other media. Here are additional examples of hypermedia:

- The visitor is a young girl who wants to play a computer game. She goes to a Web site to read the latest review; then she clicks on a picture of a game scene. It begins to download that portion of the game to her system so that she can play it locally. If she so desires she can go one step further and link with other friends on the Internet. Now she can start an on-line version of the game playing against or with others.
- A student wants to learn English. He reads an American phrase, clicks on the text, and hears the phrase spoken aloud with all the inflections and pauses included.
- A high school chemistry teacher needs some last-minute examples for the seventh period chemistry class (the students who like to sleep). She clicks on the image of a molecule, and a whole experiment comes to life. Not only will she be able to show the experiment to her students, but also the experiment comes with homework study questions (answers are found in a password-protected area for teachers).

With browser software, you can do all these things:

Look at electronic text in a variety of fonts.
Display text in bold or italics.
See paragraphs as lists, numbered lists, or in bullets.
Hear sounds.
See movies (MPEG-1 and Quicktime).
Read foreign languages (such as French, German, and Japanese).
Click on basic form elements, such as fields, check boxes, and radio buttons.
See graphics (in GIF or JPEG format) of as many as 256 colors within documents.
Have other applications control your display remotely.
See a history of the road you have traveled (the hyperlink history).
Store a list and retrieve a list of places you have visited.
...And much more.

What can you find on the Web?

Anything served through search tools.
Anything served through anonymous File Transfer Protocol (FTP) sites.
Internet phone book services.
Addresses of users on the Internet.
Newsgroups.
Anything that uses Telnet.
And much more.

How Does It Work?

The Web works within the client/server model. A *Web server* is a program running on a computer. This program "serves" documents to other computers. When a Web *client* (using a browser) makes a request for a document, the appropriate server "ships" that document to the requesting browser. The intention of this process is to give control to the visitor, to minimize network traffic, and to localize system-intensive calculations. This means that if a developer thinks that the client system is capable of running a calculation or performing an operation, the developer may send only raw data to the client; the client will interpret the data. For example, suppose a game player is on-line playing against other players. The game engine is on the clients' machines. The server sends only the location data of each player to the client machine. The client machine does all the calculations regarding the actions of the other players based on what the server passes to it.

In a different situation, a user might want to find the number of seats available at the local Dance Center for the Broadway musical *Cats*. The user would click a button on the screen that tells a server to activate a call to a database. This call directs the server to search 2 million records in a database on the server. The distribution of calculations is based on how the developer designs the client/server application.

Figure 1.2 shows a simple way of understanding the client/server model.

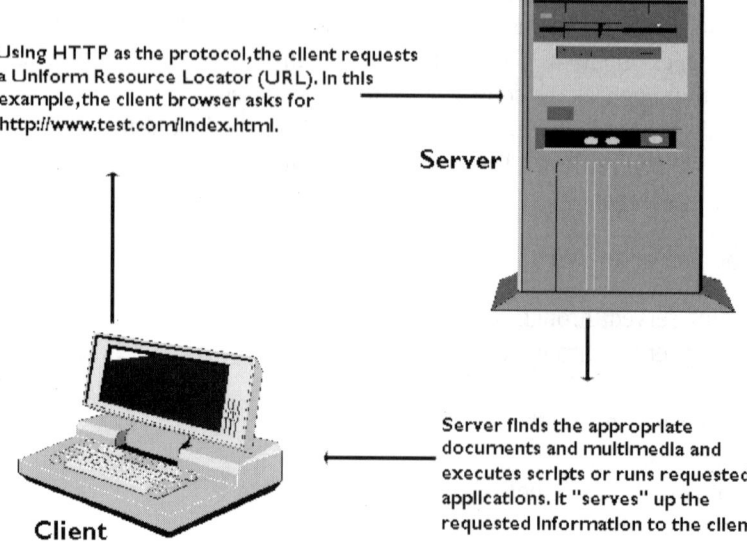

Figure 1.2 A Client/server sample.

Here's another analogy. A man goes into a restaurant to buy a burger. He is the client. He is met by a waiter. The waiter acts as the server. The server takes the client's order, determines who should build the burger (application), has it built, and then passes the burger to the client.

Let's apply this to the World Wide Web:

1. The customer runs a Web client (the browser).
2. The customer selects a piece of hypertext that connects to a text document, "The History of Hamburgers."
3. The Web client connects to a computer (the server) specified by a network address. The appropriate server takes the request.
4. The Web server acknowledges that the client wants to see "The History of Hamburgers."
5. The server responds by sending the text and any other media within it (pictures, sounds, or movies) to the client's screen.

In a conservative estimate, the World Wide Web is composed of thousands of servers that handle millions of transactions. This arrangement creates a large amount of information flow. To meet the needs of all these customers safely, Web servers use encryption and client authentication. They can send and receive secure data and be selective as to which clients receive information. The Social Security Administration (SSA) learned this the hard way. The SSA made the Personal Earnings and Benefits Estimate Statement available as an on-line service. Workers could find out how much they were entitled to receive from the program. To access personal records, a user needed only an individualís name, Social Security number, motherís maiden name, date of birth, and place of birth. The program was discontinued when concerns were raised that this information could be easily obtained by third parties, allowing them access to a personís retirement account.

Developers need to provide secure methods that cannot be broken by someone looking into public records. They must choose passwords and schemes that are not easily deciphered.

Web clients and servers talk in a language called the Hypertext Transport Protocol (HTTP). Web servers are often called HTTP servers. If the systems talk to each other in another language such as FTP, in which systems are transferring binary files, the server is called an FTP server.

The World Wide Web, then, is the network of servers speaking to each other in HTTP as well as the information housed on those servers.

If servers communicate using HTTP, how does the client communicate with the server? It is done through Hypertext Markup Language (HTML). HTML is related to Standard Generalized Markup Language (SGML). You may have seen SGML when working with other document-formatting systems. HTML is an interpreted language understood by Web browsers such as Mosaic, Netscape, Lynx, and Internet Explorer. It is technically a subset of SGML.

When a Web client "speaks" to a Web server, the main command is GET ME THE ìURL-NAMEî (the URL is explained in the following section). This process runs on top of the TCP/IP protocol (please see Chapter 7 for a further discussion of TCP/IP).

Developers write Web documents using HTML. The files are saved with a file extension of **.html** (UNIX and Macintosh) or **.htm** (Microsoft DOS and Windows). HTML documents are standard ASCII files with formatting codes. These codes contain information about hyperlinks as well as information about layout, such as text styles, document titles, paragraphs, and lists. There are many free software converters that convert standard documents (such as Word and Quark documents) to HTML.

HTML represents links to networks and hypermedia via Uniform Resource Locators (URLs). A URL looks like this:

http://www.you.com/index.html

In this example, the client requests a page called www.you.com/index.html. The text before the slashes (//) tells the server the type of access; the client is looking for a server that can talk HTTP to other servers. The second part of the address tells the server where to look for the information, in this case a Web server called you.com. The latter part of the address is the name of the document.

Here is an HTML page called **index.html**. The address could be extended with folder locations:

http://www.you.com/folder/index.html

Figure 1.3 shows two URLs and the resultant screens.

The Active Ingredients of a Well-Done Web Site 7

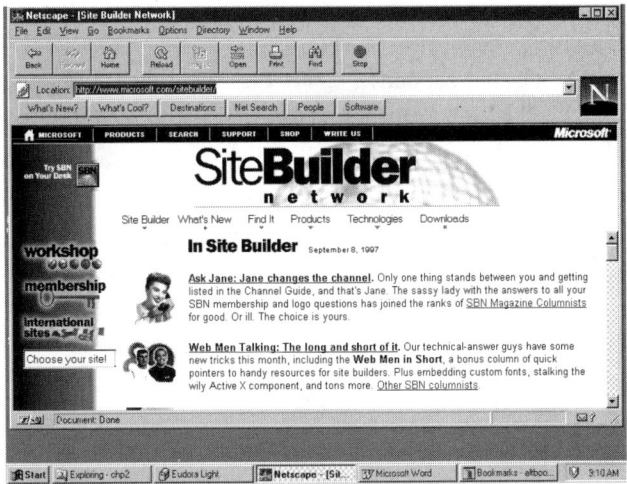

Figure 1.3a http://www.microsoft.com/sitebuilder/.

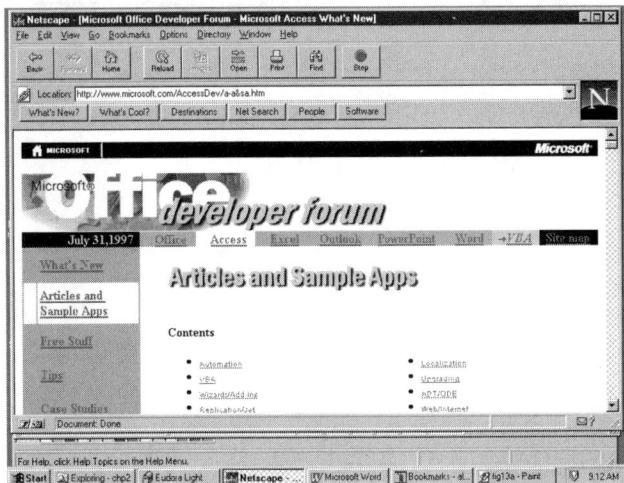

Figure 1.3b http://www.microsoft.com/AccessDev/a-a&sa.htm.

HTML Basics

HTML is a simple text file that contains *markup* tags that define the format and layout of a page. You can use a DOS editor, Notepad, or even Word to create and edit the **.htm** file. Here is a sample file:

```
<HTML>
<BODY>
<FONT SIZE=7>
Hello World! I am in font=7<BR>
</FONT>
<b>I am Bold</b>
<li> this is a bullet point
<a href="link.html>THIS IS A HYPERLINK</a>
</BODY>
</HTML>
```

Figure 1-4 shows the resultant page in a browser window.

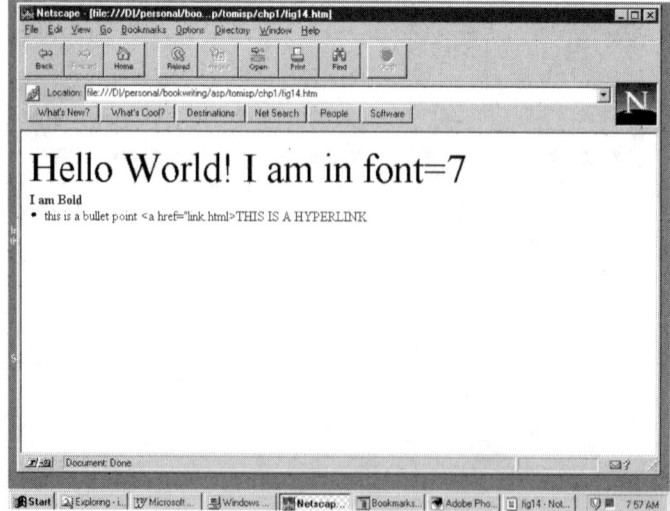

Figure 1.4 Resulting HTML file.

Tags tell the browser how to display text, images and other types of data. This tagging process usually starts with `<tag>` and ends with `</tag>`. The begin tag `<HTML>` tells the browser that the document is in HTML format and not plain text. The end tag `</HTML>` tells the browser that it has read the last of the HTML tags. The header information follows `<HTML>`; it is designated by `<HEAD>` and the appropriate closing tag, `</HEAD>`. Following the header is the main body of information. The opening tag is

`<BODY>`, and the closing tag is `</BODY>`. Within the body you will see tags such as the following:

- `<FONT>` to change font size
- `<B>` to display the characters in bold
- `<LI>` to make a bulleted list (no special numbering order)
- `<A HREF>` to create a hyperlink

You create Web pages based on HTML standards. These pages are arranged in an organized fashion to create what is known as a Web site. You can even cause a mouse click to open an e-mail window by adding the tag

`<a href="sendto:mailme@test.com">E-mail address</a>`.

You can create interactive forms. Here is the HTML (the screen appears in Figure 1.5).

```
<HTML>
<HEAD>
    <TITLE>Form Test</TITLE>
    </HEAD>
<BODY BGCOLOR="#FFFFFF" text="#000000" link="#3100BA" vlink="#260023" alink="#004C16">
<!Using the IDC/HTX method for inserting this data to a database>
<Form  method=POST   action="../oss/queries/browser.idc">
<!outer table>
<TABLE>
<TR>
<TD></TD>
<TR><TD>Databases</TD></TR>
<!first inner table>
<TD>
<TABLE>
                <TR align=left><th>
            <!make this a TABLE with a single column)
                <TD align=right>
                    <INPUT   TYPE="checkbox"   NAME="group"   VALUE="area1" Checked>
                    <font size="4">                            AREA 1
</font>
                </TD></TR>
                <TR>  <TD align=center>
                    <INPUT   TYPE="checkbox"   NAME="group"   VALUE="area2">
                    <font size="4">                            AREA
```

```
2</font>
                        </TD></TR>
                        <TR><TD align=left>
                            <INPUT   TYPE="checkbox"  NAME="C"  VALUE="area3">
                            <font size="4">                          AREA 3
</font>
                        </TD>  </TR>
                            </TABLE>
</TD>
<!second TABLE>
<TD>
<TABLE border=0>
                <TR>
                    <TD align=right>
                        <INPUT   TYPE="radio"  NAME="A"  VALUE="Title" >
                        <font size="4">                          </font>
                    </TD>
                    <TD align=center>
                        <INPUT   TYPE="radio"  NAME="A"  VALUE="Description">
                        <font size="4">                          </font>
                    </TD>
                    <TD align=left>
                        <INPUT   TYPE="radio"  NAME="A"  VALUE="URL">
                        <font size="4">                          </font>
                </TR>
<!second row>
            <TR>
                    <TD align=right>
                        <INPUT   TYPE="radio"  NAME="B"  VALUE="Title" >
                        <font size="4">                          </font>
                    </TD>
                    <TD align=center>
                        <INPUT   TYPE="radio"  NAME="B"  VALUE="Description">
                        <font size="4">                          </font>
                    </TD>
                    <TD align=left>
                        <INPUT   TYPE="radio"  NAME="B"  VALUE="URL">
                        <font size="4">                          </font>
                </TR>
<!third row>
        <TR>
                    <TD align=right>
                        <INPUT   TYPE="radio"  NAME="C"  VALUE="Title" >
                        <font size="4">                         </font>
```

The Active Ingredients of a Well-Done Web Site 11

```
                    </TD>
                    <TD align=center>
                        <INPUT  TYPE="radio" NAME="C" VALUE="Description">
                        <font size="4">                              </font>
                    </TD>
                    <TD align=left>
                        <INPUT  TYPE="radio" NAME="C" VALUE="URL">
                        <font size="4">                              </font>
                </TR>
            </TABLE>
</TD>
</TR>
</TABLE>
                    <input type=submit name=Button value="Finish">
                    <input type=reset name=Button value="Clear">

</Form>

</body>
</html>
```

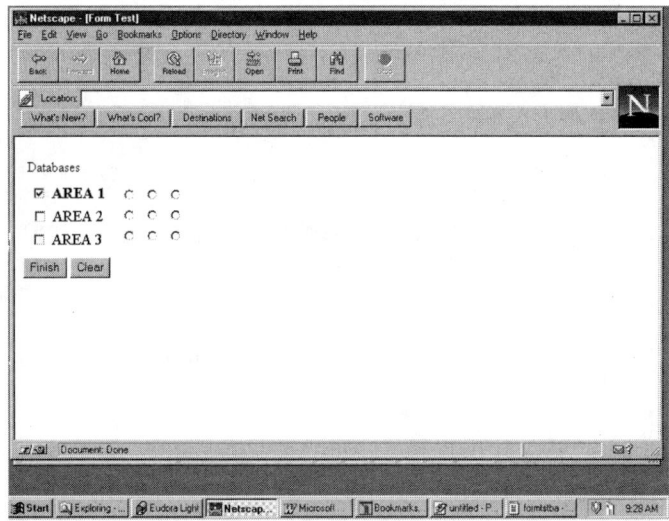

Figure 1.5 The resultant form screen.

Web browsers allow the user to specify a URL to be visited. As has been noted, when the visitor selects a hyperlink, a request is triggered to open a URL.

HTML has undergone numerous changes and now lets you include tables (see Figure 1.6), frames (see Figure 1.7), and many other useful document forms. These changes allow you to make the site more interactive (dynamic) and to more closely compete with current advertising industry publishing practices.

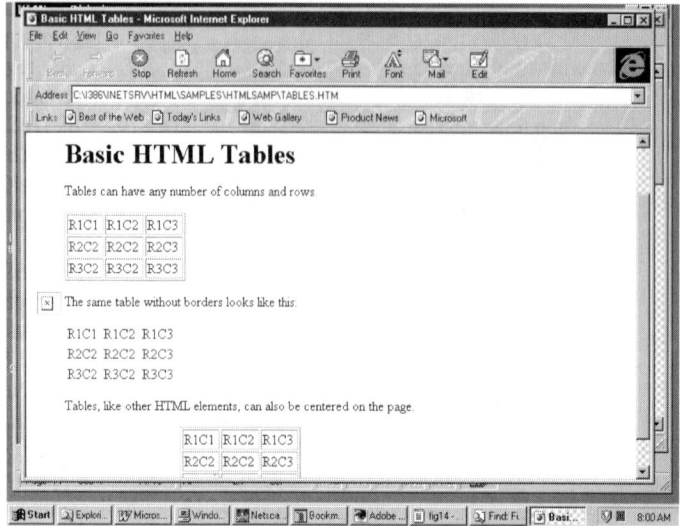

Figure 1.6 An example of tables.

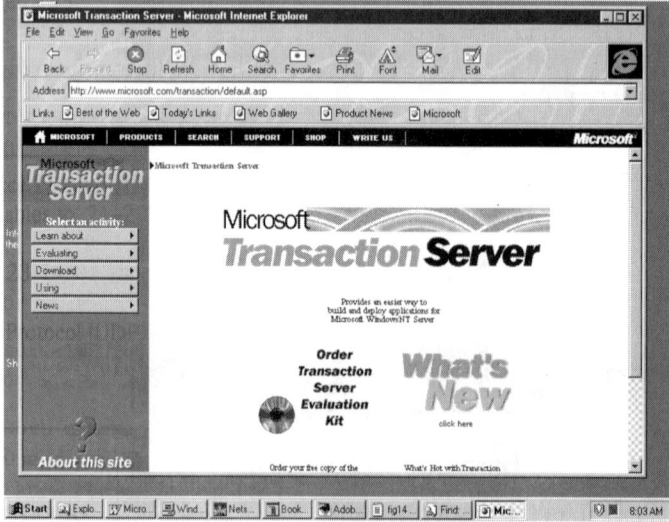

Figure 1.7 An example of frames.

The HTML specification has gone through several revisions, such as HTML 1.0, HTML 2.0, and HTML 3.2. If you write a page in HTML 3.2, the page will display the HTML 1.0 tags properly if the user visits the site with an older browser (one that recognizes only HTML 1.0 tags). Netscape and Microsoft have been working together with the W3 committees to establish a Dynamic HTML standard (please see Chapter 6 for further examples).

This compatibility between versions is wonderful. You can create pretty nice Web sites by using basic HTML and artistic design theory. But the world changes and products and services get better and better. How do you tell the world? Not through static code such as that described in HTML. With the examples given here, the site becomes somewhat interactive but not totally dynamic. You must constantly make changes to update a site. Instead, letís look deeper into the client/server world to uncover the dynamics of the active site.

WHERE DO WE GO FROM HERE?

You have learned that the Web is an ever-changing environment. Developers tend to use the latest technology to make a high-tech site, but this may not meet the needs of users. Developers need to concentrate on good Web design principles that are based on the basics of design layout theory (there are many good books on this subject) and the use of an active client/server environment (read on).

From here you should look at the following related chapters:

- Chapter 2 "Client/Server: Who Serves Whom?," to learn more about the operations within the active environment.
- Chapter 3 "The Active Platform," to learn more about the server products that make up an active site.
- Chapter 12, "How the Active Desktop Works" to understand when and where to use the tools in the client/server world.

Chapter 2

Client/Server: Who Serves Whom?

Client/server computing has come to the forefront of business development for a number of reasons. First, the maintenance of single mainframe operations has become cumbersome and expensive. Second, centralized systems are vulnerable to single-point failures, so companies have looked to fault-tolerant systems. Such systems never go down, at least from the customer's point of view; whenever a fault-tolerant system has a hardware failure, it switches immediately to backup hardware without a pause in processing. But with all that hardware and software to support, fault-tolerant systems are an expensive solution. A third problem is the difficulty of adding resources to large systems in response to changing business requirements—something that means an increase in maintenance and capital expenditures and inefficient use of company resources. For these reasons, and many others, companies have moved to the client/server environment.

CHALLENGES OF CLIENT/SERVER

Client/server is a distributed application architecture in which the desktop (client) is an extension of the host (server). The Web is a good example; a Web browser runs as a client that requests pages from a server.

The move from mainframe control to client/server architecture has created a new set of challenges. Developers find that network loads tend to be erratic as departments add systems and applications. Network engineers are sometimes left in the dark regarding what kinds of changes are being made. It is not unusual for corporate networks to become bottlenecked because one department incorrectly manages its part of the network.

Departments heads love having control over their own destinies, but from the perspective of senior management it's important that someone is minding the store. Otherwise, a lack of coordination between departments may mean that related business activities, such as billings and payables, aren't properly synchronized. A decentralized client/server solution is appealing, but some centralization is required.

Another issue is the range of hardware that developers must support. Artists and page layout specialists, for example, often use Macs, but database programmers work on PCs or a

UNIX boxes. A developer may have to figure out how to link an Excel spreadsheet with an image produced in Photoshop and use an Oracle database on the UNIX box. It's a nightmare.

How about a simpler example? Let's say Customer Service needs to create a training manual. They need artwork, documentation, help desk records, software development changes, and marketing brochures. The artwork is in TIFF format on a Macintosh, the documentation is in WordPerfect on a PC running Windows 3.1, the help desk records are in dBase on a PC set up for DOS only, the software development changes are codified in Word and Excel documents on Windows NT machines, and Marketing is using QuarkXpress on a Power Macintosh.

Once these coordination difficulties are overcome, however, companies enjoy great flexibility in data sharing along with gains in efficient use of company assets. The client/server distributed computing environment has driven the need for the network and the desktop to become transparent, as expressed in the Sun slogan, "the newtwork is the computer." Microsoft has responded with an outstanding set of networking tools that is built into Windows 95 and Windows NT.

With Windows 3.1 you had to load code and properly update your network batch files to run a TCP/IP client environment. With NT and 95, the TCP/IP, along with IPX/SPX, is transparent to the user. The operating system runs either Distributed Component Object Model (DCOM) or Remote Procedure Call (RPC) services. DCOM allows client program objects to obtain services they need from program objects on servers on the network. RPC protocol allows the system to communicate with the client and the server.

NT provides an integrated environment in the client/server model. Users need only log on once to a single server rather than to a set of servers. NT handles the relationships between primary controllers on the company network. The system administrator can run one secure administration database for each major controlled region or domain within a company. Geographically, these points of control can be down the hall or around the world. Nodes on the NT network use a conventional set of names that become transparent to the user. This arrangement even makes adding Macintoshes and their shared volumes painless.

THE BENEFITS OF CLIENT/SERVER

The client/server solution provides advantages to developers and companies, including the following:

1. Developers can deliver functionality to users quickly. Developers can deliver components, rather than whole applications, for testing and implementation. With such a release schedule, developers can modify and update new releases with minimal impact to the company. Because developers tend to use graphical interfaces when building a client/server applications, they can incorporate the most appropriate

level of functionality required for the product.
2. Client/server's rapid prototyping environment allows managers more flexibility in deploying personnel to meet changing company needs. Users and developers can work from remote locations and use a dial-up solution to update internal company systems.
3. Developers can use the client/server environment to provide companies with increased revenue, increased profit, increased market share, improved customer satisfaction, and cost savings.

Lets take a closer look at the financial aspects client/server.

Financial Benefits

Because developers can deploy client/server applications in components, development costs can be spread over multiple years. A company can implement applications and purchase hardware and software as needed. Developers may not need to upgrade licenses for database applications until the later stages of development, allowing companies to push out costs until a form of revenue or savings can be realized. Client/server tools usually include a runtime license and a developer's license, so a company need not buy a copy of the development license for every workstation. In some cases, a full development license may not be required for each developer (check the licensing agreement sent with the client/server software regarding each vendor's legal requirements). Developers can do much of the preliminary work using tools, and then launch the developer license to create the executables to run under the runtime license.

To minimize costs, it's important to monitor application development. Sometimes adding another tool can increase programmer productivity by 100%. For example, let's say a developer is running a full Microsoft shop and uses SQL Server for database development. Yet the same developer prefers having Access loaded on all of his systems so that he can take advantage of the wizards to create queries or forms when prototyping database designs. A developer can then upsize the procedures, tables, and triggers to SQL Server.

From an administrator's point of view, developers should try to minimize the number of servers and use hardware scalability where possible. Doing so will reduce overall implementation costs. In addition, developers should standardize on hardware and software releases.

With that said, developers also need to consider costs.

THE COSTS OF CLIENT/SERVER

The costs of client/server include both hardware and software resources: server hardware, server operating system, server DBMS engine, networking hardware and software, networking installation, client hardware, client operating system, client front-end tools, development of pilot programs (conversion of legacy systems), and training. Future costs include hardware and software upgrades, applications maintenance, and training for upgrades.

For example, let's calculate the cost of taking 100 users from Windows 3.1 to Windows 95.

> Windows 95 at $50 per unit plus purchasing/labor of $200 = $5,200
> Installation at 1 hour per user plus training of 8 hours per user ($50/hr)= $45,000
> Customer support at 5 hours per user ($50/hr)= $25,000
> Operating system upgrade total = $122,000
> Upgrading desktop applications to fit the new client/server environment:
>
>> Average of 3 applications per user ($100/application)= $30,000
>> Labor for installation (1 hour for 3 applications) = $5,000
>> User training (1 hour per application)= $15,000
>> Customer support (5 hours per year per user)= $25,000
>
> Total application upgrade costs = $75,000
> Total costs = $122,000 + 75,000 = $197,000

That works out to $1,99.00 per person. To some, that may seem like a lot of money. It costs money to start up or convert an existing data world to client/server. In implementing host-based applications, companies typically spend about 35% of the budget on labor (acquisition, training, and support), whereas in client/server 70% goes to labor. Client/server is labor-intensive. Developers need to be cautious when assessing moving costs.

Many of the implementation costs include both the company's networking environment and the database needs. Let's look a little deeper into these areas.

The Network

Networks can be defined by a number of methods. One approach is based on topology or physical layout; another method is based on the logical view of the network as seen by a department. In either case, a developer establishes the network to share data or applications, and the developer must consider the basic issues of data management, data synchronization, and security. Then there is the bottleneck problem. You must have a basic understanding of the network so that you can pinpoint whether the problem arises from the client or server side.

Once a client/server network is implemented, network troubleshooting can be difficult and expensive in terms of both expertise and technology. Network downtime that knocks out on-line transaction processing is more critical than problems with departmental updates of Word documents and Excel spreadsheets. In the latter situation, you can resort to using the "sneaker-net" (carrying a diskfile it over to the marketing department to update an Excel spreadsheet), but that not acceptable for a customer who lives out of town and needs an order filled.

The Active Platform is a distributed client/server computing environment. This means that the Active Platform server products need to share data and controls. The complexity of this requirement increases as a company adds clients and servers to existing legacy systems. Developers may add the latest hardware and software for application development, but many departments will be working with older systems. When you try to upgrade user software in a department, supposedly there should be no problems, but suddenly no can reach the database or get Internet access.

For these reasons, you need to learn about networking principles. You may also need to hire a network engineer who is dedicated to studying network traffic and the load implications created by each new application released.

Database Needs

Client/server database systems give users flexibility, which in turn tends to create greater demand for software products. As a result, developers require additional personnel to manage and control the data, perhaps including a database administrator. You must also institute security measures that are quite different from those needed in the early stages of development and deployment. With the success of these measures, you will find that senior management will become interested in sharing sensitive corporate data, and that will require additional development efforts.

You will also find that you must continue to add graphical user interfaces (GUIs). These interfaces improve user productivity but add development and testing time to the development cycle. Do not underestimate the time and resources necessary to implement a database GUI.

THE DYNAMIC SOLUTION

It takes two—a server and the client—to tango. But a client/server solution that is static will not meet customer expectations As things stand, HTTP is a static environment. Although you can use HTML tags to add dynamic components, such as Shockwave and embedded GIFs, this approach fails to take full advantage of Web technology to give your customers (internal and external) what they desire: dynamic data updates as changes are made to the database.

The first step in using client/server development tools to implement this feature is to understand the basic information that is tracked in a dynamic environment.

Tracking the State of a Process

To fully understand the dynamics of a Web site, you need to know what *state* it is in. No, this is not geography. Rather, a server identifies successive Web transactions initiated by a client browser by analyzing the state of the process. The Web server must distinguish between the transactions of a given client and all the other Web transactions occurring on that server at that time. By capturing the state, the Web server to maintain the history of the target set of transactions among the other Web transactions. A transaction does not have knowledge of the previous or ensuing transactions.

You can use state information to identify a particular browser and to associate certain Web requests with that browser. This means that you can keep track of a customer's preferences. For example, once customers have entered personal data on an order form, they do not want to repeat this task on subsequent forms. It is time-consuming and discourages them from returning to the page. They believe that you do not care enough about their time. They came to the Web for an interactive experience that they control not one that controls them. The same principle applies to a company network built with Web technology—an *intranet*—where worker productivity, instead of competitive pressures, is at issue.

State information lets you make a site more effective in meeting the needs of customers. For example, a customer may be asked to make choices in an opening page that will help him or her navigate through a desired area. Keeping this data in a state object can minimize the effort required for customers to get where they want to go. In addition, a company can use this data as a sales tool, guiding people to a destination that saves them money and sells more products for the company.

HTTP is a *stateless* protocol. This means that HTML does not depend on any other calls made to the Web server. According to Tim Berners-Lee, who conceptualized and defined the HTTP protocol in 1992, "HTTP is a protocol with the lightness and speed necessary for a distributed collaborative hypermedia information system. It is a generic stateless object-oriented protocol." This means that applications that use state-aware transactions need something other than HTTP.

The server must keep track of who is where and the client needs to know where a visitor is in the site. In a game, a player usually must get certain items to complete a level. In a multiplayer game, the state information would be that information that tells the server where each of the players (browser) was and what level each one had completed. Without this information, the server's only recourse would be to keep requesting that the user input the state data. This would be unacceptable.

How does the system handle state? If there is only one customer, establishing state is easy. You know that the first request received at the server is the customer's first request. The second one is the customer's second request, the third one is the customer's third request, and so on. Now suppose that a second customer comes to the site. What do you do? In a regular store, a ticket dispenser might be used. The customer with ticket #1 is known to be the first customer. The customer with ticket #2 is the second customer. In this way, the store clerks can identify the two customers.

The problem arises when we try to track their movement. Suppose the store manager asks the clerks to determine whether customer 1 has been to their departments, but forgets to tell them to mark down when the customer came through. Every store clerk can say whether customer 1 was there, but they do not know in what department order customer 1 traversed the store. That data could be important if the manager is trying to determine which part of the store to remodel to meet customer needs.

How about a simpler concern? Suppose that the manager wants to be alerted when the customer is going to the check-out area. The manager breaks the store into four departments: department A (toys), department B (clothes), department C (cosmetics), and department D (the cash register). When a customer is in an area it is marked as completed. To complete a shopping trip, customers must always pass through D, so the manager ensures that the last stop is D. For example, suppose there are four customers and they travel as follows:

```
1A—1C—1D
2C—2D
3A—3D
4A—4B—4C—4D
```

The manager need only watch the D station; when customers pass through, the manager knows they are ready to exit. When they have reached D, just as in the game example, the developer "grabs" them and assists them into the product delivery area.
You can pass this form of state information through a number of methods.

1. You can use hidden form variables. You ask the customer to enter a name on the first page; then pass that data as a hidden variable using `type=hidden` in the HTML form statement. By the way, "hidden" means that it is passed in the background but can still be viewed by someone choosing to view the source HTML. The developer must pass the hidden variable to every subsequent page; otherwise, the customer would have to reenter the data. The customer must also press a **SUBMIT** button on the form.
2. You can add a variable to the end of the URL. This technique is often used when you use a search engine. For example:

```
http://www.hotbot.com/?SW=web&SM=MC&MT=setting+up+pws+on+win95&DC=10&DE=2&RG=NA&_v=2
```

> This approach has two immediate drawbacks. First, you cannot use the `GET` command in a form document. The `GET` command limits the length of a URL that can

be sent to the server at any one time. Second, you cannot pass confidential data, because it shows up live in the browser window.

3. You can use *cookies*: small data files that are written to the hard disk of the visitor's computer. Cookies contain only text and not executable code, so they do not spread viruses. A cookie is limited to an overall size of 4K. The combined number of cookies cannot exceed 300 cookies or 1.2MB. Cookies usually have an "expiration date;" if the customer never visits the site again the cookie will eventually expire. The problem is that developers use unreasonably expiration dates.

Cookies are handled slightly differently by different browsers. If the visitor uses Netscape Navigator, the system stores the cookies in the computer's memory until the visitor quits the browser. A user can view the cookies file with a text editor. To know when cookies are being sent, the user can set the Network Preferences / Protocols in Netscape. The client uses Windows Explorer to view the following information on each cookie:

- Cookie name
- Internet address of the site that sent cookie
- Size of cookie
- Date cookie expires
- Date of last modification
- Date of last access
- Date cookie was last checked

The client cannot view the contents separately. To be notified of cookies being sent by a server, the client reads the preference in View Options Advanced.

The server does not know whether a visitor has accepted a cookie. The only problem arises when a site requires that the visitor accept the cookie to continue to move through the site. The server will continue to ask the browser for a return cookie, but if the client did not accept one there will be no return cookie and the visitor will not be permitted to progress.

The problem with cookies is twofold. First, a customer may not accept the cookie, as noted. Second, because the cookie is written to the hard disk some people are concerned about privacy and security.

NOTE

Be careful with browsers that have internal e-mail capability. Some servers can read the e-mail address of such Web browsers. This means that the IP address and the e-mail address can be obtained by the server. The recommendation is to use a separate e-mail package.

4. You can used a modified cookie approach, in which you read browser variables (including the IP address) and then enter that data into a session table. The data is

not saved to the client side but rather to the server side. Note that Internet service providers (ISPs) dynamically assign IP addresses to their customers. This means that users will not always have the same IP address on subsequent visits or if they log off in the middle of a visit and then log in again. You should use a combination of username and database functionality to verify the user.

Push vs. Pull

There is a major discussion among developers about whether client/server is best used for push or pull. *Pull* means that customers use the browser to "pull" content by asking the HTTP server for the HTML. In the case of *push*, the server does not wait for the customer's request. Instead, a customer visiting a site is asked whether he or she wants future updates. The visitor says yes. When the requested content is ready, the server delivers, or "pushes," the new pages automatically to the customer's computer.

Developers who use push compare it to the television or radio broadcast model. In the case of cable TV, a customer subscribes to certain content that is then delivered to him or her on a regular schedule. In the Web version, the delivery of those channels can be customized. Customers can order part of a program or the whole program. In radio and television, the customer must wait for the whole show, make sure that the VCR is always on taping when the television show is playing, and review the tape to obtain the desired information. A hard drive, on the other hand, is always on. The push data is sent directly to the hard drive for off-line viewing where the data can be searched and more easily used by the viewer.

A number of products, such as PointCast, are described as push technology. Actually, PointCast is a modified pull. PointCast schedules regular requests from the client to the server. Look at the updating options in PointCast; customers decide when and at what intervals to get the latest download. Another approach is to press the **Update** button. That is pull.

In a pull situation the customer's machine were always on and connected to a secure network, the server would have no problem pushing the updated data. But that is not the current state of the Web. People dial in and say, "Here I am. Send me the latest information."

If a server merely broadcasts, it is more like a pull server. Some systems, such as Global Village's NewsCatcher, broadcast using a wireless method. This means that a customer need not be connected to the Internet to get the latest information.

Push technology has the potential to help you create a dynamic site. Issues remain that need to be ironed out in how the information is regularly sent to the user.

THE FUTURE OF CLIENT/SERVER

As companies grow, their databases and systems must also grow without duplicating the problems of the mainframe world where they originated. Magnetic storage is as much as 80 times cheaper than paper, and databases are delivering data to the desktop and to decision makers. This means that many growing companies will put data somewhere in an on-line database. The ultimate goal is to transform data into useful information. A person can read about 10MB of data per day, can hear 400MB per day, and can see more than 1MB per second. What do we do with all that data? How can we efficiently retrieve a specific piece of data from all that we read, hear, and see? Database developers take each of these pieces of data and create related objects that have properties or attributes, thereby making the data available in meaningful ways.

Figure 2.1 shows an example of such a relationship. Suppose a developer owns a car; that is an *entity*, or a group of things with common characteristics. A developer is a person. That, too, is an entity. A developer has a license, and again that is an entity. These entities have *relationships* among themselves, and they also have *attributes*. An attribute of a driver's license is a birth date. An attribute of a person is a name. An attribute of a vehicle is its model. A person has a relationship with a vehicle by owning it. A person has a relationship with a driver's license in that he or she is issued one.

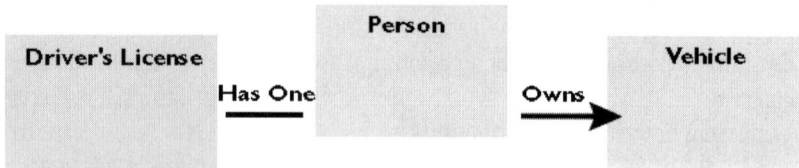

Figure 2.1 Simple entities and relationships.

This web of relationships can go on and on (please see Chapter 8 for further discussion of entities and relationships). The point here is that data has attributes and relationships and defining them adds to the complexity of client/server development.

As you develop dynamic sites using the client/server model, you must consider some basic questions.

- Who is the audience for the site? Does the customer profile change depending on the service and product offered?
- What do you want to tell the customer?
- What is the best way to give the customer the interactivity they want without a lot of graphics? Should you include audio? There are regular customer complaints of going to a site using Windows 95 or Windows NT and getting a MIDI error. The problem is that the customer does not see the error; everything happens so fast that the MIDI error window ends up on the taskbar. Then customers cannot figure out why nothing is happening in the browser window. They must relaunch the error task and then click **OK** to close out the error. Be careful about how you trap and set up error handling.

- Should you use cookies or a combination of cookies, variables, and database entries? Should the client store the information or should it be totally server-driven?
- Should you use scripting language and client-side efforts or use compiled code and server-side applications?

You must consider administrative as well as technical client/server issues while developing content for a Web site. Complexity is not decreasing but rather increasing. A good plan is essential.

Where Do We Go from Here?

The World Wide Web was built as a flexible environment to adapt to its users' needs. What is static can be made dynamic. Many developers edit their HTML pages manually; the browser uses HTTP to request the HTML files from the Web server. Then the server receives the request and sends the appropriate file to the browser. These pages are nicely formatted—but where is the interactivity? *Gateway* interfaces—programming environments that link client requests to server applications—allow for more interactivity. Examples are the Common Gateway Interface (CGI) and the Internet Service Application Programming Interface (ISAPI). As you will learn in subsequent chapters, many tools are available to assist you in developing an active, enjoyable site.

From this point, you may wish to look at the following closely related chapters:

- Chapter 8, "Active Data" where you will learn more about the data behind the scenes.

Chapter 3

The Active Platform

When we use the term active in the context of client/server computing, we're referring to an environment that uses client/server technology to adapt to user's changing needs. That could be as simple as a Web site that offers a variety of choices to every customer or as complicated as one that is programmed to recognize the specific preferences of each customer upon arrival. Microsoft's Active Platform (see Figure 3.1) is composed of client and server products designed to help developers use Web technology to make their client/server applications active. Part 2 of this book covers the server products, and Part 3 covers the client tools, which Microsoft calls the Active Desktop.

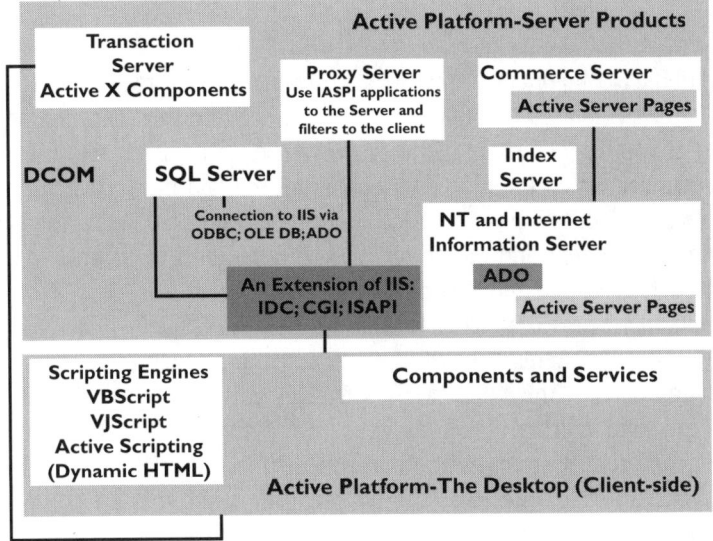

Figure 3.1 The Active Platform.

The Active Platform fully supports the client/server environment that you have been learning about. The server architecture stores data, processes client requests, administers operations, and sends the appropriate information to the client. The servers communicate among themselves via distributed components (see Appendix C for more details). You manipulate Component Object Model (COM) objects by using standard object linking and embedding (OLE) procedures and obtaining the pointer to the object's `IUnknown` interface. COM tells the system how components on a single machine can communicate. Distributed Component Object Model (DCOM) tells the system how components on a network of machines can communicate. OLE uses the COM architecture to allow objects to store data from one object (such as Microsoft Excel) in another object (such as Microsoft Word). The result is a distributed, scalable environment within the client/server world.

DISTRIBUTION OF OBJECTS

What are the problems that a distributed environment solves? Remember that developers and companies choose a client/server environment because it is less expensive than a mainframe approach. The purpose of a client/server architecture is to let you distribute functionality and applications to various servers as well as clients, thereby reducing the cost of implementation as well as reliance on a single solution. In DCOM, Microsoft takes the solution one step further by distributing objects to both servers and clients in order to run operations and services.

This approach raises some concerns regarding data management, load balancing, and network size.

- With distributed components, how does a developer keep track of and manage the data? Windows NT takes advantage of remote procedure calls to synchronize clients and servers. The client waits for the proper response before it executes code. You need to consider which products and techniques will aid in the management of the data. Microsoft's Active Server products assist in this process. Using the NT Services messaging environment and the object programming tools, you can get a handle on where the data is located and how to manage it.
- *Load balancing* means that when you add a new server or services to the distributed systems, the systems "know" how to add the new system. Using the server products described in this chapter, NT 4.0 gives you some control in sending data to and receiving data from various services. The Active Platform allows components to run on different systems without the need for the calling program to know where the components are located. You can use scripts to start components that enable application access to services and databases.
- In the client/server environment, developers must consider the size of the network. Running operations between two servers talking to 20 PCs changes radically when there are 20 servers talking to 100 PCs—and 100 Web clients are accessing the data at one time. Although the application programs do not need to know the network's physical location, the developer must decide on which system the component should run based on network bottlenecks. Transaction Server can help you in this area (see Chapter 11).

SCALABILTIY

If the distribution of objects is the major concern, why is there a need for scalability? With the burgeoning growth in the use of distributed objects, developers are determined to keep their customers happy. That means greater demand for on-line transaction processing, which in turn requires more systems or system capacity. As a result, to be successful a program must be scalable.

For individuals reading on-line newspapers or attending conferences on the Web, information processing occurs in a process as simple as e-mail. Companies are moving to the Web for cost reduction and profitability reasons. So the demand is on developers to help companies coordinate the use and distribution of the data and to put this information into databases along with implementing transaction processing servers. Here are some additional reasons:

- Items can be stored at minimal cost (see Figure 3-2).

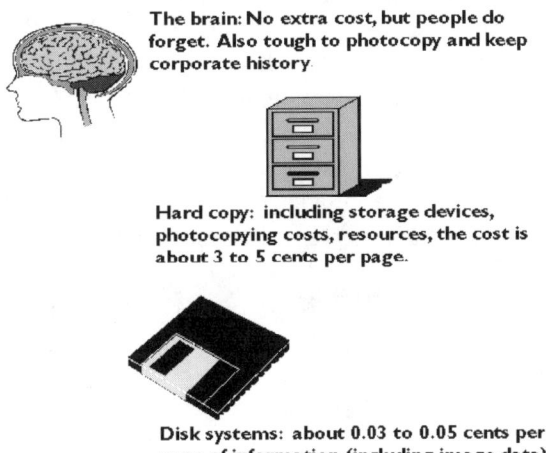

Figure 3.2 Data storage gets less expensive.

- The client/server network allows you to process information immediately or at a more convenient time.
- The distributed environment allows the data to be placed at any point in the network.
- Processes can be automated.

Chapter 3

For scalability to work the Active Platform developer must incorporate on-line databases, which require unique storage mechanisms because of the amount of data and its complex relationships. In older architectures, millions of objects were stored as simple datatypes in chunks of 100 bytes. Now you must store billions of objects in 1MB chunks, and those objects have behaviors along with rich datatypes (such as sound, images, and full documents).

In the world of the Active Platform, the devices are intelligent. Potentially, billions of clients need millions of servers. Whether clients are in a fixed location or "on the move," they are all networked to servers. As clients become faster at processing data, they will require faster servers. Servers must coordinate data, share data, communicate with other servers, and provide a decentralized model of control.

Developers must also consider the hardware processing environment. In the symmetric multiprocessor world, for example, developers have been used to building bigger and bigger systems to deal with the issue of scalability. The benefit of the single large system approach is that data is easier to manage; memory and thread management can easily be shared.

An approach being introduced by Microsoft originated at DEC. Called *clustering*, this approach (using Microsoft's Wolfpack product) eliminates the cost of a large front end as well as expensive transaction-monitoring software. This environment is built into the SQL Server and Transaction Server products at a much smaller cost than large systems running in a single-system environment. A cluster of PCs running BackOffice Server products can be built inexpensively using readily available commercial products. You can use spare modules to approximate the fault tolerance functionality. The system is expanded both in the hardware and software environment by adding modules. A cluster also allows many small on-line transaction jobs or a few large intranet client requests to run simultaneously. See Figure 3.3 for an example of the client/server cluster approach.

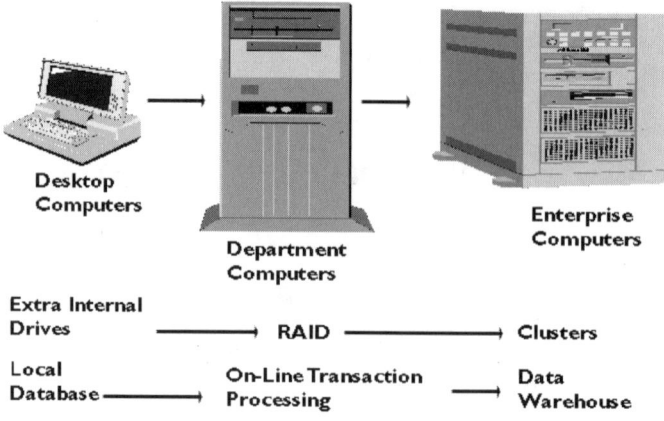

Figure 3.3 Scaling using clustering versus larger systems.

Companies need solutions that are readily available and provide off-the-shelf solutions for developers. Active Platform provides this solution through its BackOffice line of products that integrate into Windows NT 4.0 Server.

THE BIG PICTURE: PUTTING IT TOGETHER

The developer can use the various BackOffice products to implement a distributed, scalable environment. He can use SQL Server in a fail-safe mode by running RAID 5 (see Chapter 5) and the Wolfpack software. Each server, in essence, owns half the database. When one server fails, the other one takes over the shared disks using the SQL Server recovery method.

Using the Active Platform server products, you can picture your software modules as objects. For example, an object request broker (such as a transaction-processing monitor) connects the objects from the clients to the servers. You can use standard interfaces to build software plug-ins. The transaction ties the execution of a task into a single lasting, isolated unit that is processed or not processed. This all-or-nothing approach ensures data integrity in the associated databases.

The model is simple. Either a transaction is successful or it fails. There is no uncertainty. Transactions are coded as if a single user were the target user, and then Transaction Server handles the resource pooling necessary for additional users. The transaction monitor can be used to spread work among the server nodes. This distributed transaction environment allows for large databases. Transaction Server lets you build ActiveX objects on the desktop, or you can have the client download the appropriate control from the Web. The ActiveX object model becomes your structuring mechanism for development. The Commerce and Transaction Server products can be implemented to manage thread pools and to provide simple operator interfaces to shopping centers. They also let you administer the Active Platform by using GUI tools.

Active Server is an extension of Internet Information Server (IIS) 3.0, which can recognize and process Active Server Pages (ASP). ASP provides an application development environment in which a developer uses HTML, scripts (VBScript and JavaScript), and ActiveX components without the need for a compiler. The Active Server tools let you greatly expand the realm of corporate databases. You can use such varied tools as ASP, IDC/HTX, ISAPI, and Visual Basic to input and gather data. Developers who have varied programming experience can be a part of the active development team.

Another useful tool is Index Server, a full-text indexing and search engine that is integrated into Microsoft Internet Information Server. You can customize search windows to allow any Web browser to search documents for key words, phrases, or properties (such as file size). Index Server is integrated with the NT security environment. This means that if the Web pages are stored on an NT File System (NTFS) volume, the system abides by the security restrictions of the access control list (ACL), a benefit over other Web search tools that give users a "hit" on documents that they cannot view. What a frustration! With Index Server, you can customize the results to provide document abstracts as well as log all queries for review.

Proxy Server rounds out the list of Active Platform Server products by integrating tightly with Windows NT Server user authentication to ensure Web site security. Proxy Server lets you restrict user access by name or group. It uses caching to improve system response time for internal users as well as to attempt to reduce network traffic. Caching also tells you which sites are frequently visited by company users, information that can be used in analyzing company and departmental needs for external and internal data. Proxy Server is easily integrated with standard network protocols using both the Web proxy and Winsock proxy services. You can even set specific hours and days of the week for Internet access.

The Active Platform products change the way companies look at on-line transaction processing. Its object-oriented, secure programming interface provides a new programming paradigm. Databases and transactions can be componentized. Security and searching can be compartmentalized. All this ensures that customers get the latest data in a format that is essential to their business and personal needs.

WHERE TO GO FROM HERE

You may wish to look at the following related chapters:

- Chapter 8, "Active Data," where you can learn more about the place of SQL Server.
- Chapter 11, "Active Middleware Solution," will help you understand how to handle ever-increasing numbers of transactions.
- Chapter 12, "How the Active Desktop Works," introduces you to the client-side tools used to develop the sites implemented on the Active Platform.

Chapter 4

The Dynamic Server Environment: The Players

The Active Server environment is based on the Windows NT operating system. The products that make up the server side of the Active Platform were introduced in previous chapters. In this chapter, you'll get a better understanding of the servers and their tools. The Active Platform products include many of the BackOffice products that work within the IIS framework. IIS 3.0 provides the Active Server programming environment along with an Open Database Connectivity (ODBC) link to SQL Server, an extension of the operating system with Microsoft Transaction Server acting as the system-level service. Proxy Server and Index Server fit hand-in-glove with IIS (see Figure 4.1).

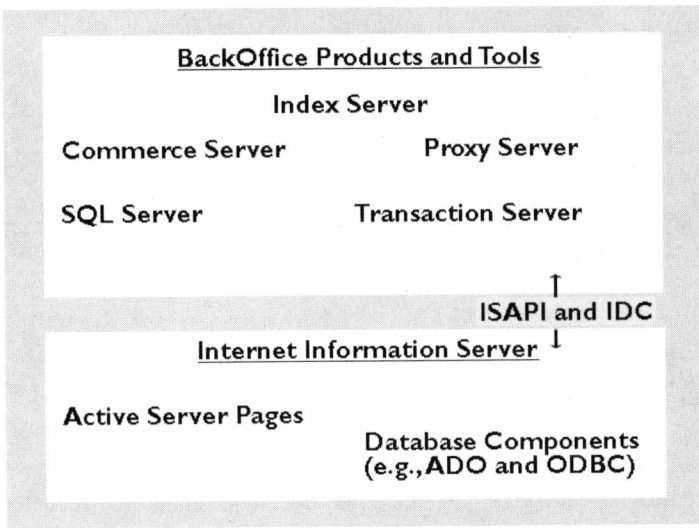

Figure 4.1 The Active Server products in action.

EXTENDING THE PLATFORM

The Active Platform operates as an extension to IIS. There are a number of benefits to using IIS as an extended platform. First, this development environment gives you a number of options. Second, extending IIS provides support for industry standards. Third, through IIS Microsoft has created an architecture that lets you leverage existing Win32 and OLE resource investments.

Internet Information Server can be extended using server tools (such as ASP, Internet Database Connector (IDC), CGI, and ISAPI) as well as through the server products themselves (such as BackOffice), as shown in Figure 4.2.

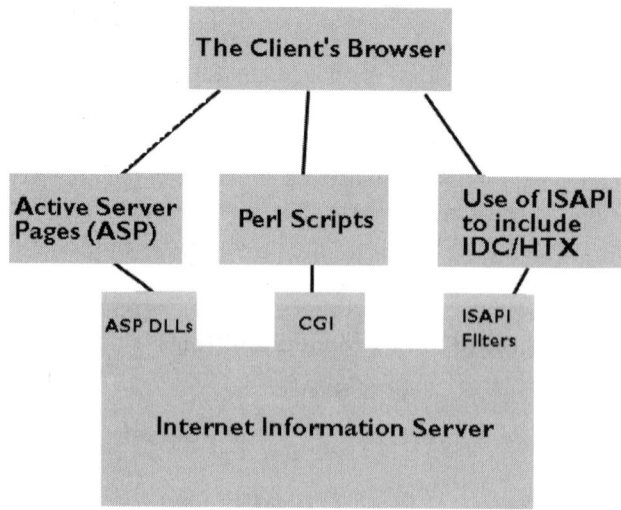

Figure 4.2 Server extensions and tools.

Lets look at some of the components of IIS.

Components of IIS

The Internet Database Connector lets you access any ODBC data source (such as SQL Server). You can produce high-performance applications that are run in-process and allow for ODBC connection pooling. IDC is a programming-free authoring environment that supports rich static and dynamic queries. This means that a developer can use IDC/HTX without having a formal programming experience. The queries provide update access to a database and can be run as stored procedures. See Chapter 6 for examples.

The Internet Service Application Programming Interface is a dynamic link library (DLL) that runs as an in-process CGI. It supplements CGI but does not replace it. The beauty of the ISAPI DLL is that it does not require process creation, as does CGI. ISAPI is a single-process thread-pooling DLL that the server calls.

ISAPIs are broken into two categories: applications and filters. ISAPI applications extend the functionality of the server. They are in-process DLLs that provide high performance. They can cooperate as plug-ins and maintain the state of their process. Multiple ISAPI DLLs can be loaded and called simultaneously.

ISAPI filters monitor the activity and behavior of the server. They can modify input and output as well as participate in intermediate actions.

CGI scripts give you full access to all the HTTP variables. These variables include the following:

HTTP headers	Remote_Host
Auth_Type	Remote_User
Content_Length	Request Method
Gateway_Interface	Script_Name
Long_User	Server_Name
Path_Info	Server_Port
Path_Translated	Server_Port_Secure
Query_String	Server_Protocol
Remote_Addr	Server_Software
URL	

(For an in-depth discussion of CGI, please see Chapter 6.)

IIS fully supports CGI applications. They are scripts based on STDIN and STDOUT and typically written in Perl. A CGI application runs as a process and can run in the context of the client or the server.

The jewel of this group, however, is ASP.

Active Server Pages

Active Server Pages are files with the **.asp** extension. They use HTML content along with script commands. ASP includes components that extend the reach of the scripts by automating server activities. ASP provides for Web-based applications with a group of **.asp** files defined in IIS by virtual directories (see Figure 4.3).

36 Chapter 4

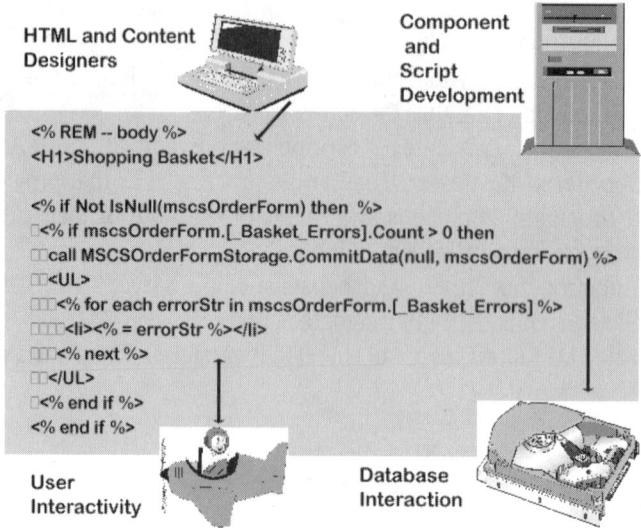

Figure 4.3 Active Server Pages in action.

ASP has a number of key benefits.

- An HTML developer can have an ASP site up and running in a matter of hours.
- The programming environment is open. IIS 3.0 runs an ActiveX scripting engine that understands VBScript and JavaScript. You can write components in Visual Basic, Java, or C++ to further extend the server.
- The environment is compiler-free. This means that you can update data, change content, and implement components without disrupting current users.
- With all these scripting and programming tools, ASP is usable with all types of browsers.

Active Server itself is made up of objects that allow you to create Web applications:

- ASP files that are HTML extensions. You can take any HTML page and add the **.asp** extension.
- Intrinsic objects. These objects provide a simple programming environment where you can track both application and session activity of the site.
- ActiveX Server components. These objects can be written in Java, C++, or Visual Basic and can be used in standard Windows application environments.
- Base components. Microsoft provides base components that allow you to install a dynamic Web site on the first day of implementation.

Within Active Server, the application flows from the client to the server, much as described in Chapter 1 (see Figure 4.4).

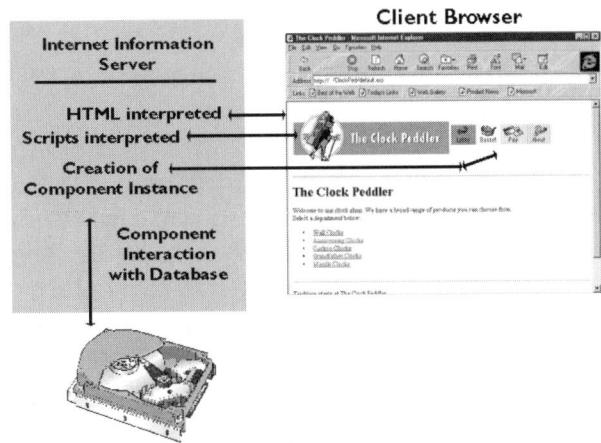

Figure 4.4 ASP flow.

Active Server, lying within IIS, receives the **.asp** request and sends the various parts to the scripting engine. The scripting engine interprets the scripts, and components are processed as delivered. Active Server uses automation interfaces in much the same way that Excel and Word use them (OLE automation). In addition, Active Data Objects (ADO) provide the automation interfaces that you can use to query ODBC databases.

With ASP, you can use inline script delimiters. The characters `<% %>` are used to delimit inline script. These symbols are used as a shorthand for outputting single expressions. For example, the following script checks the current time:

```
<% h=Hour(Now) if h<12 then %>
Good morning
<% else%>
Good afternoon
<% endif%>
The time is now <%Now%>
```

If it is before noon, the system displays **Good Morning**; after noon, it displays **Good Afternoon**. The system then prints the current time.

The default inline script language is VBScript, but any ActiveX scripting language is supported. The inline script language may be set per page using `<%@Language=Whatever%>` as the first directive. The following line notes that the code to follow is to be interpreted as JavaScript.

```
<%@Language=JScript%>
```

ASP also uses block script delimiters. The `<script>` tag can be used with the attribute `RUNAT=SERVER`, which allows scripting languages to be mixed within a page. It is commonly used to define subroutines and to do more program-oriented scripting. For example:

```
<Script Language=JScript RUNAT=Server>
functon PrintDate()
{x=ne Date ()
Response.Write(x.toString())}
</Script>
```

As previously noted, ASP has built-in objects, and they are available to the scripts. The objects include Request, Response, Server, Session, and Application. For example, the Request object gives you easy access to information from the browser. The Response object creates the output page, and the Server object creates component instances. The Session object includes cookies that permit you to maintain state information about individual clients. The Application object stores variables for a current application, and these values are global.

You can also create and use ActiveX Server components. The components, built on OLE automation, provide such capabilities as database access and the display of advertising banners.

Using ASP, content developers can create dynamic content for a site using ASP and ActiveX components (please see Chapter 5 for an in-depth discussion of ASP).

SAFETY FIRST

You can extend the safety of the Active Platform through the use of Microsoft Proxy Server. Proxy Server, as noted in Chapter 3, is a Windows NT server application that securely links a private network to the Internet. It provides for popular Internet protocols to include WWW, FTP, and Gopher.

Proxy Sever not only protects the internal network but also restricts outbound access by users, protocols, and domains. The server supports most Internet protocols and Windows socket applications. It can handle Novell's IPX/SPX as well as standard TCP/IP. It provides for Internet protocol (IP) address aggregation and Internet resource caching. It does all this to ensure a scalable, high-performance, secure environment.

The components include Web proxy and Winsock proxy (WSP). The Web proxy allows for the WWW service along with caching of often-visited sites; this service supports standard browsers. The Winsock proxy handles IPX/SPX and TCP/IP traffic issues.

The useful part about the services for developers is that they can create ISAPI filter add-ons. The filters will monitor and modify all client (or proxy) requests and responses. The Web proxy and Winsock proxy allow for logging through an ODBC database.

The Web proxy runs as an ISAPI DLL (**w3proxy.dll**). It operates as an ISAPI filter and ISAPI application. As a filter, it directs proxy requests for ISAPI applications and ignores published requests from clients. As an application, it handles user authentication, domain filter checking, and the delivery and checking of cache information (see Figure 4.5).

The Dynamic Server Environment: The Players 39

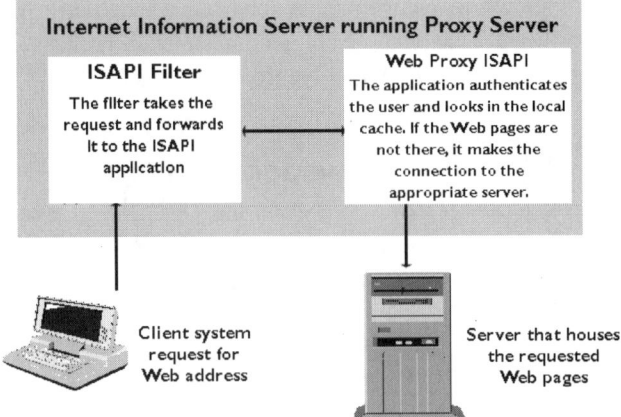

Figure 4.5 The operation of **w3proxy.dll**.

The Winsock proxy application runs on one network and communicates with a TCP/IP application on another network (see Figure 4.6).

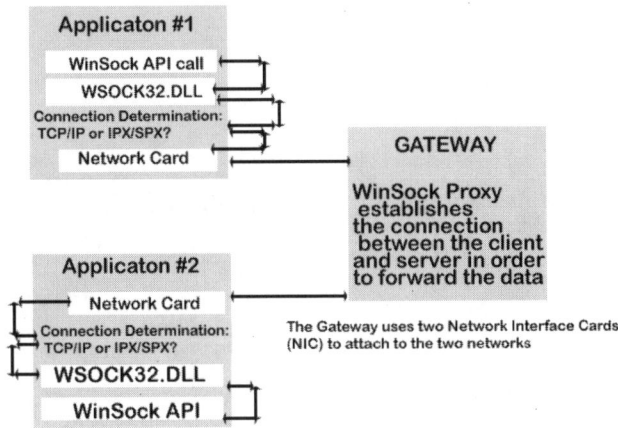

Figure 4.6 Windows sockets.

You use two network interface cards (NICs) to connect the networks. The Winsock proxy runs transparently and makes a remote call to the Winsock API. The proxy provides security and control for both outbound and inbound connections.

The Winsock proxy components include the WSP service that runs on the gateway and the WSP DLL that runs on the client. The service establishes virtual connections between client and server. It forwards data once the connection is established. The DLL intercepts

Chapter 4

Winsock API calls, as shown in Figure 4.6. It determines whether a request needs to be remoted and notifies the WSP service of connection or DNS requests. Figure 4.7 shows the TCP/IP view of the Winsock proxy and Figure 4.8 shows the Novell view.

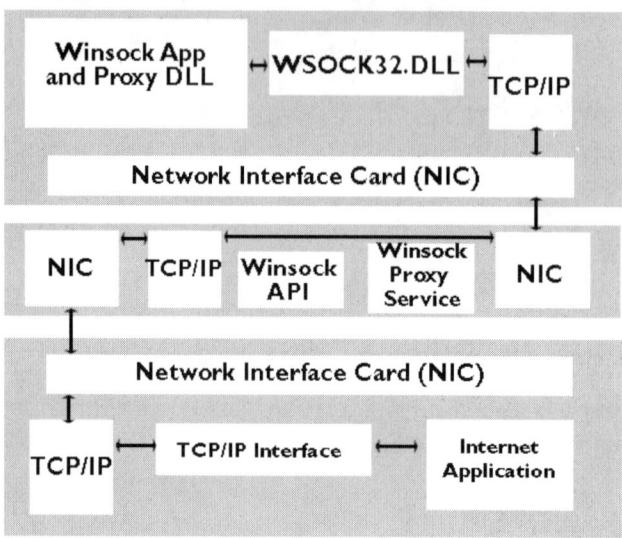

Figure 4.7 WSP architecture as seen by TCP/IP.

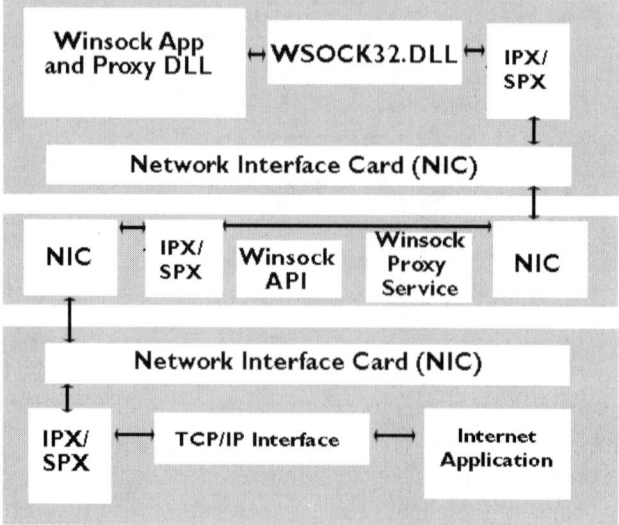

Figure 4.8 WSP architecture as seen by IPX/SPX.

The Web proxy server is easy to use. It provides secure access using IPX/SPX or TCP/IP. The caching capability means that the system need go only once to the Web to get the data.

Hardware Considerations

As noted in Chapter 3, because you're working in a dynamic environment the Web server must be scalable. The hardware, the operating system, and the Web server software must scale together.

Hardware systems can be designed to support multiple processors, accommodate several gigabytes of RAM, and provide expandable disk I/O and network subsystems.

Symmetric Multiprocessing

In symmetric multiprocessing (SMP), a server balances its load using multiple processors. These processors share memory.

Processor affinity is the method by which an operating system optimizes use of the cache. NT incorporates processor affinity by running a thread on the same CPU as a previous run in order to maximize its chance of a cache hit.

The Operating System

NT places threads in queues and assigns each queue a priority level. When a CPU becomes available, NT locates the queue with the highest priority and executes the threads inside it sequentially from top to bottom. To prevent threads from monopolizing the CPU's attention, NT determines how many milliseconds of execution remain for each thread. By splitting a single-thread program into multiple concurrent threads, NT can boost performance and provide you with faster response times.

IIS, the Web server that Active Server is based on, is integrated into NT. In addition, IIS has tools that allow you to minimize system impact. For example, you can move CGI scripts to ISAPI and thereby benefit from ISAPI's lower number of creation and termination processes. This frees memory usage and processing power.

In a dynamic environment, this means that items are changing all the time based on server input. You will need to make decisions about where you want the information to sit. Can you scale up the Web server to run all the needed database and server software, or do you need to distribute the data, the applications, and the tools to different servers? Do you add memory, processors, hard drives? Are you running RAID?

Redundant Array of Inexpensive or Independent Disks

Redundant Array of Inexpensive or Independent Disks (RAID) is used to increase the availability of data. RAID comes in a number of versions, each one designated by a number.

Chapter 4

0: data striping
1: mirroring
3: byte striping with dedicated parity
4: block striping with dedicated parity
5: block striping with distributed parity

Let's look at the most common forms: RAID 0, 1, and 5.

RAID 0, known as *data striping*, stores data across multiple disks. This method is very fast for data acquisition, but there is no data safety—no fault tolerance.

In RAID 1, or *disk mirroring*, one set of disks is mirrored with a set of similar sized disks. The operating system can use only the capacity of one set of disks. RAID 1 is very fast and provides the maximum fault tolerance. Unfortunately, the cost to implement RAID 1 is high.

RAID 5 is the most popular form of fault tolerance. It is designed so that the data and a parity value are striped over at least three disks. Both data and parity are placed on all three disks; if one disk fails, the system will remain operational. (RAID level 4 uses one drive for parity and the other drives for data.)

RAID 5 has excellent read performance but poor write performance, so it is useful for file and print server environment, where the files are small. If the drive fails, read and write performance are significantly reduced, because the system must read data from all the drives in order to compute the correct value of the requested data.

Implementing RAID 5 systems tends to cost less than implementing RAID 1 systems when the target drives are larger than 4GB.

Figure 4.9 shows the three most popular forms of RAID.

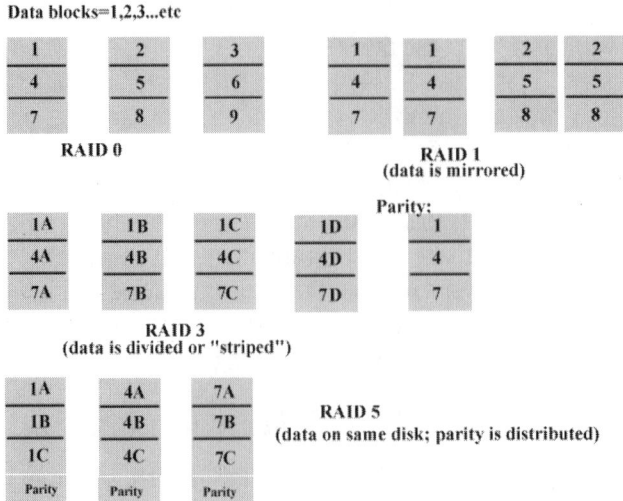

Figure 4.9 RAID.

Network Connections

Another important hardware issue is the use of Category 5 (Cat-5) cable for high-bandwidth applications. Cat-5 is a class of connector and cable that can support 100 Mbit Ethernet (100BaseT). Have you segmented the network so that only 25 people share the same "pipe" rather than all 100 employees? If they are hooked to the Internet, do they need higher bandwidth?

WHERE DO WE GO FROM HERE?

Active Server products use DCOM technology along with various server products that extend the capability of Internet Information Server.

Active Server products complement Active Desktop and ActiveX components to provide a platform for building distributed applications. Active Server products include a scripting capability for developers who like to write VBScript, JavaScript, Perl, or other scripts. These scripts are valid as long as they execute as a client or server application.

Active Server extends IIS 3.0 beyond ASP. With ASP files you can create HTML documents that contain embedded scripts, ActiveX components, and Java applets. IIS supports Internet Database Connector for ODBC access to SQL data, ISAPI, and CGI scripts. Active Server supplements IDC with ADO, which allows you to use simple Visual Basic commands to access and manipulate databases.

See also the following related chapters:

- Chapter 5, "Active Server Pages," where you will get a good overview of using Active Server Pages.
- Chapter 6, "Tools for Active Platform Servers," where you will learn more about the benefits of using CGI, IDC, and ISAPI.
- Chapter 7, "Using Proxy Server," provides you with in-depth information about how to set up a secure site.

Chapter 5

Active Server Pages

A number of different books and magazine articles have been written about Active Server Pages (ASP), but this chapter does not assume that you have read them. This chapter will be an overview of ASP. For more detailed information, please see the MIS:Press book *Active Server Pages Developerís Handbook*.

WHAT IS ASP?

Active Server Pages is a new programming environment that allows developers to create dynamic Web applications. It is based on a serverís ability to process *scripts*. The Web server does the work of generating the HTML pages to the browser.

ASP provides a browser-neutral approach to application design. Because all the application logic to generate dynamic content can be executed on the server, developers need not worry about which browser is used to view the site. Browsers "see" the results of an **.asp** file (a special HTML document with ASP code) as a normal HTML page.

As a user requests the **.asp** page, the server sends the file to the Web server and calls ASP. The server reads the requested file, passes HTML back to the browser, and runs the script that is sent by the page (see Figure 5.1).

Figure 5.1 ASP in action: The Ad Rotator component.

Chapter 5

ASP is designed to provide dynamic content. This could mean that customers get one page when they first visit a site and a different page when they return. You can use Visual Basic, Java or Visual C++ to create powerful server-side components and use VBScript or JavaScript to create client tools. ActiveX components can be created in virtually any language, including Java, Visual Basic, C++, and Delphi.

Active Server can be implemented with either Microsoft's Internet Server products (such as IIS and Personal Web Server) or O'Reilly's WebSite.

In Figure 5.1, a user comes to a site served by IIS 3.0 (with Active Server installed). The client browser requests the appropriate **.asp** page. IIS receives the request, notes that it is an **.asp** page, and sends that call to the ASP component. The ASP component interprets the page, including scripts, and sends the result to the client browser. This is a classic client/server relationship.

ASP applications are a set of HTML and ASP files that work together to perform a certain task. Each ASP application requires a virtual root in the Web server where the files are stored. All ASP pages must end in the file extension **.asp**; this lets the Web server know that the page contains ASP logic.

Active Server allows you to add programming logic to your Web pages. This logic is surrounded by special tags (and) and is interpreted by the Web server when you request a page.

ASP also provides extensive database connectivity. It connects to a database via an OLE-DB hook into ODBC. ASP pools the database connections for better performance and provides access to database cursors. Additionally, it provides for the execution of SQL statements and stored procedures. (When you're using ODBC, the availability of these features depends on the implementation of your ODBC driver.)

ASP enables server-side scripts to call an external library and provides interfaces to C++, Visual Basic, and Java. These interfaces enable access to user-session maintenance objects.

In ASP, you must create a virtual directory for the application in the Web server; then the ASP files must be moved into the appropriate directory. Microsoft ASP has Visual InterDev, a powerful development environment for developing ASP applications. It includes wizards for database access and site management tools.

ASP consists of text, HTML tags, and script commands. Special tags must be used to enclose server-side code in ASP. Because ASP supports multiple scripting languages, server-side tags take two forms: the <% %> tags and the <SCRIPT></SCRIPT> tags. The <% %> tag uses the default language (this can be set for the whole server or a whole page), whereas the <SCRIPT></SCRIPT> tag allows you to specify which language the script is written in. (ASP currently supports JavaScript and VBScript.) Here is a sample **.asp** file from the ASP files that come with IIS3.0:

```
<HTML>
<HEAD><TITLE>Creating Hello World with Incremental Text Size
Increase</TITLE></HEAD>
<BODY BGCOLOR=#FFFFFF>
```

```
<% for i = 3 To 7 %>
        <FONT SIZE=<% = i%>>Hello World</FONT><BR>
<% Next %>
<BR>
<BR>
<!--#include virtual="/ASPSamp/Samples/srcform.inc"-->
</BODY>
</HTML>
```

Guess what? This code prints "Hello World" (see Figure 5.2).

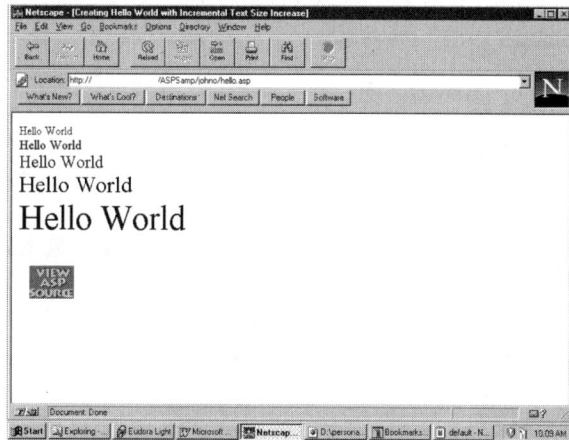

Figure 5.2 Hello World.

Now let's look at a more detailed approach with components and variables. The following example shows HTML with inline VBScript:

```
<HTML>
<HEAD>
<TITLE>Sample Web Page</TITLE>
</HEAD>
<BODY>
<P>
Hello <%= Request.ServerVariables("REMOTE_USER") %>
The time here is <%= now %>
Your browser is <% = Request.ServerVariables("http_user_agent") %>
</BODY></HTML>
```

Active Server Pages makes it easy for HTML authors to "activate" their Web pages on the server. Customized pages and simple applications can be developed immediately. Instead of writing complicated Common Gateway Interface (CGI) programs in languages such as Perl and C to generate personalized content for each user, a Web developer can use ASP to do all the work. In the following simple example, VBScript is used to display both the current time and the type of browser the client is using.

```
<HTML>
<head>
<title>Time</title>
</head>
<body>
<p>
The time is <%=now%><p>
<% Set bc = Server.CreateObject("MSWC.BrowserType") %>

Browser   <%= bc.browser   %>   <p>
Version   <%= bc.version   %>   <p>

</body>
</html>
```

See Figure 5.3 for the screen output.

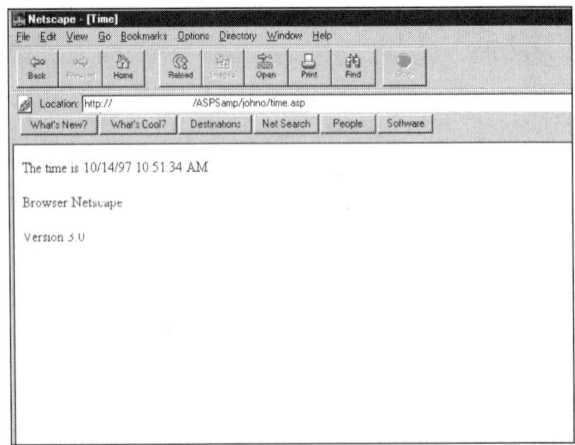

Figure 5.3 Time and browser type returned to the client.

An ASP script can assign values to variables, send an instruction to the server, or use a sequence of commands known as a *procedure*.

ASP lets you use a variety of scripting languages, because scripts can be processed on the server side as opposed to the client side. In fact, you can use several scripting languages within a single **.asp** file by identifying the script language in a simple tag at the beginning of the script sequence.

For example, the following script indicates that the upcoming script sequences are to be processed by Active Server Pages as JavaScript code and VBScript code, respectively:

```
<HTML>
<SCRIPT LANGUAGE=JScript RUNAT=Server>
<JScript code here>
</SCRIPT>
<SCRIPT LANGUAGE=VBScript RUNAT=Server>
<VBScript code here>
</SCRIPT>
</HTML>
```

One of the hidden benefits of ASP is that it allows you focus on dealing with the business logic and not the appearance or the output. Web page designers can feel free to use HTML or tools (such as FrontPage) to create and modify pages without being too concerned about where the data comes from. The scripting language brings the two processes—development and design—together. You can use scripting and components to separate the programming that accesses data in databases and applications from the design and other content of a Web page.

Before we go any further, let's look at some definitions. Please see Appendix C for a full discussion of objects and components in the Microsoft world.

Basic Definitions

As you start to use Active Server, a number of terms are thrown around. Let's define a few of the more important terms.

Component Object Model (COM) is considered by developers to be the cornerstone of Microsoft's document and component architectures. COM lets objects (components) talk to one another. OLE documents, OCX, and ActiveX controls are based on COM. COM is somewhat similar to CORBA's Object Request Broker (ORB) except for one piece of hardware.

Distributed Component Object Model (DCOM), formerly known as Network OLE, is Microsoft's technology for distributed objects. It competes with CORBA, another distributed object standard.

ActiveX is an independent program that works with the Windows environment. It, too, is based on COM. ActiveX objects can be on separate machines or used on a network (such as the Internet). ActiveX objects were designed to take advantage of the low-overhead network environment provided by the Internet. ActiveX objects are called ActiveX *controls* and ActiveX *components*. They can be as simple as a button on an application screen or as complicated as a complete application. ActiveX objects can be written in Visual C++, Visual Basic, and other languages. A developer could, for example, create an ActiveX object to grab data from a database and insert that data into a document.

Object linking and embedding (OLE) is an object-oriented document technology based on COM. OLE allows you to *embed* such items as a spreadsheet or an image in a document. The document is known as the OLE *container* (or client application), because it contains the object(s). The application that created the object is called the OLE *server*. If a user double-clicks the spreadsheet, the application launches so that the user can edit the spreadsheet. The object can be *linked* instead of being embedded. This means that the OLE container does not physically hold the object. Instead, it points to the object.

Automation is the name for the component software; automation is equivalent to ActiveX automation. *Automation client* and *ActiveX client* are equivalent terms and used to be called *OLE Automation*. An automation controller and the ActiveX client are the same. An automation server is the same as the ActiveX object.

An OLE container is the OLE client application. This is the item that holds the linked or embedded objects. It is also known as the ActiveX client.

With those basic definitions in place, let's look at the objects that make up ASP.

ASP Objects

Active Server Pages includes a number of built-in server objects and application-building objects. These objects free developers from the work of writing code to get client information, get the state of an application, or create a response.

As noted in Chapter 4, these objects include the following:

- `Request`, which provides access to information passed into the script with the HTTP request. This includes information from cookies, forms, URL queries, and HTTP headers.
- `Response`, which is used to build output to the client, including setting cookies, page expiration, and full control of the HTTP output stream.
- `Application`, which is used for handling state management.
- `Server`, which is used to allow scripts to create instances of ActiveX components.
- `Session`, which is used to handle user sessions.

The `Request` Object

The `Request` object is used to get information from the user that is passed along when the client's browser makes an HTTP request. This includes all `GET` and `POST` form data as well as cookies and HTTP header information. Various properties are built into this object.

- `ClientCertificate`. Retrieves the certification fields from the Web browser.
- `QueryString`. Retrieves form text such as a name or item of interest. Use the `QueryString` method of the `Request` object to retrieve the query string sent by a `GET` method. For example, to retrieve the address field from a query string, use

    `Request.QueryString("address")`

- `Form`. Retrieves data from an HTML form. Use the `Form` property to retrieve form data from the `Request` object sent by the `POST` method.

- `Cookies`. Retrieves the value of an application-defined cookie.
- `ServerVariables`. Retrieves HTTP information such as the server name or server software.

The Response Object

The `Response` object, which is used to send information to the user, is the counterpart of the `Request` object. The `Response` object is used to compose the data that is sent back to the browser. Developers tend to use the `Write` method as the most common function, but this object lets the developer also send cookies to the client for storage.

Its properties include the following:

- `Buffer`. When you set this property to `true`, the server will not send a response until all the server scripts on the current page have been processed. (The exception is if the developer sends a `Flush` or `End` method shown later.) If it is `false`, the server sends responses to the client as they are available.
- `ContentType`. Used to set the type of content (text/HTML, Word, and so on).
- `Expires`. Sets the expiration time for cached browser pages. The value is expressed in minutes.
- `ExpiresAbsolute`. Allows you to set the expiration date (for cached browser pages) to an absolute date and time.
- `Status`. Returns the status of the page to the client. For example, to return the status of a page not found you would use the following:

```
<% Response.Status = "404 Not Found" %>
```

The `Response` object also support some methods such as:

- `AddHeader`. Adds a header with a specified value.
- `AppendToLog`. Adds a string of data to the log file.
- `BinaryWrite`. Writes binary data.
- `Clear`. Clears the buffered HTML output.
- `End`. Stops script processing.
- `Flush`. Looks to the buffer and dumps all the data.
- `Redirect`. Sends the client to a different URL.
- `Write`. Writes a string back to the client. For example:

```
Response.write("its lunchtime")
```

The Application Object

The Application object stores variables specific to the current Web application. You can create new properties in the Application object as shown here in setting a page count:

```
Application("page_count") = 10
```

It holds its information as long as the server is running

The Server Object

The Server object supports one property: ScriptTimeout. This property allows you to set the value for the time that the script processing will time-out. It also includes the following methods:

- CreateObject. Creates an object.
- HTMLEncode. Encodes a string in HTML.
- MapPath. Maps the current virtual path to a physical directory structure.
- URLEncode. Applies URL encoding to a specified string.

The Server object has as its scope the whole server and not just an application. Here is an example of setting the variable papers_online:

```
Server("papers_online") = 200
```

The Session Object

The Session object provides the ability to save data for each user session. To set a property in the Session object, pass the Session object the property name. The following example shows the property client_name being set in the Session object:

```
Session("client_name") = "Barnaby"
```

The variables used with the Session object operate globally during the session.

The Session object supports one method: Abandon. This method stops the current Web server session, destroying any objects. The two properties for this object are as follows:

- SessionID. Contains the identifier for the current session.
- Timeout. Specifies a time-out value for the session.

ASP Object Samples

Following are code samples that use some of the items denoted earlier:

```
<HTML>
<HEAD>
<TITLE>Sample Web Page</TITLE>
```

Active Server Pages 53

```
</HEAD>
<BODY>
<P>
Hello <%= Request.ServerVariables("REMOTE_USER") %>
The time here is <%= now %>
Your browser is <% = Request.ServerVariables("http_user_agent") %>
</BODY></HTML>
```

The next example includes some Java and Visual Basic scripting to collect some user data. In this customer sign-in application, the customer enters data on the customer **.HTML** page. This information is sent to the **customer.asp** page through a POST method.

customer.html

```
<HTML>
<head>
<title> Customer Sign-In </title>
</head>

<body>

Please enter your name and address:

<form method="POST" action="customer.asp">

First Name:
<input type="text" name="firstname" maxlength="30"> <br>
Last Name:
<input type="text" name="lastname" maxlength="30"> <br>
Address:
<input type="text" name="address" maxlength="30"> <br>
City:
<input type="text" name="city" maxlength="40"> <br>
State:
<input type="text" name="state" size=2 maxlength="2"> <br>
Zip:
<input type="text" name="zip" size=5 maxlength="5"> <br>
Area code:
  <input type="text" name="area" size=3 maxlength="3"><br>
Phone:
  <input type="text" name="phone" size=8maxlength="8"><br>
Customer  Name:
<input type="text" name="username" maxlength="10"> <br>
Password:
<input type="password" name="password" maxlength="10"> <br>
<input type="submit">

</form>
```

Chapter 5

```
</body>
</HTML>
```

customer.asp

```asp
<% Response.Buffer = True %>

<HTML>
<head>
<title> Customer Registration </title>
</head>
<body>

<%
```
' The following code checks for all the information. If a customer does not provide all of the
'information, then errors are returned from the error dimensional array. It is sent back via the
'Response.write object

```vbscript
dim error
error = ""

If Request.Form("firstname") = "" Then
   error = error & "Missing First Name<br>"
End If
If Request.Form("lastname") = "" Then
   error = error & "Missing Last Name<br>"
End If
If Request.Form("address") = "" Then
   error = error & "Missing Address<br>"
End If
If Request.Form("city") = "" Then
   error = error & "Missing City<br>"
End If
if Request.Form("state") = "" Then
   error = error & "Missing State<br>"
end if
If request.form("zip") = "" Then
   error = error & "Missing Zip Code<br>"
ElseIf Not validate_zip(Request.Form("zip")) Then
   error = error & "Invalid Zip Code<br>"
End If
If Request.Form("area") = "" Then
   error = error & "Missing Area Code<br>"
End If
If Request.Form("phone") = "" Then
```

```
        error = error & "Missing Phone Number<br>"
      End If
      If request.form("username") = "" Then
        error = error & "Missing Customer Name<br>"
      end if
      If Request.Form("password") = "" Then
        error = error & "Missing Password<br>"
      End If

      If error <> "" Then
        Response.Write("<strong>The following errors were found:
        </strong><br>")
        Response.Write(error)
      Else
        Session("firstname") = Request.Form("firstname")
        Response.Redirect "mainmenu.asp"
      End if

      %>
      </body>
      </HTML>
```

Here is the Java script to validate the ZIP code (`validate_zip`):

```
      common.js
      <SCRIPT LANGUAGE=JScript RUNAT=Server>

      // validate the ZIP code
      function validate_zip(zip) {
        zip = zip + "";
        if (zip.length == 5 && isNumber(zip)) {
          return true;
        }
        else {
          return false;
        }
      }

      </SCRIPT>
```

Here is a sample output page:

```
      entry.asp
      <HTML>
      <head>
      <title> Entry Menu </title>
      </head>
```

```
            <body>

            <center>
            Welcome <% Response.Write(Session("firstname")) %> <br>
            <p>
            Please select from the following menu options
<li><ahref="store1.htm">Clothing Store</a>
<li><ahref="store2.htm">Outdoor gear Store</a
 <li><ahref="store3.htm">Toy Store</a
            </center>

            </body>
            </HTML>
```

Now that you know how to use objects to send and receive data, let's look at the component architecture of ASP.

COMPONENTS

Components are objects that run in the same process as IIS 3.0. They communicate with each other and with the server using COM. Components can talk to each other in a consistent way, using the same interfaces. They are the same thing as ASP objects but are not included as part of the specification.

ASP comes with a number of built-in components. Following is a sample of what is included.

Data Access Component

Active Data Objects (ADO) give you connectivity to compliant databases through OLE-DB. ADO lets you link and manipulate the data. The ADO component allows pages to be dynamically updated from ODBC-compliant databases.

Content Linking Component

The Content Linking component manipulates a list of Web addresses. This means that you can set up your Web site like a book, with chapters as well as pages within chapters. You can maintain a table of interrelated pages that can be updated as pages are changed. The benefit is that you need not change the navigation on the pages.

File System Component

Some scripting languages do not allow for file access. The File System component helps developers by not requiring them to write separate code to open and close files.

Browser Capabilities Component

This component is used to determine the capabilities of browsers, thereby allowing you to customize a response based on the type of browser. For example, a developer site might have one response for Internet Explorer and another one for Netscape.

Here is an example provided with the Adventure Works sample provided by Microsoft. It supports an ActiveX browser (one that sends a control) and a non-ActiveX browser (one that runs the Ad component).

```
<%
  Set OBJbrowser = Server.CreateObject("MSWC.BrowserType")
  If OBJbrowser.ActiveXControls = TRUE Then
%>
  <OBJECT
CODEBASE="/AdvWorks/Controls/nboard.cab#version=5,0,0,5"
WIDTH=460
HEIGHT=60
DATA="/AdvWorks/Controls/billboard.ods"
CLASSID="clsid:6059B947-EC52-11CF-B509-00A024488F73">
  </OBJECT>
<%
  Else
    Set Ad = Server.CreateObject("MSWC.Adrotator")
    Response.Write(Ad.GetAdvertisement("/AdvWorks/adrot.txt"))
  End If
%>
```

Advertisement Rotator Component

The Advertisement Rotator component allows you to create a list of advertisements that you wish to display over time.

Using Your Own Components

You may want to add your own functionality to a site by writing ActiveX server components. These components have access to the variables and methods in the `Request`, `Response`, `Application`, and `Server` objects that were described in the previous section. (It is beyond the scope of this book to demonstrate how to create a component.)

To use the newly created component, you must instantiate the object using the `CreateObject` method of the `Server` object. Once assigned to an object, all the methods and properties of the ActiveX Server component are available. Here is an example of implementing the Ad Rotator component:

58   Chapter 5

```
                    Set ad =
Server.CreateObject("MSWC.AdRotator")

Response.Write(ad.GetAdvertisement("ads.txt"))
```

If the added functionality needs database connectivity, you must ensure that a database is available. Next, you implement a Data Source Name (DSN). Then a `Connection` object must be created:

```
Set Conn = Server.CreateObject("ADODB.Connection")
```

Then you establish a connection to this object:

```
Conn.Open "dsn=sample_db;uid=;pwd="
```

Now you can build the SQL statements:

```
sql1="UPDATE shipping SET delivery=01/09/99 WHERE shipID=25"
```

Then you execute the statement with the `Execute` method:

```
Conn.Execute(sql1)
Conn.Close
```

You can return one row at a time and use the `MoveNext` method. This approach lets you view the next row until it is empty and `EOF=true`.

```
sql2 = "SELECT lastname FROM employee ORDER BY lastname"
cursor = Conn.Execute(sql2)
Do While Not cursor.EOF
   Response.Write(cursor("lastname") & "<br>")
   cursor.MoveNext
Loop
```

Active sites, by definition, change over time. Letís look at what matters over time: the session.

SESSIONS

In Chapter 3, you learned about the importance of keeping track of an application's state. As a refresher, let's use an example.

User 1 is connecting to the SQL database via his personal computer. User 2 is connecting to the SQL database via the Internet. User 1 could be on for a few minutes or a few hours. If the network does not remove user 1, all is OK and the server will continue to "know" that user 1 is connected. For user 2, this situation is different. Using a browser, the connection is happening for only a few seconds. It does not necessarily track the user unless it is set up to maintain and monitor sessions.

Active Server uses *sessions* to track the state of a client. The session starts as soon as the customer arrives. This is where the **global.asa** file comes into use. The **global.asa** file gives you the ability to globally enable scripts or declare objects that need session or application-level scope. Let's look at a sample:

```
<SCRIPT LANGUAGE=VBScript RUNAT=Server>
Sub Session_OnStart
                    Session("customer_id") = customer_count
                    customer_count = customer_counter + 1
END Sub
                    </SCRIPT>
```

The code in **global.asa** runs when a Web server starts or ends an application or creates or destroys a session. It has four procedures: `Application_OnStart`, `Application_OnEnd`, `Session_OnStart`, and `Session_OnEnd`. In the preceding example, `Session_OnStart` is used to set a customer ID.

LET'S CREATE A FEW PAGES

Let's build a few simple pages. Type the following:

```
<HTML>
<BODY>
<FONT SIZE=6>
Hello<BR>
</FONT>
</BODY>
</HTML>
```

Save this as **hello.asp**. You may wonder what is so special about this page. Nothing is special, but that is the point. A standard HTML page can be renamed as **.asp** and it will run fine!

Now let's post back the same ASP file that displays a form:

```
<%@ LANGUAGE="VBSCRIPT" %>
<!- FILE: login.asp -->
<HTML>
<HEAD>
<TITLE>Login Example</TITLE>
</HEAD>
<BODY>
<% IF IsEmpty(Request.Form("Name")) THEN
    Response.Write "Please enter your name"
%>
    <FORM ACTION="login.asp" METHOD=POST>
      <INPUT NAME="Name"
    TYPE=TEXTBOX MAXLENGTH=20>
```

60 Chapter 5

```
   <INPUT TYPE="SUBMIT" VALUE="Submit">
    </FORM>
<%
   ELSE
      'User verification code goes here
      Response.Write "Welcome " & Request.Form("Name") & "!"
   END IF
%>
</BODY>
</HTML>
```

Note that the data `Name` is input to `Request.Form` and is then written back as `Response.Write` with a `Welcome` tag added.

This page passes some internal variables:

```
<HTML>
<BODY>
<%For x=1 To 4%>
<FONT SIZE=<%=x%>>
This gets Bigger<br>
<%Next%>
</BODY>
</HTML>
```

This code results in a page with the words "This gets Bigger" printed in font size 1, then 2, then 3, and finally 4.

TIPS AND TROUBLESHOOTING

Here are a number of tips and troubleshooting techniques shared by various developers.

Tips

- Want to stop the client browser from caching the ASP file? Just add the following script to the beginning of the file:

    ```
    <% Response.Expires = 0 %>
    ```

- Many developers find that catching and throwing errors helps in debugging. Here is a way that one Visual Basic programmer traps errors:

    ```
    <% Response.Buffer = True %>
    <% On Error Resume Next %>
    ```

    He turned it off by setting

    ```
    <% On Error GoTo 0 %>
    ```

Troubleshooting

- I seem to not be able to use the ADO component any longer. I mean, it used to work... I think. Or I get an ASP 0115 error? Or this page was working fine on the development machine, but now that it is in production, nothing works.
Answer: The problem usually relates to permissions. What usually happens is that the administrator has restricted NTFS file permissions on various directories. The account used for anonymous login, IUSR_MACHINE, cannot access the required files.
ADO has a problem in that it depends on many DLLs that are located in various directories on the hard drive. ADO relies on many ODBC DLLs and other database drivers that are located in the **WINNT** and **System32** directories. ADO also depends on certain registry keys that may not be readable by the anonymous logon account if permissions are set incorrectly. In addition, some database drivers attempt to write to the registry, thus requiring write access for the anonymous logon account.
Try these steps:

1. Temporarily add the anonymous logon account (IUSR_MACHINE) to the administrators group. If this causes ASP to function properly, there are permissions issues. Remove the IUSR_MACHINE from the administrators group when you are finished with your tests. If that does not work, try using ADO from some other application, such as Visual Basic. If Visual Basic can use the component, it may be a permissions problem.
2. If it is a registry concern, use a registry editor to examine permissions on the various registry keys. Look at the ODBC and ADO keys. Possibly try the process on another machine. If the components work, compare the registry settings of both machines.

- I keep getting errors such as the ODBC drivers error 80004005 when attempting to open an ADO connection. Or the ASP code worked well until I moved the database to a remote machine.
Answer: Go back to the IUSR_MACHINE account. Change the anonymous logon account on the IIS server from IUSR_MACHINE to a different domain account. Make sure that the new account is seen by both machines and has proper permissions as noted earlier. If that does not seem to work, add a local account (to the remote machine) that matches the IUSR_MACHINE account. Make sure that account has proper access to the database.

WHERE DO WE GO FROM HERE?

Active Server Pages provides you with the power of server-side technology without losing the ability to run client-side scripts. ASP currently runs on Windows 95 and NT systems, allowing you to use VBScript and JavaScript. ASP has an advantage over CGI scripts, because it saves and retrieves variables per user session. You can connect to a database and pool database connections for better performance. You can even execute SQL statements and stored procedures. There are component interfaces that allow you to use C++, Visual Basic, and Java to provide extended functionality.

From here you should look at the following:

- Chapter 8 "Active Data," to discover more about the power of SQL Server.
- Chapter 12, "How the Active Desktop Works," to get an overview of the tools that can be used in preparing dynamic pages via the Active Server.

Chapter 6

Tools for Active Platform Servers

The World Wide Web is a great platform for a company to use to deliver enterprise products and information. As explained in Chapters 1 and 2, the Web was constructed to be platform-independent. This means that companies can deliver content by taking advantage of their current client/server applications.

GETTING DATA TO THE CLIENT/SERVER WORLD OF THE WEB

The Web saves companies time and money by letting customers use a simple client-based environment (a browser) to view a multitude of company information. This information can be intended for external viewing, in the case of an Internet site, or internal viewing with an intranet. Behind the Web architecture lie a number of server products that store and deliver the content. We will look at those server products in more detail in Chapters 7 through 11. For now, we'll concentrate on the basic programming environments available for full dynamic site implementation.

Microsoft introduced Internet Information Server (IIS) as its part of a company system solution. This Web server is integrated with the Windows NT operating system to provide security and Web management. Microsoft envisioned going beyond the static HTML pages, so it introduced the active environment. It extended the IIS environment to provide developers with multiple solutions that support industry standards and leverage existing developer investments. Microsoft provided five major options:

1. Common Gateway Interface (CGI). Somewhat complex in that you need a reasonable programming background even to modify CGI scripts for personal use.
2. Internet Database Connector (IDC). A simpler method than CGI for obtaining information records from company databases, but it lacks the richness desired and understood by current Microsoft application developers.
3. Internet Server API (ISAPI). A rich, extensive tool that allows you to create HTTP server extensions.

4. Active Server Pages (ASP). Allows you to use your programming skills to drill down and obtain all appropriate company data on multiple platforms in a minimal amount of time.
5. Dynamic HTML. A new client-side method for using scripts and HTML to create on-line interactive Web sites.

Let's look at each approach in more detail.

Common Gateway Interface

CGI is a set of specifications that tells a system how to pass data from the client (browser) to the Web server. The user starts a CGI application by filling out an HTML form or clicking a link in an HTML page on the Web server. The CGI application manipulates the data on the server (perhaps entering data into a database), and the results are returned in HTML to the browser. CGI applications are usually called *scripts*, because many developers write the procedure in scripting languages such as Perl. Perl is discussed in the next section.

Microsoft Internet Information Server supports CGI applications.

Figure 6.1 illustrates how a browser, a server, and a CGI application exchange information. The rest of this section discusses this five-part process.

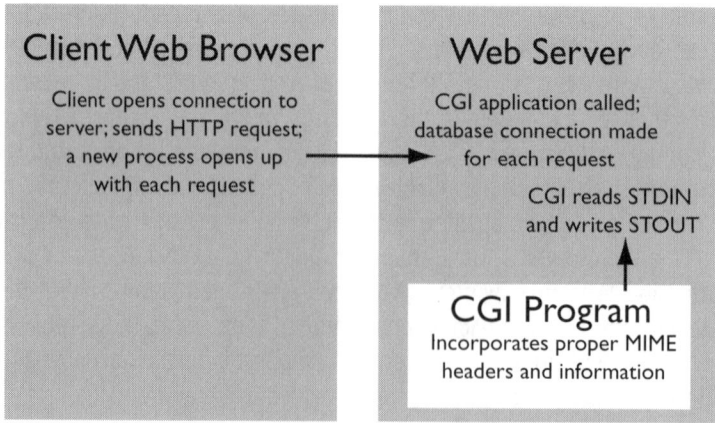

Figure 6.1 The CGI process.

Perl

Perl Practical Extraction and Report Language) has been in use for a long time by UNIX system administrators for automating administrative tasks. Perl is good for these applications, because it lets you quickly write code to handle string manipulation and match patterns within strings. In addition, it does not require memory management.

CGI programs can be written in a number of languages (C or C++, database languages, Lisp, tcl, Java, and so on), but Perl remains one of the primary choices for programming in a static environment. Letís look briefly at a Perl program and see how it runs on a server.

RUNNING A PERL PROGRAM

Perl is an interpreted language; when it runs, it is executed one line at a time. It is not compiled first. For example, typing **Perl file name** at a command line should execute the Perl instructions in the file.

Users are often insulated from knowing this detail. Most shells support the following convention: If the first line of an executable text file starts with #!, the remainder of the line identifies the interpreter for the file. All the Perl program examples given here will follow the conventional form.

Perl programs begin with the #! line:

```
#!/usr/local/bin/perl
print "Hello World\n";
```

This code tells the server to run the Perl interpreter. If it is not located in **/usr/local/bin**, that line must be changed. Comments are marked by the pound character. Text to the right of the pound character is not interpreted within Perl.

Here is an example of the comment line:

```
#!/usr/local/bin/perl
# This is a Comment that will not be interpreted
print "Hi\n"; # This is also comment
```

The output is

```
Hi
```

You use *file handles* to provide an I/O connection between Perl and the operating system. STDIN and STDOUT are file handles. STDIN and STDOUT are automatically open to files or devices established by the parent process.

Consider this example:

```
sub ReadParse {
        local (*in) = @_ if @_;
        local ($i, $key, $val);

        if ( $ENV{'REQUEST_METHOD'} eq "GET" ) {
          $in = $ENV{'QUERY_STRING'};
        } elsif ($ENV{'REQUEST_METHOD'} eq "POST") {
          read(STDIN,$in,$ENV{'CONTENT_LENGTH'});
        } else {
```

Under the form GET, the client appends data to the URL it passes to the server. Using POST, the client sends data to the server by way of the HTTP message data field. This technique overcomes size limitations that are inherent in the GET method. Under the POST method, the browser supplies it to the script on STDIN.

The good news is that the IIS environment supports the STDIN and STDOUT handlers, giving you full access to all the HTTP variables. You can process forms using both client-side and server-side efforts.

CLIENT/SERVER ACTIVITY

The user starts the CGI process by clicking on a hypertext link, a **Submit** button, an object that is retrieved with the GET method, or a search element.

On an NT system, as a browser activates a CGI script, the server compares the file name's extension to the server's script mapping registry key to find the executable it needs to start. The server has script mapping entries for the following:

- **.cmd** and **.bat** files, which start the command-line environment.
- **.idc** files, which start the Internet Database Connector (read more about this method in the following section).

To enable Perl scripts to run, make sure that the following is added to the registry key (HKEY_LOCAL_MACHINE, 'SOFTWARE\Microsoft\Resource Kit\PERL5):

.pl: REG_SZ: C:\RESKIT\PERL\BIN\PERL.EXE %s %s

The **\Reskit\Perl\Bin** directory contains **Perl.exe**.

The server passes the variables to the CGI application and launches the application. The CGI application returns the data to the server. Normally, the application writes the data to the standard output stream (STDOUT). The application must follow this format in returning data: The first line or lines must contain server directives (such as redirecting the client or sending a document) and must contain the MIME content type. This information is followed by a blank line, which is followed by the data.

The server gets the STDOUT stream and puts the HTTP headers in place. This stream (including HTTP header) gets sent back to the client.

FINAL NOTES

CGI applications are stand-alone executables and do not run as server extensions as is the case with ISAPI applications (explained later). This means that CGI scripts may run slower than comparable ISAPI applications and can consume more server resources.

CGI executables can also be a security hole, especially when you try to run batch files with CGI scripts. You should give only execute permission to virtual directories that have

CGI applications. As a general note, Web directories should be assigned read permission only. Any executable files that a developer may use for downloading should also be assigned read access only. The normal file name extension for a CGI is **.exe** or **.cgi**.

Internet Database Connector

The Internet Database Connector (IDC) gives the developer a simple tool with which to integrate database queries into HTML pages (see Figure 6.2). It has largely been replaced, however, by Active Server Pages (see Chapter 5).

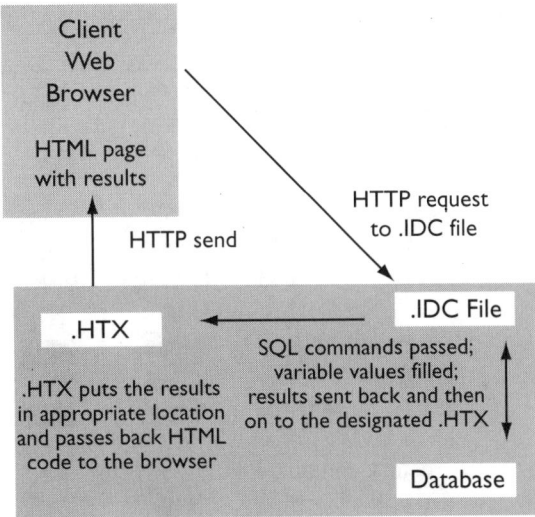

Figure 6.2 The IDC process.

Here is how it works. A user comes to a site and uses a Web browser to submit a request to the Internet server. The Internet server sends back a document formatted in HTML. Database access is provided by the IDC component.

The IDC uses two types of files to control how the database is accessed and how the output Web page is constructed. These files are Internet Database Connector (**.idc**) files and HTML extension (**.htx**) files.

The IDC files contain the necessary information to connect to the appropriate ODBC data source and execute SQL statements. An IDC file also contains the name and location of the HTML extension file. The HTML extension file is a template for the actual HTML document that will be returned to the Web browser after the database information has been merged into it by IDC.

Letís set up the database connection and then create an example IDC query.

DSN Setup

If you are a little rusty on setting up an ODBC Data Source Name (DSN), here is a brief example. First, create the system data sources. Follow these steps:

1. Launch Control Panel.
2. Double-click the **ODBC** icon (**ODBC32** in Windows 95), as shown in Figure 6.3. The ODBC Data Sources dialog box appears. You may see other data sources in the list if you previously installed other ODBC drivers.

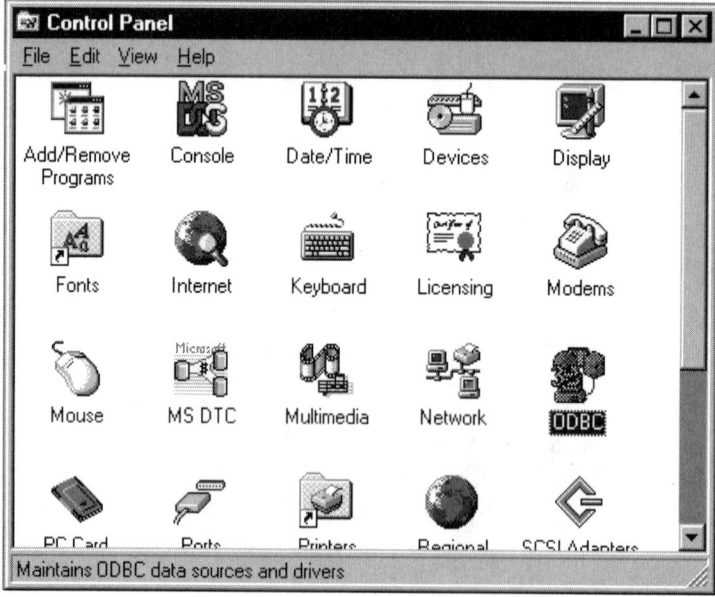

Figure 6.3 ODBC icon.

3. Click the **Machine DSN** tab. The System Data Sources dialog box appears. Important: The Internet Database Connector will work only with system (or ìmachineî) DSNs.
4. Click the **Add** button. The Create New Data Source dialog box appears (see Figure 6.4).

Tools for Active Platform Servers 69

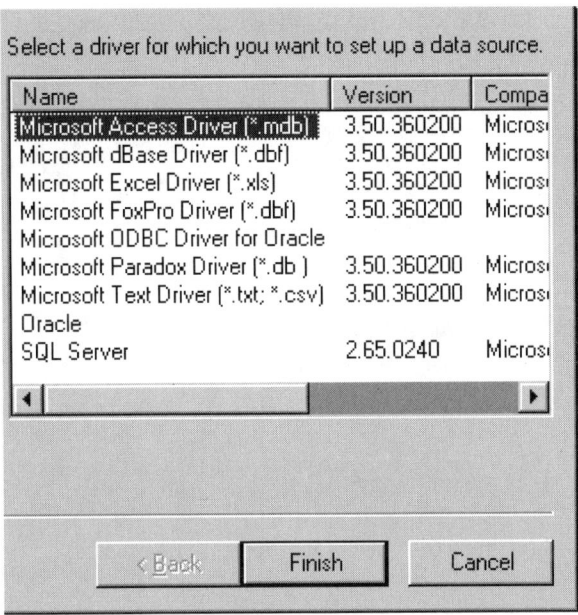

Figure 6.4 Create New Data Source dialog box.

5. Select an ODBC driver in the list box and click **OK**. A dialog box specific to your driver will appear.
6. Enter the name of the data source. The DSN is a logical name used by ODBC to refer to the driver and any other information required to access the data. DSN is used in IDC files to tell Internet Information Server where to access the data.

    For Microsoft SQL Server (see Figure 6.5), the server name, network address, and network library displayed in the Setup dialog box are specific to your installation. If you do not know what to enter in these controls, accept the defaults. For details, click the **Help** button and find the section that describes your network.

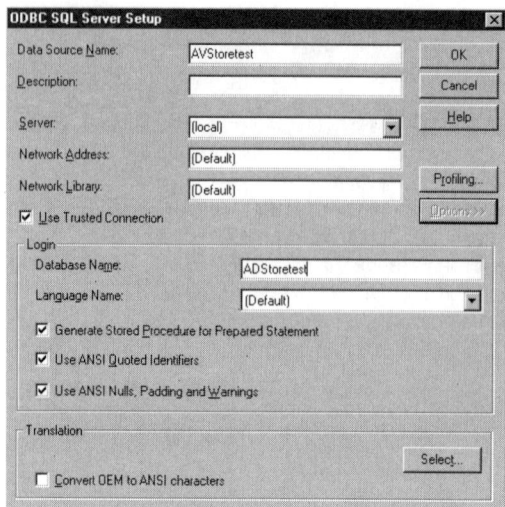

Figure 6.5 ODBC SQL Server setup example.

7. Click **OK**. The System Data Sources dialog box will be displayed again, but now it will have the name of the new data source displayed.
8. Click **Close** to close the System Data Sources dialog box.
9. Click **Close** to close the Data Sources dialog box.
10. Click **OK** to complete the ODBC and DSN setup.

A Simple Example

In this example, you will create an opening page, **Sample.htm**. A hyperlink on this page causes the server to query a SQL Server database (using a **Sample.idc** file), and that will result in a query being executed using the ODBC driver for Microsoft SQL Server. In turn the system sends back a page (**sample.htx**).

Figure 6.6 shows **Dbsamp1.htm** as it is displayed by Microsoft Internet Explorer.

Tools for Active Platform Servers   71

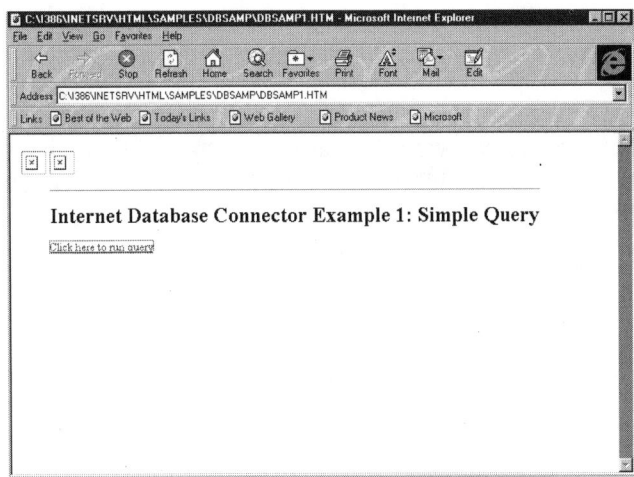

Figure 6.6 Sample query screen.

As you click on **Click here to run query**, a URL is sent to the server. The following code launches **dbsamp1.idc**:

```
<A HREF="http://webserver/samples/dbsamp/Sample.idc">Click here to run
query</A>
```

The system now completes the following steps.

1. Internet Information Server receives the URL that was sent by the browser.
2. IIS loads **Httpodbc.dll** and provides it with the information in the URL. The **.idc** file is mapped to **Httpodbc.dll**.
3. **Httpodbc.dll** reads the IDC file. Here is **Sample.idc**:

```
Datasource: Web SQL
    Username: sa
    Template: sample.htx
    SQLStatement:
    +SELECT company, client_name
    + from pubs.dbo.company
    + where sales>50000
```

This IDC file contains information in a field:value syntax. The **.idc** file needs a data source to know which database to connect to; in this example you will see this line:

```
Datasource: Web SQL
```

This Data Source Name was set up as demonstrated in the preceding section. The username must be a valid logon to the ODBC data source. Here, the systems administrator (`sa`) account is used. The HTML extension file is specified by

```
Template: sample.htx
```

The template tells the system which file to use to merge the results.

Then you will see the SQL statement section, which contains the SQL statement that the system is to execute. In this example you are looking for all the company names and sales in units from the ìpubsî sample database in SQL Server for companies that have sales of more than $50,000.

4. IDC connects to the ODBC data source. The system executes the SQL statement contained in the IDC file.
5. IDC grabs the data from the database and merges it into the HTML extension file. Once the SQL statement is executed, IDC reads the HTML extension file specified in **Sample.idc**. This is the **Sample.htx** file. The **.htx** file contains special HTML tags that IDC uses to control where and how the data returned from the SQL statement is merged. Please see the following section for an explanation of these tags.
6. The IDC sends the merged document back to IIS. IIS then sends the HTX page, with the merged data, to the client.

SIMPLE HTX

To send data to the client's browser, IDC merges the ODBC data into the **.htx** file specified in the template.

The **.htx** file is an extension of the HTML document style. It has a set of delimiter tags: `<%%>` or `<!-%%->`. IDC passes data into the variables designated by these tags. Six tags (`begindetail, enddetail, if, else, endif,` and `%z`) control how the database results are merged into the **.htx** file. The database column names are used to identify which results from the database query belong in which variable of the **.htx** file For example, let's say the IDC file had the SQL statement `select username from names` and that a database had three records under `username` with the following entries: John, Ringo, Paul.

If the **.htx** file contained

```
<%begindetail%><%username%><%enddetail%>
```

The result would be

John
Ringo
Paul

IDC fetches the username from every record in the database and inserts it into the `<%username%>` tag.

Here is the **Sample.htx** file from our sales record example:

```
<HTML>
<BODY>
<HEAD><TITLE>Companies and Sales</TITLE></HEAD>
<%if idc.sales eq ""%>

<H2>Companies with sales greater than <I>50000</I></H2>
<%else%>

<H2>Companies with sales greater than <I><%idc.sales%></I></H2>
<%endif%>

<P>
<%begindetail%>
<%if CurrentRecord EQ 0 %>

Query results:
<B>CompaniesYTD Sales<BR></B>
<%endif%>
<%company_name%><%sales%>
<%enddetail%>
<P>
<%if CurrentRecord EQ 0 %>
<I><B>Sorry, no companies had sales greater than </I><%idc.sales%>.</B>

<P>
<%else%>

<HR>
<%endif%>

</BODY>
</HTML>
```

The `<%begindetail%>` and `<%enddetail%>` tags let the IDC know where the variable inserting begins and ends. The columns returned from the query are surrounded by `<%%>`. In this example that would include `<%company_name %>` and `<%sales%>`.

HTX Passing a Value

Suppose you wanted to let the user input the value of sales. In the previous example, the select statement was hard-coded with a search resulting in sales greater than 50,000. To add the variable field, the HTML would look like this:

```
<FORM METHOD="POST" ACTION="/scripts/samples/smplenew.idc">
<P>
Enter  sales amount: <INPUT NAME="sales" VALUE="50000" >
<P>
<INPUT TYPE="SUBMIT" VALUE="Run Query">
</FORM>
```

The IDC looks like this:

```
SQLStatement:
+SELECT company_name, sales
+ from pubs.dbo.company
+ where sales > %sales%
```

The parameter `sales` in the IDC must match the variable `sales` in the HTX. As the IDC receives the **.idc** file, it will substitute the customer's value for `sales` in the `SELECT` statement.

Now suppose you have a multiple list box. For example, suppose the HTML form looks like this:

```
<SELECT MULTIPLE NAME="region">
<OPTION VALUE="Western">
<OPTION VALUE="Eastern">
<OPTION VALUE="Northern">
<OPTION VALUE="Southern">
</SELECT>
```

The **.idc** file has this SQL statement:

```
SQLStatement: SELECT name, region FROM customer WHERE region IN ('%region%')
```

If the user selected **Southern** and **Eastern**, the IDC converts the SQL statement to this:

```
SELECT name, region FROM customer WHERE region IN ('Southern', 'Eastern')
```

If numeric data is passed instead of text, no quotation marks are needed. For example:

```
<SELECT MULTIPLE NAME="year">
<OPTION VALUE="1996">
<OPTION VALUE="1997">
<OPTION VALUE="1998">
</SELECT>
```

The **.idc** file has this SQL statement:

```
SQLStatement: SELECT product, sales_year FROM sales WHERE sales_year IN
(%year%)
```

If the user selected **1996** and **1998** from the HTML form, the SQL statement would be converted to this:

```
SELECT product, sales_year FROM sales WHERE sales_year IN (1996, 1998)
```

HTX SYNTAX

Let's review the basic syntax of the **.htx** files. First there are the two tags `<%begindetail%>` and `<%enddetail%>`. They encompass that section of the **.htx** that contains output from the database query. For example, the following will list the columns `company_name` and `sales` but not `company_location`.

```
<%company_location%>
<%begindetail%>
<%company_name%>: <%sales%>
<%enddetail%>
```

Why? It falls outside the `<%begindetail%>` and `<%enddetail%>` tags.

To build in a form of `IF-THEN` programming, use `<%if%>`, `<%else%>`, and `<%endif%>`.

For example, let's look at the syntax in the earlier **Sample.htx**:

```
<HTML>
<BODY>
<HEAD><TITLE>Companies and Sales</TITLE></HEAD>
```

(portions omitted for brevity)

```
<P>
<%begindetail%>
<%if CurrentRecord EQ 0 %>

Query results:
<B>CompaniesYTD Sales<BR></B>
<%endif%>
<%company_name%><%sales%>
<%enddetail%>
<P>
<%if CurrentRecord EQ 0 %>
<I><B>Sorry, no companies had sales greater than </I><%idc.sales%>.</B>
```

76   Chapter 6

```
<P>
<%else%>

<HR>
<%endif%>

</BODY>
</HTML>
```

If there are no records (`if CurrentRecord EQ 0`), the HTX file prints "Sorry, no companies had sales greater than" to the screen with the **idc.sales** variable inserted.

The general syntax for this `IF-THEN` syntax is as follows:

```
<%if condition %>
HTML text
[<%else%>
HTML text]
<%endif%>
```

The `condition` reads as

>   value1 operator value2

and `operator` can be one of the following:

>   EQ if `value1` equals `value2`
>   LT if `value1` is less than `value2`
>   GT if `value1` is greater than `value2`
>   CONTAINS if any part of `value1` contains the string `value2`

The IDC tool is a great way to retrieve and even insert data into a database. But what if you determine that you need more flexibility and you like using C++? Then it is time to look at the Internet Server API.

ISAPI

Internet Server API (ISAPI) is a thread-safe application programming environment that runs within the Web server's process space. It supplements CGI rather than replaces it.

A developer can write an ISAPI application that redirects a user to a different page or one that manipulates a database to service a full intranet site. You create ISAPIs as DLLs that run on the Web server. ISAPI applications provide better performance than CGI scripts, because ISAPI applications are loaded into memory and are an extension of the Web server.

Unlike CGI, ISAPI does not start a separate process, so there is less system overhead. For applications such as customized authentication, access, or logging, you can incorporate an ISAPI filter, a DLL that can act on the HTTP request before the server reads the request or writes the response to the client.

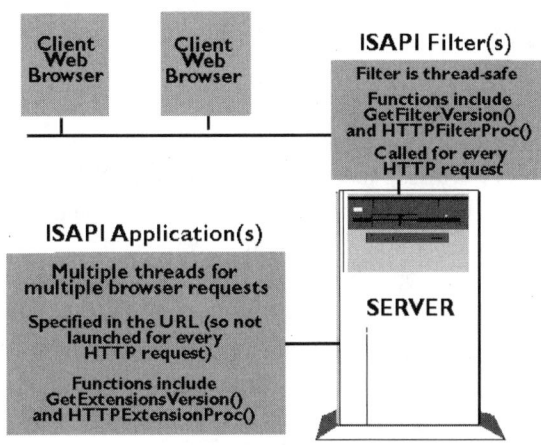

Figure 6.7 ISAPI flow.

Unlike CGI scripts, ISAPI DLLs do not require that a process be created for each hit. The advantages of using ISAPI include low overhead, speed of loading (even the first time the DLL is called), better scalability, and more efficient use of resources. In the CGI model, HTTP servers create a separate process for each request they receive. As the number of concurrent requests increases, so does the number of concurrent processes created by the server.

When a DLL is used the server loads it and keeps it in memory. This means that the server is ready to serve other requests until it determines that the DLL is no longer required.

ISAPI functions include `GetExtensionVerison()`, `HttpExtensionProc()`, `TerminateExtension()`, and `PFN_HSE_IO_COMPLETION()` along with the `EXTENSION_CONTROL_BLOCK` data structure.

`GetExtensionVerison()` is the first entry point called by a server. It is used to get the version and description. `HttpExtensionProc()` is equivalent to CGI's `main()` function. It is called once per request and can have multiple simultaneous requests called from different threads (so be sure that the DLL is thread-safe). `TerminateExtension()` is called by the server in the event that the server wants to unload the extension. `PFN_HSE_IO_COMPLETION()` returns the status of the last I/O.

`EXTENSION_CONTROL_BLOCK` contains the most commonly needed information for a request, such as pointers to server callback functions and parameters that can be obtained using callbacks. This data structure closely resembles the environment block that is passed to CGI applications.

CREATING A SAMPLE ISAPI

ISAPI applications are usually written in C or C++. Let's use the Visual C++ environment to build a simple ISAPI. Follow these steps:

1. Select **New-Project Workspace**. Choose **ISAPI Extension Wizard** as the project type, name it **Hello World**, and press **Create**. In the dialog box that appears, the default settings are already configured and MFC is dynamically linked. If the server has the MFC DLLs, you will be ok. If they are not available or you are not sure, choose to statically link.
2. Press **Finish**. Visual C++ tells you which files it is creating. It will generate a class called `CHelloworldExtension`, a descendent of `CHttpServer`.
3. Because ISAPI becomes an extension of IIS, you must stop the service from running if you want to debug the code. In addition, you must ensure that the user account that creates the ISAPI has proper permissions. To do this, go to the User Manager for Domains. Select **User Rights** from the Policies menu. Check the **Show Advanced User Rights** box. Scroll down and find the **Act as part of the operating system** selection in the Rights list. Click the **Add** button to **Add Users and Groups**. Use the **Show User** button to select the appropriate account. Click **Add**. Repeat these steps to add **Generate security audits rights** from the Rights list. Log off and log back on with the appropriate account that you used in this process.
4. Go to the IIS Manager window and stop all the services.
5. Return to the Visual C++ workspace. Open the Select Settings dialog box from the Build menu. Then click on the **Debug** tab to select **General Category**. In the **Executable for debug session** field, enter the location of the IIS executable. By default it is found in **c:\inetsrv\server\inetinfo.exe**. Type **-e w3svc** in the **Program arguments** field. Click the **Link** tab and type the path and file name where you want the compiled DLL to be placed. This information goes in the **Output filename** field. Remember that it must be accessible by the URL. If the server is called **website**, the location is **http://www.website.com/helloworld.dll**.
6. Build the project. When the build process is completed, open the browser and type **http://www.website.com/helloworld.dll?**.
   The system should generate this message:

   ```
   This default message was produced by the Internet Server DLL Wizard.  Edit
   your CHelloworldExtension::Default() implementation to change it.
   ```

TIP If the system returns an Error 500 at any point while running the DLL, the system is not running the Microsoft Foundation Classes (MFC) libraries. Make sure that you relink the project statically with MFC.

THE CODE

HELLOWORLD.CPP has this code:

```
BEGIN_PARSE_MAP(CHelloworldExtension, CHttpServer)

// TODO: insert your ON_PARSE_COMMAND() and
            // ON_PARSE_COMMAND_PARAMS() here to hook up your commands.

        // For example:

        ON_PARSE_COMMAND(Default, CHelloworldExtension, ITS_EMPTY)
        DEFAULT_PARSE_COMMAND(Default, CHelloworldExtension)

END_PARSE_MAP(CHelloworldExtension)
```

The command handler for this DLL is as follows:

```
void CHelloworldExtension::Default(CHttpServerContext* pCtxt)
{

    StartContent(pCtxt);
    WriteTitle(pCtxt);

    *pCtxt << _T("This default message was produced by the Internet");
    *pCtxt << _T("Server DLL Wizard. Edit your
CHelloworldExtension::Default()");
    *pCtxt << _T("implementation to change it.\r\n");

    EndContent(pCtxt);

}
```

Let's change this so that the DLL sends a "Hello World" message back. Remove the default code and add the new line:

```
void CHelloworldExtension::Default(CHttpServerContext* pCtxt)
{

            StartContent(pCtxt);
            WriteTitle(pCtxt);
            *pCtxt << _T("Hello World!");
            EndContent(pCtxt);

}
```

Now rebuild the project and run it. The message on the screen should look like this:

    Hello World!

One final point: Do not forget to check the file permissions on the DLL. If the user does not have execute permissions for the DLL (`IUSR_Computername` in the case of the anonymous user from the standard browser), it will not execute. Because the ISAPI runs in memory, you would have to stop and restart the WWW service to enact any permission changes.

A Word about Active Server Pages

Active Server Pages was discussed in detail in Chapter 5. ASP is mentioned here to remind you that CGI, IDC, and ISAPI methods can also be used in conjunction with ASP. For example, if you take any HTML page that has been mentioned in this chapter and change the extension to **.asp**, it will be recognized as an Active Server Page. ASP gives you the creativity to write the code in whatever script or language is appropriate for the design team. For example, if the team had a C++ programmer, a Perl programmer, and a SQL database administrator, each individual could develop Active Server Pages without learning Visual Basic or Java. The C++ programmer could write a user authentication filter as an ISAPI that is launched when the user tries to enter an area of Active Server. The Perl programmer could embed an e-mail form in that same page and point the `FORM` command to a CGI script that sends the e-mail. The SQL database administrator could put another `FORM` command on the **.asp** to grab data from a database that informs customers about the latest products available.

Dynamic HTML

Dynamic HTML gives Active Server developer the ability to extend HTML for the newest browsers. Both Microsoft and Netscape proposed Dynamic HTML standards to the World Wide Web Consortium.

With Dynamic HTML, content developers can create Web pages that have the interactivity found in many applications and CD-ROM titles. This interactivity provides users with a richer and more compelling experience. In addition, Dynamic HTML enables developers to create these applications in HTML and scripting without requiring traditional programming languages.

Overview

Dynamic HTML gives you added flexibility beyond writing programming code. The benefits include the following:

- The ability to integrate the authoring and the viewing of the data. You can see the content as you construct it on various platforms.
- You can implement and edit HTML, text, cascading style sheets, ActiveX controls, and applets.
- You should see quicker turnaround of designs, because the content runs locally and does not require server intervention.

Dynamic HTML also allows for *layers*, which appear depending on conditions that you set. This means that the HTML is sent once and is activated based on the conditions. Layering reduces network traffic and increases interactivity. There is one problem: Netscape allows designers to layer whole blocks of objects using the proprietary `Layer` tag. Microsoft uses the more standard cascading style sheets. Please see Appendix C for the Netscape and Microsoft documentation.

You learned about push technology in Chapter 3. Dynamic HTML supports those developers who are sold on using push technology.

Let's look at the Microsoft and Netscape approaches.

The Players

Dynamic HTML is supported by Netscape Navigator 4.0 (Communicator) Preview Release 3 (or later) and Microsoft Internet Explorer 4.0 Platform Preview 1 (or later).

Microsoft's Approach

Microsoft uses the Document Object Model (DOM) based on a W3C standards proposal. In this model, documents have *behaviors* and *characteristics*. DOM lets you manipulate HTML by embedding VBScript and JavaScript.

You will be able to accurately place objects on a screen using DHTML. Objects can be moved over time to simulate animation.

Customers using Dynamic HTML–enabled browsers will have control over the data sent to them. They can modify and sort data without sending requests to the server. This arrangement should reduce the complexity of database scripts written by developers. For example, a database call would look like this:

```
<TABLE DATASRC="#company_source">
    <TR>
        <TD><INPUT TYPE=TEXTBOX DATAFLD="company_name">
</TABLE>
```

The text box is bound to the `company name` of the current row of the data source control with `ID=company_source`. Each record of the database column `company_name` will be entered as a cell in a table (`<TR><TD>`).

Netscape's Approach

Netscape's approach gives developers control over content formatting such as fonts and spacing. Additionally, Netscape partially implements the Document Object Model in a way that allows a developer to use JavaScript to position and format HTML elements. JavaScript, along with other languages, can be used with the proprietary `Layer` tag to provide accurate positioning of items.

The `<LAYER>` tag allows you to build multiple layers of content. You can use x, y, and z coordinates to place objects such as images and text. If you have used Photoshop, you will find the same concept used by Netscape in its layering technology.

Problems with Dynamic HTML

Because Microsoft and Netscape have their eye on the next-generation browser, there are a few problems with Dynamic HTML as it now stands.

You would find it beneficial to create separate navigation through a site (depending on the browser) or to include both Netscape and IE tags on the same page. Separate navigation can be implemented using a JavaScript that reads the header file and determines which browser the client is using. The latter choice opens up new horizons.

On the page, use VBScript for IE coded functions. Place the VBScript first to ensure that the IE browser will see the calls. Netscape will bypass the VBScript. Then provide JavaScript for the Netscape functions. Please note that if a non–Dynamic HTML browser comes to this new site, the user will probably see JavaScript errors for any commands. For this reason, you may want to put the Dynamic HTML pages one layer deep behind an opening page that determines the version of Netscape and IE. If the user has a Dynamic HTML–enabled browser, the user will be sent down the appropriate path.

Another option is to use the ASP Browser Capabilities component to detect the browser and forward the appropriate DHTML to the user.

What Now?

Each of these tools has its place in the active development arena. As has been noted, each method has its own benefits. CGI scripts are relatively fast and are simple to write for sending and parsing strings of information, as in e-mailing form information. IDC is a simple method for querying ODBC-compliant databases but is not as robust as ISAPI, and it has been supplanted by ASP. ISAPI is a rich programming environment, but its implementation takes somewhat more programming experience. ASP and Dynamic HTML are handy ways for a developer to use scripting languages and HTML to deliver active site content.

From here you should review the following chapters:

- Chapter 8, "Active Data," where you learn more about SQL Server and its use in the construction of active sites.
- Appendix B, "Dynamic HTML Code," where you can review the features implemented by Netscape and Microsoft in their latest browsers.

Chapter 7

The Active Security Environment: Proxy Server

You may have received a letter from an organization you belong to—perhaps an automobile association, homeowner's association, or credit union—asking you to authorize a proxy vote on your behalf. A *proxy* is a mechanism by which you empower someone to transact a business affair for you.

A *proxy server* plays a similar role in an intranet and the Internet. A proxy server is a program or service that manages a company's internal requests made through protocols (such as FTP, Telnet, or HTTP) using external sources (Web site servers). It is intended to give users the illusion of "talking" directly with the external Web site while providing protection to the internal network.

Increasing numbers of companies and individuals are using the Internet as their gateway to the world of fast and unlimited communication. With the growing number of Internet-enabled computers, the need for private networks, gateways, and security is also expanding, and is assuming greater importance to network administrators and users.

As developers are building increasingly dynamic sites, new problems are emerging. These problems are related to the process of connecting an internal network, or even a single PC, to the Internet and to the use of intranets and extranets:

- The company networking group cannot change all the Internet Protocol (IP) addresses in the network to official IP address, perhaps because of a limited number of IP addresses given to the company by Internic or its local Internet service provider.
- A company policy says that users can use the Internet only if the data is encrypted. The company requires security for all the data over an Internet connection. It may be necessary to build a private virtual network, that connects to the Internet.
- The company needs to control how users are interacting with the network.
- Users complain that navigation to support sites is slow. In addition, network costs are getting too high. The company may need to incorporate proxy and cache servers.

How does a developer deal with these issues? Microsoft's Proxy Server can give Active Platform developers some of the tools they need to meet company security requirements.

This chapter will help you understand how to make Microsoft's Proxy Server a key part of an active Web site. But first let's look at general security issues.

THE ROLE OF SECURITY IN DEVELOPMENT

Network managers are in a battle to protect corporate networks, and the first rule is to know the enemy. Sun Tzu said that a person must lay out a plan and that "he who wishes to fight must first count the costs." These are good guidelines for developers who are sensitive to corporate network security issues.

Who is the enemy? Many developers believe that hackers are the primary concern. Maybe, maybe not. The "enemy" is not only external hackers but also internal violators of company security policies. Do individuals inadvertently publish corporate e-mail addresses and internal documents while they are surfing the newsgroups? Security policies as well as hackers may be at fault.

When you research Web site security, it's important to keep issues in perspective. At one level you will deal with the actual network traffic. Once that is understood, you will want to manipulate data to meet company needs—which range from a request for information to ordering a product.

Let's look at the two areas that will assist you in assessing data needs : getting to and from the site and securing the data.

Getting to and from the Site

As an individual accesses a corporate Web site, systems need to control the visitor's access to internal network resources. There are products that selectively permit or deny access based on criteria such as protocols, system names, phone numbers, and usernames. There are many types of access-limiting devices, defined generally as *firewall* schemes. A firewall—a computer network architecture that stands between the company's internal network and the Internet—lets you monitor all traffic to and from the Internet.

A firewall is only as good as the company security policy. It wouldn't do any good to install an alarm system at home and then place your wallet in an open drawer at work. If you compound the error by leaving your credit cards unattended on a counter at Nordstrom's while you hunt for your identification, you open yourself up to any thief who wanders by.

Another pearl of wisdom to consider is that firewalls can't protect against attacks that don't go through them. What if an individual removes items on a floppy or zip drive? Do they check it for viruses? Do they log the movement of data off-site? Is such a log necessary? What kinds of controls exist on dial-up modems? Maybe certain systems, such as banks, should not be hooked up to the Internet.

A firewall cannot protect against a data-driven attack in which something is mailed or copied to an internal host, where it is then executed. That is why you should put virus scanning software on a workstation as well as servers. Most viruses are transmitted via floppy disks on the company's intranet and not via the Internet. The National Computer Security Association, Carlisle, Pennsylvania, produced a report that identifies how viruses gain entry to the company network (see Figure 7.1).

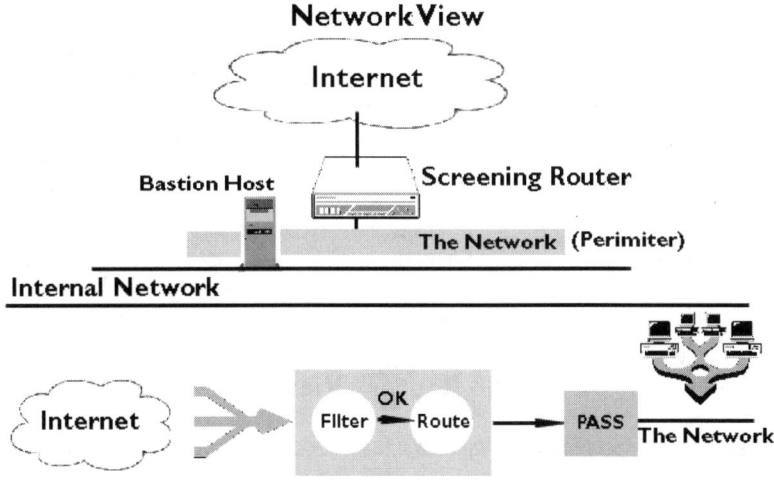

Figure 7.1 Methods of virus attacks.

Security is a real issue that requires practical solutions as well as technology-driven solutions. The next step is to understand the various security mechanisms.

Security Mechanisms

Firewall mechanisms include packet filtering, bastion hosts, perimeter networks, firewall software, dual-homed hosts, Domain Name Service (DNS), and proxy servers.

Packet Filtering

In *packet filtering*, you allow or block packets based on a company security policy. To implement a packet filtering system, you would use a *screening router*. Figure 7.2 shows an example.

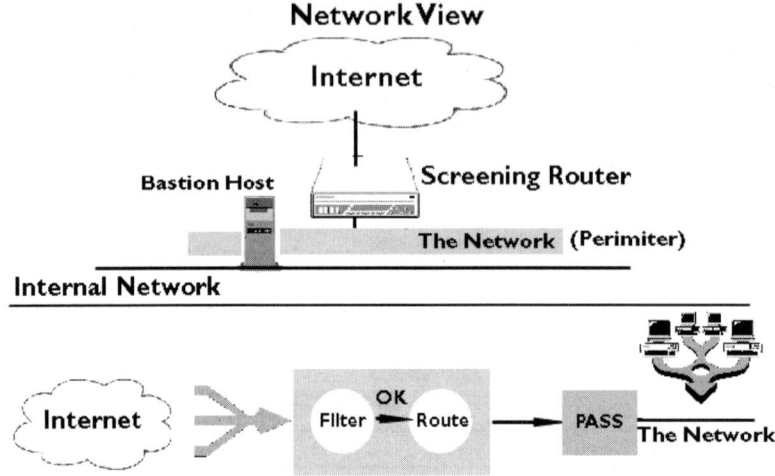

Figure 7.2 Screening router views: the network and router viewpoints.

A router handles each packet it receives, determining for each packet the least congested route in a Web-type network of paths. Packet-filtering software examines the port number associated with the network application service requested (Telnet, File Transfer Protocol, Send Mail Transfer Protocol, and so on), protocol type (such as Transport Control Protocol, Universal Data Protocol, Internet Control Management Protocol), and the source and destination addresses of the packets that arrive for forwarding through the firewall. This means that different packets that are part of the same file may travel different routes. Routers talk to each other to determine these least congested paths.

A screening router is a dedicated router or a host configured to filter packets. It can block traffic by destination or port (by protocol such as FTP). A packet-filtering router defines the route and determines whether it should send the packet. Packet filtering is transparent to users.

IP packet-level filtering is a good first line of defense. Packets bearing one of a predefined table of IP addresses are allowed to pass, and all others are turned away. The problem is that packets containing bogus IP addresses can easily be created or even hijacked. Once someone has acquired a valid IP address, it's not hard to gain passage through even the most elaborate set of IP address filters.

Cisco Routers

The Cisco router is the mainstay of the Internet world. The following example, recommended by a Cisco engineer, sets up a router for IP packet-level filtering. Lets assume our company has Class C network address 207.137.150.0. The company network is connected to the Internet via a T1 connection with a local IP service provider. The company policy is to allow everyone access to Internet services, so all outgoing connections are accepted. All incoming connections go through a mail host. Mail and DNS are the only incoming services.

In this implementation we will do the following:

- Allow all outgoing TCP connections.
- Allow incoming SMTP and DNS to mailushost.
- Allow incoming FTP data connections to high TCP port (>1024).
- Try to protect services that live on high port numbers.

Only incoming packets from the Internet are checked in this configuration. The rules are tested in order, and they stop when the first match is found. There is an implicit deny rule at the end of an access list that denies everything. This IP access list assumes that you are running Cisco IOS v. 10.3 or later. Here is the code:

```
1.  no ip source-route
 2. !
 3. interface ethernet 0
 4. ip address 195.55.55.1
 5. !
 6. interface serial 0
 7. ip access-group 101 in
 8. !
 9. access-list 101 deny ip 207.137.150.0 0.0.0.255
10. access-list 101 permit tcp any any established
11. !
12. access-list 101 permit tcp any host 207.137.150.10 eq smtp
13. access-list 101 permit tcp any host 207.137.150.10 eq dns
14. access-list 101 permit udp any host 207.137.150.10 eq dns
15. !
16. access-list 101 deny tcp any any range 6000 6003
17. access-list 101 deny tcp any any range 2000 2003
18. access-list 101 deny tcp any any eq 2049
19. access-list 101 deny udp any any eq 204
20. !
21. access-list 101 permit tcp any 20 any gt 1024
```

```
22. !
23. access-list 101 permit icmp any any   24. !
25. snmp-server community ANYTHING RO 2
26. line vty 0 4
27. access-class 2 in
28. access-list 2 permit 207.137.150.0 255.255.255.0
```

The developer has dropped all source-routed packets. Source routing can be used for address spoofing. If an incoming packet claims to be from the local net, we will drop it. All packets that are part of established TCP connections can pass through without further checking. All connections to low port numbers are blocked except SMTP and DNS. We block all services that listen to TCP connections in high port numbers. In this example, we have UNIX clients, X-Windows (port 6000+), and OpenWindows (port 2000+). Network File System (port 2049) usually runs over UDP, but it can be run over NFS, so you need to block it. Incoming connections from port 20 into high port numbers are supposed to be FTP data connections. Access-list 2 limits access to the router itself (Telnet and SNMP). All UDP traffic is blocked to protect RPC services.

The problem with this solution is that you cannot enforce strong access policies with router access lists. Users can easily install back doors to their systems to get over "no incoming Telnet" or "no X" rules. Also, network crackers install Telnet back doors on systems where they break in. You can never be sure what services they have listening to connections on high port numbers. Checking the source port on incoming FTP data connections is a weak security method. It also breaks access to some FTP sites. It makes it more difficult for users to use their back doors but doesn't prevent hackers from scanning a company's systems.

BASTION HOSTS

The *bastion host* operates as the receptionist to the company's network. Just as a receptionist must fend off salespeople so must the company's bastion host fend off spies and hackers. There are no user accounts on the bastion host. You can run whatever services you need such as FTP, HTTP and Telnet) but you should keep them to a minimum. Anything not needed becomes a possible opening for intrusion. It is best to run bastion host calls through an internal router (see Figure 7.3).

PERIMETER NETWORKS

Perimeter networks provide an extra layer of protection between the internal and external networks. This type of network is normally used in conjunction with a bastion host. Internal networks safely pass data back and forth to each other but not to the perimeter network. One NT solution is Secure Computing Firewall for NT. For literature, see http://www.sctc.com/NT/HTML/ntcontents.html or enter **Secure Computing Firewall for NT** into a search engine. According to the company, this product is a "perimeter firewall based on application gateway security technology."

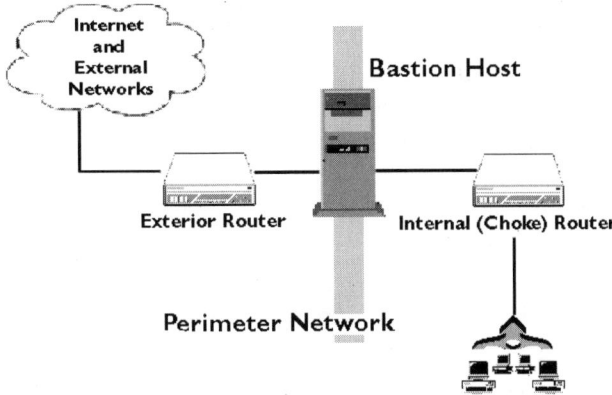

Figure 7.3 Bastion host architecture.

The configuration shown in Figure 7.4 provides three levels of defense. If the external router and a bastion host on the perimeter network are compromised, the attacker does not gain unlimited access to the internal network because the internal router is controlling access.

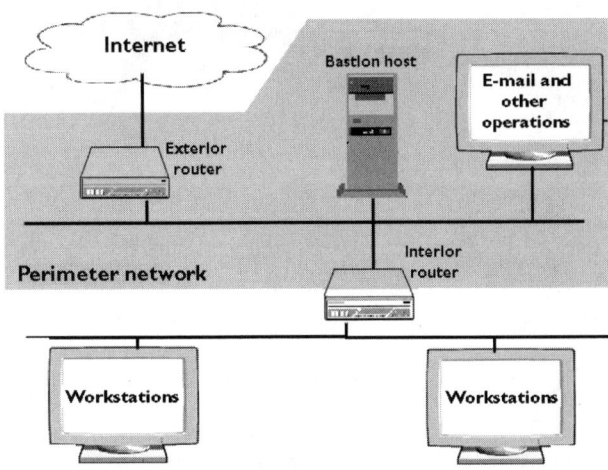

Figure 7.4 Perimeter network.

FIREWALL SOFTWARE

Misconfiguration of firewalls (or other network devices) is perhaps the biggest factor in opening security schemes to vulnerability. Although some firewalls come with configuration-checking software and others can warn of a potentially risky setup, some weaknesses will go undetected at first. It's up to net managers to track down these vulnerabilities and do something about them.

One class of firewall software is used for the virtual office: employees on business trips who need to access their electronic mail, field sales representatives who need corporate proposal data, and telecommuters working after hours and weekends from home, who must transfer files and open applications. So-called virtual private networks (VPN) are created by the use of firewalls, proxy servers, TCP/IP tunneling protocols, and data encryption to create secure communication using the Internet.

You can establish secure VPN between identified users, essentially establishing a safe intranet across the Internet. Encrypted personal communication goes through a firewall at the transmitting and receiving nodes. This type of VPN is a security solution for mobile and telecommuting employees as well as business-to-business communications and transactions.

Many organizations mix encrypting routers with conventional firewalls. The routers support interoffice communications, and the firewalls protect the customer access networks (see Figure 7.5).

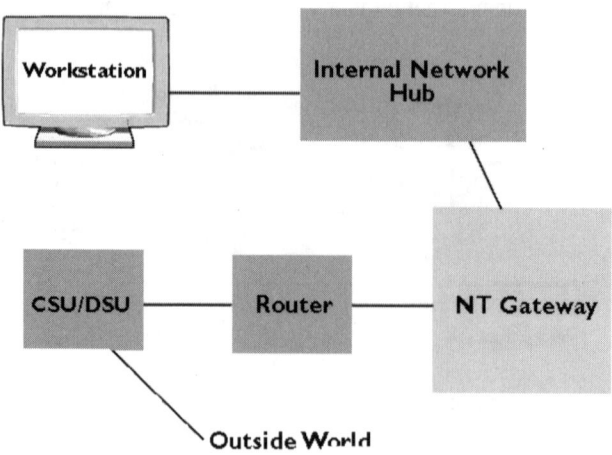

Figure 7.5 Firewall security.

For dial-in systems, you can use firewall software implementations such as remote access servers equipped with authentication schemes, including Radius (remote authentication dial-in user service) from Livingston Enterprises Inc. (Pleasanton, California) and TACACS (terminal access control access control system). Encrypting firewalls also allow users to access the corporate network via a secure Point-to-Point Protocol connection from a local Internet service provider rather than through the corporate modem pool. Dial-in is the hacker's first point of attack. Be careful not to spend a lot of money on routers and forget the back door created by the dial-in (see Appendix C for information on Remote Access Services for Windows NT).

For access-control devices to work, net managers must know ahead of time who's allowed onto the network. That makes these devices good for handling known groups of users. It also means that they're not much use when it comes to authenticating "strangers," such as customers and potential business partners. Also, these schemes typically don't provide gradations of access control: Once users gain access, they typically can reach the entire network, and that means they have too much freedom to poke around.

DUAL-HOMED HOSTS

A *dual-homed host* is a host with IP forwarding disabled (see Figure 7.6). One Ethernet card connects to the Internet, and the other one connects to the hosts on the internal net. There is no direct contact between the Internet and the internal network, but files can be made available on the gateway machine, or Internet access can be provided via an account on that machine. It can route IP packets from one network to the other, a capability that you would normally disable.

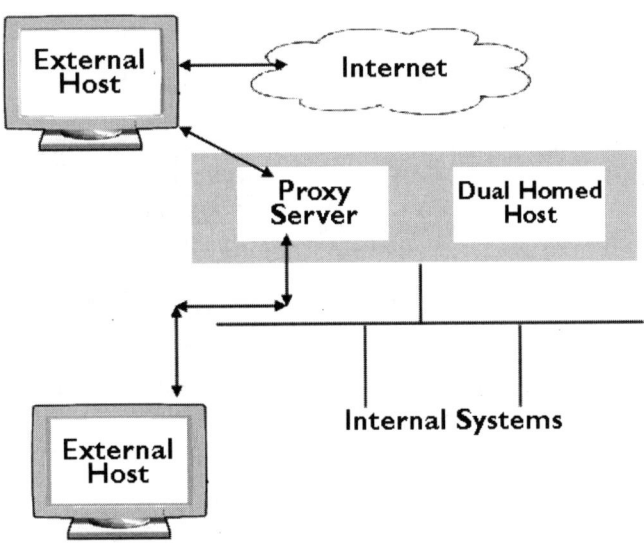

Figure 7.6 Dual-homed hosts

DOMAIN NAME SERVICE

DNS is a distributed database that translates between numerical IP addresses and domain names. (For a more detailed discussion, see Appendix C.) Here we will discuss the basics of DNS operation.

When a client needs to find out information about another host, such as the IP address for www.you.com, it queries its local DNS server. The local DNS server responds if it has the information. If it doesn't have the information, it queries other DNS servers until it either finds the information or runs out of places to look. This query forwarding is transparent to the client, which connects only to the local DNS server.

How is DNS of benefit in a security scenario? First, you set up a DNS server on the bastion host that the outside world can interrogate. You set up this server so that it claims to be authoritative for your domain. In fact, all the server knows is what you want the outside world to know, including the names and addresses of you gateway and your e-mail records (such as MX records used in setting up DNS). This is the "public" server.

Then you set up a DNS server on an internal machine. This server also claims to be authoritative for your domain and it is truly authoritative. The public system is a smokescreen to hackers. This internal server is your safe nameserver, into which you put all your regular DNS entries. This server forwards queries that it can't resolve to the public server.

Finally, you set up all your DNS clients, including the ones on the machine with the public server, to use the internal server (see Figure 7.7).

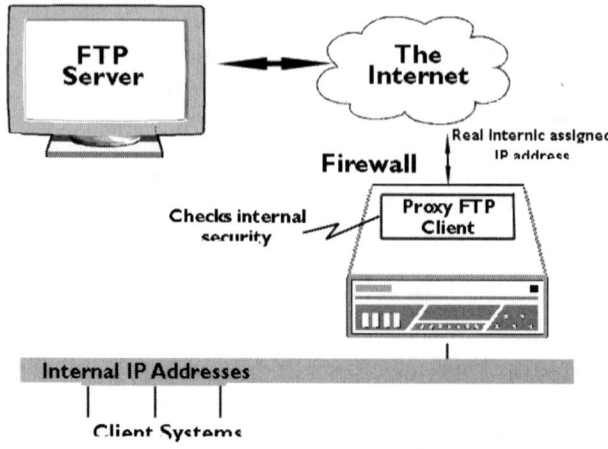

Figure 7.7 Hidden DNS.

Some companies also use wildcard PTR records in the IN-ADDR.ARPA domains. A PTR is a pointer record that is used to convert an IP address to a host name. IN-ADDR.ARPA is a special domain that supports the location of gateways and the Internet address-to-host mapping. It is similar to an inverse query of a site. If your Web site had the IP address 200.100.10.10, the entry in the IN-ADDR.ARPA domain would be 10.10.100.200.IN-ADDR.ARPA.

When you use the wildcard PTR record, an address-to-name lookup for any of your non-public hosts will return a statement such as "unknown.YOUR.DOMAIN." It does not show up as an error, so would-be hackers aren't tipped off about the company's shadow DNS.

DNS has packet-filtering and proxying characteristics. It uses packet filtering to determine where to look up the proper IP address. Let's look at you.me.us.com. (see Figure 7.8).

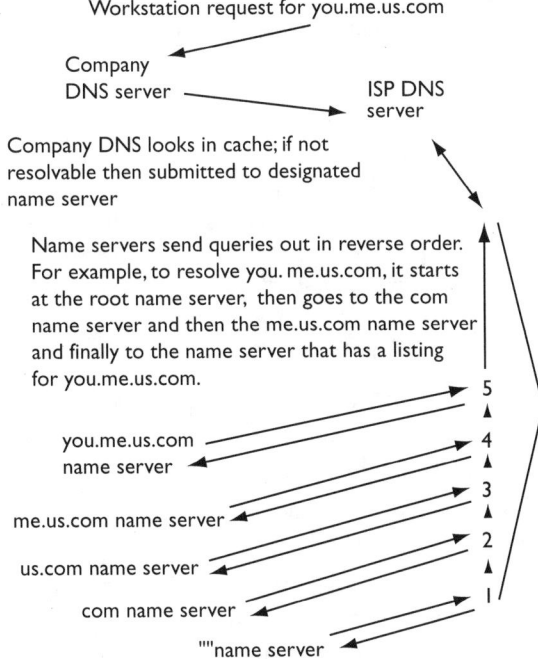

Figure 7.8 Performing DNS lookup.

Going from right to left, the DNS resolver starts with your DNS cache. If it cannot resolve the address, it points to .com, which will query and point to us.com, which will query and point to me.us.com, which will query and point finally to you.me.us.com. Your client will now receive the resolved information, and the screen will be painted with the home page for you.me.us.com.

PROXY SERVERS

A proxy server (sometimes referred to as an application gateway or forwarder) is an application that mediates traffic between a protected network and the Internet. Proxies are often used instead of router-based traffic controls to prevent traffic from passing directly between networks. Many proxies contain extra logging or support for user authentication. Because proxies must "understand" the application protocol being used, they can also implement protocol-specific security; for example, an FTP proxy might be configurable to permit incoming FTP and block outgoing FTP. Proxy servers are application-specific. To support a new protocol via a proxy, you must develop a proxy for it (see Figure 7.9).

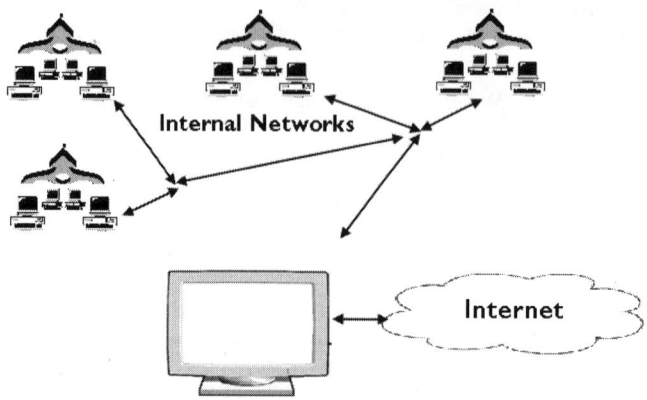

Figure 7.9 Proxy server.

As the figure shows, the user connects first to the proxy server within the firewall. The proxy client, acting for the user, sets up a session with the destination host. In this case, after verifying the connection to the FTP site, the proxy server starts the proxy FTP client.

Securing the Data

We determined how to remove unwanted access to a company's systems. Now what about those customers who want to buy the latest widget or employees who need to file a human resources training report on the intranet or Web site? The system must complete some sort of *transaction*. For this reason, you may need to know how to set up secure transactions for database record retrieval and electronic commerce.

In this case, you may not want to establish a permanent VPN between all the clients involved (as discussed earlier), so you need to consider transaction security. You can take a closer look at the transaction model in Chapter 11.

To understand these two types of basic transactions—the external purchase and the internal request—let's separate them into secure payments and internal transactions.

SECURE PAYMENTS

Secure payment methods are intended to provide an acceptable level of trust between a business and a customer. The company trusts that the customer request is valid and not an attempt to trash its database. This means that the company needs a method to authenticate a cardholder as a legitimate user of an account. The customer trusts the company not to share payment information with anyone else and to properly charge the account. This means that the method must authenticate that a merchant can accept bankcard payments through its relationship with a financial institution.

This is usually done with encryption algorithms such as DES (Data Encryption Standard) or RC-4 from RSA Data Security Inc. At the moment the dominant security scheme is Secure Sockets Layer (SSL) (Netscape Communications Corp., Mountain View, California), which encrypts a single session using RC-4. Other technologies are HTTPS and SET (secure electronic transaction), which was developed by Visa and Mastercard and several high-tech companies, including GTE Corp. (Stamford, Connecticut), IBM, Microsoft Corp. (Redmond, Washington), Netscape, and RSA.

These methods provide confidentiality of payment and ordering information and ensure integrity for all transmitted data (see Figure 7.10).

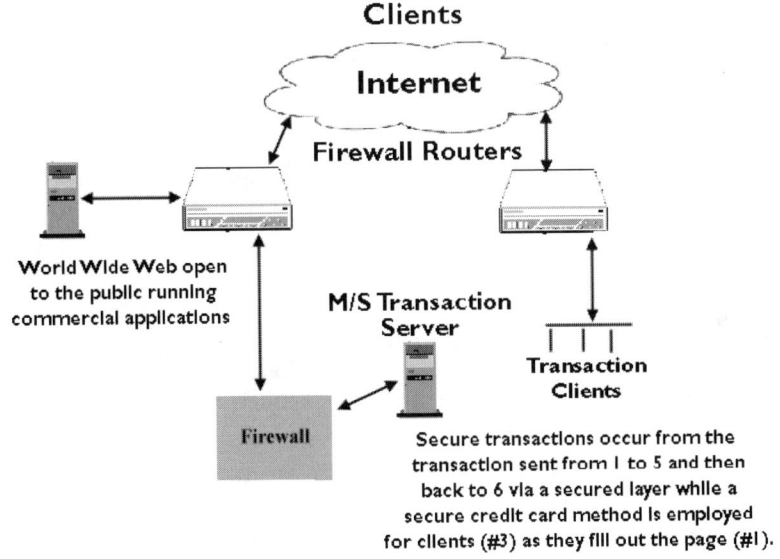

Figure 7.10 Secure payments and transactions.

Remember that these Internet methods are based on currently successful credit-card authorization networks. If a person purchases a new cellular phone using a credit card, the merchant authenticates the customer using credit-card authorization bureaus, which maintain databases with pertinent authentication data. Visa and Mastercard have installed secured Internet gateways to link more than 18,000 banks and their databases.

How do customers verify that the on-line merchant is OK? Netscape's SSL addresses this issue by having the merchant verify its identify to the customer using an RSA public key certificate, which is countersigned by RSA's spinoff company Verisign Inc. Companies request *digital IDs.*, which verify that no forgery or false representation has occurred.

SECURE SOCKETS LAYER

So what is the HTTPS:// that you may see, instead of HTTP://, when entering some Web sites? It has to do with Secure Sockets Layer. SSL provides data encryption, server authentication, message integrity, and optional client authentication for a TCP/IP connection. SSL is an open, nonproprietary protocol that has been heavily pursued and championed by Netscape. The protocol allows client/server applications to communicate in a way that cannot be eavesdropped. Servers are always authenticated, and clients are optionally authenticated. SSL is intended for protecting only application-layer data.

When a system transmits data structured in one protocol format within the format of another protocol, it is called *tunneling*. When a company is running the Novell protocol (IPX) in a TCP/IP environment, its network is tunneling.

In tunneling SSL, the proxy cannot have access to the data being transferred in either direction. Such access would be a security breach. The proxy knows the source and destination addresses and possibly the name of the requesting user.

The HTTPS protocol, then, is HTTP on top of SSL.

INTERNAL TRANSACTIONS

Internal transaction security must be far more airtight than that of simple payment schemes. With credit cards, the customer and merchant are protected by state and federal laws. The consumer's liability is minimized. With a fraudulent on-line sale, though, the developer has lost a product. In addition, when a company is handling trade secrets, personnel information, and federal tax information, it has no legal safety net. The company is totally liable. This also implies that transactions must be kept private and viewed only on a need-to-know" basis.

The amount of fraud in credit-card systems is an unacceptable level for internal transactions. Companies need better authentication schemes. One of these schemes is registration-based transactions. In this case, customers are issued account numbers and an electronic key before they can access the system. The key can be used both for authentication and to exchange additional secure keys. An advantage of registration-based systems is their performance. These systems are running a challenge-response handshake with a preregistered party.

Registration-based transactions work like automatic teller machine card transactions. The bank issues the person an ATM card, which contains some keying information on its magnetic strip. The customer can choose an additional key (the personal identification number, or PIN). If customers are allowed to withdraw money from another bank's ATM (such as the STAR network on the back of the customer's bankcard), it is called *delegation of trust*. This means that businesses must be able to trust one another and their customers (see Figure 7.11).

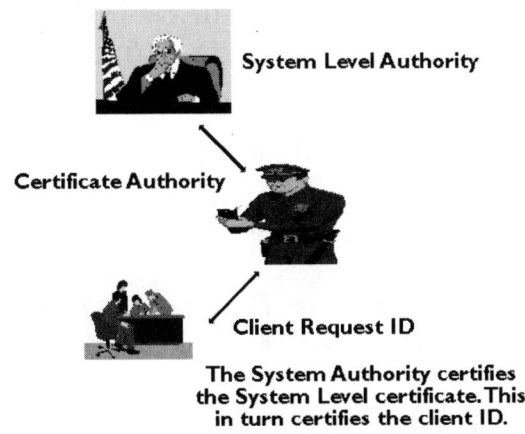

Figure 7.11 System authority certification.

Security Components of Microsoft's Proxy Server

Microsoft's Proxy Server is constructed as a firewall-class security service and has a number of add-in security features. The Proxy Server architecture is resistant to common attacks. In *IP spoofing*, (see Figure 7.12) the intruder sends messages to a computer with an IP address indicating that the message is coming from a trusted port. SATAN (System Administration Tool for Analyzing Networks) tests host systems by probing Network Information Services, Finger, NFS, FTP, TFTP, rexd, and other services. This test determines which Internet services are present and whether those services are misconfigured or contain vulnerabilities that an intruder could exploit.

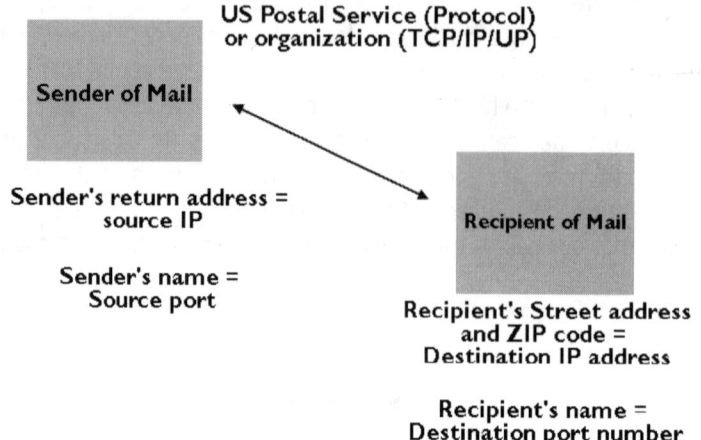

Figure 7.12 IP spoofing.

Through its IP address aggregation features, Microsoft Proxy Server ensures that an internal network's topology and addressing is never revealed to the outside network, thereby hiding the internal network structure.

The Web Proxy server supports both HTTP plain text and encrypted user authentication. WinSock Proxy client provides support for NT C2-encrypted authentication. Microsoft Proxy Server allows administrators to select a list of sites that users are exclusively permitted or denied access to. Administrators can also set detailed user and group permission lists per protocol in both the Web Proxy and WinSock Proxy components. Developers can create textual and database logs to provide a detailed audit trail. Web Proxy supports SSL tunneling to provide an encrypted path between the client and the remote server.

You can secure the company's intranet by placing a proxy server between the main corporate LAN and a secure private LAN. This arrangement allows administrators to control user access between network segments if they do not wish to use a hardware switch/router solution.

A summary of these features can be found in Table 7.1.

Table 7.1 Microsoft Proxy Server 2.0 Features

PERFORMANCE	FIREWALL SECURITY	MANAGEMENT
Hierarchical caching	Dynamic packet filtering	Internet service management
Distributed caching	Reverse proxy	HTML-based administration
FTP caching	Server proxying	Command-line administration with scripting
40 % better performance	Real-time alerts	Array administration
HTTP 1.1 Support	VPN support	Configuration backup and restore

C2 Security

You may see a lot of sales information regarding C2 security. What is it? C2 is a security standard that tells an administrator that a product, when configured in a certain way, has certain features responsibly implemented. That configuration is a stand-alone workstation with no diskette drive.

C2 does not necessarily close all the holes that may exist in a company's security. It will log those cases it cannot solve. For network testing, you would use the TNI (Trusted Networking Interpretation) evaluation.

Although Windows NT does a good job of incorporating the C2 specs in Proxy Server, it has no real protection against malicious hosts on the network. This includes those systems that can actively or passively tap an NT-NT conversation. To address these issues, you need to look at confidentiality and integrity-related encryption methods.

In any case, you can go to the NT Resource Kit CD-ROM and load **c2config**. This program can help you ensure a tighter security model.

What Is the Best Solution?

To determine the best security system, you need to select the items that work best for your operation. First, you need to understand your network's topology and accessibility and determine which systems are mission-critical. It is a good idea to install network management tools that allow you to review traffic on the network and design it to fit the needs of the users. Segment traffic for the various departments and create zones and domains.

Now let's look at the basic services on Proxy Server and find out how you can use them to protect your dynamic Web site.

Proxy Server: The Heart of Its Services

Many companies are beginning to use Web servers to manage internal company information. The point-and-click nature of the Web makes it simple for computer novices to perform their jobs. A Web interface is also the perfect environment for disseminating information. It's a tricky task to open a Web server or any Internet server (such as FTP and Telnet) to the outside world if the network where the server resides does not have valid Internet addresses.

Proxy Planning

When setting up Proxy Server, you will install components, set the cache drives, define the Local Address Table (LAT), configure client setup information, and set access control.

Although details regarding Proxy Server are beyond this book's scope, we want to highlight the major issues regarding its setup.

THE SETUP

Two major software requirements must be met before Microsoft Proxy Server will run correctly. The first is that the Internet Information Server must be running. The only IIS component that must be installed is the Web Server. The second software requirement is that a connection method must be used.

The IIS Web Server is required for Microsoft Proxy Server to operate properly. If you want to use Proxy 2.0, you will need to load Service Pack 3.

Remember that if you use Proxy Server and Microsoft IIS together for external Web publishing, it is highly recommended that you use different computers to run Proxy Server and IIS. Proxy Server is installed on a server that already has IIS installed. During Proxy Server setup, IIS is automatically configured so that it does not listen to Internet requests (requests sent to the IP address of the server's network adapter card that is connected to the Internet). In this default configuration, requests from Internet clients are ignored.

The Proxy Server computer requires at least one network adapter card connected to the internal network plus one network adapter, modem, or integrated services digital network (ISDN) adapter card to connect to the Internet. When you're setting TCP/IP properties for any network adapter card, remember to enter a permanent reserved IP address for the Proxy Server computer and an appropriate subnet mask for your local network. Dynamic Host Configuration Protocol should be disabled, because it attempts to reset the default gateway you selected for Proxy Server.

Microsoft Proxy Server is usually set up to run on the same machine as Internet server applications. This arrangement poses no problem as long as the Web server in use is the Microsoft IIS Web Server, the only application that is required by Microsoft Proxy Server. This is because Microsoft Proxy Server works in conjunction with the listening services of the IIS Web Server on port 80. In this way, Proxy Server picks up on LAN requests that are destined for the outside world. Any other Internet server applications can be run on an NT machine that also runs Microsoft Proxy Server. Microsoft Proxy Server's Web Proxy and WinSock Proxy services are implemented so that port conflicts are not an issue on the server.

Other proxy servers operate by listening to ports that other server applications listen to. This arrangement causes a conflict, because no two applications can respond to the same TCP/IP port traffic.

TCP/IP: PAVING THE ROAD TO PROXY SERVER

Before we go any further at the packet level and proxy issues, you should understand the pavement used on this information highway. TCP/IP is a system of protocols for the packet-switching network that is the foundation of the Internet. TCP/IP takes a message to be transmitted to a remote computer, breaks the information into chunks called *packets*, and sends the packets to the remote computer, where they are reassembled into the original message. Each packet contains a piece of the information (document, sound, or image) plus an ID tag that contains information such as the addresses of the sending and receiving computers and where the packet fits in the total message.

The movement of IP packets is similar to that of postal mail. The IP has a sender and a receiver address along with the names of those involved in the sending, receiving, and transfer (see Figure 7.13).

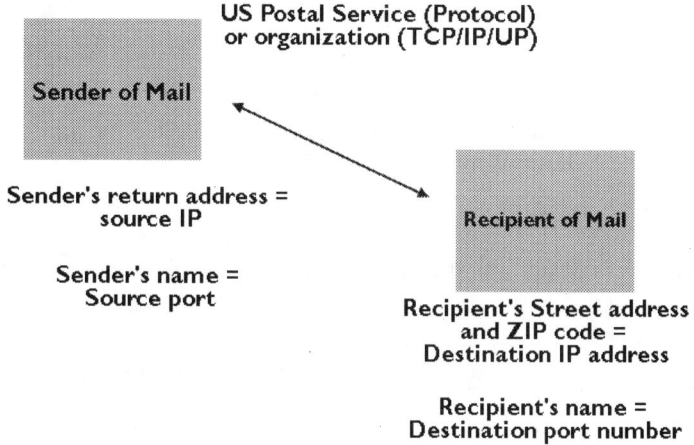

Figure 7.13 Similarity between sending personal mail and the movement of IP packets.

Packet switching takes advantage of the appearance of a large number of circuits, called a *virtual circuit*. A virtual circuit is a communication path between devices that is used only during a specific message transmission. Even though packet switching allows several different terminals to be interconnected on the same communication circuit (like a party line), it appears to the user as though there are many dedicated circuits.

This arrangement is in opposition to circuit-switching services that are used for phone systems in which a dedicated channel—a circuit—is set up between two nodes (phone callers in a phone system) for the duration of the call. The amount of bandwidth is fixed, and that usually does not work well for handling bursts of traffic. The virtual circuits used for circuit switching have only one route, without the alternative paths available in packet switching. For applications, such as multimedia, that need fixed, guaranteed bandwidth, circuit switching is a better method.

Because each packet has its own addressing information, it can travel independently in a network. Because the Internet is a network (not a hierarchy) of interconnected computers, each packet may travel a different path to reach its destination. The packets may arrive out of order or may be damaged and require resending. The sequencing information allows the receiving computer to reconstruct the message.

The architecture of the TCP/IP model contains four layers, and each layer performs a different task. When a layer receives a data packet, it performs its task and sends the packet to the next level.

The first layer, the network layer, establishes virtual paths between nodes in a network. Examples of this layer include X.25, Ethernet, Asynchronous Transfer Mode (ATM), and Frame-Relay.

The second layer is the Internet level: IP (Internet Protocol). IP is a connectionless protocol that describes how to find the one computer out of millions of interconnected computers; it defines standards to transmit messages from one computer to another. Different networks can use IP to talk to each other.

The third layer is the transmission level, which is responsible for transporting packets between network nodes. Here we have the TCP (Transaction Control Protocol), which concerns itself with acknowledgments, error checking, and error recovery protocols. Another packet at this level is the UDP (User Datagram Protocol). It is a connectionless transport protocol that does not contain an error recovery attribute. UDP is used for transmitting IP address information and also used for many multimedia applications in which loss of data may result in a temporary reduction in the quality of the image or sound (static).

The fourth layer is the application level, which identifies client/server application protocols, including the following:

- Hypertext Transport Protocol (HTTP), which is used in the World Wide Web.
- Simple Mail Transfer Protocol (SMTP), which is used to deliver e-mail on the Internet.
- File Transfer Protocol (FTP), which is used for file transfer and directory management of remote computers.
- Telnet, which is used to establish virtual terminals that connect you to any authorized computer connected to the Internet.

Data is organized in IP packets with destination addresses. TCP/IP packets have headers that Proxy Server uses to implement its level of security.

How do you handle these conflicts? Microsoft Proxy Server resolves these conflicts by using two services: Web Proxy and WinSock Proxy.

The Basic Services

With standard proxy requests (WWW, FTP, and Gopher), the IIS Web Server first fields all traffic through a special filter DLL (ISAPI) that determines whether the traffic is local or destined for the outside. If the traffic is not to be picked up by the WWW server itself,

Microsoft Proxy Server takes over the traffic and passes it outside. TCP/IP traffic that is not covered by the Microsoft Proxy Server Web Proxy Server (any traffic on a port other than 80) is handled by the Microsoft Proxy Server WinSock Proxy service.

WEB PROXY SERVICE

The Web Proxy service supports all popular Internet browsers and the HTTP, Gopher, and FTP. Also, the Web Proxy service supports the HTTP-S protocol for secure sessions using SSL connections.

The Web Proxy service stores copies of requested Internet URLs in a dedicated cache. Subsequent requests for these objects can be serviced from the server disk rather than by issuing the request over the Internet. Proxy Server employs active caching. This means that Proxy Server can be set to automatically connect to the Internet and download certain Internet objects based on their popularity, without client initiation. Active caching improves browser response time, thereby reducing the demand on an Internet connection.

The Web Proxy service uses caching to maintain a local copy of HTTP objects. Not all objects that pass through the Web Proxy service can or should be cached. Some objects are dynamic and change frequently, and some objects change every time they are accessed. Other objects require authentication of the requesting client and cannot be cached for security reasons.

Reverse proxying is the ability to listen to incoming requests for an internal Web (HTTP) server computer and respond on behalf of that server (see Figure 7.14).

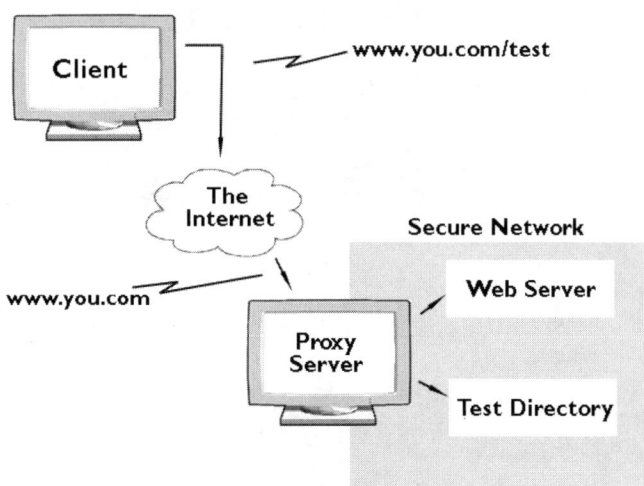

Figure 7.14 Reverse proxying.

In this way, an insecure server is made to "look" secure. *Reverse hosting* maintains a list of internal server computers that have permission to publish to the Internet, thereby

106 Chapter 7

allowing Proxy Server to listen and respond on behalf of multiple servers that are located behind it. The reverse proxying and hosting features offer great flexibility and enhanced security. Virtually any computer on your internal network that is running an HTTP server application, such as IIS, can publish to the Internet. Security is not compromised. All incoming requests and outgoing responses pass through Proxy Server first, so there remains only a single "hole" to the Internet (see Figure 7.15).

Figure 7.15 Proxy Server handles all requests.

Proxy Server can be configured to allow anonymous requests by users or to require users to be authenticated (validated) by the server. Once users are authenticated, you can determine which protocols (HTTP, FTP, or Gopher) are accessible for each user. Users can be granted access to selected protocols. You open the Web Proxy Service Properties dialog box and click on the **Security** button. This opens up the Security dialog box. Then click on the **Packet Filters** tab showing the protocols (see Figure 7.16).

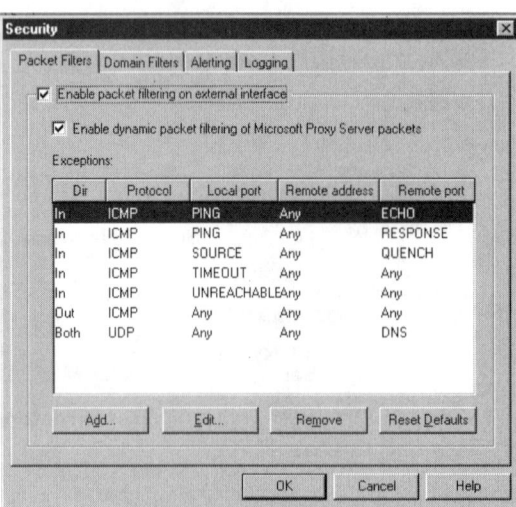

Figure 7.16 Packet filter choices.

Click on the protocol of interest (make sure that **Enable packet filtering on external interface** is checked) to see a screen similar to Figure 7.17.

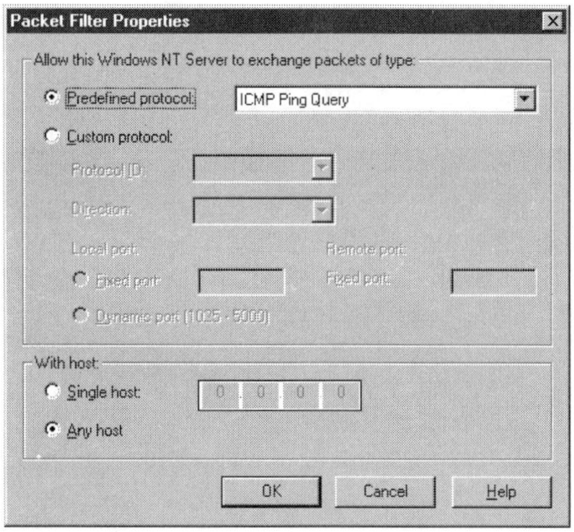

Figure 7.17 Packet filter properties.

You now manipulate packet filtering on single or multiple hosts.

The Web Proxy service provides secure, encrypted logon for those browsers that support Windows NT challenge/response authentication, and it provides basic authentication for other browsers. It also allows data encryption by means of SSL tunneling.

You can restrict access to remote Web sites by domain name, IP address, and subnet mask. Open the Web Proxy Service Properties dialog box, and choose the **Service** tab. Then choose **Security** (see Figure 7.18).

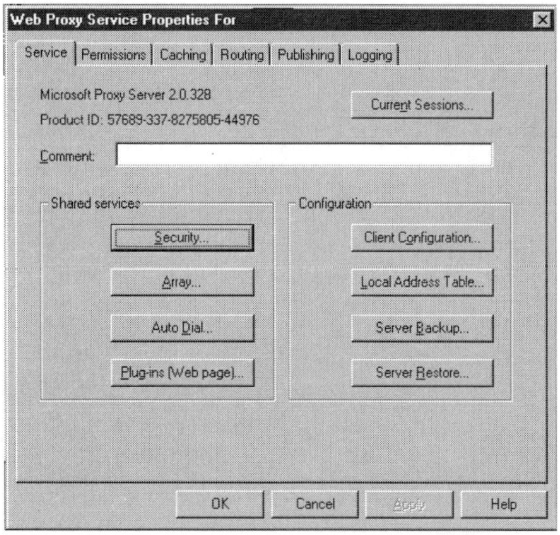

Figure 7.18 Web Proxy Service Properties For dialog box.

You will see the Security **dialog** box. By choosing the **Domain Filters** tab and checking **Enable filtering**, you can choose to grant access to all protocols except those listed or deny access to all Web sites except those listed (see Figure 7.19).

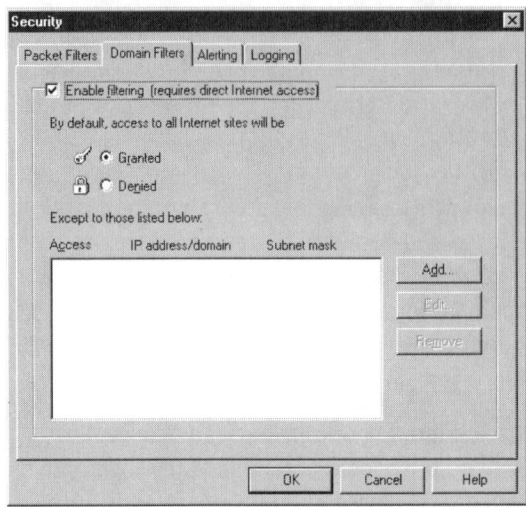

Figure 7.19 Domain Filters tab.

The settings are global and affect all users who access the Internet through the Proxy Server computer.

All requests to the Internet are made with the Proxy Server's external (Internet) IP address as the source address. This approach hides internal IP addresses and allows the use of unregistered or private addresses.

The Web Proxy service consists of two components: the Proxy ISAPI filter and the Proxy ISAPI application (see Figure 7.20).

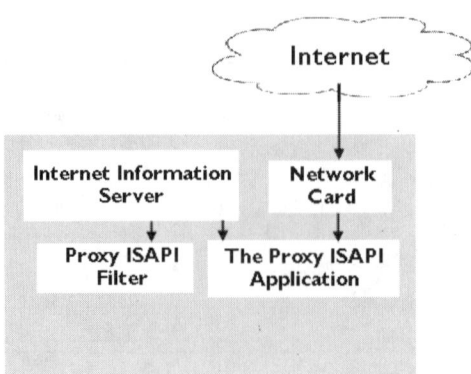

Figure 7.20 The Proxy ISAPI filter and the Proxy ISAPI application.

An ISAPI filter is called for every request regardless of such details as the identity of the resource requested in the URL. This means that an ISAPI filter can monitor, log, modify, redirect, or authenticate requests sent to the Web Server. The WWW service can call the ISAPI filter DLL's entry point at various times during a request-and-response sequence. When the ISAPI filter is loaded, it programmatically registers the notification points in which it is interested. The WWW service then starts calling the ISAPI filter DLL's entry point at each requested notification point for each HTTP request (see Figure 7.21).

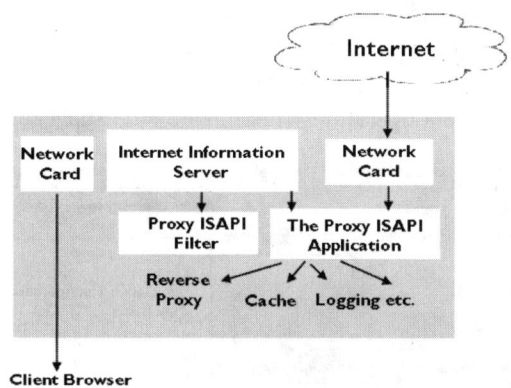

Figure 7.21 ISAPI call.

For HTTP requests, all input/output (I/O) is done asynchronously after the domain name has been resolved. If possible, the DNS is used to resolve the domain name (see Figure 7.22).

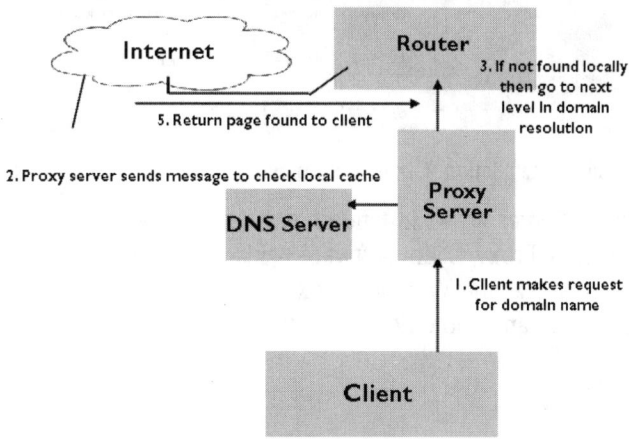

Figure 7.22 DNS resolution with Proxy Server.

WINSOCK PROXY SERVICE

The WinSock Proxy service supports communication over TCP/IP and IPX/SPX on the internal network, allowing access to Internet sites from Internet applications on the network. However, only applications that are written to use Windows Sockets over TCP/IP (Internet applications) can be redirected.

The WinSock Proxy service provides Windows NT challenge/response authentication (a secure, encrypted logon process) whether or not the client application supports it. You can use Windows NT challenge/response authentication between clients and the WinSock Proxy service to avoid sending passwords across the internal network. Once authentication is done, the WinSock Proxy service uses the logon username to verify that the user has permission to do the network operations attempted by the application (see Figure 7.23).

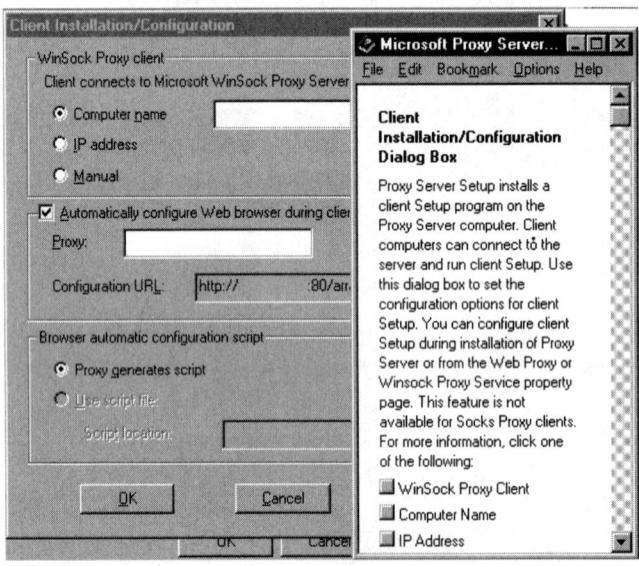

Figure 7.23 Client Installation/Configuration dialog box. Note the availability of help tools.

The WinSock Proxy Server works in tandem with the WinSock Proxy Client on the workstations. The WinSock Proxy Client software fields any local TCP/IP requests, translating the traffic to the port that the WinSock Proxy Server is listening to. This means that the WinSock Proxy Server can handle nearly any type of TCP/IP client, such as SMTP, NNTP, and Telnet, without a conflict with other Internet server software that may be running alongside Microsoft Proxy Server (see Figure 7.24).

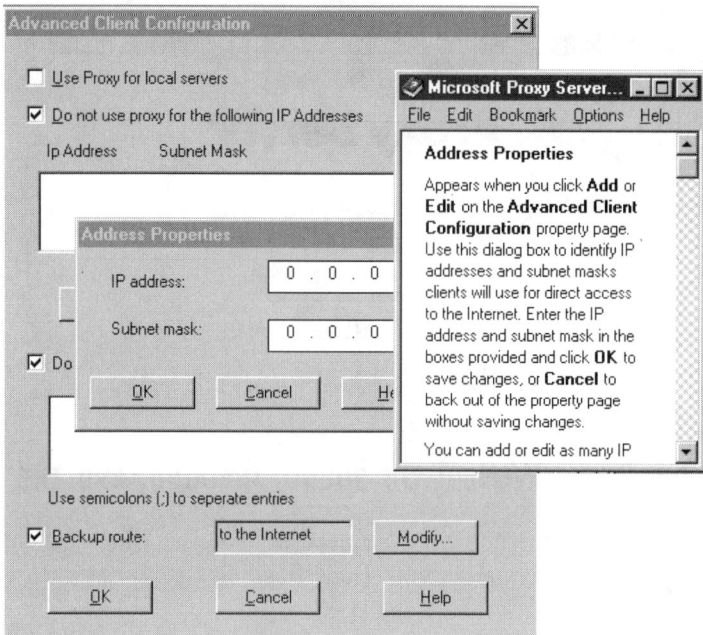

Figure 7.24 Advanced Client Configuration dialog box with Address Properties help.

The Web Proxy service configuration consists of only a few settings in Control Panel. The WinSock Proxy client-side configuration requires installation of special client software. WinSock Proxy redirection is enabled or disabled via an **INI** file.

A nice feature in the WinSock Proxy service is its ability to pass streaming audio and video, such as RealAudio and VDOLive. Other Winsock proxy servers that use Sockets version 4.0, such as Netscape Proxy Server, cannot handle streaming data. Built into the WinSock Proxy service is generic support for all protocols. In fact, you can add protocols using Proxy Server's protocol property sheets and specifying the port that the protocol calls. See Figure 7.25 for other plug-in–related information.

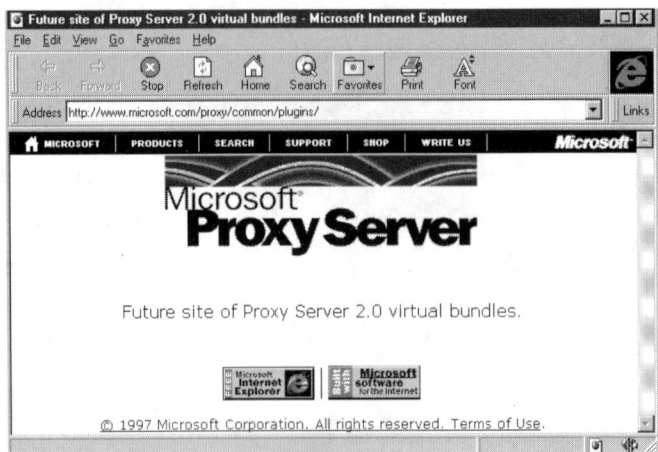

Figure 7.25 Proxy Server plug-in information screen.

ACCESS TO THE PROXY WORLD: OUTBOUND, INBOUND, AND THE GATEWAYS

In implementing access to the network, you need to understand how people access information from external and internal systems. Understanding this process can help you better develop and troubleshoot your active Web pages.

Outbound Access

Let's start with how your system handles password authentication. The three methods for password authentication in Proxy Server are the same as those for IIS: anonymous, basic, challenge/response.

ANONYMOUS PASSWORD AUTHENTICATION

The anonymous technique uses a standard logon account to provide guest access to resources on the Internet. This account, when installed under IIS, defaults to IUSR_Computername. For example, if the machine's name is Accounting5 the account is IUSR_Accounting5. If you wish to change this account, you must do so both in IIS and on the NT Primary Domain Controller (PDC) to validate future network connectivity (such as SQL database access by a guest user). FTP clients always default to using "anonymous" as their logon.

This method allows any client to access without an NT username and password, and it is a good method for guest entry to a site. The problem is that it leaves a hole for non-Windows clients.

BASIC PASSWORD AUTHENTICATION

Basic authentication uses an HTTP mechanism that sends and receives user information as clear text. Passwords and usernames are encoded but not encrypted. The client software is responsible for prompting the user for username and password credentials. If you are using a trusted domain account, the username must contain the domain name in the following format:

```
username=domain\account
```

For example, if the domain is "sound" and the account is blaster, then the format is sound/blaster.

As you can probably tell, the problem is that this method exposes the network traffic to hackers. It validates the account against the NT security database.

CHALLENGE/RESPONSE AUTHENTICATION

Challenge/Response (also called NT LM in the Proxy literature) consists of a number of messages between the client and the server. In this sequence, the client computer uses its established user logon information to identify itself to the server. The client software does not prompt the user to enter any data. Instead, the information is available after the user first logs on to a Windows NT-based computer.

Not all browsers support this method. Internet Explorer, of course, supports it.

NOTE If you are is using Microsoft Internet Explorer 3.02, Windows NT challenge/response authentication does not work with the Web Proxy service for SSL connections. You must use basic authentication for all SSL connections.

WHAT IS THE BEST METHOD?

If you choose all three methods, the Web server returns all authentication methods in a header to the Web browser. The Web browser then chooses which authentication method to use. Because the Windows NT challenge/response protocol is listed first in the header, a browser that supports the Windows NT challenge/response protocol will use it. A browser that does not support the Windows NT challenge/response protocol will use basic authentication. If the browser does not support basic authentication, it will use the anonymous login.

To increase security there are a few things you can do.

1. Do not give the IUSR_computername account, the Guests group, or the Everyone group any right other than **Log on Locally** or **Access the computer from this network**.
2. Use the NT User Manager to set bad logon policies.

3. Always use NTFS disk partitions instead of File Allocation Table (FAT). Set NTFS permissions for the individual files.
4. Make sure that all of NT's password control features have been implemented. Employ **PASSFILT.DLL,** which comes with SP2 and SP3. It forces strong password choices on users.
5. The default Administrator account is a target for most intruders. Create a new account that has all the administrator privileges. Leave the old administrator account enabled but remove the rights and permissions.
6. Enable auditing on all NT systems.
7. Disable NetBIOS over TCP/IP network bindings where possible.
8. Block all nonessential TCP/IP ports, both inbound and outbound. In particular, at least block UDP ports 137 and 138 and TCP port 139.
9. Revoke the **Access From Network** right (using User Manager) for users who don't need to connect to that particular NT system.
10. Do not leave NT workstations turned on and unattended. Depending on how your network is set up, a hacker can start looking for any kind of opening on the network, including an idle modem connection.
11. Disable the Simple TCP/IP services.

Next, you need to control the physical dial-up access in and out of the network.

The Remote Access Service (RAS) in Windows NT is used on the server computer to manage dial-up sessions and connect to a service provider. The primary purpose of RAS is to provide a dial-in feature for outside users of a network. However, it can also operate as a dial-out service for local users to connect to other networks. RAS can also be used to dial out and connect to the Internet. Under NT 4.0 the outbound capability of RAS is found in the **Accessories** folder as Dial Up Networking. If a RAS connection is not used within 20 minutes, NT will shut it down. The NT time-out value can be disabled by editing the Autodisconnect key in the registry.

To start the NT registry editor, open a command prompt and enter the command **REGEDT32.EXE**. Locate the following key:

```
HKEY_LOCAL_MACHINE

  System
  CurrentControlSet
   Services
    RemoteAccess
     Parameters
      Autodisconnect
```

The Autodisconnect key is a hexadecimal key and is set to 14 (14 in hexadecimal notation = 20 in standard decimal notation). Editing this value and setting it to 0 will disable the time-out value for RAS connections. Be careful when editing the registry. Making incorrect changes will sometimes render NT unbootable, and only a reinstallation of the system will take care of the problem.

Microsoft Proxy Server can automatically dial a provider if the Internet connection is not currently available when a proxy client requests a connection. This capability is known as Auto Dial, and it is Configured through an external application found in the **Microsoft Proxy Server** folder. This application can be used to specify which ISP is dialed and what times of the day the ISP can be dialed. By default, Auto Dial is not enabled and the administrator is responsible for making the connection from Microsoft Proxy Server to the Internet.

Microsoft Proxy Server requires that TCP/IP be installed on the NT machine on which it is running. To make a successful connection to a TCP/IP UNIX host, TCP/IP must be installed first. Connections to LAN workstations do not have to be made through TCP/IP; Microsoft Proxy Server WinSock Proxy will function via the IPX/SPX protocol. The Web Proxy portion of Microsoft Proxy Server will function correctly only via TCP/IP. When IPX is the transport protocol between workstations to Microsoft Proxy Server, all Internet requests from workstations are handled as though they were external requests and WinSock Proxy server will manage them all.

For IPX/SPX to be successfully used as the primary workstation transport method, the WinSock Proxy client software (provided with Microsoft Proxy Server) must be installed on all workstations that will access the Internet. Applications that would normally use the Web Proxy Server (such as Netscape and IE 3.0) must use the WinSock Proxy Server instead, because the Web Proxy Server can communicate with clients only via a direct TCP/IP link.

Except for these minor points, Microsoft Proxy Server is very flexible when it comes to operating via either TCP/IP or IPX/SPX.

NOTE Under rare conditions, it is possible for external packets to slip into a LAN that is connected to the Internet. This opens the possibility for unauthorized external users to have access to resources within the network. The following minimum conditions would have to be met before LAN security would be compromised. Keep in mind that this issue has nothing to do with Microsoft Proxy Server, which only directs internal traffic outward.

- An external user must send directed packets into the LAN and know ahead of time the IP address of the system to connect to.
- The target system must be running a server application that the outsider is attempting to connect to.
- Network security must be breached. If the target resource has a password assigned to it (in the case of a Windows 95 or Windows for Workgroups system), the outsider must know the password. If the target resource is an NT resource the outsider will be challenged to provide valid NT security credentials **IP Forward** on the NT machine connected to the Internet must be enabled.

Disabling IP forwarding is another method you can use to prevent passing IP packets between internal networked systems and the Internet. To disable IP forwarding, follow these steps:

1. Open Control Panel.
2. Select the **Network** icon.
3. Select the **Protocols** tab.
4. Select the **TCP/IP** protocol.
5. Select **Properties**.
6. Select the **Routing** tab.
7. Uncheck Enable IP Forwarding.

Inbound Access

When Microsoft Proxy Server is installed, two elements of NT are altered so that security is enhanced. First, **IP Forwarding**, a setting found within the TCP/IP settings, is turned off. It controls whether NT will forward IP packets between network interfaces in managers (such as a network card and a RAS connection to an Internet provider). If a dedicated, full-time Internet connection is available to a network and if each workstation on the LAN is configured for its own direct Internet access, IP forwarding must be enabled for workstations to pass their packets to the Internet and vice versa. This arrangement will halt all inbound traffic at the NT server, which is connected to the Internet.

Second, Microsoft Proxy Server disables listening on all TCP/IP ports that do not have permissions set for them. This means that any Internet server application (such as an FTP server, a Telnet server, or a POP3 server) running on the connected NT server will not be able to hear any external inbound traffic until permissions are set for the associated protocol in the WinSock Proxy. The Web Proxy listens only to port 80 for traffic. If permissions are set for any of the supported protocols in the Web Proxy, port 80 will be listened to for inbound traffic. If you want to set your network security at a very high level for proxy access, one approach is to set up the NT server running Microsoft Proxy Server as a primary domain controller of its own domain. A one-way trust relationship can then be established between the Proxy domain and the network domain. The Proxy domain would be set to trust the network domain, but the network domain would not trust the Proxy domain. This arrangement will further limit access between Proxy Server and all other systems on the network domain.

This arrangement also works well when the network is set as a workgroup instead of as a domain. The NT server running Microsoft Proxy Server can be set on a primary domain controller of its own domain, and that will give greater security control and allow easier expansion for future growth.

If you do not have any name resolution service available on this network, the network administrator must hard-code the IP address location of Microsoft Proxy Server into each workstation.

Handling Increased Loads

Keep in mind that for Microsoft Proxy Server 1.1, separate proxy servers do not work in concert; they do not share cache data, security settings, log files, and filter settings. Each server operates independently. Setting up a group of Web Proxy Servers in a multihomed group under Window Internet Name Service (WINS) helps to automatically distribute the workload between all servers when it doesn't matter which server fields a client request for Internet access. If you want to control which clients access which proxy server when there is more than one proxy server for a network, you must reference each proxy server independently.

The arrangement of which workstations access which Microsoft Proxy Server is a configuration element set up on each workstation. After you install Internet Explorer 3.0 or higher, a new control icon is placed in the Control Panel of Windows 95 machines. This icon is the access point for configuring all vital Internet settings for a Windows 95 workstation, including proxy settings. To control whether Windows 95 will use a proxy for its Internet connections, select the Connection tab.

The Proxy as a Gateway

Microsoft Proxy Server gateways can be used just as normal gateways can be used. Most company installations of Microsoft Proxy Server gateways use limited connections, such as analog modems. On LANs that have Internet access, multiple Microsoft Proxy Servers are more common than gateways.

Proxy Server gateways can also spread out the Internet load. A network administrator can implement multiple proxy servers, each server dedicated to servicing only a certain type of connection (such as FTP). Another way to balance the load is to set different groups of LAN users to use different Microsoft Proxy Servers.

As you implement various gateway load balancing techniques, you should be aware of FTP demands. FTP access tends to be more demanding of a connection than WWW access. FTP access involves lengthy file transfers, and the transmitted data is not stored in the Microsoft Proxy Server cache (remember the active caching for HTTP in Proxy Server).

One of the best features of Proxy Server is its multiprotocol support. You can access Proxy Server not only over IP but also over IPX/SPX. This built-in gateway support provides you with a couple of important features. You can use your current LAN topology, and Proxy Server does not need a dedicated IP address at the Internet service provider.

But even Microsoft admits that Proxy Server is not meant as firewall alternative. Proxy Server does not filter at the packet level. If you want to install IP at each client, you must use Microsoft's TCP/IP stack, which is set up in Network Control Panel on NT and

Windows 95. The reason for this is that the WinSock Proxy Client installation modifies the IP stack, and Microsoft does not support anyone else's stacks.

CONTROLLING THE PROXY

Internet Service Manager (ISM) can be started from either the **Microsoft Internet Server** folder or the **Microsoft Proxy Server** folder, because the ISM that is used to administer Proxy Server is the same as that used in IIS. Note that when you stop or start the Web Proxy service, the WWW service (of IIS) is also stopped or started. However, ISM does not this. You must press **F5** to refresh the ISM screen.

As noted in the Microsoft Proxy Server on-line documentation, ISM allows the developer to do the following:

- Set server parameters: configure for each server the dial-out schedule, caching properties, internal IP addresses (via the Local Sddress Table or LAT), and back up files
- Set security policies: configure password authentication (Anonymous, Challenge/Response, and Basic), along with disabling IP fowarding and monitoring unknown network activity.
- Configure multiserver environments: configure Proxy Server arrays along with Proxy Servers that operate with other network servers.
- Administer clients: configure client applications to include Web Proxy and Winsock Proxy applications.
- Troubleshoot and monitor server performance: use service logs as well as system logs to identify system bottlenecks and performance issues.

In addition to ISM, you can use the HTML Tool administrative tool (which resembles the user interface for ISM) and command-line inputs.

The developer needs to understand the key items of caching, LAT, client services, and logging.

Where Is the Cache?

Proxy Server uses caching to store local copies of Internet objects, or URLs. *Cache* is a military term that has been borrowed by the computer industry. A cache is a collection of equipment, weapons, or food resources that is brought to the front lines to support the troops. A cache is large enough to supply the front lines for a sustained battle but not as large as the major stores kept in a warehouse. The same concept is used in a cache for Proxy Server. You create and allot hard disk space for a cache to allow subsequent client systems to take advantage of the places others have visited. This speeds the delivery of Web pages to your client systems (see Figure 7.26).

The Active Security Environment: Proxy Server 119

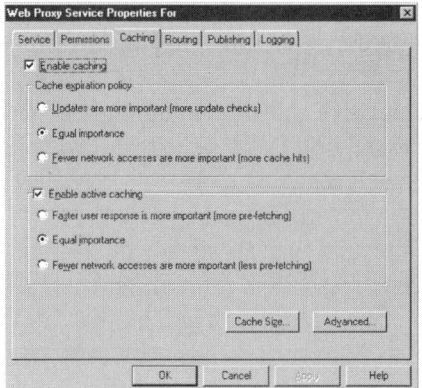

Figure 7.26 Security dialog box, **Cache** tab

With Proxy Server you can set both passive and active caching. *Passive* caching allows all objects returned to Proxy Server by Internet servers to be stored in a cache. Proxy Server has a time-to-live (TTL) parameter for all objects in the cache. When an object's TTL has expired, the next request for the object is served from the Internet instead of the cache.

Active caching automatically goes to the Internet for an object without client prompting. With active caching, the freshness and availability of popular objects are ensured. Note that active caching is disabled during those times set in Auto Dial when Proxy Server is not allowed to dial out to the Internet.

Making certain that Microsoft Proxy Server has a large cache for WWW objects will also help ensure that connections to the Internet seem to be as fast as possible. The Microsoft Proxy Server cache should be configured for 100 MB, plus 0.5 MB of disk space per Microsoft Proxy Server user of disk space (see Figure 7.27).

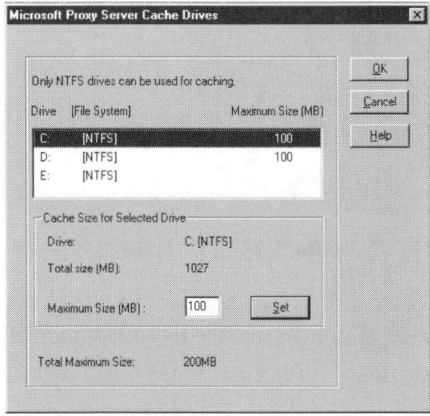

Figure 7.27 Microsoft Proxy Server Cache Drives dialog box.

If you have many LAN clients accessing many different places in the outside world, it might be a good idea to increase Microsoft Proxy Server's cache so that it can maintain local copies of most outside objects.

You initially set up caching size and location during the Proxy setup routine. Once it is configured, administer the cache using ISM. Note that if you choose to decrease the cache size on a selected drive, some cached data on that drive may be deleted. If you set the cache size for a selected drive to zero, all cached data is deleted. If you increase the cache size on a drive, there is no effect on the data already cached on that drive.

The Web Proxy service is responsible for both normal caching and active caching of Web pages. Normal caching takes place when you browse the Web by storing pages to the Proxy cache as you load them. For active caching, you can explicitly name sites to hold the objects or let the server's caching algorithm load what it determines to be necessary. Two sliders control how often Internet sites are polled to refresh the cache. You can specify the amount of disk space you want to dedicate to the Proxy cache. Generally, the larger the cache, the better chance you'll have of finding a page without reloading it. Standard cache sizes range from as little as 200 MB to 1 GB. Monitor both the system performance and client acceptance level to determine the best cache size for your operation.

LAT or Longitude?

During installation you will add internal network IP addresses the LAT. You do not add external IP addresses (see Figure 7.28).

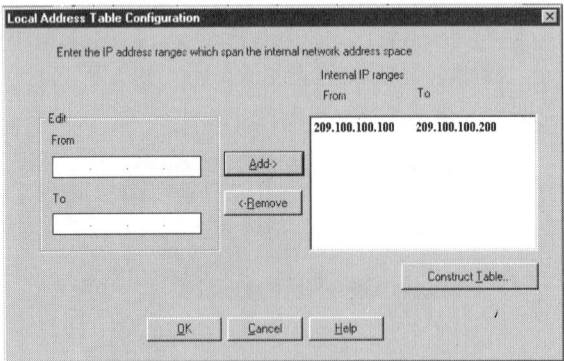

Figure 7.28 LAT dialog box.

You do not add any IP addresses that are associated with external servers running Proxy Server. If you added external addresses to the LAT, it would allow external addresses to appear as internal addresses, permitting security breaches. In addition, internal clients trying to reach those addresses would not be redirected through Proxy Server, making them unavailable. Once LAT is installed, you can modify it by using ISM or by using a text editor to edit the **Msplat.txt** file (located by default in the **C:\Msp\Clients** directory).

Client Services

You must also identify how client systems will access Proxy Server by using the Client Installation/Configuration window. Note that if you use the **DNS name** button in the **WinSock Proxy Client** section, you must ensure that you have a name resolution service running DNS or WINS (see Appendix A for detailed discussion of name services). Otherwise, you can click **IP Address** (**IP Addresses** in Proxy 1.0) or **Manual** to add selected IP addresses. You would choose this option if you do not have a name resolution service running (see Figure 7.23).

Logging without Carrying the Wood

Proxy Server has a minimum of three service logs that monitor the Web Proxy, WinSock Proxy, and Sockets Proxy services. Proxy Server logging should always be enabled; running Proxy Server without logging should not be considered a secure operating condition.

These logs can be stored in a text file or in an ODBC-compliant database table. By default, all information is logged to a text file. It is recommended that you log to a database. It is worth the extra effort because of the ability it gives you to generate reports using the Active Platform environment. You can simply create an Access table or SQL Server table, use the included wizards (Access or Webdb for SQL), and create customized reports. You can go the extra step and create ActiveX components or ISAPI filters that monitor log activity and issue warnings based on prefiltered entries. To log to a database, follow these steps:

1. In Internet Service Manager, do one of the following:

   If you want to log service information, double-click the server name next to the Web Proxy, WinSock Proxy, or the Sockets Proxy service.
   If you want to log packet filter information, double-click the server name next to any of the Proxy Server services.

2. In the Service Properties dialog box, do one of the following:

   If you want to log service information, click the **Logging** tab.
   If you want to log packet filter information, on the **Service** tab, under **Shared Services**, click **Security**. In the Security dialog box, click the **Logging** tab (see Figure 7.29).

122 Chapter 7

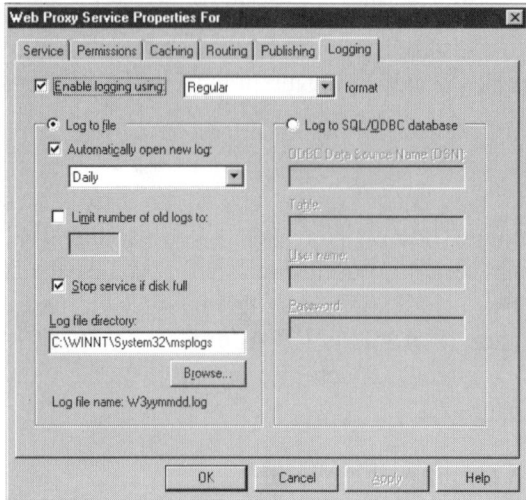

Figure 7.29 Web Proxy Service, **Logging** tab.

3. Make sure that the **Enable logging using** check box is selected. Click either **Regular** or **Verbose** from the drop-down list.
4. Click **Log to SQL/ODBC Database**.
5. In **ODBC Data Source Name (DSN),** type the system DSN that you have created for the database logging.
6. In **Table,** type the name of the table that you will be logging to.
7. In **User name** and **Password,** type a username and password that are valid for the database.
8. Click **Apply** and then click **OK**.

PROXY PERFORMANCE ISSUES AND ADDITIONAL FEATURES

It's important that the Microsoft Proxy Server on a LAN be set up as efficiently as possible to handle outbound and inbound Internet traffic. By default, NT gives quite a bit of CPU attention to any task that may be executing in the foreground on the server. If no user tasks are being executed, the priority NT gives to foreground execution is not an issue. However, if a Microsoft Proxy Server will also be used as a network workstation, you should lower the application performance boost time to ensure that Microsoft Proxy Server traffic is not slowed.

To alter the boost time NT gives to foreground applications, follow these steps:

1. Open Control Panel.
2. Select the **System** icon. The System applet will execute, and the System Properties dialog box will open.
3. Select the **Performance** tab. Adjust the **Boost** slider as needed. By default, the slider is set to the maximum value, giving a great deal of extra CPU time to any foreground application. Moving this slider to the left decreases the boost time.
4. Moving the slider all the way to the left (**None**) forces NT to handle background and foreground tasks equally. The best value here should be **None**.
5. Select **OK**. For the new settings to become effective, the NT server must be restarted

Proxy Server Connections

The number of internal connections Microsoft Proxy Server must support is also a factor in the amount of memory NT needs. The more connections Microsoft Proxy Server must maintain, the more memory is required. TCP/IP is a memory-intensive protocol. Because Microsoft Proxy Server requires that TCP/IP be installed on the NT server it is running, less than 32 MB of memory will most likely be too little to provide adequate performance.

The on-line documentation for Proxy Server recommends that in all except the most extreme cases, disk caching is optional. Disk caching will increase the number of users who can be served from a single proxy because of the local availability of HTTP and media resources. Memory and cache recommendations include the following:

- Small companies with fewer than 300 desktop units: Pentium 133, 32MB RAM, <2GB cache.
- Medium companies with 301–2,000 units: Pentium 166, 64MB RAM, 2–4GB cache.
- Large companies with 2,001–3,500 units: Pentium 200, 128–256MB RAM, 8–16GB cache.
- ISPs (1,000 simultaneous dial-ups): 300MHz Alpha or Pentium 200 Pro, 128–512MB RAM, >16GB cache.

Screen Savers and Other Ugly Items

Some final notes regarding what seems to be overlooked by many people: the screen saver. The bottom line is that screen savers should not be used. On any server product, the high-end screen savers of NT 4.0 can be CPU hogs. The Open GL screen savers, such as Pipes, drain (pun intended) server performance. If you need to password-protect your screen you should just log off. In fact, NT servers perform better when no one is logged on to them (resources consumed by the Explorer shell are freed when no one is logged on). Take some time to watch the system through the Task Manager window. You might be surprised about which services and applications are running and how much they drain system performance.

Speaking of excessive services, take a look at the network services. When new NICs are set up under NT, it automatically binds all appropriate installed services to the cards. These services range from actual protocols to services such as WINS. NT assumes that all NICs are destined to be full network interfaces. The purpose of Microsoft Proxy Server is to establish Internet connections to the outside world for LAN workstations. Certain protocols and services can be unbound from the NIC that Microsoft Proxy Server will use to channel Internet-destined data from the network. This technique will improve network performance over the Internet channel.

Unbinding base elements from a NIC may cause higher-level services to fail. When a base element (such as protocol) is unbound from a NIC, make certain that no dependent services are still bound to that NIC.

SHORTCUT

You can alter network bindings through the Control Panel via the **Network** icon. To access the bindings dialog box, follow these steps:

1. Open Control Panel.
2. Select the **Network** icon.
3. Select the **Bindings** tab.

All bindings on the Internet NIC that are not related to TCP/IP can be disabled (unbound).

RAS can be treated like regular NICs for binding purposes. If RAS is used for dial-in access to a LAN, make certain that inbound callers can get by with just TCP/IP. If RAS callers will need other protocols and services on the RAS channel, the bindings can still be adjusted to move them to TCP/IP high in the priority chain.

To streamline an NT server to operate as an Internet gateway, you should remove all nonessential services or move the services to another NT server on the network. Many NT administrators make the mistake of overloading an NT machine with all network services simply for the ease of having all services in one centralized location that is easier to manage. An efficient network is one that has network services such as WINS, DHCP, gateway, DNS, WWW Servers, and RAS spread out over as many NT servers as possible.

NOTE

When You're Setting Up an ISP

ISPs need to tune the variables shown in Table 7.2 (for approximately 1,000 simultaneous users, as noted in the Microsoft documentation).

Table 7.2 Variables to Be Tuned by ISPs

Variable	Path	Default Value	Range	Description	Recommended Setting
MaxPoolThreads	\LocalMachine\System\ CurrentControlSet\ Services\W3Proxy\ Parameters	10	0–0xFFFFFFFF	Specifies the number of pool threads to create per processor. Each pool thread watches for the network request and processes it.	500.
PoolThreadLimit	\LocalMachine\System\ CurrentControlSet\ Services\W3Proxy\ Parameters	250	0–0xFFFFFF	Specifies the maximum number of pool threads that can be created in the system. Each pool thread watches for the network request and processes it.	1,000*
DnsCacheSize	\LocalMachine\System\ CurrentControlSet\ Services\W3Proxy\ Parameters	3,000	0–0xFFFFFF	Specifies the maximum number of cache entries the server maintains before it cleans up the least used entries to make space for new entries.	10,000.
MaxPoolThreads of the WWW Service	\LocalMachine\System\ CurrentControlSet\ Services\W3Svc\ Parameters	10	0–0xFFFFFFFF	Specifies the number of pool threads to create per processor. Each pool thread watches for the network request and processes it.	64.

*Adjust this number by increments of 500 if additional processors are available in the system.

Automatic detection of these values will be a feature of Proxy Server version 2.

126　Chapter 7

When the Microsoft Proxy Server connection to the Internet becomes heavily used or overloaded, clients may begin to see errors such as "Unable to Resolve Host Name" or "Connection Timed Out". These errors stem from packets being delayed in transit so that the client believes the connection to have been broken.

If these errors are cropping up on a network and the Microsoft Proxy Server connection is not overloaded by LAN clients, the ISP itself may be overloaded. Check with your ISP regarding your network connection and evaluate your need to upgrade the connection.

You may be familiar with the standard Performance Monitor on NT servers. When you install Proxy Server, the following counter objects are installed:

- Web Proxy Service
- Web Proxy Cache
- WinSock Proxy Service
- Sockets Proxy Service
- Packet filters

See Figure 7.30 for an example of adding a chart to Performance Monitor.

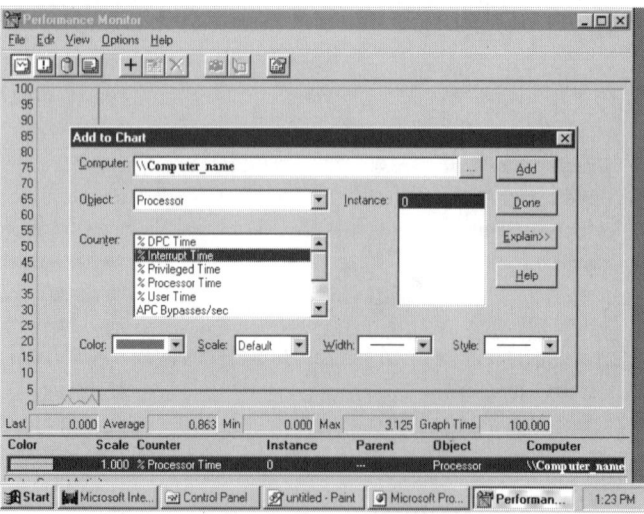

Figure 7.30 Performance Monitor screen: adding interrupt time of processor to chart.

The following counters are useful when you're tracking the performance of a Microsoft Proxy Server. This useful counter tracks the amount of time that the CPU is busy:

```
Object: Processor Counter: percent Processor Time
```

A consistent load of 70 % or higher may indicate the following:

- The computer on which Microsoft Proxy Server is running on needs a faster CPU and memory.
- Too many other services are being run on the NT machine. Some services should be removed or moved to other NT servers on the network.

This counter tracks the amount of CPU time devoted to service hardware interrupts (IRQs):

`Object: Processor, Counter: percent Interrupt Time`

If this counter is at 70% or higher, it may indicate the following:

- an piece of hardware is demanding too much CPU time.
- A serial port is causing performance problems. This is true if your (data terminal equipment speed (DTE; also known as port speed) is not high enough to handle the connect speed of the modems. A 28.8Kbps modem should have a port speed of at least 57.6Kbps (the preference is 115.2Kbps). If the port speed is too low, the serial port must constantly interrupt the CPU to offload incoming data from the modem.
- Improving a serial port to a 16550 UART—or, if possible, the newest 16650 UART—will also help relieve interrupt problems.

This counter tracks the total bytes going in and out through the HTTP server:

`Object: HTTP Service, Counter: Bytes Total/sec`

Microsoft Proxy Server uses the HTTP server for most proxied WWW, FTP, and Gopher data. This means that this counter is a good indication of the workload of Microsoft Proxy Server.

The preceding counter also tracks HTTP requests to the local WWW server. The connection is being overused if the total bytes per second counter is near the maximum number (for example, 2,900 to 3,200 for a 28.8Kbps modem) for the speed of the Microsoft Proxy Server connection to the Internet.

This counter is similar to the preceding counter except that it shows just the amount of data being passed to and from the Internet by Proxy Server:

`Object: Inet Proxy Service, Counter: Inet Bytes Total/sec`

Figure 7.31 shows how to choose the Web Proxy Server service.

128 Chapter 7

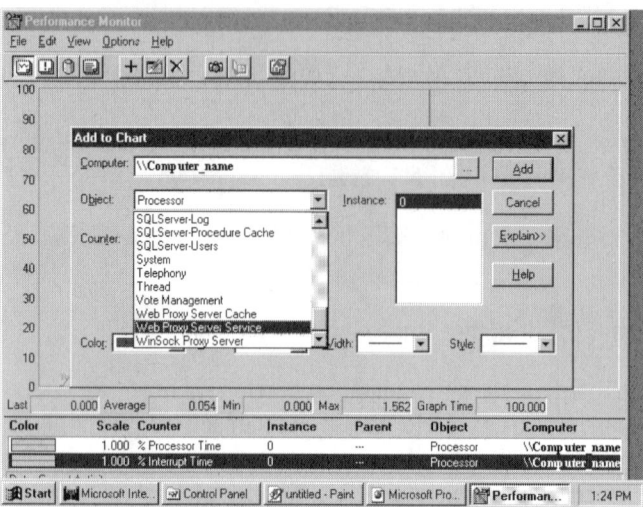

Figure 7.31 Adding Web Proxy Server service monitoring to the chart.

As you might guess, this counter shows the maximum number of users that have been (or are) connected to Proxy Server:

```
Object: Inet Proxy Service, Counter: Maximum Users
```

It is calculated over the displayed time period.

The RAS port counter is useful in tracking the performance of RAS connections:

Object: RAS Port, Counter: *

It deals with connection errors and port overruns. A network engineer or the developer can use this counter to debug physical connection problems. For example, if the error counts are high, the problem may be in the quality of the connection line or the port hardware. You need to contact your ISP and may need to reboot the connecting hardware. In addition, this object can show the exact amount of data being passed through a RAS port. This counter tracks information concerning disk performance:

```
Object: LogicalDisk, Counter: *
```

This is logical disk information and not physical disk information. Note that more than one logical disk can be held on one physical disk.

A busy disk means that the server is pulling a large percentage of its data from its cache and not having to go to the Internet to get it. This could be better news than a bad or busy connection.

The Charts

In the **Microsoft Proxy Server** folder, you will find a chart that details the basic performance counters that pertain to Microsoft Proxy Server's operation (see Figure 7.32).

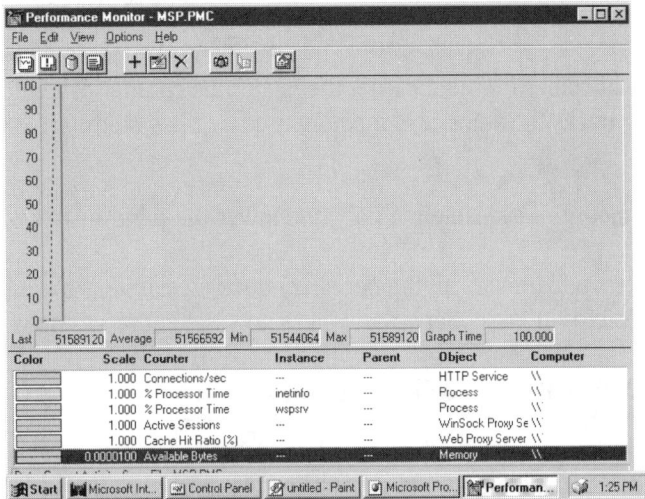

Figure 7.32 Performance Monitor of **MSP.PMC**.

You can load this chart by clicking **the Monitor Microsoft Proxy Server Performance** link in the **Microsoft Proxy Server** folder. This link runs Performance Monitor and automatically loads the chart **MSP.PMC**. This chart should be found in the **C:\MSP** directory with the other Microsoft Proxy Server files.

The following counters are part of this chart. This counter tracks the number of HTTP connections per second that are made to the HTTP server:

```
HTTP Server/Connections per Second
```

Because Microsoft Proxy Server runs as a subservice of the main HTTP server, this counter is useful in seeing the stress load of the HTTP server in general.

This counter tracks the percentage of processor time devoted to the INETSRV process:

```
Processor/percent Processor Time: INETSRV
```

The INETSRV process is the general process that drives the HTTP server.

This counter tracks the percentage of processor time devoted to the WinSock Proxy Service process:

```
Processor/percent Processor Time: WSPSRV
```

This counter tracks the number of active connections maintained by the WinSock Proxy Server over the tracking period:

`WinSock Proxy Server/Active Sessions`

This counter tracks the percentage of cache hits to extra data retrieval:

`Web Proxy Server Service/Cache Hits Ratio percent`

The more data that comes from the cache, the higher the counter percentage.

This counter tracks the amount of memory used by the system:

`Memory/Available bytes`

The lower the amount of available memory, the lower the performance of the system as a whole.

These counters will provide all the necessary tracking elements to let you see the basic performance of Microsoft Proxy Server as well as how the entire system is performing.

TROUBLESHOOTING PROXY SERVER ISSUES

All developers run into problems when installing and maintaining systems, especially as we develop active content and attempt to protect that content from intruders. Here is a list of issues and suggestions that Web site developers have found to be useful for maintaining Proxy Server.

1. If you have a problem with dial-up connections hanging up, check whether your ISP supports both PPP and SLIP. Although PPP tends to be "better" than SLIP because it provides built-in authentication and muiltiprotocol support, you may have transmission problems with your ISP. In addition, there has been discussion of known firmware problems with certain classes of modems. Contact your ISP to check on the connection.
2. Ping uses the ICMP protocol to communicate. Proxy supports only TCP and UDP packets. Ping will resolve the DNS name but go no For example:

```
D:\>ping www.microsoft.com
                Pinging www.microsoft.com [207.68.137.36] with 32 bytes of data:

Reply from 158.59.99.2: Destination net unreachable.
                Reply from 158.59.99.2: Destination net unreachable.
```

Note that you cannot ping or traceroute through a proxy server.
3. Remember that if you connect to another ISP at home or off-line at work, you must disable the proxy in your Web browser's settings. You must enable it again when you are connected to your internal network.

4. When RAS delivers the disconnect event, the line may not really be disconnected yet. This event means that you have started to disconnect. Depending on the server and the network connection, that can take minutes.
5. What about RealPlayer and security? Progressive Networks' RealPlayer is a popular program that launches and plays audio and video. To implement RealAudio in a firewall environment, consult the following Web sites:

   RealAudio Firewall Proxy Kit: http://www.real.com/help/firewall/proxyform.html
   Configuring the player to work behind a firewall: http://www.real.com/help/firewall/config.html

6. If you have a problem in Windows 95 enabling RealAudio clients, try the following:

   Install the WinSock Proxy Client on Windows 95.
   Enable access control in WinSock Proxy and grant permissions for the RealAudio protocol. Install the RealPlayer and leave the Proxy Server configuration settings in the RealPlayer blank.

7. If you have Auto Dial set up to use an entry in the Dial Up Network address book and you get an immediate message such as "12207 Proxy dialout connection failed," check the username and password. You may have to retype them
8. Are you considering getting a class "C" IP license? Proxy Server allows you to hide IP addresses, and that can save you from having to set up a network based on real IP addresses. At the same time you may have other requirements. Remember that Proxy Server handles certain protocols (TCP, UDP, and ICMP) and not all protocols.
9. When you filter out sites that you do not want your users to see, you receive a canned error command "access code invalid." An error code is returned, such as "12202: The specified URL is denied by the proxy server." To create a different page, create an **ErrorHtmls** directory (it is already available in Proxy 2.0) and create the appropriate page that you want the Proxy Server to feed the client. For example, in the case of a 12202 error, you would create a **12202.htm** file with your note.
10. What if you want to provide a backup mechanism to your Proxy Server environment? Proxy 1.0 does not support chaining. In chaining, if one Proxy Server cannot serve a request, another Proxy Server grabs the request. Proxy 2.0 solves this problem. If you are in a Proxy 1.0 environment, consider pointing some of the browsers to the other Proxy Servers.
11. If you are running Proxy Server 1.0 and try to connect to a secure SSL site through Web Proxy (using HTTPS://), you may be prompted for a password three times and receive an access-denied message. Go to the Microsoft Knowledge Base Web site and find the article Q170666.

12. If you get a Proxy message that the error log is full, that may not be the case. Instead, the system event log may be full.

Where Do You Go from Here?

This chapter should have given you a basic understanding of the need for proper security in the active environment. Although the Active Platform introduces you to fun and exciting technology, there are those who want to destroy the new site. It's a fact of life.

To assist in minimizing the pain, this chapter has discussed the following items.

- The basics of network security. We recommend you review all the different mechanisms and use a combination that works for the company site. Do not forget the obvious items that can compromise network security, such as locking the server room door!
- Two services—WinSock Proxy and Web Proxy—provided by Microsoft Proxy Server. These services help developers to protect the local site.
- The basics of NT security.
- Control of the Proxy process by properly using caching and the Local Access Table.
- Use of the NT Performance Monitor to diagnose traffic and proxy performance issues.

From here, you should refer to the following chapters:

- Chapter 11, "Active Middleware." Transaction Server teaches more about data security.
- Appendix A. Setting up IIS and NT to learn more about the naming services (such as DNS).

Chapter 8

Active Data

As noted in Chapter 1, the client/server world is one in which developers can solve many of the problems found in a host-based environment (such as the high cost of implementing solutions) and a LAN-based environment (such as network bottlenecks and slow performance).

By choosing client/server as the database solution, developers can improve system performance and system availability, which are essential in the world of dynamic content. The Web site owner is in competition for customers both on and off the Web (classic market distribution channels). The developer is in competition with all the other developers trying to keep their sites in demand.

As you have been learning, the Active Platform environment gives you a tremendous arsenal of tools and server products to meet increased demands. Content is king not only in film and games but also on the Web. How does a developer access and manage content? One essential key is the database, which is at the heart of the content wars.

THE DATABASE

Data is best handled when you have a method—known as a *data model*—for storing, editing, managing, and using it. Just as a model airplane is not the airplane but rather is a replica of the plane, a data model is not the physical data but a replica of how the data is organized. A data model also is a set of guidelines, or rules, for representing this logical organization of data.

A data model is made up of the named *logical unit* (record type, data item) along with the relationships among the logical units. A *data item* is the smallest logical piece of data. One instance of this data is called a *data item value*. A *record type* is a group of data items. This means that one instance of a record type is a record.

Like a building with multiple stories, a database has multiple levels that you need to be aware of when writing code.

The Three-Story House of Databases

The three-story house of databases is the framework for all the data concepts that have been defined.

- The external level (the user's view) is where Structured Query Language (SQL) is used.
- The conceptual level (community view) holds data as it really is and not as the customer sees it. Applications are written in this level to handle data integrity and security.
- At the internal level (storage), utility applications are written to handle physical storage issues (but not device-dependent issues). Data integrity and security are bypassed.

Figure 8.1 illustrates the three levels.

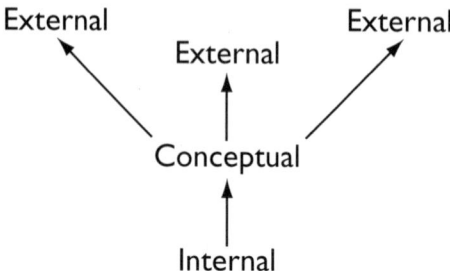

Figure 8.1 The three levels of a database.

In this chapter we focus on the external level.

Types of Database Models

Database systems can be built on various types of models based on system requirements and mathematical representations of the data. For simplification, let's look at three basic models:

- The *hierarchical* model. Think of this as the parent-child model. The family tree has a root (parent) that has branches that have branches that have more branches. This is a useful model, but it does not allow for the case of a child having multiple parents or no parent.
- The *network* model. In this model, the child has multiple parents or no parent. The complexity of relationships increases, but system performance does not necessarily improve.
- The *relational* model. Developers spend most of their time and effort on this model. It has data structures (tables), rules for data integrity, and data manipulation operators (such as `Select`, `union`, and `join`). You have much more flexibility using this model.

What Is a Relational Data Model?

The idea of a relational database originated in IBM research laboratories in the late 1960s. A researcher, E.F. Codd, wanted to use mathematics to handle database issues. His work with algebraic and calculus algorithms led to the relational data model.

The relational data model is the basis of the logical model described earlier. Relational databases consist of *tables* that have *rows* and *columns* (see Figure 8.2).

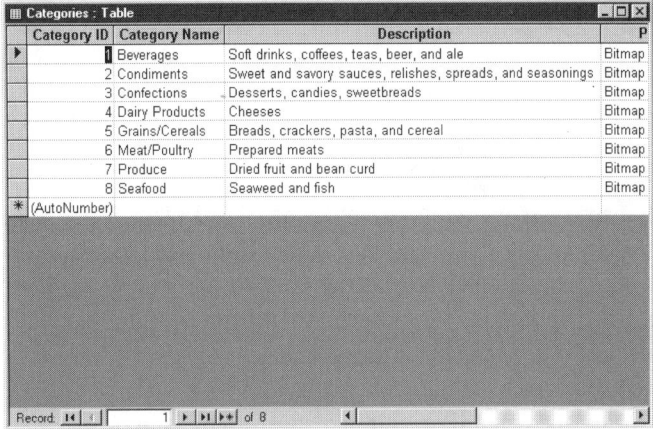

Figure 8.2 A relational database.

This Microsoft Access table has columns such as Category ID and Category Name. One row is labeled 1, 2, and 3 with data entered.

The table is a form of information. Codd helped define operators for accessing this data, and that resulted in the development of SQL. SQL Server uses the relational data model as the basis for its operation.

Variations on the Database Models

The concept behind the Active Platform is the ability to deliver dynamic content to a specified user in the most transparent way available. This means that relational systems, such as SQL Server, work in a client/server environment. Guess what? There is a client/server process model.

Some people argue that the client/server model is separate from a discussion of relational modeling. Other developers see it as a fourth model. Here you need only understand that Active Platform development is based on a client/server environment. This means that you are continually determining where to split the workload by asking yourself a series of questions. Is the application client-driven or server-driven? If it is server-driven, how many servers are available to run the application? Can you split the application into components that are handled on various servers?

This kind of analysis results in a process architecture that leads to the client/server process model. Relational databases use stored procedures and triggers to run these processes. A *stored procedure* is a set of precompiled SQL statements that execute on the server. They can be called from the client. *Triggers* are a set of SQL commands that automatically operate when an insertion, deletion, or update occurs on a table. `Insert` is a SQL command that inserts data into a designated table. `Delete` removes data from a table, and `Update` inserts the latest data into the specified row and column of a table. The commands can be column-specific or row-specific. This means that you can change a specific *cell* (row and column) or a whole row or a whole column of data.

What Is a Relational Database Management System?

A *relational database management system* (RDBMS) is a piece of software that structures data in accordance with the relational data model discussed in the previous sections. An RDBMS has a collection of tables (consisting of rows and columns), indexes, and views. *Indexes* are created by developers to reduce the amount of time that it takes to search for records in a database. For example, suppose that you create a table for automobile parts. The column headings are car make, car model, car year, and car engine number. If you know that car make and model are queried most often, you would index the database based on the car make and model. The database system creates a temporary table indexed on those columns with pointers to the actual data.

SQL statements are used to create new tables and views, add new data, modify existing data, and perform other functions. Figure 8.3 shows examples of a *view* on a relational database table.

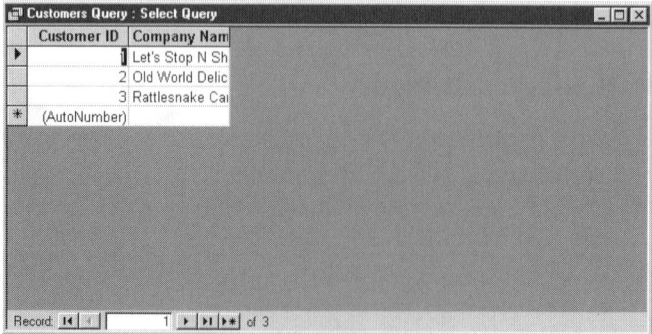

Figure 8.3 Creation of a view based on selection of the first two fields.

An RDBMS provides a means for storing, retrieving, and updating data. By structuring data, the system simplifies the job of managing interaction with the data. An RDBMS also provides data management, including the capability to define and manipulate data.

An RDBMS has several advantages. First, it handles the formal data model, letting you structure difficult issues in a logical architecture. This means that multiple users can share data even in a distributed (client/server) environment. And because this model is the abstract and is easy to apply to data, it promotes data independence.

To handle the data requires the use of a data definition language (DDL) and data manipulation language (DDM). This arrangement assists you in defining data structures and handling the data, tasks that SQL handles well.

Ensuring Data Integrity

When customers come to your interactive Web site, they ask for information or want to buy something. If that interaction is with a database, it is a *transaction*. Each transaction normally requires a number of interactive operations with the database before the process is complete. How do you ensure that it all happens correctly—especially if there are many users making input and asking for items? You can follow a set of principles often abbreviated as CIDA. Let's look at what it means.

CONSISTENCY

C stands for consistency. This means that if the transaction fails, the system must roll back the process. For example, suppose a person buys a product, his or her charge card gets credited, and then the system goes down without releasing the product order. The customer will not be happy to pay for a product that is not delivered. If at any time the transaction fails, the system must roll back the activity. A consistent system is one in which the database is never left in a corrupt state. Logs assist you in rolling back failed transactions and ensuring consistency.

ISOLATION

I stands for isolation: the ability of a system to prevent deadlock. Let's say that client A wants the same record as client B. The database system must first lock the record for A and then complete the transaction, unlock the record, and then lock it for B. If this process is not handled properly, the system is deadlocked. Isolation sounds rather simple, but it can get complicated.

Suppose client A locks record 121 and client B locks record 120. No problem. There is no conflict. Now A is finished and wants record 120. Oops. The system has another client, client C, who has locked record 122. So what? The problem is that B, when finished, wants record 122. There is a *concurrency* problem. What happens if there are hundreds of users? The system, to handle concurrency properly (to ensure isolation) must make a decision to return an error to one of the clients to resolve the problem. Which client receives the error depends on the rules of the database system.

DURABILITY

D is for durability. Durability means that something can last. The more durable it is, the longer it lasts. The more durable it is, the more punishment an object can take and survive.

Sometimes database systems crash. What happens when they reboot is the measure of durability. Without an adequate level of durability, the database is of no use to the developer. Does the database system roll back all the records within a certain time frame of the crash? Does the operator have the ability to intervene in that rollback to make changes?

Atomicity

A is for atomicity. When the database system rolls back a transaction, does the system handle this process properly? Does the system commit or not commit? This all-or-nothing commit process is known as atomicity. Without it, a developer cannot be assured of data integrity in the database. Again, a log helps you in this process to ensure integrity.

Now let's look at the logical and physical aspects of an RDBMS.

The RDBMS Logical Data Model

The logical data model is a conceptual model. A developer (or database administrator) maps objects to the relational data model by defining entities, their relationships, and their attributes. For example, if you wanted to build a relational database of vehicle drivers and their information you might use the following.

- A driver, a vehicle, and a driver's license are all entities.
- A driver has the following attributes:
  A driver is a citizen of some country.
  A driver has an age (18 and older for this database).
  A driver is male or female.
  A driver has or does not have a job.
  A driver has or does not have insurance.
  A driver has or does not have tickets.
- A vehicle has the following attributes:
  A state license plate.
  A registration number.
  No axle (motorcycle), two axles, or more than two axles (large trucks).
- A driver's license has the following attributes:
  A number.
  A picture.
  A donor organ area.
  Address information.
  Phone information.
  An expiration date.
  A note if the driver needs corrective lenses.
  A medical note area (to include handicap requirements).

The relationships are as follows:

- A driver can have one or more vehicles.
- A vehicle can have one or more drivers.
- A driver can have one driver's license.
- A vehicle has no driver's license.
- A driver's license is related to the vehicle type by axle count.

This is only a sample but should give you a sense of all the entities, attributes, and relationships that you could define. From this you create entity-relationship diagrams. A sample is shown in Figures 8.4 through 8.9.

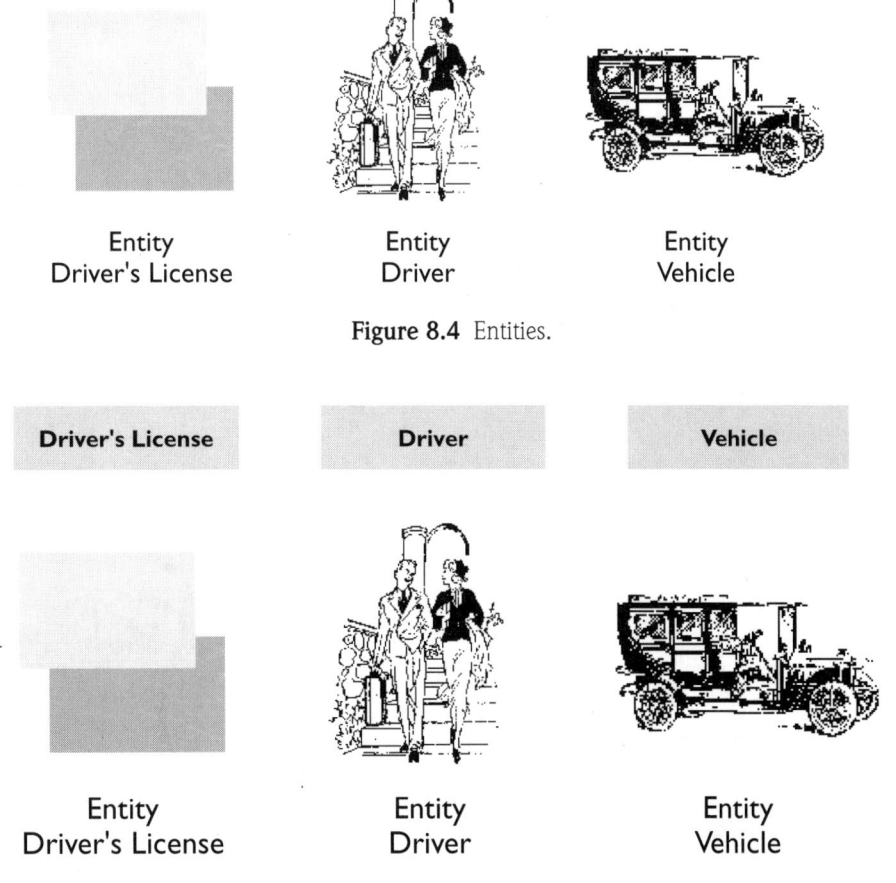

Figure 8.4 Entities.

Figure 8.5 The entity diagram.

140 Chapter 8

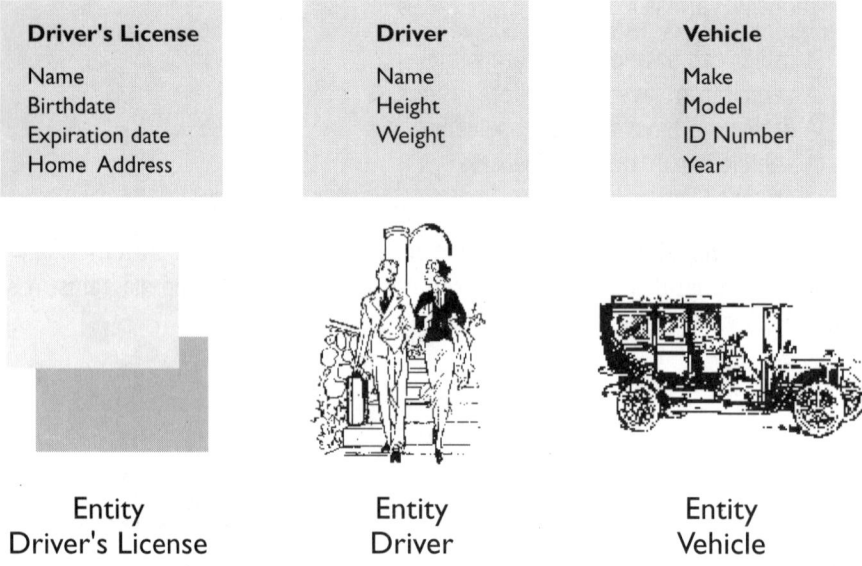

Figure 8.6 Entity attributes.

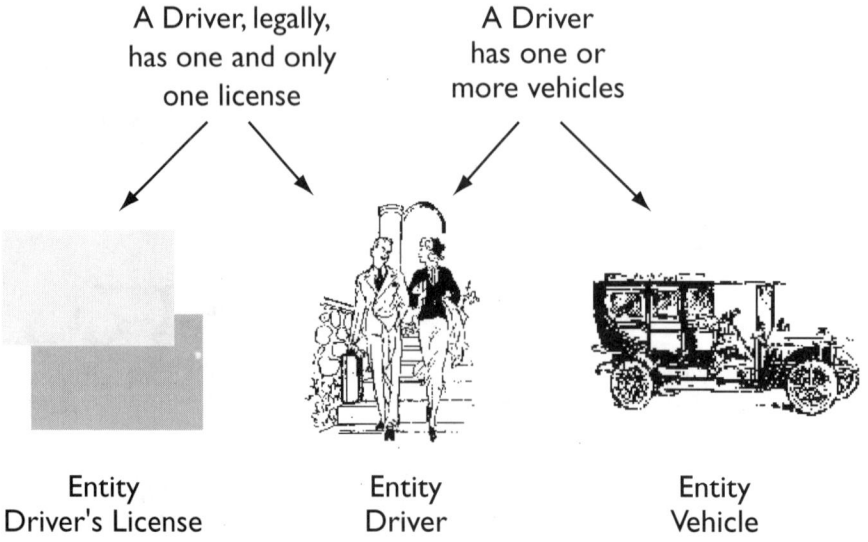

Figure 8.7 Entity relationships.

Active Data 141

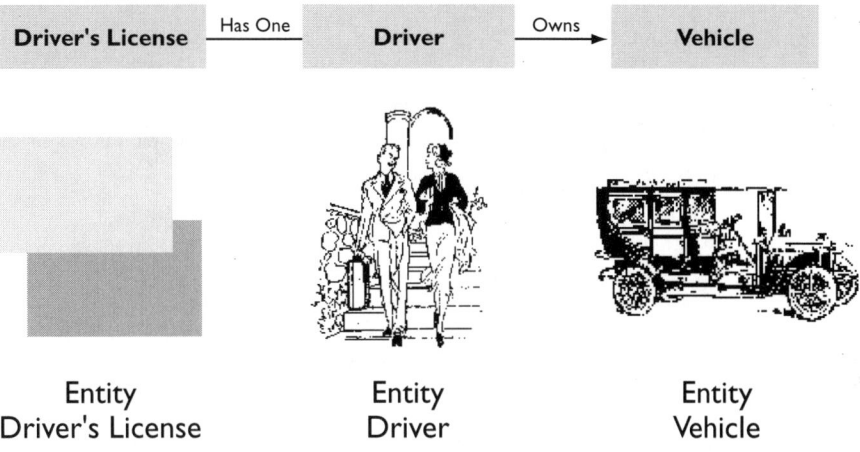

Figure 8.8 Diagrammed relationships.

This creates the business rule where
1. A driver can own one or more vehicles.
2. A vehicle can be owned by one or more drivers.
3. A driver has one and only one license.
4. A license has one and only one owner.

This results in the cardinality drawing where:

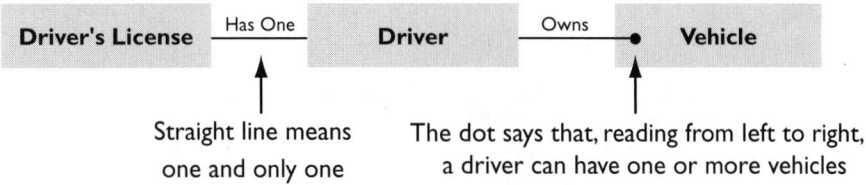

Straight line means one and only one

The dot says that, reading from left to right, a driver can have one or more vehicles

Figure 8.9 Business rules.

The intent of a logical model is to help reduce duplication of data. Suppose you created extra tables to establish the relationships between entities rather than trying to minimize the number of tables. This solution could create a nasty database performance issue.

142 Chapter 8

For simplicity, you can think of each entity, at its base level, as a table. Each attribute is a column or field in that table.

NOTE Microsoft's Access is a wonderful tool to use in prototyping a SQL Server database. Access comes with a set of visual tools that display the entities and their relationships. Using this tool, you can properly design the tables and consider the physical modeling requirements.

RELATIONAL TABLES

In a relational DBMS, data is a collection of time-varying, normalized, independent relations of assorted degree and cardinalities. Wow—that is a mouthful. We will discuss each of these concepts in this chapter. For now, let's look at the big picture. A database is made of tables that have rows and columns. For example, let's say that you want to create a car table and relate car identification numbers to their makes and models. You have just created a relational database (see Figure 8.10). Tables can also be related to one another (see Figure 8.11). Here, you want to track the color and license plate of the vehicle. Now you have created a relationship between two tables through the key called the car identification number.

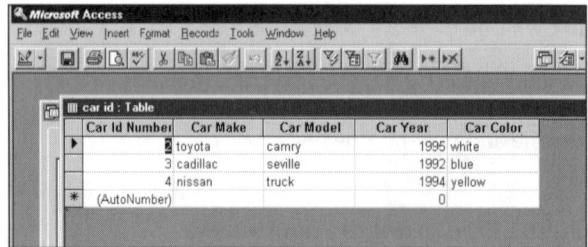

Figure 8.10 Car ID table.

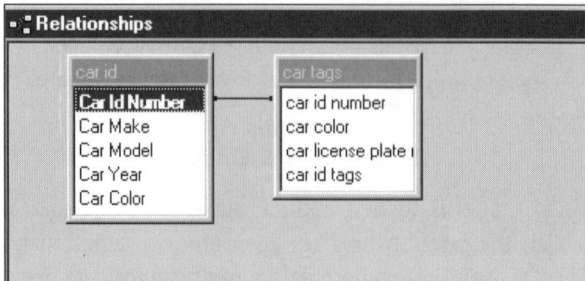

Figure 8.11 Table relationships.

RDBMS Physical Data Model

The physical model of a database is different from its logical model, because the way machines operate is different from the way people think. Suppose that the developer knows, by a quick rule change, that in California a driver can get a certain kind of driver's license under the age of 18. Physically, that data could be located anywhere on the hard drives. Logical models consider the business rules; physical models consider the physical resource requirements for housing and using the data that is manipulated by the business rules.

The physical model must consider the network, the number of servers, and the servers' attributes (such as their processor count, their processor speed, their hard drive count, and so on). The physical model allows the developer to tune a database's performance by changing those server attributes just mentioned and also helps with potential networking issues.

Now that you understand data integrity and know how to develop a database in an efficient manner, it is time to discuss the use and manipulation of that data through SQL.

Using SQL

Structured Query Language (SQL) deals with the relationships, as noted earlier, of entities. SQL looks like an English-type language. For example, here the developer is selecting every row from the `authors` table of the `publication` database:

```
SELECT * FROM publication.authors,publication.dbo.authors
```

The following statement inserts the values given into the `titles` table:

```
INSERT titles
    VALUES('ax555', 'Faster!', 'newbie', '1389',
        NULL, NULL, NULL, NULL, 'yes', '06/19/89')
```

SQL allows you to define (in the DDL, as noted in the opening section) the structure of the RDBMS to include the following:

- Table (entity) names.
- Column (field) names.
- Datatypes such as number, character, short integer, and long integer.
- User privileges such as administrator privileges, table-level privileges, and column-level privileges.

SQL allows you to manipulate the data (using the DDM, as noted in the opening section). You can do the following:

- Select data that you need from the database.
- Insert data into the database.
- Update the database with the latest data.
- Delete data from the database.

144 Chapter 8

To provide efficient selection of data, SQL provides a WHERE clause as a portion of the SELECT statement. This WHERE clause acts as a filter to get the appropriate data to the customer. See Figure 8.12 for an example.

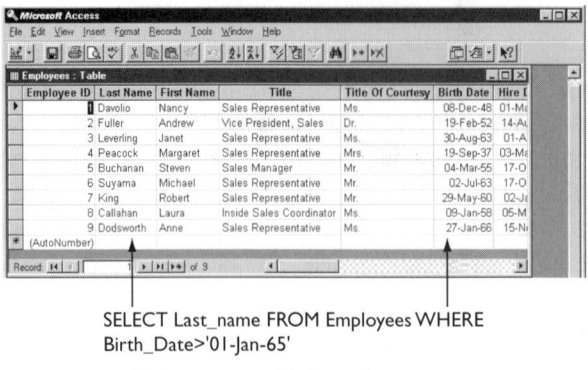

SELECT Last_name FROM Employees WHERE Birth_Date>'01-Jan-65'

results in one return: Dodsworth

Figure 8.12 SELECT example.

NOTE

It is always more efficient to filter data at the server than to send it to the client and filter it in the application. This also applies to columns requested from the server. An application that issues a SELECT * FROM statement requires the server to return all column data to the client whether or not the client application has bound these columns for use in program variables. Selecting only the necessary columns by name will avoid unnecessary network traffic. It will also make your application more robust in the event of table definition changes, because newly added columns won't be returned to the client application.

You can extend SQL by adding RDBMS-specific SQL statements. Transact-SQL, an extension of SQL Server, is an example. Please see the discussion of Transact SQL later in this chapter to see some of these additions.

Before diving into the theory and use of SQL Server, you need to understand more about how companies choose database technologies.

DATABASE TECHNOLOGY

To this point this chapter has assumed that the developer will be handling the implementation of the database server on the active site. Is the developer the best person to do this? Is there another way?

As databases are becoming more and more complex in the client/server environment, companies need to expand the role of developers who handle data content. This means that the developer will be taking over the role of, or hiring, a database administrator (DBA).

The Role of the Database Administrator

The DBA handles the company's data by establishing data management principles as well as assisting the technology departments with hardware purchases, installation of data manipulation software, and determination of personnel requirements. To provide data management input to the entire organization, the DBA should report to senior information systems management.

Organizational size can influence the decision of who is assigned to do the work of the DBA. In many small organizations, the DBA responsibility often becomes the job of the programmer who has the greatest need to solve data management issues. In some organizations the networking department performs the DBA role. As companies grow, management often recognizes the need to create a team of people to perform the DBA responsibilities.

These tasks fall into two categories: management and technical. Management functions deal with administrative aspects of a database, such as standards and security policies. Technical functions deal with corporate physical resources such as hardware and software.

MANAGEMENT RESPONSIBILITIES OF A DBA

The DBA is responsible for the following management tasks:

- Preparing the database environment, which involves dealing with the organization's personnel and with vendors and includes selecting RDBMS products. In some organizations, a DBA is expected to negotiate the deal.
- Managing the operation of the database.
- Developing standards and procedures. For example, the DBA develops security policies and is the "security guard." This task includes capacity management. For example, the DBA must validate who is allowed to view, use, and update the data. The user management process extends beyond just security and includes capacity management. The DBA must determine when to increase system capacity to meet the need of increased user demand. Also in this category are backup and archival procedures, including making a copy of the database at regular intervals. In case of database failure, the DBA is responsible for recovery. Similarly, disaster recovery procedures may include off-site storage of copies.

TECHNICAL RESPONSIBILITIES OF A DBA

The DBA must monitor the operational life-cycle of the database. This life-cycle includes the product development phases and the support phases.

The four development phases are design, build, quality assurance, and release. Databases can be in all four phases during their life-cycle. For example, when a DBA releases version 1.0 of the database application to the release phase (following a successful quality assurance phase), the DBA has received new user inputs that need to be incorporated into a version 1.1

that should now be in the design phase. As soon as version 1.1 moves through the build phase to the quality assurance phase, market changes and new customer demands create the need for version 2.0 (a major rewrite of the database application to possibly include new table design) to start in the design phase. A successful product follows this phased-process throughout its life. At least one software engineer takes the design criteria and creates a sample module which can be tested. This module should run on its own without adversely affecting normal company operations. As the design grows and the developer makes changes, he will add new modules. The DBA helps to determine which modules will be moved to the build server and which move on to the quality assurance phase.

NOTE

Database design is the topic everyone loves to debate. Is a DBA a database designer? Does DBA know how to design databases? The answer needs to be yes. The reason is because a good administrator knows how the object was designed. They need to know all of the customer requirements and the developer's programming environment. If the DBA does not become proficient at database design, the application developers will lose respect for the individual and the customer will never get their problems solved. DBAs are typically the chief database designer in companies. The DBA should be responsible for the design decisions that determine which processes will execute on the different database servers. To accomplish this, the DBA should understand such technology as the distributed client-server architecture, data modeling, and object-oriented design.

When the application has an agreed upon level of features and functions, then it is sent to the quality assurance phase. In this phase, developers can fully test each module under various stress conditions. For this reason the developer may require a separate test server. The decision to require a separate test server depends upon the availability of the development server and scheduling implications. Many companies have found that it is less expensive to add another piece of hardware to expand the developer's resources. This extra server significantly reduces the chances of a delayed release schedule for the database applications. The DBA needs to ensure that the schedule is not delayed due to resource limitations.

The application never seems fully ready to release. It is much like writing a book. Since the author can always find a better way to succinctly make his point he wants to keep revising. The publishing company needs the book on the shelves to meet an agreed-upon release date to generate revenue. These same pressures arise during the database application development phases. The developer want to continue adding new features and functions that will benefit the company. The company needs the application in place in order to take advantage of the data. The DBA can assist by making a decision when to move the application to the operational server.

The DBA should be involved in the decision making process for when the product moves from each phase. The DBA must ensure that there are systems and space available for each group to complete his portion of the development process. For example, developers in the design phase generally need less hard drive space than those developers in the build phase. The support phases include resource management, system tuning, and maintenance.

Resource management including monitoring storage parameters, the size of the rollback segments, storage area and space utilization. The DBA should also keep abreast of development tools that may be of use to the developer during each of the development lifecycle phases. For example, the DBA may become aware of a design tool that would ensure proper implementation of object-oriented programming.

Once the application has been released for company use, real-life situations occur where the network has changed or additional users need access. These changes often lead to declined application performance. The problems persist requiring the need for performance tuning. Performance tuning is similar to car maintenance. When the engine runs rough, a mechanic gets under the hood, listens, uses test equipment and modifies engine parameters (e.g. changes the spark plug gap, modifies the timing) to see what may increase performance while maintaining fuel economy. The DBA must also open the hood to get into the system and the database to determine what parameters need to be modified to increase performance. Please note that tuning a system for testing is different than tuning a system for the product-release server. There are many more system demands on the product-release server than what is normally required of the test server. Is the database fragmented? With the increased need to distribute the database environment, the storage and allocation of data becomes premier. Fragmentation can occur which will negatively affect performance. The DBA should monitor the database objects by looking at both disk fragmentation as well as data block layout.

Once the application is in the release phase, many developers want to move on to new projects. The developer has the desire to create the latest and greatest software applications using the most advanced tools. Quality assurance developers want to get more involved in the design phase of the next project. With all those demands, the DBA still needs to ensure that the current application is maintained and in working order. Sometimes the DBA fills in on the current projects and has to organize user concerns and changes that will be sent to the developers and QA.

In addition to new personnel and new responsibilities, a developer needs to reconsider the definition of the data modeling environment.

The Enterprise Data Model

To best meet the needs of the entire company and its production systems, you must perform enterprise data modeling. The concept here is to logically create a single large database for the company. Now you consider not only rules of the departments but also the departmental interrelationships as well as corporate rules.

Enterprise data modeling is best handled by implementing modules, or components: applications that are needed to help the company function properly. For example, you may build an accounts receivable application to meet the needs of the accounting department. You would like to complete that process by building the other application modules needed by the entire accounting department, but time and money may not permit that to happen immediately. Instead, you may have to start building a new customer transaction tool. The benefit of completing the AR application even though the accounting department database is not finished is that the new customer tool can take advantage of immediate billing through the AR application. In other words, you may need to build in increments.

With the enterprise model comes the need to distribute data that may be housed in multiple geographic as well as hardware locations. The distribution services of the RDBMS must synchronize the data in multiple locations by replicating it.

DATA WAREHOUSES AND PROCESSES

Now let's look at data warehouses and processes and discuss their relationship with creating and implementing a dynamic Web site.

Data Warehousing

Data warehousing is the ability to get the data to the customer in an informative and timely manner. Data warehousing assists the developer in dealing with differences in data between applications. In our vehicle and driver's license example, the payment system for keeping track of valid licenses stores the sex as *M* or *F*. However, the ticket application designers need a full definition and so store the data as *Male* or *Female*. The data is not consistent and needs to be resolved. Data warehousing also allows companies to provide large database transactions within the company intranet as well as on-line transactions for hundreds of customers.

Data warehousing has been very effective in the retail industry, where databases can range to 100GB in size. The problem is that as soon as users can get good data, the demand increases. Some industry estimates are that user needs double every year. As a result, companies must evaluate new hardware and software technologies, including the following:

- Symmetric multiprocessing (SMP). These systems run 2–48 processors, which share memory and the memory bus. The problem lies in the physical bottleneck of the bus.
- Clusters. Heavily promoted during the early VAX days and now in Microsoft's Wolfpack product. You cluster a number of machines, including SMPs, to remove the bus bottleneck.
- Massively parallel processors (MPP). This is the next step up in scalability. SMP clusters end up using a logically single connection that also can become a bottleneck. MPP allows the bandwidth to grow as you add systems.

To get data from these data warehouses, you can use query tools, on-line analytical processing tools (OLAP; discussed next), and data mining tools (to be discussed at the end of this section). No matter what tool you use, you are always under the gun to increase performance. This is the reason that data marts have come of age.

Data marts are small data warehouses. Each major department on the intranet has its needs. The developer may need to separate the requirements based on network traffic and resource issues and give each departmental group its own data mart. This approach breaks up the monolithic data warehouse and makes an Active intranet site more pleasing to company users, who get what they need when they need it.

On-Line Transaction Processing and On-Line Analytical Processing

Data can be managed and stored according to its intended use. This is where on-line transaction processing (OLTP) and OLAP come in. These are two different types of databases.

OLTP databases are designed for high-volume, repetitive processes. These databases are built to support company operations that normally generate short records. Implementations include airline travel sites, ticket sales for concerts and musicals, and ATMs. OLTP databases are sometimes called *production systems*. They are transactional in nature and provide around-the-clock information. The transactions are predictable and must be processed immediately to reflect customer requests. There is total security from unauthorized use of the database. The OLTP database designer knows that the data transactions occur on a regular basis.

On the other hand, OLAP databases are designed for decision-making processes. Data warehouses handle the building of ad-hoc queries. OLAP databases support decision support systems (DSS) applications. OLAP tools use what is known as the *star schema*. In this model, you build one large database of the company's products; it would be the center of the star. Then you build a number of smaller tables that extend from the center in a star configuration. These smaller tables may hold sales or marketing information by region. The problem here is that developers get confused when a logical model is described in physical terms (star). The data may not literally be distributed as a star!

Developers need to be familiar with these two types of databases, because performance issues vary. For example, you should design an OLTP database to handle large amounts of incoming transactions in short periods of time. You should design an OLAP database to create user output as rapidly as possible. OLTP is intended for input, and OLAP is for output. As company officers gather data to make decisions, they must use these databases wisely.

In the case of OLTP, the Web can be a great resource. The Web is server-oriented, and this can help your handling of transactions. The client software is standard, and this assists you in developing user interfaces for all types of customer client systems. The drawback is the unreliability of Web connections. You should consider your transaction policy regarding real-time rollback or commit. The Web is a great medium, but be aware of this transaction integrity issue. Airline reservation systems, for example, are off-line less than an hour per year! Transaction monitoring is essential. Please see Chapter 11 regarding the Active Transaction environment available in the BackOffice suite.

Data Mining

Data mining is the method by which a DBA or developer drills down into the data and pulls out what is essential.

Currently, developers tend to use simple methods for getting data they need from a database. They may even use wizards (such as SQL Wizard for SQL Server) to prepare the data as needed. The point is that most developers are developing interfaces and applications based on a knowledge of what they are looking for. They are merely verifying the process. Data mining follows a more discovery-based approach. The developer uses data mining tools to follow a pattern match to uncover data relationships that lead to the ability to make predictions. Tools are available that use *rules* (for linear data) or a type of *fuzzy algorithm* (for data that has some values missing) called *neural networks*.

In practical terms, what use is data mining? Banks can use it to predict who will have poor or good credit. They can also use it to uncover fraud where normal pattern-matching algorithms have failed. As would-be thieves get smarter, the developer must take advantage of new technologies that prevent theft. Companies can use this technique heavily in the area of so-called backdoor losses. If a customer no longer buys from a company and the marketing department does not know why, it is called losing them "out the back door." A marketing department could start using data mining tools to help analyze why customers are leaving.

With all of these data management chores to be done and all the tools available, where can you turn to keep your data active? In other words, what product can you use to update the data regularly on the Web site? The tool of choice is Microsoft's SQL Server.

WHY SQL SERVER?

Microsoft's SQL Server is based on the client/server architecture that you have been learning about. SQL Server, as the name implies, is the server side of the architecture. The front end comes in various application forms, from SQL client tools to Web ODBC-based applications. SQL Server resembles Sybase SQL Server, because Microsoft worked with Sybase (and Ashton Tate) in 1988 to develop Microsoft SQL Server. Originally designed for OS/2, SQL Server has become a huge success on Windows NT.

SQL Server, now in release 6.5, has an enterprise management tool called Enterprise Manager (see Figure 8.13).

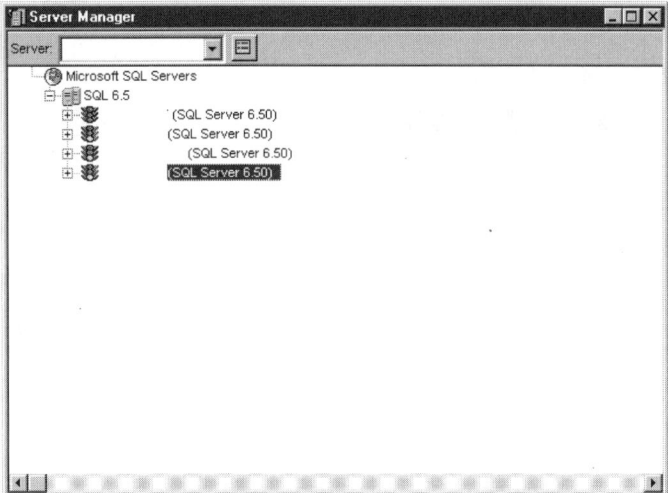

Figure 8.13 Enterprise Manager.

This tool allows you to schedule processes, handle alerts, and deal with replication.

The SQL Server Tools

What happens when you need to get copies of the data to multiple sources in different locations? What if you need to implement scaling methods on various SQL Servers? Enterprise Manager allows you to synchronize and distribute the data, including text and image datatypes. The server recognizes ODBC-compliant databases for the replication process. This means that you are not limited to replicating to SQL Server but can include Oracle and Access databases.

With SQL Enterprise Manager, a DBA or developer can manage SQL Servers anywhere on the enterprise network from a single computer running Windows NT or Windows 95. The manager allows you to create server groups to organize the SQL Servers and manage all the resources from one location. What if you have more than one person assisting in the administration? No problem. That individual can run SQL Enterprise Manager on a different computer and set up his or her own set of server groups to reflect a different view of the network.

Enterprise Manager allows you to perform multiple operations:

- List the devices and databases defined on a SQL Server (see Figure 8.14).
- List the tables, indexes, stored procedures, and other objects defined for a database (see Figure 8.15).
- View the structure of a table (see Figure 8.16).
- List the definition of a stored procedure or trigger.

Chapter 8

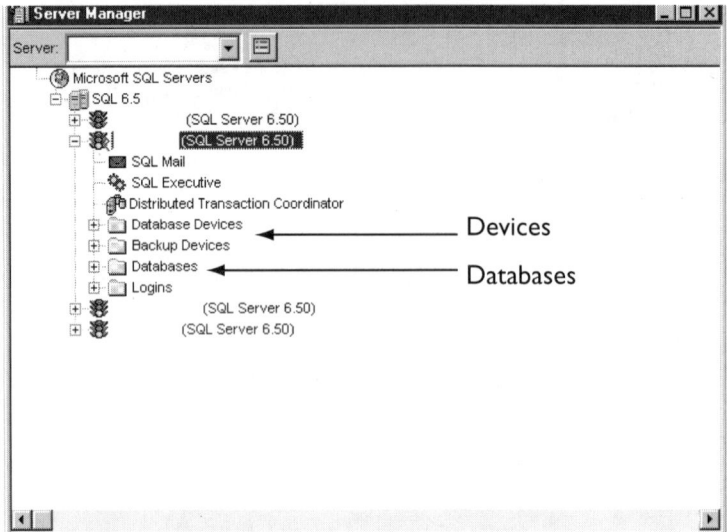

Figure 8.14 The devices and database tools.

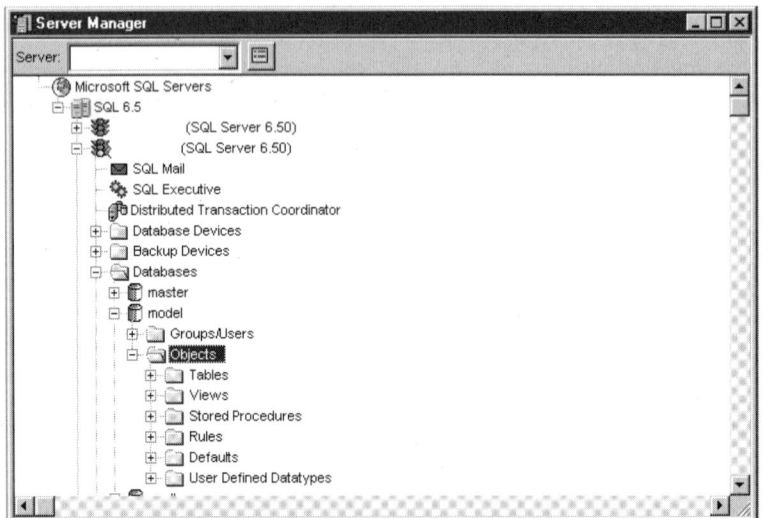

Figure 8.15 Tables and stored procedure location.

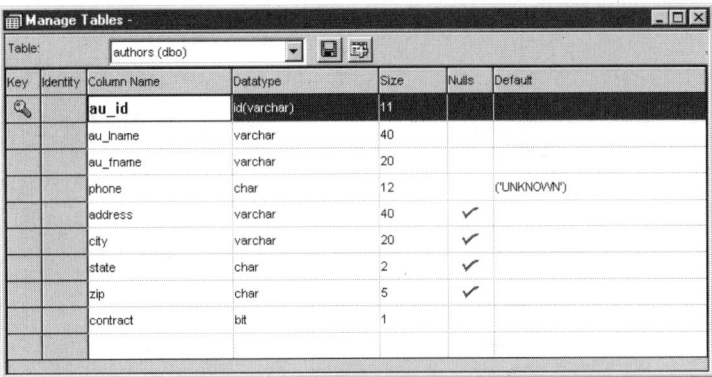

Figure 8.16 Table structure view in SQL Server.

Enterprise Manager has a component called SQL Executive. It enables replication and provides scheduling of SQL Server events, Database Consistency Checker (DBCC) operations, and other administrative maintenance tasks. In addition Enterprise Manager displays the tasks, schedule, and status of SQL Executive. DBCC is a command that checks on the internal consistency of databases or individual tables by comparing the information in SQL Server's internal system tables with the actual physical database. It tries to determine whether there is consistency in both locations. If there is a mismatch, DBCC attempts to make repairs. DBCC can also be used to set trace flags.

OTHER AVAILABLE TOOLS

Other tools available include the following:

- A SQL Web page wizard. This wizard guides you through the creation of a Web page that uses field and table information from the SQL database. A sample walkthrough is shown later in this chapter.
- Microsoft Query. This easy-to-use query tool has been available in the past as part of Microsoft Office but can also be used as a stand-alone query tool.
- Microsoft Distributed Transaction Coordinator (MS DTC), as further detailed in Chapter 11, is an extension of COM. It allows developers to create an application that creates a transaction object. The resource manager (SQL Server in this case) completes the transaction.
- Declarative Referential Integrity (DRI) tool. The developer defines data integrity restrictions for a table and relationships between tables; DRI ensures that related key

values are consistent. In addition, DRI will make changes to the database consistent with the business logic. SQL Server uses indexes for this process. To learn more about indexes, please see the discussion later in this chapter.
- Object Manager. This tool allows developers to view the database structure and definition, including tables and all objects associated with them.
- ISQL and ISQL/W. These tools allow you to execute command-line commands. ISQL, which stands for Interactive SQL, is a DOS utility, and ISQL/W is the Windows-based utility (see Figure 8.17). The developer can enter commands and run scripts. Both tools are a great way to test SQL queries.

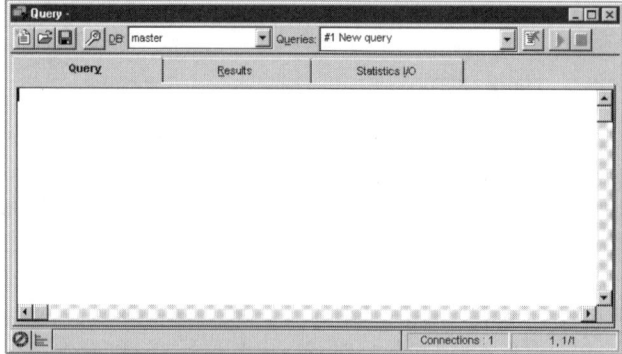

Figure 8.17 ISQL/W tool.

- Bulk Copy Program (BCP). BCP is available to make bulk transfers of data. It is similar to SQL Transfer Manager (discussed in the following section). Many developers choose Transfer Manager over BCP because of its added Windows interface. The bulk routine is a good method for restoring data to individual tables when you're loading them into non–SQL Server databases. Note that when you're using BCP it is recommended that you run the program with the -p option. This option causes the code to run slower because of the added multiple checkpoints, but it prevents the log files from filling up.

Administrative Aspects of SQL Server

SQL Enterprise Manager provides the developer or DBA with many capabilities. You can manage logins, access privileges (including user groups), devices, databases, scripts, database logs, transaction log backups, and various components (such as tables, views, stored procedures, triggers, indexes, rules, defaults, and user-defined datatypes).

SQL Enterprise Manager includes a Database Maintenance Plan wizard. The wizard allows you to create a routing maintenance plan as well as schedule tasks that SQL Executive controls.

Active Data

SQL Transfer Manager, unlike the command-line BCP, is a graphical way to transfer data and objects into and out of SQL Server. Transfer Manager allows you to move data among SQL Servers running on different platforms. For example, you can transfer information from a SQL Server running on an Intel processor to a DEC Alpha box.

SQL Enterprise Manager also has tools for setting up user accounts as well as granting them privileges.

You learned earlier in this chapter that stored procedures can help run processes. These processes include system procedures. The predefined system procedures include

- `sp_who`. Who is logged in.
- `sp_help`. Detailed information from sysobjects, syscolumns, and systypes tables.
- `sp_lock`. Current locks.

Note that the stored procedures have names beginning with `sp_`.

SECURITY

Companies must protect the data stored in their databases. Some personnel can view data only on a need-to-know basis. Other data may be less critical. For this reason, SQL Server comes with the Security Manager program.

SQL Server supports three security models: integrated, mixed, and basic. The mixed and integrated security models offer the capability to use Windows NT user accounts for access to SQL Server. If the developer chooses one of these models, SQL Security Manager is used to help manage accounts (see Figure 8.18).

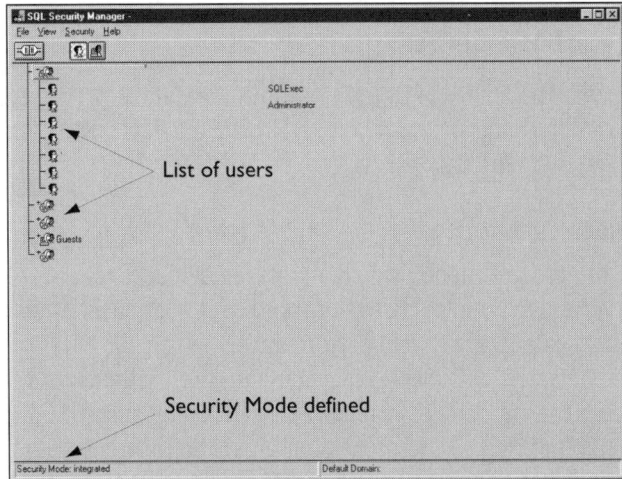

Figure 8.18 Security Manager view.

SQL Server provides database protection at various levels in the logical model. You can secure each identifiable element of data, including tables, rows, columns, and individual fields.

The user or group can be granted these privileges: select, insert, update, delete and execute. The developer is setting up a security matrix (see Figure 8.19).

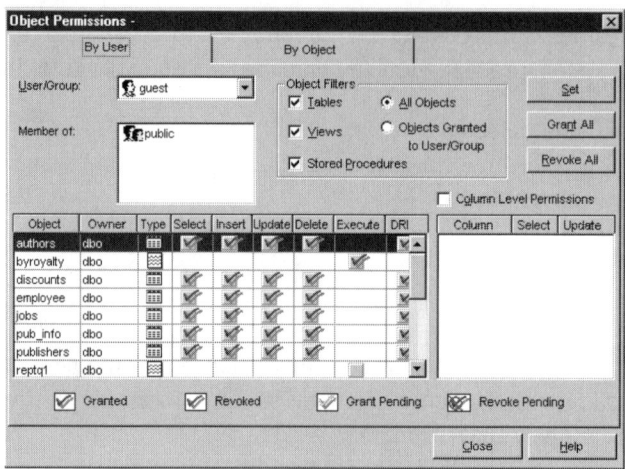

Figure 8.19 Object permissions to authorized users.

Each data element can be assigned privileges by user. As you can see, the rows represent tables, the columns represent data elements, and the cells indicate the permitted operations.

Logical Aspects of SQL Server

SQL Server gives you the ability to determine how the data is processed and moved. For example, you must determine when, where, and how the data will be distributed. In addition, you must know why the data exists.

THE PROCESS MODEL

As noted before, the process model is a client/server model. Because SQL Server is based on the client/server model, it allows developers to deal with such issues as network bandwidth, maintenance, data integrity, and performance.

Regarding the network, SQL Server lets you consider methods for reducing query size as well as reducing the number of results. You can use Transact-SQL (T-SQL) to create complex statements that reduce the processing effort. You can also use stored procedures instead of large SQL batch queries. Additionally, you can incorporate SQL warehouse methodologies to minimize the amount of data sent back by the query. It is better to present aggregate results rather than run all the data back to the customer's workstation.

Maintenance requires the developer to think through an implementation plan. Sometimes, putting a process on the server side rather than the client side will reduce problems. Running DBCC, as noted before, can cause great drains on the system. It is best to run this process during off hours.

SQL Enterprise Manager allows you to set *constraints*, whereas T-SQL provides rules, defaults, and indexes (discussed later) to handle data integrity. An example of a constraint is a primary key constraint, in which all the values in a table are unique and there are no `nulls` in the primary key. Rules and defaults deal with datatypes and columns. Indexes deal with columns other than the primary key. Constraints tend to be faster than the T-SQL methods, because constraints are loaded into memory. If you are dealing with multiple tables, you are better off with T-SQL methods.

You need to consider the placement of tables and data based on system performance constraints. Here, the logical model must be kept in sync with the physical reality. Do not forget to keep track of the number of client sessions that the database will endure. You may be able to use SQL Enterprise Manager to distribute resources to assist with increased use.

Note that each of these items assists you in making process model changes during the implementation and tuning phase. Now let's look at the tools SQL Server provides for data handling.

Data Distribution

Do SQL Server and its tools assist you in properly locating the data? The answer is yes, but first you need to understand the complications of data distribution. You must know the capacity of the system, how the data is stored and delivered, and how redundant data is handled.

Because data exists in many forms and in many locations, capacity can become a major issue. Databases grow as users find what they are looking for and demand more information. You may need to place the data in multiple locations. SQL Server supports multiple distribution as well as remote replication of data (see Figure 8.20).

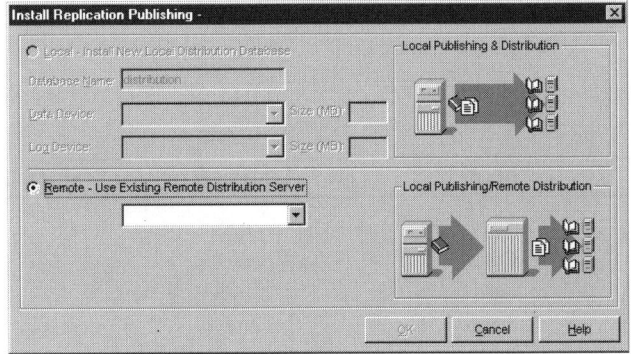

Figure 8.20 Using the distribution database.

So the data, in these cases, is split among both locations and possibly multiple servers in each location.

Another issue is data storage and delivery. In handling storage issues, you see the process as defining devices that you initialize and then creating databases to use those devices. Delivery depends on the needs of the user. If there are multiple users of the same data in multiple locations, it may be appropriate to replicate the data to reduce delivery times, something that introduces the need for database synchronization. You can accomplish much of this administration using Enterprise Manager. As long as you have given the SQL Executive account log-on privileges to each of the major servers, you can use the replication services within SQL Server.

For SQL Server, data distribution means spreading the database over multiple physical disk drives to improve performance. It is also best to put the log for a database on a separate physical disk from the data portion of the database. The data portion should be *striped* across multiple physical devices to achieve maximum throughput. Striping is easy to configure using the disk management facilities built into the Microsoft Windows NT operating system. Striping usually yields equivalent performance to placing database tables and indexes on specific devices, at a fraction of the effort. Windows NT also offers disk configurations (RAID levels) that can protect a database against the failure of a hard disk. All SQL Server databases should take advantage of these capabilities.

Normalization: The Implementation of the Logical Data Model

Normalization is used to reduce redundant data. For example, suppose that you build a database of fictitious cars and car manufacturers. You load data from the GMA manufacturing company and the Taury make, the Camer make, and the Hondu make. To prevent repetition of the makes of cars, a *first normal* database of the manufacturers has more than one entry per make.

MANUFACTURER	MAKE
GMA	Taury
GMA	Camer
GMA	Hondu

Now add the FORU manufacturing company and its three lines of cars along with another piece of information, the location.

MANUFACTURER	MAKE	LOCATION OF MANUFACTURER
GMA	Taury	Chicago
GMA	Camer	Chicago
GMA	Hondu	Chicago
FORU	Premier	Los Angeles
FORU	Adoba	Los Angeles
FORU	Pint-O	Los Angeles

The key here is the manufacturer and make. To create a *second normal* form (2NF), you must break this data into two tables. Why? The location has nothing to do with the make. It is related to the manufacturer.

MANUFACTURER	LOCATION OF MANUFACTURER
GMA	Chicago
FORU	Los Angeles

MANUFACTURER	MAKE
GMA	Taury
GMA	Camer
GMA	Hondu
FORU	Premier
FORU	Adoba
FORU	Pint-O

What if the make is location-dependent? Then you use a *third normal* form (3NF), in which you relate the manufacturer to the make and the make to the location.

MANUFACTURER	MAKE	LOCATION OF MANUFACTURER
GMA	Taury	Chicago
GMA	Camer	San Francisco
GMA	Hondu	New Orleans
FORU	Premier	Los Angeles
FORU	Adoba	Las Vegas
FORU	Pint-O	Philadelphia

That becomes the following.

MANUFACTURER	MAKE
GMA	Taury
GMA	Camer
GMA	Hondu
FORU	Premier
FORU	Adoba
FORU	Pint-O

MAKE	LOCATION OF MANUFACTURER
Taury	Chicago
Camer	San Francisco
Hondu	New Orleans
Premier	Los Angeles
Adoba	Las Vegas
Pint-O	Philadelphia

A measure of logical modeling effectiveness can be found in the level of normalization.

For this discussion, you should attempt to normalize data to the third. *Denormalizing* a database takes it from a higher level of normalization to a lower number, such as from 3NF to 2NF. Some developers do this to improve performance, but you must be careful. You could find worse problems later.

Data warehousing tends to denormalize the database environment. This is usually OK, because the intent of this database is to provide ad hoc reports and not heavy transaction management.

When you're using normalization in concert with SQL Enterprise Manager, you can break the system into departmental components. This approach can be helpful in the step-by-step process of building the enterprise model.

Physical Aspects of SQL Server

Indexing can be a vital part of the implementation of a database. SQL Server gives you two ways to build indexes: clustered and nonclustered.

A *clustered* index is one in which the indexed order of the rows is the same as the physical order of the rows. The lowest level of a clustered index contains the actual data. Clustered indexes have a direct relationship to the physical data, and that enhances data retrieval speeds.

There can be only one clustered index per table. When you want to create a clustered index, you must determine to which columns you should apply the clustered index. The system generates the clustered index for the columns that uniquely identify each row, or what is known as the *primary key*.

But suppose you need to search the columns in a sequence or you want to index by values. In that case you can apply the clustered index to columns other than those representing the primary key. A clustered index is shown in Figure 8.21.

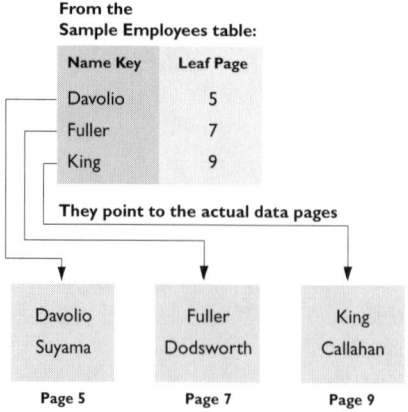

Figure 8.21 A clustered index.

A *nonclustered* index adds another level with an index row for every table row (see Figure 8.22).

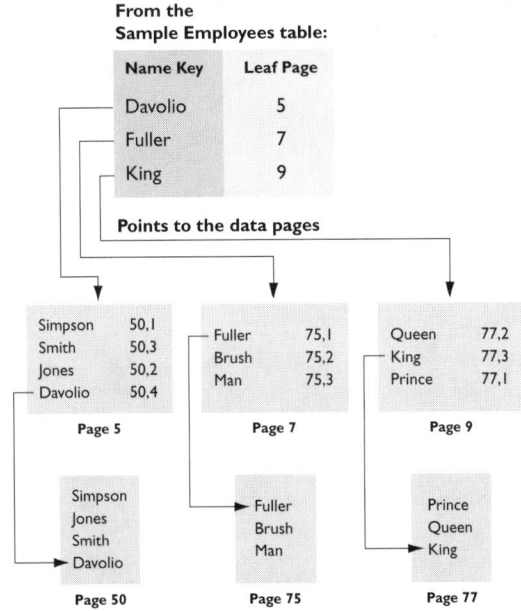

Figure 8.22 A nonclustered index.

As you might guess, nonclustered indexes are faster than clustered indexes when key values are being added or updated. Clustered indexes beat nonclustered indexes in retrieval (look at the added burden of the extra level) and in minimizing storage requirements.

ACCESSING DATA FROM WEB APPS

When you connect the database server (SQL Server) to the Web server (IIS 3.0), you gain the ability to make your site active. The database can regularly update various screens or, by interacting with the client, can generate new screens based on client requests. Collecting data for orders or for marketing surveys goes beyond using a CGI script to generate an e-mail. It becomes a transaction that is stored and used to help the company better meet the needs of customers. This active site with a database now lets you store the same data for intranets, extranets, and the Internet in one logical location, thereby reducing data redundancy as well as maintenance. An active data site also provides security for conducting business over the Web as well as for internal corporate intranets. The same SQL Server applications that have been used within a company can now be distributed over the Web.

The SQL Server architecture provides you with two major advantages: a programming interface and Open Database Connectivity (ODBC).

The SQL Server Programming Interface

Standard CGI scripts require multiple lines of code to tie the form to the database. The following listing shows sample code provided by a developer linking to a database:

```perl
#!/usr/local/bin/perl

# simple_ query.pl

# make use of some existing utilities

require 'cgi-lib.pl';

# determine form method (GET or POST), parse user inputs and
# load into an associative array (using cgi-lib.pl routines)

&ReadParse;

# set a few variables for use by database calls, etc.
$DBUSER = "guest";
$DBPASSWD = "guest";
$DBAPPL = "web-cgi";
$DSQUERY = "database1";
$DBNAME = "samples";
$ENV{'SYBASE'} = "/homes/database";
$ENV{'PATH'} = "$PATH;$database/bin";
$ENV{'DSQUERY'} = $DSQUERY;
$ENV{'DBNAME'} = $DBNAME;
$NO_RESULTS = "NO RESULTS WERE FOUND MATCHING YOUR QUERY";

# specify use of perl DBlib extensions

use Database::DBlib;

# make a connection to the SQL server and establish database to use

$dbh = Database::DBlib->dblogin($DBUSER, $DBPASSWD, $DSQUERY, $DBAPPL);
$status = $dbh->dbuse($DBNAME);

# now look at the name/value(s) pairs loaded into the associative array

@mags_types[0] = $in{'btype0'};
@mags_types[1] = $in{'btype1'};
@mags_types[2] = $in{'btype2'};
@mags_types[3] = $in{'btype3'};
@mags_types[4] = $in{'btype4'};
@mags_types[5] = $in{'btype5'};

$ price = $in{'price'};

# start generating HTML output to return to client
```

Active Data

```perl
# send content-type header identifying this as HTML,
# extra newline is required!

print "Content-type: text/html\n\n";
print "<HTML><HEAD>\n";
print "<TITLE>Sample Database Query Results</TITLE>\n";
print "</HEAD><BODY>\n";
print "<CENTER><H2>\n";
print "Sample Database Query Results\n";
print "</H2></CENTER>\n";
print "<HR>\n";

# format the query

$columns = " title, price ";
$tables = " titles ";
$clauses = "type in (";
$mag_types_cnt = 0;
foreach $this_type (@mag_types) {
  $mag_types_cnt++;
  if($mag_types_cnt > 1) {
     $clauses = $clauses.", ";
  }
  $clauses = $clauses."\"$this_type\"";
}
$clauses = $clauses.") and price \< CONVERT(MONEY,'$ price') ";

$sql_query = "select $columns from $tables where $clauses\n";

# put the query into current command buffer and send to the server
# to execute

$dbh->dbcmd("$sql_query");
$dbh->dbsqlexec;

# get results information from the server and the number of
# rows of information available

$dbh->dbresults;
$num_rows = $dbh->DBCOUNT;

print "<PRE>\n";

if ($num_rows == 0) {
   print "$NO_RESULTS\nPlease try another query!\n";
}
else {
   while(@row = $dbh->dbnextrow) {
```

Chapter 8

```
    print "@row[0]    @row[1]\n";
    }
}
print "</PRE>\n";
print "</BODY></HTML>\n";
```

In this case, the developer had the program do the following:

- Determine whether the form was using a GET or POST method.
- Parse inputs to name-value pairs.
- Create a database query.
- Log in to the database.
- Submit the query.
- Get data.
- Close the connection.
- Format the output to HTML.

There is quite a bit of programming going on in this example. Any necessary modifications will take some work, especially if the database structure changes. What if a developer has open connectivity using tools and wizards? That is what Microsoft provides (see Figure 8.23).

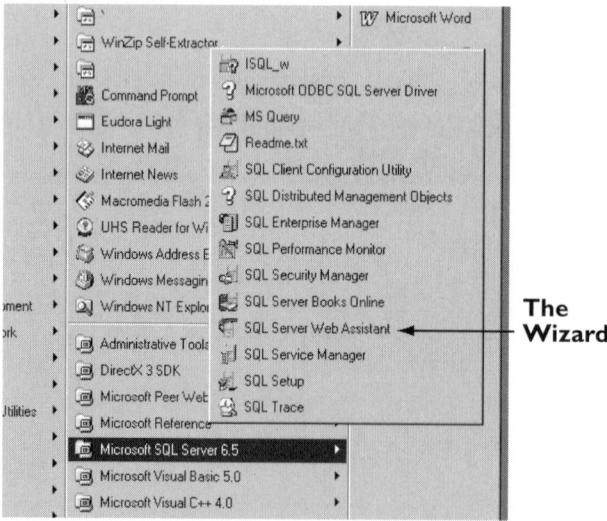

Figure 8.23 Finding the wizard.

You can use IDC/HTX (as discussed in Chapter 6) or a wizard to make a clean, transparent connection to the database. You can create an environment where the data is pulled by an activity of the client or pushed by a prescheduled trigger in the database.

Active Data   165

The SQL Web Assistant (also known as the Web Page wizard) provides you with a step-by-step process for creating database-generated Web pages. Please see Figures 8.24–8.293 for an example of the process.

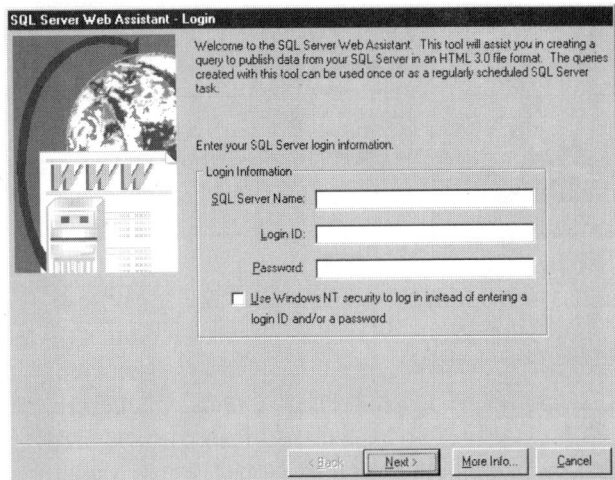

Figure 8.24 SQL Server Web Assistant opening screen.

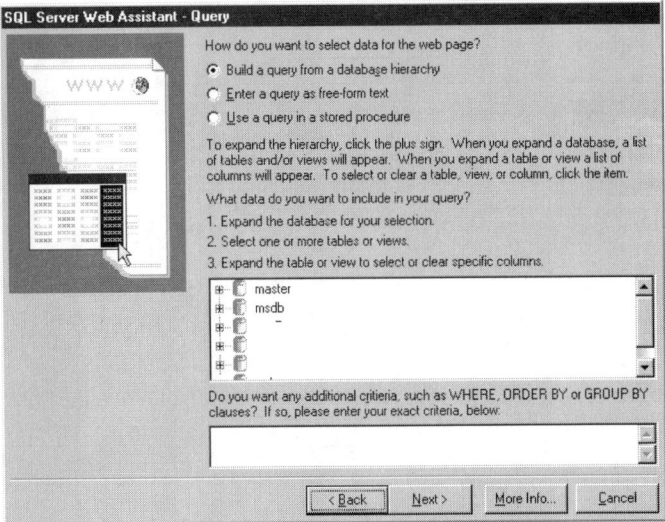

Figure 8.25 Once the developer is logged in.

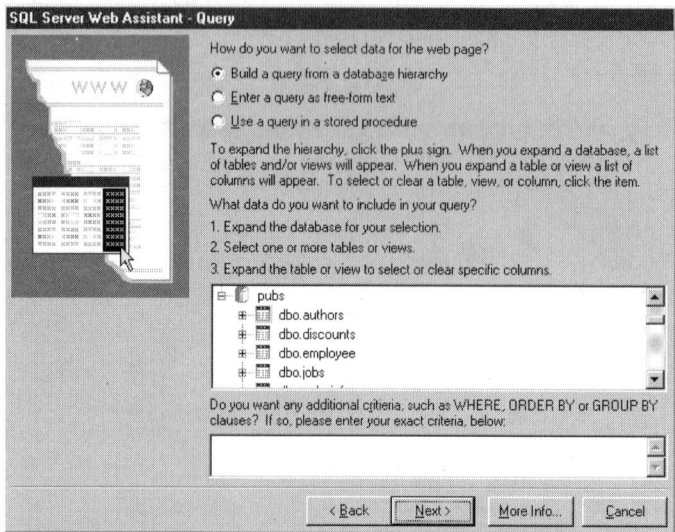

Figure 8.26 Choosing a database and table(s).

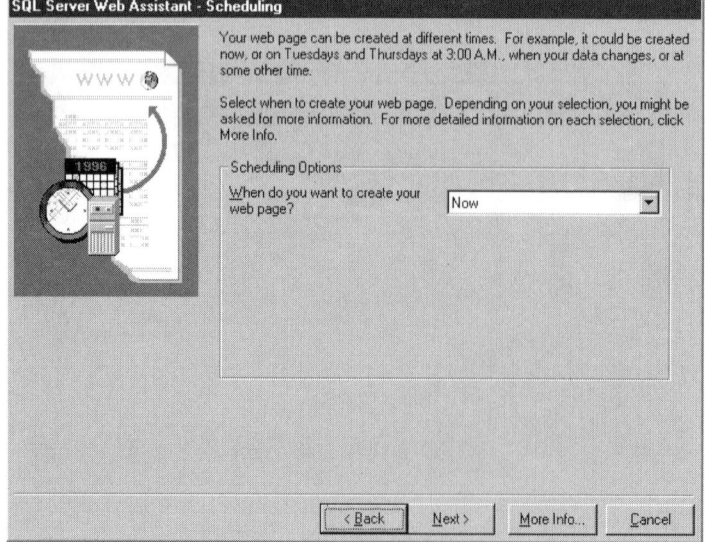

Figure 8.27 Scheduling choice.

Active Data 167

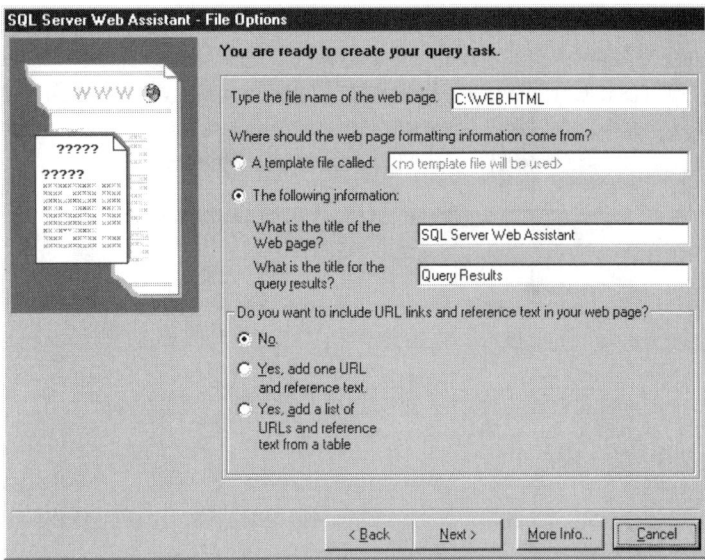

Figure 8.28 The options.

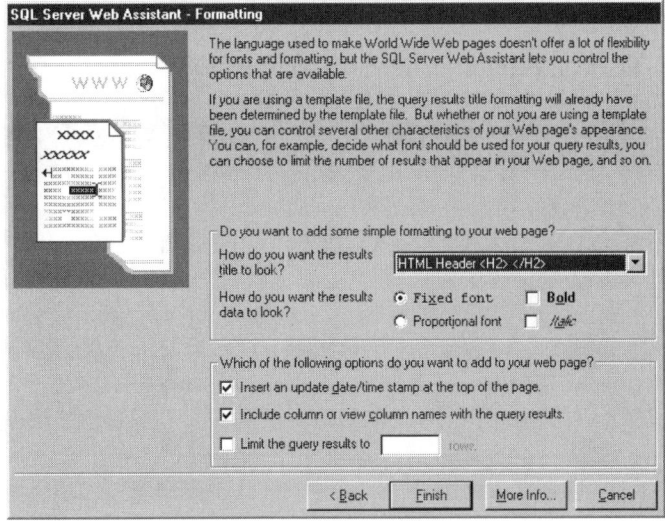

Figure 8.29 Final choices.

The nice part about SQL Web Assistant is that it executes the query only once for all the possible customers. This approach reduces resource waste. SQL Web Assistant lets you opt to have the pages updated regularly by the database.

Open Database Connectivity

ODBC is a database Application Programming Interface (API). This means that you can use standard SQL methods (such as IDC/HTX; Visual Basic in ASP) to access a driver (single DLL) that makes connections to the appropriate database. If you wish to find or replace the driver, it is **Sqlsrv32.dll** for the Win32 SQL Server and **Sqlsrvr.dll** for the Win16 driver (see Figure 8.30).

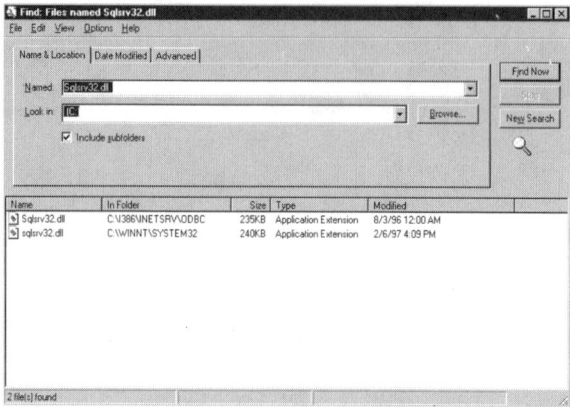

Figure 8.30 Location of **Sqlsrv32.dll**.

The IDC mentioned earlier depends on ODBC for its database connectivity. Please see Figures 8.31–8.34 for an example of how to set up an ODBC entry.

Figure 8.31 Open Control Panel; choose the **ODBC** icon.

Active Data 169

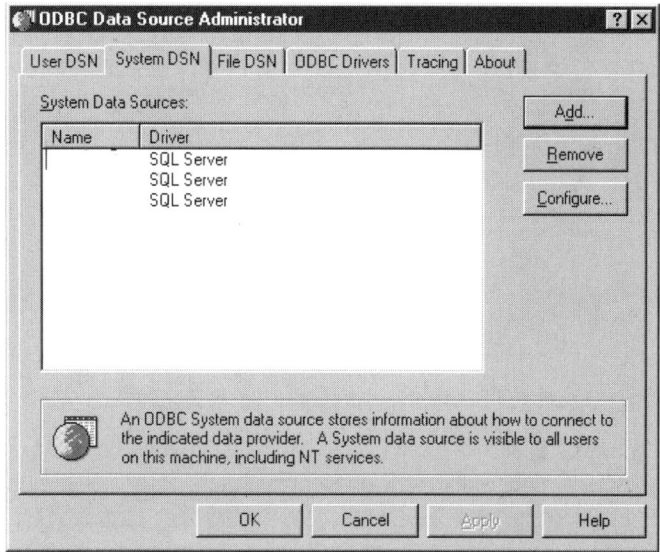

Figure 8.32 Choose the **System DSN** tab.

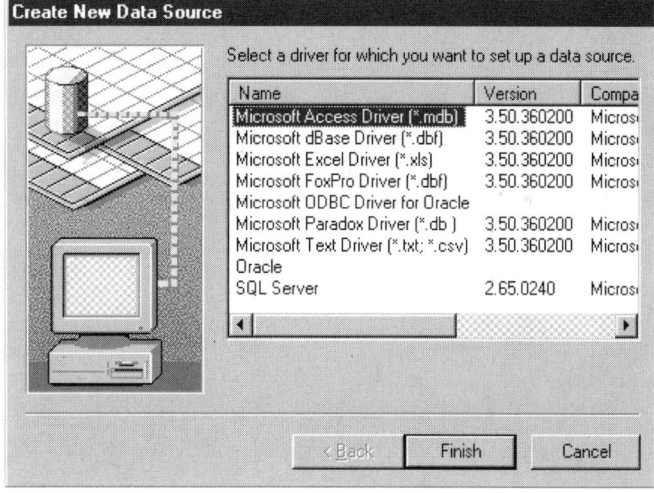

Figure 8.33 Choose **Add** and then the proper data source.

170 Chapter 8

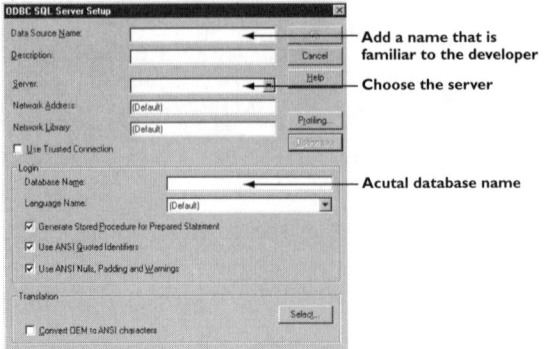

Figure 8.34 Add the appropriate database information.

What happens if you need to access a non-ODBC database but want the same connectivity interface? This is where JDBC (Java Database Connectivity) and CORBA (Common Object Request Broker Architecture) come into play. JDBC is an API that provides access to SQL databases at the object level. JDBC does not currently operate at the component level but operates instead at the object level, much like ActiveX data objects. JDBC will be reviewed further in Chapter 17.

The intent behind CORBA was to create objects that could react with other objects. The trick was that the programmer did not need to know how or where the original object was implemented. The ORB of the acronym is the software that brokers requests from the objects.

You can integrate ActiveX controls (which used to be called OLE controls, or OCX) into the programming effort. For example, you can use Active Data Objects (rather than RDO or DAO for the "older" Windows programmers in the audience) and Visual Basic or VBScript for accessing data located in a database. Please see Chapter 5 for more detailed information on these components.

The ActiveX environment provides for a `DataSource` object, as shown in Figure 8.35.

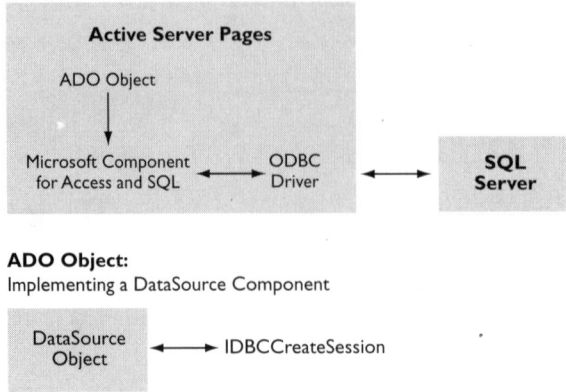

Figure 8.35 DataSource object.

The `IDBCreateSession` interface calls a `DBSession` object. The `DBSession` object has a number of interfaces to include the `IDBCreateCommon`. An application that accesses a SQL data source will connect to `IDBCreateCommand` to create the `Command` object. The `Rowset` object is equivalent to SQL results or DAO recordsets. It is the result of the query.

The Warehouse

SQL Server provides an ideal environment for implementing data warehouse activities (see Figure 8.36).

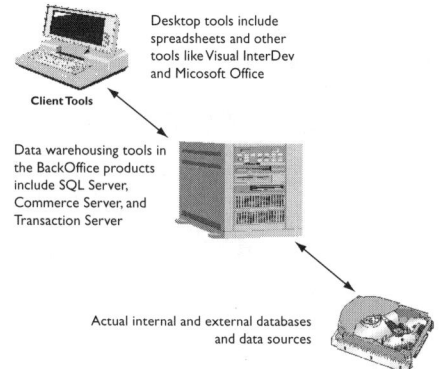

Figure 8.36 Data warehousing.

Microsoft reports that at least 26% of SQL Server clients are using SQL Server in data warehousing activities. If we include the decision support users, the percentage grows to 51%.

SQL Server provides data warehousing functionality through a number of features, including the following.

- Parallel transaction execution, data indexing and loading, and integrity checking.
- A cost-based optimizer.
- Parallel data scanning for improved performance of ad hoc decision support queries.
- OLAP query extensions—`CUBE` and `ROLLUP`—allow a query to return detailed data and aggregates across multiple dimensions, simplifying information retrieval for analytical purposes.
- Data pipe capability, which allows SQL Server to retrieve information from multiple data sources and populate SQL Server tables with the results.
- High-speed parallel backup and restore that support as many as 32 disk or tape drives.
- `Insert Exec` now enables results from remote or extended stored procedures to be stored in tables.
- Backup and restoration of individual tables (parallel backup as well as bulk load).
- Index rebuilding without dropping and re-creating the index.

Chapter 8

- Asynchronous I/O.
- Integrated security to protect your decision support data from intrusion.
- Centralized database management with scheduling and exception handling.
- Built-in support for symmetric multiprocessing.

As you build your data warehouse architecture, be sure to watch how data is moved. A data mart (a local subset of the data warehouse) is implemented within a company's enterprise model. This means that you will cross business boundaries with the data marts. Take a look at extraction tools such as Platinum or Informatica to assist in the effort. A sample implementation of this warehouse schema is shown in Figures 8.37 and 8.38.

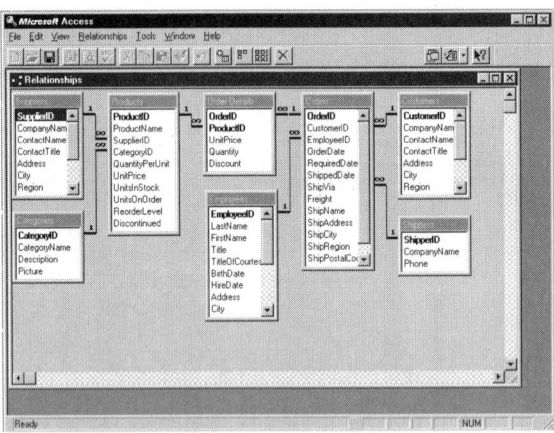

Figure 8.37 Classic table relationships.

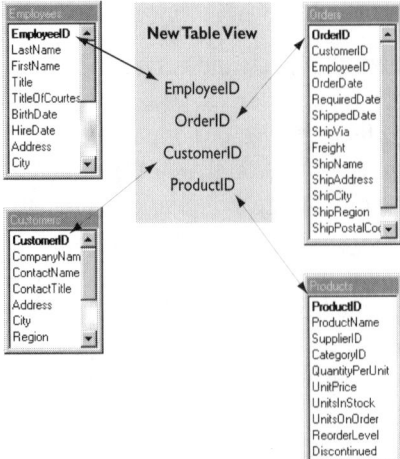

Figure 8.38 The new table view.

The developer will populate each dimension based on knowledge of when and where to find the appropriate data.

The star schema query is used to drill down into the data with a minimal use of table joins (see Figure 8.39).

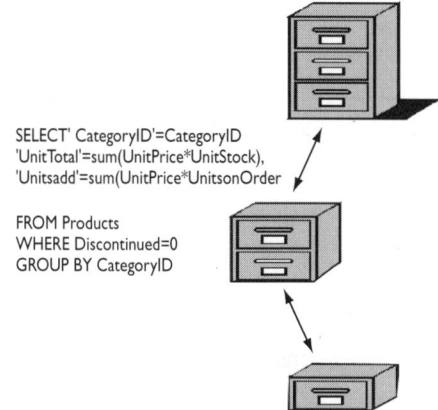

Figure 8.39 Sample drill down into the Products table.

The `rollup` and `cube` commands are used to total appropriate column data. For example, suppose that a developer uses a standard query to show the number of four-door and two-door cars sold in Nebraska. A rollup would provide the same results plus a total of all cars sold in Nebraska. A cube will look at the same process as a rollup but will not generate values for missing combinations. The next section has an example of rollup and cube.

Microsoft plans to add further data warehousing features in a future release of SQL Server. These features include the following:

- An improved SQL loader and optimizer.
- Integrated Excel connectivity (an extension of what is now available in SQL Server 6.5).
- Additional data analysis and Web administration tools.

The concept and implementation of data warehousing can be very difficult. The best way to understand some of these characteristics is to look at the data manipulation tool itself.

THE DATA RETRIEVAL METHOD: TRANSACT SQL

Transact-SQL is the language used by developers to manipulate and handle data. An extension of SQL, it is a language made up of a number of English-type statements. The following example uses the tables from the normalization discussion.

Manufacturer	Make
GMA	Taury
GMA	Camer
GMA	Hondu
FORU	Premier
FORU	Adoba
FORU	Pint-O

Make	Location of Manufacturer
Taury	Chicago
Camer	San Francisco
Hondu	New Orleans
Premier	Los Angeles
Adoba	Las Vegas
Pint-O	Philadelphia

Suppose we want to know all the locations of vehicles:

`SELECT * FROM Location`

Notice that we start with a verb and then identify the column. (In this case, the wildcard * means all columns.) Then we specify the table using the clause FROM `table_name`.

That is the basic SQL statement. Although you can write complex queries in SQL, this chapter will not cover that. Instead, the space is limited to identifying the extensive use of T-SQL in `nulls`, `joins`, and `cubes`.

Nulls

A `null` does not mean that the value is zero. Instead, it means that the value is unknown or not entered. Let's look at this from a Boolean point of view in a Null Truth Table:

And	True	Unknown	False
True	True	Unknown	False
Unknown	Unknown	Unknown	False
False	False	False	False
OR	True	Unknown	False
True	True	True	True
Unknown	True	Unknown	Unknown
False	True	Unknown	False
NOT			
True	False		
Unknown	Unknown		
False	True		

If you creates a table called NULL_table and put two variables in place (A = null and B = 5), what values are returned by these statements?

```
SELECT 1 FROM  NULL_table WHERE A=B

SELECT 1 FROM NULL_table WHERE A<B

SELECT 1 FROM NULL_table WHERE A<>B        (A is greater or less than B)

SELECT 1 FROM NULL_table WHERE A!>B        (A is not greater than B)

SELECT 1 FROM NULL_table WHERE
(A>= 0 OR A<=0)
```

Not one case returns 5. Do not be fooled by the meaning of null.

Microsoft SQL extends the NULL in the area of IS NULL and =NULL. For example, ANSI SQL allows

```
SELECT * WHERE make IS  NULL
```

but not

```
SELECT * WHERE make=NULL
```

Yet ANSI SQL allows

```
UPDATE make SET type =NULL
```

and not

```
UPDATE make SET type TO NULL
```

SQL Server extends =NULL to be the equivalent of IS NULL. Either form is usable with T-SQL.

JOINs

T-SQL supports the standard SQL implementation of INNER, OUTER, LEFT, RIGHT, and CROSS JOINs. The OUTER JOIN in T-SQL preserves nonmatching rows along with the new syntax allowing you to specify whether the criteria are applied before or after the JOIN operation. The JOIN order is important for OUTER JOIN.

CUBE

The data cube is the basis for OLAP or data warehousing. It is the way T-SQL supports multidimensional data structures (see Figure 8.40).

176   Chapter 8

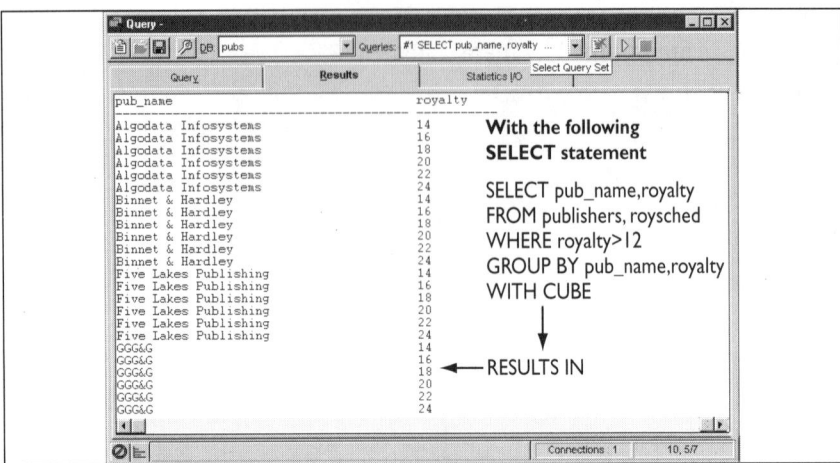

Figure 8.40 An example of a data cube.

The CUBE allows you to view different slices of the data depending on user needs.

Why not use the GROUP BY operation? For example:

```
SELECT location FROM location_table GROUP BY location having city="Chicago";
```

The problem is that users want historical records in a diagram form along with totals and subtotals. The common response is, "Well, go build some kind of report. For example, drill-down reports and rollup reports." That action does not get to the correct data!

The CUBE command in T-SQL allows you to aggregate row information to give the company decision makers accurate and timely data.

Transact-SQL supports the developer's need to implement mission-critical applications. Additionally, it reduces the need for developers to use complex programming languages (such as Visual C++) to provide company management with accurate and detailed data. The enhancements that we've briefly reviewed provide a strong extension to SQL that increases system performance and protects referential data integrity.

Where Do You Go from Here?

SQL Server is a deep and rich environment that extends well beyond what has been covered in this chapter. Numerous books and Web sites are dedicated to SQL Server.

Let's end by highlighting a few tips discussed in this chapter.

- Sometimes data is too large to house on one server. If the physical model calls for multiple servers, there is usually a need to move data between servers. SQL Server provides full replication tools to move this data. Replication assists in the scaling of

applications and SQL databases.
- Do not forget to use the wizards provided by SQL Server. Remember that the SQL Server Web Assistant makes it easy to put pages on the Web. Triggers and schedules allow for page refreshing.
- SQL Server provides stored procedures that let you extend T-SQL. The system lets you create DLLs that can call functions on Windows NT and other servers.
- SQL Server provides the tools and functionality that allow a developer to implement a data warehouse and its associated data marts.

From here you may want to spend time in the following chapters:

- Chapter 1, "The Active Ingredients of a Well-Done Web Site," for more information on the client/server world.
- Chapter 6, "Active Server Pages," to learn more about IDC and HTX.
- Chapter 17, "Java and JavaScript," to learn more about using JDBC.

Chapter 9

Active Search: Index Server

Every site—whether Web site or intranet site—is competing for visitors. If you can draw people to your Internet site, you can draw advertising. If you can attract customers to your company's Internet site, you can create sales opportunities. If you can persuade people to use the company intranet, you can justify the investment of resources you need to make the company more competitive in the global market.

As dynamic sites predominate, it's important to make your site's changing content easily available to visitors. It's no longer enough simply to place the content on the site and expect customers to sift through it to find the information they're looking for. Whether your visitors are using the site for business or pleasure, time is valuable to them. Just as they use an index and catalog system at the library, site visitors expect to use search tools at your site.

NOTE
Security becomes an issue when you support search capabilities. The "best" active sites would allow customers and employees to search for all product information. Adding product pricing information would make searching the site much easier, but the developer must be aware that competitors will be reviewing the site to establish their market. In this case, you may want to create an extranet site for selected marketplaces and selected clients. An extranet is an externally accessible intranet.

You are probably familiar with various Internet search engine sites, such as Yahoo, Infoseek, Hotbot, Excite, and Alta Vista. A well-known search site that covers the entire Internet is shown in Figure 9.1.

An example of a vendor's internal search site is shown in Figure 9.2.
All search engines are based on three basic concepts:

- Finding all the appropriate documents designated by the server.
- Building an index of the contents and properties of these designated files based on filtering properties (such as removing all the occurrences of *and*).
- Placing the index information in a catalog like the card catalogs used in libraries.

An alternative version of indexing is used by sites such as thesite.com (see Figure 9.3).

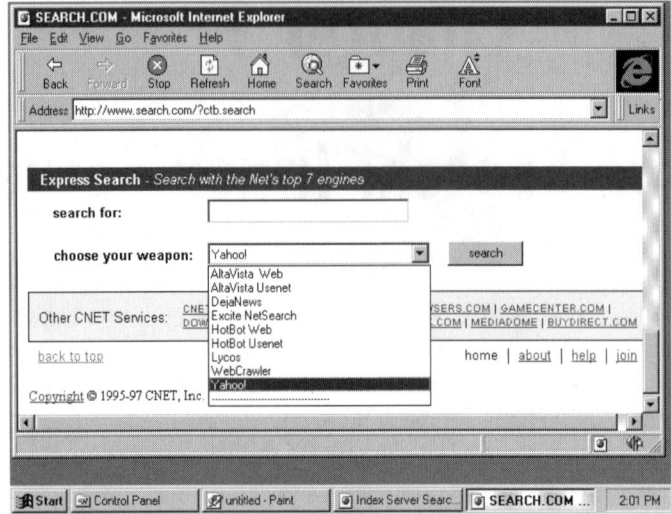

Figure 9.1 The search.com Web site.

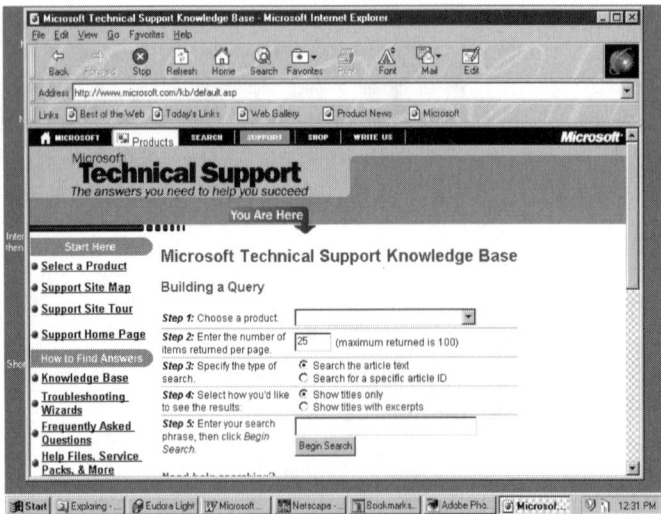

Figure 9.2 Microsoft's internal Knowledge Base.

Active Search—Index Server 181

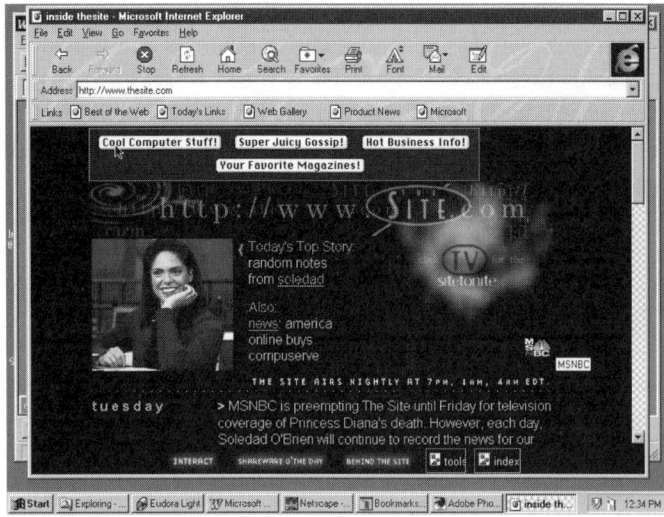

Figure 9.3 WWW.thesite.com.

In the case of thesite.com, the developers provide an actual index based on user needs (see Figure 9.4).

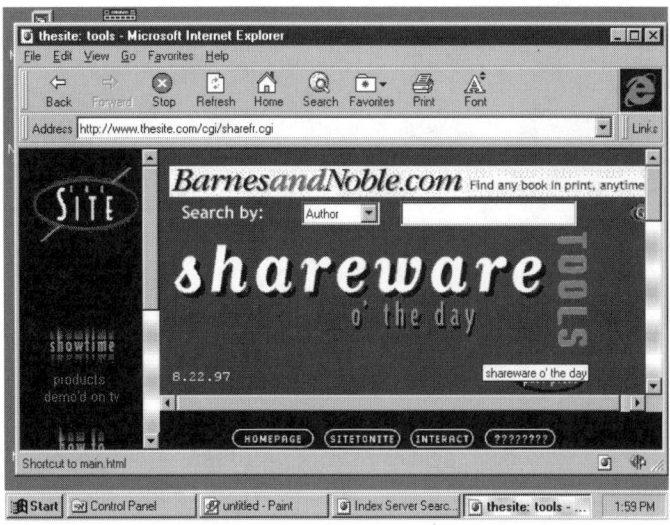

Figure 9.4 Personal search choices at thesite.com.

Microsoft's Index Server helps you create a virtual library for your site visitors. When a user queries Index Server, it finds the appropriate documents and provides search tools for the user to use within these documents. Then Index Server creates and indexes the desired contents. Finally, it builds a catalog of the content and the indexes.

This chapter describes how Index Filter works and how you can use it to provide library services at your site. You'll also learn how to develop your own filter interfaces for filtering special document types and how to administer Index Server to maximize its performance. Then we'll discuss various approaches to indexing databases.

THE QUERY PROCESS

Queries are made up of query scopes (where to search), restrictions (what to search for), and the results (what information to view). Figure 9.5 illustrates the process.

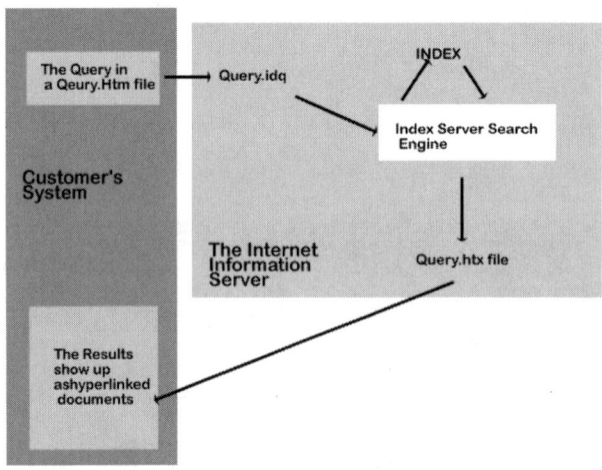

Figure 9.5 Query process.

The scope tells the query engine where to look when searching. It describes the set of documents to be searched within the collection of documents and HTML pages. The restriction tests to see whether a document should be returned. A restriction is a set of terms that can be combined by various operators. The result set defines the information returned from a query.

With regard to scope, Index Server indexes documents based on sites. An administrator can index all the sites on a server or select a subset of sites to index. Queries can be run against multiple sites, against a single site, or even against a single physical directory within a site. A customer query can include HTML, Microsoft Word, Microsoft Excel, Microsoft PowerPoint, and plain text documents. In addition, with the proper filters a customer can search for Adobe Acrobat and other types of documents. Index Server lets the developer search for multiple words and phrases. A content filter (Ifilter, which is discussed later in this chapter) reads a proprietary document format and produces text, which is indexed by Index Server.

Query restrictions include operator, free-text, vector-space, and property value restrictions. Operators are based on Boolean, proximity, relational, wildcard, and word-stemming algorithms. Free text lets customers enter any set of words or phrases, or even a complete sentence, as the query restriction. Vector space lets a person match a list of words and phrases. Property value queries can be used to find files that have property values, such as file name and file size, along with ActiveX properties (for example, `DocTitle= Title of Document`).

Standard Query

The user is presented with a standard query form (see Figure 9.6).

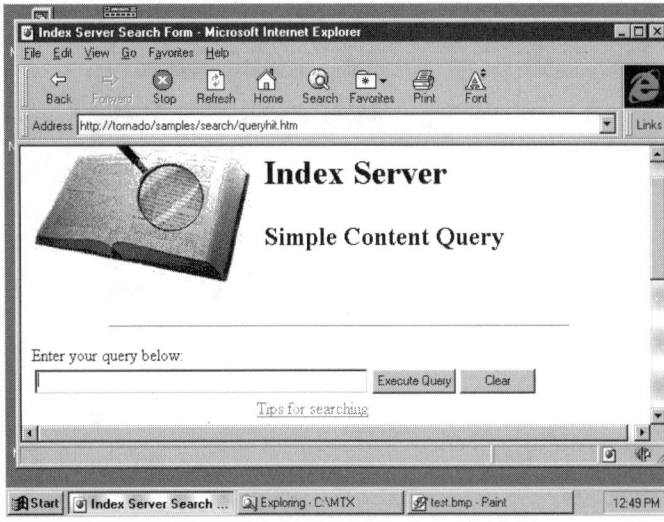

Figure 9.6 Simple query.

Here the user enters words and phrases to query against. The query language is similar to standard search engine query languages. For example, if a customer is searching for all occurrences of *visual* and *basic*, Index Server will find all the pages that contain both words. See Figures 9.7 and 9.8 for the results of a "*visual basic*" query.

184   **Chapter 9**

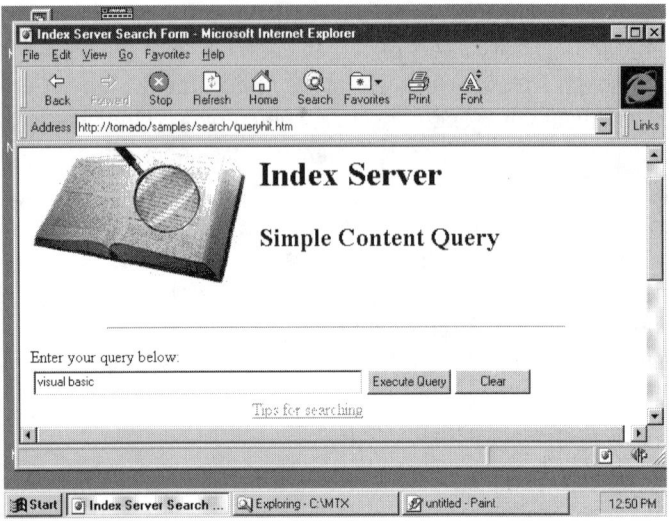

Figure 9.7 Search for documents containing "visual basic".

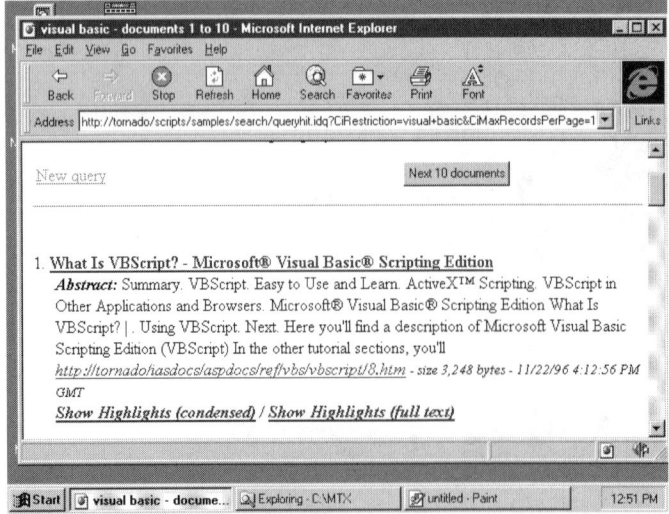

Figure 9.8 Results of search for documents containing "visual basic".

The query form determines the number of results to send per page. You can limit the maximum number of hits returned to the client, or you can configure a form to let the client specify the number of hits to be returned.

Now let's look at the syntax of the query language.

Query Language Operators

To understand the query language, you need to understand the basic operators and searches available to the user.

BOOLEAN OPERATORS

Boolean operators tie together strings of characters using AND, OR, and NOT.

Using AND, the user is looking for both words on either side of the operator. As in the previous example, entering **"visual AND basic"** means that the user wants all pages with *visual* and *basic*. See Figure 9.9 for an example of this query.

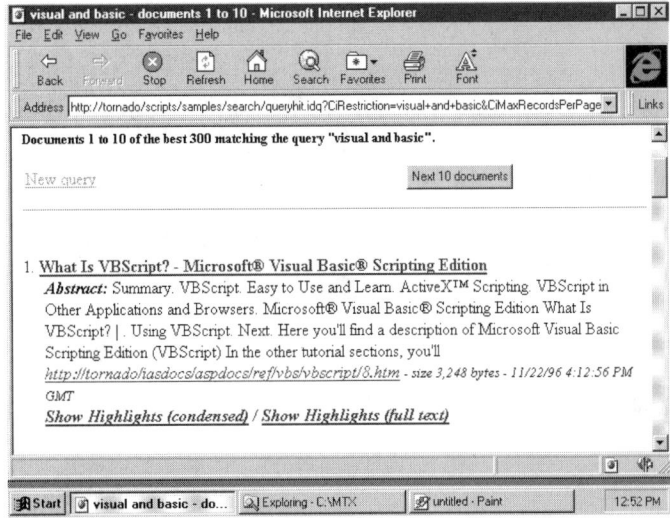

Figure 9.9 Results of search for documents containing "visual and basic".

OR means that either of the two words on either side of the operator should be found. If the user enters **visual OR basic**, the search will find all the pages with the word *visual* or the word *basic*. See Figure 9.10 for an example of this query.

186   Chapter 9

Figure 9.10 Results of search for documents containing "visual or basic".

Using the NOT operator, the user is specifying the first word and excluding the second word. In the example, if the user enters **visual NOT basic** the search engine will find all occurrences of *visual* and not the word *basic*. See Figure 9.11 for an example of this query.

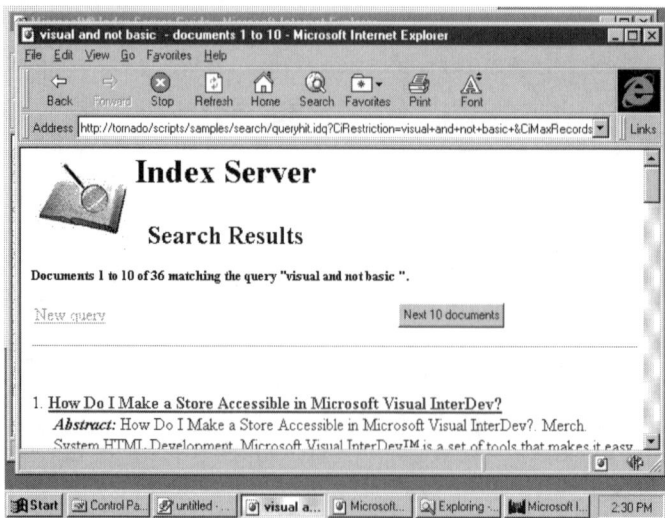

Figure 9.11 Results of search for documents containing "visual and not basic."

Active Search—Index Server

NOTE

Multiple consecutive words are treated as a phrase; they must appear in the same order within a matching document.

Queries are case-insensitive, so the customer can type the query in uppercase or lowercase.

To search for a word or phrase containing quotation marks, enclose the entire phrase in quotation marks and then double the quotation marks around the word or words you want to surround with quotes. For example, "World Wide Web" or ""Web"" searches for World Wide Web or "Web."

PROXIMITY OPERATORS

Proximity operators let you specify terms with a number of words. For example, in "visual and basic" the system returns all documents that contain *visual* and *basic*. But what if the user wants to see documents that have *visual basic*, as in the programming language? See Figure 9.12 for an example of this query.

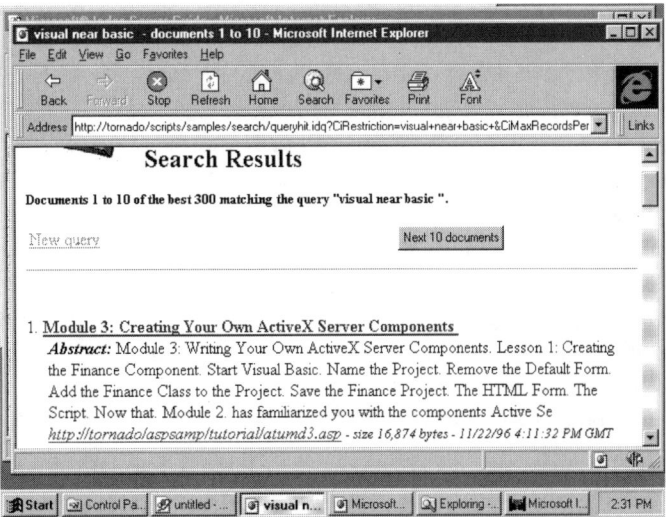

Figure 9.12 Results of search for documents containing "visual near basic".

NOTE

A customer cannot specify how far apart the two terms can be.

The results of this query have a ranked value. The closer together the two words are in the document, the higher the ranking. If the words are more than 50 words apart, the ranking is 0.

Words in the exception list are treated as placeholders in phrase and proximity queries. For example, if a customer searched for "Word for Windows," the results could be "Word for Windows" and "Word and Windows," because *for* is a noise word and appears in the exception list.

Punctuation marks such as a period (.), colon (:), semicolon (;), and comma (,) are ignored during a search.

To use specially treated characters such as &, |, ^, #, @, $, (, and) in a query, you should enclose your query in quotation marks (").

WILDCARD OPERATORS

The wildcard operator (*) is used for word stemming.

In *word stemming*, the engine strips query words of their common suffixes that indicate plurality, verb tense, and the like. For example, word stemming on the word *run* would look for *running, runner, runs*, and so on. If a customer enters **vis***, the system matches *visual, visually, vision, visit, visiting*, and so on. It is matching words with the same first three letters. Using two wildcard characters (**) gives a result of words based on the same stem word and not just the letters. So in the case of *vis*, if the customer entered **vis****, it would result in *visually, visual, visualizing*, and so on.

Use double quotes (") to indicate that a Boolean or NEAR operator keyword should be ignored in the query. For example, "Abbott and Costello" will match pages that contain the phrase and not pages that match the Boolean expression. In addition to being an operator, the word *and* is a noise word in English.

The NOT operator can be used only after an AND operator in content queries; it can be used only to exclude pages that match a previous content restriction. For property value queries, the NOT operator can be used apart from the AND operator (see Figure 9.13).

Types of Queries: Free Text, Vector Space, and Property Values

Free-text queries match nouns and noun phrases. You build a normal sentence prefaced with $contents. For example, **entering $contents Tutorials on visual basic** causes the server to parse the words as *Tutorials, visual*, and *basic* and to find documents with the most matches of all three words. As you will see in Figure 9.14, the search engine will search for the exact phrase following the variable $contents.

Active Search—Index Server 189

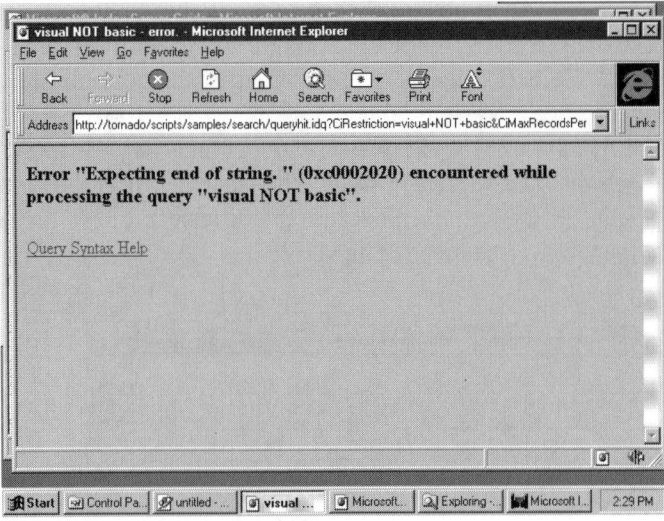

Figure 9.13 Error results in content query with "visual not basic".

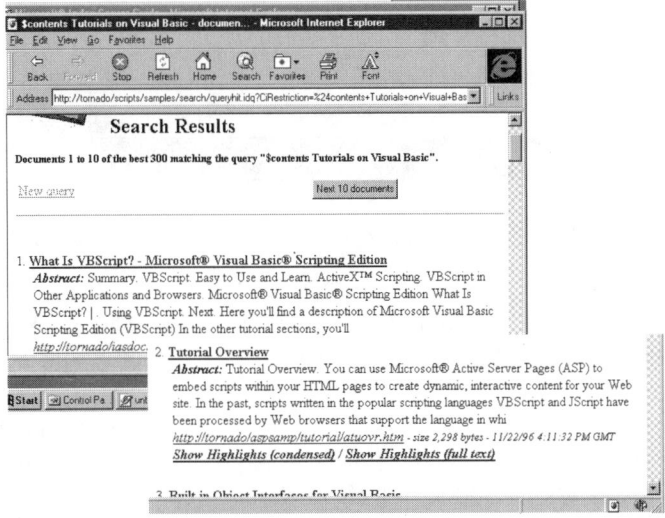

Figure 9.14 First two results for "$contents Tutorials on visual basic".

Chapter 9

Vector-space queries give a rating of how well each page matches the query. For example, using *visual basic* gives the customer a list of ranking of pages with *visual* or *basic*. The benefit of using vector space is that the developer can assist the customer in pinpointing content that has changed since a previous edition.

Typing **Visual[100], basic[75]** in the search window finds pages in which the word *Visual* has a greater weight than the word *basic*. This approach may assist in returning more-accurate documents for the customer, because the developer knows that all the new documents highlight the word *Visual* (see Figure 9.15).

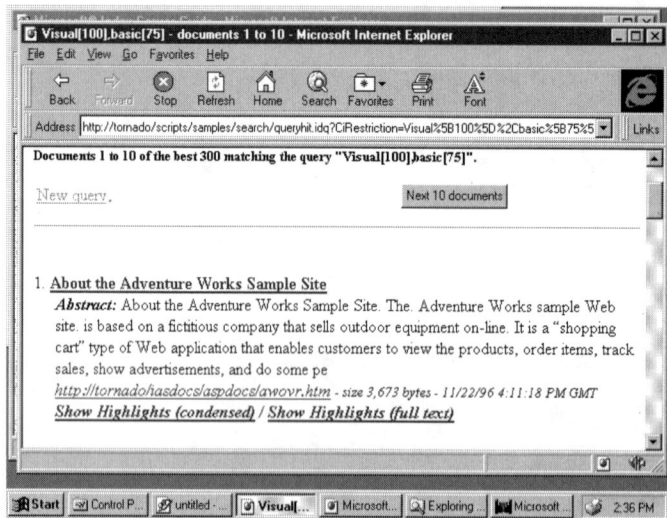

Figure 9.15 Results of search for documents containing "Visual[100] basic[75]".

Note that components in vector queries are separated by commas and that weighting uses the [weight] syntax. The engine does not return pages returned by vector queries matching every term in the query. The search engine uses vector queries to rank results based on the customer's weighted values.

Using property value queries you can find files based on file names, file sizes, and Active X properties. For example, to find all the files larger than 50K put the following query in the standard area: @size>50000. See Figure 9.16.

To find all the Quicktime files, you would enter **#filename*.mov**.

To find all documents authored by George Washington, you would enter **@DocAuthor=George Washington**.

Active Search—Index Server 191

Properties that can be queried are shown in Table 9.1.

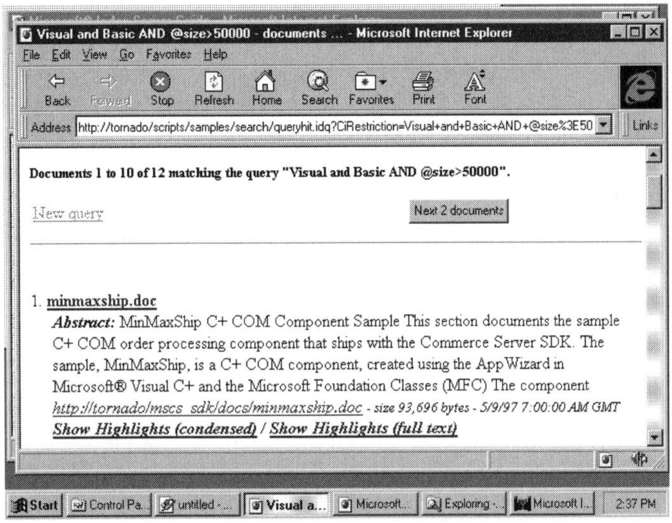

Figure 9.16 Results of a search for documents containing "Visual and Basic AND @size>50000".

Table 9.1 Sample Properties That Can Be Queried

Name	Property
Access	Last time file was accessed.
All	Searches every property for a string. Can be queried but not retrieved.
ClassId	Class ID of object—for example, WordPerfect, Word, and so on.
DocAuthor	Author of document.
DocCompany	Name of the company for which the document was written.
DocLastAuthor	Most recent user who edited document.
DocPageCount	Number of pages in document.
DocWordCount	Number of words in document.
HitCount	Number of hits (words matching query) in file.
Path	Full physical path to file, including file name.
Size	Size of file, in bytes.

Property names are preceded by either the ÒatÓ (@) or number sign (#) character. Use @ for relational queries and use # for regular expression queries. If no property name is specified, `@contents` is assumed.

Chapter 9

Table 9.2 shows some of the properties available for all files.

Table 9.2 Table of Property Names

PROPERTY NAME	DESCRIPTION
All	Matches any property.
Contents	Words and phrases in the file and textual properties.
Filename	Name of the file.
Size	File size
Write	Last time the file was modified.

Relational operators are used in relational property queries. To search for file sizes, use the following syntax (working from the previous example on a size of 50,000 bytes or 50K):

```
@size <= 50000 (less than or equal to 50K)
@size = 50000 (equal to 50K)
@size != 100 (not equal to 50K)
@size >= 100 (greater than or equal to 50K)
@size > 100 (greater than 50K)
```

With regard to property values, the developer has a number of choices (see Table 9.3).

Table 9.3 Property Values

TO SEARCH FOR	EXAMPLE	RESULTS
A specific value	@DocAuthor = Bill Barnes	Files authored by "Bill Barnes"
Values beginning with a prefix	#DocAuthor George*	Files whose author property begins with "George"
Files with any of a set of extensions	#filename *.l(exel,dlll,sysl)	Files with **.exe**, **.dll**, or **.sys** extensions
Files modified after a certain date	@write > 96/2/14 10:00:00	Files modified after February 14, 1996, at 10:00 GMT
Files modified after a relative date	@write > -1d2h	Files modified in the last 26 hours
Vectors matching a vector	@vectorprop = { 10, 15, 20 }	ActiveX documents with a vectorprop value of { 10, 15, 20 }
Vectors in which each value matches a criterion	@vectorprop >^a 15	ActiveX documents with a vectorprop value in which all values in the vector are greater than 15
Vectors in which at least one value matches a criterion	@vectorprop =^s 15	ActiveX documents with a vectorprop value in which at least one value is 15

With this understanding of the syntax, we can now build a sample query.

Sample Query

The query operation functions in much the same way that IDC and HTX (see Chapter 6) perform for SQL manipulation of an ODBC-compliant database.

The Internet Database Connector (IDC), a feature of IIS, converts a query from a Hypertext Markup Language (HTML) form into a search that works with ODBC. This feature lets you query any database that ODBC-compliant database, such as SQL Server. When a database receives a query, it returns the results, which IDC converts into an HTML page and displays on the user's screen.

The **.idc** files help IDC (which is a DLL) convert queries sent from the HTML forms. Working with **.idc** files, **.htx** files specify how the results are formatted and displayed. Similarly, with Index Server, **.idq** files help convert queries. Working with **.idq** files, advanced **.htx** files format the query results. These advanced **.htx** files include extensions to handle the unique features of Index Server query results (see Figure 9.17).

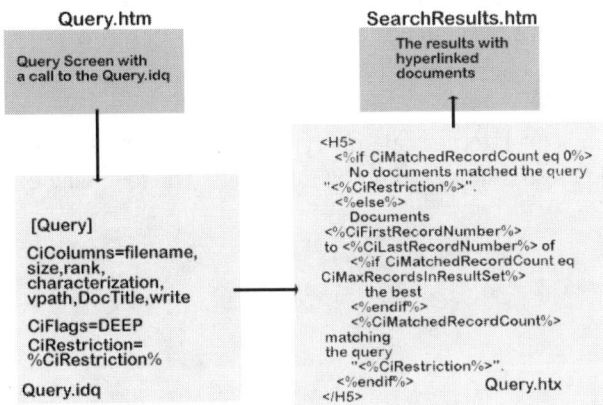

Figure 9.17 Querying: IDQ and HTX.

With a query form, a user can conveniently search for a word or phrase anywhere in a set of documents. Just fill in the blanks on the form and execute the query. In the following sample **.idq** and **.htx** files, a user wants to search for all documents containing the phrase *visual basic*.

You create a query form in standard HTML format, just as you would create any Web page. If you know how to write pages in HTML format, you can put together a simple query form.

194   Chapter 9

Here is the sample query:

```
<FORM ACTION="/scripts/bkdemo.idq?" METHOD="POST">
```

Enter the query:

```
<INPUT TYPE="TEXT" NAME="CiRestriction" SIZE="60" MAXLENGTH="100" VALUE=" ">
<INPUT TYPE="SUBMIT" VALUE="Excecute Query">
<INPUT TYPE="RESET" VALUE="Clear">
</FORM>
```

There are two lines of interest here. First, the line beginning with `<FORM ACTION. . .>` tells you where to find the **.idq** file that goes with this form. An **.idq** file helps process an Index Server query form. Therefore, every Index Server query form must specify a corresponding **.idq** file. Second, the line beginning with `<INPUT TYPE="TEXT". . .>` defines a variable called `CiRestriction`. This variable is preset to accept whatever text is typed into the query. For example, if someone types **visual basic** in this field, `CiRestriction` holds the text "visual basic".

When the **Execute Query** button is clicked, the data in the text field is sent to IIS and processed. IIS locates the specified **.idq** file and passes the query data ("visual basic" in the example) and the **.idq** file to the Index Server program.

INTERNET DATA QUERY FILES

The **.idq** file (IDQ stands for Internet data query) defines query parameters, including the scope of the search, any restrictions, and query result sets. The following example shows a basic **.idq** file:

```
[Query]
CiColumns= CiColumns=filename,vpath,DocTitle
CiFlags=DEEP
CiRestriction=%CiRestriction%
CiMaxRecordsInResultSet=100
CiMaxRecordsPerPage=10
CiScope=/
CiTemplate=/scripts/test.htx
CiSort=rank[d]
```

Let's look at each line of the sample **.idq** file. This line tells the server that a query follows:

1. `[Query]`

This shows the kind of information to return in the result:

2. `CiColumns=filename,vpath,DocTitle`

This line tells the query to search all subdirectories within the scope:

Active Search—Index Server   195

```
3. CiFlags=DEEP
```

This line indicates the query terms to search for:

```
4. CiRestriction=%CiRestriction%
```

This line sets the maximum number of results to be returned. Here, the maximum is 100.

```
5. CiMaxRecordsInResultSet=100
```

This line tells the server to send back 10 results on each page:

```
6. CiMaxRecordsPerPage=10
```

This line tells the server where to start the query. Here, it starts at the root.

```
7. CiScope=/
```

This line tells the server which template to use to return the results:

```
8. CiTemplate=/scripts/test.htx
```

This line tells how to sort the results. Here, [d] means to use a descending order.

```
9. CiSort=rank[d]
```

When the results are returned in raw format, Index Server formats the results according to the **.htx** file specified in the `CiTemplate` parameter.

HTX

The HTML extension (**.htx**) file is an HTML file that contains variables that refer to data in the query results. The following code defines a page header that displays the query restriction and the documents displayed on the page the user sees. This file is written to work with the variables indicated in this sample **.idq** file.

```
<%if CiMatchedRecordCount eq 0%>
<H4>No documents matched the query "<%CiRestrictionHTML%>".</H4>
<%else%>
<H4>Documents <%CiFirstRecordNumber%> to <%CiLastRecordNumber%> of
<%if CiMatchedRecordCount eq CiMaxRecordsInResultSet%>
the first
<%endif%>
<%CiMatchedRecordCount%> matching the query
<%CiRestrictionHTML%>".</H4>
<%endif%>
```

> **NOTE** In the case of IDC/HTX and ASP, Index Server uses the <%%> delimiters to send variables to the engine.

The text in the sample **.htx** file produces the following:

```
Documents 1 to 10 of the first 150 matching the query "visual basic".
```

Through this example, you can see that the **.htx** file is a template that formats how results are returned to the user. The file is written in HTML format with some extensions supplied by IIS and Index Server. These extensions include variable names and other codes for processing results.

Here are the basic rules, according to the Index Server documentation, for formulating queries:

- You can search for any word except those in the exception list (for English, this includes *a*, *an*, *and*, *as*, and other common words), which are ignored.
- You can use Boolean operators (AND, OR, and NOT) and the proximity operator (NEAR) to specify additional search information.
- Free-text queries can be specified without regard to query syntax.
- Vector space queries can be specified.
- ActiveX and file attribute property value queries can be issued.

Now that you can write a sample query, you need to understand the "rules of the syntax road." The basic rules for query syntax include the following:

- Any character except asterisk (*), period (.), question mark (?), and vertical bar (|) defaults to matching only itself.
- Regular expressions can be enclosed in matching quotes (") and must be enclosed in quotes if they contain a space ( ) or closing parenthesis ()).
- The characters *, ., and ? behave as they behave in Windows; they match any number of characters, match (.) or end of string, and match any one character, respectively.

You know how to build simple queries and to manipulate information via the syntax. But to obtain document content, the query process needs an index to operate on.

INDEXES

Indexes are data structures that hold the content and property information taken from documents. Storing this information using the `CiDaemon` process (a process created by the index engine) is called *indexing*. This is what the server uses to conduct queries (see Figure 9.18).

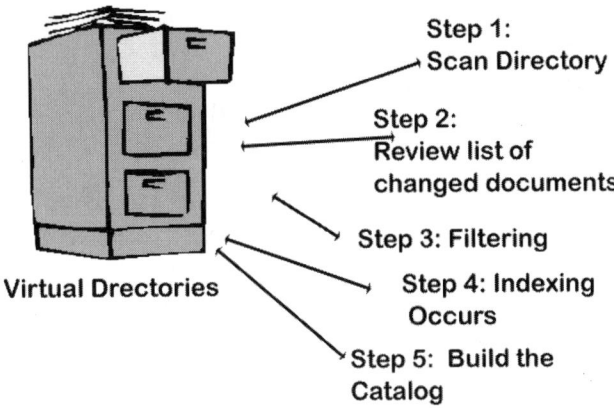

Figure 9.18 The indexing process.

Indexing is the method used for optimizing queries. In some cases, the index is bypassed by a query.

The Microsoft Index Server saves system resources by awaiting notification of file system changes. Because indexing is a resource-intensive process, it is desirable to perform this operation in the background and only when necessary. This is why IIS and Index Server are tightly integrated into the NT operating system.

Figure 9.19 shows three types of indexes: word lists, shadow indexes, and a master index. The entire process of using these indexes is transparent to the user, who sees only the results of the query.

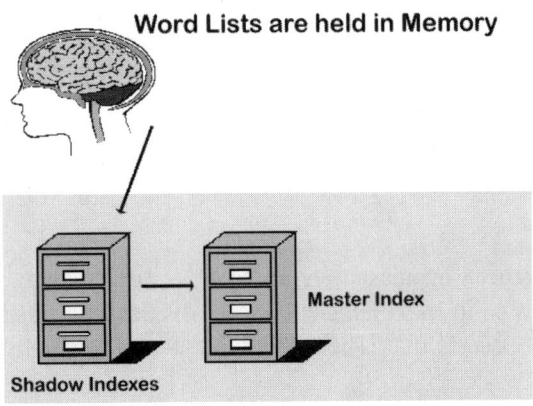

Figure 9.19 The various indexes.

Because word lists are stored in memory, they are called *nonpersistent*. The other two types of indexes are called *persistent*, because they are stored on disk and therefore continue to exist even if memory is filled or purged.

Word Lists

As soon as a document is filtered, its data is stored in a word list. Filters break documents into words (known as *keys*) and create word lists. The word lists are small indexes that are stored in memory.

The architecture of Index Server creates word lists quickly. These lists act as temporary staging areas for index data that will be used for shadow indexes. This process is called *merging* (see the following section).

To control word list behavior, the developer turns to the following registry settings:

```
HKEY_LOCAL_MACHINE
\SYSTEM
 \CurrentControlSet
  \Control
   \contentindex
```

The parameters include the following:

- `MaxWordLists`. The maximum number of word lists at any one point. If the number exceeds this, a shadow merge will be performed. The range is from 10 to 30, and the default is 20.
- `MaxWordlistSizeMaximum`. The recommended size of a single word list. If the size of a word list exceeds this value, a new one will be created. This is an internal value and must not be changed. Unit values can range from 10 to infinity, with 14 being the default. Each unit is 128K (for example, 20 = 2.5MB).
- `MinSizeMergeWordlists`. If the combined size of all word lists exceeds this number, a shadow merge will be performed. The measurement is in kilobytes, with the default being 1024K or 1MB.

PERSISTENT INDEXES

Persistent indexes are stored on disk; they survive the server being stopped and the machine being shut down. To make efficient use of disk space, persistent indexes are stored in a highly compressed format. There are two types of persistent indexes: shadow and master.

A *shadow* index is created when word lists and other shadow indexes are merged into a single index.

Active Search—Index Server

A *master* index contains the indexed data for a large number of documents. It is usually the largest persistent data structure. There should be only one master index present. This would be true if there were no shadow indexes or word lists.

A master index is created when the server merges all the shadow indexes and the current master index (if any) into a new master index. This process is called a master merge. Queries tend to be more efficient, because the source indexes are deleted and only the new master index is left.

The total number of shadow indexes and master index in a catalog cannot exceed 255.

Indexes are created by merges. Let's look at the different types of merges and why they are used.

Merges

A merge occurs when the system combines data from multiple indexes into a single index. It's like merging two lanes of traffic into one lane. This process should free system resources and clean up redundant data. The goal is to have fewer indexes in order to resolve queries. There are three types of merges: shadow, annealing, and master merges.

SHADOW MERGE

A *shadow* merge occurs when the system combines multiple word lists and shadow indexes into a single shadow index. The purpose of a shadow merge is to free memory used by word lists. In addition, it takes the nonpersistent word lists and makes this filtered data persistent by storing it to disk.

The source indexes for a shadow merge are usually word lists.

NOTE

Shadow indexes are also used as source indexes during an annealing merge. Please see the next section for a detailed discussion.

The server performs a shadow merge under one of the following conditions:

- The number of word lists exceeds the registry parameter `MaxWordLists`.
- The combined size of `WordLists` exceeds the threshold set by the registry parameter `MinSizeMergeWordLists`.
- Before starting a master merge, a shadow merge is performed to merge all existing word lists into a shadow index.
- An annealing merge operation will be performed (see the next section for more information).

If the total number of shadow indexes exceeds `MaxIndexes`, some of the shadow indexes are also used as source indexes. `MaxIndexes` is found in the registry by following this path:

```
HKEY_LOCAL_MACHINE
 \SYSTEM
  \CurrentControlSet
   \Control
    \contentindex
     \MaxIndexes
```

The `MaxIndexes` parameter can range from 10 to 150, with 50 being the default maximum number of persistent indexes in the catalog. This means that if the developer has set `MaxIndexes` to 60, the server will automatically perform a shadow merge when it "sees" that the shadow and master indexes total 61 or greater (see Figure 9.20).

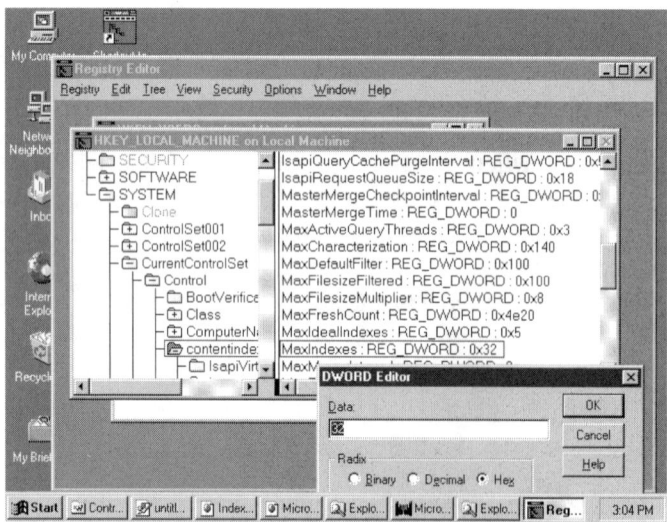

Figure 9.20 Registry setting for MaxIndexes.

ANNEALING MERGE

An *annealing* merge is a special kind of shadow merge. It occurs when the system is idle for a specific length of time and the indexes have reached a maximum value. That idle time is evaluated by two registry parameters: `MaxMergeInterval` and `MinMergeIdleTime`.

`MaxMergeInterval` is set as follows:

```
HKEY_LOCAL_MACHINE
\SYSTEM
 \CurrentControlSet
  \Control
   \contentindex
    \ MaxMergeInterval
```

`MaxMergeInterval` is the sleep time between merges and is set in minutes. The default value during installation is 10 minutes.

The second idle parameter, `MinMergeIdleTime`, is found in the following registry area:

```
HKEY_LOCAL_MACHINE
\SYSTEM
 \CurrentControlSet
  \Control
   \contentindex
    \ MinMergeIdleTime
```

`MinMergeIdleTime` is calculated by the system when it checks the average system idle time for the last merge check period. The values are calculated and registered in percentage of CPU. The default value is 90% of CPU time. In the default case, this means that the system will perform an annealing merge if the average system idle time since the last merge is greater than 90% of the CPU time.

The server not only checks time parameters but also ensures that the persistent indexes have exceeded the `MaxIdealIndexes` registry parameter before performing the annealing merge. `MaxIdealIndexes` can be found in the following registry tree:

```
HKEY_LOCAL_MACHINE
\SYSTEM
 \CurrentControlSet
  \Control
   \contentindex
    \ MaxIdealIndexes
```

Microsoft says that `MaxIdealIndexes` is the maximum number of indexes "considered acceptable in a well-tuned system." The question is, what is a well-tuned system? The number of indexes allowed by this parameter ranges from 2 to 100, with 5 being the default set by the system. Leave it at the default setting unless you are truly monitoring performance of the indexing model for your searches.

The purpose of an annealing merge is to reduce the number of shadow indexes, and that should improve query performance. Again, be aware that in the case of the annealing merge you need to monitor closely a number of registry combination settings to ensure this performance increase.

Master Merge

To perform a *master* merge, the server merges existing shadow indexes and the current master index into what Microsoft calls a "single target master index." This is like two major freeways that merge into each other to create a main freeway, whereas a shadow merge (including annealing) is like a four-lane freeway merging into three lanes. Using the freeway analogy, the number of lanes and the location of lane merges are based on registry settings.

While performing the master merge, the server, as in the previous merges, deletes redundant data. Be aware that the master merge, because of the size of its process, takes up a great many system resources. This means that you would hate to lose this merge when a system hangs or a server stops. The good news is that Microsoft knows about this concern. If the merge fails or the server shuts down or stops, the system sets a pointer. When the server is made available, the master merge will continue from where it stopped previously. In addition, you can go to the event log to review any errors during the interruption.

There are both administrative and system reasons for starting a master merge:

1. Performing regular maintenance. As with any computer system, the administrator sets certain times to clean up records and perform backups. In essence, that is what you can do by setting the registry parameter `MasterMergeTime`. The setting is found in the following registry area:

```
HKEY_LOCAL_MACHINE
\SYSTEM
 \CurrentControlSet
  \Control
   \contentindex
    \ MasterMergeTime
```

   `MasterMergeTime` is the number of minutes after midnight when the server should perform the merge. Choose a time when the company is not running system backups, virus checking, or other CPU-intensive procedures.

2. Setting a value for checking the number of changed documents since the last master merge. As the number of changes increases, memory is consumed. The registry parameter is `MaxFreshCount`:

```
HKEY_LOCAL_MACHINE
\SYSTEM
 \CurrentControlSet
  \Control
   \contentindex
    \ MaxFreshCount
```

Active Search—Index Server

`MaxFreshCount` is the maximum number of files that have been indexed but are not in the master index. The default is set at 5,000 files, with the allowable range being 1,000–40,000. When the server notes that there are more than 5,000 indexed files that are not in the master index, the system will start a master merge. Following the master merge, the parameter `FreshCount` is set to zero.

3. Checking disk space usage. Two parameters can be checked. First, the server will check to see whether the disk space remaining on the catalog drive is less than `MinDiskFreeForceMerge`. This parameter is measured by percentage of disk space used. The available values range from 5% to 25%, with 15% being the default. Then the system checks to see whether the cumulative space occupied by shadow indexes exceeds `MaxShadowFreeForceMerge`. This parameter is also measured in percentage of disk space used. The allowed values and default value are the same as those for `MinDiskFreeForceMerge` . Next, the server checks the total disk space occupied by shadow indexes. If that value exceeds `MaxShadowIndexSize`, a master merge is started. This parameter is measured in percentage of disk space. The values range from 5% to 100%. The server gives this condition higher precedence than the previous check.

4. Using the administrative Web pages. A master merge, when completed, will make queries run faster. Therefore, you may wish to activate a master merge when you believe that queries are taking longer than normal. But do not jump on this solution. There are many variables involved.

Property Cache

It was noted earlier that queries can be performed on properties as well as document content. Index Server provides a *property* cache, a separate persistent storage area that is used for indexing document properties. Properties include `Path`, `Abstract`, `Title`, `Attributes`, `Last Write time stamp`, and `File Size`.

The property cache is comparable in size to the master index. To control the amount of this memory cache, the server uses the registry parameter `PropertyStoreMappedCache`.

```
HKEY_LOCAL_MACHINE
\SYSTEM
 \CurrentControlSet
  \Control
   \contentindex
    \PropertyStoreMappedCache
```

The value is from 0 to the amount of space available, measured in 64K page units. The default is 16. The rule of thumb is to start the process with `PropertyStoreMappedCache= 16`. Increase it as the size of the Index Server increases.

WARNING If the system shuts down unexpectedly, the property cache may become corrupted. The system will run a consistency check when you restart the computer. The system should correct any property cache irregularities. If there are irreparable inconsistencies, all existing index data is thrown out and documents automatically re-index. Check the event log for any further information.

Indexing Process

The preceding section described the structure of indexes and merges. But what data should be included in the indexes? That is determined by the filtering process in Index Server. Filtering takes data from document files and puts it into content indexes. Index Server uses content filters to break documents into words (keys) and to create word lists. Filtering is a three-step process:

1. Index Server runs a filter DLL to extract text and properties.
2. Index Server parses text using a word-breaker DLL.
3. Index Server removes noise words (such as *and*, *you*, and *the*).

NOTE The CiDaemon process, working as a child process, filters the documents by obtaining the list of documents and identifying the correct filter DLL and word-breaker DLL with the specific document.

CiDaemon operates in a background mode and releases a document when another process is writing to that document. If Index Server closes before finishing, it will retry filtering on non-networked shared files.

FILTER DLLS

The server typically stores documents in a private file format. This means that WordPerfect files and Microsoft Word files are stored differently. It is like having a proprietary system for reading each document format. A filter extracts text and properties from the acceptable document types. Preinstalled filter DLLs cover the following document types: HTML, Word, Excel, PowerPoint, plain text, and binary. In the case of the binary files, there is a `Null` filter (discussed later). You can use `IFilter` ActiveX tools to build your own filters, as Acrobat has done to create the PDF `IFilter`.

The `CiDaemon` process uses this `IFilter` interface to extract the text from a document. It is recommended that you edit the registry to avoid filtering documents with no useful content. The filter extracts what are called *text chunks* (discussed later) from the document and passes them to Index Server in a format the system recognizes.

Indexing starts with content filtering. Content filters handle objects embedded within a document. For example, if an Excel spreadsheet is in a Word document, Index Server will index both the text of the object (Excel) and the document.

After filtering, the next element is the process of breaking up the words (parsing the text).

> ## Default Filter
>
> The default filter will treat the file as a sequence of characters. It filters both the system properties and the contents of the file. The server will implement this default filter during either of the following situations:
>
> - There is no association to be found in the registry.
> - The value of the registry setting `FilterFilesWithUnknownExtensions` is 1.
>
> The registry tree for this latter setting is as follows:
>
> ```
> HKEY_LOCAL_MACHINE
> \SYSTEM
>   \CurrentControlSet
>    \Control
>     \contentindex
>      \FilterFilesWithUnknownExtensions
> ```
>
> The `FilterFilesWithUnknownExtensions` registry key can be either 0 or 1. Yes, this is a Boolean setting, like true or false. The default value is 1, meaning that all file types (registered and unregistered) are to be filtered.

Let's go through a sample process using an Excel worksheet (see Figure 9.21). The class registry information is located under

```
\HKEY_LOCAL_MACHINE
  \Software
    \Classes
     \Excel.Application
```

The first step is to determine the class identification number (see Figure 9.22). This is the folder called **CLSID** (software class ID). The registry setting is found at

```
HKEY_LOCAL_MACHINE
  \Software
    \Classes
     \Excel.Application
      \CLSID
```

Chapter 9

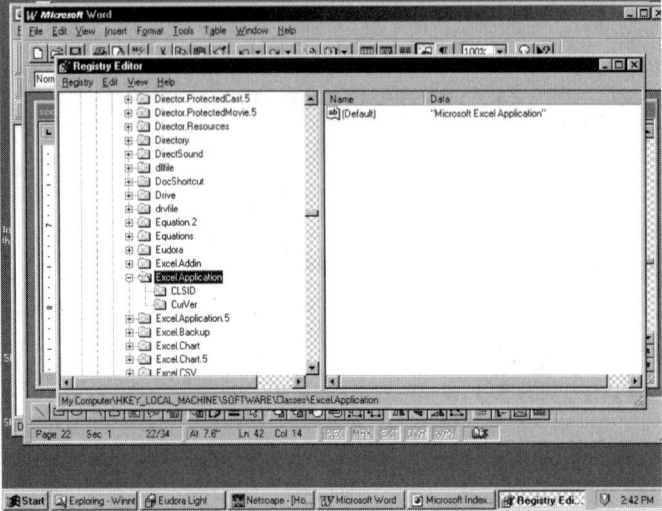

Figure 9.21 Registry setting for Excel.Application.

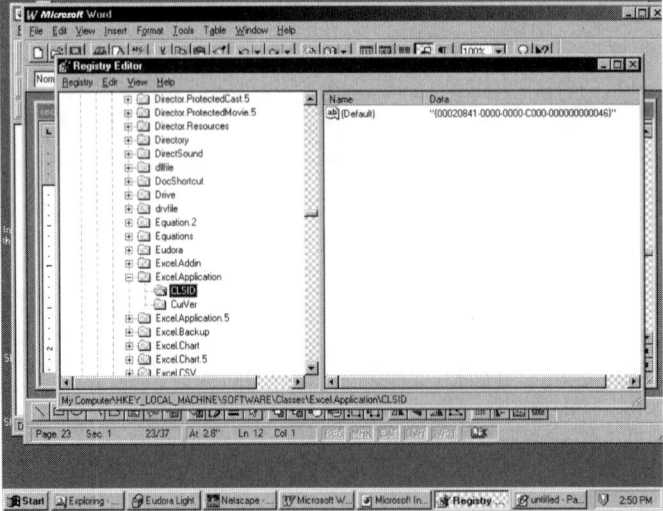

Figure 9.22 CLSID setting.

Active Search—Index Server

The number you would find in the system running this example is 00020841-0000-0000-C000-000000000046.

Now you can use this number to determine the persistent handler. Open the registry tree:

```
HKEY_LOCAL_MACHINE
  \Software
   \Classes
    \CLSID
     \00020841-0000-0000-C000-000000000046
      \PersistentHandler
```

NOTE If you do not find the persistent handler key, you have not properly registered Ifilter interfaces. Re-install Index Server or make sure that you are editing the registry on the machine running Index Server.

The `PersistentHandler` entry is 98de59a0-d175-11cd-a7bd-00006b827d94. This number is now used to identify the global unique identifier (GUID) for Excel worksheets.

To find the GUID (see Figure 9.23), look under the following tree:

```
HKEY_LOCAL_MACHINE
  \Software
   \Classes
    \CLSID
     \98de59a0-d175-11cd-a7bd-00006b827d94
      \PersistentAddinsRegistered
```

The number you would find in the system running this example is 53524bdc-3e9c-101b-abe2-00608c86.

The final step is to look up the registry entry for the `InprocServer32` key under the `Ifilter` GUID you determined in the preceding step (see Figure 9.24). Look at the following registry tree:

```
\HKEY_LOCAL_MACHINE
 \SOFTWARE
  \Classes
   \CLSID
    \ 53524bdc-3e9c-101b-abe2-00608c86
     \InprocServer32
```

Chapter 9

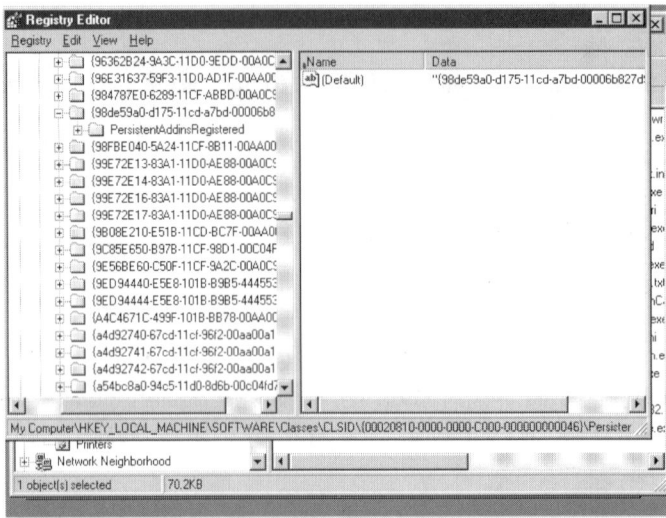

Figure 9.23 PersistentAddinsRegistered setting.

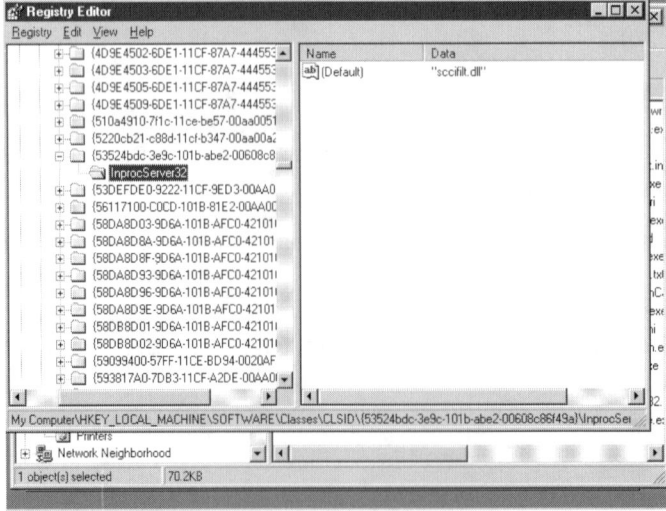

Figure 9.24 InprocServer32 setting.

The filter is **sccifilt.dll**. This is the filter DLL used when filtering Excel worksheets.

Associating File Types

What if you want to associate a file with an existing file type? For example, you know that **.htx** and **.html** files can be read the same way. How can you associate the **.htx** with an existing **.html** file type?

Let's assume that your system has the following current association of file types with **.html**:

```
\HKEY_LOCAL_MACHINE
\SOFTWARE
\Classes
   .htm
        = REG_SZ htmlfile
   .html
        = REG_SZ htmlfile
   .stm
        = REG_SZ htmlfile
```

You can add the **.htx** extension to the **.html** file type. To do so, you need to add a registry setting for the new file (**.htx** in this example) that associates a setting with the known file type (**.html**). Therefore, you would add this association:

```
\HKEY_LOCAL_MACHINE
\SOFTWARE
\Classes
   .htx
        = REG_SZ htmlfile
```

Null Filtering

What happens when binary files such as sound (**.aif**) and video (**.avi**) need to be filtered? If a file type is registered, the Server uses a `Null` filter. Here is a list of registered binaries:

.aif,.avi,.cgm,.com,.dct,.dic,.dll,.exe,.eyb,.fnt,.ghi,.gif,
.hqx,.ico,.inv,.jbf,.jpg,.m14,.mov,.movie,.mv,
.pdf,.pic,.pma,.pmc,.pml,.pmr,.psd,.sc2,
.tar,.tif,.tiff,.ttf,.wav,.wll,.wlt,.wmf,.z,.z96,.zip

The `Null` filter only retrieves file system properties (such as file name and file size) and does not filter the content.

If a file is unknown, you can add it to the registry. For example, many active sites use Shockwave, which is a director file that has been converted to a smaller, faster format for the Web. This format carries the **.DCR** extension. You would edit the registry as follows:

Chapter 9

```
\HKEY_LOCAL_MACHINES
 \Software
  \Classes
     \.dcr
        = REG_SZ BinaryFile
```

When Index Server sees the class `BinaryFile`, it needs to use the `Null` filter for its `IFilter` implementation.

WARNING If the extension for which you want to use the Null filter already has a, do not change it to BinaryFile. If you do, it could damage the Windows NT installation. Instead, you should determine the file type; determine the CLSID; determine the persistent handler; and set the IFilter persistent handler. For example, to follow this procedure for an **.exe** file you would do the following:

1. Determine the file type.

   `\HKEY_LOCAL_MACHINE\Software\Classes\exefile`

2. Determine the CLSID.

```
HKEY_LOCAL_MACHINE\Software\Classes
     exelfile
          = REG_SZ Application Extension
          CLSID
               = REG_SZ {08c524e0-89b0-11cf-88a1-00aa004b9986}
```

3. Determine the persistent handler.

```
\HKEY_LOCAL_MACHINE\Software\Classes
     CLSID
          {08c524e0-89b0-11cf-88a1-00aa004b9986}
               PersistentHandler
                    = REG_SZ {098F2470-BAE0—11CD-B579-08002B30BFEB
}
```

4. Set the IFilter persistent handler.

```
\HKEY_LOCAL_MACHINE\Software\Classes
     CLSID
          {098F2470-BAE0—11CD-B579-08002B30BFEB }
               PersistentAddinsRegistered
                    {89BCB740-6119-101A-BCB7-00DD010655AF }
                         = REG_SZ { C3278E90-BEA7-11CD-B579-
08002B30BFEB }
```

Removing Filter DLLs

To remove a filter DLL, you must remove the `IFilterPersistentAddinsRegistered` and `InprocServer32` keys. If you don't know the keys for the filter DLL you wish to remove, you can follow the same process we followed in the beginning section.

For example, to remove the installed **Htmlfilt.dll**, the following two entries must be removed:

```
\Registry\Machine\Software\Classes\CLSID
    {EEC97550-47A9-11CF-B952-00AA0051FE20}
        PersistentAddinsRegistered
            {89BCB740-6119-101A-BCB7-00DD010655AF}
                = REG_SZ {E0CA5340-4534-11CF-B952-00AA0051FE20}

\Registry\Machine\Software\Classes\CLSID
    {E0CA5340-4534-11CF-B952-00AA0051FE20}
        = REG_SZ HTML Filter
        InprocServer32
            = REG_SZ htmlfilt.dll
```

You should also be aware of a number of other items in dealing with filter DLLs. First, you should check the event log or run the administration tool for unfiltered files. The unfiltered **.idq** has the following code:

```
[Names]
Unfiltered (DBTYPE_BOOL) = 49691c90-7e17-101a-a91c-08002b2ecda9 7

# This is the query file for the unfiltered document query
#

[Query]

# The CiCatalog variable must point to where the catalog (index) files
# are stored on the system.  The developer will probably have to change this
# value.

CiCatalog=C:\

# These are the columns that are referenced in the .htx files
# when formatting output for each hit.

CiColumns=vpath, path, write

# The CiRestriction is the query — all files not filtered

CiRestriction=@unfiltered=TRUE

# Display CiMaxRecordsPerPage hits on each page of output

CiMaxRecordsPerPage=100
```

```
# CiScope is the directory (virtual or real) under which results are
# returned.  If a file matches the query but is not in a directory beneath
# CiScope, it is not returned in the result set.
# A scope of \ means all hits matching the query are returned.
CiScope=/
# This is the .htx file to use for formatting the results of the query.
CiTemplate=/scripts/srchadm/unfilt.htx
# Setting CiForceUseCi to true means that the index is assumed to be
# up to date, so queries that might otherwise force a walk of the
# directory structure (find files older than X), will instead use
# the index and run more quickly.  Of course, that means that the results
# might miss files that match the query.
CiForceUseCi=true
```

If you see a note regarding unfiltered files in the event log or you get results from the preceding IDQ, it may be caused by a corrupt file or bad Ifilter interface.

If you need to filter a directory (that means to add its properties to the index), set the following registry key:

```
HKEY_LOCAL_MACHINE
 \SYSTEM
  \CurrentControlSet
   \Control
    \contentindex
     \FilterDirectories
```

UNKNOWN EXTENSIONS

A file with an extension that does not have an association in the registry is treated as an unknown extension. The behavior of Index Server depends on the registry setting FilterFilesWithUnknownExtension. If this value is set to 0, the Null filter is used to filter those files. Otherwise, the default filter DLL is used to filter the contents.

FILTERING DIRECTORIES

By default, directories are not filtered and will not appear in query results. To filter directories, set the registry key FilterDirectories to 1. When directories are filtered, their system properties are filtered.

CHARACTERIZATION

The CiDaemon process can automatically generate summaries or characterizations (also called abstracts) for documents. If the registry key GenerateCharacterization is set to 1, the characterization will be automatically generated. The maximum number of characters in the generated characterization is controlled by the registry key MaxCharacterization.

PREINSTALLED FILTER DLLS

The list of document types for which filter DLLs are preinstalled is as follows: HTML 3.0 or lower, Microsoft Word, Microsoft Excel, Microsoft PowerPoint, plain text, and binary files.

Word Breaking

When a filter does its job, it sends a stream of characters, but the user wants words and not a stream of characters. In addition, different languages handle characters, word breaks, and punctuation in dissimilar ways. For this reason, Index Server has language-specific *word breakers*, or modules that know the syntax of a particular language. The following languages are included in Index Server: English, French, German, Spanish, Italian, Dutch, and Swedish (see Figure 9.25).

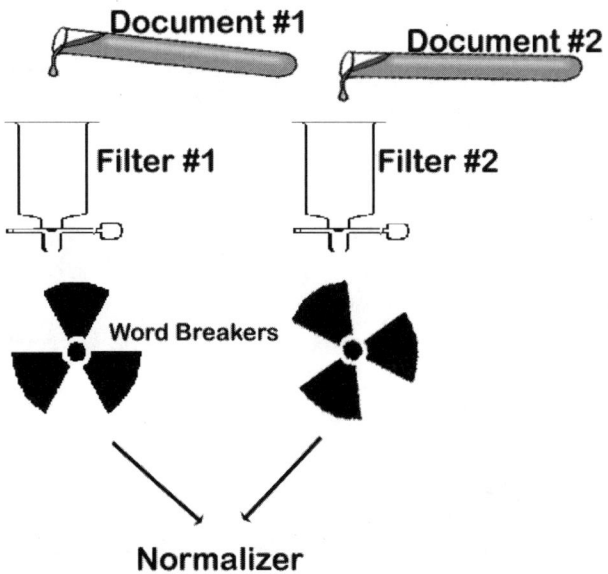

Figure 9.25 Word breaking.

Index Server is based on component technology. This means that you can create your own word breaker component, based on Microsoft specs, for a foreign language of choice.

The last step is to clean up the noise words.

Cleanup

The final step "cleans up" the words created by the word breaker. It handles capitalization, punctuation, and the removal of noise words. Noise words are utility words, such as prepositions and conjunctions, that help in both speech and writing but aren't central to a topic in a search. Examples include *the*, *of*, *and*, and *you*.

References to these words are not stored in the content index. The administrator can customize the list maintained by the system. This cleanup process can reduce index sizes by as much as 50%.

The noise word file for a particular language is specified in the registry under this key:

```
HKEY_LOCAL_MACHINE\SYSTEM
\SYSTEM
 \CurrentControlSet
  \Control
   \ContentIndex
    \Language
     \<language>
      \NoiseFile
```

For example, the noise word file for English_US is listed as this registry key:

```
HKEY_LOCAL_MACHINE\SYSTEM
\SYSTEM
 \CurrentControlSet
  \Control
   \ContentIndex
    \Language
     \English_US
      \NoiseFile
       \noise.enu
```

Following cleanup, words are put into the content index.

UNMASKING THE IFILTER

The Ifilter, as you may guess from the syntax, is a COM interface that extracts data from documents. An Ifilter scans for text and attributes (such as properties). See Figure 9.26.

Active Search—Index Server 215

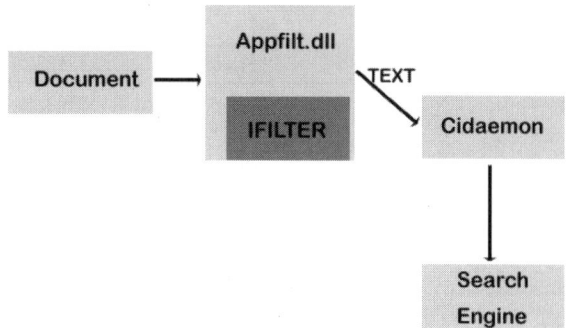

Figure 9.26 Ifilter Interface.

Appfilt.dll runs the `Ifilter::GetText` function to generate words that are cleaned up and stored into an index. Objects are broken into *chunks*. A chunk is defined as a "linear, sequential flow of text that has the same attribute and locale." The DLL uses the `Ifilter::GetChunk` function, which sets a break type, an ID, the state (flag), locale, and attributes. The function sets a pointer at the beginning of the next chunk.

Let's look at an example developed by Microsoft engineers at the 1996 Professional Developer's Conference. Take the following text:

```
The small detective exclaimed, "C'est finis!"
Confessions
This room was silent for several minutes. After thinking very hard about it the
young woman asked, "But how did you know?"
```

Chunks are broken down as shown in Table 9.4.

Table 9.4

ID	Text	Break Type	Flags	Locale	Attribute
1	The small dete	N/A	CHUNK_TEXT	ENGLISH_UK	CONTENT
2	ctive exclaimed,	CHUNK_NO_BREAK	N/A	N/A	N/A
3	"C'est finis!"	CHUNK_EOW	CHUNK_TEXT	FRENCH_BELGIAN	CONTENT
4	Confessions	CHUNK_EOC	CHUNK_TEXT	ENGLISH_UK	CHAPTER_NAMES
5	Confessions	CHUNK_EOP	CHUNK_TEXT	ENGLISH_UK	CONTENT

Chapter 9

Table 9.4 continued

ID	Text	Break Type	Flags	Locale	Attribute
6	The room was silent for several minutes.	CHUNK_EOP	CHUNK_TEXT	ENGLISH_UK	CONTENT
7	After thinking very hard about it, the young woman asked, "But how did you know?"	CHUNK_EOS	CHUNK_TEXT	ENGLISH_UK	CONTENT

From this table, note the following:

- Each chunk gets an ID number that is unique, like a primary key in a database. This ID stays with each chunk until the Ifilter is released by the server.
- The break types are based on the current chunk and the previous chunk. For example, the Chunk_no_break means that no break is placed between the chunk and the previous chunk. Figure 9.27 summarizes the process.

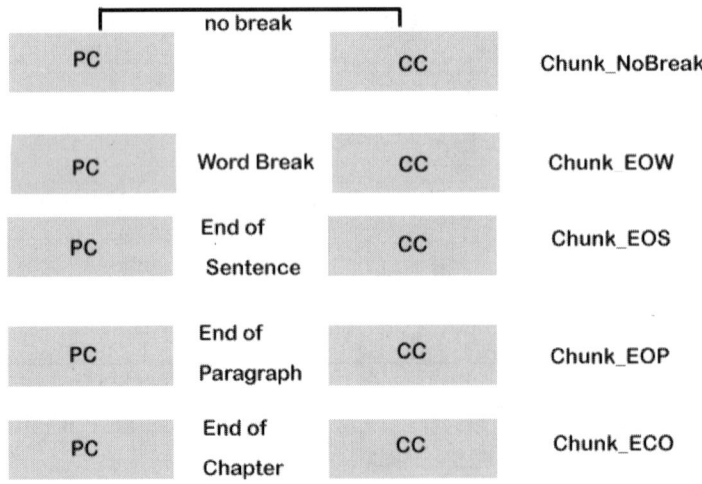

Figure 9.27 The chunking process.

- The flag indicates that the chunk is text (use Ifilter::GetText) or a value (use Ifilter::GetValue), such as a file property.
- The locale is the language.

The attribute is a property that Index Server can use for separate searches. Note that the attribute for *Confessions* has two attributes created by the `Ifilter`. Attributes include content types, external published properties (such as the `<BODY>` tag in HTML), and attributed text. Attributed text identifies a special portion of the contents.

For extensive information regarding the development of `Ifilter` interfaces and the functions, go to http://www.microsoft.com/ntserver/info/indexdeveloping.htm. There you can download the `Ifilter` software development kit (SDK).

THE CATALOG

A *catalog* is a directory of files that Index Server uses to maintain the properties and indexes for virtual roots. To create a virtual root, go to the Internet Service Manager, double-click on the WWW services in question (this opens the Properties window), and choose the **Directories** tab. Here you will find the current list of directories logged by the WWW. To add a virtual root, click the **Add** button. This brings you to the Directory Properties dialog box, as shown in Figure 9.28.

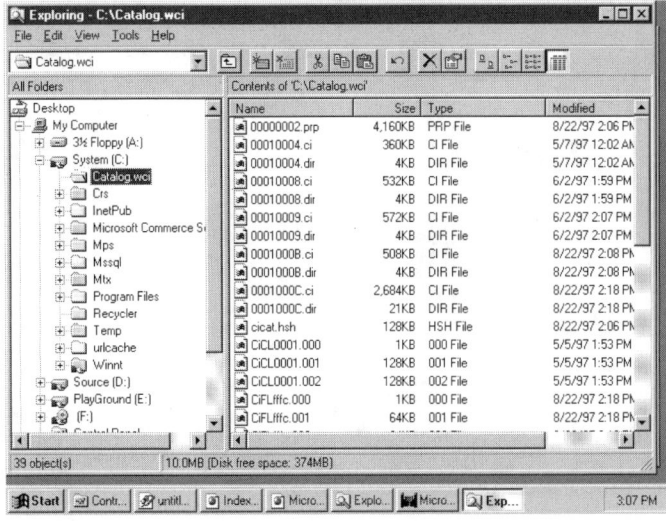

Figure 9.28 Directory Properties dialog box.

You can add both physical and virtual paths. To add the virtual root that you want Index Server to index and scan, add the physical address as well as the virtual address that you prefer. Click **OK** and you now have a virtual root.

Chapter 9

WARNING Do not delete any files under the Index Server Catalog directory.

To inventory or catalog the virtual roots is called scanning. The documents that have been determined to be filtered are added to a list of changed documents. In the background, a `CiDaemon` process is running. `CiDaemon` is an Index Server child process that Index Server uses to filter the documents (filtering is discussed in the next section).

NOTE If the CiDaemon process stops, it will be restarted automatically by the Index Server engine.

The content and property information is passed to the indexes. There it is collated, compressed, and stored in a catalog (see Figure 9.29).

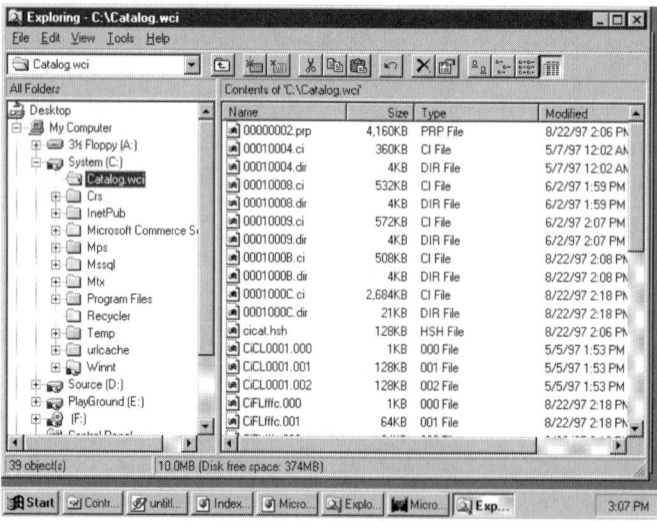

Figure 9.29 The catalog.

The catalog directory is **Catalog.wci**. In a standard installation you should find it on the **C** drive. The files found in the catalog directory have the properties shown in Table 9.5.

Table 9.5 The Access Control List for Catalog Files

Permission Level	Notes
No Access	Prevents the user from accessing that directory or files
List (RX)	The user can view file names and change to subdirectories but cannot access files
Read (RX)	Can do the same as List plus access files
Add (W)(X)	Can add files to a directory but cannot access files
Add & Read (RWX)(RX)	Can do the same as Read plus add files
Change (RWXD)(RWXD)	Can do the same as Add & Read plus change data in files and delete files
Full Control (All)(All)	Means what it says, including taking ownership of files

The catalog directory is not indexed. In the catalog directory you will find the document filter list (**CiSL0001.***) and a list of the physical scopes that are indexed (**CiSP0000.***). Because you are running the catalog in an NTFS directory, all the common access control lists (discussed later) are available to you.

What if you need to support a number of servers or remote virtual roots? What if you want to create a more extensive search system for internal company users (intranet users)? What if the performance of your system seems poor? You can create multiple catalogs.

To create additional catalogs, follow these steps:

1. Choose the desired location for the additional catalog. As with the default setup, create a directory named **Catalog.wci** in that new location.
2. Set the catalog permissions. You want to prevent unauthorized users from seeing the contents of the catalog (although the catalog is in a form that would be difficult for a novice to understand), and you want to allow access for administrators and for the System account. Remember that Index Server runs as a service, so system access is required.
3. Modify the CiCatalog parameter of the **.idq** and **.ida** files. Remember that the CiCatalog parameter is set to tell the files that the catalog location is different from the registry settings or from the CiScope setting (the starting directory for the search). This means that if you create a new catalog at **F:\IntranetX\Search\Catalog.wci**, CiCatalog is set to F:\IntranetX\ Search\.

WARNING

Before editing the registry, make sure that you have a backup. Also make sure that you are 100% confident of the syntax of all the entries you will make. If you make a mistake, your NT system may not boot or Index Server may not start up. It is best to modify parameters by using Control Panel, the system policy editor, and other such utilities before actually modifying the registry.

4. The initial query against the new catalog will start the indexing process. See the section "Managing Resources" for a discussion of virtual root indexing.

WARNING
Although multiple catalogs seem very useful, be careful. Index Server does not support queries that span multiple catalogs. You can index only a single machine, even though a single IIS Web server can host multiple Web sites. This means that you cannot query everything on your intranet or Internet site. Additionally, using multiple catalogs can impair the use of the default catalog. This means that you cannot support multiple IP-address–specific default catalog locations.

Performance will improve if you restrict your query to a subscope, because the gain in using multiple catalogs is based on reducing false hits or queries outside the scope.

Catalogs and Registry Settings

As you deal with catalogs, you need to understand how to best use NT registry settings. As you know, the registry is a database of configuration settings for the NT system. In the initial catalog setup you will find the following registry setting:

```
HKEY_LOCAL_MACHINE
  \System
  \CurrentControlSet
  \Control
  \ContentIndex
  \IsapiDefaultCatalogDirectory
```

This registry value is used by all **.idq** and **.ida** files.

To associate catalogs with specific virtual servers, follow these steps:

1. Go to the registry and add this entry:

```
HKEY_LOCAL_MACHINE
  \System
  \CurrentControlSet
  \Control
  \ContentIndex
  \IsapiDefaultCatalogDirectory
```

In the previous example, you added a catalog in **F:\IntranetX\Search** that contains virtual roots accessible only from IP address 200.200.200.100. The registry entry would be

```
HKEY_LOCAL_MACHINE
  \System
  \CurrentControlSet
```

```
\Control
\ContentIndex
\IsapiVirtualServerCatalogs\200.200.200.100= F:\IntranetX\Search\
```

2. Stop and restart Internet Information Server.
3. Issue a query against the catalog for 200.200.200.100. This will start the indexing process.
4. Update the **.idq** and **.ida** files to reflect the `CiCatalog` parameter changes.

What if you need to set up multiple catalogs for multiple virtual servers? In this example, you have 200.200.200.100 as the IP address and the following paths: **F:\IntranetX\Search**, **F:\IntranetX\Search\Scripts**, and **F:\IntranetX\Search\Reports**. Follow these steps:

1. Create a directory **F:\IntranetX\Search\Catalog.wci**. If **F:** is a Windows NT File System (NTFS) drive, set an ACL on it giving full access to `System` and `Administrators` accounts only.
2. Add an entry in the registry under the key

```
HKEY_LOCAL_MACHINE
  \System
  \CurrentControlSet
  \Control
  \ContentIndex
  \ ISAPIVirtualServerCatalogs
    \200.200.200.100= F:\IntranetX\Search
```

Note that key value does not include the directory **Catalog.wci**.

3. Copy all the query forms (**.htm**) files from the default installation to **F:\IntranetX\Search \Samples\Search**. (Create the directory hierarchy if necessary.)
4. Copy all the query script and administration files (**.idq**, **.ida**, and **.htx**) from the default installation **to F:\IntranetX\Search\Scripts\Samples\Search**. (Create the directory hierarchy if necessary.)
5. Modify the `CiCatalog` variable specification in all the **.idq** and **.ida** files in **F:\IntranetX\Search\Scripts\Samples\Search** to point to **F:\IntranetX\Search**. Make sure that it does not contain any comments. (It should look like `CiCatalog= F:\IntranetX\Search`. Again, note that **Catalog.wci** is not included in the specification.)
6. Modify the `CiTemplate` parameter in the **.idq** and **.ida** files to point to **/Scripts1/samples/search**. Note the change from **Scripts** to **Scripts1** for the virtual root.

7. Modify the **.htm** files in **F:\IntranetX\Search\Samples\Search** to point to the appropriate **.idq** and **.ida** files. You may have to change the path from **/Scripts/Samples/Search** to **/Scripts/Samples/Search**.
8. Issue a query by connecting to **http://200.200.200.100/samples/search/query.htm**. This will start indexing for the virtual server 200.200.200.100.

You can customize the query forms to restrict access to specific scopes. You may also have to modify the administration forms separately.

If you need to change the location of a catalog on a site because of company network or server changes, follow these steps:

1. Stop the Internet Server.
2. Move or delete the **Catalog.wci** directory.
3. Review all the **.idq** and **.ida** files to make sure that there are no references to nonexistent catalogs. Make the appropriate changes.
4. Update the relevant registry entries `IsapiDefaultCatalogDirectory` and `IsapiVirtualServerCatalogs`.
5. Restart Internet Server.

That is it. You now know how to build sample queries, content indexes, filtering mechanisms, and the catalog of properties.

Managing Resources

To keep Index Server running efficiently, you need to administer it by managing system resources, scripts, and virtual roots. Let's look at each of these elements.

Basic Administration

Administration of Index Server requires that you go beyond the typical understanding of NT server architecture and dealing with day-to-day performance issues. At a minimum, you will be working with the server, handling security, monitoring performance, and logging queries.

Working with the Server

The Index Server Administration tool built into Index Server (see Figure 9.30) allows you to do the following:

- Calculate the number of indexes.
- Determine the status of the indexing in progress.

- Find out the number of documents indexed.
- Handle other operational criteria, including retrieving lists of virtual roots and their indexed state.

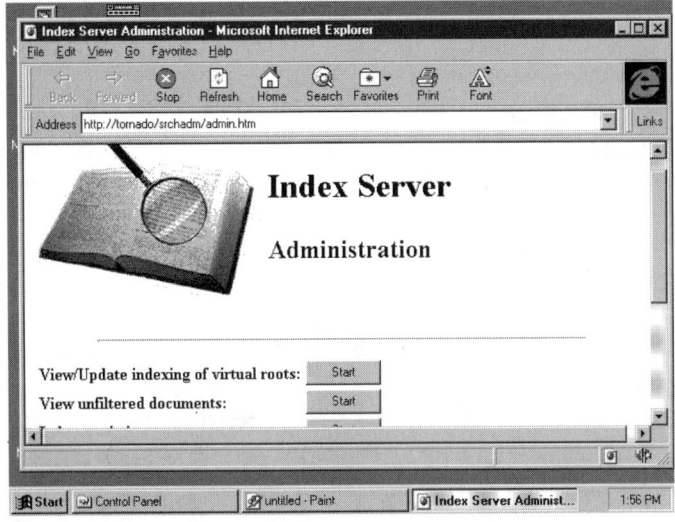

Figure 9.30 The Index Server Administration screen.

Handling Security

Index Server works in tandem with IIS and the NT operating system. It uses an access control list that allows only system administrators and system services access.

An ACL is a level of Windows NT permission that you can set on a file or folder. This setting allows some users to access the file or folder while other users cannot access it. As documents are filtered, any access controls on a document are kept in the catalog. They are checked against client permissions as a query is processed. If the client does not have access to a document, the document will not be included in any of the client's query results. In addition, there will be no indication by Index Server that the document exists. This is a useful feature if you want to index your files but need to limit access to an extranet.

Note that Index Server lets you use the access control list to limit use of an **.idq** or **.htx** file used in a query.

Monitoring Performance

You can monitor performance using Performance Monitor or by running an **.ida** script. The information available to you is nearly identical; the difference lies in how the data is retrieved. Both solutions can be used locally or over the network from a remote client. Here are two differences:

- Performance Monitor provides the automatic refreshing of data; additionally, it gives you the ability to chart the results.
- The **.ida** script gives you more choices in formatting the output via the **.htx** files; this means that the network client could be on a Macintosh, running Netscape, sitting in another country.

Please see Figure 9.31 for an example of Performance Monitor.

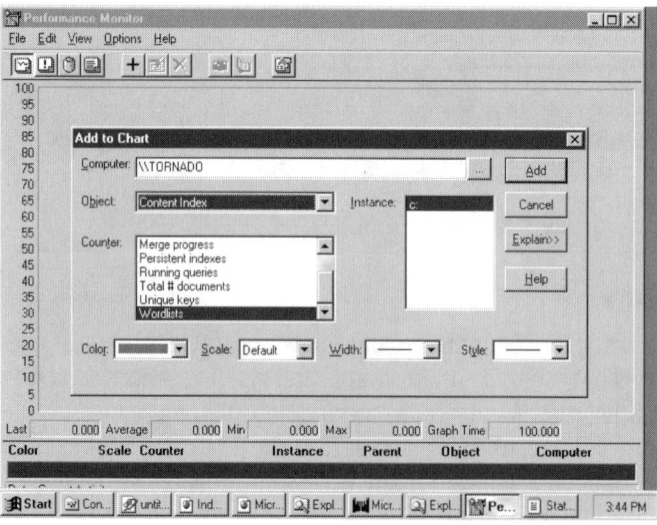

Figure 9.31 Performance Monitor.

In the script method, you create an **.ida** file with CiAdminOperation=GetState (see Figure 9.32).

Active Search—Index Server 225

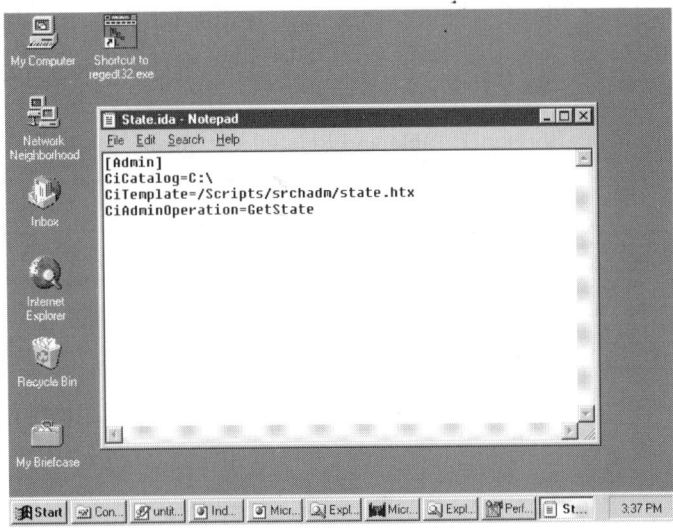

Figure 9.32 The .ida file.

The sample page is shown in Figure 9.33.

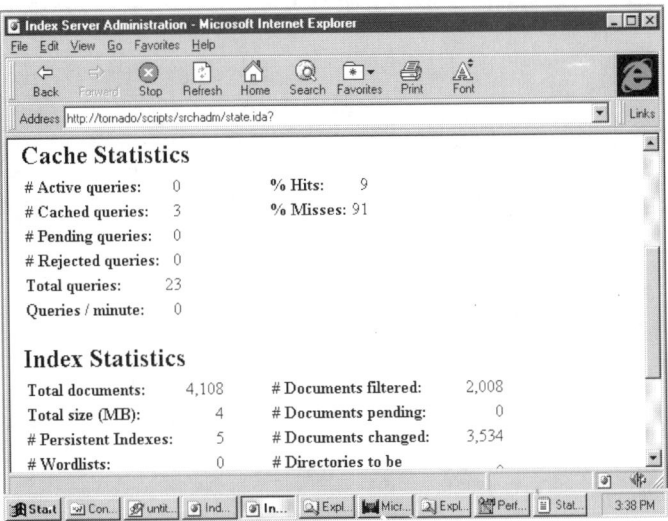

Figure 9.33 The results.

Table 9.6, created from Microsoft documents, lists the **.htx** variables available for statistics. Variables starting with `CiAdminIndex` are in the `Content` Index performance object. Variables starting with `CiAdminCache` are in the `Http Content` Index object.

Table 9.6 **Microsoft's Performance Table and Related Variables**

.HTX VARIABLE	PERFORMANCE MONITOR FIELD	DESCRIPTION
CiAdminCacheActive	Active queries	Number of queries being executed.
CiAdminCacheCount	Cache items	Number of cached queries.
CiAdminCacheHits	% Cache hits	Percentage of HTTP requests that use an existing cached query.
CiAdminCacheMisses	% Cache misses	Percentage of HTTP requests that execute a new query.
CiAdminCachePending	Current requests queued	Number of pending queries waiting for execution.
CiAdminCacheRejected	Total requests rejected	Number of queries rejected because the query engine was too busy.
CiAdminCacheTotal	Total queries	Number of queries executed since the Web server was started.
CiAdminIndexCountDeltas	n/a	Number of documents that have been indexed or deleted since the last master merge.
CiAdminIndexCountFiltered	# Documents filtered	Number of documents filtered since Index Server was started.
CiAdminIndexCountPersIndex	Persistent indexes	Count of shadow indexes and master indexes in catalog.
CiAdminIndexCountQueries	Running queries	Count of queries with open cursors against the catalog. Will differ from the number of active queries in the cache because some cached queries may be enumerated (nonindexed), and some quiescent cached queries may still hold cursors open.
CiAdminIndexCountToFilter	Files to be filtered	Number of documents that have been added or modified since the last time they were filtered.
CiAdminIndexCountTotal	Total # documents	Number of documents in the catalog.
CiAdminIndexCountUnique	Unique Keys	Number of unique words in the catalog. Updated only after a master merge.
CiAdminIndexCountWordlists	Word list	Count of word lists in catalog.
CiAdminIndexMergeProgress	Merge progress	Percent of current merge completed. Will be 100% when no merge is in progress.
CiAdminIndexSize	Index size (in megabytes)	Size in megabytes of index. Includes both in-memory word lists and on-disk shadow indexes and master indexes. Does not include property cache.

Table 9.6 continued

.HTX VARIABLE	PERFORMANCE MONITOR FIELD	DESCRIPTION
CiAdminIndexStateAnnealingMerge	n/a	True if an annealing merge is in progress.
CiAdminIndexStateMasterMerge	n/a	True if a master merge is in progress.
CiAdminIndexStateScan Required	n/a	True if the catalog needs to be rebuilt, which happens automatically when appropriate.
CiAdminIndexStateShadowMerge	n/a	True if a shadow merge is in progress.

LOGGING QUERIES

Index Server uses the Internet Information Server logging mechanism for logging queries. Please see Appendix A for detailed information about how to use the IIS logging method. A sample logging screen is shown in Figure 9.34.

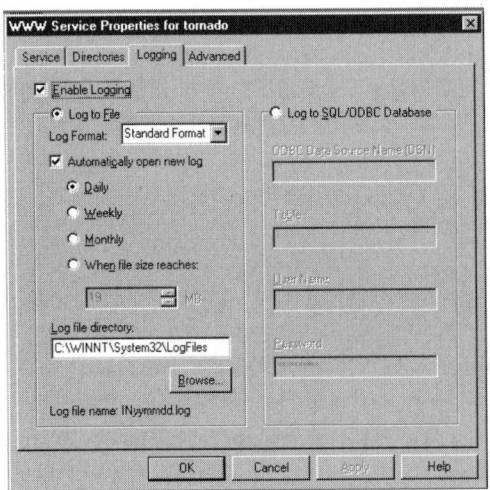

Figure 9.34 Logging window.

Managing System Resources

Be aware that if the disk space drops below 3MB, the server will pause the filtering process. If this occurs, free disk space to allow filtering to restart. In addition, indexing and merging are temporarily paused if memory load is very high. The system will retry any process that has failed in its initial attempt. If available disk space is low, shadow merges will stop and master indexes are paused. In any of these efforts, if you are looking for disk space do not touch the files in the **Catalog.wci** directory.

Managing Scripts

The system provides **.ida** files for storing administrative requests. These requests are similar to queries but are stored in **.idq** files. You can set the following parameters in an **.ida** file:

- `CiCatalog`. Specifies the location of the catalog; if it is not found, the system uses the default specified in the registry.
- `CiTemplate`. Specifies the template to use if administration operation is successful.
- `CiAdminOperation`. Defaults to `GetState`. Otherwise, you can set the value to `UpdateRoots`, `GetState`, `ForceMerge`, or `ScanRoots`.
- `CiLocale`. Defines the locale used to issue the query.

Managing Virtual Roots

You can run an **.idq** with `CiScope= VIRTUAL_ROOTS` and `CiRestriction=non-null` to retrieve a list of virtual roots. Here is a sample of an **.idq** for listing roots:

```
[Names]
# Query Metadata propset
MetaVRootUsed(DBTYPE_BOOL, 1)       = 624c9360-93d0-11cf-a787-00004c752752 2
MetaVRootAuto(DBTYPE_BOOL, 1)       = 624c9360-93d0-11cf-a787-00004c752752 3
MetaVRootManual(DBTYPE_BOOL, 1)     = 624c9360-93d0-11cf-a787-00004c752752 4
MetaPropertyGuid(DBTYPE_GUID, 36)   = 624c9360-93d0-11cf-a787-00004c752752 5
MetaPropertyDispId(DBTYPE_I4, 1)    = 624c9360-93d0-11cf-a787-00004c752752 6
MetaPropertyName(DBTYPE_WSTR, 15)   = 624c9360-93d0-11cf-a787-00004c752752 7
StorageType(DBTYPE_UI4)             = b725f130-47ef-101a-a5f1-02608c9eebac 4
[Query]
CiCatalog=f:\
CiColumns=vpath, path, metavrootused, metavrootauto, metavrootmanual

CiRestriction=#vpath *

CiMaxRecordsInResultSet=100

CiMaxRecordsPerPage=%CiMaxRecordsPerPage%

CiScope=VIRTUAL_ROOTS

# This is the .htx file to use for formatting the results of the query.
CiTemplate=/scripts/srchadm/admin.htx
```

```
#not up-to-date, so set it to false
CiForceUseCi=false
```

The detail section of the **.htx** looks like this:

```
<table>
<%begindetail%>
    <INPUT TYPE="HIDDEN" NAME="PROOT_<%vpath%>" VALUE="<%path%>">
    <tr>
        <td><%vpath%></td>
        <td><%path%></td>
<%if metavrootused ne 0%>Currently indexed<%endif%>></td>
    </tr>
<%enddetail%>
</table>
```

If `metavrootused` is true, the table displays the value of `Currently indexed`. Otherwise, it is left blank.

WARNING If you index remote virtual roots, the documents on that root may be unintentionally disclosed to unauthorized clients. This is because the username and password supplied by the Web administrator (in the Directories property sheet of Internet Service Manager) are used for all access to that remote share.

You can turn virtual roots on or off using a group of settings. You need only specify `CiAdminOperation=UpdateRoots` in the **.ida** file. You need to send one or two variables in a `GET` command. The variables are `PROOT_virtual root` or `INDEX_virtual root`.

If the home directory is **F:\\Testroot**, then `PROOT_/=f:\testroot`. If `INDEX_virtual root` is true, indexing is turned on. If there are new virtual roots, Index Server compares this set with the existing entries.

Here are the four choices available to you:

1. Enable indexing.
2. Modify the virtual or physical mapping.
3. Disable indexing.
4. Do nothing (if the new root state matches the existing index state).

If you make changes of type 1 and 2, it will cause files under the virtual root to be re-indexed. If you make change 3, it will remove files under the virtual root from the index.

Now let's look at dealing with remote systems.

Setting Up a Remote Virtual Root

You will need to log in to the remote area. Specify the domain name and the username, separated by a backslash (\):

domain\username

If you do not give the domain name, Microsoft Index Server will not index the remote virtual roots.

Make sure that the user IDs associated with the remote virtual-root setup have interactive logon permission on the computer running Microsoft Index Server. For example, let's say that the virtual root /Testing1 on Herbert_server points to \\Localcomputer\testing\testing123. If the user ID is mydomain\Barneytheuser, then mydomain\Barneytheuser must have interactive logon privilege on Herbert_server. You can do this by adding mydomain\Barneytheuser to the Guests group on Herbert_server.

DATABASE SEARCHING

Integrated Active Platforms take advantage of the ODBC-compliant databases, such as SQL Server. How do you get to the data buried in a SQL database? Here are three approaches. Items 2 and 3 are demonstrated in Chapter 20.

1. Use available ODBC search tools, including engines such as Verity and DTSearch.
2. Implement an IDC/HTX page that uses the methods shown in Chapter 6 to retrieve the data.
3. Implement a SQL Server stored procedure and trigger. The procedure and trigger create Web pages for each record in the specified tables of a database. Then you can index the pages as you would with any HTML formatted page.
4. Implement an ASP that accesses Index Server.

WHERE DO YOU GO FROM HERE?

In this chapter, you have learned the following about active searching:

- The basics of a search engine and how to build a customer-friendly query.
- How to build indexes to track old and new content on a site.
- How to properly filter what is needed in a search that will meet the customer's needs.
- The world of catalogs and how to build one that takes advantage of the index.

- Simple system tricks and techniques to keep Index Server performing in a manner acceptable to the clientele.

The following chapters will assist you in rounding out your active search experience:

- Chapter 6, "Tools for Active Platform Servers," where you can learn more about IDC/HTX.
- Chapter 20, "Case Study Site," where you will see database searching in action.
- Appendix A, "Setting Up IIS and NT," where you will learn more about IIS logging techniques.

Chapter 10

Active Money

As you probably know, the Internet was originally created as a way for the government and private researchers to share data. As a not-for-profit network, it was a success. Its growth was measured by the increasing number of hosts—eventually including for-profit companies—that were able to share useful data. But its success wasn't a matter of numbers as much as a matter of value-added information.

Now that has changed. With the development of the World Wide Web, a graphics standard was introduced, making it easier to access and use the Internet. Increasing numbers of people can communicate their ideas successfully without knowing very much about the technology. The Internet has become a global collection of thousands of different networks and hosts that communicate using TCP/IP, a standard communications protocol. The use of e-mail is burgeoning. The Internet is a huge niche market, and Internet service providers (ISPs) are targeting commercial users as much as—or more than—individual users.

For example, PSINet, a major provider whose Internet roots go back to the late 1980s, has more than 20,000 corporate customers. This amounts to more than 35% of all commercial Internet accounts. Through its efforts and those of many others, PSINet is overseeing a change in how people obtain information and products. Commerce is not just a matter of using a certain platform for purchasing goods; rather it is a sociological process that people go through to fulfill family and personal needs.

Suppose you want to buy a car for work and play. Will you go on-line to buy it? Maybe, but let's say that you will not. Why? Because a car is a significant enough purchase that most people want to see and feel what they are buying. It is an emotional as well as financial investment. But you may be willing to learn more about the car you're interested in on-line. While you are perusing detailed product and consumer information on the vehicle, a banner may flash or a button may be available for simple payment calculations. Or maybe there is a button for free auto insurance quotes. You may follow that lead (banner or button) to pursue additional information. You may fill out a form and get a price listing for the car to take to the local dealer, making you a more informed consumer. You may even receive a discount coupon via e-mail for your first year of car insurance. Has commerce transpired? Yes.

As you have learned, the role of the Active Platform is to involve the customer in the site-building and evolutionary process. With the Active Platform, developers have a suite of tools and resources that allow them to build, maintain, and grow a site that will encourage customers to return often. What if the developer wants to sell products on the site? That is where Microsoft Commerce Server comes into play.

This chapter covers the basics of electronic commerce (e-commerce): how to implement Commerce Server, create a start-up store, and program ASP tools in the commerce environment. We will also look at tips on increasing sales.

E-Commerce

To begin our discussion of an active site that promotes commerce (and some money moving through the local "store"), let's look at the basis of electronic commerce.

Most people think that e-commerce means on-line shopping, but buying a book or bottle of fine wine on-line is a small part of the e-commerce world. E-commerce also means buying and downloading software or getting additional information on products. E-commerce includes businesses buying from other businesses to meet immediate stocking requirements at a reduced cost.

Here are definitions of a few of the terms shared by developers implementing e-commerce systems.

- Certification authority (CA). A third party that individuals trust to create and sign key certificates.
- Cryptographic key. Data selected from a very large range of possible values. This data is used to change the effect of an encrypting/decrypting algorithm.
- Digital signature. A mechanism, somewhat like a fingerprint, used by the recipient of the data ton ensure that the data is from a reliable source.
- Electronic cash (e-cash). On-line money. Banks use digital cash numbers as a representation of the actual money.
- Electronic wallet. A payment scheme, such as Microsoft's Wallet, that stores the customer's credit card numbers (encrypted) on the customer's hard drive.
- Encryption. The process by which a system can change user-readable data to an unreadable form to protect the data content. Decryption is the process used to return the data to a readable format.
  Extranet. A portion of a company's internal site that is viewable to a limited number of customers, subcontractors, and product suppliers.
- Multipurpose Internet Mail Extensions (MIME). The protocol used to attach binary files to an e-mail message.
- Pretty Good Privacy (PGP). A tool for securing e-mail and computer files by using encryption.
- Private key. One of the two keys used in public key cryptographic systems. The private key is known only to the key holder.

- Public key. The "other" key used in public key cryptographic systems. The public key is widely publicized.

Is Anyone Making Money?

ActiveMedia, a company that investigates the Internet marketplace, says that more than 30% of the on-line merchants are making a profit from their sites. Whether or not that is an acceptable number, do not forget that the availability of information on-line promotes sales via other channels (such as stores and mail order catalogs). If you are not dealing with a recognized brand name, it can be a little tougher. It all depends on the company's cross-promotion efforts.

Is it Safe for Merchants and Customers?

E-commerce systems remove some potential security problems by using encryption algorithms. This approach tends to be safer for merchants than running a local storefront that is subject to weather ills and robbery.

Transactions can be encrypted using Secure Sockets Layer (SSL), a protocol that creates a secure connection to the server, protecting the information as it travels over the Internet. As noted in Chapter 7, SSL provides data encryption, server authentication, message integrity, and optional client authentication for a TCP/IP connection. SSL uses public key encryption. Many e-commerce devices support secure electronic transaction (SET) to authenticate the two parties involved in the transaction.

The customer can determine that the connection is secure using two methods:

- The Web site address starts with https:// rather than http://.
- Netscape products have an unbroken key on the lower-left corner of the browser window. Internet Explorer displays a padlock on the lower-right portion of the screen.

NOTE

Merchants must also consider the issue of collecting sales taxes. The U. S. government is debating the issue, and many states are awaiting the IRS ruling. The smart step is to treat Web purchases like mail-order sales. This means that the company collects taxes if it has a significant presence in the state where the buyer resides.

How Big Is the Potential Market?

E-commerce represents a very small percentage of total commerce. Many research groups, including Jupiter Communications and Forrester Research, have noted that about 10% to 20% of Internet users use e-commerce. The interesting point is its growth. Forrester says that e-commerce sales will amount to $8 billion by 1998, with a projection of more than $500 billion by 2001.

The average buyer is more than 30 years old and earns more than $65,000 per year. Men are the majority of buyers, but the number of women buyers is increasing.

Here are a couple of simple scenarios for the use of e-commerce. Developer 1 wants to set up a purchasing system for buying office supplies on-line. This system will reduce turnaround time for office supplies to days rather than weeks. This means that personnel will buy what they really need and not what they think they will need in a few weeks. Silicon Graphics and Microsoft have incorporated such a function in their systems. Silicon Graphics calls its system Silicon Junction; Microsoft's is MS Market. The developer needs to make sure that the system has the following functionality:

- Each individual must be authenticated by a login ID.
- Prenegotiated purchasing department catalogs must have the highest priority. The user should be presented with the best deal based on company purchasing department needs and not individual needs. The purchasing department must have the freedom to negotiate with suppliers based on items such as payment terms and return authorization.
- Company cost information must be integral to the order for proper departmental tracking.
- Order tracking must start as soon as the user presses the submit order key.

The Microsoft Active Servers can easily meet these needs using Microsoft Internet Explorer as the client software and using BackOffice servers such as Commerce Server, SQL Server, Transaction Server, and Exchange Server. The developer could create an order form that manages orders, a virtual mall that lists approved vendors and catalogs, and an internal e-mail system for delivering orders and products.

Suppose developer 2 wants to use the Internet for direct marketing. The developer has a request from marketing to include the following functionality:

- Customers can click on banner ads and not leave the site.
- Preferences are kept for the customer to choose from.
- The customer can choose the form of payment.
- The customer can personalize chosen items.

The developer can implement this solution using Internet Explorer as the client solution and BackOffice (SQL Server, Transaction Server, and Commerce Server, especially the Wallet application). In addition, the developer can include the client-side Buy Now software in Commerce Server.

Can any size business be successful on the Web? A large company (more than 1,000 employees) can put large amounts of money into e-commerce sites, but what about a small business? With the proper tools, the developer of a small site can include much of the functionality found on the larger sites. What you need to consider is which features to include. A local pizza shop may not benefit from trying to incorporate a full Active Server solution for selling $5 pizzas; it would do better to get its name out via on-line cooperative advertising or merchandise. However, an Amish country store would find a huge demand in the niche of the Internet marketplace. Not everyone can travel to Pennsylvania Dutch country to buy these quality-made items.

Troubles with E-commerce

Commerce on the Web is not without pitfalls. First, customers are worried about credit card theft, maintaining the privacy of their personal information, and unreliable network performance. What if the system goes down or the network connection is broken during a transaction? Does the credit card get entered and the account charged but no product delivered? That does not happen when the customer is in a real store! To minimize uncertainty, the answer is to educate customers about security precautions, including the use of firewalls and proxies, and to incorporate sound business rules into your e-commerce activity.

Another drawback is that screens can be hard to understand, and there may not be a real directory of products. The problem arises when you do not add all the product pricing information to a site's search tools because you are concerned about competitors obtaining price information without buying. The solution is to better design the site and incorporate extranets for valued customers.

Customers also find that there is no easy way to pay for purchases. SET hopes to be the standard that will help reduce confusion. The credit card companies support the SET standard, and their influence may prove beneficial.

Finally. businesses do not always integrate commerce applications properly. Businesses may not be sharing their concerns as openly as consumers are, but their concerns are real. For example, companies may not be able to properly share data between the ordering system and the billing system, something that can be disastrous in customer billing. A solution may be to quit implementing technology as it shows up (for example, Java and ASP), instead planning an integrated database transaction solution.

SECURE TRANSACTIONS

Before going much further, you need to understand how to provide your customer with secure transactions. You may have seen https:// on a URL instead of the normal http://. The https identifies a secure server environment.

You can obtain such security through a *digital certificate*. These certificates are based on the Pretty Good Privacy security model.

PGP is an application that lets you digitally sign documents to make them tamper-proof. PGP uses *keys*, which come in three flavors.

To begin the process, two people agree to a single *private* key to be used to lock and unlock a message. A *public* key is used in advanced cryptographic systems such as PGP. These systems mathematically generate public and private keys at the same time; the two keys are related by the private key, which decrypts a message that has been encrypted with the related public key. The third flavor is the *session* key, which is used in complex cryptographic systems to add an extra element of secrecy. PGP uses a session key to encrypt the message, and the message and the session are bundled together. The public key is used to encrypt the session key. Finally, the package is sent to the recipient.

A digital certificate begins with information such as this:

```
MIIBOjCB5QIBADCBgDELMAkGA1UEBhMCVVMxEzARBgNVBAgTCllvdXIgU3RhdGUx
FjAUBgNVBAcTDVlvdXIgTG9jYWxpdHkxFTATBgNVBAoTDFlvdXIgQ29tcGFueTES
MBAGA1UECxMJWW91ciBVbml0MRkwFwYDVQQDFBBZb3VyIE5ldCBBZGRyZXNzMFsw
DQYJKoZIhvcNAQEBBQADSgAwRwJAXpEjiQ65wxVlKuhlCA5hx5WUMhsD21/Sap+G
EJFPyy1A35OmzNCYn2MiUoGExkdQPsNF3xZ8A4wWNcVTMyJLiQIDAQABoAAwDQYJ
KoZIhvcNAQEEBQADQQBQVyUMkM8XNHDW6j5koSgXH3crG+uJSnQW9Y/43hnUu43R
U9EZVm0O+T7D34nqyryS/0tg8uzTIgG9UdeE46zg
```

This random set of alphanumeric characters and symbols is the system's *fingerprint*, which is used to send your information over a secured layer, SSL. You can read more about SSL in Chapter 7.

Commerce Server operates within the integrated NT/IIS environment. This means that you have the standard NTFS security as well as HTTP basic authentication. In addition, Commerce Server supports personal or digital certificates using SSL.

There are a number of security issues that you must consider. As you install Commerce Server, SSL must be supported on the client-side application. In this case, it is a browser that must support SSL. Using NTFS, you can protect various directories rather than the whole site. For example, you could create a set of Web and FTP pages that allow for limited access. You could add a virtual directory called *extranet1*, giving it a second virtual name, *intranet5*. The *extranet1* directory is secured; *intranet5* is not. By telling certain customers about *extranet1*, you give them access to limited pieces of insider information that they need. Field managers are given the *intranet5* directory for unlimited access.

In addition to SSL, Commerce Server supports the SET payment protocol. SET was created jointly by Visa and Mastercard. Since then, American Express and the Discover card have also embraced this protocol. SET is intended to use encryption along with digital certificates to ensure a safe transaction.

SSL is the bridge from one safe haven to the other. SET is a protocol (like a gate to the bridge) for payment methods.

SET is based on the use of a public and private key pair. You generate these pairs and obtain authorization from a third-party certificate authority. If there is any compromise in the public-private key pair, SET revokes and reissues safe certificates.

How is a cardholder protected? The system provides a one-way protected card number (like a one-way mirror) with an expiration date. The system software also generates a secret value to ensure privacy. The only way that the cardholder can prove that this is his or her "card" is by having the account information. The current account applications are similar to those used in banks. Personal and business information is required for proper account setup.

Many companies are starting to incorporate digital certificates, but it will be some time before the average consumer will find the process user-friendly. For now, messages from the client to the server are fully encrypted, whereas return messages regarding order fulfillment or delivery date are not encrypted.

A transaction is a two-step process. In the first step, the client issues a certificate. The server receives it, checks its authorization, and returns the server's certificate. In this response the server sends the merchant public key, the payment processor's key, and a unique identity for this transaction. If the client application wants to continue the process, it sends the order with the unique identity. A dual signature is set up without either party seeing the other party's data. This system is much like that for accessing a security box in a bank, in which two signatures and two keys are required to open the box.

In SSL, the procedure is similar. The server has a key and the client has a key. They exchange keys to decipher each other's data. Two communication layers—HTTP and SSL—operate in HTTPS. The client makes a normal request via HTTP. The server grabs the information and sends the response encrypted via the SSL. Once the keys are exchanged and the communication channel is opened via SSL, SSL encrypts and decrypts the data flowing between client and server. The only difference is that on the client side the system is using the server-sent key to handle the SSL operations.

In a sense, the server is offering a proxy key to the client to use until finished.

Getting the Keys

The first step is to generate the key request. The developer sends the request, receives the key, installs it, and establishes the secure connection.

GENERATING THE REQUEST

To generate the request, go to IIS and the Key Manager dialog box, where you will choose the appropriate server (see Figure 10.1).

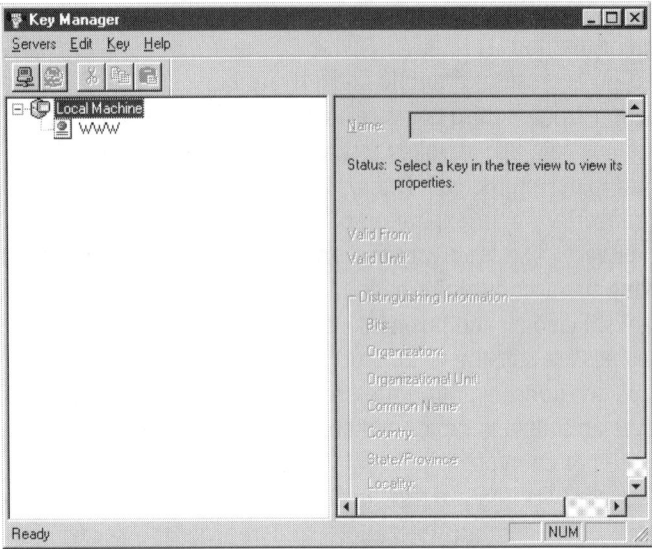

Figure 10.1 Key Manager dialog box.

Key Manager will make a connection to the server. If it is available, it will show up in the window. If you cannot find the server, try its IP address. Once the server is found, create the key by highlighting the server (use a right-mouse button click) and choosing **Create Key Request**. The dialog box lets you choose various parameters, as shown in Figure 10.2.

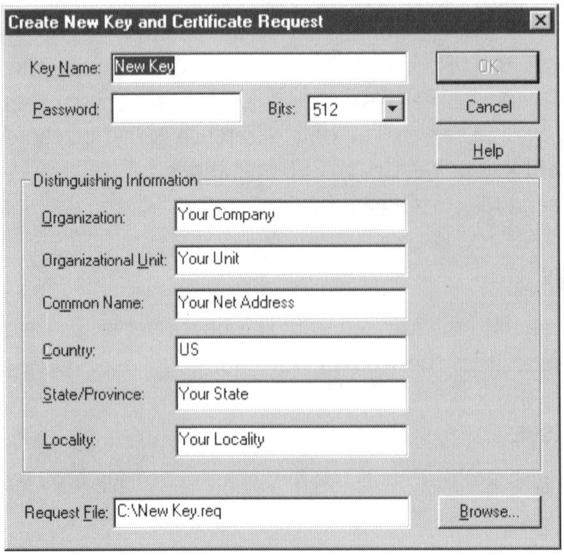

Figure 10.2 Key parameters.

Verisign, the third-party authority used by many developers, recommends that you fully spell out cities and states. In addition, you should use no apostrophes, because the key leaves the server as one string of characters that Verisign will parse appropriately.

Next, set and confirm a password. You will see the key file in the right-hand pane of the Key Manager window. This is what is sent to the certificate authority for signing, which produces the counterpart key for your site.

Send the Request

In the following examples, we will be using Verisign. There are a number of other vendors.

Verisign recommends that developers fax and mail a letter on the company letterhead to ensure proper authentication, as an individual would do to request a bank security box or obtain an ATM card. The letter should state who is authorized to operate the software and the name of the server and server software you are using (Internet Information Server in this case). For more information, read the legal agreement at http://www.verisign.com/microsoft/legal.html.

The signed certificate is e-mailed to you. Note that certificates normally last for one year. Just as a company renews its domain name, so must it renew its certificate.

INSTALLING THE CERTIFICATE

Save the certificate as a text file. The following lines must appear at the beginning and end of the certificate:

```
----------BEGIN CERTIFICATE----------
MIIBOzCB5gIBADCBgDELMAkGA1UEBhMCVVMxEzARBgNVBAgTCllvdXIgU3RhdGUx
FjAUBgNVBAcTDVlvdXIgTG9jYWxpdHkxFTATBgNVBAoTDFlvdXIgQ29tcGFueTES
MBAGA1UECxMJWW91ciBVbml0MRkwFwYDVQQDFBBZb3VyIE5ldCBBZGRyZXNzMFww
DQYJKoZIhvcNAQEBBQADSwAwSAJBAME+8oavGx4qAYMh9uBHr3rEE/+gxHSCmgyE
6f0bAaJyNoZnqjzboEWMi3O5cMGGZYBOnSp1PmwX2EbhIslbMI0CAwEAAaAAMA0G
CSqGSIb3DQEBBAUAA0EALLPYzJ9/P51utYkmx8Allr1ZWJi+rfXUw5t1GbiL0wu7
B05BGNe1psWzxlnwxozfuKY8TI6MrSyAZ0gHcxcwFg==
----------END CERTIFICATE----------
```

This information assists Key Manager in registering the certificate. Key Manager opens with a new "unvalidated" certificate marked with a red line through it. Right-click on the key request and select **Install Certificate**. Select the file and provide Key Manager with the password. Apply the certificate systemwide (choose the **Default** setting) or choose the **IP Address** option in the Server Connection window. You have successfully applied the certificate to the site.

To remove the certificate, right-click on the certificate entry and select **Delete**.

To apply the certificate to specific directories, go to IIS Manager. Double-click the **WWW** service and choose the **Directories** tab. You can now apply the SSL flag on a directory-by-directory basis.

ESTABLISHING A SECURE CONNECTION

Early in this section, you set up the virtual directories **extranet1** and **intranet5**. You should now have the **intranet5** user access the site using an HTTPS entry in the address area of the browser. This will start the HTTP and SSL process.

Microsoft Wallet

Microsoft Wallet has two ActiveX controls called Address Selector and Payment Selector. To install the appropriate Active X controls, go to the **Microsoft Commerce Server\Server\Images\Controls** folder. There you will find **Mswallet.cab** (for Intel machines) or **Mswltalp.cab** (for DEC machines).

The Netscape plug-ins are located in the same folder (**Microsoft Commerce Server\Server\Images\Controls**), where you will find **Actpaynp.exe**. In addition, you will need the **Empty.adr** and **Empty.wlt** files from the **Microsoft Commerce Server/Server/Images/Navclient** folder.

The Address Selector control is an interface for address entry and storage for billing records. The Payment Selector gives the user an interface for payment entry, secure storage, and on-line payment methods. You can look at this setup just as if you were sharing a personal wallet or purse. In that wallet, you would have a place for credit cards, addresses, and identification. Remember, though, that you are sharing the wallet.

This means that customers can use the wallet (the Payment Selector control) to enter payment method types (American Express, Visa, Mastercard, or Discover card) and the card number that they want to use. In addition, the wallet must hold proper identification. This secure information is stored on the local computer. The payment information is password-protected, because this information can be edited off-line. Additionally, you can use the software development kit to edit the Wallet to add other types of credit cards and payment methods. You locate the controls on the Web page as selections that allow customers to add, edit, and delete information. In addition, customers can choose address and payment information.

You use the Address Selector to allow the customer to ship and bill purchases to alternative locations. For example, an individual may want the bill sent to the office but the product shipped to his or her home address. The customer can store these multiple addresses in the Wallet and select them as needed, perhaps labeling the office as Jim's Office and the home as Jim's Abode.

Wallet controls (Address and Payment) can be used in a combo box. This means that the customer sees a text box and a drop-down list. An example of the two control inputs is shown in the Commerce Server product information (Figure 10.3) and the sample Volcano Coffee Shop (Figure 10.4).

Active Money 243

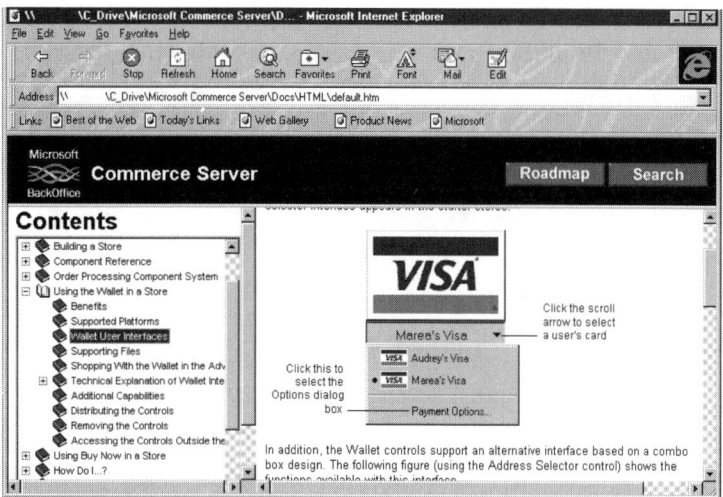

Figure 10.3 Drop-down example in Commerce Roadmap.

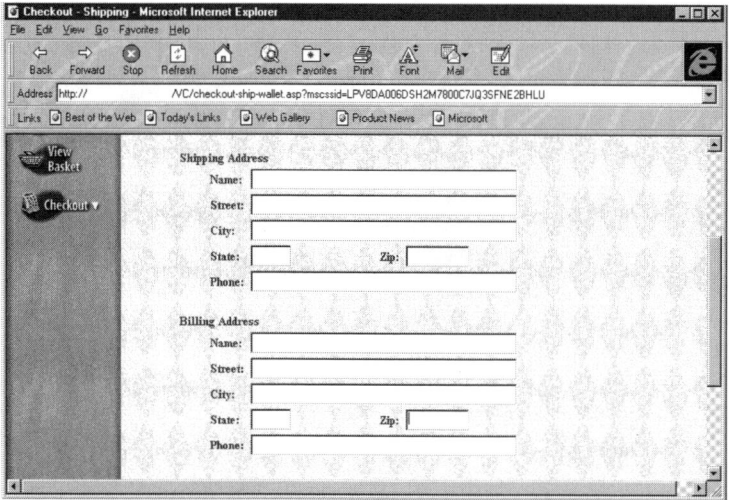

Figure 10.4 Shipping information in text boxes.

This means that you can capture both the payment and the address information at the same time. You set this option by setting the UseComboBox parameter to True. The following example is from the Microsoft Buy Now example shipped with MCS. In this example, you will see the listing for **Payment.asp** found in folder **Microsoft Commerce Server\Stores\Aw\Shop\BuyNow**. This example is for Internet Explorer:

```
<OBJECT ID=paySelector
    CLASSID="<% =
MSWltIEPaySelectorClassid() %>"
    CODEBASE="<% = MSWltIECodebase()
%>
    HEIGHT=30
    WIDTH=192>
    <PARAM
NAME="AcceptedTypes" VALUE="<% = strMSWltAcceptedTypes
%>">
    <PARAM Name="UseComboBox" Value="True">
>
```

This example is for Netscape Navigator:

```
<EMBED
    NAME="paySelector"

SRC="<% = "http://" &
Request.ServerVariables("SERVER_NAME")
%>/MSCS_Images/navclient/empty.wlt"
    PLUGINSPAGE="<% =
MSWltNavDwnldURL("plginst.htm") %>"
    VERSION="<% =
strMSWltDwnldVer %>"
    HEIGHT="<% = strBuyNowControlHeight
%>"
    WIDTH="<% = strBuyNowControlWidth %>"

ACCEPTEDTYPES="<% = strMSWltAcceptedTypes %>"
    TOTAL="<%
= MSCSDataFunctions.Money(CLng(mscsOrderForm.[_total_total])) %>"

USECOMBOBOX="True"
>
```

If you create the store using the MCS Store Builder wizard, the Wallet control scripting is included. This means that any store built using the wizard will properly load address and payment information into a database. The good news is that consumers need not add name, telephone number, and address information every time they shop. The Wallet stores that data.

MCS comes with Active Server Pages to help integrate the implementation of Commerce Server and the developer's active site. For example, the Wallet contains ASP files for storing pages during the shopping process.

Money in Action

Let's go shopping with the wallet. Go to http://host_name/aw/default.asp (host_name is the proper name of the computer where you are running Commerce Server). Click the **New** button. Register in the store. If the Wallet is not loaded on the client side, an Authenticode Security box will appear. The customer will download the files that were noted in the preceding section for example, **Mswallet.cab**).

THE ADDRESS SELECTOR CONTROL IN ACTION

Next, the registration page displays the Address Selector control. If there are no stored values, click **Add Address** and add an address record. Registration is required. If you do not add a new address, the system will generate an error and will not allow you to proceed.

Registration requires that you supply a name, e-mail address, phone number, street address, city, state, ZIP code, and country. When completed, this page sends values to the shopper table.

Commerce Server provides a new shopper ID. After you add a first name in the **Add A New Address** box, the Address Selector control puts the name in the **Display Name** box. Complete all the boxes and click **OK**. The box closes and sends you to the registration page. Click the **Start The Adventure** button.

This process causes a control to launch the Security Information box. Click **Yes** to "release" the shipping address information to the Adventure Works Store. The Address Selector control shows up again during the purchasing process, so that you can select a shipping address. The control will show the address information that was entered during registration. You can add, edit, or delete the address information.

Add items to the shopping cart. Click **Check Out** to purchase the items selected. The Address Selector control handles the shipping information. Use the control to change address information as needed. The Security Information box should appear as data is posted.

THE PAYMENT SELECTOR CONTROL IN ACTION

The next page uses the Payment Selector control to display the credit card information. Click **Add Card** and select a card type. As noted before, the system accepts Visa, Mastercard, American Express, and Discover card. Click **Agree** to continue.

This process starts the Add A New Credit Card wizard. Here, you enter card information and the billing address, and you create a password to safeguard the payment information. Click **Next** to go to the Credit Card Information.

In the Credit Card Information dialog box, enter the card username, expiration date, card number, and the display name. Note that Commerce Server uses display names in numerous dialog boxes to provide easy-to-remember names. Enter your first name. The **Display Name** field is updated with the name and card type. Click **Next**. The control checks the credit card number for proper format. This prevents you from proceeding if you entered a wrong number.

The Credit Card Billing Address dialog box should appear. Previous addresses are listed in a list box; select an existing address or click **New Address** to add a new billing address. To protect against unauthorized use, the Credit Card Password dialog box prompts you to enter the password correctly and then re-enter it to confirm the process.

Click **Finish** to close the wizard and proceed to the purchase. The wizard is needed again only if you use a different credit card. The good news is that the credit card information is stored on your computer. To access it, choose **Purchase Now** and type the password.

Clicking **Purchase Now** lets you view the amount that you are authorizing the store owner to charge against the card. Type the password and click **OK**. This action completes the purchase and submits the order to the store.

Data is sent to the shopper table database. The store credit card payment processing component receives the payment information.

THE ROLE OF ASP

ASP files invoke the Wallet control. The ASP files are **I_selector.asp**, **I_mswallet.asp**, **Payment.asp**, and **Shipping.asp**. To create the ASP files, you should run the Store Builder wizard. The system comes with blueprint files to allow the wizard to convert the templates **I_selector.ast**, **I_mswallet.ast**, **Payment.ast**, and **Shipping.ast**, respectively.

The blueprints are in the **Store Builder Blueprints** folder of the **Computer_name/Store Builder Wizard** path. The ASP files generated in this process will be found in the **Shop** folder of the store.

Note that the starter stores have files beyond those mentioned here. For further discussion of these additional files, refer to the Microsoft literature following installation

Now you have many methods to ensure customer security. Let's look at operating the store.

HOW COMMERCE SERVER WORKS

Commerce Server runs integrally with Active Server (IIS 3.0) and an ODBC-compliant database. The database can be anywhere on the network (see Figure 10.5).

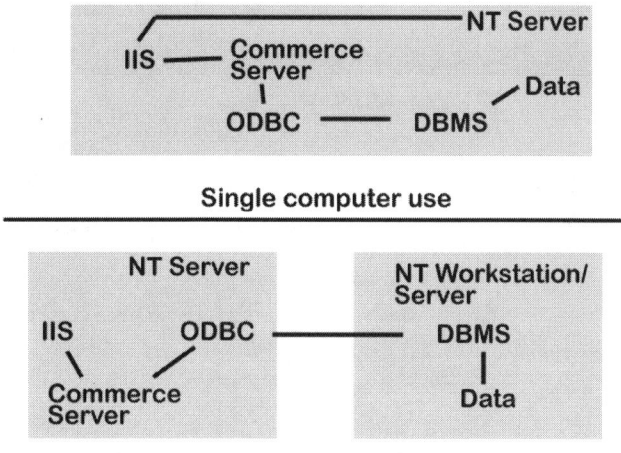

Figure 10.5 Commerce Server is integrated with IIS and an ODBC-compliant database.

Commerce Server was developed with the Active Server environment in mind. As you learned earlier, ASP provides a server-side scripting for dynamic Web site development. The Microsoft Web commerce products break down into the following parts:

- Commerce Server components. These components are used to create on-line stores.
- Order processing pipeline components. This part of Commerce Server is like a pipeline; orders flow in, and products flow out. The components manage orders, product data, merchant data, and shopper data throughout the ordering process.
- Tools for store creation and management.
- Client-side controls for managing credit cards, other payment schemes, and address information.
- The Buy Now wizard for fast purchasing.

The elements operate as shown in Figure 10.6.

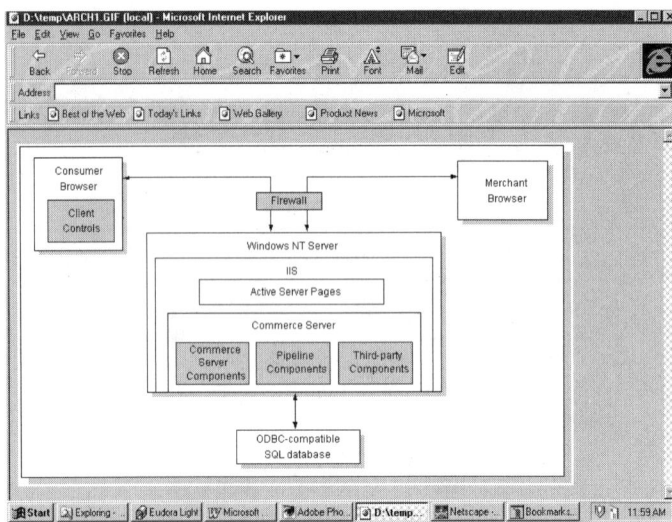

Figure 10.6 Microsoft's Web commerce product elements (from Microsoft documentation).

Commerce Server Components

The Commerce Server components provide a run-time environment for on-line stores. As with ASP, these components are ActiveX server components. A sample of the components is shown in Table 10.1.

Table 10.1

Component	Description
Content	Simplifies the developer's store interaction with the database management system. It provides a cache in which the developer can store string variables that are associated with data source names and SQL queries.
Data Functions	Supports data conversion and data validation.
Datasource	Executes SQL queries. Developers usually pass a string variable that is associated with the Content component.
DB Storage	Provides the developer with database interactivity.
MessageManager	Used to store messages to display to store customers.
OrderForm	Used to add and delete purchase items.
OrderPipeline	Loads the pipeline configuration file (**.pcf file**) that provides the order processing method for each store.
ShopperManager	Used to create, delete, and retrieve the unique shopper identifier.

Commerce Server components register as ActiveX servers. This means that they support methods and properties that you call and set from server-side VBScript or JavaScript.

This chapter describes the Commerce Server components and includes definitions of the methods and properties that they support. For a tour of on-line stores that use these components, see "Building a Store" later in this chapter.

The components can be long-lived or short-lived. You ensure better performance by keeping certain components in memory. The Content component is an example of a memory-resident, or long-lived, component. The Page component is an example of a short-lived component, which is loaded and executed every time a shopper makes a connection.

Order Processing Pipeline

The Commerce Server processing component is a pipeline made of stages of execution modes. This pipeline allows you to institute business rules for order processing. Figure 10.7 shows the stages of the order processing pipeline.

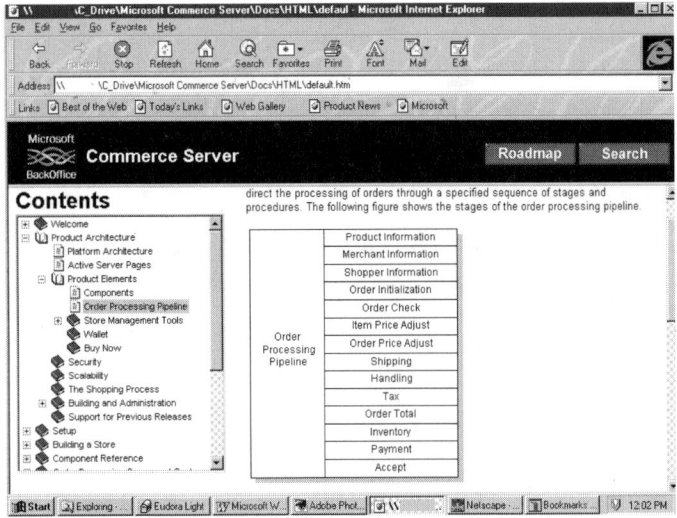

Figure 10.7 The order processing pipeline (from the Microsoft documentation).

The difference between ASP components and Commerce Server components is that Commerce Server components handle tasks across multiple sessions. Using one set of components, a developer can store content in a database, log traffic for marketing and diagnostic purposes, and automate the processing of order data through the order processing pipeline.

The Commerce Server order processing pipeline is a set of Component Object Model (COM) components that support order processing functions at various stages in the purchasing process. The pipeline supports interfaces to allow access to some of its functionality from C++ and other languages.

Many pipeline components are provided for these stages. For example, a shipping component that performs fixed-rate calculation is provided for the shipping stage of the pipeline, and the inventory stage includes a component that reduces local inventory. However, the pipeline components shipped with Commerce Server are optional and can be integrated with legacy systems or replaced with components supplied by third parties. Depending on a store's configuration, there may be one or more components at a particular stage.

After a shopper has placed an order with a Commerce Server–based store, Commerce Server retains the order data in the order form. The order form's storage is passed from stage to stage and component to component in a sequence determined by the pipeline configuration file. (A pipeline configuration file is created using Pipeline Editor, one of the Commerce Server tools.)

Each component modifies the contents of the order form by reading data from it and writing data to it. To transfer order form data to a legacy system for further handling, the merchant can configure the pipeline to run a component that captures order form data for the transfer.

To extend the pipeline's functionality, developers can create custom pipeline components. For information about developing custom components, see the Commerce Server SDK for header files, libraries, sample components, and documentation describing the interfaces of the pipeline components.

Store Builder Wizard Tools

The Store Builder wizard is intended to hide database schema issues by giving you a step-by-step approach to designing a store. The first step is to create a store foundation by using the Store Foundation wizard.

In the Store Builder wizard you will handle these tasks:

- Provide merchant information such as address and telephone information.
- Determine the locale that is used for display of items such as time and currency.
- Identify product characteristics such as size, color, and sale prices.
- Determine shipping methods as well as shipping and handling charges.
- Handle tax collection information such as state and amount.

The wizard allows you to go back and forth throughout your entries. When you're finished, you click **Finish**. Then the wizard creates the store files, defines the database schema, creates the order processing pipeline, generates sample data, and loads the data directly into the database.

The wizard is an ASP-based application that can be accessed from a Web browser.

Client-Side Controls: The Wallet

The Wallet, available either as an ActiveX control or as Netscape plug-in, has a Payment Selector control and the Address Selector control. The Payment Selector controls payment entry, payment storage, and payment methods for making on-line purchases. The Address Selector controls address entry, address storage, and use of addresses for shipping and billing during on-line order entry.

Buy Now Wizard

If you want to help impulse buyers complete purchases quickly, you can use the Buy Now wizard. The shopper launches the Buy Now wizard by clicking a product name or a banner .The customer starts and completes the shopping process without leaving the context of the page containing the link. Customers can even use Netscape 2.0 to access the Buy Now box.

Buy Now is integrated with the Wallet and the server database. This means that when the advertisement is clicked, the wizard opens a dialog box that includes the following:

- A title bar containing the name of the store and product images.
- An **Options** section for choosing product color, size, and quantity.
- Navigation buttons.

THE SELLING PROCESS

To sell products, you must assist the consumer in shopping. The first step is to build the store.

Building a Store

A Commerce Server store is a set of Active Server Pages. The store begins operation as soon as the customer's browser makes a request for product information.

The server creates the pages as text files that have the **.asp** extension. The pages contain HTML characters as well as scripting expressions enclosed in the delimiters <% and %>. The four starter stores shipped with Commerce Server use server-side VBScript.

Web page serving operates the same here as in all other cases. As the server receives an HTTP request for the file, the server reads the HTML code and VBScript. The result is an HTTP response that paints the appropriate information on the customer's browser.

The developer sets up a database and Data Source Name (DSN) during the initial installation. A sample is provided by Microsoft. All actions of Commerce Server are intended to be integrated with a database, and this initial setup allows the **.asp** files to be filled with information that is queried from those established databases. Note that the databases contain store information such as inventory data, product descriptions, pricing, shopper information, tracking data, promotions, and pointers to product images.

A Commerce Server on-line shopping site is integrated with the IIS via the use of virtual directories. As you know, an IIS virtual directory maps a directory to a logical name. For an on-line store, you map the store name to the directory (see Figure 10.8).

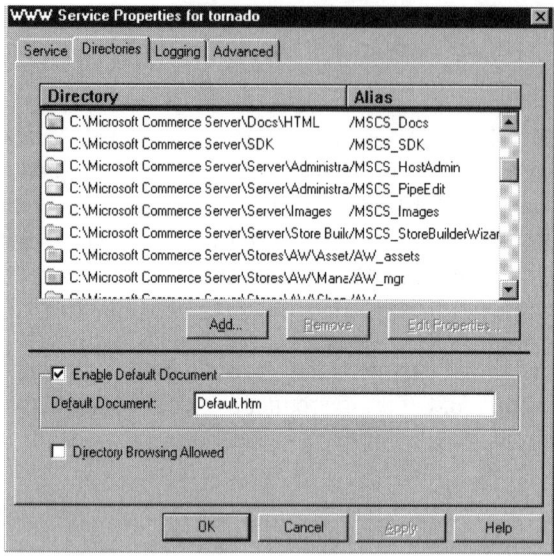

Figure 10.8 The sample virtual directories.

An on-line store needs an IIS virtual directory that maps to the **\Stores\storename\Shop** folder. For example, the Clock Peddler store, provided by Microsoft, has the following virtual directory:

> Directory: **C:\Microsoft Commerce Server\Stores\Clockped\Shop**
> Alias: **/ClockPed**

Microsoft recommends that you provide two additional IIS virtual directories for each store. These directories map to the **Assets** and **Manager** folders. For example, the Clock Peddler store is shipped with the following two additional virtual directories:

> Directory: **C:\Microsoft Commerce Server\Stores\Clockped\Assets**
> Alias: **/ClockPed_assets**
> Directory : **C:\Microsoft Commerce Server\Stores\Clockped\Manager**
> Alias: **/ClockPed_mgr**

The good news is that when you use the Store Foundation wizard or the Starter Store Copy wizard, the wizard creates these virtual directories for the new store.

For information about IIS virtual directories, see the IIS documentation.

The server includes two main configuration files. The **\Shop\global.asa** file initializes the store application, and the pipeline configuration file, **pipeline.pcf**, sets up the order processing pipeline for the store. All these elements are related. When you design and build the store database, you must consider where the data will appear in the **.asp** files. You must also consider how the system will retrieve the data. Remember all that you have learned regarding performance issues and network bottlenecks. If you do not have a plan for the logical and physical design of your system (please see Chapter 8 for an in-depth discussion of this subject), then changes made to the **.asp** files and components can have adverse effects. With the incorporation of **.asp**, you have the **global.asa** entries. As noted before, these entries initialize the store application. When you make changes, you must follow that effect throughout the database design and **.asp** implementation. See the following section to learn more.

In addition to the databases used with Commerce Server, there are **.asp** files that use the Content object (see the **global.asa** file example in Figure 10.9) to display dynamic information to the consumer.

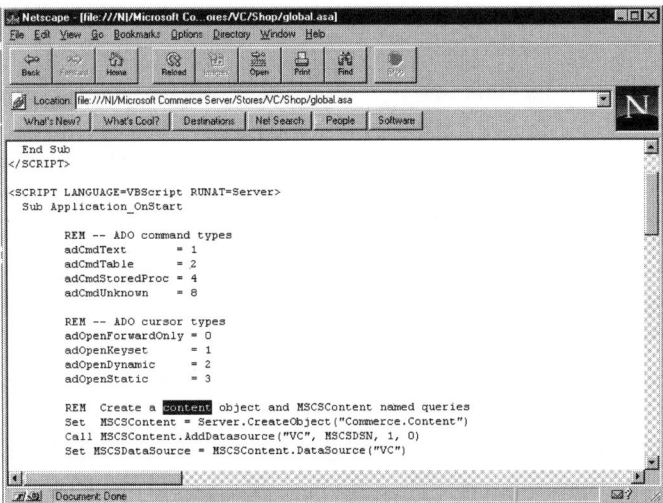

Figure 10.9 The **global.asa** file.

The system also provides ASP templates for creation of store display pages. These templates use standard scripting expressions, and that allows you to make simple store changes.

Commerce Server is an object-based environment. The store template scripts just described actually call the objects. The objects, in turn, handle all the calculations and functionality, including the creation of new shoppers, adding orders to a shopping cart, and closing out the order. Please see the following section for further discussion of the use of objects on each commerce page.

Chapter 10

Commerce Server comes with four examples of how to implement stores and their components. Coverage in this chapter is limited to an overview of component operation. Please review the Microsoft examples to learn more details about the interaction of the components.

USING GLOBAL.ASA IN STORE DEVELOPMENT

As is the case with most ASP development, the **global.asa** file can be a great way to initialize components. This is true with the Commerce Server object environment.

In the Adventure Works store provided by Microsoft, the objects created by **global.asa** are stored as variables in the Web server Application object (see Figure 10.10).

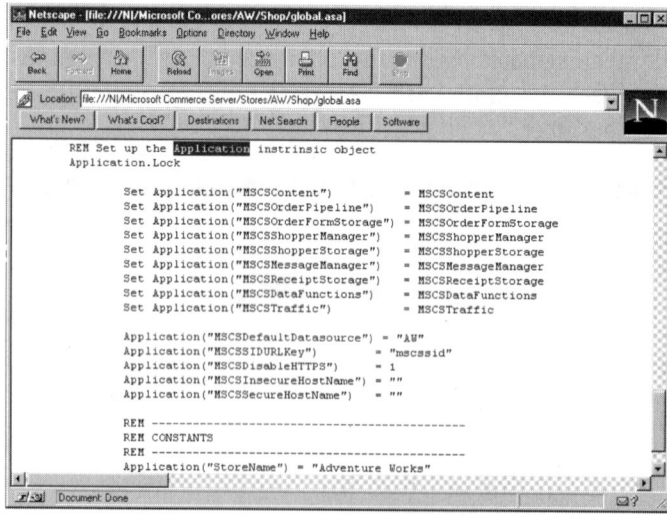

Figure 10.10 Application object used in the Adventure Works store.

The following listing is found at the end of each sample store's **global.asa** file. It creates the Application variables.

```
REM Set up the Application instrinsic object
Application.Lock
    Set Application("MSCSContent")          = MSCSContent
    Set Application("MSCSOrderPipeline")    = MSCSOrderPipeline
    Set Application("MSCSOrderFormStorage") = MSCSOrderFormStorage
    Set Application("MSCSShopperManager")   = MSCSShopperManager
    Set Application("MSCSMessageManager")   = MSCSMessageManager
    Set Application("MSCSDataFunctions")    = MSCSDataFunctions
```

```
REM Set Application("MSCSShopperStorage")   = MSCSShopperStorage
   REM Set Application("MSCSReceiptStorage")   = MSCSReceiptStorage
   REM Set Application("MSCSTraffic")          = MSCSTraffic

Application("MSCSDefaultDatasource") = "ClockPed"
   REM — uncomment the next line if you use "url" for ShopperManager above
   REM Application("MSCSSIDURLKey") = "mscssid"

Application("MSCSDisableHTTPS")          = 1
   Application("MSCSInsecureHostName") = ""    ' use this host
   Application("MSCSSecureHostName")   = ""    ' use this host
Application.Unlock
```

USING OBJECTS IN STORE DEVELOPMENT

In the starter stores, there are OrderForm and Page objects. Commerce Server comes with a **shop.asp** file located in every page template. This file creates an instance of the Page object. The reference is to a DSN that is found in the **\Shop\global.asa** file.

As the shopper adds items to the electronic basket, the system creates the OrderForm object. It is created in the **xt_orderform_additem.asp** file. The LookupData method or the GetData method creates an instance of the OrderForm object, and the order form data is read.

Figure 10.11 shows these page-level objects as used in the Adventure Works starter store. You can assign any name to these objects.

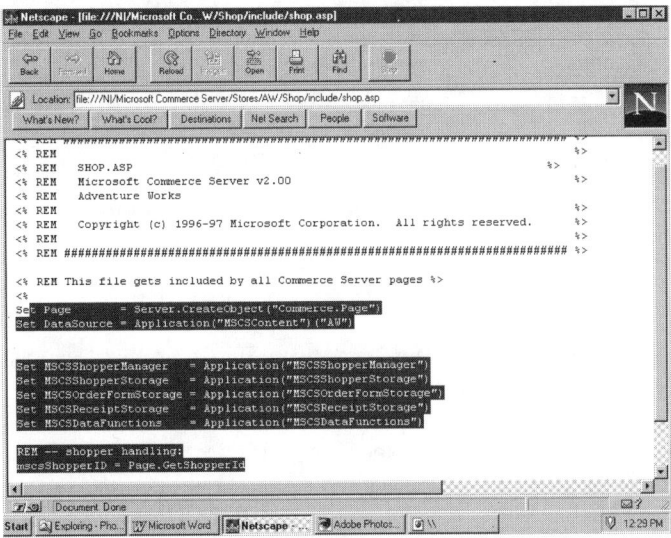

Figure 10.11 Page-level objects in the Adventure Works store.

Note that in the **\Shop\Include\shop.asp** file, page-level variables are set to corresponding objects. These objects are stored in the Application object in the **\Shop\global.asa** file:

```
Set DataSource = Application("MSCSContent")("AW")

Set MSCSShopperManager = Application("MSCSShopperManager")

Set MSCSShopperStorage = Application("MSCSShopperStorage")

Set MSCSOrderFormStorage = Application("MSCSOrderFormStorage")

Set MSCSReceiptStorage = Application("MSCSReceiptStorage")

Set MSCSDataFunctions = Application("MSCSDataFunctions")
```

GETTING TO AND FROM THE DATABASE

Database interactivity is based on the ActiveX component environment. Therefore, the Commerce Server objects use Active Database Objects (ADO) to talk with ODBC data sources (see Figure 10.12).

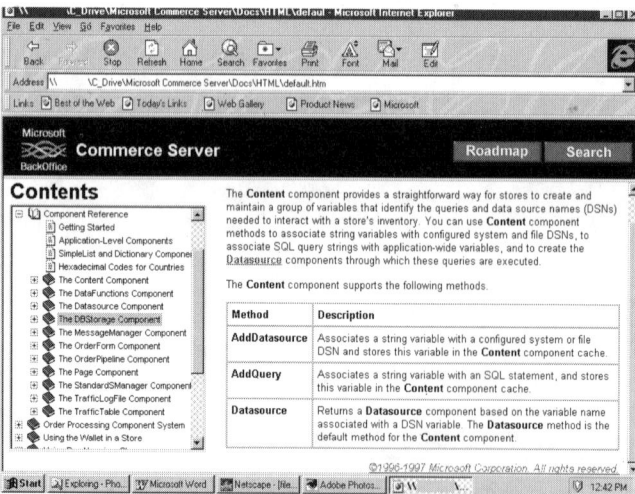

Figure 10.12 The DBStorage component.

The system initializes the DBStorage objects using the Datasource object. The Datasource method creates the Datasource object using the Content object's appropriate connect string.

THE ORDER FORM

The order form is the same object as the shopping basket. In a sample starter store, such as the Clock Peddler, the shopper goes to a product page, selects a product, and clicks **Add** to Basket. This action creates an instance of the order form or OrderForm object. The system writes the product information to the order form. The system then processes the order by using the DBStorage object to commit the data to storage. This results in the display of a new ASP file, a shopping basket page (**basket.asp**). The **basket.asp** file has the system retrieve storage data and put it into the order form.

The next step is still a page-level activity. The Page object's Page RunPlan method takes the data and passes the order form through the first 12 steps of the order processing pipeline. This process is executed through the OrderPipeline object.

The result is that the OrderPipeline object gives the OrderForm object current calculations on subtotals, totals, shipping, handling, and taxes. What happens if the product page price (placed_price) and database price (list_price) are different? An error is generated by the OrderPipeline object. It sends an error code to a MessageManager object, which in turn sends the appropriate error string to the pipeline and order form objects.

The DBStorage object created in **global.asa** stores the OrderForm. An example of the ordering process and object interaction is shown in Figure 10.13

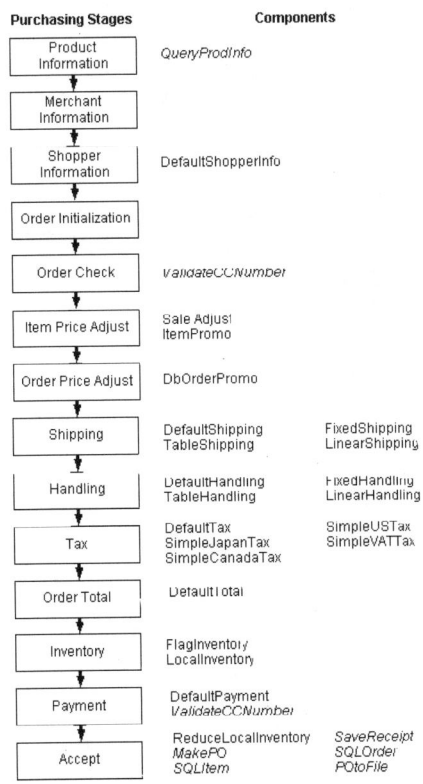

Figure 10.13 Pipeline and objects (from the Microsoft documentation).

258 Chapter 10

When the consumer makes a purchase, the Page object's RunPlan method goes through the previously identified 12 steps in the pipeline. If there is a pricing error, the error is kicked back to the order form. If there is no error, the order form data is cleared and the purchase is completed. Note that at this point the Clock Peddler displays only a confirmation page. The other stores use an accept step, in which the data is committed to the DBStorage object. This is known as *receipt storage*.

The order form is a collection of name/value pairs that stores the shopper ID, items selected for purchase, shipping and billing address information, and payment information The system stores the values as pointers to lists. For example, recall our previous discussion about error strings; a Purchase_Errors variable points to a list of error strings that are generated by the OrderPipeline object. An example of these lists is shown in Figure 10.14.

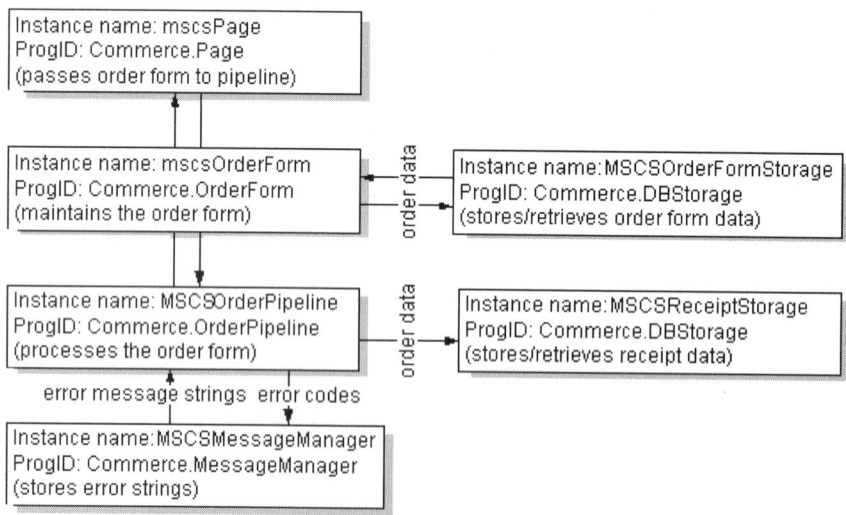

Figure 10.14 Purchase errors stored in MessageManager.

The Page object processes the order form by using its RunProduct, RunPlan, and RunPurchase methods (see Figure 10.15).

Active Money

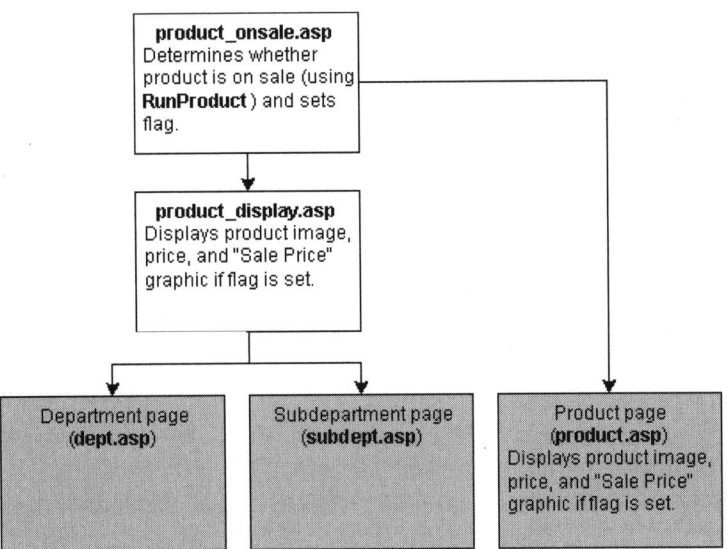

Figure 10.15 Microsoft sample of RunProduct in the Sales example.

LOCATION OF KEY FILES

With all these discussions regarding sample stores, **.asp files**, and **global.asa** files, let's look at where they can be found (see Figure 10.16).

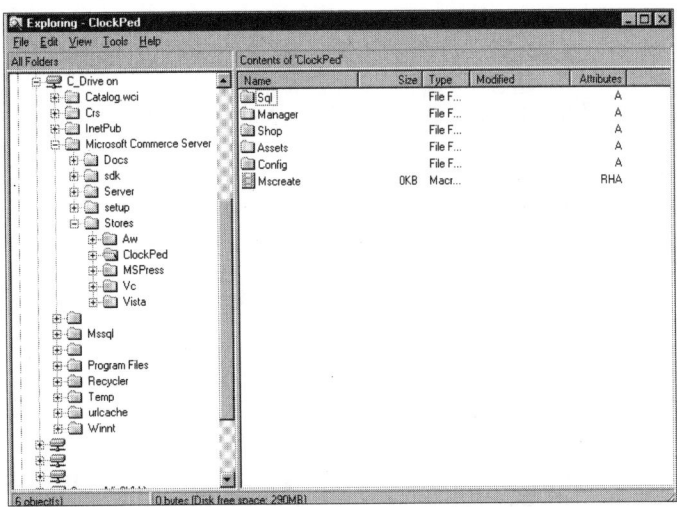

Figure 10.16 Directory structure for the Clock Peddler sample store.

The directory breakdown is as follows:

- **Assets** folder. This folder contains the images and other multimedia files used in store development.
- **Config** folder. This is where you will find the **pipeline.pcf** file, which is needed for the store's order processing pipeline.
- **Manager** folder. These are the files for the store's Manager application (discussed in following section). They are kept separate from the shop files for security reasons.
- **Shop** folder. It contains the actual on-line shop files.
- **Sql** folder. As mentioned earlier, you must create databases for each of the on-line stores. This folder contains the SQL scripts that create the databases. In some cases, you will find data for populating sample entries.

The Store Application

The store, as you know by now, is a collection of **.asp** files and applications. The customer can travel through the store, buying products or just browsing. Appropriate data is captured in on-line databases.

Commerce Server comes with four basic stores, each with its own level of complexity. The Clock Peddler is the simplest store (it has no accept step), and the Adventure Works is the most complex store. Here are the default locations:

- Clock Peddler: http://hostname/clockped/default.asp
- Volcano Coffee: http://hostname/vc/default.asp
- MS Press: http://hostname/mspress/default.asp
- Adventure Works: http://hostname/aw/default.asp

The simple Clock Peddler starter store has these characteristics:

- It is designed for all Web browsers that can handle tables and cookies. The store works with any screen resolution.
- It has only two levels: department and product. In the product area, the store sells only one type of product. This means that each product has a price and a description.
- Because of the limited number of products, it provides no searching capability.
- Because customers do not register when they enter, shipping addresses must be entered for each order.

You can review the full store's layout, **.asp** templates, queries, **global.asa** entries, and database schema following installation of Commerce Server. This review will assist you in developing a working knowledge of how a store operates.

THE MANAGER APPLICATION

In addition to creating a store, you must be able to manage the store activities. They include adding products, removing products, opening the store, and closing the store. This is the reason for the Manager application. You can reach each store's Manager screen from the Administrator screen. See Figure 10.17 for a sample Manager screen.

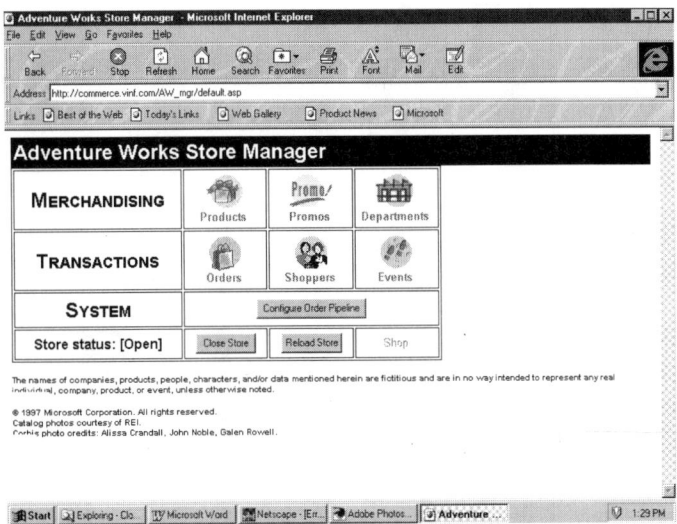

Figure 10.17 Sample Manager screen.

The Manager files are located in a different directory from the store files. This arrangement ensures that you do not accidentally allow unauthorized access to the management screens.

Following are the locations of the Manager applications of each sample store.

- Clock Peddler: http://hostname/ClockPed_mgr/default.asp
- Volcano Coffee: http://hostname/vc_mgr/default.asp
- MS Press: http://hostname/mspress_mgr/default.asp
- Adventure Works: http://hostname/aw_mgr/default.asp

For example, the Clock Peddler Manager application is an **.asp** file that manages the Clock Peddler store. You should look in the **\Stores\ClockPed\Manager** folder for the templates.

To start the Clock Peddler Store Manager, open your browser and use the following URL: http://hostname/ClockPed_mgr/default.asp. The Manager page requires a username and password for proper operation.

HOST ADMINISTRATOR

You can manage multiple stores by using Host Administrator, a Commerce Server application for creating and deleting stores. See Figure 10.18 for the Host Administrator screen.

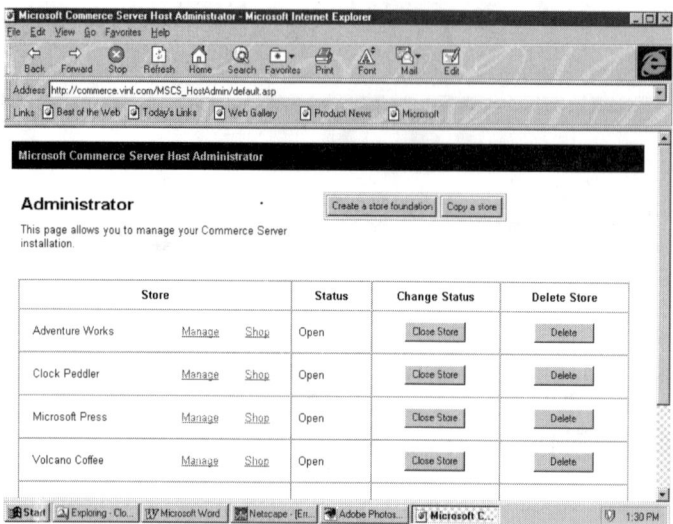

Figure 10.18 Host Administrator.

To connect to Host Administrator, use the following URL: http://hostname/MSCS_HostAdmin/Default.asp. The Host Administrator page requires a username and password for proper operation.

Host Administrator creates its list of stores by doing the following:

- Host Administrator looks in the **\Stores** folder and generates a list of the store name folders. For each name in the **\Stores** folder, Host Administrator ensures that there is an IIS virtual directory (**\Stores\storename\Shop**).
- Knowing the **\Stores** folder and virtual directory information, Host Administrator parses the **\Manager\Include\dsn_include.asp** file. If it passes, then the store is listed and is valid to use. If this process fails because of a bad file or no file, the store is listed as invalid.
- Once the store is listed as valid, Host Administrator determines the status of the store by searching the **storename\Shop** folder. It is looking for the **global_opened.asa** file. If the file is not present, the status of the store is set to "closed." The Manager will use the Manager application to "open" the store.

To access the Store's Manager application, Host Administrator displays each store name, as shown in Figure 10.18. There is a hyperlink to that store's Manager application.

The store must use the appropriate directory structure (see Figure 10.19).

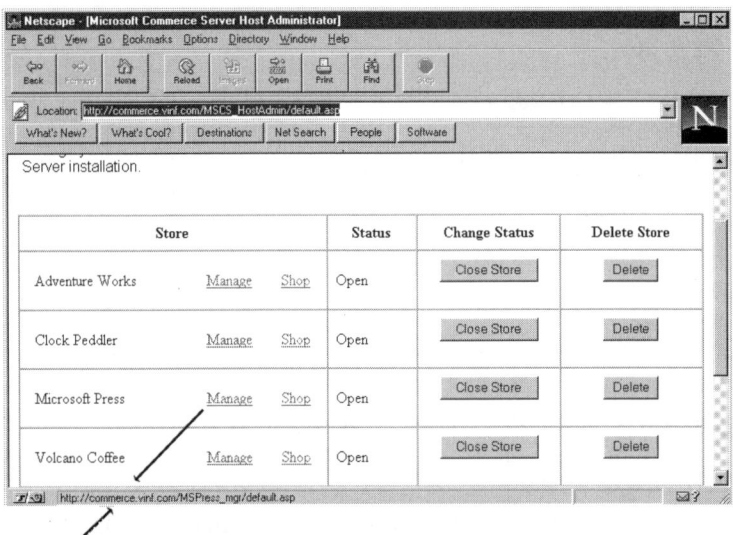

Figure 10.19 Link to the virtual directory.

For the link to work properly, the Manager application for each store is located in the **\storename\Manager** folder. If it is not in the proper location, the link will not work.

Setting Up a Store

There are two ways to set up a store:

- Build a new store. You create a new store by using the Store Foundation wizard to build the virtual directories and directory structure. Then you use Store Builder to generate the store and add it to the foundation.
- Copy a starter store. You go to the Administrator screen and copy one of the starter stores (Adventure Works, Clock Peddler, Volcano Coffee, or MS Press). The structure and components are available; you must rename and personalize the store.

The starting point in either case is Host Administrator (see Figure 10.18).

You may want to create a host service provider (HSP) on a separate server. The HSP would host the foundation of the stores. The merchant would use the Store Builder wizard to build the store and save it to the HSP.

BUILDING A NEW STORE

Host Administrator allows you to build the foundation for the new store. The store foundation includes

- A store directory structure along with IIS virtual directories and a connect string for the new store's database.
- The Microsoft Windows NT store manager account along with the Manager application for the store.

When the Store Foundation wizard has created the foundation, it displays the first page of the new store's Manager application. At this point, this page is blank except for a link that starts the Store Builder wizard. Based on the merchant's input, the Store Builder wizard generates the **.asp** files for the new store and saves them into the foundation.

An HSP can provide the URL for the new store's Manager page to the merchant, who can then connect to the page and run the Store Builder wizard to generate the new store.

COPYING A STARTER STORE

To create a copy of a store, follow these steps:

1. Use a browser and enter the following URL: http://hostname/MSCS_HostAdmin/Default.asp. (If an authentication dialog box is displayed, enter your username and password.)
2. In Host Administrator, click the **Copy a store** button (see Figure 10.20).

Active Money 265

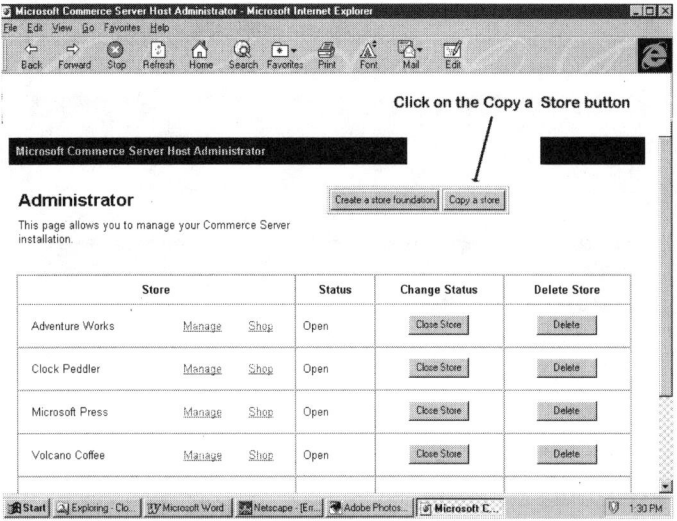

Figure 10.20 Choosing the **Copy a store** button.

3. On the Welcome page, click **Next** (see Figure 10.21).

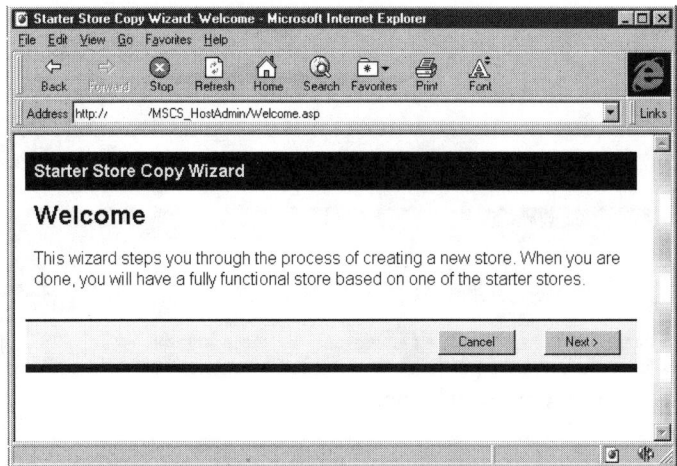

Figure 10.21 The Welcome page.

4. On the Choose A Store Template page, select the store you want to copy and click **Next** (see Figure 10.22).

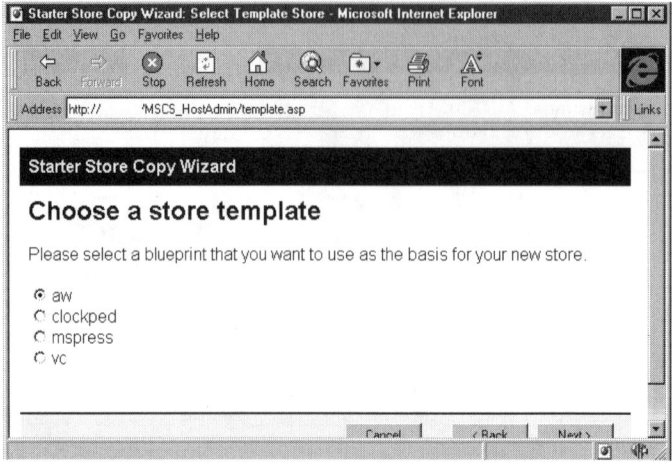

Figure 10.22 Choosing a store template.

5. Enter a unique **Short Name** and **Display Name** for the new store and click **Next**. You cannot use the same name as an existing store. The display name is used for display on the generated pages. The short name is used for creating the IIS virtual directories, the store directory, and the database tables. For example, if you enter **mine** for the short name and base the new store on Clock Peddler, the new basket table is named mine_basket (see Figure 10.23).

Figure 10.23 Adding a store name.

Active Money 267

6. Select the appropriate driver for the database. Then click **Next** (see Figure 10.24).

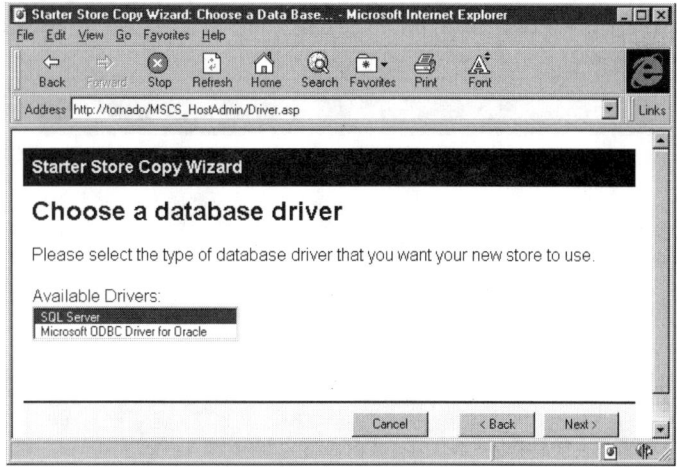

Figure 10.24 Choosing a database driver.

7. Specify the connect string. The connect string contains the DSN, the database name, and the username or password. Click **Next** (see figure 10.25).

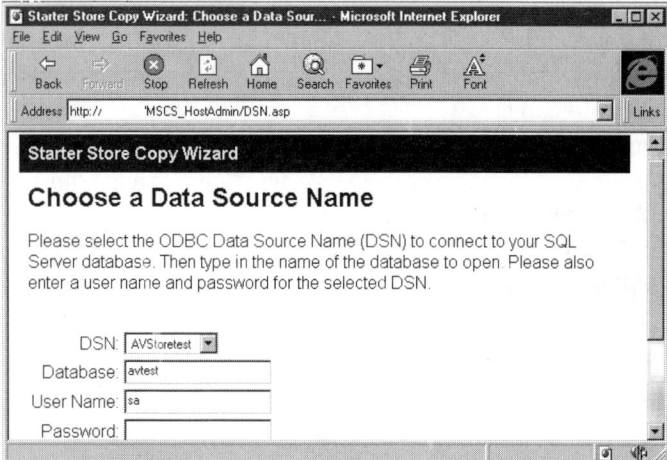

Figure 10.25 Choose a Data Source Name.

8. Select a Windows NT account, as shown in Figure 10.26. This provides Manager application access. Click **Next**.

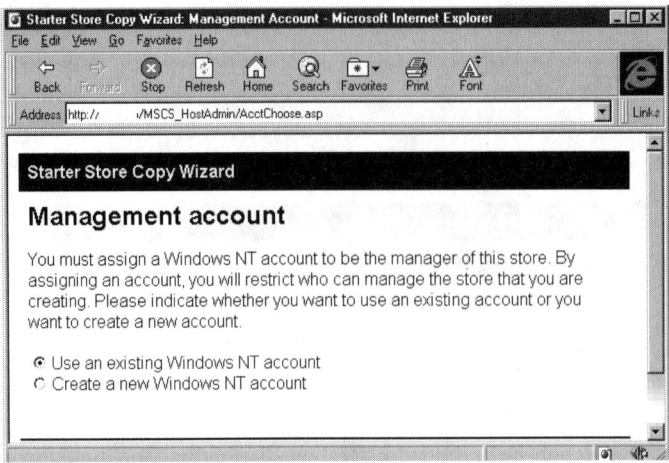

Figure 10.26 Assigning the manager's account.

9. Click the **Finish** button.

The Starter Store Copy wizard creates the store. Host Administrator will now have a valid link to the store's Manager application.

DELETING A STORE

To delete a store, you must provide Host Administrator with the store's connect string (DSN, username, password, and database name). Look in the **\storename\Manager\Include\dsn_include.asp** file.

For you to use Host Administrator to delete a store, the **dsn_include.asp** file must have exactly the same format as those of the starter stores. The file must be located in the **\storename\Manager\Include** folder.

Also look for **Uninstall.sql** in the **\storename\Shop\Sql\Oracle** or **\storename\Shop\Sql\SqlSvr** folder. This file allows Host Administrator to delete the store's database.

That is all it takes for you to use Host Administrator delete a store.

Buying Assistance in Commerce Server

Remember that you have the use of the Wallet and Buy Now components to assist in immediate customer purchases.

As a reminder, the Wallet is a pair of ActiveX controls that you can use to register payment and shipping information. This data is conveniently stored on the client's system for future use.

Buy Now lets the customer make quick purchases. Clicking on a special advertisement opens the Buy Now wizard. Remember the intent is to meet the customer's needs. The Buy Now component works in concert with the Wallet (for the client) and the order processing pipeline (for the server). Commerce Server comes with a sample store-based implementation of the Buy Now component.

The Customer Shopping Process

The shopping process begins when a consumer clicks on a link that activates an on-line store. New shoppers are prompted to register in the registration page. Shoppers then enter the store and begin browsing through departments and looking at the products. The server provides a traffic component that monitors users as soon as they have entered the main page; marketing department personnel are provided with immediate consumer information.

You can easily create an **Add to Cart** or **Add to Basket** button to allow the consumer to purchase a product. This is the electronic shopping cart. The resultant page is in HTML format and gives the consumer a chance to review and change the product listed. If all is OK, the consumer clicks on a **Check Out** button. This process should be similar to other ordering sites that the consumer has encountered.

This process calls up the address and payment selector information, which is displayed for the consumer to enter. Note that this information is password-protected. The consumer now reviews the totals and all the information. If satisfied, the consumer clicks the **Submit Order** button. The system then follows an encrypted method via SSL to the on-line credit card transaction company. When the amount clears, Commerce Server processes the order by providing a confirmation page and order ID tracking number. This ID tracking number will allow both the consumer and the developer to track any lost or undelivered orders.

Microsoft provides a chart, shown in Figure 10.27, to outline the shopping process.

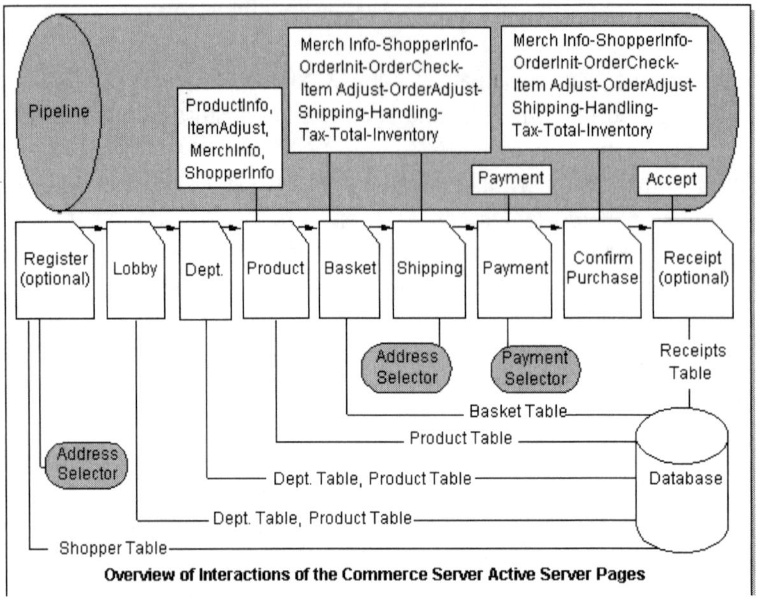

Figure 10.27 Microsoft's shopping process.

TIPS FOR INCREASING SALES

Commerce Server provides store management tools, wizards, and a scaleable architecture that help you create a site that can increase product sales. Without the proper tools, a good product may go unnoticed. If a consumer is happy with the product and with customer support (that starts with the buying process), then that person will refer people to your site. That is the essence of Web sales: getting references.

It is essential for you to understand the usefulness of the tools and wizards for creating an enjoyable shopping process.

Tools

You can choose to create a store without using the tools available, but the complexity of maintenance increases dramatically. Here is a summary of the tools.

- Commerce Server Host Administrator. This browser-based tool lets you become more than a site administrator. You become a store manager. Think of what it takes

to run a ROSS or Clothestime or REI store. A manager must maintain resources (personnel), keep inventory in place (products), and adjust prices based on seasonal changes (make database changes). The manager must also make sure that the store is opened at the proper hours and closed for inventory counting and restocking. Host Administrator assists you in all of these areas.
- Pipeline Editor. The method used by the store manager to process orders may change based on a variation in product mix or geography. To assist in this task, you can turn to Pipeline Editor. You can launch this tool as a Windows application or as an Active Server Page. You use this editor to change component and stage configuration based on company and user needs.
- Starter stores. Commerce Server comes with a sample template of ready-to-run stores. It's like buying a food franchise with the napkins and cups already delivered and sample dishes already prepared. You are free to use the stores to test and run your own commerce environment. (Note that the artwork is for demonstration purposes only; the licensing agreement for Commerce Server does not allow a developer to use Microsoft-owned resources.) Each of the stores provides a different level of merchant capability. In addition, you can study these stores to understand the internal workings of Commerce Server.

Wizards

- Store Foundation wizard. The Foundation wizard produces a foundation for an on-line store. Just as a contractor needs a strong foundation on which to build a lasting home, so the developer needs a strong foundation for a store. The Foundation wizard allows you to set up the store's data source name (used by ODBC and ADO), virtual directories (for proper store application and management tool placement), and file system structure (to allow for proper security management). Once the foundation is laid, you can use the Store Builder wizard to create the store.
- Store Builder wizard. Now that you have laid the "concrete" and "walls" for the store, you must design the layout. Where will the products go? How much will they sell for? Do you need to incorporate specials? The Builder wizard lets you create the store structure along with the database schema and page layouts.
- Starter Store Copy wizard. Commerce Server comes with a set of starter stores. You can use the Store Copy wizard to copy a standard store and modify it to meet your requirements, thereby reducing store development time significantly.
- Buy Now wizard. Do you need to hear any more about this wonderful component? You can create bargain basements, special purchases, and "blue light" specials just by linking to the Buy Now wizard.

Scalability

Now you have the tools and wizards to get stores on-line quickly. Commerce Server can also support the movement of stores and managers over multiple computers. If you need to bridge several pieces of hardware, you will need to install IIS 3.0 and Commerce Server on each computer. Microsoft recommends that you use the DNS round-robin technique to balance the load of incoming consumer requests. This technique routes consumers to a single store Web address (URL) (see Figure 10.28).

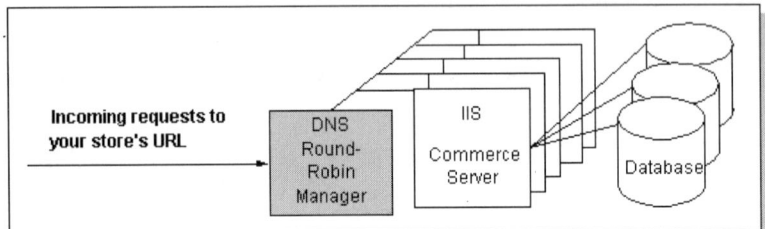

Figure 10.28 Microsoft's round-robin diagram.

To monitor the performance of each server, Commerce Server provides its own set of counters for the Windows NT Performance Monitor. In this manner, you can track the number of shoppers (old and new) in the processing pipeline.

Where Do You Go from Here?

The goal of any store is to make more sales and keep the customer happy. You have learned not only that the consumer shopping process can be a great way to make money on the Web but also how to ensure a level of technological success. You must be aware of the consumer's security concerns and implement the appropriate solutions, such as digital certificates. Commerce Server provides a component environment that is Active Server-friendly. This ASP component package, along with the wizards and tools, makes Commerce Server a satisfying solution to the developer building a dynamic money-making site.

From here you should look at the following chapters:

- Chapter 7, "The Active Security Environment: Proxy Server", to learn more about system and network security.
- Chapter 8, "Active Data", to understand the essential back end of the store.
- Chapter 16, "Java and JavaScript", to obtain a basic understanding of one of the great programming tools for the storefront pages.

Chapter 11

Active Middleware

With the increased use of the Internet for electronic commerce (e-commerce), Web databases and applications must be scalable. As you learned in Chapter 10, e-commerce means more than someone buying flowers or sending a birthday card on the Internet. It includes such things as reviewing on-line bank records, stock transactions, and personal medical records. When you're considering electronic transactions for a site, you should think about these issues:

- How safe is the transaction? Should you give the user alternative methods for the transaction?
- What facilities should you provide for the consumer who wants to learn more about the product and purchase it via other distribution channels (such as stores, fax delivery, phone call, or catalogs)?
- What items must you track? Many people think about storing customer data, logging a sold item in inventory, and similar items. But what about taxes? The federal government and state governments haven't determined how to handle the issue. Developers need to consider whether it is worthwhile to add a method for tracking taxes even if they are not currently assessed.
- Which items are being sold on-line? Does the company need a simple way to manage different inventories of products sold on-line versus those sold off-line?
- Does the on-line transaction feed a subcontractor or vendor? Do you need to provide a paper trace of the process? Does the subcontractor use on-line data entry or data entry personnel?
- Does the company currently have Java applets and Visual Basic programs that have been collecting data but not depositing it into a database?

How do you adequately deal with these issues? The first step is to understand the state of the art of transaction management. Then you need to formulate a solution. Here, it is simple: Microsoft Transaction Server. Once the solution is found, you need to understand its components and learn how to build an application that operates within safe bounds of the transaction model. Finally, you must handle basic administration of the transaction infrastructure and deal with issues of scalability.

The Methodologies

The current approach for database transactions is two-tiered, but the future of transactions lies in the use of middleware (see Figure 11.1).

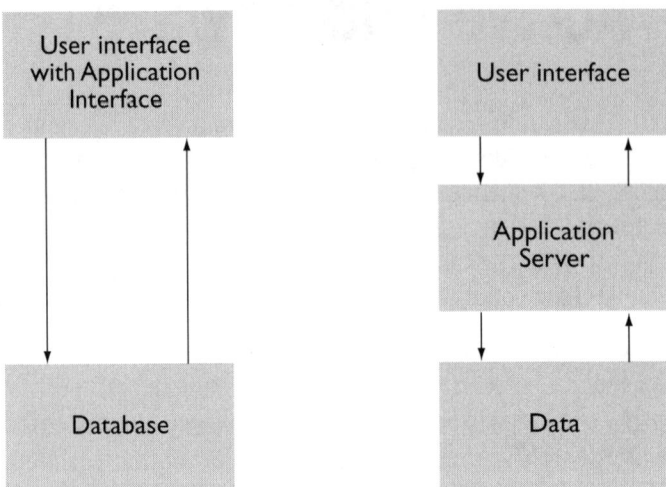

Figure 11.1 Transaction architectures: current (left) and future.

In Figure 11.1, the application server in the middleware solution assists with security, database connectivity, application logic, resource management, and thread safety. The two-tier database, on the other hand, was the first method that most developers learned and still is successfully used to create dynamic Web sites. Let's look at it first.

Two-Tier Database

Many Active Platform developers have become proficient in writing client-based applications. These applications tend to let users select data from and insert data into a database using joins and other SQL statements. As demands on the server increase and response time decreases, these developers increase memory, CPU speed, the number of CPUs, and disk space. Many of them even go so far as to install RAID. As requirements are added or changed, the increasing complexity of such systems means that the developer begins to lose track of how best to implement a fully functional solution in a limited time. Developers have application skills in their areas of expertise, such as inventory system development, business accounting, bookstore management, and order control processing. As departments become more decentralized and must support a "global" requirement, these skills must be intermixed. After customers have visited a Web site, they expect the ordering system to know them when they return even if they have cookies turned off.

Developers learn to live with the three-sided nature of software development (see Figure 11.2).

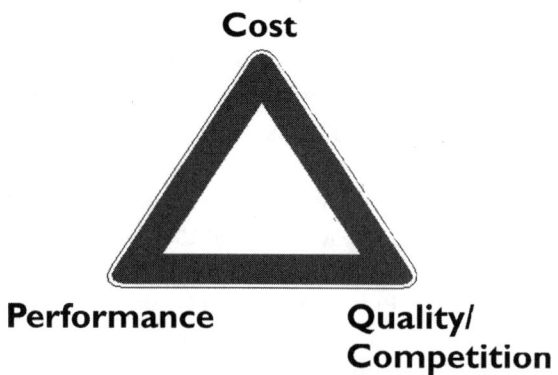

Figure 11.2 Development decisions.

The development triangle remains in equilibrium as long as the appropriate tension is maintained among the three corners: cost, performance, and competition. A developer acquires an understanding of the level of competition and then creates a plan based on the cost of creating a product having an appropriate level of performance. Suppose that the competing product is available via an intranet site (supporting the Microsoft Internet Explorer browser), an Internet site (supporting all types of browsers, the least common denominator being AOL 2.5 on a Windows 3.1 box), an extranet site (supporting IE or Netscape), and a CD-ROM. Instead of seeing the competition as a software company or a developer writing FoxPro database applications for a local bookstore or code for a huge hotel database, the developer recognizes that, in this case, the level of competition is based on the delivery mechanism.

Planning efforts are therefore devoted to considerations of cost versus performance. Many developers are trying to cut costs and improve performance by using so-called open solutions, but often these solutions are not tightly coupled. As multiple systems are added to a network, developers and administrators lose control over performance management and capacity planning.

That's why developers are turning to the UNIX model: the three-tier, or middleware, solution.

The Middleware Solution

In the middleware solution, an application's functionality is shared among the users. This means that the system can be managed efficiently.

- Applications are always available, and data is reliable. Application availability takes into account server hardware and software problems as well as networking and application problems.
- Servers are scalable to the point that client requests are served on demand. This means that the server must support high-level, on-demand concurrency.
- Security for both users and data items is transparent. Client security includes authorizing and authenticating customer data files. Data item security includes networking location, passwords, and access privileges that are shared among distributed systems. You can locate your applications and tools on various resources to make the new "site" immediately available. You are not looking for a mainframe solution.
- Transaction processing (TP) monitors not only support multiple databases (as in the two-tier approach) but also are tightly integrated with resource managers (those that monitor transaction queue messages).
- Administrative capabilities include recovery and database rollback.

How can a Microsoft Active Server developer implement the middleware solution? Three possibilities come to mind:

1. DCOM is a primitive approach. DCOM allows COM-based applications, built in languages such as Visual Basic and Visual C++, to link via RPC (Remote Procedure Call) mechanisms to database sources.
2. You could use a TP monitor device (see Figure 11.3). Microsoft provides a TP monitor environment within the Transaction Server infrastructure. Microsoft Transaction Server (MTS) uses DCOM as well as Message Queue Server (MSMQ, codenamed Falcon) to accomplish the middleware functionality. MS DTC was released as a transaction manager on SQL Server 6.5 and incorporated in the first Transaction Server release to assist in the TP monitoring activity.
3. You could implement an Active Server environment with a full integrated Web, database, and Transaction Server environment. This is the intent of the current release of Transaction Server (see Figure 11.4). With the ActiveX component functionality built into the Microsoft Web products and MTS, you can now provide both the channel and the dynamic push environment for safely attaching the client to your databases.

Active Middleware   277

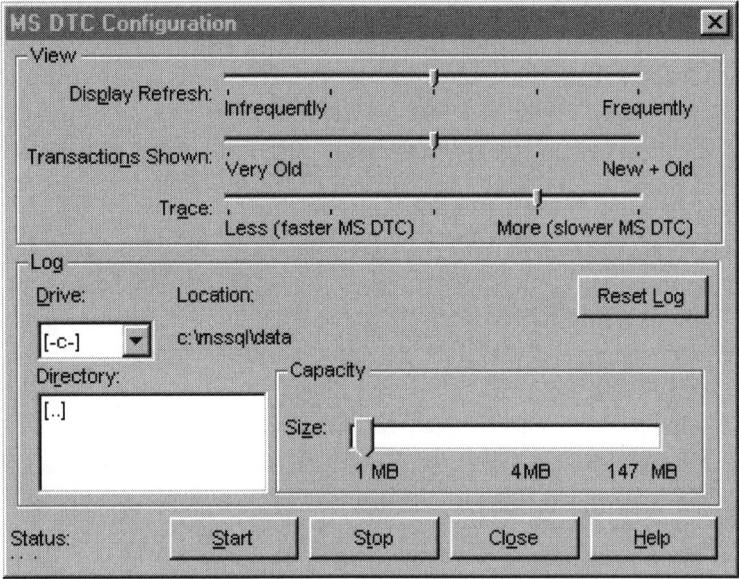

Figure 11.3 Transaction process monitoring.

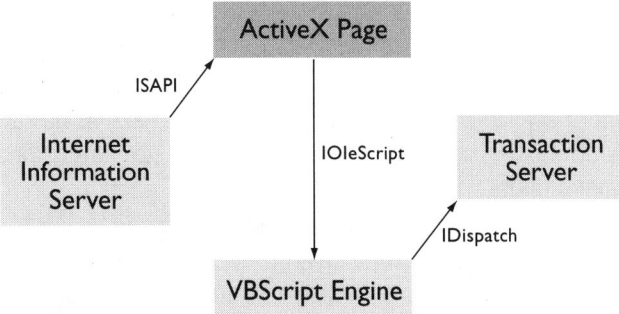

Figure 11.4 MTS and ActiveX.

Transaction Server

For many applications, a database is enough for the sharing of data. The challenge for the developer is to increase performance as more users come on-line. One of the key items to monitor is the *hotspot* (a record in the database that is frequently accessed), where customer transactions wait in line, as in a bank on payday. The problem is that throughput declines dramatically.

To design an avoidance method for hotspots, look at the access patterns of clients and determine how many transactions are trying to share records. For many applications you will find that the database has enough capability, with its built-in tools, for sharing data. For example, you can spread the work among various systems or redesign the tables to allow access to the data.

You must also consider that some failures are acceptable in a transaction environment. For example, suppose that a customer is purchasing a book at a bookstore and the Internet slows or the local customer machine hangs because of modem problems. If the order hangs longer than 15 seconds, the order may need to be canceled. The customer must then re-enter the data or resubmit the order to get a confirmation number. This level of failure may be acceptable to the average consumer.

Another approach is analogous to picking a number. Suppose you enter a customer service department at Target after the holidays. You find a ticket dispenser and a digital number counter on the wall. Each customer obtains a unique number that increases as a ticket is pulled from the dispenser. The customers await their turns. When a customer service representative is free, he or she pushes a button that advances the digital number counter. If the number changes and the customer does not respond after two requests, the representative advances the number counter and serves the next customer.

Developers can design database environments to follow the same principle. They allocate numbers in a unique manner, increasing as each customer arrives to perform a transaction. No numbers are repeated. When the server is ready to perform the transaction, it notifies the customer application that the time for the transaction has arrived. If the customer application does not respond in a reasonable time, the transaction is deemed a failure. The server moves to the next customer.

The problem is that you must provide a unique number for each transaction. This number may match the order number or may be a primary key set as an identity in SQL Server. Why? The system cannot have duplicate numbers! If your only approach to implement the "take a number" solution is to use database technology, the database record does not scale. Each transaction locks the record, and this means that only one transaction is allowed at any time. That is too limiting if your site has multiple customers. In the sample application installed with Transaction Server, you will find the SampleBank application, which contains the `Receipt` component. Here is a portion of the Visual Basic code:

Active Middleware 279

```
Public Function GetNextReceipt(ByRef strResult As String) As Long

' Get object context
    Dim ctxObject As ObjectContext
    Set ctxObject = GetObjectContext()

On Error GoTo ErrorHandler

' If Shared property does not already exist it will be initialized
    Dim spmMgr As SharedPropertyGroupManager
    Set spmMgr = CreateObject("MTxSpm.SharedPropertyGroupManager.1")

    Dim spmGroup As SharedPropertyGroup
    Dim bResult As Boolean
    Set spmGroup = spmMgr.CreatePropertyGroup("Receipt", LockSetGet, Process, bResult)

    Dim spmPropNextReceipt As SharedProperty
    Set spmPropNextReceipt = spmGroup.CreateProperty("Next", bResult)

    Dim spmPropMaxNum As SharedProperty
    Set spmPropMaxNum = spmGroup.CreateProperty("MaxNum", bResult)

Dim objReceiptUpdate As Bank.UpdateReceipt
    If spmPropNextReceipt.Value >= spmPropMaxNum.Value Then
        Set objReceiptUpdate = ctxObject.CreateInstance("Bank.UpdateReceipt")
        spmPropNextReceipt.Value = objReceiptUpdate.Update(strResult)
        spmPropMaxNum.Value = spmPropNextReceipt.Value + 100
    End If

    ' Get the next receipt number and update property
    spmPropNextReceipt.Value = spmPropNextReceipt.Value + 1

    ctxObject.SetComplete          ' we are finished and happy

GetNextReceipt = spmPropNextReceipt.Value

Exit Function

ErrorHandler:

ctxObject.SetAbort             ' we are unhappy
    strResult = Err.Description    ' return the error message
    GetNextReceipt = -1            ' indicate that an error occurred

End Function
```

Make sure that you set a maximum number that can be assigned to a transaction. A next number is allocated by the server and cannot exceed the maximum number (spmPropMaxNum.Value = spmPropNextReceipt.Value + 100). When the system gets close to the maximum number, make sure that a transaction occurs that advances the maximum number. When the server is restarted, it should start at the previous maximum number.

The drawback of this approach is that if a transaction stops it will lose the numbers, because the aborted transaction has failed to use them. They were already allocated. If the system crashes, the system loses the numbers; if the maximum number is very high, the system loses a lot of numbers. You could keep the next number in a database and avoid losing any numbers, but this technique is not scalable.

If the data is used and quickly discarded—if it is not durable—performance is a critical issue. If your database is subject to ODBC pooling, the database may not be sufficiently large. With Transaction Server, you can use Shared Property Manager to assist with these problems (see Figure 11.5). See the section "Resource Dispensers" for more details.

Transaction Server uses a component-based programming environment. MTS is integrated into Active Server Pages (ASP) using VBScript or JavaScript to invoke Transaction Server components.

Transaction Processing

Dr. Watson, as you probably know too well, is a utility that logs information about applications that fail in NT and Windows 95. What can you use to help prevent similar errors that occur when customers order at your site? Transaction Server is made up of various elements that should help prevent users from seeing major errors while placing orders. These elements include the following:

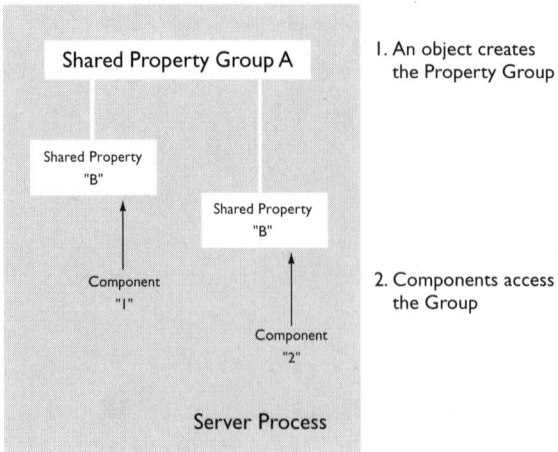

Figure 11.5 Shared Property Manager.

- Active components, which implement the application function.
- Transaction Server Executive, which provides the run-time services used by the application components.
- Server processes, which provide surrogate process environments to host the application components.
- Resource managers, which manage the application's durable state. Examples include relational database systems and transactional message queues.
- Resource dispensers, which manage nondurable shared state (data) for components within a process. Examples include database connection pooling.
- Microsoft Distributed Transaction Coordinator (MS DTC), which allows transactions to be coordinated across multiple resource managers, resource dispensers, and application components.
- Transaction Server Explorer, a graphical interface for administering Transaction Server systems.

Active Components

Transaction Server's components are used to implement a company's business rules. The banking example shipped with Transaction contains an Account component, written in Visual Basic, that lets you debit or credit an account number (see Figure 11.6).

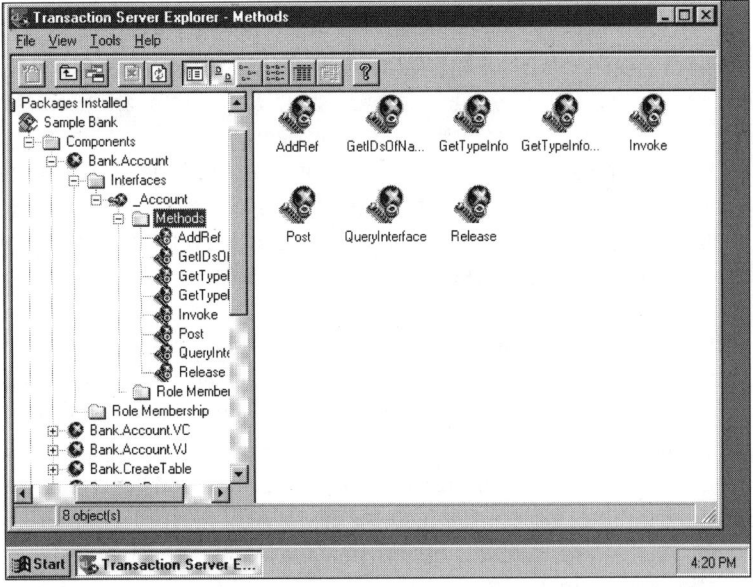

Figure 11.6 Account component.

The MTS components are business objects based on the COM DLL. Developers can write the components in Visual C++, Visual J++, or Visual Basic or by using ActiveX toolkits. Component properties are MTS-specific and are hosted in the MTS server process. The package used by MTS is a set of related components. The package defines components that run in the server process and establishes trust boundaries and the deployable unit. See the section "Building a Sample Application" to learn more about the development and deployment of packages.

Server Objects

Transaction Server objects behave like COM objects. If they hold their state, they are considered *stateful*; otherwise, they are *stateless*. The Transaction Server object has multiple interactions with a client. If it maintains its internal state, it is stateful. Whether an object is stateful or stateless when a transaction is committed or aborted, the object is deactivated and becomes stateless. This arrangement ensures that each transaction is isolated and that the database is kept consistent. *Isolation* means that each client's transactions are prevented from interfering with the application's state. Additionally, the process reduces resource overhead and improves system performance. In other words, it provides scalability.

Transaction Server Executive

Transaction Server Executive is a DLL. In a DLL, as in a subroutine, functions are compiled, linked, and stored separate from the process in which they are used. Components run in MTS under run-time services that are provided by Transaction Server Executive. The Transaction Server Executive run-time environment manages threads and context. Threads are the basic unit to which the operating system allocates CPU time slices.

Components should not create threads; Transaction Server Executive should be the only DLL handling threads. Each component has a `ThreadingModel` registry attribute (see Figure 11.7).

The attribute determines whether the component's objects are assigned to the main threading model or the apartment threading model (discussed soon). The single-threaded component can become deadlocked if it is stateful (see Figure 11.8). The solution for this problem is to create stateless objects and call `SetComplete`.

Interestingly, SQL Server has no problem with this situation, because the process is considered two different transactions, which can be thought of as T1 and T2.

To make distributed programming easier, Transaction Server implements activities and makes the location transparent.

```
CLSID222
InprocServer32=Test.dll
Threading Model="See the table below"
```

Threading Table

blank	This means SingleThreaded
Apartment	Apartment
Both	FreeThreaded which MTS treats as Apartment
Worker	This where every instance runs on any thread

Figure 11.7 `ThreadingModel` registry attribute.

Single Thread	All calls run on the same thread (COM main thread); Not recommended due to deadlock problems
Apartment Thread	Calls run on their own thread; Not recommended for application scope ASP; great for page scope ASP
Worker Thread	Each call runs on a different thread when called and re-called; used for background tasks

Source: MSDN library CDs

Figure 11.8 Threading table.

An activity is a single logical thread. A calls B, B calls C, C calls D, and so on. Only one component is running at a time in an activity. Transactions live inside an activity; even if an activity is distributed, there is a single logical thread. A component instance is the same as an object. There is a one-to-one relationship between a Microsoft Transaction Server object and an activity. The activity is recorded in the object's context, which is the object's relationship to its surroundings. A context affects the way an object appears or behaves.

Take, for example, the English word pronounced "too." It can be spelled three ways: *two*, *to*, and *too*. The spelling depends on the context of the sentence. If a person utters the sentence "I am going "too" the house," the spelling is *to*. If a person utters the sentence "I would like "too" hamburgers," the spelling is *two*. Context determines how the word is spelled in each of the sentences. Similarly, context is important in Transaction Server. Without the proper context, an object does not know how to behave.

A Transaction Server object is a single instance of an application component. Transaction Server maintains a context for each object. The context contains object execution information, including the object's creator. The context is created before the object is created and is destroyed after the object is destroyed.

In the multithreaded apartment model, the server has activities that set boundaries. These activities enable concurrent transactions without causing a deadlock of the record.

The apartment threading model provides significant concurrency improvements over the main threading model. Activities determine apartment boundaries; two objects can execute concurrently as long as they are in different activities. These objects may be in the same component or in different components.

Components cannot tell where they are running. In other words, they cannot tell whether the caller is in process, local, or remote. Configuration (location) of components is stored in a catalog. Developers administer the catalog using the Microsoft Transaction Server Explorer. The Executive DLL is loaded into the processes that host application components and runs transparently in the background.

As noted before, the single-threaded component can become deadlocked. A solution to this problem is to program stateless components. This means that the component must issue the `SetComplete` method of the `IObjectContext` function.

`SetComplete` declares that the current object is done and now must be deactivated, as shown in the following code sample:

```
#include <mtx.h>

IObjectContext* pObjectContext = NULL;
HRESULT hr;

hr = GetObjectContext(&pObjectContext);
// Do some work here.
// If the work was successful, call SetComplete.
if (SUCCEEDED(hr)) {
   if (pObjectContext)
      pObjectContext->SetComplete();
}
// Otherwise, call SetAbort.
else {
   if (pObjectContext)
      pObjectContext->SetAbort();
}
```

Let's assume that you have a birthday cake-making component (see Figure 11.9).

Active Middleware   285

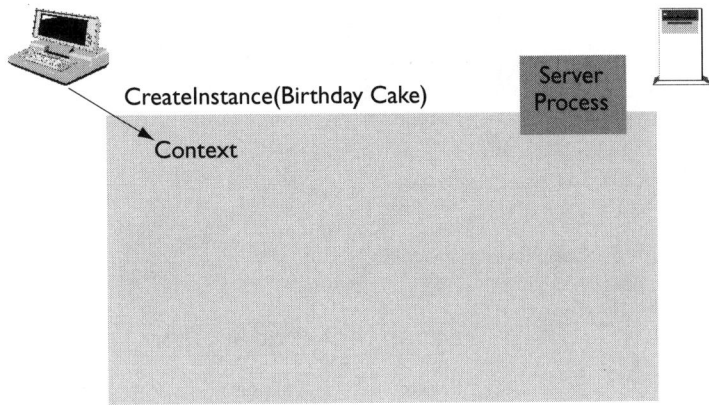

Figure 11.9 The birthday cake.

In Figure 11.10, note that the component has four categories:

Shape = round, square, bundt
Cake flavor = chocolate, vanilla, lemon
Frosting flavor = vanilla, chocolate, strawberry
Candles = yes or no

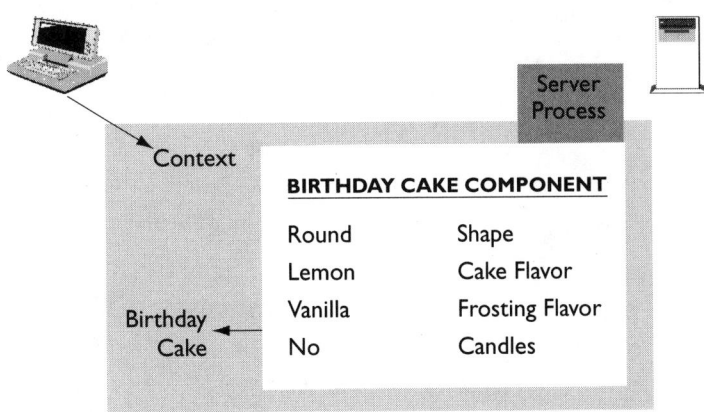

Figure 11.10 The choices.

286 Chapter 11

As shown in Figures 11.11–11.20, the customer sets `cakeshape`, `cakeflavor`, and `frostingflavor`, and specifies to include or not to include candles. Now the set is complete, and the system builds the birthday cake. The system then returns to the default settings to build standard birthday cakes until a new `Setshape` instance occurs.

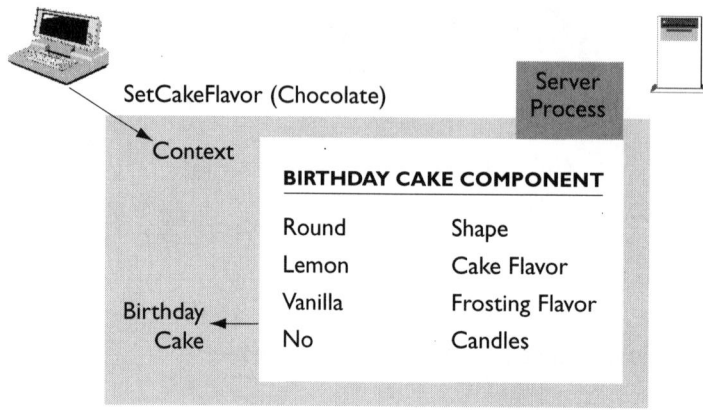

Figure 11.11 Setting the flavor.

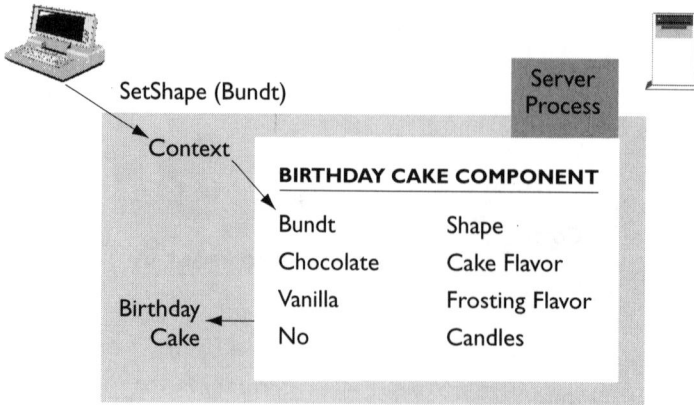

Figure 11.12 Flavor complete.

Active Middleware

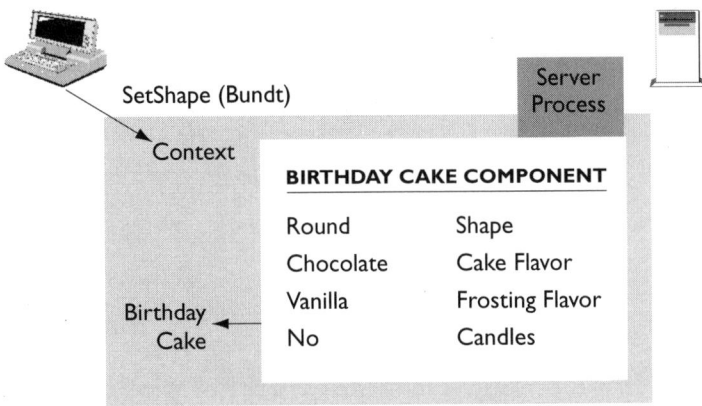

Figure 11.13 Choose the shape.

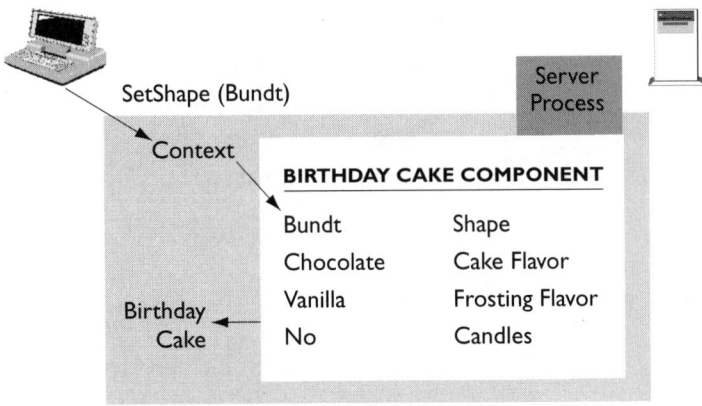

Figure 11.14 Shape complete.

288   Chapter 11

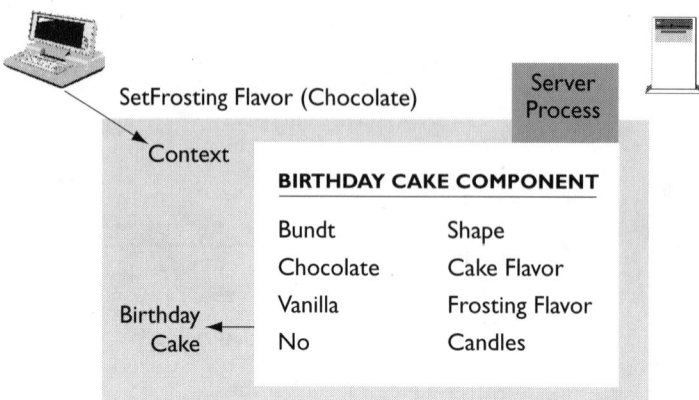

Figure 11.15 Choosing the frosting.

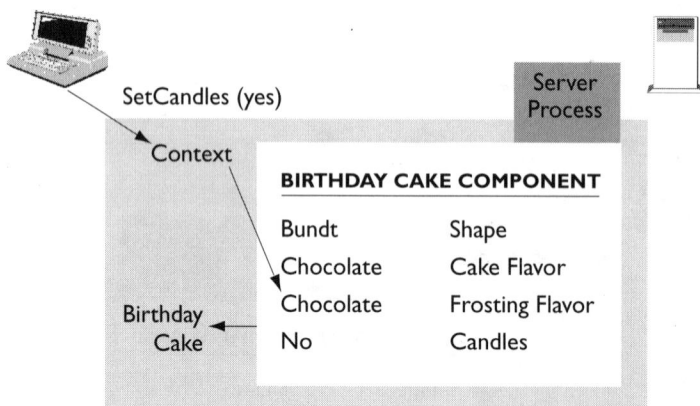

Figure 11.16 Frosting type complete; choose candles.

Active Middleware 289

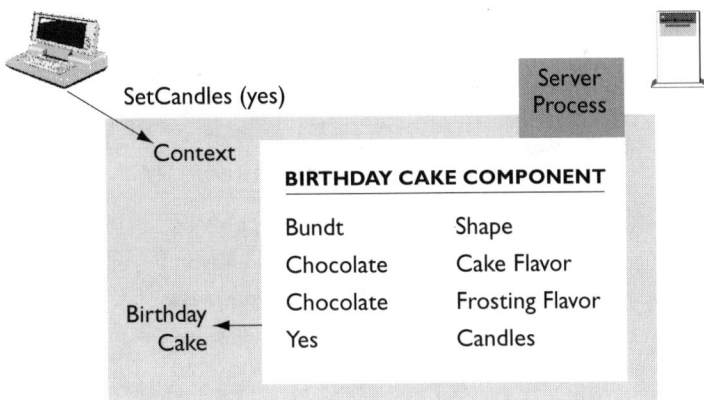

Figure 11.17 Candles complete.

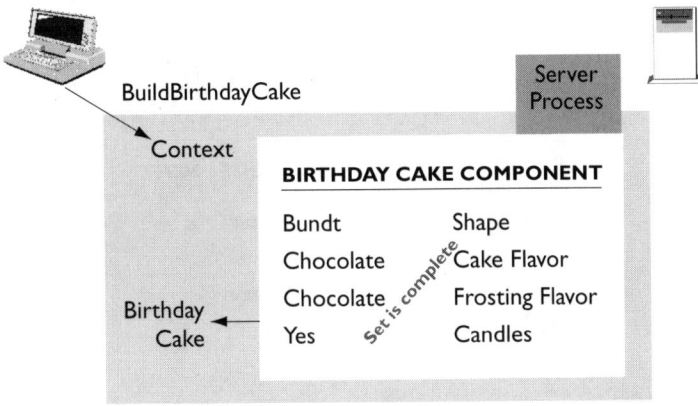

Figure 11.18 Completion of a set.

Chapter 11

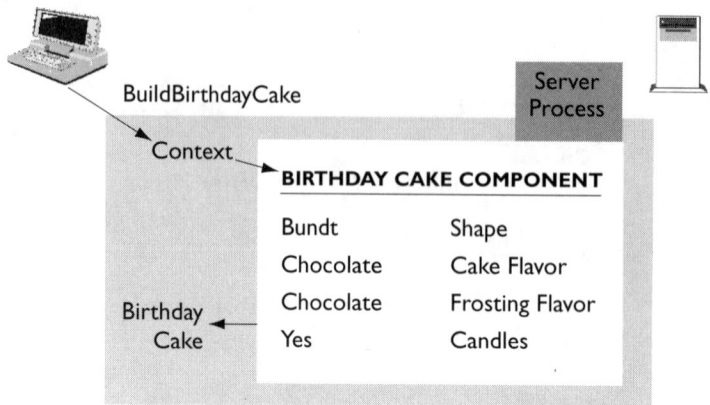

Figure 11.19 Building the cake.

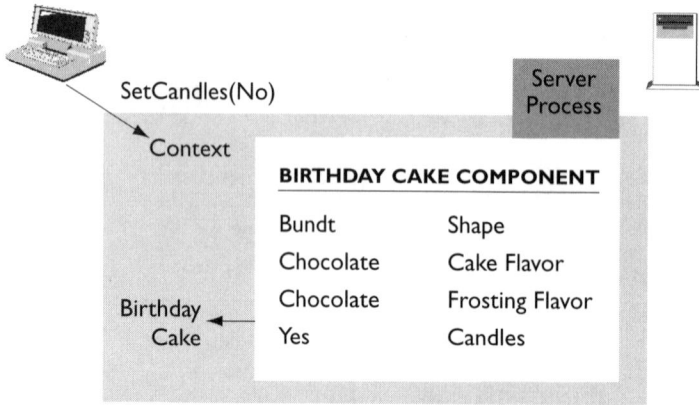

Figure 11.20 A new request.

Server Processes

Transaction Server manages two types of models: the object-oriented behavior model, which is state-oriented, and on-line transaction processing, which is the stateless model discussed in the preceding section.

A server process is a system process that handles the execution of the application component. A component is called by a client issuing a DCOM or COM request to the server process (see Figure 11.21).

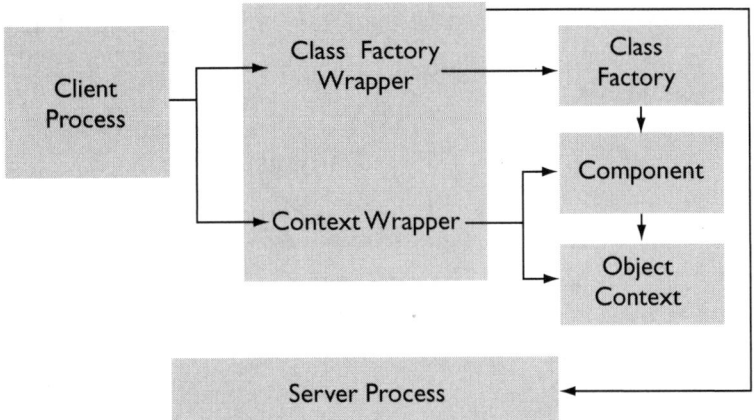

Figure 11.21 Server and client processes.

The call is made to the context wrapper, which receives and forwards calls to the context, as well as to the class factory wrapper, which tells the component's class factory to start. In object-oriented programming, a class defines object properties as well as class behavior methods. The practical implication is scalability. For example, if a pool is empty and a transaction needs more copies of an object, it will use a component's class factory to create an additional object needed by a transaction.

Microsoft Transaction Server spawns multiple screen processes to ensure scalability. The component runs in a server process, in client processes, or directly into SQL Server and IIS.

Resource Manager

As you might guess, Transaction Server uses transactions as the basis for all processes. This means that data access is protected at the transaction level. A resource manager handles data that survives system shutdown. Items that are durable and thereby last over time include current orders, inventory, accounts receivable, and accounts payable. A Distributed Transaction Coordinator (DTC) resource manager helps coordinate commit and rollbacks along with isolating client transactions. Resource managers include SQL Server and persistent messages. Microsoft Distributed Transaction Coordinator provides the actual transactions and is the transaction manager.

In a transaction the customer is involved in a commit or no commit situation; the transaction occurs or is aborted. There is no gray area. Think of a Boolean statement. The answer is true or false; there is no in-between. The same principle applies to a transaction in order to maintain data and system integrity.

A resource manager is a subsystem, such as a database, that keeps the transaction data protected. Because it is coordinated by the local DTC, questionable transactions are resolved locally. Therefore, DTC can override questionable transactions and free locked records (see Figure 11.22).

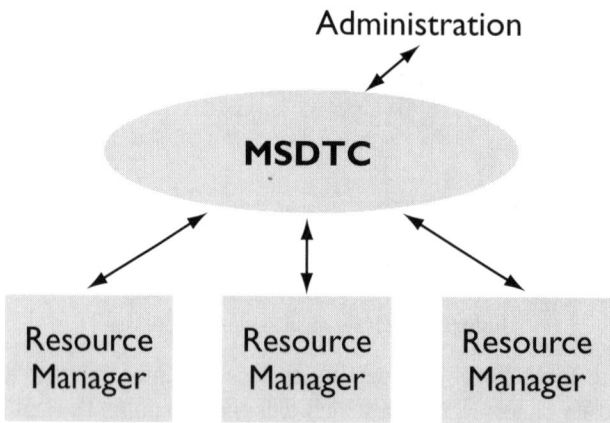

Figure 11.22 MS DTC and the resource managers.

Consistency ensures database usefulness by validating the position of each record occurrence and checking the integrity of the data.

The resource managers handle the isolation of uncommitted records during an active transaction.

Durable data survives system failures. To assist in the durability effort, Transaction Server logs activities to allow you to recover the data. In-between states of a transaction are not seen outside the transaction itself. This means that concurrency is not an issue for the developer.

Resource Dispensers

Resource dispensers are similar to resource managers. The difference is that resource dispensers do not guarantee the ability to roll back the transaction to a previous state or guarantee that the data is kept alive after a system failure. The two resource dispensers in Transaction Server are the ODBC Resource Dispenser and Shared Property Manager. A toolkit is provided for developing resource dispensers.

ODBC Resource Dispenser

ODBC Resource Dispenser manages database connections pools (see Figure 11.23).

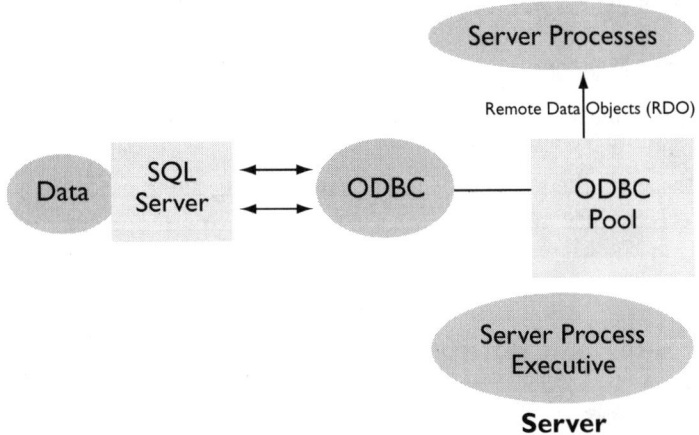

Figure 11.23 ODBC Resource Dispenser.

Any component running in the Transaction Server run-time environment uses ODBC directly or indirectly, and the component automatically uses ODBC Resource Dispenser. The dispenser automatically reclaims and reuses the connections (see Figure 11.24).

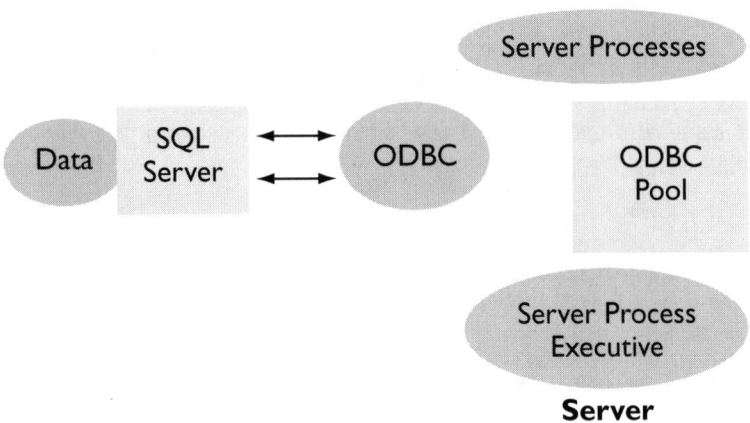

Figure 11.24 Efficient reuse of the connection.

The ODBC Data Source Names must be configured separately on each system. The connection pooler will detect whether the database is XA-compliant or an OLE transaction within the Microsoft products. The XA interface is a bidirectional interface between a transaction manager and resource managers. This standard has been agreed upon for all major databases in the X/Open committee.

SHARED PROPERTY MANAGER

Shared Property Manager (SPM) is used to share state across transactions. For example, suppose that you create Web page hit counters and receipt numbers (to avoid database hotspots). In this case, the state needs to be shared among the transactions.

SPM interfaces use these COM interfaces: IsharedPropertyGroupManager, ISharedPropertyGroup, and IsharedProperty (see Figure 11.25).

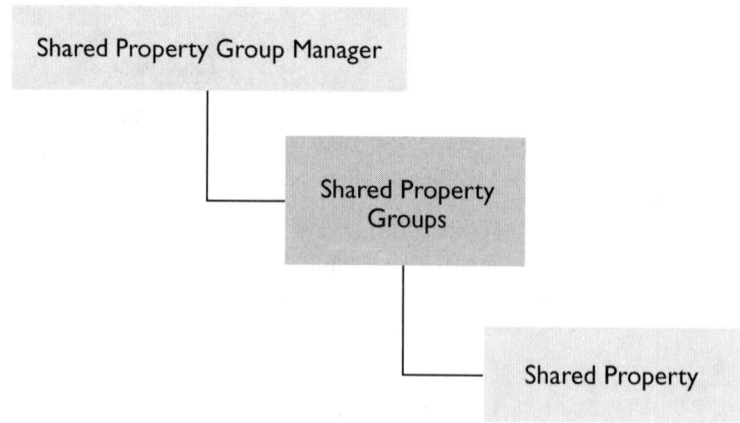

Figure 11.25 The shared properties.

To initialize a shared property, each customer call creates a shared property group. Here is the appropriate Visual Basic code:

```
Dim spmMgr As SharedPropertyGroupManager
Dim spmGroup As SharedPropertyGroup
Dim spmPropNextNumber As SharedProperty
Dim bExists As Boolean
Dim iNextValue As Integer

' Create the SharedPropertyGroupManager,
' SharedPropertyGroup, and SharedProperty.
Set spmMgr = CreateObject _
   ("MTxSpm.SharedPropertyGroupManager.1")
```

```
Set spmGroup = spmMgr.CreatePropertyGroup _
   ("Counter", LockSetGet, Process, bExists)
Set spmPropNextNumber = _
   spmGroup.CreateProperty("Next", bExists)

' Get the next number and increment it.
iNextValue = spmPropNextNumber.Value
spmPropNextNumber.Value = _
   spmPropNextNumber.Value + 1
```

Be careful when using Shared Property Manager. You must assume that there will be a set of concurrent processes that access a shared database. The problem is to maintain database consistency, which may be violated as a result of interleaving database operations. This is known as a *concurrency anomaly*.

Microsoft Distributed Transaction Coordinator

MS DTC is a service that coordinates transactions that span multiple resource managers.

The client sees a transaction as a single event. It happens (commit) or does not happen (abort). If a customer wants to credit money to one account and debit money on another account, as in a transfer between checking and savings, then both the customer and the developer want to ensure that both accounts change or neither account changes. The problem is what to do with the client's event if there is a system failure. The concept of Transaction Server is that it prevents the loss of the events by tracking and logging them.

For example, when a person goes to a store and wants to buy a product, the salesperson will not only handle that transaction but will also customize it to meet the customer's need. Suppose that the person, Mary Smith, is a regular customer at the local espresso bar. The food server will usually begin the transaction as soon as Mary enters the building. The food server may ask whether Mary is using a check, credit card, or cash. If Mary wants a house coffee today and not an espresso, she will have to redirect the transaction. If she forgot her cash, checks, and credit card, the food server may cancel the transaction.

A transaction follows this same basic principle: Several independent entities must agree. If any party disagrees, the deal is off. Once they all agree, the transaction can occur. MS DTC performs this transaction coordination role for the other components of the COM architecture.

The salesperson's role is called the transaction manager. The customers in the transaction that implement transaction-protected resources, such as relational databases, are called resource managers. The transaction occurs as shown in Figure 11.26.

The two-phase commit is a process by which MS DTC coordinates data updates on multiple servers (see Figure 11.27).

As shown in Figure 11.28, the DTC on SQL Server computer A is the coordinator for committing the transactions. The process follows sequentially from computer A through computer D. Phase 1 of the two-phase commit is finished, and computer A has a committed record in the log. The call from B to C has failed, resulting in an unresolved state. Next, the system administrator forces a commit on computer C. C will now try to pass the commit to D. D commits and forgets the transaction. This passes a message back to C to forget the transaction. The problem is that B and C are still not talking, so B must remember the transaction. The system administrator forces B to forget the transaction. B communicates with A to forget the transaction. During the transaction, the DTC coordinates all multinode transactions.

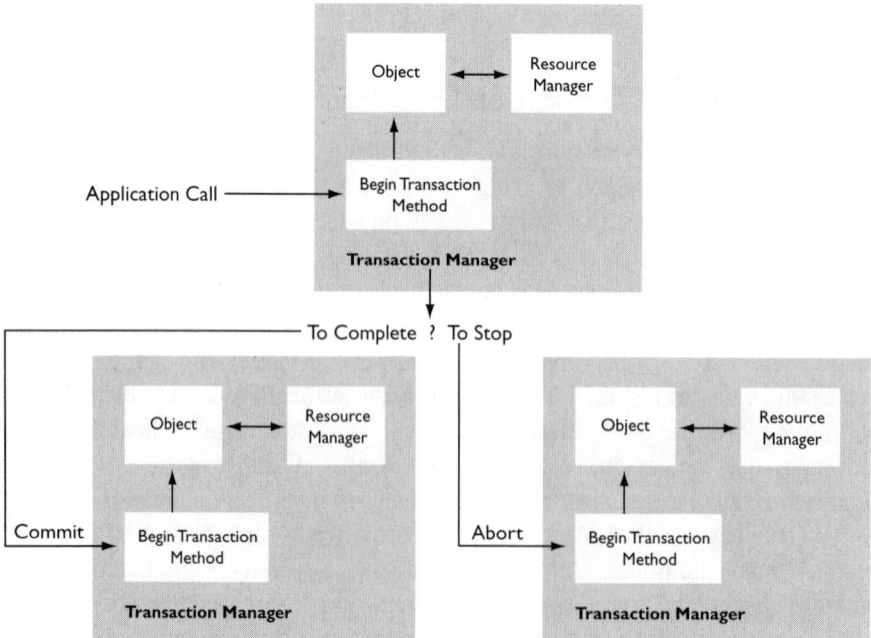

Figure 11.26 The two-phase commit: Either commit or abort the transaction.

One of the DTCs is the parent and acts as the coordinator, so the system may have a tree of DTCs. The resource manager implements the two-phase commit to the transaction manager (DTC). The application communicates with the DTC to begin, commit, or abort the transaction (see Figure 11.29).

Active Middleware

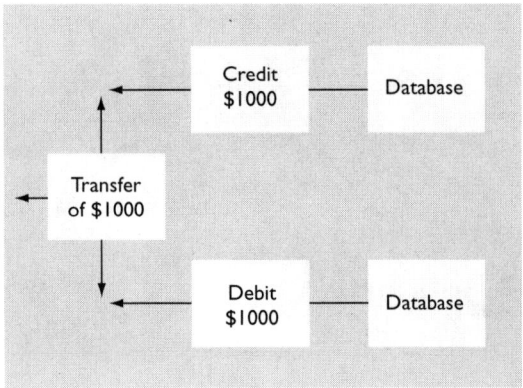

Figure 11.27 Transactions simplified: The credit must equal the debit.

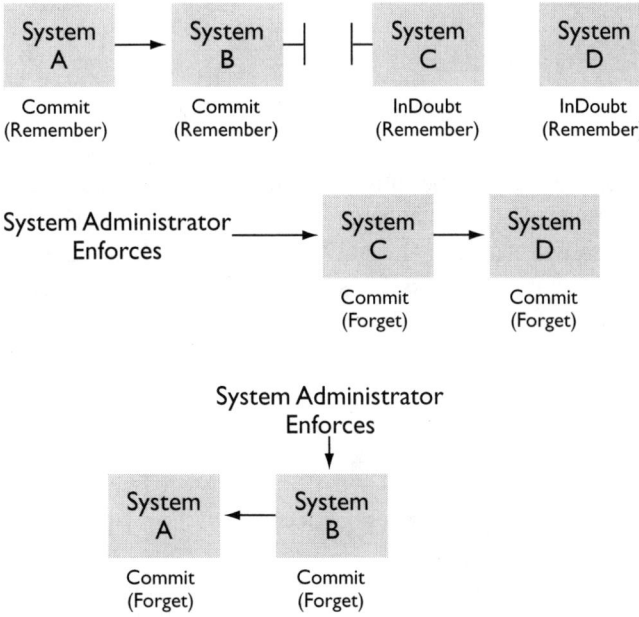

Figure 11.28 Multinode transactions.

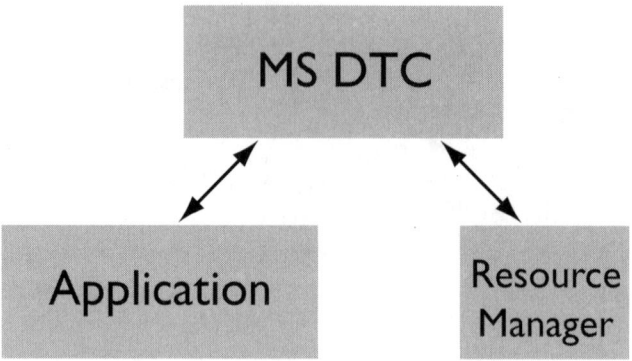

Figure 11.29 MS DTC communication cycle.

To begin a DTC transaction, the system calls `TransactionObject`. Here is an example using C++ code:

```
Hresult hr;
ItransactionDispenser* pDtc;
Itransaction* pTc;
hr= DtcGetTransactionManager(NULL, NULL)
```

The system first gets `TransactionDispenser` and then calls the `BeginTransaction` method.

The XA protocol is used to perform the transactions. The point is that Microsoft is meeting the database transaction standards that bridge NT to the UNIX world. The DTC becomes an XA resource manager and an XA transaction manager. As a result, you can implement multiple heterogeneous databases in the Transaction Server environment (see Figures 11.30a and 11.30b).

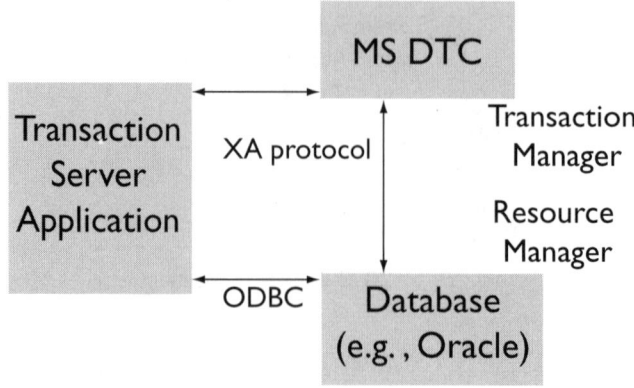

Figure 11.30a Transaction view by the transaction manager.

Active Middleware 299

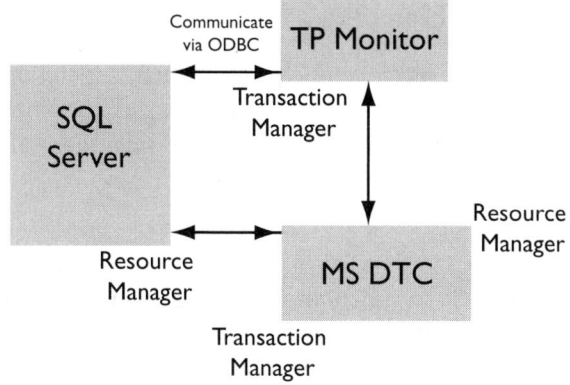

Figure 11.30b Transaction view by the resource manager.

Transaction Server Explorer

Transaction Server Explorer helps you package, deploy, and administer your applications. MTS applications consist of one or more *packages*: a set of components that performs related application functions that are organized into one deployment unit. You can use MTS Explorer's graphical user interface to perform development, deployment, and administration tasks on your package files. The MTS Explorer hierarchy depicts how the items in the run-time environment are organized so that you can manipulate your applications on the package, component, interface, and method levels. Its interface lets you perform tasks ranging from creating a new package to providing a brief description of a method on an interface for administrators to reference (see Figure 11.31).

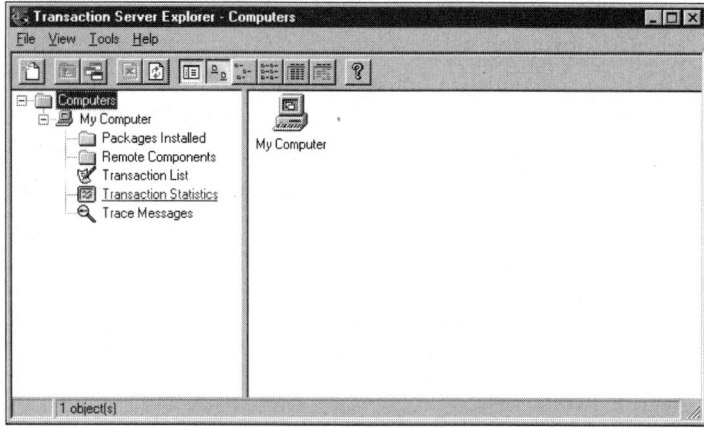

Figure 11.31 MTS Explorer.

Server and Client Issues

As you consider designing and implementing successful transactions, you must understand client and server issues. On the client side, the goal is to give customers what they expect (such as automatic refreshing of the data). On the server side, the goal is to minimize network traffic and increase system efficiency.

The Client Side

You must determine basic client functionality as well as minimize response time. For example, you may want to provide regular updating of data. In a Windows application, you can use dynamic data exchange (DDE) technology. In DDE, any Windows program can share data with another Windows program through a link. In an on-line database, you must consider how many calls to make to the server, increasing IIS resource needs versus embedding all functionality into SQL Server.

You may want to view as much of the database as possible and provide the user with small sections at a time. This arrangement is similar to Index Server, which returns ten records at a time. This approach minimizes communications traffic over the Internet connection and gives the customer reasonable response times.

If a Transaction Server object A uses Transaction Server object B, then A is called a *client* of B. It becomes a *base client* if the object is outside the direct control of the Transaction Server run time.

Careful attention should be given to lookup lists in client applications. Lookup lists, possibly containing tens or even hundreds of records, usually reside on multiple screens. They are loaded every time a screen is loaded into memory. Although guaranteeing data currency, this architecture can slow the network in systems that have a large user base. System designers should investigate whether it is feasible to load these lists once and cache the results to be used throughout the program. This strategy speeds up the client and reduces network traffic. Additionally, the type of data residing in data lookup lists is usually fairly static, so keeping data current is often not as important in practice as it is in perception. When the data is less static, two alternatives would be to consider a user-initiated refresh function or to construct MTS servers capable of evaluating data changes and returning data only when it has changed.

One of the greatest benefits of MTS is that the servers are easy to interact with through code. If you have ever programmed an application that uses an ActiveX-based server, you already have all the experience needed to access MTS servers. Calling an MTS server is as simple as the following Visual Basic code:

Active Middleware 301

```
Dim obj as object
Set obj = CreateObject("Projects.clsProjects")
obj.Method
Set obj = Nothing
```

MTS handles all the complex issues, shielding the client developer. The only criterion to which the client developer must adhere is that the MTS server application be registered on the client machine. Depending on where the ActiveX-based server resides, COM (if local) or DCOM (if distributed) will handle the call from the client to the server.

The Server Side

To understand how to manage the server side during design, there are two areas of importance: Transaction Server Executive and the run-time environment.

TRANSACTION SERVER EXECUTIVE

Transaction Server Executive is a DLL that provides the run-time services for Transaction Server components. These services include thread and context management. This DLL is loaded into the processes that host application components and runs transparently in the background.

Let's look at the context. In Figure 11.32, note that each object has a ContextObject, which is provided by Transaction Server. The client, interfacing to the object via IObjectContext, uses the GetObjectContext API and makes a call to the object's context, as shown in Figure 11.33. The information in context provides both transactional data and the security identity. The ObjectContext interface (IObjectContext) is detailed in Figure 11.34. Note that the interface is obtained via the GetObjectContext call, as noted in the API in Figure 11.33.

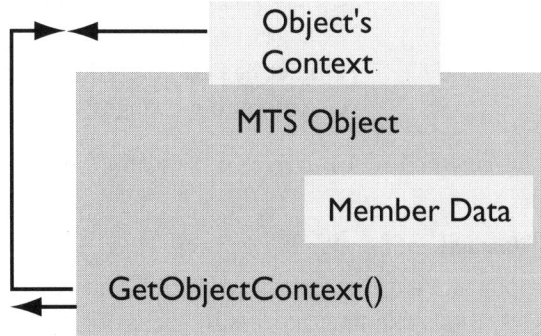

Figures 11.32 An object's context.

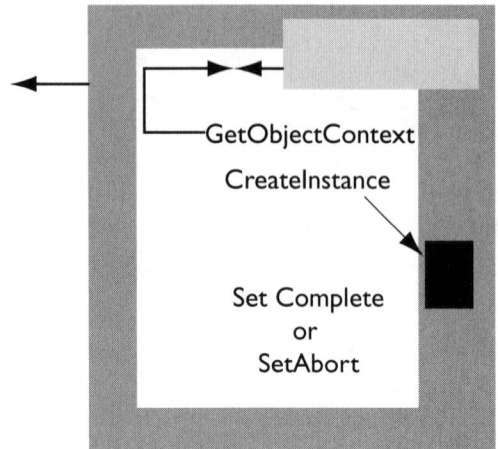

Figures 11.33 Using the `GetObjectContext` API.

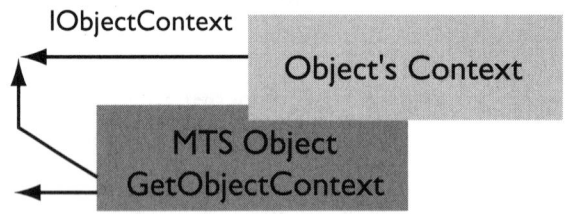

IObjectContext:

    Create Instance = Launches a new object (inheritance)

    SetComplete = Object has complete its effort
                              Changes are OK

    SetAbort = Object has completed its effort
                             Unacceptable changes: abort

Figures 11.34 `IObjectContext` interface.

MTS Run-Time Environment

MTS application components execute in the MTS run-time environment. Transaction Server Executive assists in this run-time process by managing system resources (such as processes, threads, and database connections) and managing server component creation, execution, and deletion as well as initiating and controlling transactions. This approach allows the server application to scale and ensures application reliability. Transaction

Server Executive also provides security and tools for configuration, management, and deployment.

In the run-time environment, components access databases via ODBC, as shown earlier in Figure 11.23. This run-time environment can best be seen in Figures 11.35–11.45. In this example, you will see the basic run-time environment when two clients access six records in a database.

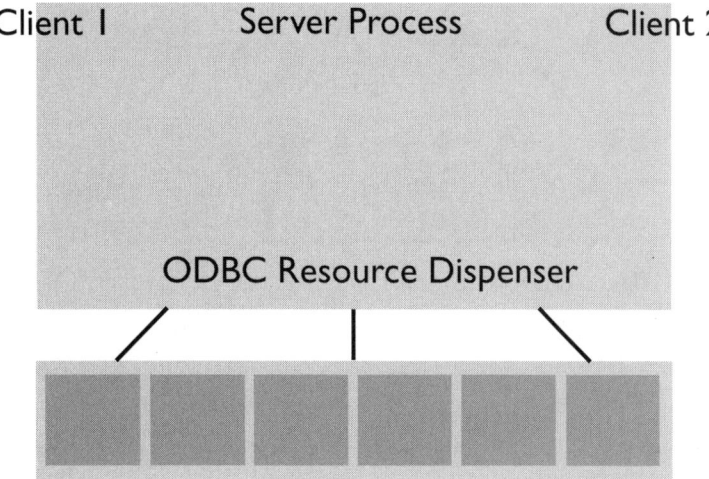

Figure 11.35 Database with six records, three ODBC connections, and two clients.

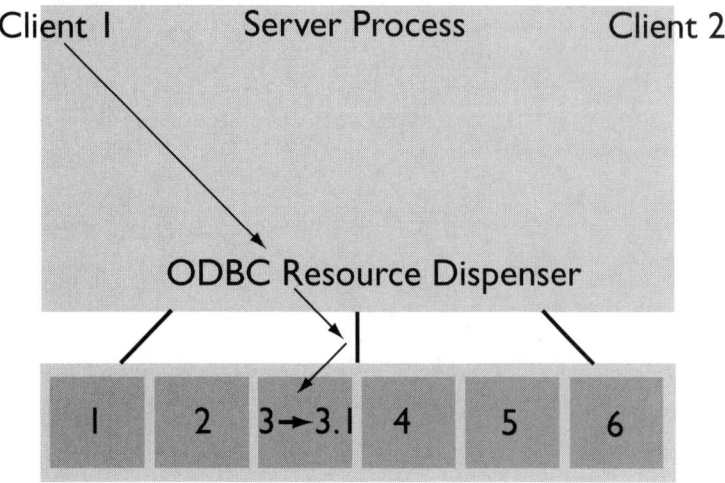

Figure 11.36 Client 1 accessing data.

Chapter 11

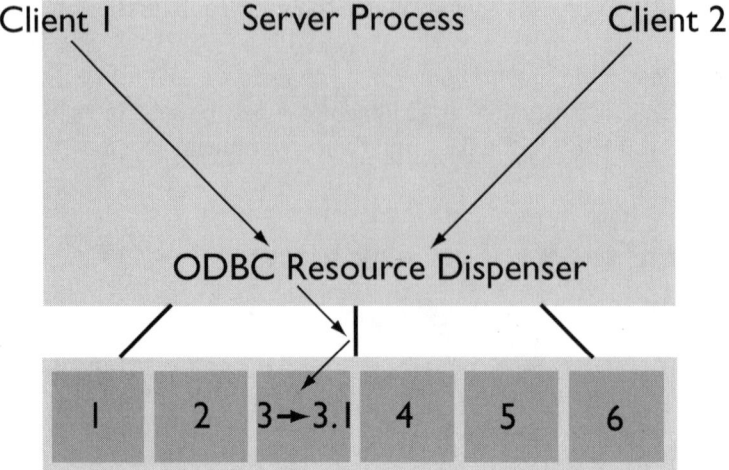

Figure 11.37 Client 1 updates record; client 2 accessing data.

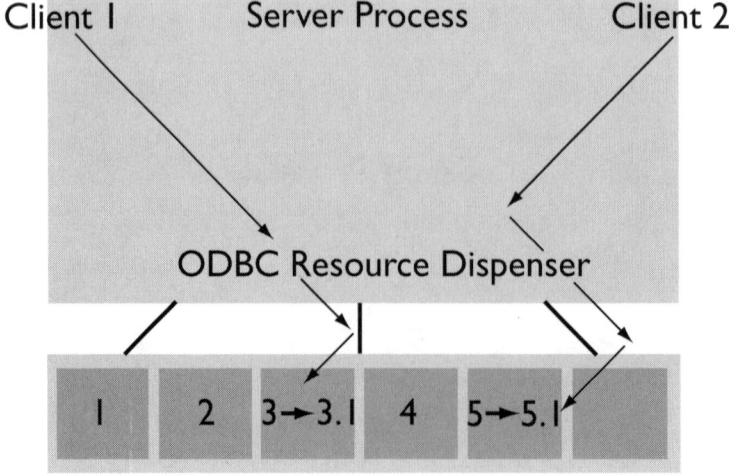

Figure 11.38 Client 2 accesses data.

Active Middleware 305

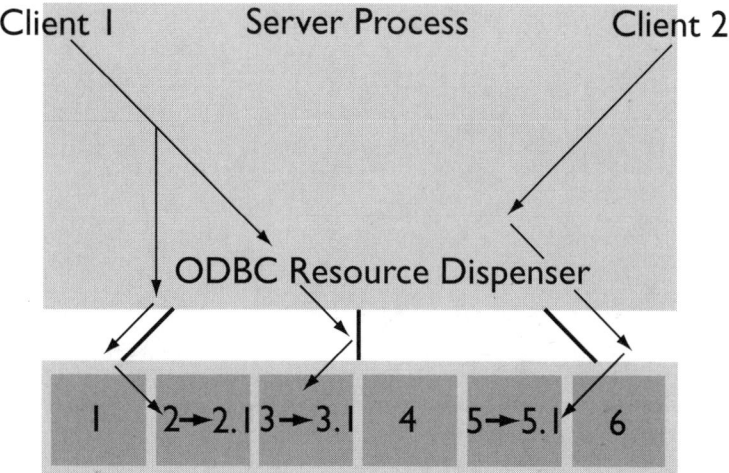

Figure 11.39 Client 1 is back while client 2 still in records.

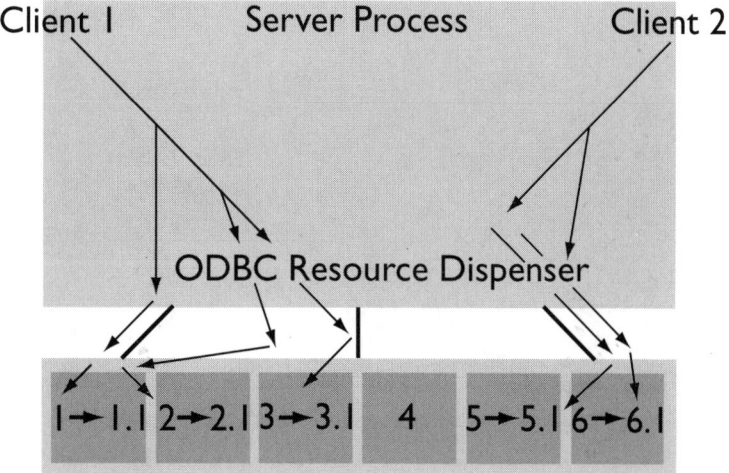

Figure 11.40 Client 1 and 2 updating more records.

Chapter 11

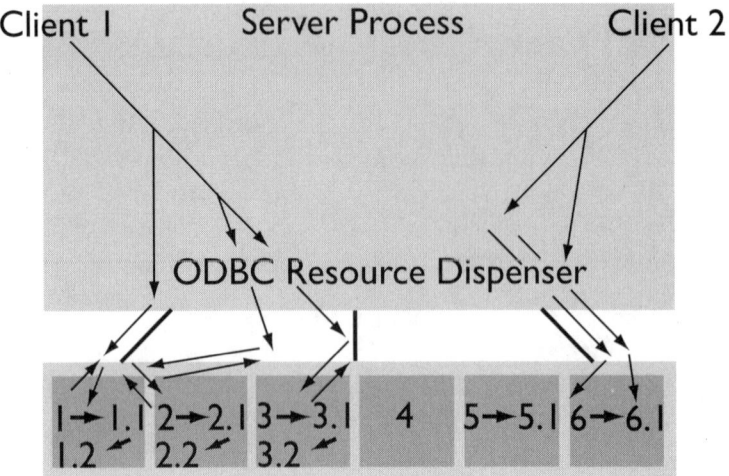

Figure 11.41 New updates to records.

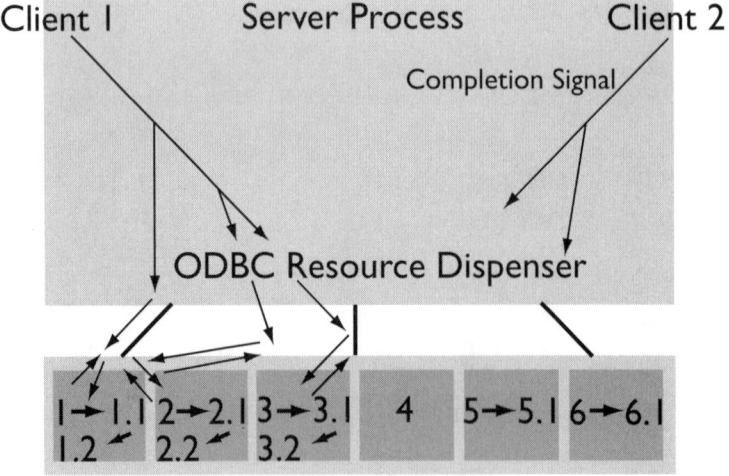

Figure 11.42 Client 2 is complete.

Active Middleware 307

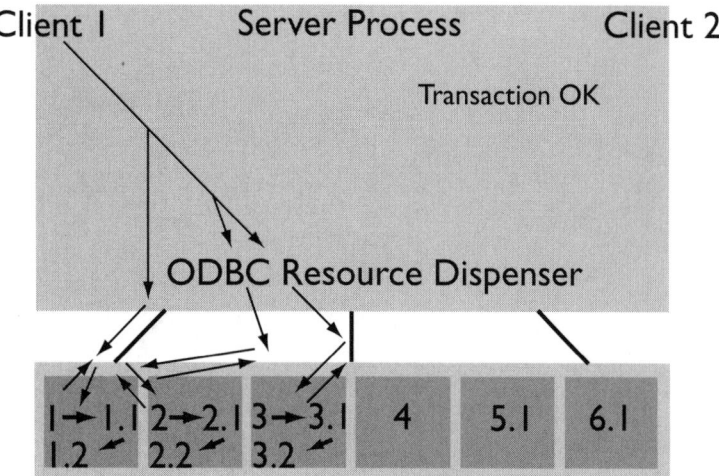

Figure 11.43 Transaction succeeded for client 2.

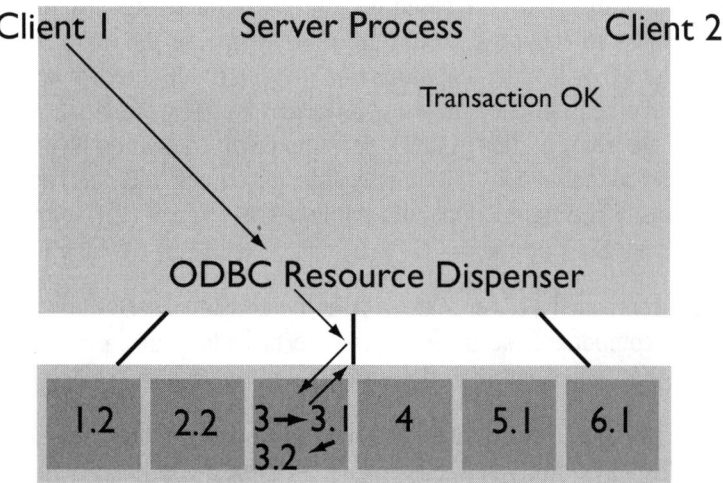

Figure 11.44 Client 1 finishing updates.

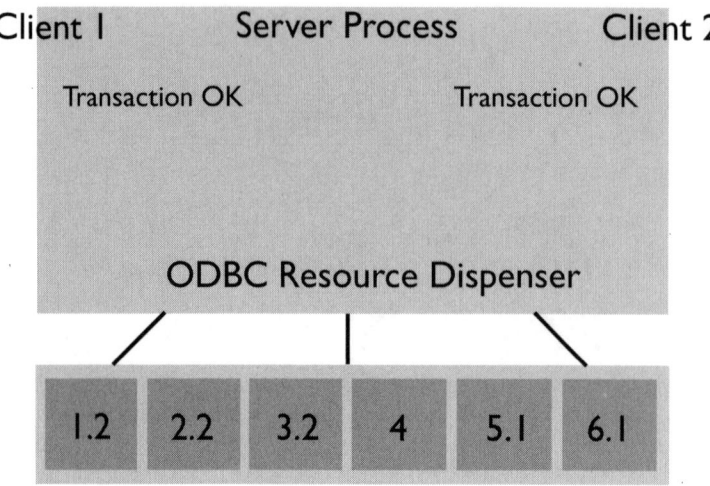

Figure 11.45 Transaction succeeded for client 1.

APPLICATIONS

The application-building process is based on integral resource sharing, making a scalable transaction. To build an application using the MTS approach, you build components for a single user. The server will scale as appropriate. You determine the component state (stateful or stateless) following completion. Using interfaces (such as Icontext and Iobject (as discussed in the preceding section) allows the components to be reusable.

You can write code that does not directly share resources; you need not concern yourself with that issue. The transactions and context are automatic. This method is implemented for two reasons:

- To make components easier to develop and maintain and therefore robust.
- To make components scalable in order to provide high performance and server availability for one client or 100 clients.

As noted before, the developer creates transaction components using the same tools (such as Visual Java, Visual C, and Visual Basic) as in ActiveX development. You can write the code focused on the user and not on the system issues. You can compile the code as a DLL and install the DLL into MTS via the MTS Explorer. Related components are put into packages. The executables are put in a location for client-side testing (see Figure 11.46).

Active Middleware 309

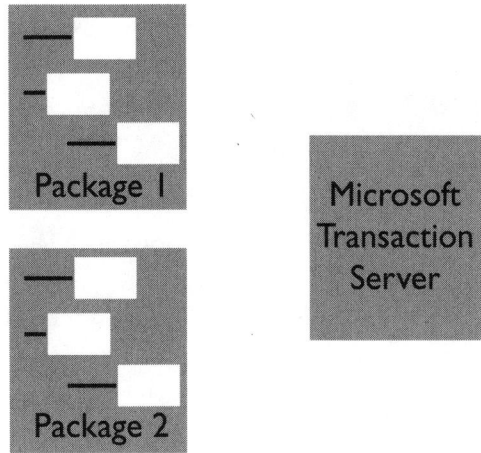

Figure 11.46 Building the package.

The packages are the method of deployment. You install the package on the server (see Figures 11.47 and 11.48) and set the server identity used to access external resources. You map roles and authority to NT users and groups. The final step is to configure client machines with authentication or allow the server to call the client.

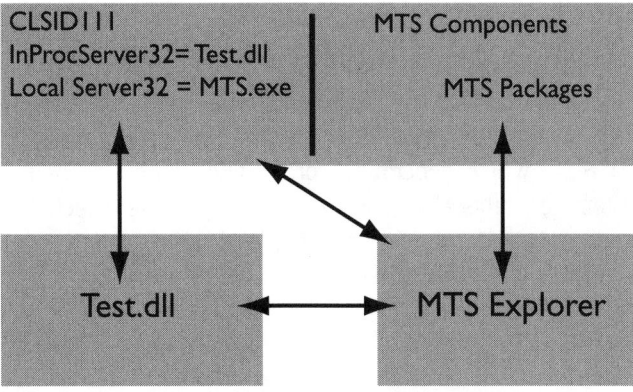

Figure 11.47 Installing a component.

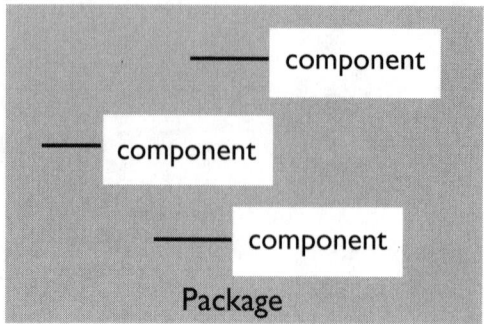

Figure 11.48 The package.

What about database connections during this process? A database connection is opened at the beginning of a normal SQL Server client/server application, thereby allowing rapid response to the customer. In Windows applications as well as in the Web implementation, the database is used only a small percentage of the time. The problem arises when tens to hundreds of customers want to get to the same database and hold those connections. MTS handles these problems on an as-needed basis by using the ODBC resource dispenser discussed previously. This also means that very little of a client application needs to be running on the client's machine. To deal with the limiting use of resources, MTS uses a just-in-time activation method.

Just-in-Time: ..How to Activate and Deactivate Objects

Just-in-time (JIT) activation is shown in Figures 11.49–11.59. JIT is the method that MTS uses to activate and deactivate objects. As a customer makes a request, Transaction Server runs `CreateInstance`, which generates a proxy and context. When the transaction is complete, the system generates a `SetComplete` to recycle the object. The proxy and context are left in place. This is As Soon As Possible (ASAP) deactivation.

Active Middleware 311

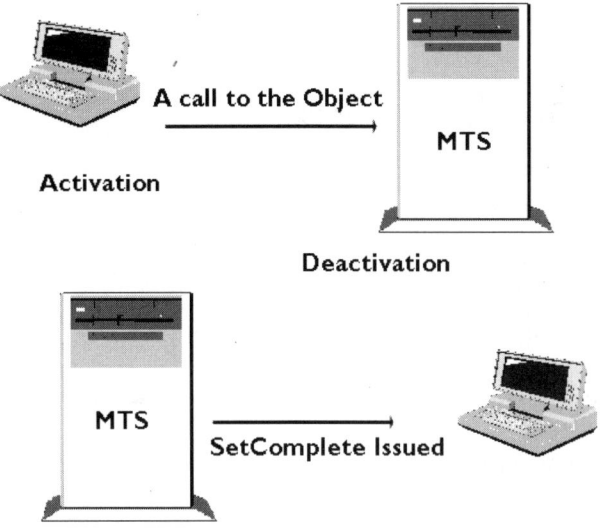

Figure 11.49 Activation and deactivation.

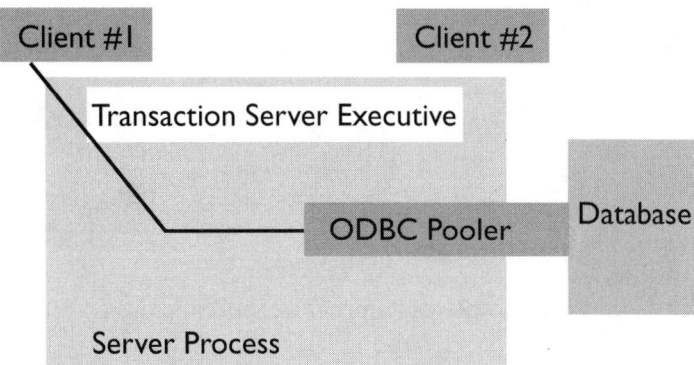

Client 1 issues a call, which gets an ODBC connection

Figure 11.50 Client #1 issues the call for data.

312 Chapter 11

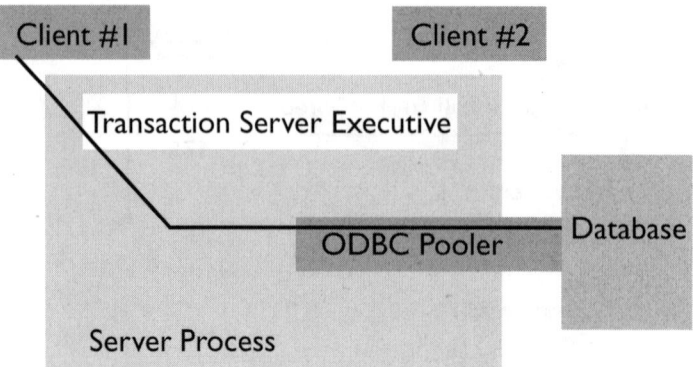

Client # 1 makes a connection to the database

Figure 11.51 ODBC activated and deactivated as needed.

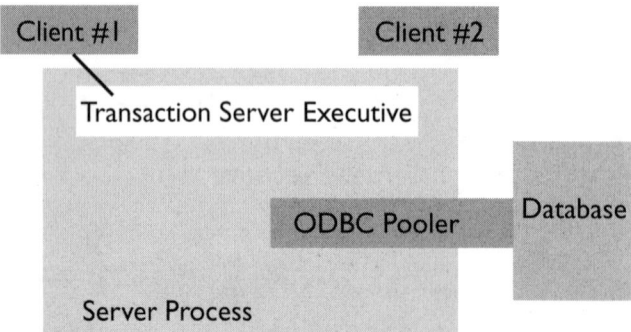

Client # 1 completes its process: SetComplete so that the object is deactivated

Figure 11.52 Client #1 completes its process.

Active Middleware 313

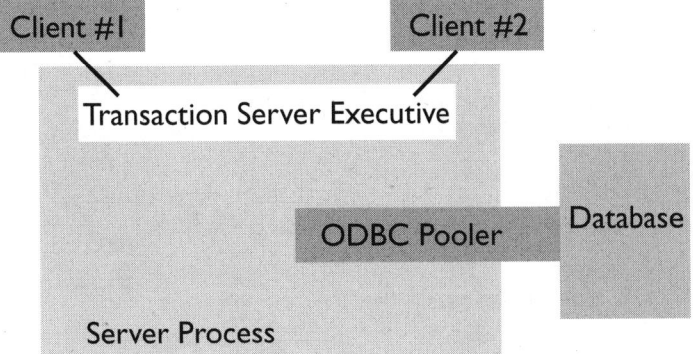

Client # 2 issues a call, which gets an ODBC connection

Figure 11.53 Client #2 issues a call.

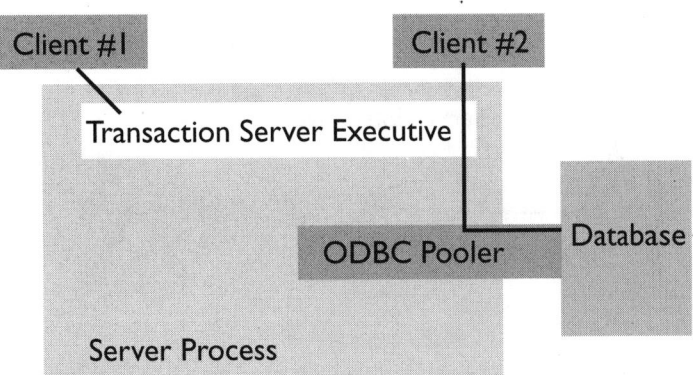

Client # 2 makes a connection to the database

Figure 11.54 Client #2 makes a connection.

Chapter 11

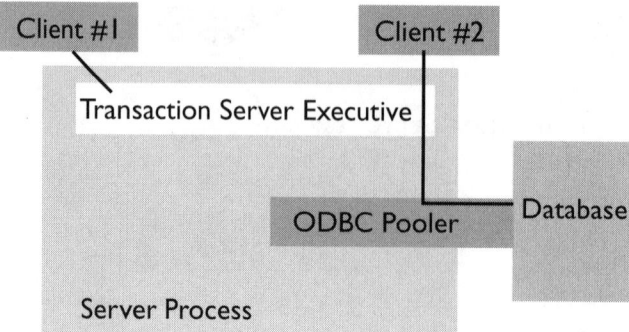

Client # 2 completes its process: SetComplete so that the object is deactivated

Figure 11.55 Client #2 completes its process.

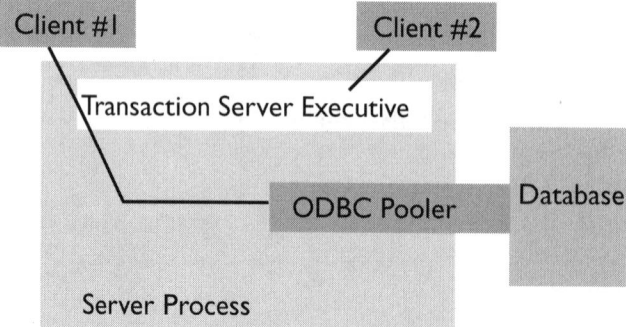

Client 1 issues a second call, which gets an ODBC connection (connection reclaimed)

Figure 11.56 Client #1 issues a second call.

Active Middleware 315

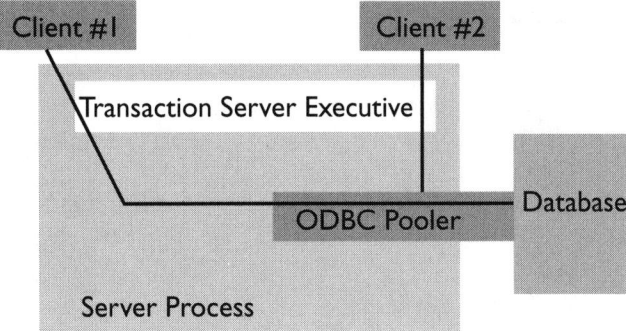

Client #1 makes a connection to the database
Client #2 issues a second call (connection reclaimed)

Figure 11.57 Client #1 makes a connection; client #2 issues a call.

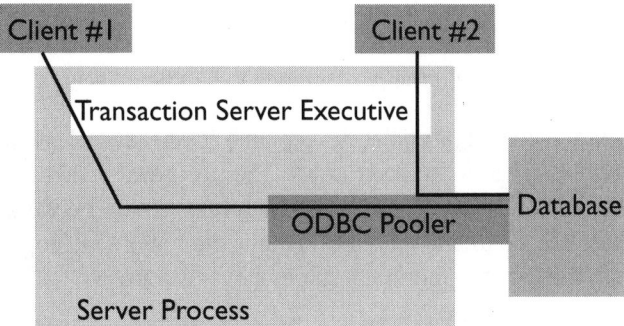

Client #1 making further recorded changes
Client #2 makes a connectioin to the database

Figure 11.58 Client #1 gets more data; client #2 makes a connection.

316   Chapter 11

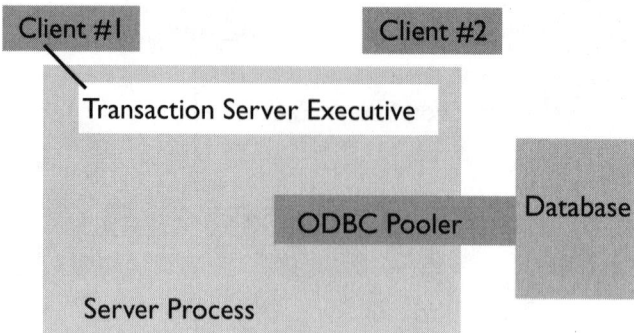

Client #1 completes its process: SetComplete so that the object is deactivated
Client #2 completes its process: SetComplete so that the object is deactivated
All resources reclaimed.

Figure 11.59 Both are complete.

Instead of JIT, you can use two alternative methods to handle objects.

1. Create, use, and release an object every time it's needed. This method conserves server resources. That is the good news. The bad news is that it decreases system performance and scalability, especially if the servers are on networked machines.
2. Maintain a reference to an object throughout the life of the program. This method is faster than the first one, but it consumes server resources.

The inability to properly scale in method 1 and the resource consumption problem in method 2 means that neither method works in a large distributed system.

This is where JIT activation and ASAP deactivation come into play. When an object is deactivated, it becomes available for reuse by other clients. What happens if the client has a valid reference to the object while being deactivated? MTS will continue the deactivation process (ASAP), but it will "remember" the reference. When the client calls another method, the reference is automatically bound to a new object (JIT). The client does not know that it is a new object.

MTS also has a security mechanism based on user roles. *Roles* are names for logical groupings of users. They are defined during development and assigned at deployment time. The administrator restricts components or particular component interfaces through role assignment.

Building a Sample Application

You can use object-oriented programming to take advantage of components in building applications. To accomplish this, it is best to build the sample component, Account, that is shipped with Transaction Server.

In the following sections you will learn how to do the following:

- Create the Account component. Create a project (**Account.vbp**) with a class module (**Account.cls**). A module is a procedure that acts, or performs functionality, on an object.
- Create the Bank package using Transaction Server Explorer.
- Install the Account component in the Bank package using Transaction Server Explorer.
- Run and monitor the Account component using the bank client and Transaction Server Explorer.
- Modify the Account component to add a database connection.

Create the Component

NOTE

You are assumed to have a basic understanding of Visual Basic. Do not try to install an executable file (**.exe**) in Transaction Server. Remember that TS runs DLLs.

You can create the Account DLL using **Account.vbp** or **Account.mdp** (Java or C++). Here is an example of the post method for Visual C++:

```
// CAccount.cpp : Implementation of CAccountApp and DLL registration.

// Microsoft Transaction Server Sample Application
// Copyright (C) 1996 Microsoft Corporation
// All rights reserved.

#include "stdafx.h"
#include "Account.h"
#include "CAccount.h"
#include <stdio.h>
#include <mtx.h>
#include <sql.h>
#include <sqlext.h>

#define RETURN_BUF_SIZE    512
/////////////////////////////////////////////////////////////////////
//
```

```
#define SQLSUCCEEDED(rc) (rc == SQL_SUCCESS || rc == SQL_SUCCESS_WITH_INFO)
//
//    Post: modifies the specified account by the specified amount
//
//    pbstrResult: a BSTR giving information.  NOTE: this can be set even on an error!
//    plRetVal   : -1 if success, 0 if not
//
//    returns:   S_OK or S_FALSE
//
STDMETHODIMP CAccount::Post(
   IN long lAccount,
   IN long lAmount,
   OUT BSTR* pbstrResult,
   OUT long* plRetVal)
{
   HRESULT hr = S_OK;
   RETCODE rc = SQL_SUCCESS;
   HENV henv = NULL;
   HDBC hdbc = NULL;
   HSTMT hstmt = NULL;
   SQLTCHAR szSqlStmt[300];

   *plRetVal = -1;
   *pbstrResult = SysAllocStringLen(NULL, RETURN_BUF_SIZE);
```

Create the Bank Package

To run the DLL you must create a package. As you know, the component just created is a business object that runs as a COM DLL. It can be written in ActiveX technologies, including Visual Basic, Visual C++, and Visual J++. It has MTS-specific properties and is hosted in the MTS server process.

A package is a set of related components (see Figure 11.60). It defines components that run in a server process with a trust boundary. It is the deployment unit.
In this example, you will work with one component of the Bank package. You will create a package called Bank that will contain the Account component. To create the Bank package, follow these steps:

1. On the Start menu, choose **Programs** and then choose **Microsoft Transaction Server**. Click **Transaction Server Explorer**.
2. Create a new package named Bank. In the Set Package Identity dialog box, select **Interactive user** (see Figure 11.61).

Active Middleware 319

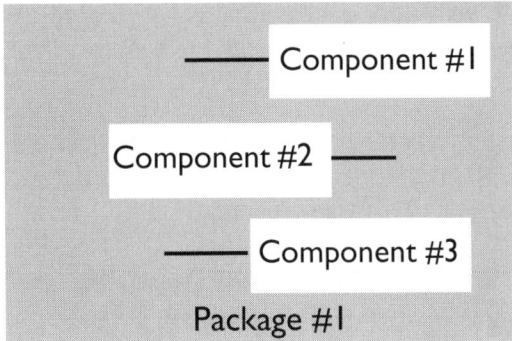

Related components that are deployed as a unit

Figure 11.60 The package.

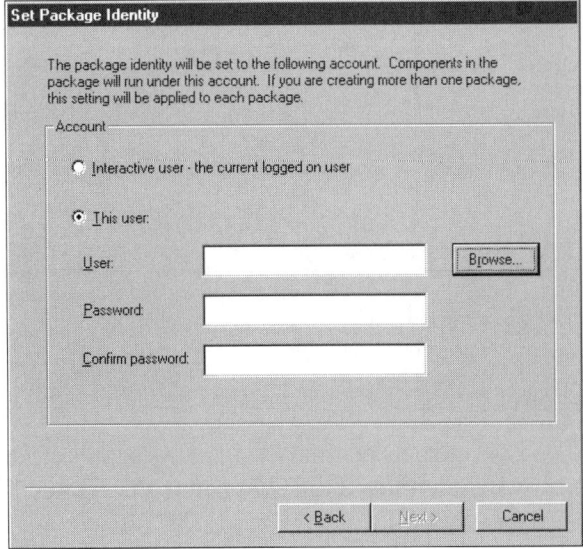

Figure 11.61 Package identity.

3. In the left pane of Transaction Server Explorer, select the computer for which you want to create a package. Open the **Packages Installed** folder for that computer. On the File menu, click **New** (see Figure 11.62).
(You can use the Package wizard to install a prebuilt package or create an empty package. If you create an empty package, you must add components and roles before it will be functional.)

4. Click the **Create an empty package** button (see Figure 11.63). Type a name for the new package and click **Next**. Specify the package identity in the Set Package Identity dialog box and then click **Finish**.

Please note that the system sets the default selection as the current user. This is the user who was logged into NT on the machine that is running the package. If you wish to change this default, choose the **This User** option.

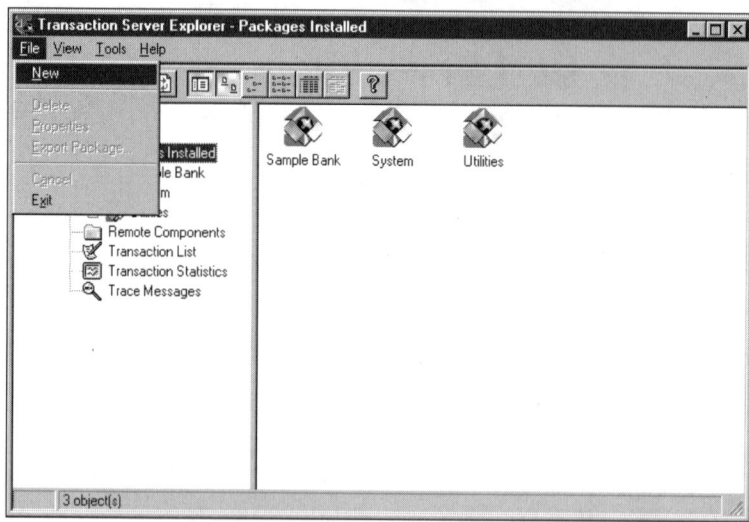

Figure 11.62 New package installation.

Install the Component

Now let's install the Account component into the Bank package. Use the Account component that you built in **\Mtx\Samples\Step1\Account.VB\VBAcct.DLL**. Follow these steps:

1. In the left pane of Transaction Server Explorer, select the computer where you want to install the component.
2. Open the **Packages Installed** folder and select the package where you want to install the component.
3. Open the **Components** folder.
4. On the File menu, click **New**.
5. Click the **Install new component(s)** button.
6. In the dialog box that appears, click **Add Files** to select the files you want to install (see Figure 11.64).

Active Middleware   321

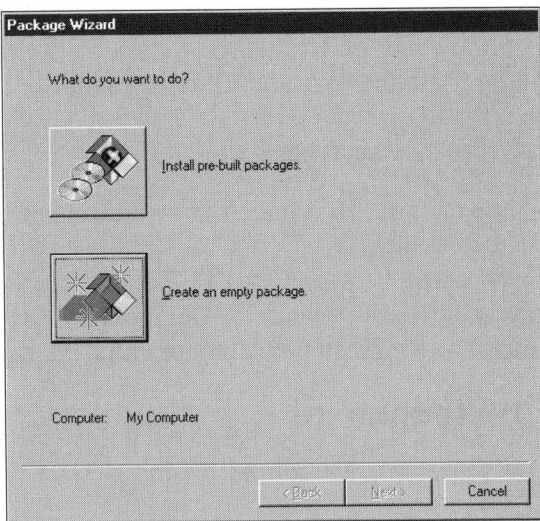

Figure 11.63 Package wizard.

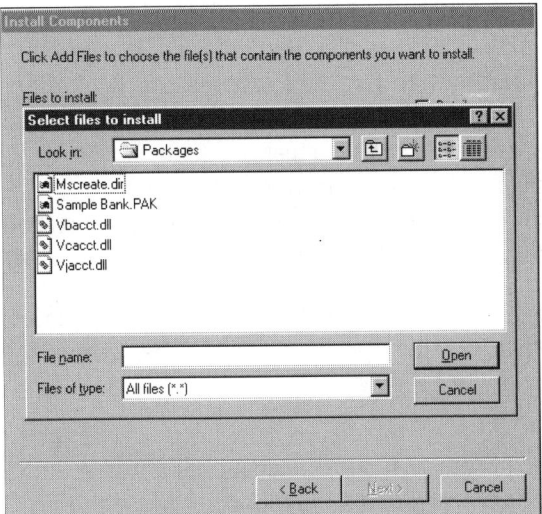

Figure 11.64 Selecting files to install.

You may not see the DLLs in the Component wizard Add Files box if you forgot to set the File attributes to **Show All**. Go to the Windows Explorer; choose **View** and then **Options**. Choose **Show all Files**.

7. In the dialog box that appears, select the file(s) you want to add and click **Open**. If the component's type library isn't found, you will not see the component in the list. Optionally, to remove a file from the **Files to install** list, select it and click **Remove Files**.
8. Click **Finish** to install the component.

Note that you will not see the methods or interfaces for the imported components in the Transaction Server Explorer window.

You can install a component by dragging a **.DLL** file from the Windows NT Explorer to the right pane of Transaction Explorer while the **Components** folder is open. This technique works the same as using the Install **new component(s)** button.

Run and Monitor the Component

To run and monitor your component, follow these steps:

1. In the left pane of Transaction Server Explorer, click the **Components** folder where you installed the `Bank.Account` component.
2. On the View menu, click **Status** to display usage information for the `Bank.Account` component.
3. On the Start menu, point to **Programs**, point to **Microsoft Transaction Server**, point to **Samples**, and then click **Bank Client**. It is recommended that you now arrange the windows so that you can see the Bank Client window and the Microsoft Transaction Server Explorer window simultaneously. The form will default to credit $1 to account number 1.
4. In the Bank client, click the **Account** component.
5. Click **Submit**. You should see the response **Hello from Account**.
6. In the Bank client, change the iterations from 1 of 0 to **1 of 100** and click **Submit**.

In the right pane of Microsoft Transaction Server Explorer, you should see the values under the **Objects** and **Activated** columns change to **1** and then change back to **0**.

To Maintain Integrity

Whom should a customer trust? If an individual does not have integrity, would you trust that person with your new car? Your family? Your wallet with cash? Trust is important to individuals and in business transactions.

For example, a bank must be trusted to track all credits and debits on a customer's bank account. Failing to perform these transactions correctly will cause a bank to lose customers ... fast!

Active Middleware

A computer may be reliable to a certain certifiable level, but developers are people, and they are trying to keep track of increasingly complex data resource issues. Companies are demanding faster, smaller, distributed applications in order to compete.

In the business model, a developer would need to ensure that debits equal credits; it would be an integrity constraint. If the action fails, the transaction aborts. This accounting object would call `HRESULT IObjectContext::DisableCommit ( )`. Example C++ code is as follows:

```
#include <mtx.h>

IObjectContext* pObjectContext = NULL;
HRESULT hr;

hr = GetObjectContext(&pObjectContext);
hr = pObjectContext->DisableCommit();
```

The object is stateful, so integrity is verified before the final commit. If there is an error, the system aborts, preventing an incorrect cash flow entry. In other words, the system will not credit $100 without debiting $100.

SECURITY AND ADMINISTRATION

The world economy is increasingly dependent on computers connected through networks, often the Internet. As a result, secure, distributed, transactional computing is important to the consumer, to corporations, and to governments.

With MTS, the unit of trust is the package, where everything trusts its cohorts. Packages run inside a process and are assigned a user ID when installed. Windows NT uses a package user ID to secure access to resources, such as database tables. The logical groups of users are assigned at development time. They are independent of Windows NT groups until deployment (see Figure 11.65).

When a package is developed, you define its role and provide an access list for components and interfaces. When the package is deployed, the roles are bound to the Windows NT group.

Access can be declared at the package level, where rules are set for all possible users of the package. At the component level, you can set the rules for all possible users of the component. At the component level interface, you can establish rules for all possible users of a specific interface implementation.

Security is not checked within a package but rather is checked when crossing a package. The calls have the client's identity or package identity. If you must allow for special needs, such as a person having approval process for capital goods over $1,000, you can use programmatic security.

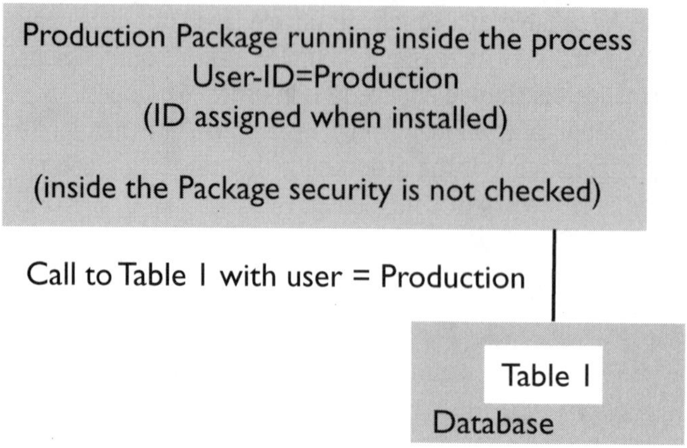

Chapter 11

```
┌─────────────────────────────────────────────────┐
│  Production Package running inside the process  │
│              User-ID=Production                 │
│          (ID assigned when installed)           │
│                                                 │
│   (inside the Package security is not checked)  │
└─────────────────────────────────────────────────┘

    Call to Table 1 with user = Production
                                    │
                            ┌───────────────┐
                            │    Table 1    │
                            └───────────────┘
                              Database
```

Figure 11.65 The Human Resources package.

In development, the package and component can be partitioned to ensure security and fault isolation. You should establish security roles as well as assign roles to components and interfaces. You can use programmatic security to establish detailed authorization rules as well as authentication levels.

In deployment, you install packages on the servers and set the server identity. You configure client machines using authentication (channel security) and authorize the server to call the client.

Suppose you are creating an accounting application that has unchanging application data. For example, a company's account number tends to stay consistent. Some accounts, such as an office products supplier, are always active. Accounting regulations specify many of the business rules needed for the application and the components.

For these reasons, you may want to cache the data. In this way, the system need not read the database very often and the data is readily available in memory. You would use the ability of the shared property manager to assist in this effort.

Data would be accessed through the components. You would create interfaces to provide appropriate functions. The component would modify and read data as well as update the database and ensure that data survives any system failures. SPM would cache the invariant data (see Figure 11.66).

Active Middleware 325

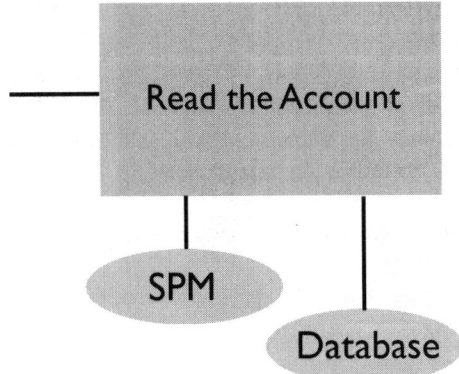

Figure 11.66 Data access.

You must make sure that data is not "remembered" during the writing process to prevent cached data from being incorrect if the transaction aborts. Therefore, you will cache only committed data. The whole point is to encapsulate access to the data. Let the senior programmers deal with building the component wrappers and the younger programmers develop the interfaces. Use the database to hold the data and spread out the access to avoid hotspots. When you find hotspots, build the transaction as the application model. Remember, as shown in Figure 11.67, the problem you are solving is to create reliable distributed applications. In Figure 11.67, this simple example reminds us that the transfer of $1000 must happen in accordance with what is secure and trustworthy to the customer. You cannot afford to lose that $1000.

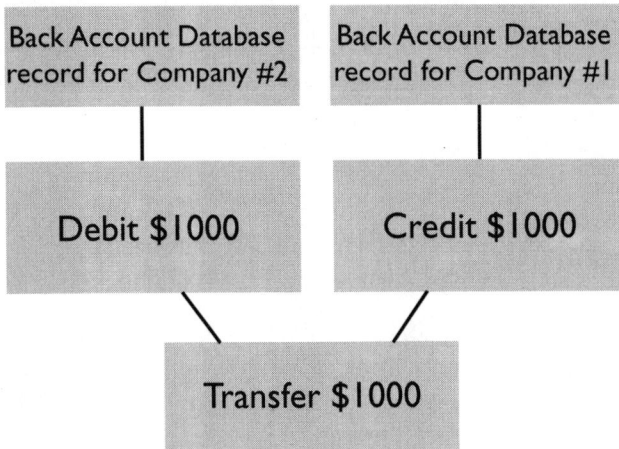

Figure 11.67 Reliability is important.

WHERE DO YOU GO FROM HERE?

You have learned how to determine the best method for implementing reliable and secure transactions at your active Web site. You have learned the basic component structure of the MTS environment and how to implement simple business rules in the environment. From here, you can explore the following chapters:

- Chapter 5, "Active Server Pages," to better understand components and their use in the transaction environment.
- Chapter 8, "Active Data," to learn about the SQL Server that sits on the server side of the middleware development.
- Chapter 10, "Active Money," to incorporate commerce transactions on your active site.

Chapter 12

How the Active Desktop Works

The Active Desktop as described in this book is the client side of the Active Platform client/server environment. The user can use a dynamic browser, such as Internet Explorer 4.0 or Netscape 4.0, that interprets dynamic HTML or can use Internet Explorer 3.0 and Netscape 3.0 to view client applications that are written with CGI or Web scripting languages.

THE CLIENT

In the case of Microsoft Internet Explorer, the Active Desktop is implemented in two layers. The *icon layer* allows the user to get to all the normal desktop shortcuts. Internet Explorer 4.0 creates a **desktop.htm** or **home.htm** file for capturing *HTML layer* information. This HTML file contains tags for each desktop object, an ActiveX control for moving and resizing objects, and a reference to the background wallpaper.

Using scripting, you can increase the interactivity on your site. Let's review how scripts work.

As a customer types a URL to visit a site, the browser requests the Web page from the server. The browser then interprets the HTML code. If there is a <SCRIPT> block in the HTML, it identifies the enclosed code as a script. If the tag is <SCRIPT LANGUAGE=VBScript>, the browser knows to find the DLL-based VBScript interpreter. In the case of Netscape, a customer would need a plug-in. An Internet Explorer browser understands VBScript.

There are many tools that you can to assist in the creation of dynamic Web sites. In the following sections, you will learn about a few of them.

ACTIVEX

ActiveX is a set of technologies based on the Component Object Model. COM specifies how components on a single machine communicate. ActiveX is OLE without all of the normal interfaces. (Object linking and embedding technology allows you to share data among programs.) This means you can take the HTML and add components that are accessible via scripting, CGI calls, or ISAPI.

This technology is available for Internet Explorer 3.x as an integral part of the browser. Netscape Explorer 3.0 (or later) requires a plug-in. As a person enters, for the first time, a Web site that has ActiveX components, the browser downloads the appropriate controls (components). The ActiveX component is saved on the client's system. Java applets, by comparison, must be downloaded every time a client visits the Web site. This also means that Java does not run a binary file that can cause harm on the client's system. Let's look specifically at the controls and the security issues.

ActiveX Controls

ActiveX controls are OLE controls with reduced overhead (see Appendix C for a further discussion), resulting in a smaller file that is of an acceptable size for the Internet. An ActiveX control is also intended to "fit" the browser. If a feature is not implemented in the browser (the container), the control reduces its behavior to meet the need of the browser.

ActiveX controls can be created using various methods, including using Visual C++ and the Active Template Library (ATL). ATL is a set of template-based C++ classes that you can use to create small COM objects and ActiveX controls. If you follow common Visual C++ development practice and create an ActiveX using Microsoft Foundation Classes (the library of C++ classes that assist you in providing user interface controls and customized application windows), the download time for the control could be rather long (in minutes) because of the size of the DLL that supports MFC. Some developers have turned to ATL to can remove the need for MFC and the C++ run-time library.

The `BaseCtl` method, shipped with the Microsoft ActiveX development kit (ADK), is a framework with which you can delve into component development. The advantage of using `BaseCtl` is that the controls will be small and effective. The disadvantage is that you need a stronger background in COM and ActiveX than you need if you're using ATL.

Speaking of the ActiveX development kit, you may want to pay attention to Microsoft's updates to this kit. For example, ISAPI started in the ADK and a new release of the kit will supposedly include the Java Virtual Machine (JVM: the specification that Java is written in to run on a target machine; here that would be Internet Explorer) as a control.

In addition, the ADK lets you incorporate a developer license with your ActiveX control. If you include the license feature, the control can only be used in runtime mode once it has left his development area. That is nice for trying to protect original coding efforts.

SECURITY

ActiveX controls are binaries. On a client's machine, they can do great things or do great damage. The security of ActiveX and Java are sometimes compared with that of Java. Java applets run as interpreted code. They are compiled before reaching the client. An applet cannot call another applet or run files on a client's system. ActiveX controls run outside this so-called sandbox.

To address the security controversy, Microsoft introduced the Authenticode digital signing method. Authenticode is a method by which you can verify that the component you sent is yours and has not been tampered with. As a user may guess, this method does not protect a client from a virus. The originator of the code could be an unsavory person, and Authenticode will not prevent such a person from damaging a client machine using an ActiveX control.

This makes ActiveX a great tool for intranets but may still be a concern for the Internet. You need to seriously consider these security issues before distributing ActiveX controls on your site.

ACTIVE TEMPLATE LIBRARY

ATL is a group of C++ templates that allows you to create controls without having to link to the C run-time library. ATL helps eliminate some of the coding necessary to implement COM, but a user of ATL should have a good knowledge of COM to use this library appropriately.

JAVA

Java is an object-oriented programming language. Java tends to be used by developers to create push buttons and controls for such things as games and interactive sites and to create graphics and animations.

Java has been well accepted on the Internet because of its built-in networking abilities and its resemblance to C++. Many early Internet developers came from a strong C++ and networking background in the UNIX world. The good news is that, unlike C++, Java does not use pointers and memory allocation. Java applets are compiled to a Java virtual machine specification and sent to browsers to be interpreted.

Hello World in Java

Here is the classic Hello World program written in Java.

```
//Hello.java
import java.awt.*;
import java.applet.*;
class HelloWorld extends Applet {
    public void init() {
        resize(150,25);
    }
    public void paint(Graphics g) {
        g.drawString("Hello World!", 50, 50);
        }
}
```

You would save this program—let's call it **Hello.java**—and then type the following in a command line:

```
javac Hello.java
```

The result is a file called **Hello.class** that has the binary code needed for the applet. If you have a Java-enabled browser, you can create the following HTML page:

```
<HTML>
<HEAD>
<TITLE>Hello, World!</TITLE>
</HEAD>
<BODY>
Its me!

<APP CLASS="HelloWorld">
</BODY>
</HTML>
```

This creates a 320 × 240 window that displays **Hello World!**

Let's look closer at the code. In the first two lines are libraries. (AWT is discussed in the next section.)

```
//Hello.java
  import java.awt.*;
  import java.applet.*;
```

The following line declares a new class named `Hello`. This class inherits functionality from the `Applet` class and will extend its capabilities.

```
class HelloWorld extends Applet {
```

In the next line, `public` means that other objects outside this class can use it.

```
public void init() {
```

Rhe next line, resizes the window to 320 × 240

```
resize(320,240);
```

The following line replaces the current `paint` method

```
public void paint(Graphics g) {
```

The final line draws **Hello World** at point 50,50

```
g.drawString("Hello World!", 50, 50);
```

The AWT Library

AWT, affectionately known as Another Window Toolkit, actually stands for Abstract Window Toolkit. It allows you to create graphical user interfaces. The AWT library contains controls that allow you to make buttons and edit areas, fonts, images, check boxes, and so on. The library also has several different containers that you use to arrange your controls on the screen, along with many other features.

Here is an example of the `Button` class being used:

```
import java.awt;
import java.applet;

class MyButton extends Button {
   public MyButton(String label, String name, Window w)
   {
      super(label,name,w);
   }
   public void selected(Component c, int pos) {

   }
}

class testButton extends Applet {
   MyButton button = new MyButton("my button", "atest", item.parent);
   protected void init() {
      button.move(20,20);
      resize(320,240);
   }

   public void paint(Graphics g) {

      button.map();
   }
}
```

Images and Animation

One benefit of Java is that it provides automatic memory management. In C++, a developer must use memory management libraries such as Free. Java uses a multithreading environment for eliminating objects when they are no longer needed. Memory management is especially beneficial when you're producing animations. Here is a sample animation applet:

```
import java.applet;
import java.awt.Graphics;
import java.awt.Image;

class ClickAnimation extends Applet implements Runnable {
   Thread animationThread = null;
   protected int cycles = 0;
   Image frame[] = new Image[15];
   int cur = 0;
```

```
protected void init() {
    resize(50,50);
    String cyclesTemp = getAttribute("CYCLES");
    if (cyclesTemp != null)
        cycles = Integer.valueOf(cyclesTemp).intValue();
    for(int i = 0; i < 10; i++)
        frame[i] = getImage("frame"+i+".gif");

}
protected void start() {
    animationThread = new Thread(this);
    animationThread.start();
}
public void run() {
    for(int i = 0; i < cycles; i++) {
        play(sound);
        for(cur = 1; cur < 15; cur++) {
            repaint();
            for(int j = 0; j <5000; j++);
        }
        cur = 0;
        repaint();
    }
}
public void paint(Graphics g) {
    g.drawImage(frame[cur], 0, 0);
}
public void mouseDown(int x, int y) {
    animationThread = new Thread(this);
    animationThread.start();
}

}
```

Note these lines halfway through the code:

```
}
protected void start() {
    animationThread = new Thread(this);
    animationThread.start();
}
```

A method called *start* creates a new *animationThread* so that the animation can start. Each thread runs for a period of time, and when it is finished the next thread launches. This is one example of introducing multithreading to the Java environment.

JavaScript

With the need for speed Java has been extended into a scripting environment. JavaScript is a client-side scripting language supported by most browsers.

To create the script you could use a notepad or HTML editor. Java and JavaScript share the same base, but they are not the same. Some functionality was removed from JavaScript in order to meet the needs of a scripting environment. For example, JavaScript is object-based but not object-oriented. It has no classes, and there is no such thing as inheritance.

Like Java, JavaScript allows a developer to add graphics and controls. In addition, Java can be used to interface with databases, determine the browser type, and provide the user with an interactive adventure. Here is Hello World in JavaScript:

```
SCRIPT LANGUAGE="JavaScript">
<!--
        function print (s) {
                document.write(s)
        }
// -->
</SCRIPT>
<TITLE>Hello World</TITLE>
</HEAD>

<BODY>
<H1>A simple example of JavaScript</H1>
<SCRIPT LANGUAGE="JavaScript">
<!--
        msg = "Hello World";

        }
// -->
</SCRIPT>
</BODY>
</HTML>
```

Running scripts is much easier in JavaScript than in Perl. With Perl, the interaction is with the server; with JavaScript, the process is happening in the browser. That is good news and bad news. It is good news to be able to run a local process and reduce network bottlenecks. The problem is that all data must have a home if it is to be of any value. The server is the best place for that data. Until the JavaScript-enabled page makes a call to the server, the data is temporary on the client side. A good mix of client-side (JavaScript) and server-side (Perl, ISAPI, IDC/HTX) pages will be of most benefit to a developer.

Visual Basic and VBScript

Visual Basic is a programming language in which you create forms and objects that provide interactivity. You create a project that has forms, classes (you define classes and their characteristics), modules (declarations and procedures), and resources. In the following sample, the developer created a set of control buttons and a text box. Then the developer created code for the buttons.

Here is the code for building a button set with Hello World. The object CmdHello:

```
Private Sub cmdHello_Click()
    tbxDisplay.Text = "Hello Wonderful"
End Sub
```

Object CmdClear:

```
Private Sub cmdClear_Click()
    tbxDisplay.Text = ""
End Sub
```

Object CmdExit:

```
Private Sub cmdExit_Click()
    Beep
    End
End Sub
```

Object Form:

```
Private Sub Form_Load()
End Sub
```

Pressing on the **Display Hello** button, which is controlled by CmdHello, displays **Hello Wonderful**, as shown in Figure 12.1

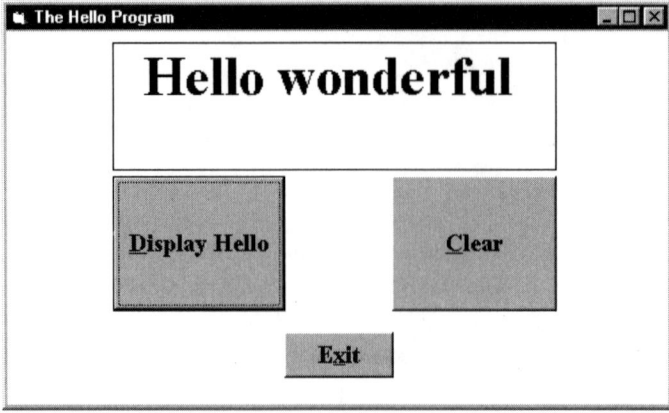

Figure 12.1 Hello World.

VBScript

VBScript is an extension of Microsoft's Visual Basic; the scripts look like Visual Basic programs. VBScript has a number of differences from Visual Basic,.= such as the inability to handle declarations. The point is that VBScript is made for the Web. VBScript is interpreted at the browser via the VBScript interpreter. This means that there is no compiling on the server side. The benefit is that the developer is not running an executable on the client's system, thereby promoting the security aspect of the developer's site.

Here is a sample of Hello World in VBScript:

```
<SCRIPT LANGUAGE="VBScript">
            Sub BtnHello_OnClick
                    MsgBox "Hello, world!" "
            End Sub
      </SCRIPT>
```

or

```
<SCRIPT LANGUAGE="VBScript">
            Document.write "Hello,wold!"
      </SCRIPT>
```

To connect to a database is as simple as defining the DSN and putting the code on the page that needs the access as in this example:

```
<%
                        Conn.Open "DSNsource"
                        Set RS = Conn.Execute("SELECT * FROM Customers")
                        Do While Not RS.EOF       .
                        RS.MoveNext
                        Loop
                        RS.Close
                        Conn.Close
                        %>
```

Or you can add a connection in the **global.asa**:

```
                        SUB Session_OnStart
                        '---- Open ADO connection to database
                        Conn.Open "DSNsource", "userlogin","userpassword"
                        END SUB
```

The **global.asa** sits in the root of each application and can provide for global events. The developer can set four events in the **global.asa** to include: `Application-Start`, `Application-End`, `Session-Start`, and `Session-End`.

It is useful to learn VBScript is useful to learn because Microsoft is using it not only in Active Server but also in Active Desktop (as can be seen in Internet Explorer 4.0). VBScript allows the use of conditional statements, as in `If-Then-Else`, which allows you to execute different portions of the script based upon a user environment. The latest version of VBScript, version 2.0, provides some new objects. Version 1.0 had only the `Err` object to catch errors in code. Now Microsoft has added `Dictionary` (an object for handling arrarys), `CreateObject` (lets you tap into automation servers such as Index Server), `FileSystemObject` (lets you create and open text files on the file system), `GetObject` (lets you open other objects such as an Excel spreadsheet), and `TextStream` (gives you sequential access to text in a file). In addition, it adds `DateDiff` and `DateAdd` functionality, which some database developers like to use to verify that a customer's order is current.

Visual Basic and VBScript provide developers with an exciting new way to create dynamic Web sites that can be updated by company databases full of information.

Where Do You Go from Here?

It is probably obvious that each of the following chapters in Part 3 provides a deeper discussion of the topics in this brief overview of tools. In addition, you should look at these related chapters:

- Chapter 20, "Real Life Security Issues," to ensure that not only your code but also your company's policy for security protect the rights to the data
- Appendix A, "Setting Up IIS and NT," to obtain an overview of the NT environment.

Chapter 13

ActiveX

ActiveX is not a programming language but rather a group of technologies that allows you to distribute content over the Web. An active Web site includes multimedia effects, applications, interfaces to databases, and other enhancements that should be downloadable via the Internet. ActiveX makes this—and more—possible.

WHAT IS ACTIVEX?

ActiveX is based on the Component Object Model (COM) and Microsoft's object linking and embedding (OLE). Let's review these technologies.

COM is an object architecture that provides standard interfaces, giving developers the ability to write applications that use these interfaces to pass data in and out without knowing the COM code itself. COM code is a binary that executes or stops execution on its own. These features make the use of COM beneficial, because programs can be upgraded with ease. If you are using legacy applications, that is OK with COM. Each version of the module maintains an interface for earlier versions (see Figure 13.1).

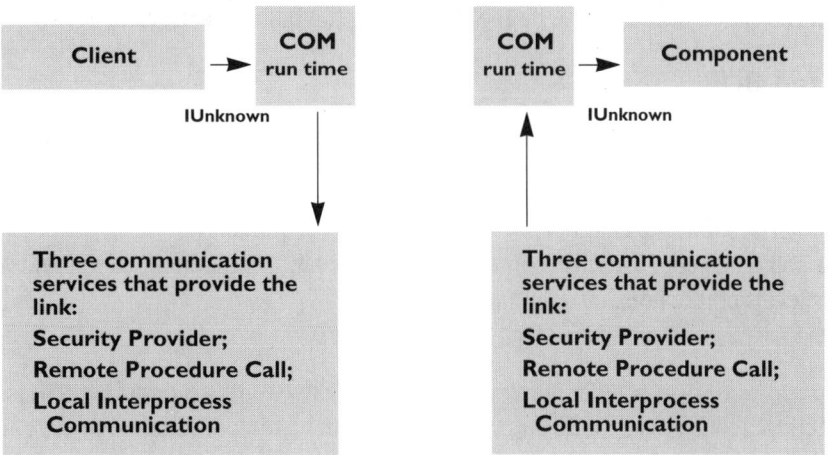

Figure 13.1 The COM architecture.

Because COM, like the framework of a building, is an architecture, you can create applications and modules that use that architecture. Microsoft introduced OLE as one such implementation of COM. OLE adds object linking, controls, automation, drag-and-drop capability, monikers, and much more (see Figure 13.2). COM modules called *controls* are self-contained, have upgrade interfaces and handle a level of network activity as well as security.

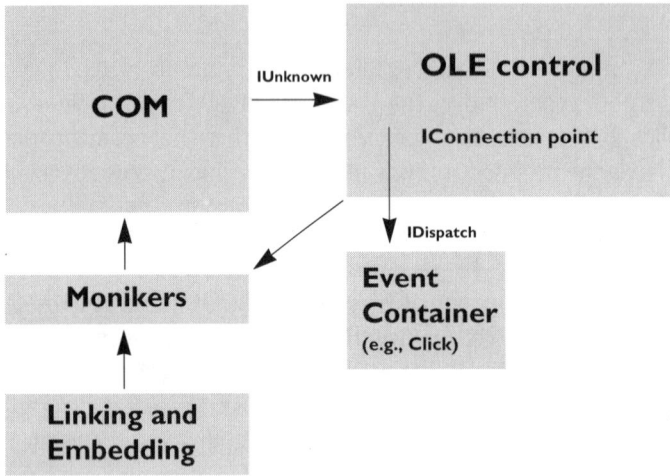

Figure 13.2 The OLE world.

A simple example of an OLE implementation is the ability of a user to embed an Excel spreadsheet into a Word document. The Excel spreadsheet still has a link to the original Excel application, so a user can change the sheet using the built-in features of Excel.

ActiveX and OLE

ActiveX is a newer implementation of OLE, so it has a number new features, including the following:

- An interface that the client can use to serve object requests.
- The ability to support multiple interfaces. In this way, a component can provide various levels of functionality.
- The ability to be dynamically loaded and executed.

ActiveX controls are one popular implementation of ActiveX. In a network such as the Web, an ActiveX control can send output from application to application. For reasons of security (discussed later) the control needs a trusted source.

ActiveX can define how one program or control should interact with another program or control. So is ActiveX another name for OLE? Not quite. ActiveX incorporates the functionality of OLE, but there is one simple difference: size. Let's take another look at the example of embedding an Excel spreadsheet into a Word document. Word is the OLE *container*, and the spreadsheet is the OLE control. The objects communicate through OLE (on the Internet, it would be ActiveX). Go to Explorer and look at the size of both files before embedding. Then embed the Excel spreadsheet into the Word document. The size of the final document is greater than that of the two files added. Why? OLE carries a lot of overhead. In some cases, the DLLs are in the hundreds of thousands of bytes. This may be OK in an office intranet but is unacceptable on the Internet.

ActiveX requires fewer interfaces than OLE requires. That can be a blessing and a curse. The blessing is that the functionality is similar to what developers have seen from Microsoft in the past. The size is smaller, so they are more apt to use it. The curse is that it is not efficient. By cutting up the OLE design, you do not have a tool that was specifically designed for the Internet.

To properly run ActiveX you need a container, usually a Web browser, to provide a place for ActiveX controls to run. As a person goes to an HTML page that has ActiveX controls, the browser downloads ActiveX objects as well as graphics. The objects could be spreadsheets, programs, or documents.

Database Interactivity

With ASP, developers have been introduced to Microsoft's component, or object, methodologies. One of those components is ActiveX Data Objects, now known as Active Data Objects (ADO). ADO is an ActiveX-based wrapper around OLE-DB. ADO lets you get to three objects within Active Server: `Connection` objects (which link ASP to an ODBC data source), `Command` objects (which handle items such as SQL queries and stored procedures), and `Recordset` objects (which provide access to the rows and columns in the database).

The benefit for the developer is that these three objects operate a little differently than in the earlier Data Access Objects (DAO) implementation. In DAO each of these objects worked in conjunction with the others. In ADO, you can create a `Connection` object that is totally independent of a `Recordset` or `Command` object.

Let's now take a look at the tools.

THE ACTIVEX TOOLS

The ActiveX tools include the controls and ActiveX Control Pad, a way to add controls and functionality.

Controls

You can write ActiveX controls using C++, Visual Basic, and other languages. You can take advantage of the Active Template Library to create these controls (see Chapter 14) or use the ActiveX Control Pad to add controls to the Web page.

As noted before, the control needs a container. The standard container for the Web is a browser. In the case of ActiveX, that is Internet Explorer (IE). IE includes the following controls:

- Chart. Lets you display seven types of charts, including bar, line, pie, and column charts.
- Label. Lets you display a string of text as a label, allowing you to manipulate it by, for example, rotating it at an angle.
- Marquee. Lets you put marquees across the page.

Please note that ActiveX is compiled code. It is a derivative of OLE, so it works well with a Microsoft browser. Other browsers need plug-ins. A Netscape plug-in is available from NCompass Labs at http://www.ncompasslabs.com/products/scriptactive.htm.

How to Install a Control

In many cases, you need only put the control on the page; the client's browser downloads it, and the control should self-install. The user must make sure that Internet Explorer is set to install the controls. If it is not, here is a quick list of what the customer should do (you could list this on a FAQ page for customer support):

1. While running IE 3.x, choose **View**, then **Options**, and finally **Security**.
2. Choose **Certificates**. Select **Sites**. You may want to double-check the list to make sure the sites are trustworthy. Now select **Publishers**. Check the list to be sure they are trusted publishers.
3. Look at **Active Content**. Select all the check boxes.
4. Click **Safety Level** and set the level based on your personal acceptance standards. Normally, users set the level to **High** until they trust a site and then reset the level. On an intranet, the level may be set by the administrator to **Low** because the company has its own internal security standards.

Once you have a control you wish to use, add it to the HTML page using the <OBJECT> tag. The tag includes a set of parameters such as this:

```
<OBJECT "IDLabel" CLASSID="CLSID:978C9E23-D4B0-11CE-BF2D-00AA003F4D0"
 <PARAM NAME="Caption" VALUE="Customer ID">
        <PARAM NAME="Size" VALUE="3493;600">
        <PARAM NAME="FontCharSet" VALUE="0">
        <PARAM NAME="FontPitchAndFamily" VALUE="2">
    </OBJECT>
```

The parameters (defined with the PARAM tag) affect the behavior and appearance of the control. You can use any text editor to add the ActiveX information to the Web page. Using the ActiveX Control Pad, though, is much simpler and can help you add ActiveX scripting.

CONTROL PAD

The ActiveX Control Pad is a tool that lets you add both ActiveX controls and scripting to the page. Control Pad includes the following:

- A text editor for editing HTML source code.
- An object editor so that you can place the controls in the appropriate location. It also allows you to visually set control properties.
- A Script wizard to help Web designers who do not program but want to add VBScript or JavaScript code to a page (see Figure 13.3).

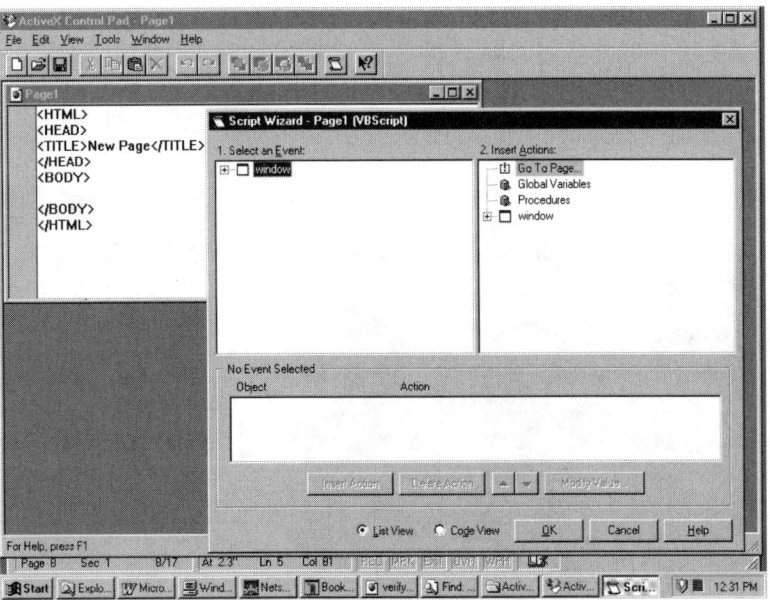

Figure 13.3 Control Pad and Script wizard.

Control Pad is free from Microsoft and is slightly less than 3MB in size. The screen interface gives this tool the appearance of a text editor. It is not an HTML editor, because many HTML tags are foreign to Control Pad. In addition, you cannot preview what you have done unless you launch a browser.

Control Pad uses VBScript or JavaScript to activate the components. Download a sample control (many controls can be found at the Microsoft Web site). From the Edit menu, select **Insert ActiveX Control**. Look through the list to find the control that was downloaded. Click on it. Click **OK** to insert the control into the HTML page (see Figure 13.4).

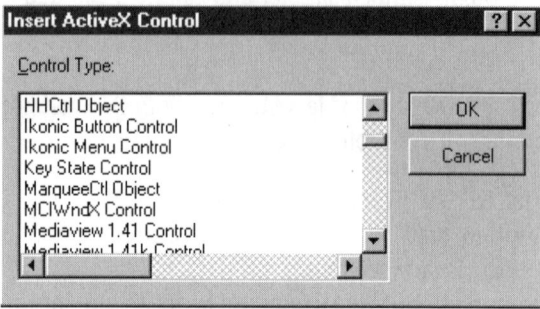

Figure 13.4 Inserting a control.

Now two windows should appear. The left pane lets you arrange the control's visual design. The right pane is the Property window, where you can set the control's properties. Let's say that you want to change the caption. Double-click on the **Caption** property in the right pane. Now edit the text and then press **Enter** or click **Apply** (see Figure 13.5).

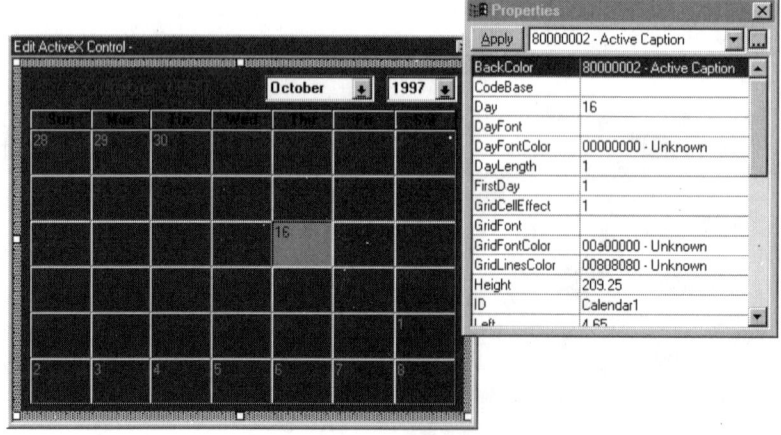

Figure 13.5 Setting the properties.

You should always check the `Codebase` property. This property tells the client's browser where to download the control if the user does not have it. For example, the Button Menu control is at http://activex.microsoft.com/controls/iexplorer, so the `Codebase` property is `http://activex.microsoft.com/controls/iexplorer/btnmenu.ocx#Version=4,7 0,0,1161`.

The entry might be

```
<OBJECT
            ID="Button Menu control"
            ...
            CODEBASE=" http://activex.microsoft.com/controls/iex-
plorer/btnmenu.ocx#Version=4,70,0,1161.
" >
            </OBJECT>
```

Now press **Close**.

To use the scripting tools to set up the look of the control, choose **Tools**. Then choose **Script Wizard**.

Let's allow for the control to provide a drop-down menu for jumping to another site. A dynamic page means that items change over time. VBScript is designed to operate based on events happening over time. The two events of interest here are `OnLoad` and `OnUnload`. The Windows `OnLoad` event tells the browser to load an object, image, or application, and `OnUnload` tells the browser what to do as the page is unloaded.

To work with the `OnLoad` event, double-click the **Window** object. Click **OnLoad**. Click the **Code View** button (see Figure 13.6).

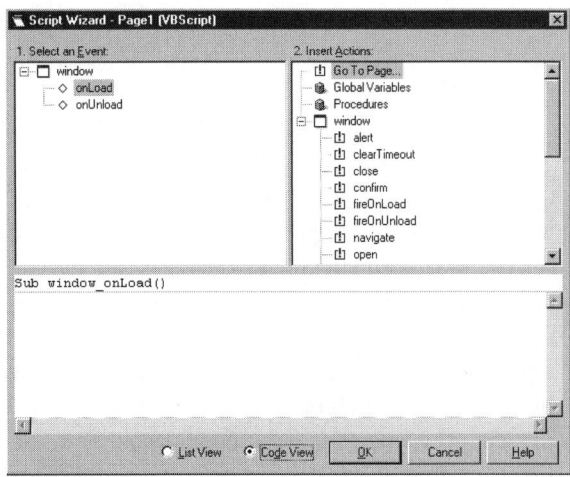

Figure 13.6 The `OnLoad` event.

Now you can type code in the **Actions** window. Insert this code:

```
            Sub window_onLoad()
                pmenu1.AddItem "Thesite.COM"
                pmenu1.AddItem "Disney.COM"
                pmenu1.AddItem "@home.COM"
    [End Sub]
```

Click **OK**. This code will now run when the page is loaded.

The preceding code creates a drop-down menu. How does the user select an item? For the system to respond to the Button menu's `Select` event, you must write some more code. Notice that this code must pass an argument. Here it is called `item`. This `item` designates which site noted earlier (Thesite.com, disney.com, or @home.com) is chosen:

```
Sub pmenu1_Select(item)

Select Case item
  case 1
  Window.location.href = "http://www.Thesite.com"

  case 2
  Window.location.href = "http://www.Disney.com"

  case 3
  Window.location.href = "http://www.@home.com"

End Select
```

Choose **File** and then **Save**. Now you can try this page and see whether it works.

We've looked at ActiveX and a method to incorporate controls in a Web page. Now let's turn to the issue of security.

SECURITY

ActiveX has come under scrutiny because of the increased concern for security on the Internet. In this area, developers tend to compare ActiveX to Java. Interestingly, though, the comparison is somewhat correct; remember that, like Java, an ActiveX control can be written using Java. But ActiveX is a technology and not a language. With that said, let's look at a security comparison.

ActiveX controls are native executable programs. This means that they can access the hard disk, system memory, and system services of the machine on which they execute. Java applets run via the Java Virtual Machine (JVM). This "machine" operates as a *sandbox* in which the Java byte code must operate, so the code cannot go to other parts of the system. No applet can launch another applet, for example, nor write information to your hard disk (although this is changing with the latest release of Java).

Because of security concerns, Microsoft introduced *code signing*, in which a digital "signature" is embedded in the control. The signature guarantees that the control will reach the user's browser untampered. It can also reveal who wrote the control. The problem is that a digital signature does not guarantee that the code runs properly nor that it does not contain a virus. The code may still cause harm to the user's system. Rather, the signature means that the code went from one point to another without being changed. This digital signing is known by Microsoft as Authenticode.

If you are a regular user of IE, you will have seen, in the past year, a note that comes up on your browser asking whether you want to install Authenticode 2.0, the latest release. You need to be aware of which controls you are using.

On Microsoft's site at http://www.microsoft.com/intdev/security/desrev-f.htm, the documentation states: "While not guaranteeing bug-free code, Authenticode technology is designed to identify the publisher of the code and to assure end users that software has not been tampered with before or during the download process."

Could a developer register a buggy piece of code and then get it signed under a false name? Sure. The code signing process also costs money, because someone must keep track of the developers and their signatures. A VeriSign Digital ID costs about $400 per year, and that adds to a developer's overhead.

You can run an ActiveX control that is not signed. If your system is set up with security at a proper level, the browser will ask whether you want to download the control. If you click **Yes**, the control will be downloaded. It is your decision. If you believe you need the controls to enjoy the site or to get the information you need, you will enter at your own risk. Otherwise, site traffic diminishes because the security warning drives visitors away. It all comes down to what Microsoft believes are trusted sources. The question is whether the user trusts the source.

A user can change the level of trust in IE or can say **No** to a downloaded control prompt. Figure 13.7 shows the choices offered by Internet Explorer.

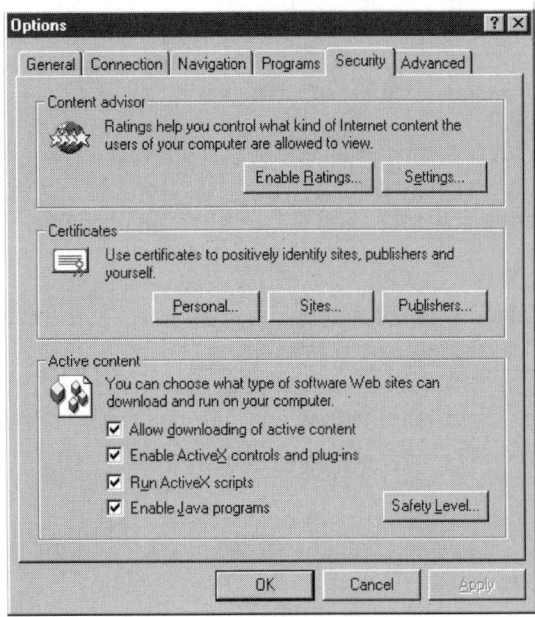

Figure 13.7 Security choices.

346   Chapter 13

The user gets to this screen by choosing **View, Options,** and then the **Security** tab. This action sets the browser's behavior regarding ActiveX controls. The level chosen tells the browser to disallow unsigned controls, display a warning prompt of an unsigned control, or send all controls through.

Internet Explorer will check the source of the ActiveX control each time the browser encounters the CLSID. The browser will check the control against a list of trusted publishers. If the source for that control does not appear on the list, you will receive a prompt.

A user can choose to trust all controls from an author by listing the author in the List of Trusted Publishers. A user could also set the security to accept all controls registered with VeriSign.

Clicking the **Advanced** button will bring up a dialog box that contains a list of all the trusted sources. Users can remove any that they no longer want there or no longer trust. The check box that says **Consider all commercial software publishers trustworthy** means exactly what it says. Be careful. This option may work OK for an intranet but would not be recommended for the Internet.

TIPS FOR THE ACTIVEX DEVELOPER

Let's look at a number of tips that developers have been sharing over the Internet.

1. If you are concerned about security and want to protect yourself or if you do not use plug-ins, you should do the following in IE:

    - Click the **View** menu option and select **Options**.
    - Click on the **Security** tab.
    - In the **Active** content panel, uncheck the **Enable ActiveX controls and Plug-ins** option.

    Otherwise, leave the default setting, leave security set to **High**, and pick **No** whenever a control is presented for downloading.

2. Most developers will want to use already existing ActiveX controls rather than create new ones from scratchActiveX controls can easily be included in a Web page using the `<OBJECT>` tag. The control has a number of common components, including the following:

    - `CLASSID`, the unique number assigned to each ActiveX control when it is registered. No two ActiveX controls can have the same CLASSID number.
    - `ID` is a shortened name, or nickname, for the `CLASSID`. Using `ID` helps reduce the long listing to reference a control everywhere in a page.

- `Position` gives the height and width of the control.
- Parameters depend on the control itself.

Remember that if you type the `CLASSID` incorrectly, the control will not work properly. It is recommended that you use Control Pad for page layout of controls.

3. With all the requirements to determine how to react to each browser that comes to a site, you may want to consider using some code to identify the browser. This code checks the browser name and version:

```
<SCRIPT LANGUAGE="JavaScript">
<!--
document.writeln("The browser name is " +
navigator.appName+'<br>')
document.writeln("The version number is " +
navigator.appVersion+'<br>')
// -->
</SCRIPT>
```

Netscape 3.0 will send back the value of `appName` as `Netscape` and the `appValue` as 3.0. IE 3.0 will send back an `appName` of `Internet Explorer` and an `appValue` of 3.x. Now you can enter scripts that lead the Netscape viewer to a non-ActiveX area and the IE user to ActiveX pages.

4. The IE HTML marquee tag runs only right or left. The ActiveX control sets up the marquee property to run left, right, up, or down. To go up and down, set `ScrollPixelsX` to zero. Here is a sample of the code:

```
<OBJECT ID="Marquee1" WIDTH=250
HEIGHT=490
CLASSID="CLSID:1A4DA620-
6217-11CF-BE62-0080C72EDD2D">
<PARAM NAME="_ExtentX" VALUE="40">
<PARAM NAME="_ExtentY" VALUE="50">
<PARAM NAME="ScrollPixelsY"
VALUE="90">
<PARAM NAME="ScrollPixelsX"
VALUE="0">
<PARAM NAME="szURL" VALUE="file:
//c:\scrolltst.html">
```

Play with the `ScrollPixelsY VALUE="90"` to see what happens if the number is negative.

5. Using the `WriteLn` method, you can modify the page code within the browser's memory. This means that you can use this method to redirect a user to a page for another browser:

```
<SCRIPT LANGUAGE="JavaScript">
<!--if (navigator.appName== 'Netscape')
{document.writeln('<a href= \netscape.htm>
Click here for a special page for Netscape browsers!</a><b>') }// -->
</SCRIPT>
```

WHERE DO YOU GO FROM HERE?

The ActiveX technology takes advantage of the complex component architecture within Microsoft's client/server world. It is intended to give the added functionality desired by developers who have used OLE applications in Windows development. The concerns with ActiveX are how to limit the size of the control and how to ensure security. Review each area before deciding on ActiveX.

You should also review these chapters:

- Chapter 14, "Active Template Library," where you can learn about another tool for creating ActiveX controls.

Chapter 14

Active Template Library

The Active Template Library (ATL) is a set of template-based C++ classes that developers can use to create small COM objects and ActiveX controls. Available in a usable source code format from Microsoft, ATL provides built-in support for many of the fundamental COM interfaces. One of those interfaces, IDispatch, is the center of OLE automation. OLE controls are driven by calls to their virtual function tables or by using the IDispatch interface.

WHY USE ATL?

After reading this description of IDispatch and realizing the ease of use of ASP, you may wonder why someone would want to do all this to build components. Why not just use the built-in ASP components?

Furthermore, why build more C++ components when you can use VBScript or JavaScript to enhance the interactivity of a page and take advantage of off-the-shelf components? Does the developer have to write CGIs, ISAPIs, and Visual C++ applications linked to the Microsoft Foundation Classes (MFC) libraries? Perhaps you thought all that was gone with the introduction of the ASP.

There is some truth to these concerns. Let's take a brief look at the script world of ASP and determine when ATL might be of use.

ASP Scripts

VBScript and JavaScript are wonderful tools, and this book covers them in Chapters 15 and 16. You can use the scripting tools to develop Web applications faster than you can develop new components using C++. Also, debugging, tends to be less cryptic.

Experienced developers find that there is a need to customize the off-the-shelf components or create new components with functionality that fulfills the needs of the company Web site. Off-the-shelf components give you only certain amount of functionality. Eventually, you need to expand the component's capabilities. So must you use Visual C++ to do all the work? No. Visual Basic 5 provides the functionality needed to write components. As with Visual C++, Visual Basic 5 can handle memory management and create apartment threaded objects (see the later overview of thread). This is a change from Visual Basic 4, which could handle only single-threaded objects. The drawback is that Visual Basic 5, like VBScript, cannot properly access the operating system.

Then there is Java and Visual Java++. Again, Java provides great functionality, and it can, like C++, give you access to the operating system. A problem is that some Windows APIs need pointers and Java does not use them. That can be a problem when you're interfacing the component with some applications.

There are good reasons to use C++. First, you can hide your code in a C++ application. The problem with VBScript is that everyone can see it. By using C++, you can own your code. Second, C++ is faster than interpreted languages (such as VBScript and JavaScript), and you can directly access the system registry. A C++ application can also be run as a Windows application or made into a component. This means that you can leverage your product in multiple markets. C++ can also be used to write components, which are easier to distribute to different locations on the company's network.

When to Use ATL

You need to understand that writing any component takes time. You may find it faster to create the functionality in an ASP rather than write a component. Try building the page first using other methods, such ASP or IDC/HTX. Then see whether the performance is acceptable. If it is, you may not need to write a component.

If you do choose to create a component, you can generally use two methods: MFC and ATL.

MFC has a lot of built-in functionality. If you are familiar with using the libraries, you should continue to do so. ATL, on the other hand, provides a more compact code sample. If you do not need all the MFC functionality, you may find it easier to use ATL. If you have a good handle on COM, then ATL is a good choice. Otherwise, the MFC wizard may be more applicable.

You need to weigh the development time in building and debugging a component. What if you need to build the component? Are there benefits to using ATL? Yes. When you're writing the component in C++, ATL provides small, fast code that supports the COM threading models. ATL supports the IDispatch interface and provides a COM error mechanism. ATL gives you better control of COM features, including implementations of the IUnknown and IClassFactory interfaces and ActiveX controls.

How to Use ATL

ATL works like a macro. Developers write macros to reduce the number of keystrokes or amount of effort needed to repeat a task and to expand an application's capability. You can use ATL to broaden your code's use of COM, thereby meeting the need of current distrib-

Active Template Library

uted applications. Be careful not to let the code get bloated. ATL does not give every developer what he or she needs. It does not operate as a C++ class library, in which you derive from the class the functionality you need. ATL creates an instance of a class from a template. In addition, ATL does not currently provide ODBC support. There is no document model as used in MFC. You use ActiveX controls to deal with user interface objects.

BUILDING A SAMPLE

The simplest way to create a project that you can then modify is to use the ATL COM AppWizard. It is available in the Visual C++ section of Microsoft's Web site.

To create a project using the ATL COM AppWizard, open Developer Studio. Click **New** in the File menu. Click **Project Workspace**. Click **OK**. Choose **ATL COM AppWizard** (see Figure 14-1). Enter the project name.

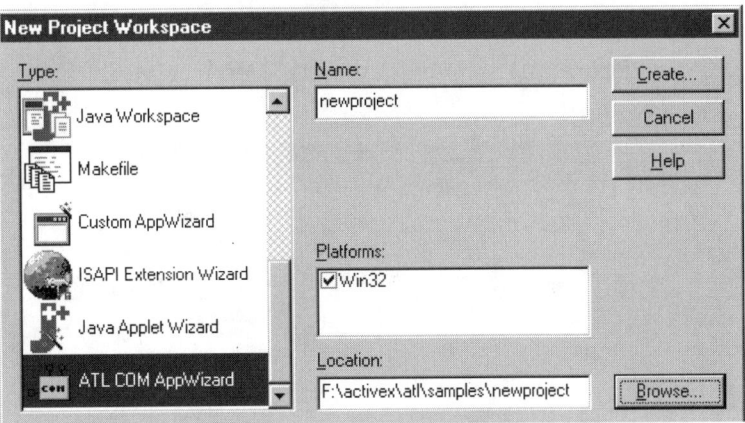

Figure 14.1 New ATL COM project.

Now click **Create**. This action opens a dialog box (see Figure 14.2).

Note the choices. Choose **Dynamic Link Library** for the in-process server (a DLL is an in-process server because it operates in another object's process area as a client). Choose **Executable** for the out-of-process server (an out-of-process server runs locally, as in the case of an executable piece of code). Choose **Service** if you want the code to run in the background as a service (a service, as defined by Microsoft, is a "set of interfaces that perform related tasks").

If you require marshaling interfaces, choose **Allow merging of proxy/stub code**. If you need MFC support (for example CString), check **Support MFC**.

Click **Finish** to generate the New Project Information page (see Figure 14.3).

Chapter 14

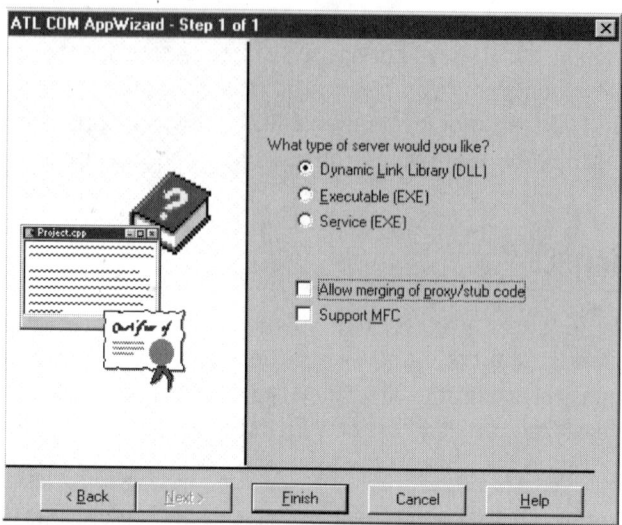

Figure 14.2 Step 1 of 1 in the ATL COM AppWizard.

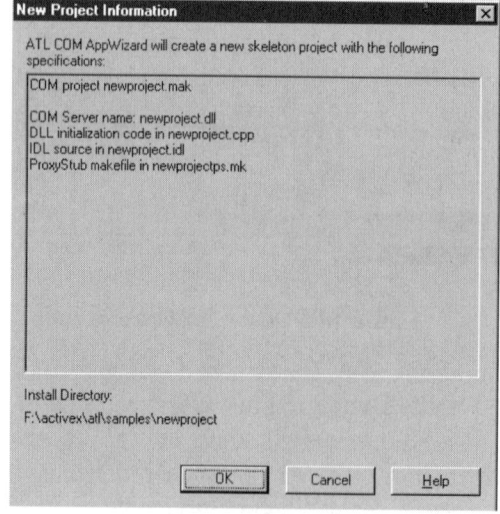

Figure 14.3 New Project Information.

Active Template Library

Various files are generated by the wizard (see Figure 14.4).

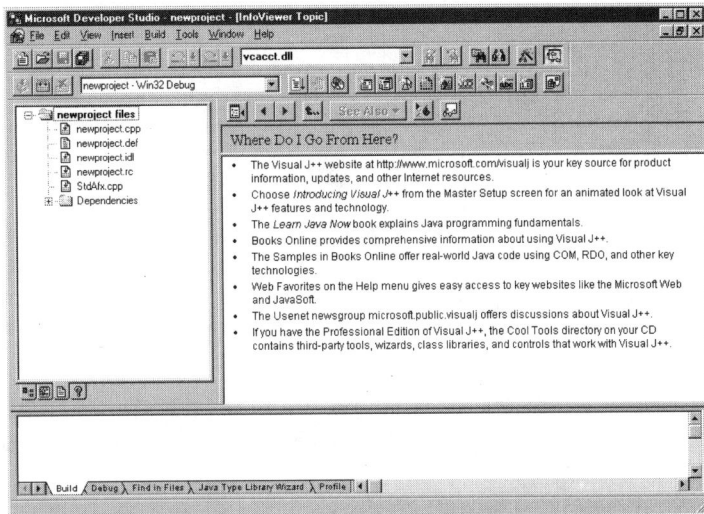

Figure 14.4 Microsoft Developer Standard Projects.

Note the files generated:

- **newproject.cpp**. This file has the DLLs for the in-process server. This includes WinMain for the local server. If you chose Service, this file has the service management functions.
- **newproject.def**. Created only for the in-process server.
- **newproject.idl**. Contains the definition for the interfaces.
- **newproject.rc**. Has the project resource information.
- **StdAfx.cpp**. Includes the ATL header files (**StdAfx.h**).

To add a component, choose **Component** on the Insert menu (see Figure 14.5).
 This opens Component Gallery. Here, you can select the **ATL** tab (see Figure 14.6).
Now choose **ATL Object Wizard** to open the ATL Object wizard. From here you choose to create objects or controls.
 The ATL Object wizard opens. There are two windows. Click in the left window on **Objects**. In the right window, double-click **Simple Object**. If you have Visual C++ 5.0, choose **ActiveX Server Component**.

Chapter 14

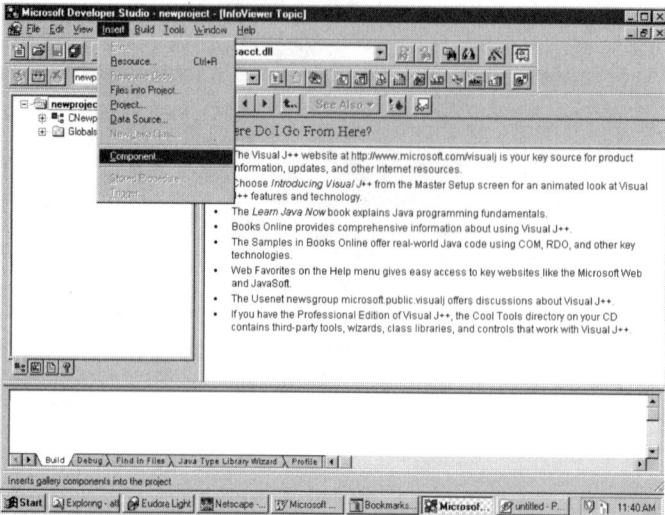

Figure 14.5 Creating a component.

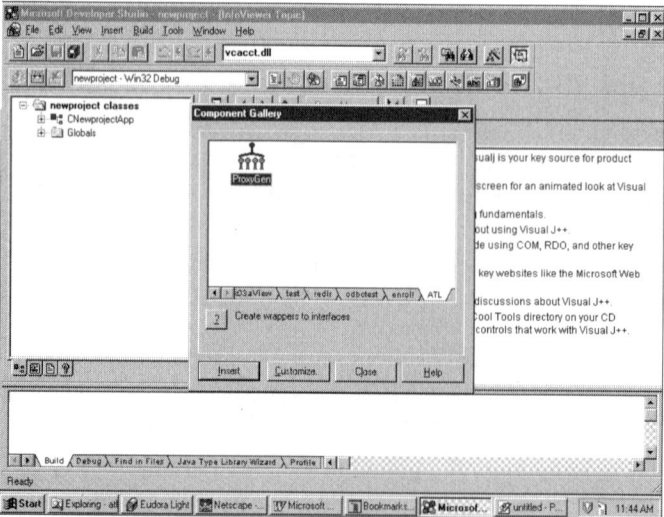

Figure 14.6 Component Gallery.

The next box is the ATL Object Wizard Properties. Type the abbreviated name in the **Names** tab. The system fills in the other names.

You can change the Threading Model to **Both** on the **Attributes** tab.

In Visual C++ 5.0 there is an **ASP** tab. Here you can set ASP *intrinsics*, or built-in objects: Application, Session, Server, Request, and Response. To use the intrinsics, you must use the OnStartPage and OnEndPage event-handling methods. When an ASP is called by the Web browser, the ASP calls these two methods. One opens the page, and the other closes it.

From here you can now modify the new project files to implement your component.

Let's take a brief look at one type of component: the control.

ActiveX Controls Implemented by ATL

ActiveX controls used to be known as OLE controls or OCX controls. They are objects (components) that you can insert into a Web page or an application. The ActiveX controls for Internet Explorer 3.0 provide formatting and animation capabilities. Other sample controls include the following:

- A Web browser control that displays HTML pages, ActiveX controls, and ActiveX documents.
- A Microsoft Forms 2.0 **Option** button that allows users to choose between multiple options.
- An ActiveMovie control that displays streaming and nonstreaming media such as video, sound, and synchronized images with sound.

You can write ActiveX controls using MFC, ATL, and other tools. In this chapter, we will look at the ATL implementation method.

The ATL is C++ templates allow you to create small, efficient controls. You need not link in the C run-time library. As mentioned earlier, the templates can assist with development of OLE functionality, but the developer needs a good understanding of COM.

Some developers would say that using ATL requires a deeper knowledge of how OLE controls communicate with their containers. There are at least 12 OLE interfaces (such as Idispatch and IScriptingContext) to consider.

The Benefit of Using ActiveX Controls

The advantage of using ActiveX controls compared with applications such as Java applets and Netscape plug-ins is that ActiveX controls can also be used in Windows applications other than Web browsers.

ActiveX functionality ranges from the simplest timer to an integrated video control. The controls are scaleable and reusable. When a person comes to a page that has a control, the control is downloaded into an ActiveX control cache located in the **\windows\occache** directory.

You add ActiveX controls to a Web page by using the standard HTML <OBJECT> tag. The <OBJECT> tag includes a set of parameters that you will use to determine which data the control should use. You will also designate the control's appearance and behavior.

When building a control, you are allowed to choose a *MinDependency* option. This means that the resulting DLL (or EXE) is completely self-contained. When you release your control to the Web, it will rely only on standard system DLLs such as KERNEL32, USER32, GDI32, OLE32, OLEAUT32, and ADVAPI32. You must distribute other DLLs only if you build a proxy/stub DLL that is not a part of your server DLL.

Sometimes a developer releases a control that must remain a certain size in the browser. This may be true with multimedia controls, such as animation controls. A developer shared the following technique to prevent the resizing of the control. In this case, the developer set the following in the control's constructor known as FinalConstruct:

```
// Don't allow a resize
m_bAutoSize = TRUE;
// Set the original size
SIZEL size = {48, 48};
AtlPixelToHiMetric( &size, &m_sizeExtent );
// Make sure the natural extent is the correct size too
m_sizeNatural = m_sizeExtent;
```

Internet Explorer 3.0 (and later) comes with a set of ActiveX controls. These controls do the following:

- Simplify and automate the authoring procedures. For example, a Web designer can set a date for an image to expire and no longer show up on the page.
- Display data in charts or rotated to different angles (for example, at a slant to the page).
- Add timers, animation, and background downloading.

These ActiveX controls are automatically installed when the customer installs Internet Explorer 3.0, making it convenient if you have who has an intranet to support. You can choose Internet Explorer as the standard client tool and build simple, dynamic Web pages that use these embedded controls. As soon as a user comes to your page, the client's control activates.

Netscape Navigator users will need a plug-in. It is available from NCompass Labs at http://www.ncompasslabs.com/products/scriptactive.htm.

Do not forget to visit the Microsoft ActiveX site for controls. The standard free controls include the following:

- Two small components—Simple and Power—each written in ATL, MFC, Java, Visual Basic 4, and Visual Basic 5, so that you can compare and contrast their implementations.
- A Registry Access component (ATL).
- A Page Counter component (ATL).
- A Permission Checker component (ATL).
- An HTML Database Table formatting component (Java).
- A Text Formatter component (parallel implementations in ATL, Java, and Visual Basic 5).

Now let's look at the thread models.

THREADING

There are four thread models: single threading, apartment threading, free threading, and both (a combination of apartment threading and free threading). A thread is a single process flow with a beginning, a sequence of events, and an ending.

When we talk about multithreading, we mean that a program can run concurrent processes to perform various tasks. A simple example is in Windows 3.1 running Notepad versus Microsoft Word. Notice that the executable that runs Notepad allows only one file open at a time, whereas Microsoft Word allows a number of windows to be open at one time.

In a *marshaling* interface, multiple clients are trying to use a main thread. The DLL may use a marshaling approach to handle each of the different client threads. For example, if thread A were calling a DLL object and then thread B called the same object, the DLL would use marshaling to put the thread B request in line behind that of thread A. When A was finished, B would be allowed to make the call.

In the single-threading model, only one thread uses COM and all calls to COM objects are synchronized by COM. ASP does not perform well with this model.

The apartment-threading model allows one or more threads in a process to use COM. As in the single-threading model, COM synchronizes the calls. Shared data must be protected. ASP performance is acceptable with this model.

The free-threading model also has one or more threads in a process using COM. The difference from the first two models is that the objects automatically synchronize the COM objects.

The Both-threading model means that the objects include the apartment and free-threaded models. ATL defaults to this environment.

Objects must be thread-safe. This means that data is properly protected as each of the client threads makes a call to the object handling the data. Without thread safety, a DLL may return the wrong data to a client and the data itself may become out of sync during updates.

Where to Go from Here

In this chapter, you have learned a little more about ActiveX and its component architecture. ATL provides a way to add functionality to an active site, but it is not always the best method. Weigh the other tools of the Active Desktop before diving into ATL. It can quickly plunge you into murky waters.

From here, you should look at these chapters:

- Chapter 13, "Active X," if you are not totally familiar with ActiveX controls.

Chapter 15

Visual Basic and Its Scripting Environment

Developers can use Visual C++ to produce wonderful interactive applications, but they turn to Visual Basic when they want a rapid development environment for developing Windows applications that also implements an event-driven environment. Developers find it very easy to build client/server and database applications using Visual Basic. This chapter will focus on the use of VBScript because of its use with ASP and ActiveX controls. If you wish to learn more about the Visual Basic environment, there are a number of great books on that subject.

OVERVIEW

The benefit of Visual Basic (VB) is that it gives the developer more power than the older sequential processing versions of BASIC. For example, let's say you build a database of employees. In that database is a table holding employee names and addresses. With the older versions of BASIC, a user would have to enter the name, the street address, the city, the state, the ZIP code, and so on. At the end, the BASIC program would verify the user's input and then ask whether the user was ready to move on. If the user gave the BASIC application an affirmative statement, all the data would be entered. If the user said no, he or she would probably have to start over. With a Visual Basic form, the user fills everything in, makes corrections, and clicks a **Submit** button. Visual Basic also provides a great Windows interface.

Visual Basic is a 32-bit tool for building Windows applications. It has a good remote data access and OLE-based toolset, and can use the Jet database engine. It can ensure referential integrity and has database support for cascading updates, deletes, field-level and record-level data validation, enforcement of a primary key, caching administration of a remote data source, and password security. Microsoft incorporated a data control environment that allows a Visual Basic programmer to access any database (including Excel and dBase) that is already accessible through Jet.

In addition, VB can access clientserver data via the ODBC data sources. You can use VB to write OLE automation objects. The resultant DLLs are interpreted at run time rather than compiled (as C++ DLLs are). You use class modules to create OLE automation objects, which provide methods and properties that you can use to interface with clientserver applications.

VB supports the creation of both in-process and out-of-process servers. *In-process* servers are compiled as DLLs, and *out-of-process* servers are compiled as EXEs. To pass data between process boundaries (or between the developer's object and applications such as Word or Excel), VB uses an OLE proxy/stub mechanism. The communication between out-of-process servers carries more overhead than the communication in an in-process server. The problem with an in-process server, though, is that every OLE client would need its own copy of the server. An out-of process server can serve many OLE clients. Planning is essential when you're making these decisions.

The added benefit of an out-of-process server is that it communicates with OLE clients on a network, such as the Internet. This is known as *remote automation* in the VB world. In this instance, the proxy/stub mechanism is replaced by a mechanism that uses Remote Procedure Calls (RPC), which provide added functionality to network communications. In this way, the VB programmer gains the ability to distribute objects in the clientserver world and to properly communicate with them. The drawback is the overhead of using RPC as well as network latency issues. It is still recommended that remote OLE automation not be used in a critical area. VB is getting closer to being an object-oriented programming tool, but inheritance, which is used heavily in Java and C++, appears to be missing.

Visual Basic 5.0 appears to provide greatly increased programming code efficiency. Its integrated development environment (IDE) provides a multiple window interface that is like the Visual C++ and Visual Java ++ development environments. The layout of the main project window is similar to a file directory tree, so you can work on multiple projects at one time, something that is very useful for writing ActiveX controls. VB 5.0 will compile native code.

An Auto Complete feature lets you handle long property names and associated values. You can type the name of a built-in control object, press the period (.) key, and get a list of the object's properties and methods. Click on the property, press the equals (=) key, and the values are displayed.

Visual Basic 5.0 replaces the Office 95 macro and scripting languages. You have more control over programming user-defined events, something that is important in a clientserver world, where it is the dynamic changes (items happening over time triggered by events) that bring users to a site. Visual Basic 5.0's Active Documents technology lets you put CGI, GIFs, JPEGs, and HTML in an application and then access them through an ActiveX browser. This means that a developer could control a Web site via a browser.

All this means that there must be a way to incorporate Visual Basic in the browser environment. That is where VBScript fits in.

VBScript

VBScript, like VBA, is a derivation of Visual Basic. Although VBScript does not have all the functionality of VB (see the later discussion on the differences), it is of great use to developers. VBScript is an integral part of both Internet Explorer and Active Server.

VBScript can be used to create interactive mechanisms such as menus, calculators, and forms. You can use VBScript to run a process locally in the browser and then interact with a database, when necessary, on the server side.

Developers can access Web page elements using controls, including Active X controls and those built into the VBScript environment. Let's look at the VBScript environment first. A VBScript control would be something like a button, such as this one:

```
<INPUT TYPE=BUTTON NAME=anyButton VALUE="This is a Button!">
```

To activate a dialog box when the user pushes the button, a developer would include this code:

```
Sub anyButton_OnClick
              MsgBox "Thanks for clicking me"
              End Sub
```

Note that the button is called anyButton and has an event called OnClick. As the button is clicked, the Subroutine is executed. The MsgBox creates a dialog box.

Basic Syntax Rules

Let's look at some of the basic syntax of VBScript, including the datatypes, constants and variables, mathematical operators, and procedures and functions.

DATATYPES

VBScript has a single datatype called a *variant*. A variant tends to contain a string or numeric value. It acts like a number when used with numerics and as a string when used with strings.

A variant has what are called subtypes. The subtype can be empty (a zero or no-length string), null (no valid data), Boolean (T or F), byte (0 to 255), integer (−32,768 to 32,767), currency (−922,337,203,685,477.5808 to 922,337,203,685,477.5807), long (integers from −2,147,483,648 to 2,147,483,647), single (single-precision, floating-point number from −3.402823E38 to −1.401298E−45 for negative values and 1.401298E−45 to 3.402823E38 for positive values), double (double-precision, floating-point number from −1.79769313486232E308 to −4.94065645841247E−324 for negative values; 4.94065645841247E−324 to 1.79769313486232E308 for positive values), date (between January 1, 100, and December 31, 9999), and string (a variable-length string that can be as many as 2 billion characters in length)

Constants and Variables

A *constant* is a number or string that does not change over time. VBScript uses the Const keyword. For example:

```
Const AString = "This is a string."
        Const Bookpages= 500
```

A *variable* is an item that can change over time. Variables must be declared. VBScript uses the Dim statement, the Public statement, and the Private statement to declare variables.

```
Dim ClickCount
```

If there are a number of variables to declare, use a comma to separate them:

```
Dim First, Second, Third, Fourth
```

Variable names must begin with an alphabetic character and the name must be unique (used only once in a procedure), cannot have a (.), and cannot exceed 255 characters.

Here is how to assign a value to a variable:

```
First = 200
```

You can also declare an *array*, or a series of values for a variable. For example:

```
Dim First(5)
```

To assign values to the array, use this syntax:

```
First(0) = 10
First(1) = 20
First(2) = 30
First(3) = 40
First(4) = 50
First(5) = 60
```

You can create a two-dimensional array as a table:

```
Dim AnyTable(3, 4)
```

This table has three rows and four columns. A value would be set as follows:

```
AnyTable(1,1) = 25
```

where row 1, column 1 is 25.

Mathematical Operators

VBScript uses standard mathematical operators.

      Exponent: x^5
      Equal: x=5

Addition: x+5
Subtraction: x-5
A negative: x Not 5
Multiplication: x*5
Inequality: x<>5
And join: x And 5
Less than: x<5
Or join: x Or 5
Division: x/5
Greater than: x>5
Less than or equal to: x<==5
Modulus: x Mod 5
Greater than or equal to: x >= 5
String concatenation: x & y

Procedures and Functions

VBScript has subroutines that are called *procedures*. Here is an example:

```
Sub ConvertLength()
        time = InputBox("Please enter the length in feet.", 1)
        MsgBox "The length in inches is" & Length(inches) & "inches."
    End Sub
```

This procedure processes MsgBox and InputBox. InputBox prompts the user for information, and MsgBox returns the result as a pop-up window.

A *function* is like a procedure, but it returns a value. In this case, the developer needs to calculate the difference between feet and inches:

```
Sub ConvertLength()
        time = InputBox("Please enter the length in feet.", 1)
        MsgBox "The length in inches is" & Length(inches) & "inches."
    End Sub

Function Length(inches)
        Length = (inches * 12 )
    End Function
```

Adding to the Web Page

Note that in all the examples in this section, the variables are passed via the object.property syntax. In the second example there is an incident of orderCost.Value= Cost. This means that the object orderCost has a property of Value. This property now is set equal to the Cost.

In each of the examples, events are occurring. These events include the following:

- OnClick= when the user clicks the object
- DblClick= when the user double-clicks the object
- OnLoad= when the current page is loaded

Object tags are also used with ActiveX controls. You insert controls and objects between the <OBJECT> </OBJECT> tags. Note that there are also <PARAM> tags within the Objects. These tags identify the properties of the object or control. Object values include the following:

- CLASSID. The system registration number of each class of object.
- ID. The nickname of the CLASSID.
- CODEBASE. Where to find the control.
- HEIGHT. The height of the object.
- WIDTH. The width of the object.

Parameter values include

- Name. The object's property (such as angle).
- Value. The value of the Name just specified (such as 90, as in 90 degrees).

The <SCRIPT> </SCRIPT> tags allow you to add the VBScript to the page.

```
<SCRIPT LANGUAGE="VBScript">
         <!-
Function Length(inches)
            Length = (inches * 12 )
        End Function

->
         </SCRIPT>
```

The <SCRIPT> tag can have attributes. One of them is the LANGUAGE, which indicates the scripting language. You must specify the language, because browsers can use other scripting languages. Microsoft Explorer interprets VBScript. To run VBScript in a Netscape environment, the user will need a plug-in from NCompass Labs. The function is embedded in comment tags (<!— and —>). If the browser does not understand the <SCRIPT> tag, it will not display the code within the comment tags.

Because the example is a general function—it isn't tied to any particular form control—you can include it in the HEAD section of the page:

```
<HTML>
    <HEAD>
    <TITLE>Place Your Order</TITLE>
    <SCRIPT LANGUAGE="VBScript">
    <!—
       Function CanDeliver(Dt)
          CanDeliver = (CDate(Dt) - Now()) > 2
       End Function
    —>
    </SCRIPT>
    </HEAD>
    <BODY>
    ...
```

<SCRIPT> tags can appear anywhere, but with forms, as in CGI scripts, it is best to put the script information within the <FORM> </FORM> tags:

```
<HTML>
    <HEAD>
    <TITLE>Buttons</TITLE>
    </HEAD>
    <BODY>
    <FORM NAME="Form">
       <INPUT TYPE="Button" NAME="Buttonnew" VALUE="Click">
       <SCRIPT FOR="Buttonnew" EVENT="onClick" LANGUAGE="VBScript">
          MsgBox "This is  a button being pressed!"
       </SCRIPT>
    </FORM>
    </BODY>
    </HTML>
```

MORE SAMPLES

The following samples highlight the use of buttons and forms. Here is an interactive button:

```
            <HTML>
               <HEAD>
               <TITLE>VBScript buttons</TITLE>
               </HEAD>
               <BODY BGCOLOR="#FFFFFF">
               <H1 ALIGN=CENTER>VBScript Demo</H1>
               <P>This is a button example</ P>
               <INPUT TYPE=BUTTON NAME=newButton VALUE="!">
               <SCRIPT LANGUAGE="VBScript">
               <!—
```

Chapter 15

```
                    ' This procedure runs when  the button labeled newButton
is clicked
                    Sub aButton_OnClick
                    MsgBox "Thanks for pressing the button?"
                    End Sub
                    ->
                    </SCRIPT>
                    </BODY>
                    </HTML>
```

This code builds an order form:

```
              <HTML>
                    <HEAD>
                    <TITLE>VBScript Orders</TITLE>
                    </HEAD>
                    <BODY BGCOLOR="#FFFFFF">
                    <H1>The Order Center</H1>
                    <P>Place your order using the following form</P>
                    <P>
                    Number of reports: <INPUT NAME="orderSize" SIZE=5 VALUE=1>
                    <P><B>
                    <INPUT TYPE=BUTTON VALUE="Report Order"
                    NAME="Costs">
                    </B></P>
                    Sub Total
              $<INPUT NAME="initCost" SIZE=10>
                    Total                   $<INPUT NAME="Total"
                    SIZE=10>
                    <SCRIPT LANGUAGE="VBScript">
                    <!- Option Explicit
                    Sub Costs_OnClick()
                    Dim numReports
                    Dim Cost
                    Dim Total
                    numReports = orderSize.Value
                    Cost = 29.00 * numReports
                    Total = Cost
                    orderCost.Value = Cost
                    Total.Value = Round(Total,2)
                    End Sub
                    ->
                    </SCRIPT>
                    </BODY>
                    </HTML>
```

Visual Basic and Its Scripting Environment

The following modifies client-side image maps from the Microsoft site: http://www.microsoft.com/vbscript/us/samples/mouset/mouset.htm.

```
<SCRIPT LANGUAGE="VBScript">
    ' Remember the last location clicked.
    Dim mX, mY
    Sub Image_MouseMove(s, b, x, y)
        mX = x
        mY = y
            If InRect(x, y, 20, 30, 240, 85) Then
                Call DescribeLink("Our catalog")
            ElseIf InRect(x, y, 20, 115, 240, 135) then
                Call DescribeLink("Our Marketing page")
            ElseIf InRect(x, y, 20, 170, 240, 220) then
                Call DescribeLink("Support Page")

        Else
            DescribeLink ""
        End If
    End Sub
    Sub Image_OnClick()
        If InRect(mX, mY, 20, 30, 240, 85) Then
            location.href = "http://www.mysite.com/catalog.asp"
        ElseIf InRect(mX, mY, 20, 115, 240, 135) then
            location.href = "http://www.mysite.com/marketing.asp"
        ElseIf InRect(mX, mY, 20, 170,240, 220) then
            location.href = "http://www.mysite.com/support.asp "

        End If
    End Sub
    Function InRect(x, y, Rect_x1, Rect_y1, Rect_x2, Rect_y2)
        InRect =  x > Rect_x1 And x < Rect_x2 And y > Rect_y1 And y < Rect_y2
    End Function
    Sub DescribeLink(Text)
        TxtLinkDescription.Value = Text
    End Sub
</SCRIPT>
```

The preceding example provides a clickable image map starting on the left side of the screen. It is similar to the CGI method of client-side mapping:

```
!—webbot bot="ImageMap" rectangle=" (20,30) (240, 85)
http://www.mysite.com/catalog.asp " rectangle=" (20,115) (240, 135)
http://www.mysite.com/marketing.asp " rectangle=" (20,170) (240, 220)
http://www.mysite.com/support.asp " src="side.gif" border="0" width="640"
height="60" startspan —><MAP NAME="Map">
```

Chapter 15

```
<AREA SHAPE="RECT" COORDS="20,30,240,85" HREF="
http://www.mysite.com/catalog.asp "><AREA SHAPE="RECT" COORDS="20,115,240,135 "
HREF=" http://www.mysite.com/marketing.asp "><AREA SHAPE="RECT"
COORDS="20,170,240,220" HREF=" http://www.mysite.com/support.asp "> </MAP><a
href="_vti_bin/shtml.exe/index.htm/map"><img ismap usemap="#FrontPageMap" bor-
der="0" height="60" src="side.gif" width="640"></a><!—webbot bot="ImageMap"
endspan i-checksum="53539" —>
```

Here is a modified cookie example from the Microsoft site: http://www.microsoft.com/vbscript/us/samples/cookies/extcookie.htm.

```
<HTML>
<HEAD>
<TITLE>VBScript Sample: Maintaining State with Cookies</TITLE>
<META HTTP-EQUIV="Content-Type" CONTENT="text/html; charset=iso8859-1">
<META NAME="DESCRIPTION" CONTENT="VBScript Sample: Maintaining State with
Cookies">
<META NAME="MS.LOCALE" CONTENT="EN-US">
<META NAME="PRODUCT" CONTENT="Visual Basic Scripting Edition">
<META NAME="TECHNOLOGY" CONTENT="SCRIPTING">

<SCRIPT LANGUAGE="VBScript">
<!—

'****************************************************************
'Dimension and set the NOT_FOUND constant for the entire page
    Dim NOT_FOUND
    NOT_FOUND = "NOT_FOUND"

'****************************************************************
' Purpose: Creates or modifies the value assigned to a given
'          variable.
'
'****************************************************************

Sub SetVariable(strVariableName, varVariableValue)
        Document.Cookie = strVariableName & "=" & varVariableValue
    End Sub

'****************************************************************
' Purpose: Delete the variable with the name held in
'          strVariableName
'
'****************************************************************

Sub KillVariable(strVariableName)
```

```
        SetVariable strVariableName, "NULL;expires=Monday, 01-Jan-99 12:00:00
GMT"
     End Sub

'****************************************************************
' This section gives the developer the values of the
'variables in the string names (strVariableName).
'****************************************************************

Function ReadVariable(strVariableName)

Dim intLocation
        Dim intNameLength
        Dim intValueLength
        Dim intNextSemicolon
        Dim strTemp

        intNameLength = Len(strVariableName)
        intLocation = Instr(Document.Cookie, strVariableName)

        If intLocation = 0 Then

            ReadVariable = NOT_FOUND
        Else

            strTemp = Right(Document.Cookie, Len(Document.Cookie) - intLocation
 + 1)

            If Mid(strTemp, intNameLength + 1, 1) <> "=" Then

                ReadVariable = NOT_FOUND

            Else

                intNextSemicolon = Instr(strTemp, ";")

                If intNextSemicolon = 0 Then intNextSemicolon = Len(strTemp) +
1

                If intNextSemicolon = (intNameLength + 2) Then

                    ReadVariable = ""
                Else

                    intValueLength = intNextSemicolon - intNameLength - 2
                    ReadVariable = Mid(strTemp, intNameLength + 2,
intValueLength)
```

Chapter 15

```
                End If
            End If
        End if
    End Function

' ************************************************
'Button Code
' ************************************************

Sub btnSaveVariable_onClick
        Dim strVariableName
        Dim varVariableValue

        strVariableName = InputBox("Enter variable name")
        varVariableValue = InputBox("Enter value for '" & strVariableName & "'")

        SetVariable strVariableName, varVariableValue
    End Sub

Sub btnReadVariable_onClick
        Dim strVariableName
        Dim varVariableValue

        strVariableName = InputBox("Enter variable name to read")

        varVariableValue = ReadVariable(strVariableName)
        If varVariableValue = NOT_FOUND Then
            MsgBox "'" & strVariableName & "' not found."
        Else
            MsgBox "'" & strVariableName & "' has a value of '" & varVariableValue & "'."
        End If
    End sub

Sub btnShowCookie_onClick
        MsgBox Document.Cookie
    End Sub

Sub btnNextPage_onClick
        Location.HRef = "extcookie2.htm"
    End Sub

Sub btnKillVariable_onClick
        Dim strVariableName
        Dim varVariableValue
```

```
            strVariableName = InputBox("Enter variable name to delete")
            varVariableValue = ReadVariable(strVariableName)

            If varVariableValue = NOT_FOUND Then
                MsgBox "'" & strVariableName & "' not found."
            Else
                KillVariable(strVariableName)
                MsgBox "Variable deleted."
            End If
        End Sub
-->
</SCRIPT>

</HEAD>

<BODY BGCOLOR=FFFFFF LINK=#0033CC TOPMARGIN=15 LEFTMARGIN=20>

<!--TOOLBAR_START-->
<!--TOOLBAR_EXEMPT-->
<!--TOOLBAR_END-->

<TABLE BORDER=0 CELLPADDING=0 CELLSPACING=0 WIDTH=100%>
        <TR VALIGN=TOP>
            <TD WIDTH=200>
                <IMG SRC="product.gif" WIDTH=120 HEIGHT=13 VSPACE=2 ><BR>
                <BR>
            </TD>
                <TD ALIGN=RIGHT>
                Produts</A> | <A HREF="/product/"
TARGET="_top">Start Page</A> |<BR>| <A HREF="/support/"
TARGET="_top">Support </A> |<BR></FONT></TD>
        </TR>
        <TR>
            <TD COLSPAN=2>
                 <BR>
                <FONT SIZE=5><B>Help on  Cookies</B></FONT>
            </TD>
        </TR>
</TABLE>
<HR NOSHADE SIZE=1>
 <BR>

<!-- Horizontal line -->
```

```
<form action="" Name="Form1">
<INPUT TYPE="BUTTON" NAME="btnSaveVariable" VALUE="Save Variable">
<INPUT TYPE="BUTTON" NAME="btnReadVariable" VALUE="Read Variable">
<INPUT TYPE="BUTTON" NAME="btnKillVariable" VALUE="Kill Variable">
<INPUT TYPE="BUTTON" NAME="btnShowCookie" VALUE="Show Cookie">
<INPUT TYPE="BUTTON" NAME="btnNextPage" VALUE="Next Page">
</FORM><P>

<A HREF="/misc/cpyright.htm" TARGET="_top">&copy; 1997 Microsoft Corporation.
All rights reserved. Terms of Use. Modified for use on a separate company
page</A>

</FONT>
</FONT>
</BODY>
</HTML>
```

CONTROLS FOR VISUAL BASIC

Visual Basic allows developers to create ActiveX controls. Unlike ATL (see Chapter 14 for a full discussion of ATL), VB is not intended to support detailed ActiveX control creation. Instead, a developer using VB may find it best to add to the functionality of a current ActiveX control.

VB has an ActiveX Control Interface wizard (see Figure 15.1).

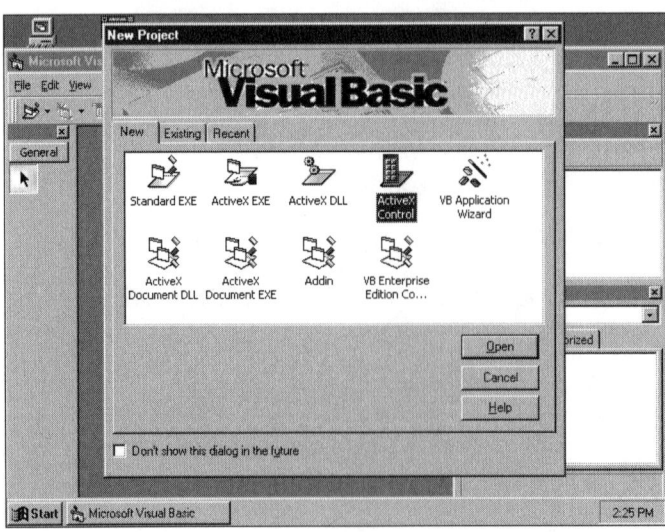

Figure 15.1 The VB ActiveX Control Interface wizard.

The wizard helps you by adding the standard and custom properties along with the events. VB gives you a user control, in essence an ActiveX control container. You can put an existing ActiveX control into a user control form and then use the wizard to align the events and properties with the control.

To create an ActiveX control you must have VB 5.0. Select **project types**. Then select **ActiveX Control**. You can build a text box on the form.

Now start the ActiveX Control Interface wizard. Select **Back Color**, **Font**, and **Text**. Now you can add custom properties, methods, and events. You can now add your own property with an event and then map the properties and events to the control. For example, you might map Back Color, Font, and Text to a Text control. The final window lets you set up the custom properties and events (see Figure 15.2).

Then you add code to the control.

Developers can use the component method in a form's environment. The form has standard and custom properties, methods, and events that are mapped to the components.

There can be a disadvantage to choosing to use VB for creating ActiveX controls. If you do not have the VB 5.0 commercial version, you cannot create stand-alone executables. The resultant control size may be small, but be cautious. To run a VB control on the client machine you must have the VB Virtual Machine DLL. This **MSVBM50.DLL** is about 1.3 MB.

The good news is that the OCXs are supported by the current version of Visual C++. This means that you can use the OCXs in any ActiveX host.

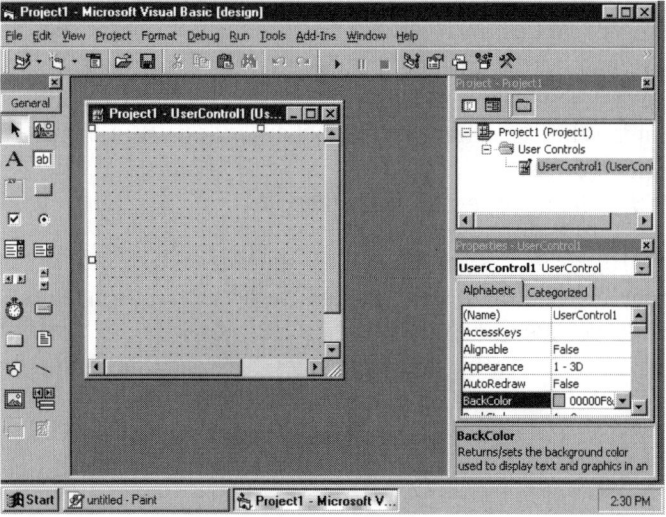

Figure 15.2 The VB design window.

VB 5.0 does not require the MFC DLLs. You can download the control run-time files (CABs) from the Microsoft site.

VISUAL BASIC TIPS AND TRICKS

Developers often share tips and new techniques over the Internet. Here are a few of them that you may find advantageous.

1. How can you incorporate multithreading? VB 5.0 comes with the AddressOf operator, which allows you to pass pointers to functions. It is the same as a callback. As in all cases of multithreaded programming, plan the effort. Here is some sample code that was shared over the Web.
2. How can you debug VBScript? Many good books describe the proper use of VBScript. In addition, you will find a large set of tools available within Visual Basic 5.0.
3. It is recommended that you not run a VB application as a Windows NT service. The first concern is thread safety. VB is not currently thread-safe. The second concern is that VB is intended to be interactive with users, but the services are not. A VB application, running as a service, might run into an error and launch an error dialog box that would not only hands the application but also lock up the server.

WHERE TO GO FROM HERE

Visual Basic and VBScript allow developers to implement powerful clientserver functionality without having to learn a difficult language such as Visual C++ or Visual Java++. The VB developer can access databases as well as develop ActiveX controls using embedded tools and wizards. VBScript extends the functionality of VB to a run-time environment within the client's browser.

From here you should review these chapters:

- Chapter 16, "Java and JavaScript," to understand the "other" scripting language (especially the one that Microsoft's Active Server Pages defaults to if you do not specify that you are using VBScript)
- Chapter 17, "Comparing the Languages," to learn more about the differences between VBScript and the other programming environments.

Chapter 16

Java and JavaScript

What is Java? It is not coffee. It is not an island somewhere in the South Pacific. Sun Microsystems calls it a revolution for both application and Internet development. Microsoft has even incorporated Java programming tools in its systems.

Java is a high-level, object-oriented programming language originally developed by Sun Microsystems in 1990 and released in 1995. Java was designed to be used on small consumer electronic devices, but eventually Sun realized that Java could be useful for much more.

Java is an interpreted language, so the development cycle can be faster than with C++. In C++ you compile the file, link it, load it, test it, find the bugs, debug, and recompile. With Java, you need only compile the project and run it. In addition, you can write the application and run it on any platform that has a Java Virtual Machine (JVM) interpreter. JVM is not really a machine. Rather, it is a set of specifications that Java code is compiled to run against. Any interpreter meeting the JVM specifications can run your code.

The Java run-time system manages memory for you. In addition, the system handles multiple threads. They are not truly concurrent—one thread runs and stops, and then the next thread runs—but it is so fast that it appears to be concurrent. This multithreading environment increases your ability to provide graphically oriented sites that do not take much time to load even with a 28.8K modem. Java uses a thread class library to handle threading issues along with a run-time system for monitoring.

You can download code to a network and run applications from any server. Security, which will be discussed further in a separate section, is of no major concern, because you compile on your server and then run applets (run-time modules) at the client.

The Java interpreter executes *bytecodes.*, which are on any machine that has an interpreter and run-time system. The client needs a Java-ready browser such as Netscape 3.0 and later and Microsoft IE 3.x and later.

During compilation, classes are linked only as needed. Any new code can be linked on demand from a local or network source. This means that Java is suitable for the developer who needs to use a clientserver development environment.

Because Java is a descendent of C++, it creates and handles objects. Java objects are modular and fit a certain architecture that is oriented to code that works over a network. Java applications are compiled into bytecodes and are targeted to run on the runtime Java Virtual Machine. The bytecodes are translated to machine code at run time. The aim is to make Java machine-independent. The drawback is that the code is not as fast as compiled C++ code. When these compiled objects are developed to run in a Web browser, they are called *applets*. They are intended to live on the server side of the Web environment. When you create an applet, the idea is for it is to be large enough to do the job but small enough to be downloaded over the Web.

A Few Definitions

- Abstract Window Toolkit (AWT). A class library that has the basic user interface widgets such as buttons and menus.
- Applet. A program that is written in Java and runs from within the browser window.
- Bytecode. The code read by the Java Virtual Machine. Java compilers translate a Java program into bytecode.
- Class. The characteristic of an object.
- Dynamic binding. The mechanism by which objects can come from even across the network.
- Java Virtual Machine (JVM). The software that interprets Java bytecodes.
- Java Development Kit (JDK). The Java development tools; Sun's applet-maker tool.
- Java Database Connectivity (JDBC). The interface that a Java developer can use to get data from databases.
- JavaBeans. Components written in Java. They are intended to perform a single simple function and are similar in function to ActiveX controls.
- JavaScript. A scripting language that uses Java-like syntax.
- Just-in-time compiler (JIT). Java compiled on-the-fly. It is much faster than bytecode but not as portable. Compilers are written to generate machine code from the bytecode.
- Object-oriented. A programming technology that relies on "things" being described as objects. This chapter discusses objects, classes and instances for this programming environment. Class is an item or type of item, such as an airplane. An object is a specific class, such as a jet An instance is a reference to a use of the class. The Jet object is an instance of class Airplane.

Basic Java Syntax

Java's similarity to C++ extends to the syntax. Let's look at three basic items: objects, classes, and instances.

A developer would use a class to define a type of thing. A car would be represented by the automobile class; a Mazda is an object. So the syntax would be Auto Mazda = new

Auto(). The object Mazda is a reference to an instance of the class Auto. So a single class, such as Auto, can be instanced a number of times.

A Java object is a container that holds variables and functions (methods). Because Java objects can be stored in variables, Java objects can also hold other Java objects. These objects have *state* and *behavior*. You can represent all these things with software constructs called *objects*, which can also be defined by their state and their behavior.

In your everyday transportation needs, a car can be modeled by an object. A car has state (how fast it's going, in which direction, its fuel consumption, and so on) and behavior (starts, stops, turns, slides, and runs into trees).

There are two types of Java objects: arrays and class instances. Let's focus on the class.

JAVA CLASSES

Java, like other object-oriented languages, has class methods and class variables. A *class variable* is a variable that is local to the class. Every object in the class that is instantiated (created) will share this variable. Here is an example:

```
class Rectangle extends Object {
        static  final int releasenum = 1;
   }
```

Note that you declare class variables and class methods as *static*. This means that every creation or instance of Rectangle will share the releasenum (short for release number).

If you declare a variable in a class definition, it is an *instance* . There can only be one instance variable per object created in a class.

Here is a class that has methods and properties:

```
class Animation {

// instance variables
private double length;
private String title;

// printer method
public void println() {
System.out.println("Title: " + title);
System.out.println("Length: " + length);
     }
//initialize variables
     public Animation(String n, double s) {
        length = l;
        title = t;
     }
```

```
public String getTitle() { return title; }
public double getLength() { return length; }

}
```

Class Animation has objects. You have declared them in the previous example. Let's now initialize the variables:

```
Animation  movie1 = new Animation("Movie1", 300),
           movie2 = new Animation("Movie2", 250);
```

What happens if you do this?

```
movie1 = null;
```

There appear to be no references to the original object. It is considered garbage. Java has a built-in ability to remove an object that has no reference.

A method is a function. For example, suppose you typed in this code:

```
movie1.setLength(350);
```

It grabs the public setLength() method, whereas the following code would grab the movie2 setLength method.

```
movie2.setLength (350)
```

That's because we previously set movie1 as Animation movie1, so that means movie1.setLength can include only members of the Animation class.

A method definition starts with the type of object that the method will return. If no object is returned, the return type is void. Remember that methods in one instance can access methods in a second instance if the method and variable are declared as public.

INHERITANCE

Let's say that you want to build a zoo project on a CD-ROM. Should you create every animal as a separate class or create a class of birds, a class of cats, a class of amphibians, and so on? Let's do the latter. In the class of cats, you can then describe cats of different sizes, perhaps a cougar and a lion. The cougar is part of the class of cats, and so is the lion. They are related. This means that the lions class and cougars class can inherit all the properties of the cats class. You can *extend* the class.

For example, let's continue with the Animation class theme. In addition to the methods and variables common to all animations, there are Quicktime animations. These animations have a revision number (revnum).

```
class Quicktime extends Animation {

      private int revnum; // revision number
      private String position = "quicktime";
```

```
public void println() {
      super.println();  // calls Animation.println()
      System.out.println("Position: " + position);
      System.out.println("Revision Number: " + revnum);
   }

public String getPosition() { return position; }

// etc.
   }
```

DYNAMIC BINDING

Java is both interpreted and dynamic. The engine links classes when needed and can download those classes from network locations. This means that a developer does not deal with the classic C++ compile and link cycle. It is a dynamically linked environment. Java methods are dynamically bound in the same way that C++ virtual functions are bound.

The good news for C++ programmers is that Java passes a symbolic reference instead of numeric values. This is one way to get around the class inheritance problem faced by C++ programmers. For example, let's say a developer creates an object A. It is defined by a class A. Then there is a class B that inherits from A. There is a class D that inherits from B, and so on. Tracking these dependencies can create many bugs for C++ programmers. That is why Java passes along the reference, and the Java interpreter (at the end of the processing pipeline) does the name resolution while linking.

Java has become a language of choice for many Web developers because of its tools, libraries, and the JVM. Let's take a look.

Java Virtual Machine

There are many technology-based reasons to like Java. One of the greatest benefits of writing to Java bytecode is that it is machine-independent. Developers write not for a PC or UNIX compiler but rather for the Java Virtual Machine. Technically, this means that a developer should be able to write it once and run it on many different systems as long as JVM exists on those systems. The intent of the Java Virtual Machine is to keep developers from having to write and port code to different environments. In C++, the developer writes code that is translated (via a compiler) to machine language (the world of ones and zeros). As a result, only one platform can run that machine language.

The Java developer produces bytecodes. The Web browser has an internal JVM, written for its platform, that interprets the bytecodes. Some Web browsers also have a just-in-time compiler. JIT performs what is called *dynamic compilation*. When a procedure or function is run for the first time, the JIT compiler interprets and compiles the bytecode. It stores the code in a binary format that it can reload during all subsequent calls. JIT compilers are machine-dependent.

Building an Applet

Building interpreted code for Web browsers means that a developer is creating an applet. There are many great resources that explain how to build applets. One of the best methods is to look at other developers' code. Samples that have been shared by a number of developers are shown in this section.

An applet can be loaded over the network or on the local system. If it comes over the network, the *applet class loader* brings it onto the local system. This means that the applet security manager must enforce restrictions. If the applet is on the local system, the file system loader handles the applet. This also means that this applet can read files, write files, load libraries, execute processes, and exit the JVM. Using the applet class loader prevents the applet from writing to the local file system or launching other applets. This arrangement is essential for deploying applets via the Internet.

Speaking of examples, here is one for saving cookies:

```
            function setCookie (name, value, expires) {
                if (!expires) expires = new Date();
            document.cookie = name + "=" + escape (value) +    <— save cookie value
            "; expires=" + expires.toGMTString() +  "; path=/"; <— set expiration date
            }                                                   and universal path
```

If the customer's name is Bob, this code saves the name:

```
var expdate = new Date ();
      expdate.setTime (expdate.getTime() + (1000 * 60 * 60 * 24 * 31));
      setCookie ("_name", "Bob", expdate);
```

This developer calculates the month using (1000 * 60 * 60 * 24 * 31) and sets the expiration date for one year. So reading the formula backwards, 31 is the number of days, 24 is the hours in a day, 60 is the minutes in an hour, the next 60 is the seconds in a minute, and 1,000 are the milliseconds in a second.

He used this function to read the cookie:

```
function getCookie (name) {
   var dcookie = document.cookie;
   var cname = name + "=";
   var clen = dcookie.length;
   var cbegin = 0;
```

Java and JavaScript

```
while (cbegin < clen) {
var vbegin = cbegin + cname.length;
if (dcookie.substring(cbegin, vbegin) == cname) {
var vend = dcookie.indexOf (";", vbegin);
if (vend == -1) vend = clen;
return unescape(dcookie.substring(vbegin, vend));
}
cbegin = dcookie.indexOf(" ", cbegin) + 1;
if (cbegin == 0) break;
}
return null;
}
```

This is used to write, for example, the name that was grabbed.

`document.write(getCookie("_name"));`

It is not as simple as Active Server, but it should give you a sense of general Java.

JavaBeans

As in the world of Microsoft's component architecture, Java comes with reusable software components: JavaBeans. They are pieces of code that run single functions. For example, if the client sees an alert screen from the printer, it could be one JavaBean that tracks the printer and another one that displays alerts. JavaBeans, which are written in Java, can work with an ActiveX control.

JAVA AND SECURITY: IS IT SAFE?

Java applets can run well over a network. Does that mean they are safe to run at all times? To answer that question, you must first be aware of your environment. Are the applets running internal to a company? Are they running in a critical corporate area? Over the Web?

In the Java business, developers call the access of applets in a page *executable content*. This means that a client runs the code. Security managers tell us that an applet must be kept from accessing file systems, controls, and devices.

To assist in delivering this level of security, there are a number of features within Java. First, unlike C++, Java has no pointers. This means that Java does not transverse memory and accidentally wipe out data. Second, the class loader checks the applet and secures it against tampering, stack overflows, and calling methods. Third, an applet cannot access a native method and therefore cannot call a C++ or Java application. In other words, applets cannot create other applets.

According to Sun's documentation, an applet can use System.getProperty(String key) to get the system properties shown in Table 16.1.

Table 16.1 System Properties Available to Applets

Key	Meaning
java.version	Java version number
java.vendor	Java vendor-specific string
java.vendor.url	Java vendor URL
java.class.version	Java class version number
os.name	Operating system name
os.arch	Operating system architecture
os.version	Operating system version
file.separator	File separator (for example, "/")
path.separator	Path separator (for example, ":")
line.separator	Line separator

On the other hand, applets cannot read the system properties shown in Table 16.2.

Table 16.2 System Properties Not Available to Applets

Key	Meaning
java.home	Java installation directory
java.class.path	Java classpath
user.name	User account name
user.home	User home directory
user.dir	User's current working directory

A couple of basic security issues often arise regarding applets: viruses and firewalls.

Viruses and Attacks

Some people say that there are viruses created by Java, but this has never been proven. The Java model for security is one in which an applet cannot call another applet. The applet is not a native executable, and it cannot affect the local system. These rumors about Java are much like the rumors regarding the possibility that an e-mail containing recipient will get a virus by reading an e-mail. There are cases in which an applet can take up a lot of system services or processor time but not one in which it trashes a hard disk.

As noted before, the Java methodology confines the applet in a sandbox. The disadvantage for developers is that the sandbox limits the capability of the applet. Sun is currently adopting changes to the security model. With the increased popularity of ActiveX, an intranet developer might not worry as much about the sandbox model. In the intranet, the developer controls the environment, and internal security issues (such as people stealing items such as laptops) are a greater problem. For this reason, Sun has announced that it is working on a version of Java that will create applets that can write to the file system.

As in the case of ActiveX, you can get a digital signature for an applet. This approach can add to the level of security that you provide to your clients.

Remember that safety is relative. Many people are concerned about the safety of applets and ActiveX controls, but they write their ATM personal identification number (PIN) on a piece of paper inside their wallet. If they lose the wallet, what good is the protection afforded by the PIN?

Using a Firewall

Let's look at an example (all names and IP addresses are fictitious in this example). Java's security manager allows an applet to communicate only with the host that runs the applet. The concern has been with DNS spoofing.

Developer A is running a set of sites; machine1.test.com has an IP address of 207.110.110.110, and machine2.test.com has an IP address of 207.110.110.115. Developer B wants to get developer A to run Destroyerapplet. To do this, developer B makes it known that he has a great new applet that saves programmers time and money at machinenew.friendly.com. The truth is that developer B's machine is realmachine1.friendly.com. Its real IP address is 100.100.100.100.

Developer B has created a DNS entry for machinenew.friendly.com that returns the following IP when queried: 207.110.110.115, 100.100.100.100. What is machine2.test.com doing in that entry? You guessed itÑthat is the machine that developer B is targeting for destruction.

Developer A gets the applet from machinenew.friendly.com. The verifier (Java Security Manager) queries the DNS and gets the two IP addresses. Remember that the Java's security manager would allow an applet to communicate only with the host that ran the applet. So the verifier thinks that the host is involved in the process and that it is OK to run the applet on 207.110.110.115, one of developer A's machines.

A group of individuals at Princeton University tested this, and it worked. For this and other reasons, Sun released a new JDK (version 1.0.1) that patched this problem.

This means that Java is not dependent on the DNS. However, some users have complained that if they are behind a firewall, they cannot run an applet because the administrator normally does not allow users access to the DNS maps. The administrator would have to run a "fake" and real DNS setup on the proxy server. The user is trying to talk to a real host and a trusted IP address, but some browsers will see this as an attack.

The documented solution is for users to point their systems to a real DNS server or use the IP address of the server housing the applet instead of the URL.

USING JAVA FOR DATABASE CONNECTIVITY

With the implications of ODBC and its ease of use in creating database sources, Java benefits from Java Database Connectivity. It allows a developer to use a windowing interface to connect to a database. JDBC does not have its own security features but rather uses Java and standard database security to ensure integrity. The developer uses JDBC to pass a SQL query to the database.

JavaSoft has created four basic groups of drivers: the JDBC-ODBC bridge driver, the Native-API Partly-Java driver, the Net Protocol All-Java driver, and the Native Protocol All-Java driver.

The JDBC-ODBC bridge driver translates JDBC calls into ODBC calls on the client machine. The Native-API Partly-Java driver translates JDBC calls to their native database API on the client machine. The Net Protocol All-Java driver uses an all-Java driver that runs on the client. It translates SQL calls into native API database calls. The Native Protocol All-Java driver communicates with the database using the database server's native network protocol.

Many Microsoft developers find the JDBC-ODBC bridge to be the most useful. A developer learning Java in a Microsoft database-oriented shop (where multiple ODBCs are set up) can use the bridge to take advantage of existing data sources. The drawback of this bridge process is decreased network performance, as suggested by the names used to describe the types of drivers: Any driver running native code will run faster. That is the reason that companies write JIT compilers for Java rather than always run an interpreter.

One reason for the network issues is that the bridge must convert Java datatypes to ODBC datatypes. Although the other drivers are faster, a number of database vendors totally support the ODBC environment. The developer will need to check with the database vendor to see whether it has a driver that does not depend on the bridge.

JavaScript

JavaScript is Netscape's version of an interpreted object-based browser scripting language that used to be known as LiveScript. JScript is Microsoft's version.

Here is a Java script:

```
aCar= "Toyota";
```

It is not much to see, but it is a script. Let's build upon it. For purposes of this chapter, the focus is on JavaScript with a comparison of the two in the final section. Lets look at the basic terms: variable, function, and object.

Variables in JavaScript

JavaScript variables are like variables in other languages; they are typeless and can be numbers, strings, arrays, or objects. This means that you do not need to declare them before using them. (Microsoft recommends declaring them as a good programming practice by using the *var* statement.)

Let's declare another car variable and its value:

```
anothercar="Cadillac";
```

Let's add to the value:

```
anothercar = anothercar + "is a nice car";
```

Now anothercar= "Cadillac is a nice car".

Variables can be global or local. You can access global variables from anywhere in the program. Globals should be used to store variables that must last for the life of the page or must be accessed from other parts of the program. JavaScript defaults to a setting of global for any variables created.

Developers use local variables for making function calls, and the variables are accessible only within the functions that create them. Developers use local variables so that the variable is destroyed when the program exits the function or if there is a need to suspend the variable while running a second function.

Functions

What is a function? Let's look at an example. Here is a function to calculate the square of a variable called number:

```
function square (number)
        {
                var result = number * number;
                return result;
        }
```

The interpreter handles each instruction one at a time until there are no more functions to execute. Now let's use the function:

```
a = 25;
b= square (a);
```

The result is 125, or 25 × 25. A function acts upon variables to provide an outcome.

What Is an Object?

An objects is a collection of variables and functions (properties and methods in JScript). The object gives you the attributes and behavior of what is modeled. If the object were a watch, the variables would be seconds, minutes, hours, and days of the week. These variables are called properties in JScript. Here are some object.property values for the watch:

```
time.hours
time.minutes
```

A function for this object might include alarm, which manipulates these variables. The function is known as a method in JScript. The interpreter creates objects when the browser loads a page with JavaScript.

Variables, functions, and objects are the building blocks of JavaScript and JScript.

Security in JavaScript

JavaScript cannot can access files except when cookies are involved. If the client allows cookies to be sent, you can write a file to the client's machine. You can read the cookie later but only if your site created the cookie. The access is there, but it's limited.

Differences between JavaScript and JScript

Here are some basic differences. Let's say you want to create a function entitled hereiam(). You would type the following for the Netscape browser:

```
<INPUT TYPE=BUTTON NAME=button VALUE="Click on the Button"
onclick="hereiam();">
```

For Internet Explorer you would enter

```
<INPUT TYPE=BUTTON NAME=button VALUE=" Click on the Button
"onclick="hereiam();"
    LANGUAGE="JavaScript">
```

The reason for the LANGUAGE tag is that IE can also handle VBScript. So you should use the second method with the LANGUAGE tag for both browsers; Netscape will bypass the tag. By the way, if you do not use the LANGUAGE tag, IE defaults to JScript. It appears that JavaScript (JScript) is the "new" accepted language of developers.

Another item to be aware of is that JavaScript is case-sensitive; Car and car are different variables. The exception is if the <INPUT TYPE=BUTTON onClick=".."> syntax is used; then Netscape is not case-sensitive.

There are also some function differences between JavaScript and JScript. Unfortunately, there is not enough space here to discuss all the current listed differences. In addition, JavaScript and JScript are evolving. Here are some sample sites from both vendors:

- Microsoft JScript tutorial:

http://premium.microsoft.com/msdn/library/devprods/vintdev/jscript/d1/jstutor.htm

- Netscape's Visual Java Script documentation:

http://search.netscape.com/eng/Tools/VisualJS/relnotes/relnotespr2.html

WHERE TO GO FROM HERE

You have learned that Java is very similar to other object-oriented languages such as C++. Java provides an acceptable security model for public network use and is a viable option to those developers concerned about implementing ActiveX technology. JavaScript and JScript allow an object-oriented programmer to write scripting tools without having to delve into Perl.

From here, you should look at these chapters:

- Chapter 13, "ActiveX," to learn about Microsoft's component technology which allows you to use Java to develop controls.
- Chapter 17, "Comparing the Languages," to review when you may want to choose Java or other languages.

Chapter 17

Comparing the Languages

In this chapter you will learn a little more about the similarities and differences between C++ and Java; Java and JavaScript; VBScript and JavaScript; VB and VBScript; and ActiveX and Java. A number of issues come to mind when we compare languages. First is the assumed knowledge level of the reader. Second is the bias of the reader, and third is the bias of the writer. Regarding the first issue, my assumption is that you have some programming knowledge and are attempting to learn more about the different languages available in developing usable applications. In the case of the second issue, that is one that you will need to take into account. In the case of the third, my bias has been in C++ but I have had to open my eyes to the benefits of each of the languages. For that reason, there is not just one language that I could recommend for an individual to learn. Each reader needs to determine the needs and the knowledge of his or her own development team.

Please note that each section is titled as a comparison rather than one language versus another language. Developers have found that each language has its place in development. For example, many people take the stand that using Visual Basic is better than using Visual C++. They talk about the ease of developing applications with VB. Visual C++ proponents, on the other hand, talk about the efficiency of C++ code. Both stands are correct. That does not mean the two languages cannot coexist in a development environment. For example, one development team that was totally driven by Visual C++ application development has found it enjoyable to write ASP using VBScript and to test some of the pages using VB applications. When they write components, they tend to use Visual C++ and MFC because of their need to write to the registry and run the executables as services. There is a great marriage in a language that has a scripting version to ease rapid development, but Visual Basic would be inappropriate for a multithreaded application that must run as an NT service.

Another area of discussion among developers is the comparison of scripting languages with compiled programming languages. A scripting language relies on working with components that have been designed and built in a programming language such as C++, Visual Basic, or Java. A scripting language has its place, and so does a compiled programming language. For example, if a developer is writing a query to a database in VBScript, it can be easy to implement. Because it is an interpreted language, the Web server does not need to be stopped and restarted each time a change is made. The developer, though, might need to go beyond pulling data from the database, developing an interactive tool to operate within the order processing pipeline in Commerce Server. This tool would best be written in C++.

Now let's look at the comparisons in detail.

Java and C++

Java is similar to C++ in that Java is an object-oriented language, but there are some differences between the two.

1. C++ programmers are very familiar with the pointer world. Java lets the developer set the size of arrays by using an operator called new.
2. C++ programmers usually use system-level calls to run certain system functions. For security reasons, that is not available in Java. A Java developer can use Java libraries to accomplish the same purpose.
3. If you look at a sample of Java code when setting up classes and then look at the opening C++ line with its #includes and #defines, you will notice a difference. Java uses only an import command to "include" a class.
4. Java includes a Boolean datatype.
5. Java does not use typedef and structs. Again, these constructs were removed to maintain a new level of network security within Java.
6. C++ programmers are used to using catch and throw for exception handling. For example:

```
try
{
//code that is being executed is put here
}
catch(error variable)
{
//code is put here for handling errors
}
throw (the string)
```

Java has its own exception handling method, with internal verification of the bytecode as well as exception handling.

7. Java, like C++, handles multithreading. Java adds the synchronized (expression) statement to handle potential cases in which different pieces of code are trying to modify the same objects.

8. Java provides for the garbage collection of objects that are not being used. This arrangement helps reduce the problem that some C++ programmers run into with memory leaks in those systems that have not reallocated memory with unused objects. This feature runs within Java only when the microprocessor is available, so be careful when writing code that does not give the system time to reallocate memory.
9. Java does not allow global variables or global functions.
10. Java has specific classes for networking (for example, TCP/IP and UDP).
11. Java does not allow multiple inheritance (as in C++). For example, to derive a class from a class you use public class AString extends String{} instead of the C++ treatment of inheritance as shown here:

```
Class Atthetop {
public: top(xy now, xy before){}
}

class belowthetop : public Atthetop{
public: bottom(xy now, xy before){}
}

class athtebottom: public belowthetop{
public bottomtop(xy now, xy before){}
}
```

Java is intended to be network-friendly (with its compact code environment) as well as network-secure. This is the reason that developers see a major difference in portions of Java as compared with C++.

JAVA AND JAVASCRIPT

Java and JavaScript are based on object-oriented principles, in which you use components and object behaviors to create the final application. There are two major scripting languages similar to Java: JScript and JavaScript. Some of their differences were discussed in Chapter 16. In this chapter, JavaScript will be used as the generic term for these scripting languages.

Many developers find scripting languages to be great for developing a way to link major components that have been developed by a major vendor (such as Microsoft) or a third party. The reason for this preference is that scripting languages do not require the variable to work correctly. For example, in a scripting language the variable newvariable could represent an integer in one area of the code and a string of characters in another part of the code. In addition, many developers find that they can develop an interactive Web site with a commerce area and heavy database access more quickly using scripting languages.

Developers like to use JavaScript for identifying users and their capabilities based on a cookie: a text file that is written to the client's machine to keep track of information that a developer wants to pass along. The intent of the cookie is to make it easier for a developer to assist a user in surfing a site and meeting the customer's needs.

Java can be used to create components that JavaScript can interface with or to create an applet (running in its own browser window) that it can call. As you learned in Chapter 16, applets are downloaded by the client to provide interactive functionality. The code is sent separately by the server and is then embedded in the HTML. Java also is a way for developers to hide proprietary code, because it is built into an interpreted form on the server side. JavaScript can be seen within the browser window. Java does not have very much built-in functionality to interact with the browser.

JavaScript depends on what the user does in the browser window. It is intended to wait and watch for a user event (such as a mouse click), whereas Java is designed for stand-alone applications that can run over the network (such as clientserver database applications).

Java objects and classes tend to follow strict syntax guidelines. A variable must belong to a class; a function must be a method of an object that is a class. These variables are declared and given a type (such as integer). JavaScript allows the developer to create functions and variables that are typeless, as discussed earlier. For example, JavaScript allows the following:

```
x= 21
y =41
z= x+y
```

The Java compiler would have a problem, because the variables, x, y, and z were not declared and given a type. Java would require this code:

```
public Addition (x,y,z){
x=21;
y=41;
z=x+y;
}
```

This would even be tougher in Java if y were a string variable and not an integer, whereas JavaScript would allow the following:

```
x=21
y="hi"
z=x+y
```

Note that JavaScript is interpreted. Java can be interpreted or compiled at run time. A compiler takes a program and writes the code so that a specific piece of hardware can run it.

Interpreted code is easier to change and rerun within the development environment, but it is generally not as fast as compiled code.

JavaScript can run on servers such as Netscape's SuiteSpot and Microsoft IIS 3.0. Again, this capability may be very useful for a developer who wishes to protect the code or needs a more direct link to the databases within a Web server environment. In addition, a developer can use Netscape's Navigator 3.0 to link a script to an applet or an applet to an applet.

Note that JavaScript-enabled browsers will not necessarily run Java, because they require different interpreters.

So if you need to create a Web page that requires user input for the interactivity, a scripting language such as JavaScript would be useful. If the intent is to create applications that can run on a Windows machine and across the Web, maybe Java or a combination of Java and JavaScript would be best.

You have learned that scripting languages can be of benefit in generating some nice Web pages quickly. Let's look at VBScript.

VBSCRIPT AND JAVASCRIPT

Scripting tools can help you create Web sites that in the past took a lot of programming language knowledge. With the incorporation of Active Server and its component architecture, you can write scripts, in a single page, that will pass information among databases, rotate a group of ads, and redirect a user to appropriate pages based on the browser being used.

Two major scripting tools are used by active site developers: VBScript and JavaScript. JavaScript, as noted in the preceding section, is similar to Java, a language loved by many Web application developers. VBScript is an extension of Visual Basic, a popular desktop application development language. JavaScript is fully object-based, whereas VBScript is not. Both are good scripting languages, and you must determine which one has the strengths you require.

JavaScript allows for the creation of Web pages that will update as the requested data is updated. You can create scripts to determine the browser that is attempting to load the page and then send the appropriate page to that browser. In this way, you can have separate parts of the site for Microsoft Internet Explorer users, Netscape users, and those whose browsers do not support frames. If you do not want to use the AdRotator component in Active Server, you can use JavaScript to rotate a set of ads. You can read and write to cookies as well as launch a Java applet.

VBScript may not have the object orientation of JavaScript, but VBScript is very useful when you're dealing with currency calculations and conversions along with large arrays and ActiveX controls.

JavaScript, for example, uses operators that are familiar to the C/C++ crowd. For this reason, you will find that JavaScript has more operators to work with. Both scripting tools have an operator for handling exponents and string concatenation, but JavaScript also includes bitwise operators. Bitwise operators treat everything as a set of bits (0 or 1) and not as decimals. So the number 5 equals 101. Bitwise operators act on this bit representation but return numerical values such as A left shift = a << b, which shifts b bits to the left.

For mathematical operations, JavaScript excels in the area of trigonometry. For example, VBScript does not contain a function such as this method:

```
acos
```

It returns the arc cosine (in radians) of a number. The proper syntax is

```
Math.acos(number)
```

The number is a numeric expression between -1 and 1 or a property of an existing object. Here is an example:

```
function getAcos(x) {
   return Math.acos(x)
}
```

This returns the arc cosine of the variable x. If you passed the value x=-1, the function would return pi, or 3.14159.

Along with math comes the need to move data in and out of the server. VBScript gives you a lot of flexibility in the type of buttons and dialog boxes available. The gain with JavaScript is the ability to more easily read and write cookies. It all depends on your needs. You could easily incorporate both scripts on a Web page.

If your interest is in string manipulation, VBScript is the winner. You can use a set of filters to search text and strings for replacement or editing of characters, as with UNIX tools such as grep. With arrays, again the comparison is close. JavaScript supports the sort function, but VBScript allows for large arrays. JavaScript supports time zones in the data area, but VBScript allows you to add dates and calculate differences in dates. This capability is essential in analyzing database transactions when you need to ensure that the record you are retrieving matches the proper client.

With regard to databases, developers find that data conversions are essential. JavaScript allows you to grab a URL string and convert it to a form used by the Web server. VBScript allows you to convert the data to ASCII code and convert strings to currency. This capability can be useful for things such as passing data from a Web page to a commerce component on Commerce Server.

Which language should you use? You can use both in an Active Server Page. By setting the LANGUAGE attribute of the <SCRIPT> tag, you can take advantage of the strengths of both languages.

VB AND VBSCRIPT

Because VBScript is a scripting environment, some Visual Basic functionality was changed to make VBScript operate efficiently on the Web. Let's look at a few of the differences. Note that many of these differences were noted by VB users who looked at my scripts and noticed what could not be used in VBScript. In addition, a number of notes on this subject have been posted in the newsgroups.

When a variable is defined, it is declared in programming languages. VBScript has apparently removed the property declarations that were used in VB, because VBScript does not allow for class creation. It is not an object-oriented language. So, for example, Property Get and Property Set would not be allowed. There is a debate about whether private and public variables are yet supported; I could not confirm this in VBScript 2.0. VBScript does not support optional arguments such as ParamArray, but it supports constants (such as Const) in VBScript 2.0. There is a set of Boolean constants with a value of true or false. VBScript is great for large dimensions, but the Dim function cannot be used with the array method (Dim Array).

The Format command is not allowed in VBScript, but other developers are using a set of string manipulation functions to build formatted strings. This also means that Str and Val are not supported in VBScript. Nor are any of the line labels (such as on—Go to) supported. A number of other commands may now be supported in VBScript 2.0. Please check the Microsoft site for further information.

Recall that for VBScript you have the ActiveX Control Pad to help use controls that will add functionality to the page. This is not the same thing as adding a component to an application using VB or C++. The comparison is similar to that between Java and JavaScript. VBScript is intended to glue the components together. VB is great for creating a stand-alone Windows application.

If you have a background in having to write Perl to get form data from a customer to a company or to try to enter database information, VBScript is a great relief. It is not as cryptic as Perl, and what you learn can only help in trying to build VB applications. Also, Microsoft has built a number of page layout controls into VBScript to take advantage of Dynamic HTML.

Some developers have said that using VBScript is child's play compared with learning VB. A number of C++ developers have proven that wrong. These hardened veterans, who have lived through memory management and lost pointers, have seen that VBScript can be a great addition to the Web programming arsenal. VBScript is not intended to be the end-all in development. That is why Microsoft created the component environment. You can let your team members use their favorite programming language.

With VB, you have an extensive tool set with IDE. When using VBScript, you may choose to use Notepad or ActiveX Control Pad. Most developers move to Control Pad because of its built-in functionality.

ActiveX and Java

Is it reasonable to compare ActiveX and Java applets? Not totally, because ActiveX is a group of technologies that can be implemented using a number of languages, including Java. Let's look at some comparisons from a technology point of view.

The first major battle is usually fought over security. Microsoft is trying to ease the fears of many people, because even though it supports Java, Microsoft wants ActiveX, a stripped-down version of OLE to be a hit. ActiveX is useful, especially in an intranet, where you can require the use of a Microsoft browser and you trust the code developers. But the problem is that when security is violated, it is usually violated by internet personnel. If a developer wanted to ruin a company's systems, ActiveX would be a good tool to choose. The developer using ActiveX has access to the client's system resources, which includes the ability to destroy hard drives. Java, on the other hand, has a more secure model. Sun Microsystems has started to change some of that, though, in response to the market that ActiveX has created. Sun has released newer versions of Java that will run under the new browsers in a limited manner, allowing some access to system resources. The decision is the developer's when it comes to security. It's a trade-off between security and features.

When you're moving code from system to system, the portability race is won by Java. If you use the Java Virtual Machine, the bytecodes become hardware-independent. But Sun does not stop there. Because there has been a demand for faster code on some systems, developers can buy Java compilers—called just-in-time compilers—to bypass the interpreted level and run Java compiled code. ActiveX has persistence —the code needs to be downloaded only once—whereas the Java applet must be downloaded each time. The problem is that an ActiveX control must be rather large to provide the same functionality as a Java applet.

Both Java and ActiveX have a number of new tools and libraries that are helping to make development much easier. Microsoft created the Visual J++ development suite to complement its Visual InterDev product. ActiveX has a VB Control Creation Edition that can help with developing code as well as the ActiveX Template Library for Visual C++. The tools are there for you to learn.

The decision is in your hands. The choice can be a matter of the environment that you are comfortable with as well as the issues noted in this section.

Where to Go from Here

You have been exposed to a number of programming and scripting languages and their relationship to one another. To ask which tool is best for your career would be a difficult question, and there is not enough space here to properly address it. The point is that you must determine what best fits the needs of your company and crew. As many developers have learned, it is important to expand your programming background to venture into those areas that were originally considered unthinkable. For example, one development crew spent six months finding every C++ solution to its problems until one person actually learned some Visual Basic and VBScript. Now the whole crew is excited about blending the two technologies in their future Internet and intranet sites. Developers need to be open to new languages and approaches.

From here you may want to review the following chapters:

- Chapter 5, "Active Server Pages," where you can learn more about how the active environment operates.
- Chapter 19, "Web Site Case Study," where you can see how one team learned to change a site based on new technologies.

Chapter 18

Creating and Managing a Next-Generation Web Site

Does "next generation" mean "new technology"? Yes. Does it mean a new way of looking at sites from a designer's point of view? Yes. But it is more than that. The next generation means business. If you have not had to deal with business issues yet, the time has come to deal with them.

Let's use the four P's to manage this site: purpose, plan, prototype, and promote.

OVERVIEW

The purpose of a site must be established by the person or organization that owns the site. Without a full level of commitment, many sites are doomed to fail. This is especially true with the maturing of the Web. The next generation will be more dynamic, mainly because of the demand for changing data. The film industry has proven that content is king. The content in Web sites is the company's data.

This means that the developer must know the audience. Does the customer need an application to see the best parts of the site? Is that acceptable? If you are providing applications as a business at the site, what is the knowledge level of the audience? Do visitors need additional frequently asked questions (FAQ) pages? What will keep people returning to the site? Is it technology, data, or a combination of both? Does the site contain a "call to action"? An example would be, "Realtor saves millions using this site." After you have the visitor's attention, you must produce an adventure that meets the expectations you have set.

Does this sound like a vision? That is what these questions about the site's purpose should define.

To plan means to get organized for success, and success must start with the vision and be accepted throughout a team. Even if you cannot afford individual personnel for each of the major tasks (such as artwork, HTML coding, and application development), the team must be defined. This will assist in managing the effort as the team is built. You may end up being the only person who thinks of building a corporate infrastructure for supporting this effort. Because a Web site becomes a company product, you should develop a design plan that determines both company and customer needs. Then build a few small examples to show the company and test customers to ensure an understanding of the issues.

A prototype reflects a plan for the content as well as a method by which you will build and launch the site. What does the road to the company's future look like (at least online)? Determine what the content is and how it fits into the navigation of the site. It is recommended that you require the design to be on paper if not in mockup form in the computer to ensure that notes and changes are not missed. Include revision levels on both the physical and the digital documents. This is no different from what is required to release a major piece of code that others use.

Arrange the resources (such as graphics, text, and sound) in a location that makes sense. You might create a server file called **Newsitev1**. This means that it is version 1 of the new site. Then create a set of folders below this directory level. These folders should make sense even when using a DOS format of eight-letter file names (**Graphics** and not **Graphics for version 1**). What is the graphical theme? When do you use the GIF format versus JPG? Lay out the navigation plan. Does it meet the vision stated in the purpose phase? Put together the final artwork and HTML needed. Do you need custom programs, components, or objects for this site to operate? Is there more than one path through the site (for a Netscape browser versus a Microsoft Internet Explorer browser)? Test, test, and test again. The quality assurance questions should really be asked during the purpose phase.

Promotion includes not only the marketing of the site but also regular updates and maintenance. What is the change cycle process? When someone finds an error, does it get corrected immediately? Is there a review cycle, in which product changes received by a certain date each week are incorporated by a certain date the following week? For example, all changes received by Wednesday are guaranteed to be incorporated by the following Wednesday. How will the site use search engines? Will someone regularly test the site's location using various search terms on the more popular engines? Does it matter? What about newsgroups and mailing lists? Which ones are important to surf and learn from? Newsgroups and mailing lists are a great way to learn more about how to promote a company site as well as get involved. Once involved, Web surfers can add a signature to their e-mails that note the company's Web site. This whole process involves understanding Netiquette (discussed later in this chapter).

Now let's look at each of these areas in detail.

Purpose

The pressure from foreign competition and a growing technologically superior work force have caused companies to embrace the World Wide Web. This means that most developers will be forced to deal with some form of Web development.

Many developers, once they look at the infrastructure of the Internet, believe that the Web is just another client/server architecture. That is a true statement. What some people miss is that it is a powerful way to communicate company ideas and promote company products to the market. Additionally, developers learn that they can distribute business applications over an internal Internet, known as an intranet. Tools and applications can be bought off-the-shelf to reduce the time to bring a product to market. With time, these tools and applications have become more and more component-oriented so that developers can modify them to meet the specific company needs.

For this reason, companies see the Web as a way to reduce the cost of deploying and maintaining products. Customers, both internal and external to the company, can use a standard browser to view and use the products. A browser is often integrated into the new hardware or operating systems that are delivered to the client. This means that marketing and sales organizations can dream up new products that do not require the company to provide the whole client application side for implementation.

Additionally, when you need to upgrade a product, the logic can be changed on the company server rather than on the clientís system. Web pages on the server can have text and graphical objects that run as a PowerPoint presentation or as an interactive CD-ROM. This new capability and excitement on the part of marketing organizations mean that developers must follow a different design process. Let's take a more detailed look at this new design process.

PLAN

Planning involves an understanding how the client/server architecture changes the design process.

Although the Web server and customer browser act, in effect, as a client/server environment, there are a few differences. If you were building a client application using Visual C++ or Visual Basic, you would create an interface that would meet the needs of that development environment. With the inclusion of the Web, you must pass information back using an HTML wrapper. The Microsoft Internet Information Server (IIS), in this case, is the server side.

Table 18.1 compares the two environments.

Table 18.1 Comparison of Classic Client/Server and Web Client/Server Environments

CLASSIC CLIENT/SERVER	WEB CLIENT/SERVER
1. The network is internal to a company. Security is an issue but not a primary driver.	1. The network is open to the world unless applications run on an extranet. Security is a primary consideration.
2. Application logic runs on the desktop.	2. Application logic runs on the server.
3. The application talks to the DBMS on the server.	3. The application talks to the DBMS on the server.

Chapter 18

4. Client/server connections tend to survive over time (they are persistent), so a transaction processor can be embedded in the database design.

4. Client/server connections are short-lived. Transaction server functionality must be built into the server environment. Resource locking can be an issue.

In a client/server company environment, the application makes a call over the internal network to the local database. The local application deals with data interpretation and any display formats specific to the application.

In the Web implementation, a browser page must send the request to the server database. The database sends back the request via a process (such as ISAPI, IDC/HTX, CGI, or ASP), and, depending on the technology used, the data is wrapped into an HTML page for display.

With the client/server company solution, the developer can bury a lot of logic in the client application and not worry about network bottlenecks. In the Web solution, the immediate concern must be network bottlenecks. The good news is that scripting languages (such as VBScript and JavaScript) and controls (such as ActiveX and Java applets) can be integrated into the client application to provide client logic functionality.

Another issue relevant to design is salability. With the local company client/server solution, the developer is assured of a persistent connection. That connection tends to be available to the client 24 hours a day if needed. If you want to add more users, you must install another copy of the application on the client system. If the network slows, you plus that new clientís computer into a new networking switch or hub to reduce bottlenecks. With the addition of Web clients, you know that the transactions will increase. This means that you must consider changing the server environment. You cannot do any physical rewiring to reduce network bottlenecks. You must locate the database's hot spots.

As you enter the design portion of the process, you must recognize that the Web provides an open architecture. You should follow these steps:

1. The Web solution has a number of components, and you must determine what they are They include the Web itself, the user interface (somewhat known because of the various browsers that users might use to visit the site), business rules and logic (found by reviewing documents and interviews), and the data itself (a continuation of the business rules and logic).
2. Determine how the information flows (AS-IS) and how it should flow (TO-BE). Determine how the current departments, customers, and managers get the data that is important to them. This includes mapping the current digital and manual flow of data.
3. Build test components that implement the TO-BE environment. Build and test often, even while you're designing. You may not use the actual tools in this phase that you will use in the final product, but you must give management and a beta

group of customers a look at your interpretation of their needs. We tend not to listen as well as we think we do. Maybe you have seen the cartoon in which a person tells three departments to build a tire swing for kids to use at a local park. The quality assurance department creates a drawing with ropes tied to all parts of the tire. It is safe, but no child can fit into the tire tube, let alone swing in it. The manufacturing department creates a drawing with a huge strip of tire that touches the ground. They thought that they were supposed to create a tire string, not swing. The marketing department creates a picture of a tire set up like a hammock. They thought they were supposed to create a tired swing. Words mean things to people. The best way to test what we hear is to show a person what we heard him or her say. You can do this by building a simple example of the application and the user interface.
4. Determine how to tie the test components and user interfaces to the server products being used. Is the company going to install all the BackOffice products? Is this a phased-in approach whereby you are to create some Active Server Pages communicating to the SQL Server and then to determine where Commerce Server and Transaction Server have a place?

These steps should help you uncover poor design decisions early in the process. The architecture is different from what many developers are used to when implementing local client/server applications. The environment is distributed, and data is being requested in a nonsequential manner. As the benefits of this environment are achieved, management will want more products and applications brought to this new client/server world. Anticipate these in the design. For example, if you are releasing a product that will be ordered on-line, take a look at other products that may be added in the next 12 months. It may be time to create a commerce design for the site.

Leverage the skills of the crew with discretion. If the developers available for this project are strong in Visual C++, you may be able to use ISAPIs to implement basic interactivity. Or maybe it is time for some of them to learn a little Visual Basic to take advantage of ADO and Active Server Pages.

If you do not have a graphics design background, find an experienced marketing and advertising group. Web design principles are not much different from television and magazine design principles. The Web just adds to the possibilities of demonstrating good design skills.

With a purpose and design in hand, it is time to create a prototype.

PROTOTYPE

Surf the Web and look at other sites. You should join the various usergoups and mailing lists for the tools you use and want to use. Here you will learn of sites that have been successful in implementing interactivity with those tools. In addition, you will learn about the problems developers encountered.

Look at commercial sites that are advertised on television and in magazines. Navigate through them and try to determine how the developers built the site. Many sites are confusing and are slow to load. They were poorly designed or poorly implemented.

The nice part about a Web site is that it is never really finished. That is also the drawback of the prototyping phase. You must decide on an initial release date, acceptable look, and appropriate functionality to get the site on-line. You can always add components or add a page or acquire better artwork. Be sure that the site is functional. Many Fortune 500 companies on the Web this past year have discovered that the more money spent on artwork, the less traveled the road to their site. Why? The concept is no different than with commercials or magazine ads. A good look will attract an audience, but if the product does not deliver, most people will walk away. In addition, dissatisfied customers will tell others to walk away.

As you gather the design documents and components to build the site, keep in mind that the site must appear to be integrated. Do not build the site as if it were a car built by four different people in different locations who did not talk to one another. Do not forget to take a step back often and see how each of the components communicates with the others.

You should implement a toolbar on the site just as you would with a local client/server application. Make the icons easy to understand, like the international traffic symbols that represent *yield*, *stop*, and *go*. Do not forget the audience. Keep looking at how different browsers interact with the various components over different network connections. For example, could a person use a portion of your site if it were behind a firewall?

Build a site that fits logically into the vision determined in the purpose phase. Does the site layout follow a product layout or a content layout? Make it easy for customers to order products. That may have been stated over and over during the design phase, but it surprises a number of developers to find that customers cannot find the order button on the site. Worse yet, the button operates incorrectly.

Learn how current successful organizations draw a crowd. Walk through the supermarket and toy stores to see how they implement navigation. How do they implement new technology? Do you know that bar coding got its greatest use in inventory management before being used for price control? Supermarkets learned how to use the technology properly. Look at your tools in the same manner. Maybe it is time to access the database using ASP rather than a group of CGI Perl scripts or ISAPIs running .

Notice how good supermarkets and toy stores make customers feel that there is a lot for them to do without getting them lost. Lets use a game analogy. The Web site must be built so that it operates as an arcade version of a game. Customers will be there for a short time; if they spend money, it is minimal. The intent is to hook customers, making them want to come back and buy the CD-ROM version of the game to play for weeks. At the Web site, customers should get what they need during a brief morning or lunch break.

Then they should see enough intriguing content to draw them back to spend evenings and weekends at the site. Successful sites make it easy for a customer to grab the needed item, but they also manage to introduce the customer to promotional messages as well as information that describes the productsí benefits. It is a tough line to walk as a developer. People want the free information, but they also want it to be easy to find. That is why more sites are displaying a **Search** button on the home page.

Speaking of buttons, it is OK to implement text versions of graphical buttons. They tend to load faster and work with all browsers. Some developers argue that the more data a site has, the fewer graphical buttons it should have. They believe that a text list better meets the needs of customers, separating the items more succinctly than graphics do. For example, consider are the various technical support and product pages at http://www.cisco.com. If these items were put into a graphical toolbar, it would be too big and too confusing to place on various pages. If you build the site with a toolbar, remember to provide text links for the same functionality. Your site will support all types of browsers and will allow the customer to navigate the site before all the graphics load. Customers will feel as if they are in control. That is an important concept. If they control the journey, they will come back for more information.

On each page of your site, you should follow a simple font format and layout just as you would if you were publishing a book or magazine article. There are headings and body text. There are titles, subheads, styles, headers, and footers. Still, individual pages can be implemented differently. For example, one section might allow for a more humorous or light-hearted look. That is OK if the transition in colors and layout is subtle or is broken by an obvious change in theme. You might use a visual change in layout or possibly an interim change via a script that takes the customer on a different and welcomed journey.

Build the site using the hardware and networking connection that works best for you, but have other people regularly test the site using various pieces of hardware, different browsers, and different connections for example, dial-up). Ask these testers to comment on the screen layout. What colors do they see? If possible, visit some customers and watch how they navigate the site as well as what they see on their screens. This process is enlightening. First you learn more about how customers move through the site. Second, they are impressed that you asked them to help, and they are more likely to recommend your site.

Create forms that allow people to easily contact you. Ask for feedback regarding company products, information, and Web site layout. You can gather customer demographics if the required forms do not waste the customerís time and offer some benefit. You might offer a free product, notoriety for helping in the development process, special e-mail updates, so on. Be sure that you do not misuse the demographic information. Customers can handle a target-marketed effort but not a shotgun approach.

When reviewing each section of the site (at the page level), be aware of how much time it takes to load each page. If the customer-support pages take longer to load than the product pages, maybe the customer-support area should be broken into sections. Or maybe there is not enough product data. As you reproduce the site theme on each page, make sure to reevaluate which types of images should be used. You may have used a number of GIFs in the marketing area, but maybe the products area would be better served with JPGs of the actual products. Do not forget that once a graphic is cached on the client's system, you should reuse it as much as possible, thereby reducing the number of graphics to be downloaded. You could use technology, such as Java, to create a JPG animation rather than build an animated GIF. Or you might want to use Macromedia Flash or Director to build an interactive area.

As more pages are added to the equation, the file layout structure becomes important. You may have to change your directory tree as the number of pages increases or the feedback changes the vision. Think of the process as cleaning a bedroom. Everything may initially get thrown on the bed so that you can vacuum the room, but eventually items must be categorized and organized to reduce future cleanup efforts. Also, do not be afraid to trash items that are not needed. Keep backups on disk separate from the server.

Here is one example layout:

> C:\Newsite = **index.html** or **default.asp**
> C:\Newsite\gfx = graphics for first page
> C:\Newsite\gfx\cussup = graphics for customer support
> C:\Newsite\html = HTML pages and subfolders
> C:\Newsite\asp = ASP pages and subfolder
> C:\Newsite\cgi = CGI scripts
> C:\Newsite\bin = executables such as ActiveX
> C:\Newsite\scripts = IDC/HTX scripts, ISAPI, VBScripts, JavaScripts

It is OK to redesign while going through the prototype phase. All developers tend to provide the best. That is admirable. The problem is that what the developer thinks adds great functionality to the site may cost more in time and money than it is currently worth. When you have the desire to redesign, look at the following list to make sure that the current design meets the minimum standards:

- Check for spelling and grammar errors. Just as in writing this book, we all wish we could continue to rewrite sections and chapters. We should continue to improve our grammar.
- Graphics can always be tweaked to load faster and look better. Determine an acceptable level of compromise.
- Test various navigation methods. A site is not like a movie; it is more like a CD-ROM. The process that a customer follows is nonlinear. Can you provide a better link to the customer-support area? Does **Search** mean the company's site search engine or a convenient link to a Web search engine?

- Be careful of the tag. It is a designerís best friend for laying out a page like a magazine, but remember that the table does not appear until the browser gets through the end tag, . A solution is to consider smaller tables or a different layout.
- Do not be afraid of including a table of contents (site overview) and index (site map).
- Can you further simplify the site? Can you remove graphics that just show off someoneís use of Photoshop instead of helping give customers information they need? Study how some companies have redesigned their sites over time. Print copies of the pages and keep a record to see what the bigger companies have learned.
- Do not be afraid to use the technology for assistance. Maybe a script will assist with creating a small navigation window for certain users who have browsers equipped with that script interpreter. In that way, you meet the needs of more advanced users.

As you put it all together, you are ready to launch the site. Set a release date and meet that date. Companies will continue to make changes, but you should attempt to get version 1 up and running at an acceptable level. If marketing is not happy with some of the forms, maybe they can be moved to version 1.1. You should continue to remind company personnel that you want feedback regarding the future of the site.

So the site is up and running. How do you help people get there? Promote.

PROMOTE

Consider the various methods for promotion:

- Tap the resources of your internal marketing departments and literature.
- Cross-promote with other literature and fellow developers. Do not forget to add the site name to business cards.
- Visit newsgroups and mailing lists that fit both hobbies and work-related issues. Get to know who is out there. Eventually, you can add a signature line in the e-mail so that when you post a response, the world ìjust happensî to see the site.
- Use search engines and take the time to learn how they operate. Before submitting the site, you need to recognize that there are developers who run the search engines. Respect their knowledge of the Web and technology. Learn from them. Ask for their help in how to best list the site. Respect their time. Do not waste it just to get listed.
- Itís OK to solicit a review of the site to get listed by certain on-line newspapers and organizations. Visit those sites regularly to learn how to get listed. Talk via e-mail to the authors of on-line magazine articles. Get their feedback. If they like what they see, they will tell the world Here are some sites to visit:

http://www.usatoday.com/life/cyber/ch.htm. *USA Today*'s hot sites.
http://www8.zdnet.com/zdimag/makeover. *ZD Magazine*'s redesign of sites.
http://www.pointcom.com. One of the ìratingî sites.
http://www8.zdnet.com/pcmag/special/web100/_open.htm. *PC Magazine*'s top 100 sites.

Just as you surf to learn in the planning and prototype phases, you should continue to do so in the promotion phase. You need to be ìseenî on-line by communicating with other developers and designers. People respect a developer who has been out there for some time looking and learning more than an e-mail saying, ìHey, I got a great Web site—list me!î

Share, share, share. What you learn, you should share in the newsgroups and mailing lists. Truly compliment others on what they have done. Correct with gentleness. The good news is that a spelling correction on the Web can be made in minutes whereas correcting a print ad would mean rerunning thousands of issues. Customers are forgiving—to an extent.

Understand what fails on the Web. Look through the magazine racks in the local bookstore to see what is being touted as successful. Then get on-line and see whether the Webmaster or developer can be found. Converse with them to learn what is really happening on a site. Even the most successful sites will fail sometimes. Learn from the mistakes, rebuild the site, and go out and promote it.

How do you determine which other developers have the credentials to teach this Webology? Watch over time. The hype tends to show through quickly. If a developer is merely passing along the latest buzzwords, the recommendations will eventually be hollow. People who take the suggestions such of a person usually need to get burned once before they become savvy. This is not a get-rich-quick scheme. This is development. If you review what has happened in the last few years on the Web, some things remain constant:

- Good developers can still create great back ends in the client/server model.
- Good developers keep learning the new technologies and are not afraid to change an opinion when confronted with the truth.
- Fortune 500 companies are still trying to understand the benefits of the Web world.
- Technology will continue to change. Those who have experience taking a product from cradle to grave will survive.

Now that you have a good handle on the current site, it's time to add multimedia. First, you need to become familiar with the various formats. There are the standard formats (WAV, MOV and MPEG) as well as the new streaming technology from RealAudio. There are Java-based products such as Emblaze and scripting-based tools such as Director (using the Lingo scripting language for interactivity). You need to learn which file types can run on any server and which ones require server software.

Do not forget your customers. Can they ìseeî and ìhearî this new multimedia using their current browsers?

Let's review a few of the standards. Most browsers support audio files in these formats: AIFF (Audio Interchange File Format), AU (Audio), and WAV (Waveform Audio). If you are looking for stereo quality, be careful with WAV and AIFF. If the quality setting is too high during development, the files are large. Streaming audio includes RealAudio and XingMPEG. The developer needs server software (or the knowledge to use a linked server), and the client needs the player software. Quality, though, tends to be high in both cases.

When it comes to video, Quicktime (**.MOV**) has the greatest acceptance. Microsoftís AVI comes in a close second, because there are many PCs that have the Windows Media Player. Streaming video includes products such as VDO, Real Video, and VivoActive. These choices also require you to deal with both a server-side engine and a client-side player (plug-in) that may not be currently loaded on customers' systems.

If the plug-ins and server engines are not a concern, what about server response time with various multimedia formats? First, you must contend with the issue of network bandwidth in this type of implementation. As most developers know, people tend to use all the space they are given. If you increase the local server bandwidth from 128 Kbps to 1.56 Mbps, it will not be long before someone will help fill the pipe. As the file size and the number of system transactions increase, so will the need for operating system processes. Could the system run short of resources? Yes, it could. Try this on a local workstation. Open a number of network connections, including the Internet. On some of these connections, make sure that a browser is hitting a Java applet as well as some Shockwave files. The workstation will reach a point at which collisions continue to occur and the system has processing problems.

Test file size and network response time. You may be surprised at how a simple doubling of file size raises major network traffic and system processor issues.

A number of Java applets are available that will test your system for various numbers of hits. You can calibrate the applet to simulate 1 to 1,000 hits per second. It is an eye-opening exercise.

Now introduce streaming, and all bets are off as to what may happen. The server is running normal services as well as trying to deal with a streaming piece of audio or video. The network channel is being hit not by bursts—as it was in the case of standard formats being downloaded—but rather by a continuous load. Many rock concert sites have noted that they could fill a T1 line with fewer than 80 attendees. This number is not very many users when you consider the cost of running the T1 and associated equipment.

As a result of all this, you need to run regular monitoring tools on the network and the servers. Many of the Microsoft BackOffice products take advantage of the NT performance monitor. In addition, there are third-party and after-market tools for adding monitoring for servers such as SQL Server and Commerce Server. *Network sniffers* are software applications that can be ran on a laptop and put anywhere in the network architecture. Additionally, by using standard routers and smart hubs you can use the factory-shipped network tools to determine which leg of the server network is handling the most traffic.

WHERE TO GO FROM HERE

A developer must implement a full production cycle in the development, release, and maintenance of a next-generation Web site. It is important to understand the purpose of the site to ensure that the goal is kept in front of the development team. The next step is to plan a tactical and strategic outline that fits the company's vision. Following planning is the prototyping phase, when you build, redesign, and rebuild the full Web site. Deadlines must be set to establish the release of this product. Yes, a Web site is a product. It is a living product, one that changes over time. The final step is the promotion of the site. This means that you make others aware of the new site, obtain market feedback and start a whole new product cycle of determining the purpose of the next version of the Web site.

The following chapters would be of use to the developer:

- Appendix A, "Setting up the IIS", to review how the NT Web server is installed.
- Appendix B, "HTML Code", where you can review standard HTML as well as Dynamic HTML.

Chapter 19

Web Site Case Study

In this chapter, you will learn from a sample case study the basic process that a development team followed during a 12-month implementation of Internet, intranet, and extranet sites at three geographic locations. Many of the items discovered during this implementation led to the investigation of the client and server material covered in this book. This chapter is broken into three sections: the layout of the sample site, the code samples, and the lessons learned. Some figures are included to give you an idea of the basic layout. The code listings are only samples of what was actually used on the sites. One site alone had more than 200 pages of material along with 30 applications running for database retrieval and interactive site updates.

LAYOUT

The sites were created under these requirements:

- The development crew had to use current hardware and software installations. No new equipment was to be purchased for six months. The external user base was mainly business users running Windows 3.1 and AOL browsers. Internal use was a combination of Macintosh, UNIX workstations, Windows for Workgroups, Windows 95, and Windows NT. Browsers included Netscape 2.0 and later as well as Internet Explorer 3.0 and later.
- A prototype had to be created in less than three months to show investors and management what could be done.
- The development team members had various backgrounds with strengths in UNIX (C++, Java, shell scripts, Perl, and TCL) and Windows (Borland C++, Visual C++, and JavaScript). Very few of the crew had experience in Visual Basic. Database backgrounds included dBase, FoxPro, Access, Oracle, Informix, and Illustra.
- There was an agreed-upon direction to move from a heavy emphasis on UNIX solutions to Microsoft BackOffice products and finding off-the-shelf solutions.

The sample sites were created for a group of companies that needed to provide information on the Internet for people who were browsing as well as an area where customers could log in and run reports or obtain a library of information. The first site was built using IDC/HTX on an NT server as well as running Perl scripts on a Solaris (UNIX) Web server. The two sites were linked via a hotlink buried in an IP address. The initial e-mail server sat on the UNIX box and eventually was moved to the NT environment. A search tool was added on the NT server so that users at both locations could search for text files (see Figure 19.1).

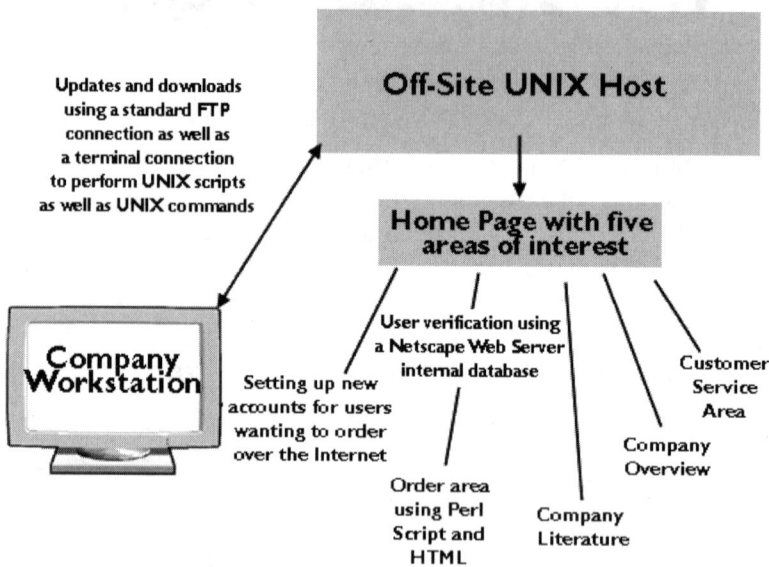

Figure 19.1 Initial site layout, phase 1.

Next, the developers used ISAPI to implement additional functionality along with JavaScript and SQL Server as the collective database engine for both sites. Stored procedures were created on the NT server to allow for dumping of SQL database data to the search tool. ISAPI was launched via the NT server, but the actual Web pages resided on the UNIX server running Netscape's server products. Because the site was being moved from UNIX to a total NT environment, Microsoft Commerce Server was added and ASP was adopted for some of the coding needs. Components for the various Microsoft BackOffice server products were written in C++.

This is why the following section has code samples in IDC/HTX, ISAPI, VBScript, and JavaScript. A later section will show sample code rewrites based on more than 36 worker-months of design, development, and deployment.

The main page consisted of a number of tags and labels built on a toolbar running down the left side of the screen. For simplicity, this bar will not be replicated in the remainder of the code.

The opening page allows a user to choose from the following:

- Creating an account.
- Logging in under an account.
- Reviewing standard corporate material.

CODE SAMPLES

The coding process followed a four-phase implementation plan. Phase 1 would incorporate known UNIX solutions to provide a minimum of interactivity. Phase 2 would include a move to database programming tools that required very little C++ involvement. Phase 3 would incorporate ISAPIs, and phase 4 would introduce BackOffice products.

The databases were often prototyped in Access and then scaled up to SQL Server.

Phase 1

Let's look at the initial Perl script for setting up forms and e-mail delivery for hand entry of orders.

E-MAIL AND PERL

```perl
#!/usr/local/bin/perl
#Includes cgi-lib file; if cgi-lib doesn't exist, returns malformed
#header error
do "cgi-lib.pl" || die "Fatal Error: Can't load cgi library";
#Sets up e-mail program
$mailprog = '/usr/lib/sendmail';
#calls the subroutine in the cgi-lib.pl library
#to read in the variables from the form and set them up
#as key=value pairs in the array @in
&ReadParse;
#set up starview as the recipient
$recipient = 'user@connection.com';
#do a simple check to make sure the necessary fields are
#completed.

$name = $in{'comp_name'};
unless ($name gt 0) {
  #tells http server incoming data is text html
  #sends back NO-GO for order form
  print "Content-type: text/html\n\n";
  print "<HTML>";
```

Chapter 19

```
   print "<HEAD><TITLE>Cannot process order</TITLE>";   print "</HEAD><BODY>";
print "</HEAD><BODY bgcolor=\"#ffffff\">";
print "<IMG SRC=\"../gfx/logo1.gif\" ALT=\"HEIGHTS Information Expressway
logo\">";
print "<H2>HEIGHTS <i> Solutions</I></H2>";

  print "<H1>Sorry\!</H1>";
  print "We are unable to process your order at this\n";
  print "time because we do not know your company...please\n";
  print " return to fill in the Prepared For information.\n";
  print "<P>";
print "<hr>";
print "<font size=4>Press the BACK button </font> on your browser";
print "<HR>";

 # print "<H3>Back to the <A HREF=\"../index.html\">";
 # print "Front Page</A></H3>";
 # print "<H3>Back to the <A HREF=\"/order.htm\">";
 # print "Order Form</A></H3>";
  print "</BODY></HTML>";
  #quit the script - not enough information was present to
  #place an order.
  exit;
}

$cont_name = $in{'cont_name'};
unless ($cont_name gt 0) {
  #tells http server incoming data is text html
  #sends back NO-GO for order form
  print "Content-type: text/html\n\n";
  print "<HTML>";
  print "<HEAD><TITLE>Cannot process order</TITLE>";   print "</HEAD><BODY>";
print "</HEAD><BODY bgcolor=\"#ffffff\">";
print "<IMG SRC=\"../gfx/logo1.gif\" ALT=\"HEIGHTS Information Expressway
logo\">";
print "<H2>HEIGHTS <i> Solutions</I></H2>";

  print "<H1>Sorry\!</H1>";
  print "We are unable to process your order at this\n";
  print "time because we do not know who you are...please\n";
  print " return to fill in the Prepared For information.\n";
  print "<P>";
print "<hr>";
print "<font size=4>Press the BACK button </font> on your browser";
print "<HR>";
```

```
# print "<H3>Back to the <A HREF=\"../index.html\">";
# print "Front Page</A></H3>";
# print "<H3>Back to the <A HREF=\"/order.htm\">";
# print "Order Form</A></H3>";
  print "</BODY></HTML>";
  #quit the script - not enough information was present to
  #place an order.
  exit;
}

$email = $in{'email_deliv'};
unless ($email gt 0) {
  #tells http server incoming data is text html
  #sends back NO-GO for order form
  print "Content-type: text/html\n\n";
  print "<HTML>";
  print "<HEAD><TITLE>Cannot process order</TITLE>";  print "</HEAD><BODY>";
print "</HEAD><BODY bgcolor=\"#ffffff\">";
print "<IMG SRC=\"../gfx/logo1.gif\" ALT=\"HEIGHTS Information Expressway logo\">";
print "<H2>HEIGHTS <i> Solutions</I></H2>";

  print "<H1>Sorry\!</H1>";
  print "We are unable to process your order at this\n";
  print "time because we do not know your e-mail address..please\n";
  print " return to fill in the e-mail field.\n";
  print "<P>";
print "<hr>";
print "<font size=4>Press the BACK button </font> on your browser";
print "<HR>";

# print "<H3>Back to the <A HREF=\"../index.html\">";
# print "Front Page</A></H3>";
# print "<H3>Back to the <A HREF=\"/order.htm\">";
# print "Order Form</A></H3>";
  print "</BODY></HTML>";
  #quit the script - not enough information was present to
  #place an order.
  exit;
}
$proper_addname = $in{'proper_add'};
unless ($proper_addname gt 0) {
  #tells http server incoming data is text html
  #sends back NO-GO for order form
  print "Content-type: text/html\n\n";
```

```perl
  print "<HTML>";
  print "<HEAD><TITLE>Cannot process order</TITLE>";  print "</HEAD><BODY>";
print "</HEAD><BODY bgcolor=\"#ffffff\">";
print "<IMG SRC=\"../gfx/logo1.gif\" ALT=\"HEIGHTS Information Expressway
logo\">";
print "<H2>HEIGHTS <i> Solutions</I></H2>";

  print "<H1>Sorry\!</H1>";
  print "We are unable to process your order at this\n";
  print "time because we did not receive the proper address.\n";
  print "<P>";
print "<hr>";
print "<font size=4>Press the BACK button </font> on your browser";
print "<HR>";

# print "<H3>Back to the <A HREF=\"../index.html\">";
# print "Front Page</A></H3>";
# print "<H3>Back to the <A HREF=\"/order.htm\">";
# print "Order Form</A></H3>";
  print "</BODY></HTML>";
  #quit the script - not enough information was present to
  #place an order.
  exit;
}

$city_name = $in{'proper_city'};
unless ($city_name gt 0) {
  #tells http server incoming data is text html
  #sends back NO-GO for order form
  print "Content-type: text/html\n\n";
  print "<HTML>";
  print "<HEAD><TITLE>Cannot process order</TITLE>";  print "</HEAD><BODY>";
print "</HEAD><BODY bgcolor=\"#ffffff\">";
print "<IMG SRC=\"../gfx/logo1.gif\" ALT=\"HEIGHTS Information Expressway
logo\">";
print "<H2>HEIGHTS <i> Solutions</I></H2>";

  print "<H1>Sorry\!</H1>";
  print "We are unable to process your order at this\n";
  print "time because we did not receive the site city location.\n";
  print "<P>";
print "<hr>";
print "<font size=4>Press the BACK button </font> on your browser";
print "<HR>";

# print "<H3>Back to the <A HREF=\"/index.html\">";
```

```
  # print "Front Page</A></H3>";
  # print "<H3>Back to the <A HREF=\"/order.htm\">";
  # print "Order Form</A></H3>";
   print "</BODY></HTML>";
   #quit the script - not enough information was present to
   #place an order.
   exit;
}

$state_name = $in{'proper_state'};
unless ($state_name gt 0) {
   #tells http server incoming data is text html
   #sends back NO-GO for order form
   print "Content-type: text/html\n\n";
   print "<HTML>";
   print "<HEAD><TITLE>Cannot process order</TITLE>";  print "</HEAD><BODY>";
print "</HEAD><BODY bgcolor=\"#ffffff\">";
print "<IMG SRC=\"../gfx/logo1.gif\" ALT=\"HEIGHTS Information Expressway
logo\">";
print "<H2>HEIGHTS <i> Solutions</I></H2>";

   print "<H1>Sorry\!</H1>";
   print "We are unable to process your order at this\n";
   print "time because we did not receive the proper state location...please\n";
   print " return to fill in the Subject Information.\n";
   print "<P>";
print "<hr>";
print "<font size=4>Press the BACK button </font> on your browser";
   print "<HR>";

  # print "<H3>Back to the <A HREF=\"../index.html\">";
  # print "Front Page</A></H3>";
  # print "<H3>Back to the <A HREF=\"/order.htm\">";
  # print "Order Form</A></H3>";
   print "</BODY></HTML>";
   #quit the script - not enough information was present to
   #place an order.
   exit;
}

$zip_name = $in{'proper_zip'};
unless ($zip_name gt 0) {
   #tells http server incoming data is text html
   #sends back NO-GO for order form
   print "Content-type: text/html\n\n";
   print "<HTML>";
```

```perl
      print "<HEAD><TITLE>Cannot process order</TITLE>";  print "</HEAD><BODY>";
   print "</HEAD><BODY bgcolor=\"#ffffff\">";
   print "<IMG SRC=\"../gfx/logo1.gif\" ALT=\"HEIGHTS Information Expressway
   logo\">";
   print "<H2>HEIGHTS <i>Information Solutions</I></H2>";

     print "<H1>Sorry\!</H1>";
     print "We are unable to process your order at this\n";
     print "time because we did not receive the proper ZIP...please\n";
     print " return to fill in the ZIP information.\n";
     print "<P>";
   print "<hr>";
   print "<font size=4>Press the BACK button </font> on your browser";
   print "<HR>";

    # print "<H3>Back to the <A HREF=\"../index.html\">";
    # print "Front Page</A></H3>";
    # print "<H3>Back to the <A HREF=\"/order.htm\">";
    # print "Order Form</A></H3>";
     print "</BODY></HTML>";
     #quit the script - not enough information was present to
     #place an order.
     exit;
}
$county_name = $in{'proper_county'};
unless ($county_name gt 0) {
    #tells http server incoming data is text html
    #sends back NO-GO for order form
    print "Content-type: text/html\n\n";
    print "<HTML>";
    print "<HEAD><TITLE>Cannot process order</TITLE>";  print "</HEAD><BODY>";
   print "</HEAD><BODY bgcolor=\"#ffffff\">";
   print "<IMG SRC=\"../gfx/logo1.gif\" ALT=\"HEIGHTS Information Expressway
   logo\">";
   print "<H2>HEIGHTS <i>Information Solutions</I></H2>";

     print "<H1>Sorry\!</H1>";
     print "We are unable to process your order at this\n";
     print "time because we did not receive your County location...please\n";
     print " return to fill in the Subject information.\n";
     print "<P>";
   print "<hr>";
   print "<font size=4>Press the BACK button </font> on your browser";
   print "<HR>";

    # print "<H3>Back to the <A HREF=\"../index.html\">";
```

```perl
# print "Front Page</A></H3>";
# print "<H3>Back to the <A HREF=\"/order.htm\">";
# print "Order Form</A></H3>";
  print "</BODY></HTML>";
  #quit the script - not enough information was present to
  #place an order.
  exit;
}

# Do any error checking you need here
$round = $in{'num_round'};
if ($round < 1) {
  $round = 0;
}
$square = $in{'num_square'};
if ($square < 1) {
  $square = 0;
}
$tri = $in{'num_triangle'};
if ($tri < 1 ) {
  $tri = 0;
}
#assigns process id to $pid
$pid=$$;
#opens up comment file for writing
open(ORDER,">./tmp/order_info.$pid");
#enter the form data into the file to be mailed
#print ORDER "           HEIGHTS Order Form\n";
#print ORDER "- - - - - - - - - - - - - - - - - -\n";
#print ORDER "    Account #:  $in{'account_#'}\n";
#print ORDER "    Contact name:  $in{'contact_name'}\n";
#print ORDER "    SARRI type: $in{'sarri_type'}\n";
#print ORDER "    SARRI: $in{'sarri_rad' }\n";
#print ORDER "    RET: $in{'ret_type'}\n";
#print ORDER "    Sandburn: $in{'sandburn'}\n";
#print ORDER "    Loc name: $in{'loc_name'}\n";
#print ORDER "    Street Address:  $in{'street_address'}\n";
#print ORDER "    City: $in{'city'}\n";
#print ORDER "    PO Number:  $in{'po_num'}\n";
#print ORDER "    Rush Service:  $in{'rush'}\n";
#print ORDER "    Message: $in{'message'}\n";
print ORDER "- - - - - - - - - - - - - - - - - -\n";
print ORDER;
#print ORDER "$in{'contact_name'} ordered:\n";
```

```
#print ORDER "     $round $in{'r_size'} Round Widgets\n";
#print ORDER "     $square $in{'sq_size'} Square Widgets\n";
#print ORDER "     $tri $in{'tr_size'} Triangular Widgets\n";
print ORDER;
print ORDER "- - - - - - - - - - - - - - - - - -\n";
#close out file to be mailed
close COMMENTSFILE;
#sends comment file as mail to user

#opens up comment file for writing
open(MAIL,"|mail user\@connection.com");
#enter the form data into the file to be mailed
print MAIL "From : $in{'fromaddr'}\n";
print MAIL "            HEIGHTS MAIL Form\n";
print MAIL "- - - - - - - - - - - - - - - - - -\n";
#print MAIL "   Account #:  $in{'account_#'}\n";
print MAIL "   If Default is on...see the acct info:  $in{'default'}\n";
print MAIL "   Company Name: $in{'comp_name'}\n";
print MAIL "   Contact Name: $in{'cont_name'}\n";
print MAIL "   Company address: $in{'comp_add'}\n";
print MAIL "   Company City: $in{'comp_city'}\n";
print MAIL "   Company State: $in{'comp_state'}\n";
print MAIL "   Company Zip: $in{'comp_zip'}\n";
print MAIL "   Contact Phone: $in{'comp_phone'}\n";
print MAIL "   Contact FAX: $in{'comp_fax'}\n";
print MAIL "   Proper ID: $in{'proper_id'}\n";
print MAIL "   Undeveloped: $in{'undev'}\n";
print MAIL "   Proper Address: $in{'proper_add'}\n";
print MAIL "   Cross Street Address: $in{'cross_st'}\n";
print MAIL "   Direction $in{'direct'}\n";
print MAIL "   Distance: $in{'distan'}\n";
print MAIL "   Proper City: $in{'proper_city'}\n";
print MAIL "   Proper State: $in{'proper_state'}\n";
print MAIL "   Proper Zip Code: $in{'proper_zip'}\n";
print MAIL "   Proper County: $in{'proper_county'}\n";
print MAIL "   Proper Latitude: $in{'latitude'}\n";
print MAIL "   Proper Longitude: $in{'longitude'}\n";
print MAIL "   SARRI Ordered: $in{'sarri'}\n";
print MAIL "   Extended Radius: $in{'radex'}\n";
print MAIL "   Special Delivery Notes: $in{'deliv_notes'}\n";
print MAIL "   Delivery Options: $in{'dops'}\n";
print MAIL "   E-mail Delivery Address: $in{'email_deliv'}\n";
print MAIL "   FAX Number for Delivery: $in{'fax_num'}\n";
print MAIL "   FED EX account number: $in{'acct_num'}\n";
```

```
print MAIL "   Bill to Fed Ex acct:   $in{'fedbill'}\n";
print MAIL "   Message: $in{'message'}\n";
print MAIL "- - - - - - - - - - - - - - - - - -\n";
print MAIL;
#print MAIL "$in{'contact_name'} MAILed:\n";
#print MAIL "     $round $in{'r_size'} Round Widgets\n";
#print MAIL "     $square $in{'sq_size'} Square Widgets\n";
#print MAIL "     $tri $in{'tr_size'} Triangular Widgets\n";
print MAIL;
print MAIL "- - - - - - - - - - - - - - - - - -\n";
#close out file to be mailed
close MAIL;

#$command='mail user@connection.com < /tmp/order_info.$pid';
#system($command);
#erases temp file
#unlink("/tmp/order_info.$pid");
#tells http server incoming data is text html
#acknowledges receipt of information
print "Content-type: text/html\n\n";
print "<HTML>";
print "<HEAD><TITLE>Thank You\!</TITLE>";
print "</HEAD><BODY bgcolor=\"#ffffff\">";
print "<IMG SRC=\"../gfx/logo1.gif\" ALT=\"HEIGHTS Information Expressway logo\">";
print "<H2>HEIGHTS <i>Information Solutions</I></H2>";
print "<H2>Thank you for submitting your order\!</H2>";
#print "According to our information, you ordered:\n";
#print "<PRE>\n";
#print "     $round $in{'r_size'} Round Widgets\n";
#print "     $square $in{'sq_size'} Square Widgets\n";
#print "     $tri $in{'tr_size'} Triangular Widgets\n";
#print "</PRE>\n";
#print "<P>";
#print "We will contact you by phone for payment\n";
#print "instructions\n";
#print "<P>";

print "<hr>";
print "<li><font size=4>Press the BACK button </font> on your browser to return\n";
print "to the order form while retaining previously entered information";
print "<HR>";

#print "<li><font size =4>Return to the   <A HREF=\"/order.htm\">";
```

```
#print "Order Form</A></font> <b>without</b> retaining previously entered
information";
print "<p>";
print "<li><font size=4>Return to the <A HREF=\"/index.html\">";
print "Home Page</A></font>";

print "</BODY></HTML>";
```

Moving from this initial site in phase 1, the next step was to incorporate database control of company information. SQL Server was introduced, as was testing of an ODBC-Perl connection. See the next section as well as Figure 19.2, which shows this phase 1A addition.

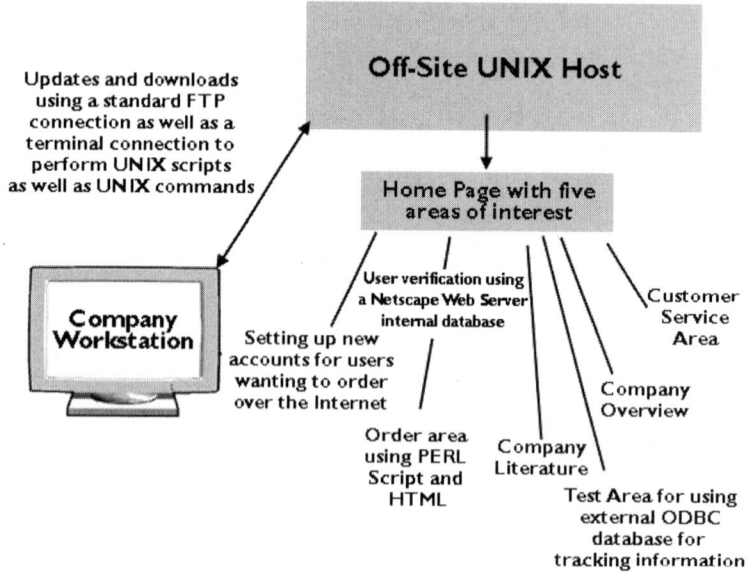

Figure 19.2 Initial site layout, phase 1A.

Phase 1A: Simple Addition to the Database Using Perl

```
<HTML>
<TITLE>Add a group of items</TITLE>

<BODY  BGCOLOR=#FFFFFF>

<P>

<A HREF="http://www.yourcomputer.com/"><IMG SRC="/someone.gif" ALT="A test
site" ALIGN=RIGHT BORDER=0 WIDTH=67 HEIGHT=92></A>
```

```
<NOBR><A HREF="/"><IMG SRC="/gifs/logo/iftech.gif" ALT="Iftech.com" BORDER=0
WIDTH=68 HEIGHT=16></A><A HREF="/"><IMG SRC="/gifs/control/topbar/tophome.gif"
BORDER=0 ALT="Home" WIDTH=52 HEIGHT=16></A><A HREF="/iti/"><IMG SRC="/gifs/con-
trol/topbar/topabout.gif" BORDER=0 ALT="About ITI" WIDTH=69 HEIGHT=16><A
HREF="/isapi/guestbook.dll?"><IMG SRC="/gifs/control/topbar/topguest.gif" BOR-
DER=0 ALT="Guestbook"WIDTH=84 HEIGHT=16></A><A HREF="/search/"><IMG
SRC="/gifs/control/topbar/topsearch.gif" BORDER=0 ALT="Search ITI"WIDTH=58
HEIGHT=16></A></NOBR><BR><IMG SRC="/gifs/control/topbar/blackbar.gif" WIDTH=427
HEIGHT=1><BR><NOBR><A HREF="/oltc/"><IMG SRC="/gifs/control/topbar/oltcbar.gif"
ALT="Online Training Center" BORDER=0 ALIGN=BOTTOM WIDTH=135 HEIGHT=16></A><A
HREF="/help/oltchelp.stm"><IMG SRC="/gifs/control/topbar/helpbar.gif"
ALT="Help" BORDER=0 WIDTH=100 HEIGHT=16></A></NOBR>

<H1></H1>
<H3></H3>

<HR>

<FORM METHOD=GET ACTION="/cgi-bin/data.pl">
<h1>Form to add data to the database</h1>
Please enter your information:
<P>Name:    <INPUT NAME="name" TYPE=text SIZE="30">
<P>City:    <INPUT NAME="city" TYPE=text SIZE="30">
<P>State:   <INPUT NAME="state" TYPE=text SIZE="30">
<P><INPUT TYPE=submit value="Add">  <INPUT TYPE=reset value="Reset">
<p><a href="/cgi-bin/list.pl">
Click Here</a> to see the contents of the database.<p>
</FORM>
</body>
</html>
```

with the data.pl being

```
# add.pl
# This script adds the name city and state data found on
# the form to the database.

require NT_ODBC;
require "cgi-lib.pl";

ReadParse(*data); #get the data from the form

$o = NT_ODBC->new("DSN=Test");
$o->sql("insert into table1 values (\'$data{'name'}\',
\'$data{'city'}\', \'$data{'state'}\')");
$o->sql("select * from table1");

# Process the form's data.
print PrintHeader();
```

Chapter 19

```
print HtmlTop("Add results");
print "Your IP address: ", $ENV{REMOTE_ADDR}, '<p>';
print "The following data has been added to the database:", '<p>';
print 'Name: ', $data{'name'},'<br>';
print 'City: ', $data{'city'},'<br>';
print 'State: ', $data{'state'},'<br>';
print HtmlBot();
```

The next test was to start building pages based on a user's needs. In some cases, Shockwave pages were added to provide training material for internal personnel. The use of Java applets was investigated to determine their usefulness. JavaScript was used to determine how many new clients needed this added interactivity.

Phase 1B: Java for Browser Detection

```
SCRIPT LANGUAGE="JavaScript">

<!— Hide from primitive browsers
document.write("<TABLE BORDER=2 CELLSPACING=1 CELLPADDING=5 VPSACE=5 HSPACE=5>");
document.write("<TR>");
document.write("<TD><FONT FACE='Palatino'SIZE='2'><B><CENTER>Data Name</CENTER></B></FONT></TD>");
document.write("<TD WIDTH='40%'>");
document.write("<FONT FACE='Palatino'SIZE='2'><B><CENTER>Value Returned</CENTER></B></FONT></TD>");
document.write("<TD>");
document.write("<FONT FACE='Palatino'SIZE='2'><CENTER><B>JavaScript used to return this value</B></CENTER></FONT></TD>");
document.write("</TR><TR>");
document.write("<TD><FONT FACE='Palatino'SIZE='2'>Code Name</FONT></TD>");
document.write("<TD>");
document.write("<FONT FACE='Palatino'SIZE='2'>");
document.write(navigator.appCodeName);
document.write("</FONT></TD>");
document.write("<TD><FONT FACE='Palatino'SIZE='2'>document.write(navigator.appCodeName);</FONT></TD>");
document.write("</TR><TR>");
document.write("<TD><FONT FACE='Palatino'SIZE='2'>Browser Name</FONT></TD>");
document.write("<TD><FONT FACE='Palatino'SIZE='2'>");
document.write(navigator.appName);
```

```
document.write("</FONT></TD>");
document.write("<TD><FONT
FACE='Palatino'SIZE='2'>document.write(navigator.appName);</FONT></TD>");
document.write("</TR><TR>");
document.write("<TD><FONT FACE='Palatino'SIZE='2'>Browser
Version</FONT></TD>");
document.write("<TD><FONT FACE='Palatino'SIZE='2'>");
document.write(navigator.appVersion);
document.write("</FONT></TD>");
document.write("<TD><FONT
FACE='Palatino'SIZE='2'>document.write(navigator.appVersion);</FONT></TD>");
document.write("</TR><TR>");
document.write("<TD><FONT FACE='Palatino'SIZE='2'>Browser UserAgent
Header</FONT></TD>");
document.write("<TD><FONT FACE='Palatino'SIZE='2'>");
document.write(navigator.userAgent);
document.write("</FONT></TD>");
document.write("<TD><FONT
FACE='Palatino'SIZE='2'>document.write(navigator.userAgent);</FONT></TD>");
document.write("</TR></TABLE>");
//end hiding-->

</SCRIPT>
```

It was determined that the greatest need was to create the internal site in a test mode that could be accessed by outside users, including engineers and sales personnel. Therefore, a second domain name was obtained from Internic.

Phase 2

Phase 2 encompassed the use of phase 1 pages for the company clients as well as the building of the internal test site. The intent was to move the site internally by phase 4. Phase 2 would open the development crew to building IDC/HTX pages for interactive database applications. This decision was based on the company's desire to develop a true database warehouse scheme for the hundreds of databases that it had been tracking for many years. These original databases were in all kinds of formats, including FoxPro, dBase, Revelation, Access, and SQL Server. It was determined that Access or SQL Server would be used for the final database layout. Databases built in Access would be scaled up to SQL Server. See Figure 19.3 for a brief overview of the flow.

Chapter 19

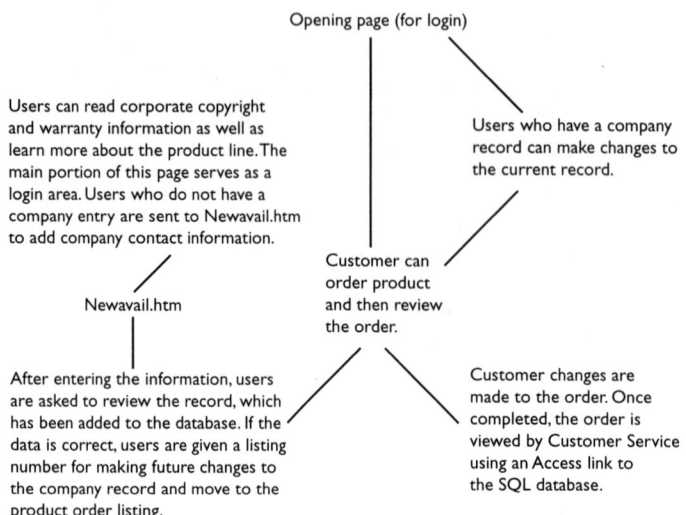

Figure 19.3 Phase 2: IDC/HTX sample site.

The following was put in **login1.htm**:

```
<html><head><title>The test Login Screen</title>
</head><body bgcolor="#ffffff"><center>
<h1>Welcome to the TEST<i>Express</i>Login </h1>
<a name="top">
<h2>Please enter your name and password for access</h2>
<p>
<h3>If you are new then please click <a href="NewAvail.htm">
HERE</a> to open a new account
<p>

<h3>Please do not forget to review the Warranty Information
...please click
<a href="#warranty">HERE</a>

<FORM METHOD="POST" ACTION="/ocs/Queries/Availj.idc">

<hr>
<pre>
Company name    : <INPUT TYPE="text" NAME="Company" VALUE="" Size="10"
Maxlength="50">

Password        : <INPUT TYPE="Password" NAME="Password" VALUE= "" SIZE="10">

Customer ID     : <INPUT TYPE="CustomerID_test" NAME="CustomerID_test" VALUE=
"" SIZE="10">
</pre>
```

```
<INPUT TYPE=submit VALUE="SUBMIT">
<INPUT TYPE=reset VALUE="No, no, start over">
<p>
</form>
<hr>

<p>
<hr>

<p>

<p>

<p>
</form>

<a name="warranty"><h3>WARRANTY INFORMATION</h3>
```

xxxxxxxxxxxx
xxxxxxxxxxx
xxxxxxxxxxxxx
xxxxxxxxxxxxx
xxxxxxxxxxxxxxx
xxxxxxxxxxxxxxxx
xxxxxxxxxxxxxxxxxxxxxx
xxxxxxxxxxxxxxxxxxxxxxx
xxxxxxxxxxxxxxxxxxxxxx

```
<h2>TO RETURN to the login page please click <a href="#top">HERE</a></h2>
</center>

</body></html>
```

Then **newavail.html** was used:

```
<HTML>

<HEAD>

<TITLE>New Customer </TITLE>

</HEAD>

<BODY BGCOLOR="#FFFFFF">

<P>
<center>
<h2>Welcome....this is where you may enter your new Record</h2>
</center>
<hr>
<P>

<FONT FACE=ARIAL SIZE="3"> <B>Customer Information</B> </FONT>
```

Chapter 19

```
<P>

<FONT FACE=ARIAL SIZE="2">

<!--This form calls the NewAvail.idc, which contains the
template for an insert query to add a new customer
record to the database. NewAvail.htx is the template
 used to display the results.-->

<FORM METHOD="POST" ACTION="/ocs/queries/NewAvail.idc">

<BR>

<P>

<!--Input boxes for the user to input data. The HTML
MAXLENGTH corresponds to the field size in the database.
The HTML SIZE specifies the size of the input area on the
form.-->

<INPUT type=hidden NAME="CustomerID_test"
value=<%NewAvail.idc%>><P>

Company: <INPUT NAME="Company" SIZE="34" MAXLENGTH="50" ><P>

Address: <INPUT NAME="Address" SIZE="35" MAXLENGTH="255" ><P>

City: <INPUT NAME="City" SIZE="15" MAXLENGTH="50"> <P>

State: <INPUT NAME="State" SIZE="2" MAXLENGTH="50"> <P>

Zip Code: <INPUT NAME="Zip" SIZE="10" MAXLENGTH="50"> <P>

Phone: <INPUT NAME="Phone"  SIZE="10"
MAXLENGTH="50" > <P>

Fax: <INPUT NAME="Fax"  SIZE="10"
MAXLENGTH="50" > <P>

Contact name: <INPUT NAME="Contact_name"  SIZE="10"
MAXLENGTH="50" > <P>

E-mail address: <INPUT NAME="Email"  SIZE="10"
MAXLENGTH="50" > <P>

<!--The password entered by the user is stored along with
the record. Users can change or update the record
only if they know the password. This is a simplistic security
 scheme designed to prevent a user from changing someone
else's record.-->

Enter a password for this listing. You will need to provide
 this password in order to update the listing.<br>
```

```
Password: <INPUT TYPE="Password" NAME="Password"  VALUE= "" SIZE="10"
MAXLENGTH="50" > <P>
<P>

<!--Graphic for a line-->
<hr><P>

<P>

<P>

<!--Submit and Reset buttons-->
<INPUT TYPE="SUBMIT" VALUE="Submit"> <INPUT TYPE="RESET">

</FORM>

<P>

<!--Graphic for a line-->

</BODY>

</FONT>

</HTML>
```

To **newavail.idc**:

```
Datasource: New
Template: NewAvail.htx
DefaultParameters:
RequiredParameters: Company, Contact_name, Email, Password
SQLStatement:
+INSERT INTO Customer_test ( Company, Address, City, State,
+Zip, Phone, Fax, Contact_name, Email, Password, dateeval)
+VALUES ( '%Company%', '%Address%', '%City%'
+,'%State%', '%Zip%', '%Phone%', '%Fax%', '%Contact_name%', '%Email%'
+, '%Password%',getdate());
```

newavail.htx:

```
<HTML>

<HEAD>

<TITLE>Customer Record Listing</TITLE>

</HEAD>

<!--The HTML page produced by this template serves a dual
purpose: 1) to allow users to confirm the data they entered
and 2) to act as an intermediate step to providing the user with
the customer number. The NewAvail.idc file,
which calls this template, generates the insert query that
```

adds the new customer record to the database. The primary key
for the record, CustomerID_test, is an identity field
generated by SQL Server. It does not exist until
the insert statement is executed. In order to retrieve CustomerID_test,
which is the listing number, we must initiate another query.
This second query is generated when the user responds to
this form by choosing whether or not the listing is correct.
Hidden HTML fields on the form generated by this template are
used to store enough information about the record to uniquely
identify it, because we do not yet know the primary key.
In addition, we need to use a query in the SQL Server
database to limit the choices to those records created in the last hour.-->

<BODY BGCOLOR=FFFFFF>

<!-- Graphics for banner and line below it.-->

<FONT FACE=ARIAL SIZE="2">

<B>Your customer record has been posted. Please review for accuracy.</B><P>

<!--The resultant HTML page contains two form sections;
the user selects the first if the customer record is correct and the
second if the customer record needs to be changed.-->

<!--If the listing is correct, the user clicks on the button for
"Listing is Correct," which passes the ListID.idc file to httpodbc.dll.
The values from the hidden fields below are plugged into the SQL
statement template in ListID.idc.
 We use a getdate call to test for those records submitted
in the last hour. ListID.htx, the template specified by ListID.idc,
is used to generate the return page that contains the listing number.-->

<FORM METHOD="POST" ACTION="/ocs/Queries/ListID.idc">

<!--Hyperlink graphic button for correct listing.-->

<INPUT TYPE=IMAGE SRC="/ocs/images/rndbtn.gif " ALIGN="Top"
WIDTH=18 HEIGHT=18 BORDER=0>Listing is correct<P>

<!--The values for these hidden HTML fields are coming from
NewAvail.idc. NewAvail.htm, the form used to take the user
input for the job listing, passes the values to NewAvail.idc,
which in turn calls this template, NewAvail.htx. The idc. prefix
for the plug-in variable represents values coming from the .idc
file rather than the record set returned from the database.-->

<INPUT TYPE="HIDDEN" NAME="CustomerID_test" VALUE="<%idc.CustomerID_test%>">

<INPUT TYPE="HIDDEN" NAME="Company" VALUE="<%idc.Company%>">

```html
<INPUT TYPE="HIDDEN" NAME="Address" VALUE="<%idc.Address%>">
<INPUT TYPE="HIDDEN" NAME="City" VALUE="<%idc.City%>">
<INPUT TYPE="HIDDEN" NAME="State" VALUE="<%idc.State%>">
<INPUT TYPE="HIDDEN" NAME="Zip" VALUE="<%idc.Zip%>">
<INPUT TYPE="HIDDEN" NAME="Phone" VALUE="<%idc.Phone%>">
<INPUT TYPE="HIDDEN" NAME="Fax" VALUE="<%idc.Fax%>">
<INPUT TYPE="HIDDEN" NAME="Contact_name" VALUE="<%idc.Contact_name%>">
<INPUT TYPE="HIDDEN" NAME="E-mail" VALUE="<%idc.Email%>">
<INPUT TYPE="HIDDEN" NAME="Password" VALUE="<%idc.Password%>">
</FORM>

<!--If the customer record is not correct, the user clicks on the
button for "Change/Update Listing," which passes the Chg_Avai.idc
file to httpodbc.dll. The values from the hidden fields
are plugged into the SQL statement template in Chg_Avai.idc.-->

<FORM METHOD="POST" ACTION="/ocs/queries/Chg_Avai.idc">

<!--Hyperlink graphic button for listing that needs to be changed.-->

<INPUT TYPE=IMAGE SRC="/ocs/images/rndbtn.gif" ALIGN="Top"
WIDTH=18 HEIGHT=18 BORDER=0>Change/Update Listing.<P>

<!--The values for these hidden HTML fields are coming from
NewAvail.idc. NewAvail.htm, is the form used to take the user input
for the customer record. This form passes the values to NewAvail.idc, which in
turn calls the template, NewAvail.htx. The idc. prefix for the
plug-in variable represents values coming from the .idc file
rather than the record set returned from the database.-->

<INPUT TYPE="HIDDEN" NAME="CustomerID_test" VALUE="<%idc.CustomerID_test%>">
<INPUT TYPE="HIDDEN" NAME="Company" VALUE="<%idc.Company%>">
<INPUT TYPE="HIDDEN" NAME="Address" VALUE="<%idc.Address%>">
<INPUT TYPE="HIDDEN" NAME="City" VALUE="<%idc.City%>">
<INPUT TYPE="HIDDEN" NAME="State" VALUE="<%idc.State%>">
<INPUT TYPE="HIDDEN" NAME="Zip" VALUE="<%idc.Zip%>">
<INPUT TYPE="HIDDEN" NAME="Phone" VALUE="<%idc.Phone%>">
<INPUT TYPE="HIDDEN" NAME="Fax" VALUE="<%idc.Fax%>">
```

```
<INPUT TYPE="HIDDEN" NAME="Contact_name" VALUE="<%idc.Contact_name%>">

<INPUT TYPE="HIDDEN" NAME="E-mail" VALUE="<%idc.Email%>">

<INPUT TYPE="HIDDEN" NAME="Password" VALUE="<%idc.Password%>">

</FORM>

</FONT>

<!--From here down the template is plugging in values from
NewAvail.idc to show the user the data that was entered.-->

<P>

<!--Graphic for a line-->

<hr>

<P>

<P>

<B><FONT FACE=ARIAL SIZE="3">Customer Information</B></FONT>

<P>

<FONT FACE=ARIAL SIZE="2">

<!--Status is set to open line because the listing is brand new.-->

<B>Status: </B>open<BR>

<!--Now we Plug in values the user entered in the input
form coming via the .idc file.-->

<B>Company Info:</B> <%idc.Company%>, <%idc.Address%>, <%idc.City%>,
<%idc.State%> <%idc.Zip%>

<B>Contact Info: </B><%idc.Contact_name%>  <%idc.Phone%>
<%idc.Fax%>  <%idc.Email%><BR>
<BR>

<BR>

</FONT>

<P>

<hr><BR>

<P>

<P>

<B><FONT FACE=ARIAL SIZE="3">Contact</B></FONT>
```

```
<FONT FACE=ARIAL SIZE="2">

<ADDRESS>

<!--This eliminates blank lines for name and address information
not entered by the user, If the field is blank, do nothing; otherwise,
display the value from the database.-->

<!-- Contact Name is a required field and should always be present.-->

<%idc.ContactName%><br>

<%If idc.Company EQ "">

<%Else%>

<%idc.Company%><br>

<%EndIf%>

<%If idc.Address EQ "">

<%Else%>

<%idc.Address%><br>

<%EndIf%>

<%If idc.City EQ "">

<%Else%>

<%idc.City%>, <%idc.State%> <%idc.Zip%><br>

<%idc.Country%><br>

<%EndIf%>

</ADDRESS>

<!--Display these fields regardless of whether the user entered the data. If no
data is entered, the heading will show, but no data.-->

<B>Phone: </B><%idc.Phone%><br>

<B>Fax: </B><%idc.FAX%><br>

<B>E-mail: </B><%idc.Email%><br>

<P>

<hr>
<BR>

<P>

</FORM>
```

```
<P>
<P>
</BODY>
</FONT>
</HTML>
```

To review the list, we used **list.idc**:

```
Datasource: New
Template: ListID.htx
DefaultParameters:
SQLStatement:
+SELECT *
+FROM Customer_test
+WHERE  Company='%Company%'AND
+Address='%Address%' AND
+City='%City%' AND
+State='%State%' AND
+Zip='%Zip%'
+AND Phone='%Phone%' AND  Fax='%Fax%'
+AND  Contact_name='%Contact_name%'
+AND Email='%Email%' AND Password='%Password%'
+AND datediff(hh,dateeval,getdate())<1
```

We used **list.htx** to give an updated listing number for future reference:

```
<HTML>

<HEAD>

<title>Listing Number</title>

</HEAD>

<!--This .htx template file is referenced from ListID.idc.

<BODY BGCOLOR=FFFFFF>

<!--Graphics for banner and line below it.-->
<hr>
<P>

<B><FONT FACE=ARIAL SIZE="3">Thank you for submitting your Customer Information.</B></FONT>

<P>

<FONT FACE=ARIAL SIZE="2">
```

```
Please jot down your listing number.
You will use this number along with
your listing password to update your listing.

<P>

<!--Data returned from the database is plugged
into the placeholder fields below.-->

<%BeginDetail%>

<B>Listing Number: </B><%CustomerID_test%>, <%Company%>, <%Contact_name%>,
submitted <%dateeval%>

<br>

<%EndDetail%>

<P>

<!--Graphic for a line-->
<hr>
<BR>

<P>

</BODY>

</FONT>

</HTML>
```

To change a record, we used **chg_avai.idc**:

```
Datasource: New
Template: Chg_Avai.htx
DefaultParameters:
MaxRecords: 50
SQLStatement:
+SELECT *
+FROM Customer_test
+WHERE
+Company='%Company%'AND
+Address='%Address%' AND
+City='%City%' AND
+State='%State%' AND
+Zip='%Zip%'
+AND Phone='%Phone%' AND Fax='%Fax%'
+AND Contact_name='%Contact_name%'
+AND Email='%Email%'
+AND Password='%Password%'
```

```
+AND datediff(hh,dateeval,getdate())<1
```

chg_ava.htx:

```
<HTML>

<HEAD>

<TITLE>Customer Record</TITLE>

</HEAD>

<!--This template, specified from Chg_Avai.idc,
is called if the user selects to change/update the
information in a new customer record.-->

<BODY>

<BODY BGCOLOR=FFFFFF>

<!--Graphics for banner and the navigation buttons below it-->

<hr>

<P>

<B><FONT FACE=ARIAL COLOR="#3366CC" SIZE="3">

Update - Customer ID <%CustomerID_test%></B></FONT>

<P>

<FONT FACE=ARIAL SIZE="2">

Make the appropriate changes to the listing below and then
click Submit.<P>

</FONT>

<!--Once the changes are made and the user presses
submit, Chg_UpdA.idc generates the query to update the record.
Chg_UpdA.htx is the template that generates the page confirming
the update.-->

<FORM METHOD="POST" ACTION="Chg_UpdA.idc">

<!--Submit button-->

<INPUT TYPE=SUBMIT>

<P>

<!--Graphic for a line-->
<hr>
```

```
<BR>

<P>

<!--The listing number, CustomerID_test, is used by
the .htx template that confirms the update.-->

<INPUT TYPE="HIDDEN" NAME="CustomerID_test" VALUE=<%CustomerID_test%>>

<P>

<B><FONT FACE=ARIAL SIZE="3">Customer Information</B></FONT>

<FONT FACE=ARIAL SIZE="2">

<P>

<!--Status is hard-coded, because this is a new listing.-->

<B>Status: </B>open<P>

<!--Values from the database are plugged into the placeholder fields.
The VALUE allows the data to be used as the default value for the
input boxes. Note the quotation marks. If quotes are not used,
only the first word from the
respective field in the database will show as the default for the
input box. For example, if the quotation marks were omitted and the
City is Los Angeles, only Los would show in the input box
on the form to change/update the customer record.-->

<B><FONT FACE=ARIAL SIZE="3">Contact</B></FONT>

<FONT FACE=ARIAL SIZE="2">

<P>

<!--Values from the database record are the default value for
the input boxes.-->

<!--All name and address fields are shown, even if no data
is present for a field, to allow user to update that field.-->

<B>

Name: <INPUT NAME="Company" SIZE="38" MAXLENGTH="50"
VALUE="<%Company%>"><P>

Address: <INPUT NAME="Address" SIZE="35" MAXLENGTH="255"

VALUE="<%Address%>"><P>

City: <INPUT NAME="City" SIZE="15" MAXLENGTH="50" VALUE="<%City%>">

State: <INPUT NAME="State" SIZE="2" MAXLENGTH="50" VALUE="<%State%>">
```

Chapter 19

```
Zip Code: <INPUT NAME="Zip" SIZE="10" MAXLENGTH="50" VALUE="<%Zip%>">

</B>

<P>

<B>Phone: </B><INPUT NAME="Phone" SIZE="14" MAXLENGTH="50"
VALUE="<%Phone%>">

<B>Fax: </B><INPUT NAME="FAX" SIZE="14" MAXLENGTH="50" VALUE="<%FAX%>">

<B>E-mail: </B><INPUT NAME="Email" SIZE="20" MAXLENGTH="50"
VALUE="<%Email%>"><P>

<B>Contact Name: </B><INPUT NAME="Contact_name" SIZE="20" MAXLENGTH="50"
VALUE="<%Contact_name%>"><P>

<B>Password: </B><INPUT Type=Password NAME="Password" SIZE="20" MAXLENGTH="50"
VALUE="<%Password%>"><P>

<!--Creates the list box and selects the option that matches the
value from the record returned in the database.-->
<P>

<!--Value from the record returned from the database is the default
value for the input box.-->

</FONT>

</FORM>

<P>

<!--Graphic for a line-->

<P>

<FONT FACE=ARIAL SIZE="2">

</FONT>

</BODY>

</HTML>
```

For updating a company record from a separate logon effort, we use **chg_upda.idc**:

```
Datasource: New
Template: Chg_UpdA.htx
SQLStatement:
+UPDATE Customer_test
+SET Company='%Company%',
+Address='%Address%', City='%City%', State='%State%',
+Zip='%Zip%', Phone='%Phone%', Fax='%Fax%',
```

```
+Email='%Email%', Password='%Password%', Contact_name='%Contact_name%',
+dateeval= getdate()
+WHERE CustomerID_test=%CustomerID_test%
```

Here is chg_upda.htx:

```
<HTML>

<HEAD>

<title>Listing Number</title>

</HEAD>

<!--This template, creates the HTML page to confirm changes
made to a new customer record.-->

<BODY BGCOLOR=FFFFFF>
<hr>

<FONT FACE=ARIAL SIZE="2">

<P>

<B>Thank you for submitting your customer record.</B>

<P>

Please jot down your listing number. You will use this
number along with your listing password to update your listing.

<P>

<!--The values for these placeholder variables are coming from
Chg_UpdA.idc.-->

<B>Listing Number: </B> <%idc.CustomerID_test%>,

<%idc.Company%>, submitted <%idc.dateeval%>

<br>

<P>

<hr>
<h4>Click <a href="../../login.htm">HERE</a> to go to the Login Screen</h4>
<BR>

<P>

</BODY>

</FONT>

</HTML>
```

The orders file follow. Here is **order.idc**:

```
Datasource: New
Template: order.htx
Password: '%Password%'
SQLStatement:
+Select *
+From Customer_test
+Where convert(varchar,CustomerID_test)='%CustomerID_test%'
+And Password='%Password%'
```

Here is **order.htx**:

```
<HTML>

<HEAD>

<TITLE>Order Form <%idc.CustomerID_test%></TITLE>

</HEAD>

<!--This template, creates the HTML page to confirm the customer available
listing update.-->

<BODY BGCOLOR=FFFFFF>

<FONT FACE=ARIAL SIZE="2">

<P>

<B>Customer Number <%idc.CustomerID_test%></B>
 <input type="hidden" name='Password' value='<%idc.Password%>'>
 <input type="hidden" name='Company' value='<%idc.Company%>'>
<P>

Please choose the product that you would like to order:<p>
<P>
1.    <a href="ret.idc?Password=<%idc.Password%>&
CustomerID_test=<%idc.CustomerID_test%>">Here</a> to go to the ordering area

<P>

</BODY>

</FONT>

</HTML>
```

To order an actual product requires **ret.idc**:

```
Datasource: New
Template: ret.htx
Password: '%Password%'
```

```
MaxRecords: 50
ODBCOPTIONS:  SQL_OPT_TRACE=1, SQL_OPT_TRACEFILE=john.log
SQLStatement:
+SELECT *
+FROM Customer_test
+WHERE convert(varchar, CustomerID_test)= '%CustomerID_test%'
```

Here is **ret.htx**:

```
<HTML>

<HEAD>
<TITLE>HEIGHTS RET Ordering</TITLE>
</HEAD>
<BODY BGCOLOR="#f3ffff">
<h1><IMG width=100 height=71 SRC="/gfx/logo1.gif"
ALT="HEIGHTS Information Expressway logo"> Order Form</h1>

<FORM METHOD="POST" ACTION="Ret_01.idc"  >

<p>
If you have an account number, please enter it below. Otherwise, please
call Customer Service at (800)777-7777.<p>

<%BeginDetail%>
<input type="hidden" name='Company' value="<%Company%>">
<input type="hidden" name='Password' value="<%Password%>">
<input type="hidden" name='CustomerID_test' value="<%CustomerID_test%>">

Account Number:<%CustomerID_test%>

Contact Name: <%Contact_name%>

<p><hr>

E-mail address for delivery of product: <INPUT TYPE= "text" NAME="Email"
Value="<%Email%>" size="30">

<%EndDetail%>

<%If CurrentRecord EQ 0 %>
SAY HELLOOOOOOOOOOOOOOOOOOOOO

<%EndIf%>
<p>
<hr>

SARRI: <SELECT NAME="SARRI_type">
        <OPTION Value="1">          None
        <OPTION Value="2" SELECTED>SARRI   Standard
```

```
                <OPTION Value="3">        SARRI   Enhanced
                <OPTION Value="4">        SARRI Plus Standard
                <OPTION Value="5">        SARRI Plus Enhanced
        </SELECT>  New Distance: <SELECT NAME="New_distance">
                <OPTION Value="1" SELECTED>Standard
                <OPTION Value="2">        Extend by 1/4 mile
                <OPTION Value="3">        Extend by 1/2 mile
                <OPTION Value="4">        Extend by one mile
                <OPTION Value="5">        All db to one mile
        </SELECT>

<center>
<font size=-1>New distance options apply to SARRI products only</font>
</center>

<p>
RET: <SELECT NAME="RET">
        <OPTION Value="1" SELECTED>None
        <OPTION Value="3">        RET 3
        <OPTION Value="4">        RET 4
        <OPTION Value="5">        RET 5
    </SELECT>  All RETs are delivered with maps.
<p>
Sandburn: <INPUT TYPE="checkbox" NAME="Sandburn" VALUE="1">
(Shipped via air express to your address of record unless
otherwise specified below in Special Instructions.
Rush service applies to SARRI and RET products only.)
<pre>

<hr>
Proper Name     : <INPUT TYPE="text" NAME="Site_name" VALUE="" SIZE="50">
Street Address  : <INPUT TYPE="text" NAME="Street_address" VALUE="" SIZE="50">
City            : <INPUT TYPE="text" NAME="City"    VALUE="" SIZE="50">
State           : <INPUT TYPE="text" NAME="State"   VALUE="" SIZE="50">
Zip             : <INPUT TYPE="text" NAME="Zip"     VALUE="" SIZE="50">
Purchase Order# : <INPUT TYPE="text" NAME="PO_number" VALUE="" SIZE="50">
Rush Service    : <SELECT NAME="Rush">
        <OPTION VALUE="1" SELECTED>None
        <OPTION VALUE="2"> Delivery within 24 hours for an additional $75
                </SELECT>
</pre>
<p>
Additional Information and Special Instructions:<p>
<TEXTAREA NAME="Order_inst" ROWS="5" COLS="60" Value=""></TEXTAREA>
<p>
```

```
<center>

<input type="submit" value="Transmit Order">
 <input type=reset    value="Reset Form">

</center>

</form>

<

<A HREF="index.html">[Home Page]</A>
<A HREF="mailto:user@connection.com">[Email HEIGHTS]</A>
<P><HR>Last updated October 17, 1996 by
<ADDRESS><A HREF="mailto:brad@HEIGHTSinfo.com">Webmaster,
brad@HEIGHTSinfo.com</A>.</ADDRESS>
</BODY>
</HTML>
```

To review the order or change the order, here is **ret1.idc**:

```
Datasource: New
Template: Ret_01.htx
DefaultParameters:
Password: '%Password%'
ODBCOPTIONS:  SQL_OPT_TRACE=1, SQL_OPT_TRACEFILE=john.log
SQLStatement:
+INSERT INTO Order_test ( Email, SARRI_type, New_distance,
+RET, Sandburn, Site_name, Street_address, City, State, Zip,
+PO_number, Rush, Order_inst,dateent, Password, Company)
+VALUES ( '%Email%', '%SARRI_type%', '%New_distance%'
+,'%RET%', '%Sandburn%', '%Site_name%', '%Street_address%',
+'%City%', '%State%','%Zip%'
+, '%PO_number%', '%Rush%', '%Order_inst%', getdate(),'%Password%'
+,'%Company%');
```

Here is **ret1.htx**:

```
<HTML>

<HEAD>

<TITLE>Order Record Listing</TITLE>

</HEAD>

<!--The HTML page produced by this template serves a dual
purpose: 1) to allow users to confirm the data they entered
and 2) to act as an intermediate step to providing the user with
the order number. The ret_01.idc file,
```

which calls this template, generates the insert query that
adds the new customer record to the database. The primary key
for the record, OrderID_test, is an identity field
generated by SQL Server. It does not exist until
the insert statement is executed. In order to retrieve CustomerID_test,
which is the listing number, we must initiate another query.
This second query is generated when the user responds to
this form by choosing whether or not the listing is correct.
Hidden HTML fields on the form generated by this template are
used to store enough information about the record to uniquely
identify it, because we do not yet know the primary key.
In addition, we need to use a query in the SQL Server
database to limit the choices to those records created in the last hour.-->

<BODY BGCOLOR=FFFFFF>

<FONT FACE=ARIAL SIZE="2">

<B>Your order record has been posted. Please review for accuracy.</B><P>

<!--The resultant HTML page contains two form sections;
the user selects the first if the customer record is correct and the
second if the customer record needs to be changed.-->

<!--If the listing is correct, the user clicks on the button for
"Listing is Correct," which passes the relist.idc file to httpodbc.dll.
The values from the hidden fields below are plugged into the SQL
statement template in relist.idc.
 We use a getdate call to test for those records submitted
in the last hour. relist.htx, the template specified by relist.idc,
is used to generate the return page that contains the listing number.-->

<FORM METHOD="POST" ACTION="relist.idc">

<!--Hyperlink graphic button for correct listing.-->

<INPUT TYPE=IMAGE SRC="/ocs/images/rndbtn.gif " ALIGN="Top"
WIDTH=18 HEIGHT=18 BORDER=0>Listing is correct<P>

<!--The values for these hidden HTML fields are coming from
ret_01.idc, the form used to take the user
input for the order listing, which passes the values to ret_01.idc,
which in turn calls this template, ret_01.htx.-->

<input type="hidden" name="CustomerID_test" value=<%idc.CustomerID_test>'>

<Input type="hidden" name="Company" Value='<%idc.Company%>'>

<Input type="hidden" name="Password" Value='<%idc.Password%>'>

Web Site Case Study

```
<INPUT TYPE="HIDDEN" NAME="Email" VALUE="<%idc.Email%>">
<INPUT TYPE="HIDDEN" NAME="SARRI_type" VALUE="<%idc.SARRI_type%>">
<INPUT TYPE="HIDDEN" NAME="New_distance" VALUE="<%idc.New_distance%>">
<INPUT TYPE="HIDDEN" NAME="RET" VALUE="<%idc.RET%>">
<INPUT TYPE="HIDDEN" NAME="Sandburn" VALUE="<%idc.Sandburn%>">
<INPUT TYPE="HIDDEN" NAME="Street_address" VALUE="<%Street_address%>">
<INPUT TYPE="HIDDEN" NAME="City" VALUE="<%idc.City%>">
<INPUT TYPE="HIDDEN" NAME="State" VALUE="<%idc.State%>">
<INPUT TYPE="HIDDEN" NAME="Zip" VALUE="<%idc.Zip%>">
<INPUT TYPE="HIDDEN" NAME="PO_number" VALUE="<%idc.PO_number%>">
<INPUT TYPE="HIDDEN" NAME="Rush" VALUE="<%idc.Rush%>">
<INPUT TYPE="HIDDEN" NAME="Order_inst" VALUE="<%idc.Order_inst%>">
</FORM>
<!--If the customer record is not correct, the user clicks on the
button for "Change/Update Order," which passes the rechg.idc
file to httpodbc.dll.-->

<FORM METHOD="POST" ACTION="rechg.idc">

<!--Hyperlink graphic button for listing that needs to be changed.-->
<INPUT TYPE=IMAGE SRC="/ocs/images/rndbtn.gif" ALIGN="Top"
WIDTH=18 HEIGHT=18 BORDER=0>Change/Update Listing.<P>

<!--The values for these hidden HTML fields are coming from
NewAvail.idc.-->

<input type="hidden" name="CustomerID_test" value=<%idc.CustomerID_test>'>
<Input type="hidden" name="Company" Value="<%idc.Company%>">
<Input type="hidden" name="Password" Value="<%idc.Password%>">
<INPUT TYPE="HIDDEN" NAME="Email" VALUE="<%idc.Email%>">
<INPUT TYPE="HIDDEN" NAME="SARRI_type" VALUE="<%idc.SARRI_type%>">
<INPUT TYPE="HIDDEN" NAME="New_distance" VALUE="<%idc.New_distance%>">
<INPUT TYPE="HIDDEN" NAME="RET" VALUE="<%idc.RET%>">
<INPUT TYPE="HIDDEN" NAME="Sandburn" VALUE="<%idc.Sandburn%>">
```

Chapter 19

```
<INPUT TYPE="HIDDEN" NAME="Street_address" VALUE="<%Street_address%>">
<INPUT TYPE="HIDDEN" NAME="City" VALUE="<%idc.City%>">
<INPUT TYPE="HIDDEN" NAME="State" VALUE="<%idc.State%>">
<INPUT TYPE="HIDDEN" NAME="Zip" VALUE="<%idc.Zip%>">
<INPUT TYPE="HIDDEN" NAME="PO_number" VALUE="<%idc.PO_number%>">
<INPUT TYPE="HIDDEN" NAME="Rush" VALUE="<%idc.Rush%>">
<INPUT TYPE="HIDDEN" NAME="Order_inst" VALUE="<%idc.Order_inst%>">
</form>
</font>
<B>Status: </B>open<BR>
<!--Plugging in values the user entered in the input
form coming via the .idc file.-->
<BR>
<B>E-mail:</b><%idc.Email%><br>
<b>SARRI Type:</b>
<%if% idc.SARRI_type EQ "1">
None
<%endif%>

<%if% idc.SARRI_type EQ "2">
SARRI  Standard
<%endif%>

<%if% idc.SARRI_type EQ "3">
SARRI  Enhanced
<%endif%>

<%if% idc.SARRI_type EQ "4">
SARRI Plus Standard
<%endif%>

<%if% idc.SARRI_type EQ "5">
SARRI Plus Enhanced
<%endif%>

<br>

<b>New Distance:</b>

<%if% idc.New_distance EQ "1">
Standard
```

```
<%endif%>

<%if% idc.New_distance EQ "2">
Extend by 1/4 mile
<%endif%>

<%if% idc.New_distance EQ "3">
Extend by 1/2 mile
<%endif%>

<%if% idc.New_distance EQ "4">
Extend by one mile
<%endif%>

<%if% idc.New_distance EQ "5">
All db to one mile
<%endif%>
<p>
<b>RET:</B>

<%if% idc.RET EQ "1">
None
<%endif%>

<%if% idc.RET EQ "3">
RET 3
<%endif%>

<%if% idc.RET EQ "4">
RET 4
<%endif%>

<%if% idc.RET EQ "5">
RET 5
<%endif%>
<p>
<b>Sandburn:</b>

<%if% idc.Sandburn EQ "1">
Sandburn chosen

<%else%>
Sandburn not chosen

<%endif%>
 <p>
<b>Site Name:</b><%idc.Site_name%><br>

<b>Site Address:</b><%idc.Street_address%><br>
```

Chapter 19

```
<b>City:</b><%idc.City%><br>
<b>State:</b><%idc.State%><br>
<b>Zip:</b><%idc.Zip%><br>
<b>PO_number:</b><%idc.PO_number%><br>
<b>Rush:</b>
<%if% idc.Rush EQ "1">
None
<%endif%>

<%if% idc.Rush EQ "2">
Delivery within 24 hours for an additional $75
<%endif%>

<b>Ordering Instructions:</b><%idc.Order_inst%>

</FONT>

<!--From here down the template is plugging in values from
NewAvail.idc to show the user the data that was entered.-->

<P>

<hr>

<P>

<P>

<B><FONT FACE=ARIAL SIZE="3">Customer Information</B></FONT>

<P>

<FONT FACE=ARIAL SIZE="2">

<BR>

</FONT>

<P>

<hr><BR>

<P>

<P>

<B><FONT FACE=ARIAL SIZE="3">Contact</B></FONT>

<FONT FACE=ARIAL SIZE="2">

<hr>
<BR>
```

```
<P>
<P>
<hr>
<BR>
<P>
</BODY>
</FONT>
</HTML>
```

This completed the effort, and customer service had an access screen linked to this order area of SQL Server.

Phase 3: Incorporate More Server Products and Start Building ISAPIs

At this point ISAPI was introduced to allow for creating redirects and form dumps. In addition, Index Server and Proxy Server were added to the mix.

SAMPLE ISAPIS

There was now a need to support searching of database records. The developers were able to obtain and incorporate some sample code from a Microsoft engineer. This code takes each record of the SQL table and creates an HTML page. Then Index Server is used to index the resultant HTML pages. The ISAPI samples are not shown here because of the amount of proprietary code that was written. A sample set of ISAPIs that are similar to those developed (along with credits for the people who wrote them) is on the accompanying CD-ROM.

SAMPLE SQL PROCEDURES FOR INDEXING

SQL procedures were developed for a number of system procedures. The one to note for this chapter included an extensive set of code provided by Microsoft. The development team needed to search a SQL database for various pieces of information. Microsoft engineers pointed the crew to the tips and tricks provided by the engineering staff. Some of that code is shown in this section.

The following samples were rewritten based on the code provided by the Microsoft staff. The intent was to dump each of the 2 million records to an HTML page that could be searched using Index Server. To do so required the creation of a set of stored procedures and the appropriate **.IDC** and **.HTX** files.

Here is the stored procedure. The IDC file for generating the Web page for each row is called **jonstores.idc**:

```
Datasource: NEWtest
  Username: sa
  Template: jonstores.htx
  SQLStatement:
+USE NEWtest
+DECLARE stores_cursor CURSOR
+       FOR
+       SELECT ID FROM Flagfile_CA1
+OPEN stores_cursor
+DECLARE @ID varchar(255)
+FETCH NEXT FROM stores_cursor INTO @ID
+WHILE (@@fetch_status <> -1)
+BEGIN
+       /*
+               A @@fetch_status of -2 means that the row has been deleted.
+               No need to test for this, because the result of this loop is to
+               drop all user-defined tables.
+       */
+       EXEC ('FlagCA1_id ' + '''' + @ID + '''' +
+
',@filepath=''E:\tools\johnoNew\pubs\stores'',@templatefile=''E:\tools\johnoNew\scripts\jstores.tpl''')
+       FETCH NEXT FROM stores_cursor INTO @ID
+END
+DEALLOCATE stores_cursor
```

The template file for the IDC is called **jonstores.htx**:

```
<HTML>
  <HEAD><TITLE>SQL Server Web Page Generation Example</TITLE></HEAD>
  <!BODY BACKGROUND="/samples/images/backgrnd.gif">
  <BODY BGCOLOR="FFFFFF">

  <TABLE>
  <tr>
  <TD></TD>
  <TD>
  <H2> Success!! </H2>
  </TD>
  </TR>
  </TABLE>

  </BODY>
  </HTML>
```

The template file for the formatting of each generated page is named **jstores.tpl**:

```
<html>
<head>
<title>SQL Server NEWtest, Flagfile_CA1 table</title>
<body>

  <H1>Stores Table Row</H1>
  <HR>

  <%begindetail%>
  <META NAME="ID" CONTENT="
  <%insert_data_here%>">
  <TABLE>
  <TR> <TD> <B>ID</B> </TD> <TD>
  <%insert_data_here%> </TD> </TR>
  <TR> <TD> <B>HEIGHTS</B> </TD> <TD>
  <%insert_data_here%> </TD> </TR>
  <TR> <TD> <B> FacName</B> </TD> <TD>
  <%insert_data_here%> </TD> </TR>
<TR> <TD> <B>FacStreet</B> </TD> <TD>
  <%insert_data_here%> </TD> </TR>

<TR> <TD> <B>FacState</B> </TD> <TD>
  <%insert_data_here%> </TD> </TR>
<TR> <TD> <B>NewCity</B> </TD> <TD>
  <%insert_data_here%> </TD> </TR>
<TR> <TD> <B>NewZip</B> </TD> <TD>
  <%insert_data_here%> </TD> </TR>
<TR> <TD> <B>NewCounty</B> </TD> <TD>
  <%insert_data_here%> </TD> </TR>

<TR> <TD> <B>FacCity</B> </TD> <TD>
  <%insert_data_here%> </TD> </TR>
<TR> <TD> <B>FacZip</B> </TD> <TD>
  <%insert_data_here%> </TD> </TR>
<TR> <TD> <B>FacCounty</B> </TD> <TD>
  <%insert_data_here%> </TD> </TR>
<TR> <TD> <B>EPAID</B> </TD> <TD>
  <%insert_data_here%> </TD> </TR>

<TR> <TD> <B>Finds</B> </TD> <TD>
  <%insert_data_here%> </TD> </TR>
<TR> <TD> <B>Npl</B> </TD> <TD>
  <%insert_data_here%> </TD> </TR>
<TR> <TD> <B>Cerclis</B> </TD> <TD>
```

```
    <%insert_data_here%> </TD> </TR>
<TR> <TD> <B>Cars</B> </TD> <TD>
    <%insert_data_here%> </TD> </TR>
<TR> <TD> <B>Spl</B> </TD> <TD>
    <%insert_data_here%> </TD> </TR>

<TR> <TD> <B>Scl</B> </TD> <TD>
    <%insert_data_here%> </TD> </TR>
<TR> <TD> <B>SolidWaste</B> </TD> <TD>
    <%insert_data_here%> </TD> </TR>
<TR> <TD> <B>OpenDump </B> </TD> <TD>
    <%insert_data_here%> </TD> </TR>
<TR> <TD> <B>Tris</B> </TD> <TD>
    <%insert_data_here%> </TD> </TR>
<TR> <TD> <B>Lust</B> </TD> <TD>
    <%insert_data_here%> </TD> </TR>
<TR> <TD> <B>Erns</B> </TD> <TD>
    <%insert_data_here%> </TD> </TR>

<TR> <TD> <B>Spill</B> </TD> <TD>
    <%insert_data_here%> </TD> </TR>
<TR> <TD> <B>Ust</B> </TD> <TD>
    <%insert_data_here%> </TD> </TR>
<TR> <TD> <B>RcraTSD </B> </TD> <TD>
    <%insert_data_here%> </TD> </TR>
<TR> <TD> <B>RcraGenLarge</B> </TD> <TD>
    <%insert_data_here%> </TD> </TR>
<TR> <TD> <B>RcraGenSmall</B> </TD> <TD>
    <%insert_data_here%> </TD> </TR>
<TR> <TD> <B>RcraTRANS</B> </TD> <TD>
    <%insert_data_here%> </TD> </TR>

<TR> <TD> <B> Npdes</B> </TD> <TD>
    <%insert_data_here%> </TD> </TR>
<TR> <TD> <B>Air</B> </TD> <TD>
    <%insert_data_here%> </TD> </TR>
<TR> <TD> <B>Cicis </B> </TD> <TD>
    <%insert_data_here%> </TD> </TR>
<TR> <TD> <B>PestMfg</B> </TD> <TD>
    <%insert_data_here%> </TD> </TR>
<TR> <TD> <B> PcbHandler</B> </TD> <TD>
    <%insert_data_here%> </TD> </TR>
<TR> <TD> <B>Wells</B> </TD> <TD>
    <%insert_data_here%> </TD> </TR>
```

```html
<TR> <TD> <B> SetsPRP</B> </TD> <TD>
  <%insert_data_here%> </TD> </TR>
<TR> <TD> <B>Docket</B> </TD> <TD>
  <%insert_data_here%> </TD> </TR>
<TR> <TD> <B>Raats </B> </TD> <TD>
  <%insert_data_here%> </TD> </TR>
<TR> <TD> <B>Osha</B> </TD> <TD>
  <%insert_data_here%> </TD> </TR>
<TR> <TD> <B> TSCAViol</B> </TD> <TD>
  <%insert_data_here%> </TD> </TR>
<TR> <TD> <B>FIFRAViol</B> </TD> <TD>
  <%insert_data_here%> </TD> </TR>

<TR> <TD> <B> EPCRAViol</B> </TD> <TD>
  <%insert_data_here%> </TD> </TR>
<TR> <TD> <B> Ast</B> </TD> <TD>
  <%insert_data_here%> </TD> </TR>
<TR> <TD> <B>AirViol</B> </TD> <TD>
  <%insert_data_here%> </TD> </TR>
<TR> <TD> <B>RcraViol</B> </TD> <TD>
  <%insert_data_here%> </TD> </TR>
<TR> <TD> <B> NpdesViol</B> </TD> <TD>
  <%insert_data_here%> </TD> </TR>
<TR> <TD> <B>NpdesEnf</B> </TD> <TD>
  <%insert_data_here%> </TD> </TR>

<TR> <TD> <B> Nfrap</B> </TD> <TD>
  <%insert_data_here%> </TD> </TR>
<TR> <TD> <B> RcrisOther</B> </TD> <TD>
  <%insert_data_here%> </TD> </TR>
<TR> <TD> <B>RcrisBBL</B> </TD> <TD>
  <%insert_data_here%> </TD> </TR>
<TR> <TD> <B>HmirsCarrier</B> </TD> <TD>
  <%insert_data_here%> </TD> </TR>
<TR> <TD> <B> HmirsShipper</B> </TD> <TD>
  <%insert_data_here%> </TD> </TR>
<TR> <TD> <B>HmirsConsignee</B> </TD> <TD>
  <%insert_data_here%> </TD> </TR>

<TR> <TD> <B> Dockets_Defendant</B> </TD> <TD>
  <%insert_data_here%> </TD> </TR>
<TR> <TD> <B>FlagNames </B> </TD> <TD>
  <%insert_data_here%> </TD> </TR>
```

```
</TABLE>
<%enddetail%>

</BODY>
</HTML>
```

The stored procedure in the SQL database is called `j_store_update`:

```
USE NEWtest
GO
if exists (select * from sysobjects where id = object_id('dbo.FlagCA_id') and
sysstat & 0xf=4) drop procedure dbo.FlagCA_id

GO
  CREATE PROCEDURE dbo.FlagCA1_id
  @ID varchar(12),                             -- Primary Key, id
  @filepath varchar(100),    -- Directory where to create the Web page
  @templatefile varchar(100) = NULL     -- Optional template file to use

  AS
  --
  -- This procedure creates a Web page for a row with the specified ID
  -- which is a key in the Flagfile_CA1 table.
  --
  --This was a hint given to me.....
  -- Forming the strings to give to the "EXEC" command is confusing when
  -- we have run-time variables in the string. Splitting it into variables
  -- will make it a little more readable.
  --
  DECLARE @cmd_text1 varchar(255)
  DECLARE @cmd_text2 varchar(255)
  DECLARE @file_name varchar(255)

  --
  -- Compose the file name using the primary key "ID".
  -- For example, if the ID is 3456 and @filepath is e:\New\pubs\stores
  -- the generated Web page will be e:\New\pubs\stores\3456.htm
  --
  SELECT @file_name=@filepath+'\'+@ID+'.htm'

  --
  -- Compose the sp_makewebtask command and parameters.
  -- Note that ID is being retrieved twice because we want to
  -- Use one instance for a meta tag and another for a table value.
  --
  SELECT @cmd_text1='sp_makewebtask @outputfile='''+@file_name+''',\
```

```
@query=''SELECT ID, ID,HEIGHTS, FacName,FacStreet,FacState, NewCity,
NewZip,NewCounty,FacCity,FacZip,FacCounty,EPAID,Finds, Npl, Cerclis,
Cars, Spl, Scl, SolidWaste ,OpenDump ,Tris ,Lust ,Erns ,Spill,Ust,
RcraTSD, RcraGenLarge, RcraGenSmall,RcraTRANS, Npdes, Air, Cicis, PestMfg,
PcbHandler, Wells, SetsPRP, Docket, Raats, Osha, TSCAViol, FIFRAViol,
EPCRAViol,
Ast, AirViol, RcraViol,NpdesViol, NpdesEnf, Nfrap, RcrisOther, RcrisBBL,
HmirsCarrier,
HmirsShipper, HmirsConsignee, Dockets_Defendant, FlagNames,  FROM Flagfile_CA1
\
  WHERE ID='''''+@ID+''''''+''''

--
-- If a template file is specified, use it
--
IF @templatefile <> NULL
BEGIN
    SELECT @cmd_text2=',@templatefile='''+@templatefile+''''
END

--
-- For debugging purposes
--
--PRINT @file_name
--PRINT @cmd_text1
--PRINT @cmd_text2

EXECUTE( @cmd_text1+@cmd_text2 )

GO
```

Here's the final SQL query to test all of this:

```
EXEC ('j_store_update @id='130' ',\
@filepath=' 'the location of the database' ',\
@templatefile=' 'the location of the tpl script' ' ')
```

Phase 4

At this point the majority of the BackOffice products were introduced. The emphasis was on using Commerce Server to build a general shopping environment that would allow any of the previously developed code to be implemented into a component. In addition, this store would allow other products, written in C++, to be inserted inside the ordering pipeline process.

Standard **.ASP** files were used to create the store layout, and components were developed for each of the major products. The site was moved internally to run on a full NT environment using two CISCO routers and Proxy Server for firewall protection.

LESSONS LEARNED

We learned many lessons, not only in the layout of the original site but also about security and the requirement for an extranet site for some users.

Basic Education in Site Development

As in the development of company products, many company officials still question the need or benefit of a site.

Security Issues

Security became a major issue as phase 3 was incorporated. ISAPI filters were initially used to help verify users. As the developers moved to phase 4, they incorporated a firewall approach as shown in Figure 19.4.

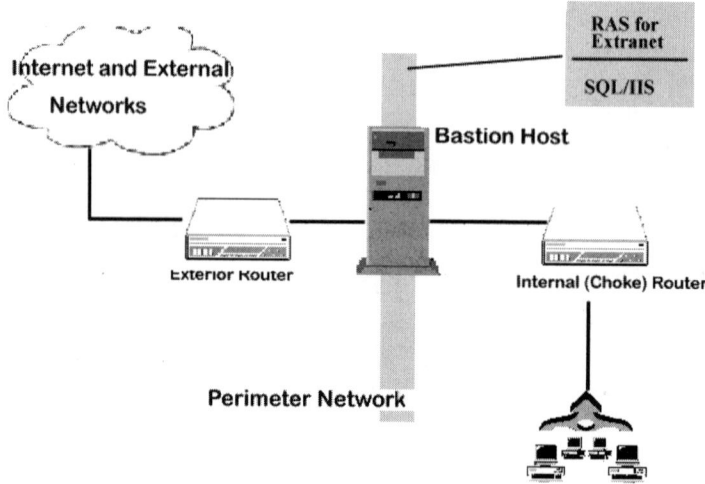

Figure 19.4 The secure network.

Extranet Requirements

During the building of phase 3, many client companies wanted to buy products on-line but did not want to give their employees Internet access. A RAS server was set up using the

NT services and IIS with ASP for the site. The current Internet site was copied to the RAS server, with the server blocking TCP/IP traffic past the computer. The RAS server had both a real IP address used by the servicing company administrator to maintain the system and a fake address that allowed for only dial-up access to that Web site. This implementation required ASP to be used as heavily as possible, because the RAS server would have its own e-mail server and access to SQL Server. The system would be not allowed to communicate openly on the interior network or to communicate to the Internet. This meant that any current ISAPI and Perl scripts would not be available to the extranet. ASP was the simplest approach for incorporating interactivity and reducing system overhead. Some of the sample code is shown in the following section.

Code Lessons

A number of code lessons were learned during this exercise. In general, the developers were able to break out of their C++ and Java molds and start using ASP files to increase interactivity without having to extend the development timeline. Following are two examples of using VBScript and ASP to replace Perl scripts, ISAPIs, and JavaScript.

COOKIES

One of the first decisions was to incorporate cookies, a standard method on Active Server sites, to serve users who had cookies turned on. If cookies were not turned on, the server sent the user to a login page, where the user would be asked to log in. The server would take this information and compare it to the records in the company table. If the user was a repeat visitor, then he or she was moved to the ordering area. New customers were sent to the ASP files that created a new database record.

Here is a sample of the cookie request:

```
<HTML>
<HEAD>
<TITLE> Cookie request</TITLE>
</HEAD>
<BODY BGCOLOR=#ffffff>

<%

For Each cookie in Request.Cookies
      If Not Request.Cookies(cookie).HasKeys Then
           ' cookie has only information, print it
%>
           <%= cookie %>  = <%= Request.Cookies(cookie)%>
<%
     Else
```

Chapter 19

```
                'print the dictionary of this cookie
                For Each key in Request.Cookies(cookie)
%>
                <%= cookie %>   (<%= key %>) = <%= Request.Cookies(cookie)(key)%><BR>
<%
                Next
        End If
Next
%>
 <BR>

</BODY>
</HTML>
```

Forms

The site used a number of forms that had originally been sent to a Perl script in phase 1 and an ISAPI in phase 3. By phase 4, a solution had been found using ASP.

```
<HTML>
<HEAD>
<TITLE> Form Processing</TITLE>
</HEAD>
<BODY BGCOLOR=#ffffff>
<CENTER>
<H1>Simple form test</H1>
Your choices<P>
</CENTER>

<B>You like:</B><BR>
<%
Response.Write(Request.QueryString("comp_name")(i) & "<BR>")
Response.Write(Request.QueryString("comp_city")(i) & "<BR>")
Response.Write(Request.QueryString("comp_state")(i) & "<BR>")
Response.Write(Request.QueryString("comp_zip")(i) & "<BR>")
Response.Write(Request.QueryString("comp_contact")(i) & "<BR>")
%>
</BODY>
</HTML>
```

There is much more code than there is room to show. For example, an ISAPI was written to allow for redirection of a page to another location on the site. It required very little modification to create an ASP that would accomplish the same process.

WHERE TO GO FROM HERE?

The programmers found that, over time, various tools were made available by Microsoft that would allow them to reduce development time considerably. The sites continue to change with the addition of Commerce Server and Transaction Server. More ASPs are being generated to take advantage of VBScript, and components are written in Visual C++.

From here you may want to review these chapters:

- Chapter 20, "Real-Life Security Issues," which will assist you in establishing a company security policy.
- Appendix B, "HTML/Dynamic HTML Reference," which will allow you to review your knowledge of HTML coding techniques.

Chapter 20

Real-Life Security Issues

Security is an issue for Internet operation as well as normal computer operations. How does a developer ensure that a machine is not compromised? What if the developer is ok but compromises a company server? Does anyone use the machine in addition to the one developer? Can a person who knows the administrator password get access to the developer's system?

This book cannot guarantee that your site and equipment will be totally safe, but this chapter offers suggestions that should be considered in terms of each operation. For example, if a company administrator is already running a firewall then software that affects this firewall needs to be approved by the network administration department.

One of the first items to be aware of is Internet etiquette, known as Netiquette.

NETIQUETTE

Netiquette is simply good manners. By staying out of arguments and obvious emotional exchanges, you can prevent others from trying to take revenge. You can get involved in such discussions at home or outside the company environment.

If you're new to the Net, watch and listen before engaging others. Get a sense of people and their attitudes. This medium is a great way to share data, but people sometimes forget that they cannot read "body language" over the Net.

Keep personal issues out of the major mailing areas and newsgroups. Use individual e-mails to handle those issues. The following symbols, called emoticons, are accepted as body language in e-mails.

:-)	Plain happy smiley-face
:-(	Plain unhappy smiley
;-)	Winking Smiley
;-(	Crying smiley
:'(	Another crying smiley
:-\	Pensive smiley
:*)	Red-nosed smiley
}:*)	Rudolph

*<:o)   Clown
:-X   Censored smiley

You can use any major search engine under the word *emotions* to find a number of sites that list the accepted standards.

CONFIDENTIAL ISSUES

Do not forget that the Internet is public! Please respect the rights of others and be very cautious about what is shared via a network connection. When a person publishes a page on the Internet, it is, in general, available to the world.

Even when using e-mail, you need to be careful about revealing company and personal data. It is not like taking a class and telling a few classmates about your hobbies or what you do at work. Rather, it can be like taking out an advertisement in the *Wall Street Journal, USA Today,* the local newspapers, and a few professional journals. At some point you're doing work for clients or a company. The point is not to become paranoid but rather not to do anything that you would not like your friends, family, and employer to see on the front page of a newspaper or hear on a national radio talk show or see on *20/20*.

You eventually may want to learn the laws of other states and other countries regarding personal use of company material and information.

Copyrighting and Solutions

Copyright has become a complex matter. Assume that everything that you see on the Internet has value to someone. You can look at how other developers build sites to learn, but take only what is offered to you or given to you. Do not take a graphic unless the developer or Webmaster has agreed to its distribution.

Written material on the Web is just like that in a magazine or book. Quotations should be referenced. If a page is hyperlinked, make sure that the original author has no problem with the link. Some major companies, such as Microsoft, enjoy developers linking to their documentation, but you should always check if you are unsure.

As with this book, be sure to give credit to other developers. Throughout this book are examples that were e-mailed to developers for use in learning and teaching others. Those examples are acknowledged as provided by other developers and not originally created by me.

If you are personally concerned about internal copyrights, you can put the information in question behind a firewall. As was discussed in Chapter 7, a firewall can provide controlled access from one network to another. Companies cannot afford to lose important information. Unfortunately, companies may forget to consider those issues until a break-in has occurred. By then, the company may have lost customers.

Programs such as System Administration Tool for Analyzing Networks (SATAN) help developers uncover security holes. The real message is to have a company security policy that specifies which systems and data are mission-critical. Backup and recovery requirements are outlined, as are the cost and timing of resource acquisition. With this information, company management can determine when to spend the funds to increase security. Customers want to be assured that the company they do business with protects customer records.

Developers will make trade-off decisions based on data being conveniently available and secure networking in place. An intranet is a great tool for companies that have multiple geographic locations, but you must ensure that you have taken the proper procedures to protect both internal and customer data.

You need to keep backups of the operating system (emergency repair disks) and essential data. Do not forget to document the original setup procedures for each of the tools and servers. You know what it means if you must reinstall DNS or SQL Server without the personal installation notes in place. One bad entry could turn an interactive site into a useless site. Be careful of adding back doors to the system. If you have it, a hacker can find it. Many hackers run their own systems to stay in touch with the technology.

Here are some basic NT security suggestions:

1. Do not give the IUSR_computername account, the Guests group, or the Everyone group any right other than "Log on locally" or "Access the computer from this network" rights.
2. Use the NT User Manager to set "bad logon" policies.
3. Always use NTFS disk partitions instead of FAT. Set NTFS permissions for the individual files.
4. Make sure that all of NT's password control features have been implemented. Employ the **PASSFILT.DLL** that comes with SP2 and SP3; it forces strong password choices on users.
5. The default Administrator account is a target for intruders. Create a new account that has all the administrator privileges. Leave the old administrator account enabled, but remove the rights and permissions.
6. Enable auditing on all NT systems, because it allows you to determine which computer may be under attack regularly.
7. Disable NetBIOS over TCP/IP network bindings when possible.
8. Block all nonessential TCP/IP ports, both inbound and outbound. In particular, block UDP ports 137 and 138 and TCP port 139.
9. Revoke the "Access from network" right (using User Manager) for users who don't need to connect to that particular NT system.
10. Do not leave NT workstations turned on and unattended. Depending on how your network is set up, a hacker can start looking for any kind of opening, including an idle modem connection.

11. Disable the Simple TCP/IP Services, because hackers will first try to penetrate a network using the simplest and most common opening.
12. Consider using private networks to tie together back-end servers. Try to use protocols that put a time stamp on a transaction.
13. Encryption is a good way to ensure client/server protection, but know that anyone who has administrative access can see one of the keys. Suppose a person is logged in as Administrator and leaves the server room for lunch, leaving the door unlocked. Anyone who walks by before a screen saver starts becomes the administrator and can look at security keys, possibly gaining Administrative group access.
14. Consider using multiple Ethernet cards in a system to split portions of the network or to remove a system from the network. Use only CD-ROMs, zip drives, and the like to update and back up the system.
15. Be careful of interesting Web sites that require a special viewer that only that Webmaster can provide. It may be a binary that compromises the NT server.

How to Prevent Hacking

You have probably heard about the various hacker problems on the Internet. The *Computer News Daily* advertised that it was getting more than 50,000 hits per day. A hacker got in and put millions of copies of chat messages on the server. This is an old trick, but it still works.

As you enhance visitors' database access, the threat of hacking is increased, especially if the site reaches a list of desirable technologists on the Internet. Someone is always trying to be the fastest gun in Dodge City.

Many hackers are long-time Internet users who do not like the new NT groups or companies selling products. It's as if someone were invading their UNIX academic world. They take it very seriously. What should you do to protect yourself?

You should become familiar with what hackers are looking for. The Department of Defense used to be the target that hackers were trying to crack. Now there are more than a million Web sites, many of them run by underskilled people. Hacking a site is sometimes like joining a fraternity or gang by showing others how well a person can hack. Some hackers are even getting jobs as security experts or consultants by showing off their skills. You should try not to make your site the target for demonstration.

Commercial sites are obvious targets. Many of them are left open or have obvious back doors. Many of them are running a DNS without knowing how to protect it. Some NT administrators keep the same standard set of groups kept by every other NT administrator. It takes little work for an NT hacker to figure out how to break the system. Original guest groups are left as open as other accounts on the internal domain. Developers run FTP and Gopher without knowing how to protect those protocols. These developers do not even consider protecting some of them with a firewall.

A hacker may try to come in at port 80, where both the Web server and the `Administrator` account run. The hacker needs only a few seconds with a client software package to try to run Administrator. To protect yourself, you need only ensure that every client comes in as a guest or anonymous.

Another possibility is the hacker who submits bogus orders in your ordering area. Do you have a way to verify proper processing of an order request? What if this process overflows the buffer? This in itself can leave a system vulnerable. Many programmers need to see whether someone can hack their scripts or ISAPIs before their sites go live.

Consider the following ways to improve security at your site:

1. Develop a strategy to protect the Web server. As simple as that sounds, bringing up the discussion may unearth some obvious holes that other developers or employees have found.
2. Try to set traps that log who is on the system. Track IP addresses. This technique will not stop the professional but can unearth an amateur.
3. Make sure that it takes at least two system bugs to bring the site down. This approach increases the odds of preventing a successful attack.
4. Be careful when encrypting a URL. If you create a site where the password is passed in that URL, what happens if a client bookmarks the file on a laptop and then loses the laptop?
5. Be careful about writing elaborate CGIs and ISAPIs. The more elaborate the code the more a hacker has to play with. If you pass an argument in the URL, a hacker can append variables to see what your script does.
6. Watch all the server ports and not just the Web port, number 80. Monitor connect times on all the ports.
7. Include all the latest service packs. That includes SQL Server as well as the Visual Development tools and the NT server. Keep the system up-to-date. Microsoft spends a lot of time and money to try to prevent security breaches. Learn from it.
8. Double-check to make sure that you need all the services that are running.
9. A reminder: Install two Ethernet cards in a single machine. Route all TCP/IP services through one card. Restrict any local protocols such as the hard-disk mounting. Route all the local protocols and services to the other card. This technique can prevent an easy break-in to the network.
10. On the router you should not accept packets that are looking for services that you have turned off. For example, one developer turned off FTP and Telnet and found that a certain IP address was continuing to try to run through the router using those protocols.
11. IP spoofing was mentioned in Chapter 7 regarding Proxy Server. It deserves to be mentioned again. A hacker may try to look as if he or she were running an IP address from within the company network. Stop this by programming the router not to allow inbound packets from a part of the network that it is supposed to control.

12. Watch the setup of the e-mail server. Take all possible precautions recommended by the vendor.
13. Do not run programs that are unknown to the development staff. Especially with Perl, make sure that you remove the control characters that are erroneously added by a user.
14. Have friends and professionals test the site. Let them simulate attacks. See whether you can determine when an attack happened and what type it was.
15. Continue to test even if things look secure. Make sure that you know when things have changed. Many people usually share the servers. Some hackers will try to change dates and go to the log files to remove traces of their entry. Back up the log files regularly and check them.
16. Participate in the security Web sites and newsgroups (such as comp.sys.security newsgroups and http://www.cert.org).

FIREWALLS

Firewalls were discussed in depth in Chapter 7, and we will review these issues here.

Client/server is a wonderful development environment, and the Web provides many capabilities. The problem is that the sites are in open traffic. As companies develop new networking plans to take advantage of this environment, they must ask some questions:

- What part of the network needs protecting? The whole enterprise from the outside world or only a portion?
- Who might the network be protected from? Is the site internal or external? Would an extranet, in which a limited number of clients come to the site, be appropriate?
- Is there confidential information on the site?

These questions and many more like them should be answered. As the questions are answered a number of solutions arise. One method used to protect a site is a firewall.

A firewall consists of a computer that sits between the internal and the external network. It may sit on a perimeter network. It can be incorporated with multiple routers that do the filtering, or the firewall can do the filtering. Many developers use firewalls successfully to secure their domains. Developers tend to implement firewalls as packet filters or application gateways.

As a packet filter the firewall deals with protocols such as TCP/IP. The software looks at the ports, the source, and the destination address to determine what can be forwarded. Filtering may happen in one direction or both directions (in and out of the domain). These filters often have a list of what is allowed. Reporting and login mechanisms tend to be minimal with this approach.

Application gateways look for who is requesting network access as well as the network application. They control the application (such as FTP), source, destination, and user. The good news is that a gateway connection appears to the outside user as if it started from the public side of the firewall and not the private side. For security reasons there is no packet forwarding from the internal (private) network to the external (public) network. Gateways allow extensive logging and reporting. They work especially well for forwarding e-mail and can eliminate the need for a separate e-mail host.

Some developers include authentication schemes with their firewalls. Gateways can be purchased with this scheme already on board.

If you incorporate your own firewall, you can use Microsoft Proxy Server on a computer. This arrangement is called a bastion host. Then you can use the router for IP packet filtering. Proxy Server would run the socks administration needed for socket protection. If you are not sure of yourself, there are a number of good NT firewall systems. No matter what solution you choose, the firewall must handle a few basic items:

1. The protocols include Telnet (the ability to log in to a remote system), FTP (for file transfers), HTTP (the World Wide Web), SMTP (for sending and receiving e-mail), NNTP (this is for newsgroups),DNS (for name resolution), and Gopher (for traversing tree structure information). The firewall must deal with both inbound and outbound occurrences of these services.
2. You must determine which authorization level to give to each user, including guest accounts. Use the NT domain method for creating users and groups.
3. Determine what services each server needs. Does everyone need NNTP? Probably not.
4. Determine whether the default setting for protocols is to deny their use unless authorized by user and group or to allow all users in a group to use the protocol.
5. Firewalls and proxy servers tend to allow no password access, a one-time setup for the password, or a new password every time the user tries to go into or out of the system.
6. Are there other company locations that need to use the firewall? If so, determine how they will enter, perhaps via a Remote Access Server (RAS).
7. What will run on the bastion host that sits in the perimeter network between the public and the private network? Microsoft IIS will be loaded. Do you want to run FTP and Gopher? Look at your answers to the previous questions. If FTP is included, then allow corporate users to get out through FTP without being authenticated, (only allow the put command. Provide an incoming and outgoing FTP folder on the bastion host. Use the NT Access Control List for proper protection of the folders. Remove files regularly from all the FTP folders.
8. Consider a dual-homed gateway, as described in Chapter 7, in which you put a minimal version of DNS on the bastion host. You could run a fake name server on the host and the real name server inside the firewall.

Protecting Commerce

Life on the Internet is measured in Web years, which are about one month in the real world. Many companies predict that the current $500 million commerce market on the Web will grow to more than $6 billion by 2000. A company can put up a store in no time. It can also get attacked in that same period of time. The developer must secure transactions by implementing Secure Sockets Layer, getting a digital certificate, and testing the server for safe implementation.

Secure Sockets Layer

Secure Sockets Layer (SSL), as described in Chapter 7, is a protocol that sits on the HTTP layer. Browsers show a digital key lock when they are in a site that starts with https://. IIS supports the SSL standard and is simple to set up.

You need to obtain a certificate that is coded with a unique identifier for your site. This operates like a Social Security number. There is a public key, an expiration date, the name of your organization, and the issuer's digital signature.

IIS comes with a process (outlined in Chapter 7) for setting up the key. Once the key is created, set up by the issuer (such as VeriSign), and installed on your system, SSL is enabled. You put the certificate in a text file and then use IIS Key Manager to install the key. This process enables SSL. HTTP uses port 80. SSL uses 443. The browser interprets the https:/ protocol and moves to port 443.

If you place the https:/ site outside the firewall, clients can get there but private network users cannot get there. If internal people need access, it is possible to run an internal protected server that runs port 443 to serve both private and public network needs.

Note that SSL takes a lot of overhead. It is recommended that you protect only the minimal number of pages to reduce overhead and network bottlenecks. SSL, as has been noted, encrypts the data stream but has no method for encrypting the application contents. For that reason, a number of other methods are being investigated.

Other Security Methods

At least three other security protocols are being used or investigated by major corporations.

Microsoft has introduced Private Communication Technology (PCT). PCT is similar to SSL in that it works on the HTTP level and so is not dependent on the application. Microsoft believes that PCT is an enhancement, because it runs encryption separately from authentication.

Enterprise Integration Technologies Inc. developed some of the earliest secure protocols. Its S-HTTP works at the application level. It encrypts the message content and then uses a public/private key method to authenticate and decode the message.

Visa and Mastercard have cooperated to create Secure Electronic Transactions (SET). This protocol safely links the Internet to bankcard processing networks. It uses a public/private key authentication method. The reasoning behind SET is that SSL (and PCT) provides the chance for a hacker with a network sniffer to get the vital credit card information. SET exposes only the order form data and not the credit card information, whereas SSL does not encrypt.

The great news for developers is that the addition of Mastercard and Visa will give credibility to Internet commerce.

Encryption

To encrypt is to convert an ordinary language into code. Encryption is the key to commerce security. People want their data protected beyond the obvious protection methods that they consider customary. Most individuals believe that they are prudent in protecting their credit card numbers from unauthorized use (unfortunately, the reality is that many of them throw credit slips into the trash can that anyone could grab). They want assurance that no one except the commerce company and a bank will "see" their cards.

The good news is that explaining the process is simple. In most commerce security systems, a pair of keys is generated. The message is encrypted with one key and can be decoded only by using the matching key. Depending on the amount of data that is sent, a key may be used to encrypt yet another key that secures the message contents. The intent is to reduce overhead and network bottlenecks while providing ultimate security.

Developers can use keys to make sure that the server they are talking to is the proper server. In what is called a *handshaking* process, the server sends the public key to the client and then encrypts a message using the private key. The client receives the message and decodes it using the public key that it now has in place.

VIRTUAL PRIVATE NETWORKS

Many developers must deal with offices all around the United States or even the world. Can they use the Internet to create a private network? They could use a set of leased lines, but that is cost-prohibitive to many companies.

That is why a number of developers are considering what is known as a virtual private network (VPN). This was discussed in Chapter 7 and will be reviewed in this section.

A VPN simulates the leased line approach to linking offices. A company uses the inexpensive Internet as the backbone for this link. This means that a developer can link any number of company local area networks. Some developers even find it useful to make sure that they use a modem or ISDN router to dial the "network" only when they need to send or receive information. Once location 1 makes a connection to the Internet, the packets end up at the Internet service provider (ISP) for location 2. The ISP dials up location 2 and sends the data. This method appears to be slower than a private network, but the costs are dramatically less.

To keep everything private, the VPN locations share an encryption method. Many vendors (such as PSINet) provide encryption tunnel devices for routing through the Internet to handle the transmission and security issues. (Tunneling is the use of software to code non-TCP/IP information so that it runs piggyback on TCP/IP packets.) Developers should consider using routers and possibly full firewall implementations to ensure proper security.

The disadvantages of a VPN is that it is dependent on the Internet. This means that any network bottlenecks may not be easily resolved. In addition, the Internet is TCP/IP-based. If a company network does not use this protocol, the developer will need to use tunneling software.

WHERE TO GO FROM HERE

You have learned that security is not just an item to be discussed after a break-in but to be thought about well before an accident or theft occurs. Marketing people know that one good referral can lead to seven other customers, but one bad referral leads to 17 lost customers. The time to learn this is not when the customers are gone. The old saying, "It's too late to close the barn door after the horse is gone," is absolutely true in this case. You need to design a system that will meet the clients' needs while protecting the site from obvious attacks.

From here you should look at these chapters:

- Chapter 7, "The Active Secure Environment: Proxy Server," to learn more about Microsoft's server solution to some of the security issues discussed in this chapter.
- Chapter 10, "Active Money," to understand how to best implement Commerce Server in a newly created secure environment.

Chapter 21

The Future of the Active Platform

How many developers have heard their managers and company officers complain about the multiple logins needed to get onto the company network? One part of the network might be using Novell and another portion NT, and then there are the UNIX and Macintosh requirements. These users want only a single login with a password. They want simple access and complete security while keeping costs down.

When administering networks and systems, you are continually looking for common ground in controlling access to files and directories while trying to give users a simple interface. For example, let's say you are running an NT-Novell network in which Novell administers printers and NT administers file sharing. Users go through a dual login process in which they must be validated by multiple systems. One solution—to force the company to move to just NT or just Novell—is unacceptable. Where do we go from here?

What about a solution that gives you a single set of interfaces for building applications that access, register, and manage multiple directory services? Open Directory Services Interface (ODSI) promises this solution. What ODBC is for relational databases, ODSI is for directories.

Microsoft sees that solving this problem requires the creation of an enterprise-oriented directory. The goal of Active Directory Interface (ADI) is to make this directory easy to use. An administrator or developer can create reusable, namespace-portable applications for common administration and end-user tasks. This means that you could add users from a spreadsheet or send a command to pause all your print jobs in marketing. Additionally, ADI provides a set of COM objects that make it easy to implement. You can access ADI from Java, Visual Basic, and Visual C++. You choose the language that meets your needs.

NOTE
A namespace is a way to segregate one type of variable name from another or a named object from another object. Namespaces are used in NT 5.0 and the Active Directory environment to allow multiple class libraries and functions to coexist. As more applications and tools are incorporated on your system, duplicate class names and function names can clash. Microsoft uses a namespace to solve this problem.

Active Directory, through ODSI, gives you a single set of directory interfaces. Let's look at the structure of Active Directory.

The programming model for Active Directory, as you might guess, is based upon the Component Object Model. Active Directory objects are COM objects. A programmer uses standard OLE procedures to provide a pointer to the object's `IUnknown` interface.

To use Active Directory as an administration tool, you are still dealing with the domain architecture. You follow the same process as you would with current NT administration: Make a list of users and add users to groups. An interesting development with NT 5.0 is that the directory services are based on a more common use of domains: the Internet's Domain Name Service (DNS). This means that you can say goodbye to WINS and hello to DNS (if you are unfamiliar with DNS and WINS, please see Appendix A).

DNS knows how to determine names and addresses of hosts. NT 5.0 continues to support the 4.0 and 3.5 directory structures. Microsoft allows developers to bridge the systems by using the Distributed File System (DFS). DFS will act as a catalog for finding files.

Microsoft's plans are for the NT 5.0 directory services to be able to display BackOffice server information (Proxy Server and SQL Server) in one management screen. Developers will find this arrangement very useful for development efforts.

Directory Service replaces the need for Security Account Manager. Before NT 5.0, the namespace was such that a developer could create a domain with users and then put the users in groups. There was a primary domain controller. With NT 5.0 there is a full enterprise of domains with trust being passed among the servers. This means that there can be a company domain overseeing department domains that oversee subdepartment domains that oversee individual domains.

PLUG AND PLAY

In Windows 95, users were introduced to Plug and Play, a system that recognized and set up various hardware configurations based on what it detected. This required very little user involvement. NT 5.0 incorporates the Plug and Play environment, which users have come to love.

This means that adding modems and network cards to NT systems will become easier. Plug and Play has matured to include the ability to control system devices and power. Microsoft integrated Plug and Play into the operating system rather than use a BIOS solution as with Windows 95. This means that developers who build drivers will not have to worry about coordinating their development with the current Hardware Abstraction Layer (HAL) that is used in NT 4.0. If you have a current driver for NT 4.0, Microsoft assures you that the driver will still work in NT 5.0.

So when a system boots up, it will recognize any system hardware changes. A manager handles device resource requests. The manager will then determine which drivers to load for each device. The support list of NT drivers is continuing to grow so that when it is out of beta most major hardware items should be included.

THE STRUCTURE

The new NT Directory Service provides for scalable namespaces based on the DNS methodology. For example, let's say that you have a company called Newco that has a number of departments along with various systems in each department and subdepartment. The DNS structure might look like this, going from top to bottom:

```
www.newco.com----marketing.newco.com---newproducts.marketing.com----tom.newproducts.marketing.com
```

In the NT 5.0 world, the namespace would be very similar. The hierarchy is as follows:

```
newco----marketing----newproducts----tom
```

This makes the system simple to expand with new departments or added users. The proposed method would tag each level this way:

```
O= newco
OU = marketing
OU= newproducts
CN=  tom
```

The system would then build the tree as O—OU—OU—CN.

The structure is based on a top end of country, then the locale, the organization, the organization unit, and local units.

This DS is object-oriented. Classes would be a valid list of objects that the DS can use. For example, you might determine that the classes are:

```
class person----class local-organization unit----class organization-unit-----class domain---organization-unit
```

This means that there is inheritance, in which an object inherits the content and structure of current objects. For example, you could create a new class that inherits the class `person`.

Every object has a security descriptor that is known as the Access Control List (ACL). Security can be inherited from class to class if you wish.

The Active Directory environment will come with interfaces that allow the user to easily use various programming languages. You can use an Active Directory Interface if you want to build administrative tools or need access to the Directory Services. With Active Directory, a client application finds and binds itself to a Directory Service object. A piece of code known as the Active Directory *provider* creates the object and translates the call into a Directory Service–specific API call. An object, in this case, is a container of COM. The interfaces are `IADsCollection` (gets properties and methods) as well as `IDispatch`.

THERE ARE WOLVES OUT THERE

With all these new directory additions, there is a current product release that even a NT 4.0 developer can use. It is the Cluster Server, also known as Wolfpack.

A *cluster* exists in the computing world when there are two or more servers that can be managed as a single system. This means that many systems can logically act as one system. Each system in the cluster is known as a *node*. Each of the systems can use the "cluster-wide" services. The nodes can be added and removed in a way that is transparent to the user.

Every machine or node in the cluster can be connected via public networks, private networks or SCSI buses. *Resources* are the basic entities known to the cluster whereas a *group* is a collection of resources. Figure 21.1 shows the components of a cluster.

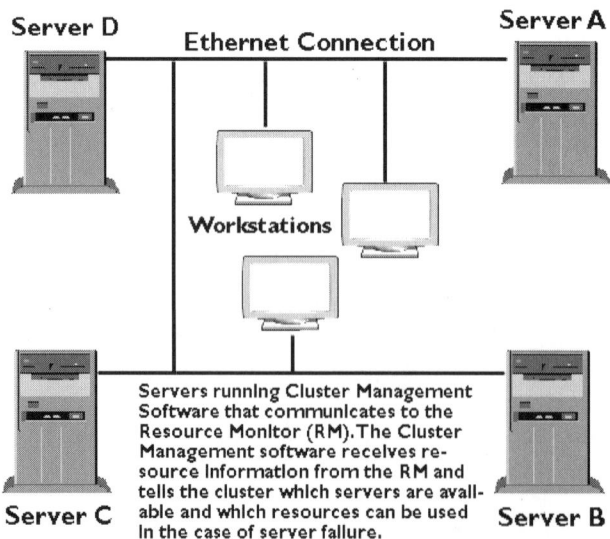

Source: Rob Short, Development Manager, Microsoft Corporation

Figure 21.1 Cluster components.

Resources, including databases and server applications, will move from one machine to another when a system fails. This includes databases and server applications. If a resource depends on other resources, the resource is brought on-line after any resource it depends on and is taken off-line before any resource it depends on. Additionally, dependent resources must move together as a failover group if there is a failure, thereby simplifying the management and administration of the network. Ownership of the group is handled via a negotiation within the nodes.

Cluster management is handled via a cluster service. This service finds and communicates with each of the nodes, knows the objects (such as nodes, groups, resources), and knows when an event occurs (such as a node state change, group location change, or resource state change). You can use a management API to create, open, and delete groups. The manager can be used to move the group and to query the group for properties.

The cluster also uses a resource monitor to provide an interface from the cluster service to resource DLLs. See Figure 21.2 for a pictorial example. The resource DLLs are resource-specific code that allow the cluster software to manage a resource, like a database. All of the resources look the same to the cluster. The function of the resource DLLs is to open resources, close resources, start a resource, bring resources off-line and on-line, and determine the resource state.

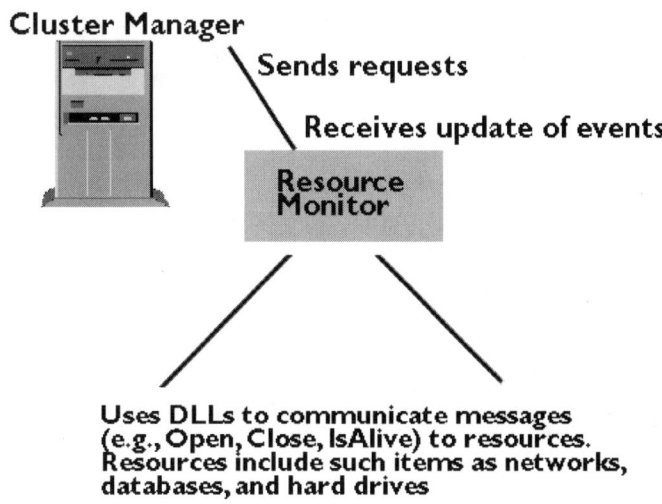

Figure 21.2 Resource monitor in action.

The system uses an API to start a resource type and verify its version. The opening function opens a resource and creates needed structures to bring the resource on-line. The closing function closes the resource and deallocates the structures. Resources generally share a resource monitor, but the resource manager can be dedicated to a single resource.

The cluster management tools monitor and manage the entire cluster. You can modify current NT tools to allow for performance monitoring of the entire cluster, administration of the disks, and logging of events. The cluster can be modified and maintained using the configuration tool.

Security

NT 5.0 will use the Kerberos security system. Kerberos, as defined in the FAQ, is "a network authentication system for use on physically insecure networks." In other words, it is a protocol to determine which users are "true" users in a distributed environment. This means that NT 5.0 will be able to safely communicate with UNIX environments.

The system will provide a ticket to systems that wish authentication. The ticket tells the computer what a system's rights are in communicating with the server. The encryption can be a public key or a shared secret. The latter approach is recommended for company internal use, because it stores a key on every system that is in the secure environment. External networks would use the public key process as used in digital certification methods.

Costs of Doing Business

As all developers have realized, the cost of doing business appears to be going up because of the need to purchase new hardware and software and hire additional workers for a project. Developers must help find ways to minimize the increase while helping companies sell more products.

With all these changes, how do you reduce the cost of implementing new solutions? Look at the overall approach that accounting (or whoever does this function) uses for funding system and application upgrades. These people need to get a handle on the costs and the potential for dramatic increase. The good news for your financial overseers is that the new generation of Microsoft server products and tools can assist in managing costs.

Windows NT 5.0 will provide a much easier setup mechanism, especially across networks, reducing the time it will take an administrative department to move to this new technology. NT 5.0 and Active Platform will allow for desktops that can be managed locally or over the network. File system complexity is reduced, and it is much easier to work with a Plug and Play environment when installing hardware.

The NT 5.0 operating system will update itself during the boot cycle. In addition, developers with a UNIX background will enjoy the fact that NT 5.0 provides the ability to boot from across the network. Developers can easily roll back any application or system updates to an earlier version.

Administrators can set up desktops using remote tools as well as provide an easy method for building a desktop that roams with the user. Desktop properties can now be assigned to groups as well as users. Users need not be involved in the application setup or installation. The system will determine whether the application is to be installed locally or launched from the network, letting you create distributed applications with real-time updates.

Administrators are familiar with having to go from workstation to workstation trying to find an original application to udpate. Each user may bury the application in a personal place on the drive. In addition, developers get involved trying to coordinate shared files when they need to track DLL versions. Finally, the user must be logged in as administrator to install current applications. With the release of NT 5.0, the application becomes a package that the operating system will install. The application is run as a service with a database that tracks the DLLs as well as the appropriate registry keys. If a workstation has an out-of-date application or operating system, it can go to the network and servers to upgrade.

To find files, users must either keep a written list or use the Find tool. Users are also normally responsible for their own backups and virus scanning. This arrangement is becoming unacceptable with increasing Internet access and shared data. Someone needs to validate the data and keep it clean. NT 5.0 uses a home directory approach for gathering and storing files. A master copy of the home directory lies on the server with a copy cached to the local workstation. This means that a developer can share home directories among users or groups.

Control Panel has a menu that allows the user to remove, review, or change the settings. The user interface will be grouped into major categories rather than just a long list of applications.

With these changes and more to come, developers and administrators can assure their financial officers and backers that upgrading to the next technology should remain painless.

WHERE TO GO FROM HERE

NT 5.0 and Active Directories are intended to help the developer find information as well as manage applications distributed over the network. The interfaces and services are component-oriented to take advantage of an object-oriented environment. Additionally, Microsoft has included the Wolfpack clustering software to ensure scalability of services.

From here you may want to read the following chapters:

- Chapter 3, "The Active Platform," to understand Microsoft's current implementation of component architecture in BackOffice.
- Appendix A, "Setting Up IIS and NT," to learn more about the current IIS environment.

Appendix A

Setting Up IIS and NT

Let's look at setting up and managing the Internet Information Server (IIS).

IIS

Before installing IIS, follow these steps:

1. Set up a computer with Windows NT Server 4.0.
2. In Control Panel choose the **Network** icon. Choose the **Protocols** tab. Make sure that TCP/IP is installed. If it is not, install it now. Additionally, make sure that the system has a legitimate Internet domain name. See the section on DNS for setting up the service.
3. Disable any previous version of IIS and its services. Stop all WWW, FTP, and Gopher services.

IIS 3.0 has Active Server as a part of its services. Find the IIS directory on the CD-ROM that you obtained or go to Microsoft's Web site to download IIS. Run **inetsetup.exe**.

The application opens with a welcome screen and then asks which options to install. Select all appropriate services. By default, all options should be checked.

The system will install IIS under **C:\inetserv**. It is recommended that you leave the default location for future upgrades.

Next, the application asks where to locate the root directory for the content. By default, the location is in subdirectories of the IIS installation directory. Some developers find that it fits their plan to use a different directory for the root location of published Web, FTP, and Gopher files. In addition, this arrangement can prevent setting improper permissions on the IIS directory.

The system will ask for the DNS domain name.

Next come the ODBC drivers (if you included that option at the beginning of the setup). Choose the appropriate drivers and then click **OK**. This should successfully install the IIS.

The services should automatically start at completion of setup. IIS Manager and the documentation are given a separate icon under the Start menu. Events are automatically logged to the Applications log.

Let's Use the Internet Service Manager

Internet Service Manager allows you to administer the IIS servers within an enterprise. If the system has Proxy Server installed, those items will also be displayed.

Internet Service Manager is shown in Figure A.1

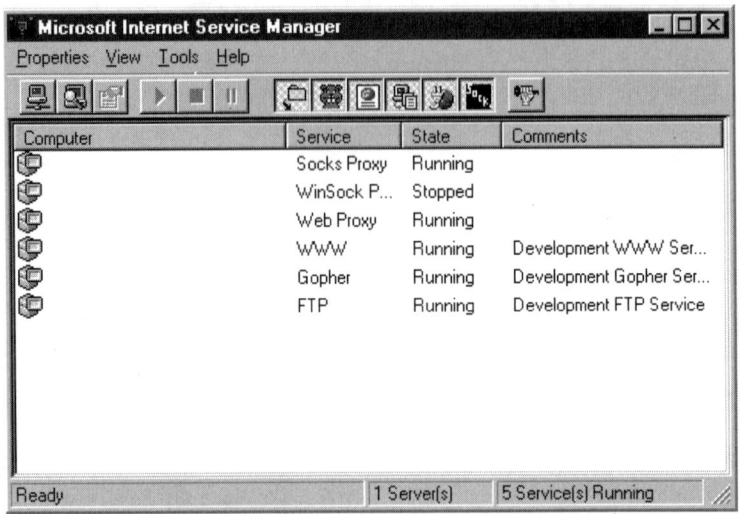

Figure A.1 Internet Service Manager.

Note that all three services are running. This interface can be used to find other IIS servers on the domain, administer the state of the servers (start, stop, and pause using the video-player-type buttons), and set up security, directories, and logging.

Internet Service Manager searches for other servers by using the Windows Internet Name Service (WINS) or the TCP/IP broadcasting method. See the following sections for a discussion of WINS and TCP/IP. Note that IIS has a difficult time finding another IIS across a router using the TCP/IP broadcast method. You can use WINS to resolve the name of the server.

Once you have found all the servers of interest, you can double-click on the server and service of interest to open a properties dialog box. You can look at information using the View menu. You are given three choices: Reports view, Servers view, and Services view.

The Reports view is the default. The servers are listed in alphabetical order. Sorting can be done by name, service type, state and comments.

The Servers view lists servers running IIS services by computer name. By double-clicking the plus sign, you can see the services ran by a server.

The Services view displays the information by service type. Double-click the plus sign next to the service to see all the servers running that service.

Setting Up IIS and NT 481

Choose the view that fits the needs of the operation. In addition, the View menu has a filters setup that will remove services from the viewing area. For example, if Gopher is not running you can filter it out.

Internet Service Manager will run on NT Workstation and NT Server. This means that you can run IIS in a remote environment. This even works across the Internet, but you should ensure that the system is running the Windows NT challenge/response authentication protocol to ensure that users must log in with a password.

You can start, stop, and pause a service by highlighting it and then choosing the VCR-like toolbar. See Figure A.2 for an example.

Figure A.2 The toolbar for IIS.

WWW

The Internet Services Manager includes a services property sheet. For example, if you double-click the **WWW** service, it opens the Service Properties dialog box shown in Figure A.3

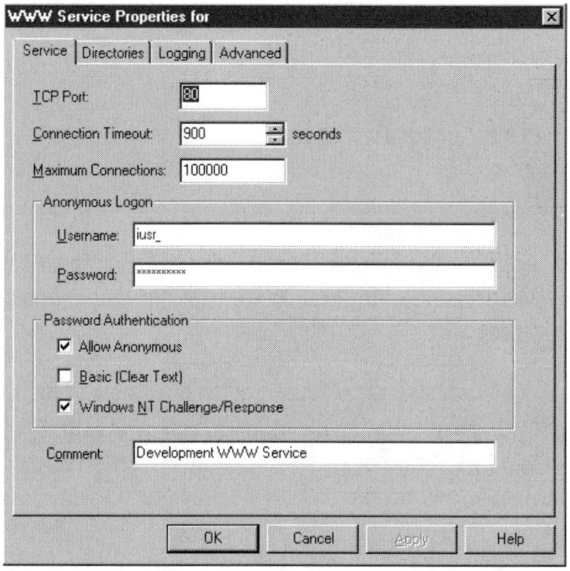

Figure A.3 WWW Service Properties dialog box.

You can choose Service, Directories, Logging, and Advanced properties.

SERVICES

The **WWW Service** tab lets you set various connection options for your WWW server. In the **Connection Timeout** box, you can specify the number of seconds that will elapse before a user is disconnected from the IIS machine. The default value is 900 seconds (15 minutes).The **Maximum Connections** box lets you limit the number of users who can simultaneously connect to the WWW service. The default value is 1,000 connections.

The **Anonymous Logon** area lets you specify both the username and the password used for the anonymous connection. The default is **IUSR_computername**. The **Password Authentication** options allow you to set the method used for authenticated logons. There are three authentication options:

- **Allow Anonymous.** If this is checked, the WWW service uses the anonymous logon ID and password set up in the prior step for authenticating all user connections.
- **Basic.** If checked, Basic authentication uses clear text to verify user connections. All browsers support the basic authentication mechanism. The problem is that sending clear text passwords over the Internet can compromise the network security. A network sniffer can capture the passwords.
- **Windows NT Challenge/Response.** If checked, uses the Windows NT Challenge/Response authentication method. This is the most secure method for user authentication.

DIRECTORIES

The WWW Directories tab can be used to set up directories for the server to use. The following items can be set:

- **Directory.** The physical directory path
- **Alias.** The path name used by users that maps to the physical path
- **Address.** An IP address of a virtual server (if the directory runs as a virtual server)
- **Error.** System errors

IIS automatically creates a home and scripts directory. The **Default Document** check box lets you identify the directory's default document to load. This helps users when they know that they are to link to a directory but do not know the name of the home page for that directory.

Directory Browsing Allowed lets you give access to files and directories under the WWW root.

If you want to add a directory, click **Add** on the **Directories** tab. Now set a new directory name in the **Directory** box or use the **Browse** button to select a directory. Please note that you must first create the directory if you choose the **Browse** button. IIS does not automatically create directories. Now choose **Home Directory** or **Virtual Directory**. If you choose **Virtual Directory**, you must specify the alias for the directory. If the directory has a network share name, you can use the **Account Information** options to specify a username and password. If the directory points to a virtual server, check the **Virtual Server** option and denote a **Virtual Server IP Address**.

For these IP addresses to be created, you must go to Control Panel and choose the **Network** icon. Then double-click the TCP/IP protocol. Find the **IP address** tab. Choose **Advanced**. Here you can add or bind multiple addresses to an Ethernet card. In this way a machine can have a number of names attached via the IP address to a virtual directory.

In the **Directories** tab there is an **Access** check box. It allows you to denote the user access permission for the directory. Choose **Read** for rights to read a directory, and choose **Execute** for items such as scripts. Remember that **Read** should not be set on executable directories.

A **Require Secure SSL channel** option allows SSL access of directories.

THE LOGGING TAB

Logging is used to store information about who has accessed the WWW service and the information he or she was looking for. The logs can be stored to files or ODBC databases.

To manipulate the log options, click the **Enable Logging** check box. This starts the logging process. Choose the **Log to File** or **Log to SQL/ODBC Database** option button. Choosing **Log to File** gives you a number of choices:

- Automatically Open New Log creates a new log that can be set for **Daily, Weekly, Monthly**, or **When File Size Reaches**. The **When the File Size Reaches** means that you can set the limit in megabytes.
- Log File Directory creates the directory name and location where the files should be stored.
- Log File Name shows the names that will be used to store the log files.

Choosing the **Log to SQL/ODBC Database** option gives you a number of other options:

- ODBC Data Source Name (DSN) tells the developer the name used to connect to the database.
- Table denotes the table name for storing the logs.
- User Name is the username for connecting to the database.
- Password is the password for connecting to the database.

Make sure that the DSN has been set by using the **ODBC** icon in Control Panel.

Advanced

This tab lets you set the access limits and control network traffic. A default option allows all users access or denies all access to IIS. After that you can specify individual computers or groups as exceptions to the default.

Select **Granted Access** for access control. By default, all computers are granted access to your IIS machine. To exclude computers from having access to the IIS computer use the **Add** button to list the computers. In the **Deny Access On** dialog box, specify the IP address of the computer or group of computers that will be excluded. If you are excluding a group, a subnet mask is used.

Use the **Edit** button to add or remove an address from the list. Click **Limit Network Use by all Internet Services on This Computer** to place a network limit. The **Maximum Network Use** box allows you to enter a limit.

FTP

To configure the FTP service, double-click on the **FTP** name. The options are as follows: Service, Messages, Directories, Logging, and Advanced.

Directories, Logging, and Advanced

These properties are similar to the settings in WWW (see the preceding section).

Service

This tab is used to set up the various connections. Click the **Service** tab.

A **Connection Timeout** box lets you set the number of seconds before a user is disconnected. The default value is 900 seconds (15 minutes). The **Maximum Connections** box can be used to limit the number of users that simultaneously connect to the

FTP service. The default value is 1,000 connections. The **Allow Anonymous Connections** options allows the developer to choose the username and password to be used in anonymous connections to FTP. The default is IUSR_computername. Many users will use the name "anonymous" and their e-mail as the password.

The **Allow Only Anonymous Connections** check box disables logon permissions for all users except anonymous logons. This can be used to prevent users who have administrative privileges from gaining access to other items beyond the anonymous permissions. FTP uses clear text for transmitting passwords. Remember that a network sniffer can read those passwords. Use the **Comment** box to denote the comment displayed by the Internet

Service Manager in the Reports view. Click **Current Session** to display users currently connected to your FTP server.

Look at the **FTP User Sessions** screen to view the currently connected users. The developer can disconnect the user by selecting them from the list and pressing **Disconnect**. **Disconnect All** means exactly that—to disconnect all the users along with ongoing transfers.

MESSAGES

This tab deals with messages you can send to users. There can be a standard welcome message when users connect to the FTP site. There can also be an exit message as they disconnect and a maximum connections message to ask users to come back when there is less traffic.

In the **Welcome Message** text box, enter the text that you wish displayed to clients when they first connect. In the **Exit Message** text box, place the message to be used when users disconnect. In the **Maximum Connections** Message text box the developer adds the message used when the users are turned away because traffic is too high.

Gopher

Double-click the **Gopher** icon. The Properties box appears with the following tabs: **Service**, **Directories**, **Logging**, and **Advanced**

DIRECTORIES, LOGGING, AND ADVANCED

These tabs are used for the same settings as those in the WWW section. Please refer to that section for further configurations.

SERVICE

The **Service** tab is for setting Gopher connection options.

In the **Connection Timeout** box, you can set the number of seconds before a user is disconnected. The default value is 900 seconds (15 minutes). The **Maximum Connections** box limits the number of simultaneous Gopher users. The default value is 1,000 connections.

The service administrator name and e-mail information is provided so that you can tell users whom to contact in case of problems or questions. The **Anonymous Logon** option allows you to set the username and password to be used for anonymous logons. The default is the `IUSR_computername` account. The **Comment** box can be used to set the comments for the Reports view.

Using Scripts

Scripts include both CGI and ISAPIs.

After building CGI scripts and ISAPIs, you can put them in the **/Scripts** directory, which was created for executables during installation. This directory needs to have execute but not read privileges. In either case, the HTML that fires off these applications can use a submit button or a hypertext link. To use scripts, remember to go to the IIS Manager window and stop the WWW service. Then restart the service to ensure that the applications are loaded for use. If you are using the Internet Database Connector (IDC) form of ISAPI, make sure that the system has **HTTPODBC.DLL**, the interface to ODBC. Ensure that it is executable by the user. Retrieve rows from a database and display it to users

TCP/IP

TCP/IP is a set of network protocols that tell exactly how data can be moved from point A to point B. When speaking of TCP/IP, the hose can be a computer or router. A gateway provides a wide area network (such as a router).

TCP/IP is a benefit for developers installing networks, because this protocol can be used over large numbers of computers where the messages are routed around the world. Using this protocol, the Internet routes packets from one computer to another. The problem is the need to know where to send the packets of information. This is where the IP address comes in. The IP address is the address space needed for each host. It is represented in the following form: 111.111.111.111. Each of the four parts has an octet (range from 1 to 254).

The computers have host names (also known as domain names) and IP addresses. How does a packet determine where it is going? The applications use Address Resolution Protocol (ARP) to resolve IP addresses. In NT there are five ways to use ARP: HOSTS file, Domain Name Service (DNS), Windows Internet Name Service (WINS), the local broadcast or LMHOSTS file. In this section the focus is DNS. WINS is covered in a following section.

Here is a sample of the instructions that come with Microsoft's DNS setup:

1. To set up DNS, select a domain name, research it to ensure that it is not already associated with another organization, and identify the IP address of the intended name servers.
2. Install the DNS Service on a name server. Run the Network application from Control Panel, select **Services**, select **Add**, select **Microsoft DNS Server**, select **OK**, and reboot the server when prompted.

3. Create a primary, forward zone. In the **Server** list, right-click the server icon for which you are creating a zone. Select **New Zone**, then **Primary**, and then **Next**. Type the **Zone Name** and select the **Zone File** text box to accept the default zone file name, or type a different one.
4. Before adding resource records to the forward zone, create a primary, reverse zone. The steps are the same as for creating a primary zone except for entering the zone name: you must type the network portion of your IP address followed by "in-addr.arpa". For example, if the name server's IP address is 10.20.30.1 and the network portion of that IP address is the first three octets (10.20.30), the name of the zone file must be **30.20.10.in-addr.arpa**.
5. Add records to the zone. In the **Server** list, right-click the name server's entry, and select **New Record**. Select the type of record and enter the appropriate information, then select **OK**. To each forward zone you must add, at minimum the following: one NS record and one A record for each other name server; one MS and one A record for each mail server (if any); and one A record for each resource server (Web server, FTP server, and so on). DNS Manager automatically creates the zone's required SOA record for you, and gives its fields the default values. The data entry dialog box for the A record also has a **Create Associated PTR Record** check box. Select this to automatically add the corresponding PTR record to the reverse zone.
6. Install the DNS service on at least one other server and configure it as the secondary name server. Install the DNS service on the intended secondary name server. On that server, start the DNS Manager utility. From the **Server** list, select the intended secondary server and right-click its entry. Select **New Zone** and then **Secondary**. Enter the zone name and the IP address of the primary DNS server.

That is a brief overview from the Microsoft documentation.

DYNAMIC HOST CONFIGURATION PROTOCOL

The Dynamic Host Configuration Protocol (DHCP) operates in a client/server environment.

DHCP consists of a scope, which is a pool of available IP addresses . As a DHCP client computer connects to the network, the DHCP server assigns a unique IP address. The server leases the IP address for a specified period of time. When that time has passed the IP address goes back into the pool (see Figure A.4).

488 ✦ Appendix A

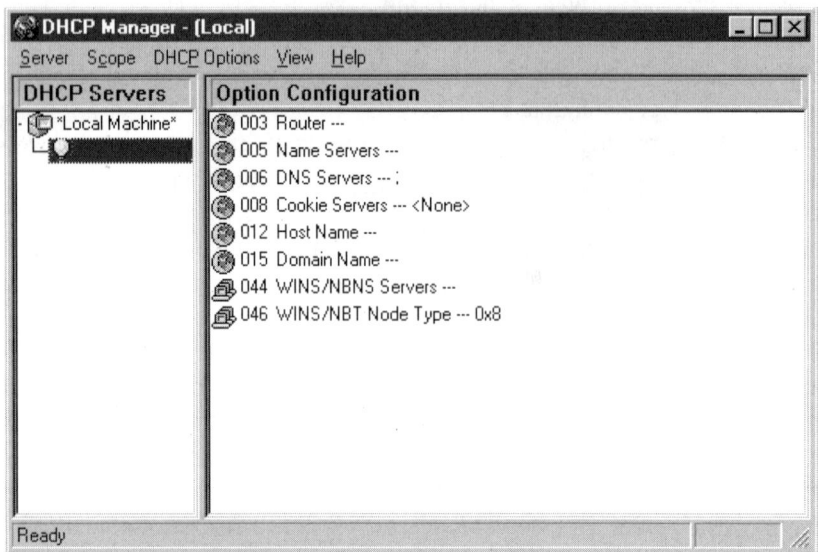

Figure A.4 DHCP Manager.

To configure the DHCP server, make sure that you know whether all the computers are clients on the network. Some systems need static IP addresses. That includes WWW servers, especially if they are multihomed, as well as routers, gateways, and many Windows 3.1 installations on a Novell/NT network. If you are running DNS and WINS, then they too should be configured in DHCP. If the network is subnetted, run a DHCP server on each subnet. The DHCP server does not share data with other DHCP servers or DNS servers, so you should determine whether there is a need for multiple scopes.

Creating a DHCP Scope

Start DHCP Manager. Choose **Scope** from the menu. The **Create Scope** box appears. Put in the IP address range for that scope. Enter the subnet mask. Enter the name for this IP address pool. Set the lease duration and activate it.

Multiple scopes can be of use when there are multiple DHCP servers handling subnets. If one server goes down, the computers can talk through the router to the other DHCP server to find a set of valid addresses.

Why DHCP?

Keep in mind that the concept behind DHCP is similar to leasing or renting a home versus buying a home. The good news is that maintenance is handled by the property owner. In this case, the DHCP server handles all the IP addressing issues, something that can reduce conflict on the network.

If a set of static IP addresses is assigned, it can mean a lot of DNS server administrative work for a user population that could be quite mobile. Many corporations are using laptops with Windows 95 and Internet connections from home. The DHCP route is the simplest and safest bet for implementing connectivity.

Users, in a sense, feel as if they are in charge of their destinies. They do not have to continually contact the developer or network administrator for valid IP addresses.

To lease addresses, the client computer logs on to the network. It broadcasts a request for an IP address. The DHCP can identify the computer, because in the broadcast contains a hardware address and computer name. The server with an available IP address will respond with the IP address, the subnet mask, the lease duration, the server IP address, and an acknowledgment of the client's hardware address and name.

The client accepts the offer and broadcasts the acceptance, ensuring that all potential DHCP servers are told of the acceptance. The server acknowledges the receipt, and a valid IP address lease is established for the client.

Setting Up DHCP

To set up options and properties, start the DHCP Manager. Choose **DHCP Options** and then **Global**. The Global dialog box opens. You can now choose any **Unused Options** by clicking **Add** to add the item to the **Active Options** box. Values are set by clicking on the item and clicking **Value**. Now add the IP addresses.

To set up the scope options go back to the main DHCP Manager screen. Click on the scope that you wish to set options for. Choose **DHCP Options** and then **Scope**. Select an option from the list of **Unused Options**. Click **Add** to add them to the **Active Options** list. Click **Value** to set the value. Enter the appropriate IP addresses.

To establish client reservations, choose **Scope** and then **Active Leases** in the main DHCP Manager window. This informs you of all current reservations. To add a new reservation, choose **Scope** and the **Add Reservations** option. Add the computer ID.

Enter the hardware address of the computer's network adapter in the **Unique Identifier** box. Enter the client name for the computer.

To configure the client in a Windows 95 box, go to Control Panel and choose the **Network** icon. Double-click the **TCP/IP** protocol to bring up the TCP/IP properties. Choose the **WINS Configuration** tab. Click on **Use DHCP for WINS Resolution**.

To see the current leases, go back to the DHCP Manager entry screen. Click on the scope and then choose **Scope** and **Active Leases**. Now you can see all the options. The list can be sorted by name or IP address. The **Reconcile** button is used to verify the list. It is best used if you think there has been a problem with DHCP or a server has crashed.

Windows Internet Name Service

Windows Internet Name Service registers the NetBIOS names used by computers when they start. WINS can help reduce the amount of broadcast traffic on a network. Name resolution is handled in a direct link from the WINS server to the clients. WINS operates across routers and so can deal with subnetting. If WINS is down, the clients can resort to broadcasting to resolve issues.

To set up WINS name registration, the WINS client is set with the WINS primary and secondary address. This can be incorporated within the DHCP parameters by configuring the optional settings, noted in the preceding section, for a WINS server. The WINS server accepts the message from the client and registers the name if there is no conflict. The registration time length is set by a time-to-live (TTL) parameter. If there is a name conflict, the WINS server challenges the old computer that has the name. If that system responds in a positive manner, the WINS server rejects the new computer's request. If the older system does not respond, the WINS server registers the new client. If the client believes that the primary WINS server is down, it tries for the second server. If the second server is down, the client broadcasts on the subnet. Figure A.5 shows WINS Manager.

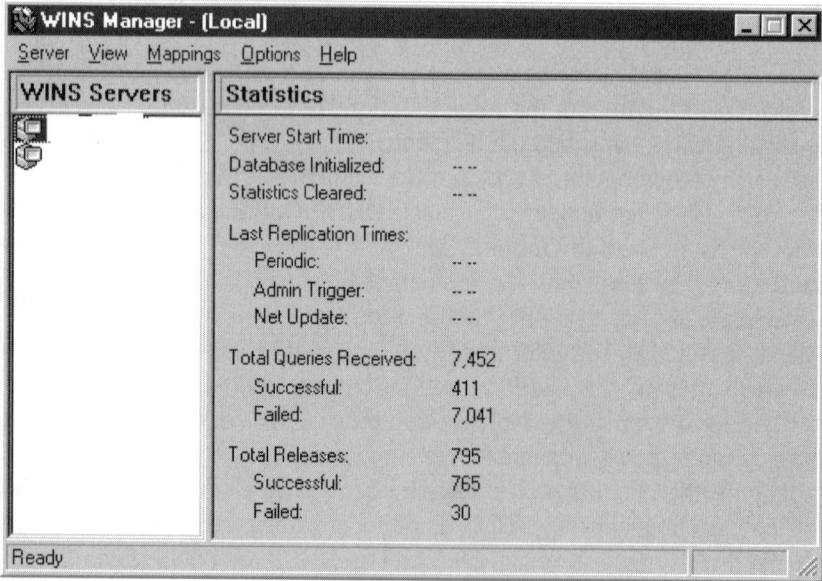

Figure A.5 WINS Manager.

Setting Up WINS

To configure the basic data, start WINS Manager. Choose **Server** and then **Configuration**. There are settings for time periods (TTL) and options. Choose **Options** and then **Preferences** to set statistic refresh rates and address display formats.

To enter a static mapping for the non-WINS clients, go back to the main screen. Choose **Mappings** and then **Static Mappings.** Choose the **Add Mappings** button. This presents an Add Static Mappings box. Enter the IP address and name to be registered.

To configure the WINS clients, go back to the WINS Manager screen. When there, choose **Mappings** and then **Show Database.** There will be a Sort Order box. Use the **Options** button to set the preferences.

To set up a WINS backup scenario, WINS Manager allows you to set up what are called push-pull partners. The push server sends its database to its partner when a certain number of changes are completed. The pull server lets you set the time to request an update. Go back to the WINS Manager screen. Choose **Server** and **Replication Partners.** Click **Add** to enter the server name that will be replicated to or from. The WINS server will attempt to reach that system. If the connection is made, the partner is added to the server list. If it is not found, the WINS server will prompt for an IP address of the other server. Assuming this is successful, click on the new server. Make the **Push Partner** or **Pull Partner** selection in the **Replication Options** box. Once the selection is made, click **Configure.** The appropriate dialog box appears.

Appendix B
Resources and the CD-ROM

This appendix lists a number of excellent Web sites and published resources you can use to learn about the various BackOffice products.

RESOURCES

Web Sites

In researching this book I became aware of several Web sites that will help novice to advanced users gain further understanding of how to build a dynamic Web site.

ASP

http://www.aspdeveloper.net/iasdocs/aspdocs/roadmap.asp

ISAPI

http://www.genusa.com/isapi/isapisrc.html

JAVA

http://webreference.com/javascript/

VISUAL BASIC/VBSCRIPT

http://www.microsoft.com/vbscript/us/vbstutor/vbstutor.htm

NETSCAPE DYNAMIC HTML

http://www.developer.netscape.com/library/documentation/communicator/dynhtml/index.htm

MICROSOFT DYNAMIC HTML

http://www.microsoft.com/workshop/author/dhtml/

Index Server

http://www.microsoft.com/syspro/technet/index.htm

SQL Server

Resources Used in the Writing of this Book

The information about how various servers and tools operate came from many sources:

1. The on-line documentation provided with Index Server, SQL Server, Proxy Server, Commerce Server, and Transaction Server.
2. Conversations with developers in the following newsgroups:

    microsoft.public.inetserver.iis
    microsoft.public.inetserver.iis.dbweb
    microsoft.public.inetserver.iis.misc
    microsoft.public.inetserver.iis.activeserverpages
    microsoft.public.vinterdev
    microsoft.public.sqlserver.server
    microsoft.public.sqlserver.connect
    microsoft.public.sqlserver.programming
    microsoft.public.sqlserver.odbc
    microsoft.public.sqlserver.replication
    microsoft.public.active.directory.interfaces
    microsoft.public.activex.controls.chatcontrol
    microsoft.public.activex.programming.control.webdc
    microsoft.public.activex.programming.control.webwiz
    microsoft.public.internet.personwebserv
    microsoft.public.java.activex
    microsoft.public.java.security
    microsoft.public.java.visualj++
    microsoft.public.microsofttransactionserver.administration-security
    microsoft.public.microsofttransactionserver.announcements
    microsoft.public.microsofttransactionserver.integration
    microsoft.public.microsofttransactionserver.programming
    microsoft.public.msdn.general
    microsoft.public.proxy
    microsoft.public.site-server.commerce
    microsoft.public.site-server.general

Resources and the CD-ROM 495

       microsoft.public.site-server.postingacceptr
       microsoft.public.site-server.publishing
       microsoft.public.site-server.site-mgm
       microsoft.public.site-server.webpost
       microsoft.public.sqlserver.clients
       microsoft.public.sqlserver.datawarehouse
       microsoft.public.sqlserver.setup
       microsoft.public.proxybeta
       microsoft.public.java.vm
       microsoft.public.merchantserver
       microsoft.public.vc.activextemplatelib
       http://microsoft.ease.lsoft.com/archives/index.html

3. Documentation provided by authors at the Microsoft 1996 Professional Developers Conference.

Other developers provided me with literally thousands of pages of material as I helped a company move from the UNIX/C++ world to the NT world of dynamic Web sites. The credit for this technical knowledge goes to those developers and the Microsoft documentation authors. I merely told the story of what I learned while installing these systems.

WHAT IS ON THE CD-ROM

On the CD-ROM you will find code in seven separate categories:

1. ASP code for:
   - A sample piece of ASP code for redirecting a user to a new index page.
   - A sample Commerce Server store created using the Commerce Server's Shop Builder Wizard. Note that all graphics are the property of Microsoft and are included only for learning purposes. You must create your own graphics if you use these samples for a company site.
2. Sample C++ code:
   - Evaluation copy of C++ code created by Quasit Technologies, Inc. (295 Greenwich Street, Suite 244, New York, NY 10007, http://www.quasit-tech.com/). This is a nice way to write streamlined CGI using C++.
   - A sample clock program written in 1995 by Tom Armstrong.
   - Sample program written using Microsoft Developer Studio. The sample program was created to test the input and extraction of data using the Microsoft Foundation Classes (MFCs).

- Form Decoder and Dumper, an Internet Information Server extension written using Visual C++.
- A sample implementation of COdbctestExtension.
- An ISAPI program to redirect users to different Web pages.
3. Sample .IDC and .HTX files used during the development of the company test Web site.
4. Sample Java to include a JScript clock and a Java Stress tester by Stuart Donovan (donovan@worldweb.net).
5. A set of image maps used during the phase 1 site in Chapter 19.

Index

A

Abandon, 52
Abstract Window Toolkit (AWT) library, 330–331, 376
Access, 142
Active caching, 119
Active Data Objects (ADOs), 37, 56, 61, 256, 339
Active Desktop, 27, 327
Active Directory Interface (ADI), 471
    structure of, 472, 473
ActiveMedia, 235
Active Platform
    distribution of objects, 28
    as an extension to Internet Information Server, 34
    hardware considerations, 41–43
    products, 33
    role of, 27–28, 31–32
    scalability, 29–31
Active Server Pages (ASP), 31, 33, 34
    application flows, 36–37
    applications, 46
    .asp files, 251, 259–260
    benefits of, 36
    block script delimiters, 37–38
    built-in objects, 38
    components, 56–58
    creating pages example, 59–60
    database connections, 46
    definitions, 49–50
    directories, 46
    extending safety, 38–41
    HTML with inline VBScript, 47
    implementation of, 46
    inline script delimiters, 37
    interfaces, 46
    objects, 50–56
    role of, 35, 45–49, 64, 80, 246
    sample .asp file, 46–47
    scripting languages, 48–49
    scripts, 349–350
    sessions, 58–59
    tips and troubleshooting, 60–61
    Web site, 493
Active Server products, 28
Active Template Library (ATL), 328, 329
    ActiveX controls implemented by 355–357
    building a sample, 351–355
    role of, 349
    threading, 357–358
    when and how to use, 350–351
ActiveX
    automation, 50
    client, 50
    compared to Java, 396
    components, 49
    control pad, 341–344
    controls, 49, 328–329, 338–339, 340–341
    controls implemented by ATL, 355–357
    database interactivity, 339
    object linking and embedding and, 338–339
    objects, 31
    role of, 49, 50, 327, 337–338
    security issues, 328–329, 344–346
    tips for, 346–348
    tools, 339–344
ActiveX development kit (ADK), 328
ActiveX Server components, 38, 49
Actpaynp.exe, 242
AddHeader, 51
Address Selector, 242, 245, 251
Adventure Works, 260, 261
Advertisement Rotator component, 57
.aif files, 209

498 Index

American Express, 238
Annealing merges, 200–201
Anonymous password authentication, 112
AppendToLog, 51
Appfilt.dll, 215
Applet class loader, 380
Applets
    building, 380–381
    defined, 376
Application gateway. See Proxy Server
Application object, 38, 50, 52
Application_OnEnd, 59
Application_OnStart, 59
ASP. See Active Server Pages
.asp files, 251, 259–260
Asynchronous Transfer Mode (ATM), 104
ATL. See Active Template Library
ATL COM AppWizard, 351
ATL Object Wizard, 353, 355
Atomicity, database, 138
Audio (AU), 409
Audio Interchange File Format (AIFF), 409
Authentication, 96–98
    password, 112–116
Authenticode, 329, 344–345
Auto Dial, 115, 119, 131
Automation client, 50
AVI, 409
.avi files, 209
AWT (Abstract Window Toolkit) library, 330–331, 376

B

BackOffice products, 30, 31, 33
BaseCtl, 328
Basic password authentication, 113
basket.asp file, 257
Bastion hosts, 90
Berners-Lee, Tim, 20
BinaryWrite, 51
Block script delimiters, 37–38
Block striping, 42
Body of information, 8–9
Boolean operators, 185–187

Browser Capabilities component, 57
Buffer, 51
Bulk Copy Program (BCP), 154
Buttons, text versions of graphical, 405
Buy Now wizard, 251, 271
Bytecodes, 375, 376
Byte striping, 42

C

Caching, 32
    active, 119
    disk, 123
    passive, 119
    property, 203–204
    Proxy Server, 118–120
Catalog, 217–222
Catalog.wci, 218, 219, 221–222, 228
Certification authority (CA), 234, 241
CGI. See Common Gateway Interface
Chaining, 131
Challenge/response password authentication, 113
Characterization, 212–213
chg_ava.htx, 436–438
chg_avai.idc, 435–436
chg_upda.htx, 439–440
chg_upda.idc, 439
Chunks, 204, 215–217
CiDaemon process, 196, 204, 212, 218
Cisco routers, 89–90
Classes, Java, 376, 377–378
Class methods, 378
Class variables, 377–378
Clear, 51
Client, role of, 4
ClientCertificate, 50
client_name, 52
Client/server
    benefits of, 16–17
    challenges of, 15–16
    comparisons between classic and Web, 401–402
    costs of, 17–19
    dynamic environment, 19–23
    example of, 4

Index 499

future of, 23–25
process model, 135
push versus pull, 23
Transaction Server, 301–310
Client services, Proxy Server, 121
Clock Peddler, 260, 261
CLSID, 205, 346
Clustered indexing, 160
Clustering, 30, 148
Cluster Server (Wolfpack), 30, 31, 148, 474–475
Codd, E. F., 134–135
Code signing, 344
COM. See Component Object Model
Command objects, 339
Commerce Server, 33
   assistance, 269
   building a new store, 264
   Buy Now wizard, 251, 271
   components, 248–249
   creating a copy of a store, 264–268
   deleting a store, 268
   global.asa file, 253, 254–255, 259–260
   host administrator, 262–263, 270–271
   how it works, 246–247
   location of key files, 259–260
   manager application, 261
   objects in store development, 255–256
   OrderForm, 248, 255, 256–258
   order processing pipeline, 249–250
   Page object, 255, 258
   scalability, 272
   selling process, 251–269
   setting up a store, 263–264
   shopping process, 269–270
   store application, 260
   Store Builder wizard tools, 250
   store building, 251–254
   tips for increasing sales, 270–272
   tools, 270–271
   wizards, 271
Common Gateway Interface (CGI), 25, 34, 47
   role of, 63, 64–67
   scripts, 35
Common Object Request Broker Architecture (CORBA), 170
Component Object Model (COM), 27–28, 249

   role of, 49, 337–338
Components
   Active Server Pages, 56–58
   Commerce Server, 248–249
   Transaction Server, 281–282
Concurrency anomaly, 296
Concurrency problems, 137
Confidential issues, 462–466
Connection objects, 339
Consistency, database, 137
Constants, 362
Constraints, 157
Content component, 248, 249
Content filtering, 204
Content Linking component, 56
ContentType, 51
Control pad, 341–344
Controls
   ActiveX, 49, 328–329, 338–339, 340–341
   ActiveX implemented by Active Template Library, 355–357
   COM, 338
   Visual Basic, 372–374
Cookies, 22, 458
   Active Server Pages object, 51
Copyrights, 462–464
CORBA, Object Request Broker (ORB), 49
C++, compared to Java, 390–391
CreateObject, 52
Cryptographic key, 234
C2 security, 101
Cubes, 175–176
customer.asp, 53, 54
customer.html, 53–54

D

Data Access component, 56
Data Access Objects (DAOs), 339
Database
   See also Relational database management system (RDBMS)
   design, 146
   integrity, 137–138
   levels, 133–134

500 Index

models, 133, 134–137, 147–148
technology, 144–148
terms, 133
warehouses and processes, 148–150, 171–173
Database administrator (DBA)
    management responsibilities, 145
    role of, 145
    technical responsibilities, 145–147
Database Components, 33
Database connections, Active Server Pages, 46
Database Consistency Checker (DBCC), 153
Database needs, 19
Data distribution, SQL Server, 157–158
Data Encryption Standard (DES), 97
Data Functions, 248
Data item, 133
Data item value, 133
Data management, distribution of objects and, 28
Data marts, 149
Data mining, 150
Data models, 133, 134–137, 147–148
Data Source name (DSN) setup, 68–70
Datasource object, 248, 256
Data striping, 42
Datatypes, 361
Data warehousing, 148–149, 160
    SQL Server, 171–173
DBStorage object, 248, 256, 257
Deadlock, 137
DEC, 30
Decision support systems (DSS), 149
Declarative Referential Integrity (DRI), 153–154
Dedicated parity, 42
Default filter, 205
Delete, 136
Denormalizing, 160
Digital certificate, 238
Digital signature, 234, 344–345
Directories, filtering, 212
Discover, 238
Disk mirroring, 42
Distributed Component Object Model (DCOM), 16, 28
    role of, 49, 276
Distributed File System (DFS), 472

Distributed parity, 42
Distribution of objects, 28
DLL. See Dynamic link library
Domain Name Service (DNS), 94–95, 472
Dual-homed hosts, 93
Durability, database, 137–138
Dynamic binding, 376, 379
Dynamic compilation, 379
Dynamic data exchange (DDE), 301
Dynamic Host Configuration Protocol (DHCP), 487–489
Dynamic Hypertext Markup Language, 64, 80–82, 493
Dynamic link library (DLL), 35
    filter, 204–208, 211–212, 213
    ISAPI, 76, 77

E

E-commerce (electronic commerce)
    potential market for, 235–237
    secure transactions, providing, 237–246
    security issues, 235
    selling process, 251–269
    terminology, 234–235
    troubles with, 237
Electronic cash (e-cash), 234
Electronic wallet, 234
E-mail
    body language symbols, 461–462
    code sample, Perl and, 413–424
Emoticons, 461–462
Empty.adr, 242
Empty.wit, 242
Encryption, 92, 93, 234, 469
End, 51
Enterprise data model, 147–148
Enterprise Integration Technologies Inc., S-HTTP, 468
Enterprise Manager, 150–153
Errors
    access code invalid, 131
    ASP 0115 error, 61
    500 error, 79
    12202 error, 131

80004005 error, 61
trapping, 60
Ethernet, 104
Executable content, 381
Expires, 51
ExpiresAbsolute, 51
EXTENSION_CONTROL_BLOCK, 78
Extranet, 234

F

File System component, 56
File Transfer Protocol (FTP), 104, 117
File types, associating, 209
Filtering
    directories, 212
    DLLs, 204–208, 211–212
    null, 209–210
    unknown extensions, 212
Fingerprint, 238
Firewalls
    bastion hosts, 90
    defined, 86
    Domain Name Service, 94–95
    dual-homed hosts, 93
    Java, 383
    packet filtering, 88
    perimeter networks, 90–91
    pros and cons of, 86–87
    proxy servers, 95–96
    review of, 466–467
    software, 92–93
Flush, 51
FORM command, 80
Form property, 50
Forrester Research, 235
Forwarder. See Proxy Server
Frame-Relay, 104
Free, 331
Free-text queries, 188
Functions
    JavaScript, 385
    VBScript, 363

G

Gateway interfaces, 25
Gateways, Proxy Server, 117–118
GET, 50, 66
GetExtensionVerison(), 77
global.asa file, 58–59, 253, 254–255, 259–260
Global unique identifier (GUID), 207
Global Village, 23
Graphical user interfaces (GUIs), 19
GTE Corp., 97

H

Hacking, preventing, 464–466
Handshaking, 469
Hardware considerations, 41–43
Header information, 8
Hidden variables, 21
Hierarchical model, 134
Host Administrator, 262–263, 270–271
Hotspot, 278
HTML. See Hypertext Markup Language
HTMLEncode, 52
Htmlfilt.dll, 211
HTTP. See Hypertext Transport Protocol
HttpExtensionProc(), 77
https, 97, 237–238, 239
.htx extension files, 67
    IDC/HTX code sample, 425–449
    passing a value, 74–75
    query, 193, 195–196
    simple example, 72–73
    syntax, 75–76
    variables, 226–227
Hyperlink, 2
Hypertext
    defined, 2
    examples of, 3
Hypertext Markup Language (HTML), 6
    Active Server Pages and, 47
    basics, 8–13
    dynamic, 64, 80–82
    .htx extension files, 67

502 Index

.htx extension files, passing a value, 74–75
.htx extension files, simple example, 72–73
.htx extension files, syntax, 75–76
versions of, 13
Hypertext Transport Protocol (HTTP), 5, 104
   HttpExtensionProc(), 77
   https, 97, 237–238, 239
   as a stateless protocol, 20

I

IBM, 97
Icon layer, 327
.ida files, 219, 220–222, 224, 228, 229
IDC. See Internet Database Connector
.idc files, 67, 193
IDC/HTX code sample, 425–449
Idispatch, 349
.idq files (Internet data query), 193, 194–195, 211–212, 219, 220–222, 228
Ifilter, 204, 214–217
IIS. See Internet Information Server
Indexes, 136
   defined, 196
   master, 198, 199
   merges, 199–203
   nonpersistent, 198
   persistent, 198–199
   property cache, 203–204
   shadow, 198, 199
   word lists, 198
Indexing
   defined, 196–198
   process, 204
   SQL Server, 160–161
Index Server, 31, 33
   Administration, 222–223
   catalog, 217–222
   characterization, 212–213
   chunks, 204, 215–217
   cleanup of noise words, 214
   filtering directories, 212
   filtering DLLs, 204–208, 211–212, 213
   Ifilter, 204, 214–217
   logging queries, 227

   managing resources, 222–230
   memory, 227–228
   null filtering, 209–210
   Performance Monitor, 224–227
   queries, types of, 188–192
   query language operators, 185–188
   query process, 182–196
   role of, 182, 183
   scripts, 228
   security issues, 179, 223
   unknown extensions, 212
   virtual roots, 228–230
   Web site, 494
   word breaking, 213
Inheritance, 378–379
Inline script delimiters, 37
In-process servers, 360
Insert, 136
Instance, Java, 377
Internet Database Connector (IDC), 34
   Data Source name (DSN) setup, 68–70
   example, 70–72
   .htx extension files, 67
   .htx extension files, passing a value, 74–75
   .htx extension files, simple example, 72–73
   .htx extension files, syntax, 75–76
   .idc files, 67, 193
   IDC/HTX code sample, 425–449
   role of, 63, 67
Internet data query (IDQ) files. See .idq files
Internet Explorer, 81, 113, 244, 327
Internet Information Server (IIS), 31
   advanced tab, 484
   benefits of, 34
   components of, 34–35
   configuring FTP, 484
   directories, 484, 485
   gopher icon, 485
   installing, 479
   logging queries, 227, 484, 485
   messages tab, 485
   products, 33, 46
   scripts, 486
   service tab, 484–485, 485
Internet Protocol (IP), 104

Internet Service Application Programming
    Interface (ISAPI), 25, 34
    advantages of, 77
    applications and filters, 35
    code sample, 449–456
    creating a sample, 78–80
    role of, 63, 76–78
    Web site, 493
Internet Service Manager (ISM), 118
IP forwarding, 116
IP spoofing, 99–98
IPX/SPX, 117
ISAPI. See Internet Service Application Programming Interface
Isolation, database, 137
ISP, setting up, 125–128
ISQL and ISQL/W, 154

J

Java
    animation in, 331–332
    for browser detection code sample, 424–425
    building applets, 380–381
    classes, 377–378
    compared to ActiveX, 396
    compared to C++, 390–391
    compared to JavaScript, 391–393
    dynamic binding, 379
    Hello World in, 329–330
    inheritance, 378–379
    objects, 376–377
    role of, 329, 375–376
    security issues, 375, 381–383
    syntax, 376–378
    terminology, 376
    viruses, 382–383
    Web site, 493
JavaBeans, 376, 381
Java Database Connectivity (JDBC), 170, 376, 383–384
Java Development Kit (JDK), 376
JavaScript
    Active Server Pages and, 46, 48–49
    compared to Java, 391–393
    compared to JScript, 386
    compared to VBScript, 393–394
    functions, 385
    Hello World in, 333
    objects, 385–386
    role of, 333, 376
    security issues, 386
    variables, 384–385
Java Virtual Machine (JVM), 344, 375
    role of, 376, 379–380
Joins, 175
jonstores.htx, 450–451
jonstores.idc, 450
Jscript, 384, 385
    compared to JavaScript, 386
jstores.tpl, 451–456
Jupiter Communications, 235
Just-in-time (JIT)
    activation, 312–318
    compiler, 376, 379–380

K

Kerberos security system, 476
Key Manager, 239–241

L

LAT (longitude), 120–121
Layers, 81
LiveScript, 384
Load balancing, distribution of objects and, 28
Local area networks (LANs), Proxy Server and, 115, 120
Logging
    Index Server, 227
    Proxy Server, 121–122
Logical unit, 133
login1.htm, 426–427
list.htx, 434–435
Livingston Enterprises Inc., 93

M

Manager application, 261
Managing resources, Index Server, 222–230

MapPath, 52
Marshaling interface, 357
Massively parallel processors (MPP), 148
MasterCard, 97, 238, 469
Master indexes, 198, 199
Master merges, 202–203
Merges, 199–203
MessageManager, 248
Microsoft Corp., 97, 236
    Distributed Transaction Coordinator (MS DTC), 153, 281, 296–299
    dynamic HTML and Internet Explorer, 81, 493
    Foundation Classes (MFC), 349, 350, 351
    Private Communication Technology (PCT), 468
    Query, 153
    Wallet, 242–246, 251
Microsoft Transaction Server (MTS). See Transaction Server
Middleware solution, 276
MinDependency option, 356
MS Press, 260, 261
Mswallet.cab, 242
Mswitalp.cab, 242
Multipurpose Internet Mail Extensions (MIME), 234

N

Namespaces, 471
National Computer Security Association, 87
Netiquette, 461–462
Netscape Communications Corp., Secure Sockets Layer (SSL), 97, 98, 235, 239, 468
Netscape Navigator, 244
    dynamic HTML, 81, 82, 493
Network(s)
    connections, 43
    model, 134
    neural, 150
    perimeter, 90–91
    principles, 18–19
    sniffers, 410
    virtual private, 92, 469–470
Network OLE, 49

Network size, distribution of objects and, 28
newavail.html, 427–429
newavail.htx, 429–434
newavail.idc, 429
NewsCatcher, 23
Next generation
    See also Web site, next-generation
    use of term, 399
NIC, 124
Noise words, 214
Nonclustered indexing, 161
Normalization, SQL Server, 158–160
NT LM, 113
Null filtering, 209–210
Nulls, 174–175

O

Object linking and embedding (OLE)
    ActiveX and, 338–339
    automation, 50
    container, 49, 50
    documents, 49
    procedures, 27–28
    role of, 49–50, 338
    server, 49
Object Manager, 154
Object-oriented, 376
Objects
    Active Data Objects (ADOs), 37, 56, 61, 256, 339
    Active Server Pages, 50–56
    Data Access Objects (DAOs), 339
    Java, 376–377
    JavaScript, 385–386
    in store development, 255–256
    Transaction Server, 282
OCX, 49, 355
OLE. See Object linking and embedding
On-line analytical processing (OLAP), 149–150
On-line transaction processing (OLTP), 149–150
Open Database Connectivity (ODBC), 33, 61
    Resource Dispenser, 294–295
    SQL Server, 168–171
Open Directory Services Interface (ODSI), 471

Operating system, 41
Operators
    query language, 185–188
    VBScript mathematical, 362–363
OrderForm, 248, 255, 256–258
order.htx, 440–441
order.idc, 440
OrderPipeline object, 248, 257
Order processing pipeline, 249–250
O'Reilly's WebSite, 46
Out-of-process servers, 360

P

Packet filtering, 88
Packets, 103
Page component, 249
page_count, 52
Page object, 255, 258
papers_online, 52
Passive caching, 119
Password authentication, 112–116
Payments, security issues, 96–98, 235
Payment Selector, 242, 245–246, 251
Performance Monitor, 224–227
Perimeter networks, 90–91
Perl (Practical Extraction and Report Language), 64–66
    and e-mail code sample, 413–424
Persistent indexes, 198–199
Personal Web Server, 46
PFN_HSE_IO_COMPLETION(), 77
Ping, 130
Pipeline Editor, 250, 271
Plug and play, 472–473
PointCast, 23
POST, 50, 53m 66
PPP, 130
Pretty Good Privacy (PGP), 234, 238
Primary key, 160
Private Communication Technology (PCT), 468
Private key, 234, 238, 239
Procedures, 48
    VBScript, 363
Production systems, 149

Property cache, 203–204
Property value queries, 190–192
Proximity operators, 187–188
Proxy Server, 32, 33, 38
    basic services, 104–105
    boost time, 122–123
    caching, 118–120
    client services, 121
    connections, 123
    controlling, 118–122
    defined, 85
    gateways, 117–118
    inbound access, 116
    increased loads, handling, 117
    LAT (longitude), 120–121
    logging, 121–122
    outbound access, 112–116
    password authentication, 112–116
    performance charts, 129–130
    screen savers, 123–124
    security components, 99–101
    setting up ISPs, 125–128
    setup, 102
    TCP/IP, 102–104
    troubleshooting, 130–132
    unbinding elements, 124
    Web Proxy, 38, 41, 100, 105–109
    WinSock Proxy (WSP), 38, 39–40, 100, 110–112
Proxy servers, role of, 95–96
PSINet, 233, 470
PTR records, 94–95
Public key, 235, 238, 239
Push
    dynamic HTML and, 81
    versus pull, 23

Q

Queries
    example, 193–194
    formulation rules, 196
    .htx, 195–196
    Internet data query (IDQ) files, 194–195
    language operators, 185–188

506   Index

logging, 227
process, 182–196
scopes, 182
syntax rules, 196
types of, 188–192
QueryString, 50
Quicktime, 409

R

Radius (remote authentication dial-in user service), 92–93
RAID (Redundant Array of Inexpensive or Independent Disks), 31, 41–42
RAS. See Remote access services
RC-4, 97
RealAudio, 131, 409
RealPlayer, 131
Real Video, 409
Receipt storage, 258
Recordset objects, 339
Record type, 133
Redirect, 51
Registration-based transactions, 98–99
Registry
    catalogs and settings for, 220–222
    editing, 219
Relational database management system (RDBMS)
    logical data model, 138–142
    physical data model, 143
    role of, 136–137
Relational data model, 134–135
Remote access services (RAS), 92–93, 114, 131, 457
Remote automation, 360
Remote Procedure Call (RPC), 16, 360
Request object, 38, 50–51
Resource dispensers, 281, 293–296
Resource managers, 281, 292–293
Response object, 38, 50, 51
Restrictions, 182
Results, 182
ret.htx, 441–443
ret.idc, 441
ret1.htx, 443–449

ret1.idc, 443
Reverse hosting, 105–106
Reverse proxying, 105
RSA Data Security Inc., 97

S

SATAN (System Administration Tool for Analyzing Networks), 99, 462–463
Scalability, 29–31, 272
Scanning, 218
sccifilt.dll, 208
Screening router, 88
Screen savers, 123–124
Script delimiters
    block, 37–38
    inline, 37
Scripting languages, Active Server Pages and, 48–49
Scripts
    Active Server Pages, 349–350
    Index Server and managing, 228
    use of term, 45, 64
ScriptTimeout, 52
Search engine sites, 179–182
Secure Computing Firewall for NT, 91
Secure Electronic Transaction (SET), 97, 235, 237, 238–239, 469
Secure Sockets Layer (SSL), 97, 98, 235, 239, 468
Security
    See also Proxy Server
    ActiveX, 328–329, 344–346
    bastion hosts, 90
    confidential issues, 462–466
    copyrights, 462–464
    C2, 101
    Domain Name Service (DNS), 94–95
    dual-homed hosts, 93
    e-commerce, 235
    firewalls, 86–96, 383, 466–467
    getting to and from a site, 86–87
    hacking, preventing, 464–466
    Index Server, 179, 223
    Java, 375, 381–383
    JavaScript, 386

Index 507

Kerberos security system, 476
packet filtering, 88
of payments, 96–98, 235
perimeter networks, 90–91
SQL Server, 155–156
of transactions, 98–99, 237–246
Transaction Server, 325–326
viruses, how they attack, 87
SELECT, 144
Selling process, Commerce Server, 251–269
Server(s)
    See also Client/server; under type of
    reading of e-mail addresses, 22
    role of, 4
    types of, 5
Server object, 38, 50, 52
ServerVariables, 51
SessionID, 52
Session key, 238
Session object, 38, 50, 52
Session_OnEnd, 59
Session_OnStart, 59
Sessions, Active Server Pages, 58–59
Shadow indexes, 198, 199
Shadow merges, 199–200
Shared Property Manager (SPM), 295–296
ShopperManager, 248
Shopping process, 269–270
S-HTTP, 468
Silicon Graphics, 236
Silicon Junction, 236
Simple Mail Transfer Protocol (SMTP), 104
SLIP, 130
SQL (Structured Query Language), 134
    commands, 136
    role of, 143–144
SQL Executive, 153
SQL Server, 33, 135
    administrative aspects, 154–155
    data distribution, 157–158
    data warehousing, 171–173
    Enterprise Manager, 150–153
    logical aspects, 156–160
    normalization, 158–160
    open database connectivity, 168–171
    physical aspects, 160–161
    process model, 156–157
    programming interface, 162–167
    role of, 150–151
    security, 155–156
    tools, 151–154
    Transact-SQL (T-SQL), 144, 156, 157, 173–176
    Transfer Manager, 155
SQL Web Assistant/Web Page wizard, 153, 165, 167
Standard Generalized Markup Language (SGML), 6
Star schema, 149
Starter Store Copy wizard, 271
State of a process, 20–23, 58–59
Status, 51
STDIN, 65–66
STDOUT, 65–66
Store Builder wizard tools, 250, 271
Stored procedure, 136
Store Foundation wizard, 271
Structured Query Language. See SQL
Submit button, 21, 66
Sun Microsystems, 375, 396
Symmetric multiprocessing (SMP), 41, 148
System Administration Tool for Analyzing Networks (SATAN), 99, 462–463
System properties, Java, 381–382

T

Tables, relational, 142
TACACS (terminal access control access control system), 93
Tags, 8
    Active Server Pages, 46
    .htx extension files, 72–73, 75
TCP (Transaction Control Protocol), 104
TCP/IP, 102–104, 486–487
Telnet, 104
TerminateExtension(), 77
Text chunks, 204, 215–217
Threading, 357–358
Timeout, 52
Time-to-live (TTL), 119
Transaction processing (TP) monitors, 276
Transactions
    establishing secure connection, 242
    generating requests, 239–241

Index

installing certificate, 241
methods for managing, 274–277
Microsoft Wallet, 242–244
security issues, 98–99, 237–246
sending requests, 241
Transaction Server, 28, 31, 33
   active components, 281–282
   Executive, 281, 283–291, 302
   Explorer, 281, 300–301
   Microsoft Distributed Transaction
      Coordinator (MS DTC), 281, 296–299
   objects, 281, 282
   processes, 281, 291–292
   resource dispensers, 281, 293–296
   resource managers, 281, 292–293
   role of, 273, 278–280
   run-time environment, 304–310
   security issues, 325–326
   server and client issues, 301–310
Transaction Server applications, 310–312
   building Account application, 319–325
   create Bank package, 320–322
   just-in-time activation, 312–318
Transact-SQL (T-SQL), 144, 156, 157, 173–176
Transfer Manager, 155
Triggers, 136
Tunneling, 98

U

Uniform Resource Locators (URLs), 6
   adding variables to, 21–22
Update, 136
Update button, 23
URLEncode, 52
User Datagram Protocol (UDP), 104

V

validate_zip, 55
Variables
   JavaScript, 384–385
   VBScript, 362
Variant, 361
VBScript
   Active Server Pages and, 46, 47, 48–49
   adding to the Web page, 363–365
   compared to JavaScript, 393–394
   compared to Visual Basic, 395
   constants and variables, 362
   datatypes, 361
   examples using buttons and forms, 365–372
   Hello World in, 335
   mathematical operators, 362–363
   procedures and functions, 363
   role of, 335–336, 361
   syntax rules, 361–363
   tips for, 374
   Web site, 493
VDO, 409
Vector-space queries, 190
Verisign Inc., 98, 241
Video, 409
Virtual circuit, 103
Virtual private networks (VPNs), 92, 469–470
Virtual roots, 217–218, 228–230
Viruses
   Java and, 382–383
   methods of attacks, 87
Visa, 97, 238, 469
Visual Basic (VB)
   See also VBScript
   benefits of, 359
   compared to VBScript, 395
   controls, 372–374
   Hello World in, 334
   overview of, 359–360
   role of, 333–334
   tips for, 374
   Web site, 493
Visual InterDev, 46
VivoActive, 409
Volcano Coffee, 260, 261

W

Wallet, 242–246, 251
Waveform Audio (WAV), 409
Web browser
   defined, 2
   examples of using, 3
Web Proxy, 38, 41, 100, 105–109

Web server. See Client/server; Server(s)
Web site, next-generation
    overview, 399–400
    plan, 401–403
    promoting, 407–410
    prototype, 403–407
    purpose, 400–401
Web site case study
    cookies, 458
    extranet requirements, 457
    forms, 458–459
    IDC/HTX code sample, 425–449
    ISAPI code sample, 449–456
    Java for browser detection code sample, 424–425
    layout, 411–413
    Perl and e-mail code sample, 413–424
    security issues, 456
Web sites
    creating, 9
    list of, 493–494
WHERE, 144

Wildcard operators, 188
Windows Internet Name Service (WINS), 117, 472, 490–491
Windows Media Player, 409
WinSock Proxy (WSP), 38, 39–40, 100, 110–112
Wizards, Commerce Server, 271
Wolfpack (Cluster Server), 30, 31, 148, 474–475
Word breaking, 213
Word lists, 198
World Wide Web
    See also under Web
    how it works, 4–7
    overview of, 1–2
    what can be found on, 3
Write, 51

X

XingMPEG, 409
X.25, 104